Introduction

The current state of architecture, as well as that of many other human disciplines such as literature, industrial design, or fashion, is so complex that critics do not always manage to explain its intricacies using clear and meaningful criteria.

This review of the architectural world over the last decade reveals a huge variety of styles and trends, which has produced undeniable riches. This diversity defines all of these projects. They have been born out of the effort of individuals and groups, who, far from trying to make their work suit already existing premises, have fought to find functional and aesthetic solutions to real problems. Originality is the child of this search.

This vast selection, largely a compilation of the most significant buildings constructed over the last ten years, is not intended to do any more than demonstrate a certain quality common to a number of these architectural projects. We did not intend to make any kind of categorical judgement of personal views, but to introduce the public to this material by highlighting trends and analyzing their characteristics, with the sole aim of offering the reader, who might not necessarily be a specialist, a broad and up-to-date vision of the scope of architecture in the world today.

This volume has, therefore, a clear

objective: to inform. It aims to orient the general reader, to bring them closer to the extensive, fertile, and hugely interesting subject of contemporary architecture.
Of course, it has not been an easy task to select the projects. The selection process was based on the proven quality and originality not only of the buildings proposed but also of the architects. In addition, we had to bear in mind that opinion is swaying towards a concrete time marker (the end of the decade and of the century), characterized by the concentration and defense of individualism. This is evidenced in the construction of buildings that are frequently personal and subjective expressions, by a heterogeneous group of master architects who establish a sincere, open, and clear dialog with architecture, the fruit of long and rich experience, as quickly as they construct strange, isolated shapes. Projects of great structural virtuosity follow, further removed and more casual than the much discussed relationship between architecture and the public. Between the two extremes, other technological or artistic contributions add to the broad range that contemporary world architecture offers us.

From among the group of buildings presented, there are some that unconditionally extend theoretical modern schemes, such as, for example, some of the Nordic projects, with their obvious tradition and significance, which are a homage to a styli-

stic and functional architectural language. In contrast, other works open the door to the future, to architecture for the 21st century, an architecture that tries to create a new reality divorced from its environment, and that gathers up all the troubled values of a uniform society controlled by international mass communication.

Once again, architecture in North America seems to be becoming the paradigm to follow. This view, however, is not yet final and will be accepted only with some hesitation and provisos.

Undoubtedly, these new departures will provide a breath of fresh air, allowing certain outmoded habits to be revised, and at the same time they will persuade people to view the current state of architecture in a new light. This is precisely the reason that, in preparing this book, a special effort has been made to include important projects built in the USA or designed by Americans.

The common thread running through all the projects here is their variety, reflecting today's multiplicity of tastes and trends: all architectural expressions seem to be accepted, as long as they produce a satisfactory and well-thought-out result, whether from the constructivist's optical point of view, or from the aesthetic or functional one. **It is a case of pragmatism carried to its logical conclusion.** This situation is certainly dependent on external

factors such as the context in which the building is located, and on internal factors such as the weight of history and the professional and intellectual experience of each of the architects involved.

The element that binds all these aspects together in determining the outcome of any project is its subject. In other words, it is not the same to design and construct a church, a museum, a communications tower, a bridge, offices, a single family dwelling, or a theater. Each of the buildings included in this book has to meet strict functional requirements that the architect cannot avoid: they have to resolve them. The architect's contribution will be to endow the finished building with special worth, subject, of course, to the external and internal circumstances already mentioned above.

The buildings presented in this volume have been designed both by architects of established reputation, with a long professional record, and by younger practitioners who are now starting to define the state of architecture today and in the near future. It is interesting to be able to compare, through the 1000 pages of this book, the work of two different generations of architects–that of Antoine Predock, César Pelli, or Michael Graves, who are all now over 60 years old, and the work of those around 40 years old, such as Studio Granda, Christian Drevet, or Enrique Norten. It can be said, however, after analyzing all the works, that there is no break between the

two. On the contrary, in some cases one can see fewer points in common between architects of the same era than between others with more than
30 years' age difference. In other words, the concerns of architects are a response not so much to their training as to their vision of reality. Ideas rush to all corners of the planet, affecting everyone equally. Architectural diversity is an undeniable reality, within which both traditionalist and frankly revolutionary attitudes coexist. A panoramic vision such as this book offers unleashes a cacophony of voices. Groups or movements do not feature strongly. Although certain materials or technical solutions are widely used, the approach to a project almost always springs from a personal and specific vision, not from the formal application of some accepted ideology or doctrine.

The publication of *The World of Contemporary Architecture* aims to give the public access to material that until now has been the province of specialists. We hope we have achieved this.

Francisco Asensio Cerver

Urban planning and transport

Talking about transport and urban planning has become an essential activity in today's culture, and in most cases it is done from a position of ignorance of the principles that govern these disciplines so closely linked to the individual in society. The purpose of the first section of this study of contemporary international architecture is to show projects that have drawn up the rules of engagement for these two architectural disciplines, with a view to shaping the basic concepts. This will provide for the reader a more rigorous and reliable approach to this vast territory, comprising those transport and urban infrastructure facilities that define our current social behavior. Transport interchanges can be interpreted as redefining the hierarchical system between cities, from the moment they are erected as emblems of the development of a territory.

The economic expansion of the 1990s has brought with it an increase in the amount of international trade and the daily movement of people. All this, together with a blurring of frontiers, explains why the most widely used means of transport are the train and the plane, objects of study in this section of the book, together with the advantages and consequences of the use of urban transport. We also wanted to make a special mention of two types of construction that fall halfway between transport and urban planning: bridges and communications towers.

The term urban planning, for its part, applies not only to the study, planning, and construction of towns and cities, but also to their relationship with the surrounding region. In any case, their ultimate objective is to design the spatial environment where man carries on social activities. In this volume we will find a series of projects (squares, streets, urban parks, peripheral parks, land art, urban property, etc.) that tries to improve the urban environment by inspiring the person in the street, by reconnecting isolated neighborhoods, and by restoring and adapting heritage areas.

Airports

There are many varied factors involved in the design of airports, ranging from atmospheric conditions to accessibility of terrestrial transport, via the possible presence of other airports in the area, surrounding obstructions, or the presence of certain aeronautical requirements. All the projects in this section share the harmonious combination of the concepts of aesthetics and functionality, demonstrating that pragmatism in the selection of materials is not incompatible with beauty, distilled into suggestive forms, subtle structures, chromatic balance, and the surrounding landscape.

Denver Airport

Curtis W. Fentress

Location: Denver, Colorado, USA. **Date of project**: 1994. **Client**: Kaiser Bautechnick. **Associates**: Reinhold Meyer (structural engineering), Kaiser Bautechnik (works supervision), Roger Preston (mechanical and electrical engineering). **Photography**: Timothy Hursley, Nick Merrick.

A long building, with a large central hall, is divided into various levels, each associated with an independent function. On both sides, there are three blocks with a number of levels for parking. The spaces between these blocks become, on arriving at the central hall, the elements that connect the terminal's different levels. The hall is covered by an enormous canvas suspended from two lines of braced pillars. Direct access from outside is via two roads for wheeled vehicles on the upper level, that flank the hall just above the parking levels. Along both roads there is an access walkway covered with the same type of canvas that covers the central hall.

Fentress's ability to translate into architecture the vast prairies of Colorado with their horizons broken by the outline of the mountains bring the traveler into the city via a most poetic series of images.

Chek Lap Kok

Foster and Partners

Location: Hong Kong, China. **Date of completion**: 1998. **Design team**: Foster and Partners (architecture), Mott Connell Ltd (engineering), BAA plc (aerial plan). **Consultants**: Ove Arup and Partners (structural engineering), WT Partnership (costing), Fisher Marantz Renfro Stone (lighting), O'Brien Kreitzberg (construction program), Wilbur Smith Associates (traffic). **Surface area**: 516,000 m² (5.6 million ft²). **Photography**: John Nye, Airphotos International.

Hong Kong's new airport has the capacity of Heathrow and JFK combined in one. With 516,000 m² (5.6 million ft²) of surface area and a length of 1.27 km (0.8 mile), the Chek Lap Kok terminal is the largest covered space ever built. What is more, before constructing the terminal, it was necessary to create the site. In 1992, Chek Lap Kok was a mountain rising out of the sea. Construction of the airport has converted this island into a flat surface four times larger than it was, and 6 m (20 ft) above sea level. The unifying element of this immense structure, which allows travelers to orient themselves in the immense halls of the terminal is the roof, which is made of a series of metal vaults. Norman Foster has developed here, on much larger scale, the same concept that he used so successfully at Stansted Airport: a light and luminous roof, an unrestricted open floor, and a basement level for housing services, equipment, and the baggage handling system.

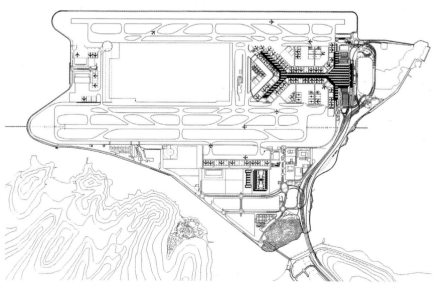

Kuala Lumpur Airport

Kisho Kurokawa Architect & Associates, Arkitek Jururancag.

Location: Kuala Lumpur, Malaysia. **Date of completion**: 1998. **Architects**: Kisho Kurokawa Architect, Arkitek Jururancag. **Surface area**: 400,000 m² (4.3 million ft²). **Scheme**: National and international terminals. **Photography**: Loo Keng Yip.

Faced with the challenge of building an airport to meet the country's economic growth, and ensure the organization of air traffic up to 2020, the Malaysian authorities saw the opportunity of turning this project into a symbol of an open door investment policy, of local industry's commitment to new technologies, and of putting money behind the national identity.

In spite of the preoccupation for developing a typically Malaysian style of architecture, which would make the building the visitor's first point of contact with the country's culture, responsibility for the project was given to the Japanese architect Kisho Kurokawa, though he did work in collaboration with the national firm Arkitek Jururancag.

The total surface area of the building is 400,000 m² (4.3 million ft²). The airport has been designed so that there is perfect symmetry between the two terminals (national and international), which are also symmetrical within themselves. The terminal building has an underground floor and five floors on a gradient. The most characteristic elements of the building are its roof and the structure of conical pillars on the top floor, the departure lounge.

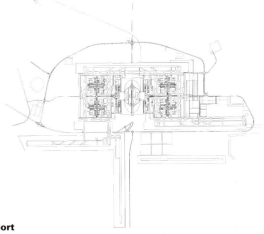

Kansai International Airport

Renzo Piano and Noriaki Okabe

Location: Osaka, Japan. **Date of completion**: 1994. **Architects**: Renzo Piano, Noriaki Okabe. **Client**: Kansai International Airport Co. Ltd. **Associates**: Peter Rice, Tony Stevens, Philip Dilley. Alistair Guthrie (Ove Arup & Partners); Kimiaki Minai (Nikken Sekkei Ltd.); Paul Andreu. Jean Marie Chevallier (Aéroports de Paris); Takeshi Kido, Misao Matsumoto (Japan Airport Consultants, Inc.). **Photography**: Sky Front, Yasuhiro Takawawa, Kanji Kiwatashi.

To build an island in the bay, with an area of more than 500 ha (1235 acres), a site had to be found that both provided enough free space and would avoid contamination. This meant that consolidation work had first to be done on the marine subsoil, which was very deep and unstable at this level. Sand was injected into the clay strata to increase strength, and then a consolidating infill was added. In less than five years the whole island was covered, using some 150 million m³ (5.3 billion ft³) of earth. Even though the degree of consolidation achieved was viable, there was still some yield, however, within acceptable limits. For this reason, the foundations had to be able to absorb any movement of the subsoil that might affect the stability of the building.

The building was designed so that, despite its huge size – it stretches for more than 1.5 km (0.95 miles) – users can orient themselves at any time when they are crossing it: the keys to achieving this are absolute transparency, and adapting the corresponding scales to each zone in the structure.

United Airlines Terminal 1, O'Hare Airport

Murphy & Jahn

Location: Chicago, Illinois, USA. **Date of construction**: 1987. **Architect**: Murphy & Jahn.
Photography: Murphy & Jahn.

United Airlines Terminal 1 consists of three areas, two of which are joined by a very long corridor running the whole length of the complex. The two basic components, blocks B and C, form two linear structures each 55 m (180 ft) long, separated by a free space of some 27 m (90 ft), which allows movement of several planes in both directions. Building C has a total of 30 boarding gates, while the other 18 gates are in Building B. The ticket area is in a large hall with 56 counters. This space has been topped with a barrel vault, which is highest at the entrance that gives onto the terminal, and slopes down towards the other end of the building.

The planning of the terminal is based on the concept of parallel volumes, a design that departs from the traditional Y shape that is prevalent at O'Hare. The walls, which are curved at the top, and the translucent roof, appear to be back lit with a wide range of colors. This gives the building a greater feeling of space.

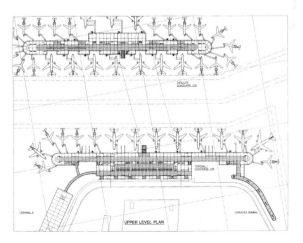

UPPER LEVEL PLAN

Terminal 2, San Diego Airport

Gensler

Location: San Diego, California, USA **Date of construction**: 1998. **Architects**: Gensler Architecture Design & Planning Worldwide (Santa Monica office). **Scheme**: Nine boarding gates, ticket sales hall, baggage collection area, shopping areas, restaurants, and services. **Surface area**: 11,000 m² (120,000 ft²). **Photography**: Marco Lorenzetti, G. Cormier.

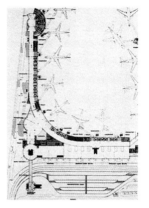

Gensler received the commission to expand Terminal 2 for the final of Superbowl XXXII.

The terminal is L-shaped, and in the angle Gensler has placed interconnecting rotundas, containing the waiting areas, cafeterias, and shops. The two arms of the L house the arrival and departure halls. The façade consists of an inclined glass plane, with a structure of heavy concrete columns supporting a metal roof that is rather evocative of the wings of an aircraft. The extensive use of glass allows one to enjoy the view out over San Diego Bay. Inside, Gensler has chosen a range of colors inspired by the local landscape: gold (sand), green (trees), and blue (sky and sea), giving a pleasing natural effect.

Stuttgart Airport

Meinhard von Gerkan

Location: Stuttgart, Germany. **Date of construction**: 1992. **Architect**: Meinhard von Gerkan. **Photography**: Richard Bryant/Arcaid.

In Stuttgart Airport, the pillars are trunks that divide into extended branches and the roof is a thick foliage that filters the light and allows only some rays to pass through. In this way some of the most emblematic symbols of technology are converted into melancholic beings and landscapes longing for the natural world.

The roof which von Gerkan designed allows both natural light to come in through skylights, and artificial light from lamps installed in boxes.

The inclined roof and the stepped levels of the hall give an impression of latent movement, in an image that has been compared with the mythical Birnam wood in *Macbeth*. In order for the roof to be better appreciated, von Gerkan placed the air-conditioning ducting over the ticket sales counters and the blocks containing elevators.

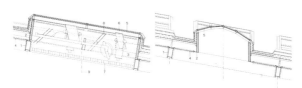

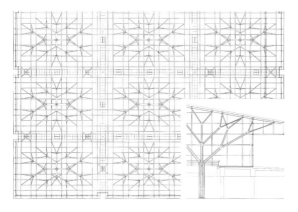

Charles de Gaulle Airport, interchange module

Paul Andreu, J. M. Duthilleul

Location: Roissy, Paris, France. **Date of construction**: 1994. **Architects**: Paul Andreu, J.M. Duthilleul. **Scheme**: Interchange module for connections between terminals. **Photography**: Paul Maurer.

The airport of Roissy-Charles de Gaulle looks like some living organism, such as a sponge under a microscope. Inside, there is constant fluid movement. There is no single concept of space in Roissy, but many different strata: scales, networks, circuits, and contrasting dimensions, into which a number of gaps break. The TGV (High Speed Train) station is part of the airport's module 2, an interchange module that will become the center of the airport when it is finished. This module allows renewal of the spatial scheme. Since its beginning (in 1974) the airport has grown as a juxtaposition of elements: Terminal 1, Terminal 2, train station, parking areas. With the advent of the High Speed Train new installations had to be built, which are now used for the internal transport system, under an immense glass roof. Roissy is a complex, yet at the same time easy to use, place which maybe reflects the sentiment of a century.

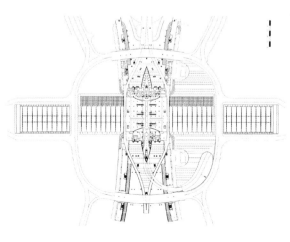

Stansted Airport

Sir Norman Foster & Associates

Location: London, UK. **Date of completion**: 1990. **Architect**: Sir Norman Foster & Associates. **Scheme**: New terminal for Stansted Airport: departures and arrivals terminals, platforms for connection with train and underground network, banks, shops, kitchens, medical facilities, offices, and services. **Photography**: Richard Davies.

In the early 1980s it had become vital to build a new terminal in the southeast of England to satisfy the urgent requirements of air traffic in the London area. The building in question is square, measuring 200 x 200 m (660 x 660 ft). The opposing sides on the southeast and northwest, which are transparent, are set back in relation to the roof. The remaining two sides are reflective in contrast to the transparency of the others. The roof complements the floor architecturally and constitutes an important structural part of the complex. It is supported over the hall by six groups of pillars, 36 m (120 ft) apart. A tree-shaped structure lends a solid configuration and the strength to bear all the technical systems: heating, ventilation, lighting, and air-conditioning. All the services included on the ground floor (banks, shops, kitchens, medical facilities, etc.), are contained in easily removable modules. With an initial capacity of eight million passengers annually, Stansted has potential for growth up to 15 million users a year.

Schiphol Airport

Benthem Crouwel NACO

Location: Amsterdam, The Netherlands. **Date of construction**: 1993–1995 **Architect**: Benthem Crouwel NACO. **Scheme**: Airport facilities, shopping center, and train station. **Photography**: Jannes Linders, Claes de Vrieselaan.

The first phase of the new Schiphol airport dates from 1967. The new facilities replaced an old airport nearby, known today as Schiphol-Oost. The project was inspired by the terminal at O'Hare (Chicago) and featured the novelty of a departures hall raised above the runways, with all-glass façades, so that passengers awaiting flights could see the planes

taking off and landing. This idea has subsequently been widely used. The architects have discovered that one of the most moving and poetic activities at an airport, surely, is to sit and watch the planes coming in and flying out.

The Schiphol terminal is an example of the relationship between the new and the modern in architecture. Two years after finishing the work on Terminal 3, the new shopping mall, Schiphol Plaza, also designed by Benthem Crouwel NACO, was opened. Built in the central

triangle formed by the different terminals, this space is the main access route to all of them, as well as to the train station. A series of metal pillars, triangular in section, supports an inclined roof garden with skylights set in it. The interior of the mall is designed like a real town square: an open and free space for people.

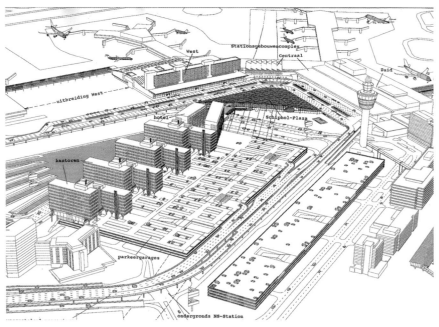

Train stations

With the dawn of the 21st century, the purpose of the railroad is changing. With the population moving from the cities to the suburbs, the train has become the means of connecting the residential periphery to the commercial center. Designers of train stations, however, often restrict themselves to planning the building in terms only of the flow of travelers and the immediate functional demands. They do not take into account the urban dynamic that can turn the station into one of the differentiating elements of a city, into the building that forms a special image, a mark of identity. The tendency is still to enclose new stations. But we have included examples that are most representative at an international level, which will help over the next few years to clarify the new image of the station.

TGV station at Lyon-Satôlas Airport

Santiago Calatrava

Location: Lyon, France. **Date completed**: 1996. **Promoter**: Lyon Chamber of Commerce and Industry and SNCF. **Architect**: Santiago Calatrava i Valls. **Associates**: Alexis Burret, Sebastien Mémet (chief architects), David Long, L. Burr (assistants). **Photography**: Ralph Richter/Architekturphoto.

In the TGV (High Speed Train) station of Lyon-Satôlas Airport, Santiago Calatrava uses his two favorite compositional mechanisms: symmetry and duality. Symmetry is provided by the desire to simplify the plan. His architecture is based on the construction; for this the essential aspect of his projects is the sectional view. For Calatrava, the plan is order and the section beauty. Duality or dialogue give tension to the project, but also give it unity. The station covers two perpendicular movements with two different structures that demonstrate that crossing point. A vaulted roof, made of an oblique mesh of white concrete beams and rhomboidal glass skylights, covers the six railroad tracks for a length of half a kilometer (one third of a mile). This roof is crossed above by a large triangular-shaped hall connecting the main entrance in one corner with the main complex and the taxi and bus terminals, and at the other end with a conveyor belt that takes passengers 180 m (600 ft) to and from the airport's passenger terminal building.

Two gigantic steel arches each rest on the corner of the triangle by the entrance and, respectively, on the two corners on the opposite side, defining the north and south façades. A structure of steel and glass sections is built on these, which rotates to improve ventilation in the hall.

TGV station at L yon-Satôlas Airport

Stockholm Bus Station

Bengt Ahlqvist, Ralph Erskine, Anders Tengbom

Location: Stockholm, Sweden. **Date of completion**: January 1989. **Client**: Municipality of Stockholm and Stockholm Railroad Company (S J). **Architects**: Bengt Ahlqvist, Ralph Erskine, Andera Tangborn. **Scheme**: Central bus station, indoor public plaza, cafeteria-restaurant, hotel, restaurant, office complex, and connection with the central railroad station. **Photography**: Kjell Appelgren.

The building is 270 m (890 ft) long and is divided into four blocks, the spaces between which correspond to existing streets. Each block consists of one tall building facing the city and a lower one that faces the outer part of the esplanade. The stair and elevator wells join these spaces to form four patios or atria with curved, transparent glass roofs. Internal connection between the patios is via a gallery located on the same level as the office complex. The first of the atria has a reception area and a panoramic view over Stockholm. The second atrium, which is the biggest, is the one that opens out onto the terminal. The third is the center of the office complex and the entrance hall of the World Trade Center. It is designed as an indoor public plaza, with a café-restaurant. The fourth atrium is the north entrance hall, with garden terraces and escalators, leading to another restaurant and the hotel included in the complex. The roof is made of sheet metal panels.

The architectural concept is based on the great classic railroad stations, and is intended to represent the apogee of the age of glass buildings; a modern version of the great passenger hall, sharing light and space with the local business premises.

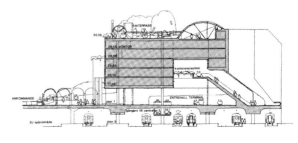

Atocha Station

José Rafael Moneo

Location: Madrid, Spain. **Date of construction**: 1990. **Architect**: José Rafael Moneo. **Scheme**: Local train station, high speed train station, bus station, subway station, parking, and remodeling the old station as an entrance hall. **Photography**: Luis Casals.

Atocha Station is in the center of Madrid, a short distance from the Reina Sofía and Prado museums. The huge glass and steel roof of the old 19th-century station had to be conserved and restored and, at the same time, the new building had to house a high speed train station and stations for local trains, buses, and the subway, in addition to a large area for parking. Moneo approached this complex program by breaking down the different elements, and playing around with different levels for each of the stations. His intention was that, in spite of the size of the building, the station should not alter the scale of the city nor of the old 19th-century structure to be converted into an entrance hall-cum-conservatory. There are very few new elements to be seen from the outside: an access rotunda and a clock tower. The other areas of the station are hidden thanks to clever sectional work.

Nagasaki Port Terminal

Shin Takamatsu

Location: Nagasaki, Japan. **Date of construction**: 1995. **Architect**: Shin Takamatsu. **Consultants**: Mitsubishi Estate A & C (building and installations). **Surface area**: 3950 m² (425,000 ft²). **Scheme**: Waiting rooms, ticket sales area, hall, offices, and services. **Photography**: Nacasa & Partners·

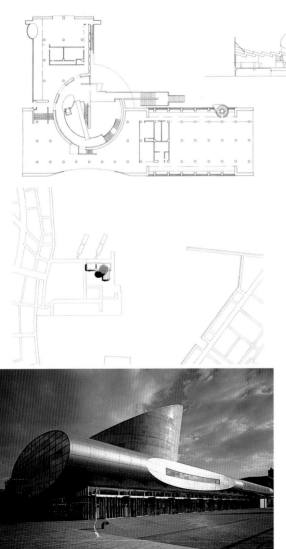

The port of Nagasaki, in the south of Japan, has historically always been very important since it was traditionally the only port open to foreign countries. A series of projects is being undertaken in Nagasaki following the Nagasaki 2001 Urban Renewal plan, supervised by locally based architect Hideto Horiike.

The ferry terminal is located in the Mofune area, in the center of the port, surrounded by mountains and sea, so that the project had to consider the distant view from both places. This privileged location makes it a symbol within new urban development. Takamatsu has planned the project as a crossroads traveled over by people from different cultural backgrounds.

Charles de Gaulle Airport, interchange module

Paul Andreu, Jean Marie Duthilleul

Location: Paris, France. **Date of construction**: 1994. **Architects**: Paul Andreu, Jean-Marie Duthilleul. **Photography**: Paul Maurer

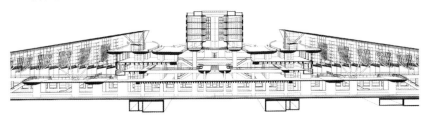

This building is a crossroads: railroads, internal communication, channels between installations. The different elements are located at different levels: the viaducts on top, and underneath, successively, are the services relating to the terminal area, the internal transport system, the hall of the railroad station, and, finally, the platforms under the first floor, forming a trench with the viaducts for taxis. Only the hotel rises between the tracks as a solid opaque mass. The glass roof and the absence of a tunnel over the train tracks means that the interchange routes are easily recognizable. Development of the visual relationships is based on the handling of the light, which is one of the main materials in this project, together with steel and concrete elements.

Liverpool Street train station

A & DG

Location: London, UK. **Date project begun**: 1979. **Date of completion**: 1991. **Client**: British Rail. **Architect**: A & DG. **Scheme**: Remodeling of an old train station: facilities, new connections with the subway, platforms, hall, ticket offices, offices, and services.

It was planned to demolish Liverpool Street station and replace it with a modern construction, but in 1979 it was agreed to remodel it, and final approval was obtained in 1983. The chief objectives laid down by British Rail (the former British state railroad company), who gave the project to A & DG, were to modernize and improve the station's facilities, and its connections with the subway and the approach roads to the station. The platforms had to be the same length (the existing ones were all different) and there was to be a new hall, respecting the historical and aesthetic demands of the existing structure. With this rebuild, Liverpool Street station has become a model for the new spirit of public-private cooperation and skillful fusion of the best of the past with the best of the future, preparing it for the 21st century.

Slependen Station

Arne Henriksen

Location: Baerum, Oslo, Norway. **Date of construction**: 1993. **Architect**: Arne Henriksen. **Scheme**: Access, train station, parking, ticket area, offices, and services. **Photography**: Jiri Havran.

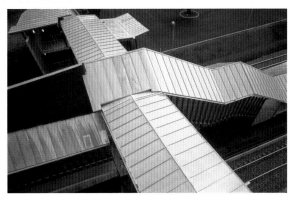

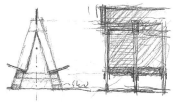

There was the chance to create an architectural milestone at Slependen Station in Baerum, outside Oslo. The landscape was highly dramatic thanks to the steep slope and the number of different levels. To connect all the existing routes with the station platforms, it was necessary to construct ramps and stairways. So Slependen Station has a large number of buildings and singular elements: two ramps, one straight and the other curved, a rotunda, a stairway, a ramp-stairway, and two bridges. The concrete represents the heavy, while the wooden structures constitute the light and active components of the design. The rotunda, with its spiral ramp constructed from elements of dark concrete, is a very special structure. Both the outer curve of the wall, and the slope of the ramp, as well as the architectural image itself, are coded in the element that constructs the rotunda.

Solana Beach Station

Rob Wellington Quigley

Location: Solana Beach, California, USA. **Date of construction** 1995. **Architect**: Rob Wellington Quigley
Scheme: Train station, parking, installation of soundproofing. **Photography**: Richard Barnes.

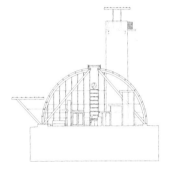

participated along with the architects in the design of the city center.

From the start, small workshops were organized which sought to reach a consensus between community and professionals on decisions about the project: the traffic, the parking, the mechanisms for soundproofing, the size of the buildings, and the relationship between commercial and residential buildings.

The station building is the first phase of an urban project of some 35,000 m² (454,000 ft²), destined to become the new city center for Solana Beach in the next few years. In addition to the station, the complex includes a large parking lot, a park, businesses, restaurants, cinemas, low-cost homes for the aged, and lofts for artists. The complex is in the form of a rectangle measuring approximately 70 m (255 ft) wide by 500 m (1780 ft) in length, bordering Route 101, which connects with the center of San Diego, and with the train tracks. The project was conceived in a completely different way from normal, more openly and democratically, since the inhabitants of Solana Beach themselves

Urban transport

This chapter is dedicated entirely to
subway and bus stations for city use.
These are projects in which architects have
found a new arena for their creativity:
places that can join streets and
underground galleries, neoclassical
façades and tunnels, in a form that
encompasses the different levels of the
city. Although bus stands are normally
mass produced, those shown here are
designed from the point of view of their
relationship to the urban context. Each of
these projects has been designed as a
particular object linked to a particular
location, as if it were a sculpture. They
clearly show a capacity to enrich the city
with minimal architectural detail–such
possibilities are all too often ignored.

Subway station in Bilbao

Norman Foster

Location: Bilbao, Spain. **Date of construction**: 1996. **Architect**: Norman Foster. **Scheme**: Access canopy, exit module, lighting, signing, roof, offices, and services. **Photography**: Luis Sans

Bilbao is a city that has traditionally been affected by the environmental consequences of its heavy industrial plants. Foster has achieved a situation in which, inside the subway, travelers sit within the earth, conscious of the singularity of the place they are in. The tunnels are the principal theme of the project. Measuring 16 m (53 ft) wide by 8 m (26 ft) high, they were dug using the Nat system (the new Austrian method of tunnel construction). To avoid weather problems, Foster wanted to create a space at the entrances to the subway that, although enclosed, was light and transparent. This gave rise to his idea of designing glass canopies with a stainless steel structure, so that, while they offer protection to passengers, by night they become enormous lamps that light up the city–inescapable landmarks.

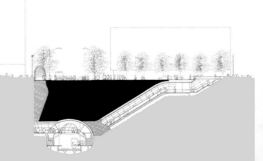

Subway station in Valencia

Santiago Calatrava

Location: Valencia, Spain. **Date of construction**: 1995. **Architect**: Santiago Calatrava. **Scheme**: Subway station, ticket offices, services, litter bins, entrance canopy. **Photography**: Paolo Rosselli.

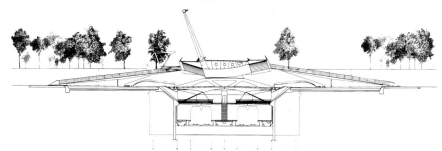

Alameda subway station is located below what was once the bed of the river Turia. Though underground, the station maintains a link with the exterior through a ribbed, translucent roof which is in turn the floor of the square above the station.

The station is divided into three levels: the entrance, the ticket offices, and the platform. The access level consists of an escalator in a steel tube at each end of the station, leading to the ticket offices, from where can be seen both the double height space of the platform as well as the shape of the roof.

The structure is of white reinforced concrete. The translucent glass skylights are supported in metal frames. In addition to allowing light and air to enter, by night the lines of skylights define the limits of the square in the busy center above ground.

Subway station in Lyon

Jourda & Perraudin

Location: Lyon, France. **Date of construction**: 1993. **Architect**: Jourda & Perraudin. **Scheme**: Subway station, offices, and equipment. **Photography**: George Fessy.

The subway station of Vénissieux-Parilly is situated in a little urbanized suburb at the intersection of a number of important roads. The mixture of different geometric shapes forms a structure of concrete arches and vaults based on diagrams of

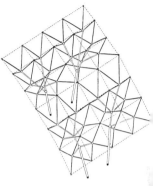

energy transmission from the ground floor to the level of the platforms. All the elements (columns, capitals, vaults, and arches) were designed according to the manufacturing techniques used: metal form-work, on-site concreting, and prefabricated vaults. This project involved underground architecture using large-scale excavation. It took advantage of the plasticity of the concrete and the expressive lines of force of the arches and the inclined side columns. Natural light penetrates thanks to two apertures in the main entrance hall.

Vuosari subway station

Esa Piironen

Location: Helsinki, Finland. **Date of construction**: 1998. **Architect**: Esa Piironen. **Scheme**: Platforms, ticket offices, and services. **Area**: 4394 m² (47,000 ft²), **Photography**: Veikko Niemelä.

Vuosari station in Helsinki evokes transparency. Esa Piironen has been concerned mainly with the roof and the glass façades, as well as with integrating the structure into the surrounding landscape. In section, two structures are superimposed one on the other: the first is of concrete, and supports the platforms, and the second is of steel and glass, forming the roofs.

As with much of the architecture of the north of Europe, transparency is identified with democracy, closeness with the citizen, and compromise with the user: a literal harmony. Clearly, this huge structure of glass and steel acts as a conservatory which, though extremely beneficial in Finland, would be unthinkable in other, more southerly latitudes.

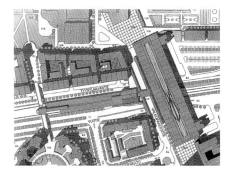

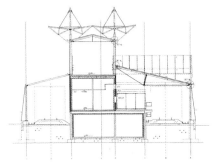

Nils Ericson Bus Station

Niels Torp

Location: Gothenburg, Sweden. **Date of completion**: 1996. **Client**: GLAB – Stefan Ekmann. **Architect**: Niels Torp AS Arkitekter MNAL. **Associates**: ABACO Arkitektkontor AB; VBB Markplanlaggare (landscaping); RF Byggkonsult (construction). **Area**: 4500 m² (48,000 ft²). **Scheme**: Terminal for the Gothenburg central bus station. **Photography**: Hans Wretling.

This project is the result of a competition held in the 1980s. It initially consisted not only of the construction of this terminal but also a new train station that had to contain a shopping mall and cafeterias, as well as a small business center. In addition, Nils Ericson square was redesigned as an urban park and became a splendid green open space, a contrast with the raucous traffic.

Passing through the rectangular entrance to the terminal one can connect with a tram stop, SJ line trains, metropolitan buses, and a taxi rank.

The scale and intimacy of this reception area relate to other parts of the complex, which retain the same importance and functionality as at the start of construction.

The main building includes an arcade which looks out onto the park outside, and gives protection from the wind and cold. It is right here that the terminal meets the city.

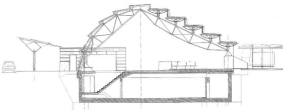

Tram station in Strasbourg

Gaston Valente

Location: Strasbourg, France. **Date of construction**: 1994. **Architect**: Gaston Valente. **Scheme**: Tram station, parking, access, commercial gallery, and services. **Photography**: Accent Visuel, Stéphane Speck, Rob Fleck, L. Locat.

The station in the Place de la Gare is the main hub of the new tram line promoted by Strasbourg's local government in order to replace traditional forms of transport with other less contaminating ones. The tram line runs at a depth of 17 m (56 ft). Gaston Valente has divided the station into four levels. The upper two are organized around an empty central plaza, where two lines of trees have been planted. This has been covered over with a structure of steel and glass. Like a classic atrium or as in one of the famous shopping arcades of the 19th century, numerous shops have been built along the perimeter on both levels. On the platforms and escalators, the American artist Barbara Kruger has installed huge concrete beams on which, in enormous capital letters, she asks travelers:

Where are you going?
Who do you think you are?
Where is your head?
Who laughs last?

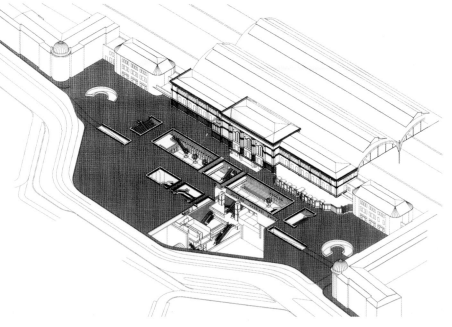

Tram station in Strasbourg 83

Stuttgart Station

Günter Behnisch & Partners

Location: Stuttgart, Germany. **Date project begun**: 1985. **Date of completion**: 1991. **Architect**: Günter Behnisch & Partners. **Associates**: Manfred Sabatke (supervisor), Ulrich Mangold, Matthias Tusker (project architects). **Scheme**: Train station, protective canopy, passenger platforms, ticket offices, pedestrian tunnel, litter bins, and remodeling of the pavement outside. **Photography**: Christian Kandzia.

It was not possible to make any major structural changes, so the architects had to adopt other less radical approaches, based on transforming existing components: in particular a defensive bunker, whose huge bulk stands out in the middle of the complex, making it the focal point of the new station/square's design. This design has cleverly integrated a number of components of great lightness of form and aesthetic value into a canopy. Two passenger platforms have been placed beside the tracks on which the local express runs, protected by pergolas of steel and acrylic. Finally, a convenient pedestrian tunnel was installed under the street that joins the city center with the autobahn.

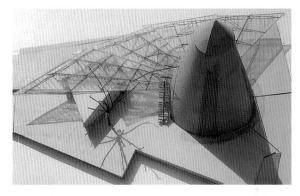

Tram station in Hanover

Alessandro Mendini

Location: Kurt-Schumacher Strasse, Hanover, Germany. **Date of construction**: 1994. **Designer**: Alessandro Mendini. **Scheme**: Canopy, signboards, and elements of urban decoration. **Photography**: Thomas Deutschmann.

In the course of the 20th century, squares and avenues have been subtly taken over by sculptures, which have become points of reference, giving their environments added meaning. Sculptures have been superimposed on buildings and embedded in the texture of façades. They present flowing images, add associations with their angles, they act as symbols.

The idea of converting bus, subway, and tram stops into singular pieces, each one conceived as an isolated and independent work of art, linked to a specific site, somehow revives the lost tradition of combining the two disciplines: sculpture and architecture. Mendini is someone who, since the 1950s when he was responsible for Casabella o Domus, has worked avidly to promote an art that is

close to society, close to the working methods of advertising and mass communications media. Mendini's popular art is based on symbolic and historical references that appeal to the collective imagination. Paradoxically, his tram station in Kurt-Schumacher Strasse turned out to be his most polemic work to date.

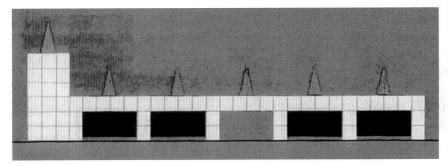

Greenwich North subway station

Alsop & Störmer

Location: Greenwich, London. **Date project begun**: 1991. **Date of construction**: 1998. **Architect**: Alsop & Störmer. **Associates**: JLE E ı M (services engineering). **Scheme**: Train station, ticket office, escalators to platforms, ventilation system, offices, and services. **Photography**: Roderick Coyne

The initial design consisted of an open station that would allow passengers to enter from the ticket sales area, located on the upper floor and facing west, through a walkway suspended from the concrete roof by cables to both sides of the station. The location of this entrance allows views to the waiting platform that connects with the entrance area by means of two passenger escalators going up and down.

The public areas (60 x 13 m, 200 x 43 ft) are open, which allows natural ventilation and good lighting. The ventilation ducts are also suspended from the roof.

The generous size and simple elegance of the structure has been emphasized by the use of ultramarine blue on walls, floor, and roofs. The air ducts and escalators are of stainless steel.

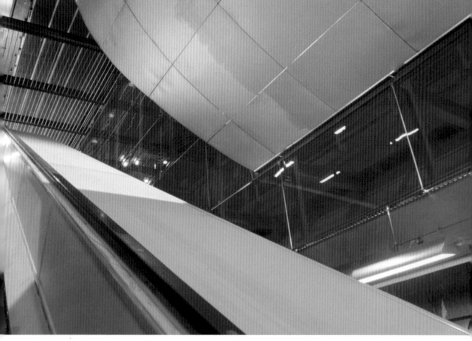

Bridges and communications towers

For a better understanding of each of the works in this chapter of *The World of Contemporary Architecture*, we must mention the complexity that accompanies the planning and construction of bridges and communications towers. They need to be a balanced combination of aesthetics and pragmatism and, at the same time, of architecture and engineering. For this reason, each of the projects included has been analyzed in terms of how it satisfies functional requirements (structures, antennas, technological elements, beams, arches, and so on) and how it meets harmonic criteria, on which the concept of beauty depends. Thus, when examining all these structures, it becomes clear that architecture and engineering cannot be separated and, consequently, architects must apply their knowledge to both disciplines simultaneously.

Normandy Bridge

Charles Lavigne

Location: Honfleur-Le Havre, France. **Date of completion**: 1995. **Client**: Chamber of Commerce and Industry of Le Havre. **Architect**: Charles Lavigne. **Associates**: F. Doyele (director of works), Quadric, Sogelerg, Eeg (viaduct), Seee (concrete structure), Sofresid (metal structure), Onera, Cstb, Eiffel, Sogelerg (wind effect), Cote (foundations), Yann Kersalé (lighting). **Photography**: S. Soane/Architekturphoto.

Just where the fresh water of the Seine meets the salt water of the English Channel, between the cities of Le Havre and Honfleur, the construction of the Normandy Bridge represents an important development that eliminates the 58 km (37 mile) round trip that used to be necessary to cross the river by the Tancarville Bridge further inland. Together with route A29, the project will establish a north–south axis that will open up the Normandy region and contribute to the development of the city of Le Havre as a logistical center. This will help in the diversification of its industrial base, reinforce its position as an important port, and encourage new activities in the estuary. The architects' most important consideration was continuity throughout the length of the bridge. The slope was not to exceed 6%. The cross section of the platform is identical for both the pre-stressed concrete sections and for the central metal section. Aerodynamic performance is improved by a blue painted aluminum cornice along the edge of the bridge which also serves to unify the two sections. The structure can withstand wind speeds in excess of 300 km/h (190 mph). Each of the A-shaped towers rises from the ground on two legs, between which the traffic passes, which then become a single anchoring mast rising to a height of 210 m (690 ft). Constructed out of pre-stressed concrete with steel reinforced tops, the towers are extremely rigid and ensure transmission of forces to the foundations. The piles, which are also of concrete, reach down deep into the banks of the Seine, while the viaducts are supported on a layer of limestone for added stability.

Höfdabakkabrú Bridge

Studio Granda

Location: Reykjavik, Iceland. **Date of completion**: September 1995. **Client**: Public roads administration. **Cost**: $1.73 million. **Architect**: Studio Granda. **Associates**: Línuhönnun (structural engineering), Landslagsarkitekar (landscaping). **Photography**: Sigurgeir Sigurjónsson.

The Höfdabakkabrú Bridge is a road interchange between a secondary road and the highway to the city of Reykjavik.

The form of the bridge is predetermined in practical terms by the precise route that vehicles must follow and by the structural logic that the engineers have laid down. In other words, in this case the architecture was not part of the origins of the project, but had to be adapted to previously made decisions and grafted on later as an additional aspect of the work. According to the architects themselves, their principal objective for this project was to smooth the impact of such a large structure on the immediate surrounding area.

The containing walls flanking the bridge follow the shape of the ground and the slopes have been planted with trees and bushes to assist this integration process.

In a contrasting strategy, brilliant black artificial stone was chosen for the finish of the walls, in order to form a background that would reflect the colored flashes of the cars speeding by. In the center of the bridge's intrados, the metal pillars have been painted in bright colors. In the darkness of the tunnel they flash like vertical brush strokes of yellow, orange, and red.

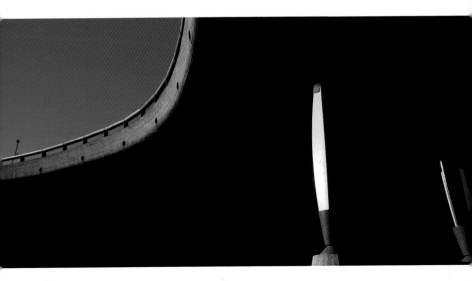

Eastern Scheldt Project

West 8

Location: Eastern Scheldt Delta, The Netherlands. **Date of construction**: 1991–1992. **Client**: Directoraat generaal Rijkswaterstaatdirectie Zeeland. **Architect**: West 8. **Associates**: Adriaan Geuze, Paul van Beek, Dirry de Bruin (model). **Scheme**: Construction of a barrier bridge as part of the Delta Project: closing the estuaries and inlets in the southwest of the Netherlands; integral landscaping project. **Photography**: Hans Werleman, Mectic Pictures Rotterdam, Bart Hofmeester.

This is the largest hydraulic engineering work of its kind in the world. In 1953, following serious floods over much of Zeeland, it was decided to return half of the land to the sea, erecting dikes along the old coastline. The construction of the final part of the project destroyed a unique

ecosystem and there was wide-scale opposition to this destruction from both ecologists and the producers of mussels and oysters. At the end of 1974, the government heeded these protests and decided that the mouth of the Eastern Scheldt would remain partially open, but provided with a system that could completely close it off in case of emergency. The integral landscaping project by West 8, following up the construction work on the barrier and its two ends, could be no less sophisticated and it was decided to form a series of enclaves in the landscape. Especially typical of this

work were the "shell beds": after flattening all the zones to the level of the surroundings, West 8 covered them with shells, produced from the neighboring shellfish beds. White and black shells were placed alternately, to form contrasting black and white designs of squares and lines. Located 13 m (43 ft) above sea level, the highway that follows the gentle curve of the delta protection barrier now offers a spectacular panorama over the watery landscape of Zeeland.

Ohnaruto Bridge

Honshu-Shikoku Bridge Authority

Location: Honshu-Shikoku, Japan. **Date of completion**: 1990. **Architect**: Honshu-Shikoku Bridge Authority. **Scheme**: Bridge connecting islands, landscaping to blend the structure in, and respect for marine fauna.

The Honshu-Shikoku Bridge Authority was formed in 1970, to be responsible for designing the rail and road networks connecting the islands of Honshu and Shikoku. This corporation considered it important to integrate the project into a magnificent landscape. For this reason it was decided to build a suspension bridge (1,629 m, 5300 ft) after considering the geological conditions of the sea bed. The most important considerations for the

design of a suspension bridge were typhoons and earthquakes. In this regard, preliminary studies were done to estimate vibrations from the wind and to construct superstructures capable of withstanding earthquakes of up to force 8 on the Richter scale. Once research into safety had been carried out, the design of the bridge was divided into two parts: the infrastructure (anchoring techniques to fix the system of cables) and the superstructure (the vertical

elements for suspending the supports). The cables are the essential part of a bridge: in total the bridge has 19,558 wires with a diameter of 5.37 mm (0.2 in), which, if joined together, would go around the world twice.

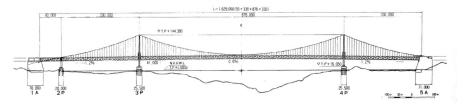

Vasco da Gama Bridge

Location: Lisbon, Portugal. **Date of construction**: 1995–1998. **Photography**: Paco Asensio.

Organization of the last World Fair of the 20th century was the driving force behind the transformation of Lisbon, through major structures such as the Vasco da Gama bridge over the Tagus. The candidature for holding the Expo in the Portuguese capital went hand in hand with the opportunity to explore location options that were both on the periphery of Lisbon and on the water. Two alternatives were proposed: one to the east and one to the west of the modern hub of the city.

The eastern option, on both sides of the Tagus, had serious infrastructure, housing, and environment problems, precisely in the place selected for the fair, bolstering the argument for regeneration. It was proposed to renovate this area and it became vital to improve all the access routes to and from the city. The most significant operation in this respect was the construction of the Vasco da Gama Bridge, which joins Lisbon to its outskirts on the peninsula over the water.

This project has provided new access into Lisbon, which before could only be reached by a bridge located a long way from the center, necessitating a much longer journey. Structurally the bridge consists of pillars from which are hung metal cables that support the elements closest to land. The central section consists of a platform on pillars with no additional support.

La Barqueta Bridge

Juan J. Arenas y Marcos J. Pantaleón

Location: Seville, Spain. **Date of completion**: 1992. **Architects**: Juan J. Arenas and Marcos J. Pantaleón. **Scheme**: Bridge connecting the island of La Cartuja to the historic center of Seville. **Photography**: Fernando Alda/ Expo '92 photo archive.

La Barqueta bridge was erected to link the historic city of Seville with the island of La Cartuja, where the vast complex of Expo '92 was developed. The triangular porticoes at the ends of the bridge platform, as well as solving the problem of stability, became a formidable entrance to the Expo site.

One of the most outstanding aspects of its design is the fact that its central arch stretches freely over the platform and that it also has, as a starting reference, a number of triangular points, heavily emphasizing its strong three-dimensional and aerodynamic nature. As to materials, steel has been used, in contrast to the general trend of using concrete or some other similar material.

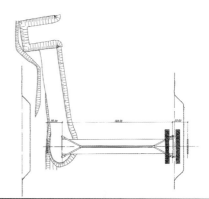

Montjuïc Tower

Santiago Calatrava

Location: Barcelona, Spain. **Date of completion**: 1992. **Client**: National Telephone Company of Spain. **Architect**: Santiago Calatrava. **Scheme**: Communications tower and surrounding gardens. **Photography**: David Cardelús

The Montjuïc telecommunications tower was erected as one of the symbols of the spirit of the Barcelona Olympics. The idea proposed by Santiago Calatrava materialized as a white figure 119 m (390 ft)

in height. Its inspiration was anthropomorphic, its attitude one of offering. The column is inclined at an angle of 17° to the vertical, which is the angle of the summer solstice in the city, so that the tower became a monumental sundial. A semicircular corona completes the tower's natural imagery.

The Montjuïc tower had to perform various functions: firstly, it had to be a node in the fixed radio communications service, as part of the infrastructure in support of small capacity short-range radio links; secondly, it had to provide

connections for automatic mobile phone services; and, finally, it had to be a substitute for the old Montjuïc Radio Station. Once the hectic Olympic games were over, it was no longer of use, and the tower has now become just a decorative element of the city landscape.

Collserola Tower

Sir Norman Foster & Ass.

Location: Barcelona, Spain. **Date of completion**: 1992. **Client**: Municipality of Barcelona. **Architect**: Sir Norman Foster & Associates. **Scheme**: Telecommunications tower, restaurant-observation platform, and parking lot. **Photography**: John Edward Linden.

The project is a mixture of a traditional television tower with a concrete column and metal masts supporting the radio antennae themselves, all passing through a high tech filter characteristic of the architect.

The tower combines three basic elements: a concrete column, 4.5 m (15 ft) in diameter and 209 m (686 ft) high; a central body with 13 platforms, the height of a 23-story building, which houses the electronic equipment; and the cables that support the structure.

This communications tower, designed by Norman Foster, involved a complex engineering operation. Situated on one of the hills in the Collserola range, the structure occupies 10 ha (25 acres) of land situated 448 m (1470 ft) above sea level. The tower itself occupies only 3.5 ha (8.5 acres), while the rest of the site is a huge parking lot.

Squares

The concept of the square as a feature planned in a single stroke is recent in the history of town planning. Moreover, an expansion of this idea has occurred in both the functional and spatial senses. A square is no longer just a wide part of the street surrounded by buildings. The word now implies more ambiguous concepts that make the square a location. In addition, many squares now have no specific use, and are intended to do no more than provide a pleasant meeting place and give some character to areas that are run down or otherwise uncared for. This chapter is dedicated to the recent design and construction of squares internationally. Here we find not only cases of rehabilitation, but also projects that create a topography or have particular uses. And there are other projects that generate their own independent arguments in respect of their surroundings and in this way revitalize space. All these have one thing in common, however: the wish to create worthwhile spaces where people can meet and just be.

Federal Tribunal Plaza

Martha Schwartz, Inc.

Location: Minneapolis. Minnesota, USA. **Date of construction**: 1996. **Architect**: Martha Schwartz. Inc. **Area**: 4,645 m² (50,000 ft²). **Photography**: George Heinrich.

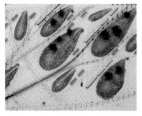

In the center of the city of Minneapolis, opposite the old city hall, this plaza has been developed in front of the new US Federal Tribunal, recently finished by the leading New York firm of Kohn Pederson Fox. The idea was to give the plaza a character that would speak for the city as a whole. It would be one large civic space that would also allow individual activities to be carried on. Elements of the actual landscape of Minnesota have been used, and these have acquired a new value when placed in the plaza. When taken out of their context, elements become sculptural, and these are capable of symbolizing both the natural features of Minnesota, and the way man has manipulated them for his own purposes. The most characteristic element of the space is a number of oblong tumuli, covered in vegetation, running east–west.

The long tree trunks used for benches are evocative of one of the state's most important economic activities: it has a long timber industry tradition. These two main elements are placed on a neutral plane that takes up nearly all of the plaza: a pavement of bands running towards the Federal Tribunal building itself.

The plaza is especially sensitive to the Minnesota climate's abrupt changes of season. In winter, the snow leaves only the edges and the central path visible. In spring and summer the tumuli are full of color. Some are permanently green, while others are covered with white narcissi or blue squills, setting off the blue banding of the pavement surface.

Schouwburgplein

West 8

Location: Schouwburgplein, Rotterdam, The Netherlands. **Date of design**: 1990. **Date of completion**: 1992–1995. **Architects**: West 8. **Scheme**: Public space. **Photography**: Jeroen Musch.

Schouwburgplein occupies a prestigious position in the center of the Dutch city of Rotterdam. Surrounded by stores and offices, and close to the central train station, it is one of the cultural centers of the city.

In addition to the municipal theater and a complex of concert halls, it now includes the recently built Pathé multiscreen cinema. What West 8's team of architects found before undertaking the project

was a place of little character, much affected by the existence of a very run-down underground parking lot below the square.

The purpose of the scheme was to encourage wider use of the square. The renovated space retains the quality of emptiness that already existed. The way the sun passes over the square throughout the day determined how it should be divided up into different sections, with different materials used for the pavement in each one. As an additional attraction, four enormous hydraulic post-cranes more than 35 m (115 ft) in height take up different positions throughout the day. People can put a coin in the control panel and direct them as they wish, thus constantly changing the appearance of the square.

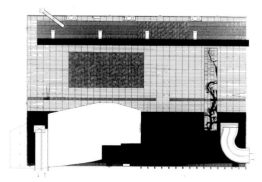

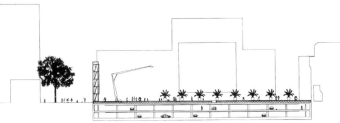

Citizens' Square

Kenzo Tange Associates

Location: Tokyo, Japan. **Date of construction**: 1991. **Architects**: Kenzo Tange Associates. **Photography**: Osamu Murai, Shinkenchiku Shashiubu.

The Tokyo Municipality's headquarters and square are located in a district of Tokyo called Shinjuku, on three adjoining blocks belonging to the Municipality that join Shinjuku park to the west, surrounded on the remaining sides by office blocks along edges of the multilevel highway.

One of the project's most important features is that this huge civic space was planned for the middle of a landscape of high-rise buildings, in a city that has hardly any parks, and where the pedestrian feels lost among huge office blocks, stores, parking lots, and urban highways. There are no other examples of squares in Tokyo and so it is inevitable that reference should be made to the historic squares of Europe, where great civic buildings traditionally have public spaces in front of them, and where an important part of city life is played out.

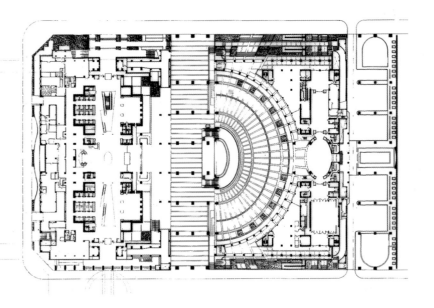

Solid Square

Nikken Sekkei

Location: Kanagawa, Japan. **Date of construction**: 1995. **Architects**: Nikken Sekkei. **Photography**: Kokyu Miwa Architectural.

Solid Square forms part of a complex of offices, apartments, and services next to Kawasaki station in the Japanese city of Kanagawa, 20 minutes from Tokyo station. It serves both as an entrance atrium for the 100 m (330 ft) high office blocks and, in the transition zone between the interior and exterior of the building, as a place for relaxation. Inside the atrium is a large pool, 27 m (90 ft) across, which dominates the space and holds the visitor's attention. Every hour, the silence of this circular sheet of water is interrupted by a gentle bubbling as the water in the pool is replaced. The sound breaks the dominant silence. The water, which is only 7 cm (3 in) deep, can be drained and the whole area converted into a large arena that can be used for other events. Apart from the water, light is the other element that plays an important role in this atrium. Up the vertical walls from ground to first floor level, a large unbroken glass surface gives an unobstructed view of the gardens outside.

Pershing Square

Legorreta Arquitectos

Location: Los Angeles, USA. **Date of construction**: 1994. **Architects**: R. Legorreta, N. Castro, V. Legorreta, G. Alonso. **Photography**: Lourdes Legorreta.

Pershing Square, more than 120 years old, is a historic plaza in the city of Los Angeles, California.
The square is a rectangle with proportions of approximately 1:2, surrounded by streets with very dense traffic. On all four sides, there were previously entry and exits ramps leading to the underground parking lot underneath. The plan was simple: locate the entrances on the four corners, away from the square, allowing easy access; concentrate vegetation around the edges in an attempt to protect the square from noise; and, at the same time, hide the cars entering and leaving the parking lot, thus freeing the central area for the enjoyment of the people in the neighborhood.

The result of these decisions is a square slightly lower than the surrounding streets and with planting all around, which separates it from the buildings. Onto this area the architects have projected a plan for a plaza as if they were founding a new city, as a metaphor for and homage to the foundation of the Spanish cities in America, and, in particular, to the origin of Los Angeles.
The first step in this development of the square was to trace out two imaginary lines in the form of a cross: the longer arm runs north–south and the smaller one east–west. On this primary plan are placed the elements of the plaza in the same way that public buildings are placed on the grid of Spanish towns in the traditional way.

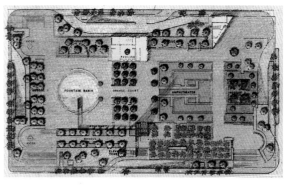

Plaça de la Constitució

J. A. Martínez Lapeña, E. Torres Tur, J. Esteban, A. Font, J. Montero

Location: Girona, Spain. **Date of construction**: 1993. **Architects**: J. A. Martínez Lapeña, E. Torres Tur, J. Esteban, A. Font, J. Montero. **Photography**: Lourdes Jansana.

In 1983 the Municipality of Girona decided to dedicate a plaza to commemorate the Spanish Constitution of 1978. For this they chose a triangular plot of land located in the outskirts of the city. Limited on one side by the Gran Vía de Jaime I and the new building of the Banco de España, on the other side it borders a college and an access ramp for an underground parking lot. The architects have built the plaza on the basis of a metaphor: "The plaza is a flowerpot in the city." The planners wanted to be faithful to this image and their first job was to think of the shape that a flowerpot might take; how it had to be able to hold fragments of nature in the middle of the city, in the same way that a flowerpot does in a house.

But walls are made not of clay but of concrete. They are not soft, smooth shapes that adapt to the hand, but have sharp angles that can harm it. These walls express the result of all the tension generated between the fragment of nature, fenced in and constrained, and the city that encircles it. These long polyhedral shapes are like tectonic folds rising from the earth that, unable to support the forces they are subjected to, break into crystalline forms that immediately solidify on contact with the air.

Place des Terraux

Christian Drevet

Location: Lyons, France. **Date of construction**: 1994. **Architect**: Christian Drevet. **Photography**: Eric Saillet.

This square is located in the middle of historic Lyons, and is the largest public space in the city. The buildings around it have grown up gradually since its creation in the 17th and 18th centuries. The project has tried to minimize the amount of work carried out on the square, with each decision prudently thought out, and full recognition given to the values of the location The first job was to slide the sculptured Bartholdi fountain gently from the middle of the square to the north façade and turn it through 90° so that it faces the Palais St-Pierre. This minimal movement achieved surprising results: it gave order and clarity to the undifferentiated space of the square and suddenly gave emphasis to the façade of the Palais St-Pierre. The next step in Cristian Drevet's reasoning was simple: change the look of the square, so that all the different elements are linked, to give some level of civic cohesion and make this public space justify its existence.

He has used only two materials to do this: water and light. Sixty-nine fountains have been set into the paving, with their jets forming a spurting forest. The murmur of the sprinklers, like the whisper of leaves, competes with the urban traffic. This is a place for strolling, chatting and relaxing.

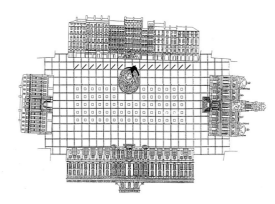

Tanner Fountain

Peter Walker

Location: Cambridge, Massachusetts, USA. **Date of construction**: 1985. **Architect**: Peter Walker. **Associates**: SWA Group. **Scheme**: Design and construction of an urban square. **Photography**: P. Walker, A. Ward.

The space chosen for the Tanner fountain was a loosely defined area where a number of paths crossed. It was an empty space between the Georgian brick buildings of Harvard, the modern science center planned by J.L. Sert, and the commemorative Victorian Gothic assembly hall. However, since it was one of the few open spaces on campus, the area was heavily used.

The challenge for Peter Walker was to make people aware of the place and its identity without restricting the usual movement through the locality.

There are 159 round stones measuring 1.2 x 0.6 x 0.6 m (4 x 2 x 2 ft) set haphazardly like cobbles in a circle 18 m (60 ft) in diameter between the asphalt and the lawn of a parterre. They are placed with no geometric relationship with each other or even with the asphalt path.

A fine mist some 6 m (20 ft) in diameter and 1.5 m (5 ft) high rises from the center of the stone circle, formed by five concentric rings of water sprinklers buried in the asphalt. In winter, when the temperature drops below zero, the water mist is replaced by steam from the heating system of the adjacent science center. The snow that falls on the ground melts at a different speed from that falling on the stones, but the resulting configuration is impossible to predict since wind and shade from the trees also have an effect. The water in its different forms becomes fire at night, when the mist or steam reflects and refracts the light projected upwards from the ground.

Plaza de Olite

Francisco José Mangado Beloqui

Location: Olite, Navarre, Spain. **Date of construction**: October 1996 – January 1998. **Client**: Municipality of Olite. **Architect**: Francisco José Mangado Beloqui. **Associates**: Fernando Redón, Arturo Pérez (supervisor). **Scheme**: Design and construction of urban plaza with access to underground galleries, street furniture, landscaping, and lighting. **Photography**: Francesc Tur.

The site is in the medieval village of Olite. The architect had to take into account the existence of old galleries constructed in the 11th and 12th centuries, of great historical importance, that were probably the entrance to the cellars of a palace. There were three problems to be solved by the architects. Firstly, they were obliged to make uniform a geometrically asymmetrical shape that had arisen from random urban growth; it was also decided that the underground galleries should be able to communicate with the outside, even though they had remained hidden for centuries. Lastly, there was the issue of the juxtaposition of old and new materials. Three sections can be seen on the ground: the steps into the plaza, the boulevard, and the plaza space itself. The geometric configuration of the boulevard is completed by street furniture, benches, lights, and fountains, laid out in a line, achieving a horizontal effect, in contrast with the verticality of the foot of the walls. As to materials, it was decided to use quarried stones with a grayish tone, a contrast with the original that confers autonomy on the new creation. With the geometrical theme continued by means of pyramids, circles, and cones, the whole layout of the complex is unified.

Plaza Berri

Peter Jacobs, Philippe Poullaouec-Gonidec

Location: Montreal, Quebec, Canada. **Date of completion**: 1992. **Client**: Municipality of Montreal. **Architects**: Peter Jacobs, Philippe Poullaouec-Gonidec. **Associates**: Beauchemin, Beaton, Lapointe Inc.; Consultants Geniplus Inc.; Montreal City Council. **Scheme**: Urban square for public use in the center of Montreal. **Photography**: Philippe Poullaouec-Gonidec.

The Place Berri is located right in the middle of the Latin quarter. This inclined plane, covered with lawn and framed by lines of silver maple trees and thorn trees, which forms a green open space like the eastern slope of Mont Royal, symbolizes the terraced foot of the mountain that the city has erased. The water that runs at an angle to the space symbolizes that other watercourse which gushes out of old terraces and disappears into the city to flow later into the invisible river. Melvin Charney's sculptures, metaphorically crossed by bridges and streets that remind one of the structure of the city, take action physically as cascades which cross the square. The main area, paved with hundreds of pink granite slabs, placed some 90 cm (3 ft) below the level of the sidewalks, leads to an immense ice rink open five months of the year. A retaining wall of polished black granite, 40 cm (1.3 ft) wide, separates the square itself and the inclined plane; 46 cm (1.5 ft) high and running the whole width of Place Berri, it is also used as a bench for eating. An area with reddish gravel, under the shade of three rows of silver maples, runs along the whole north façade. The square has become a meeting place invoking ample and diverse use of the whole space.

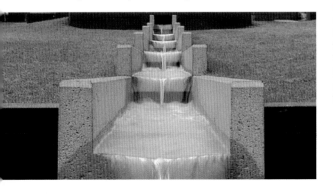

Promenades and streets

This chapter is dedicated to analyzing streets and promenades. It includes observation and interpretation of the most interesting landscaping proposals in the contemporary urban context: all those streets, avenues, promenades, or any urban roadway that makes up the city landscape. All the projects presented meet the criteria and principles that qualify them for this book: that can be summed up as the way in which they possess certain physical, cultural, historical, or humanistic characteristics. All these examples have been included because of their special attention to the resources provided by nature (light, water, vegetation) as well as for their understanding of the changing rhythms of life.

Public spaces in Nantes city center

Bruno Fortier & Italo Rota

Location: Nantes, France. **Contest**: 1991. **Date of construction (1st phase)**: 1992–1994. **Client**: Municipality of Nantes. **Architects**: Bruno Fortier, Italo Rota. **Associates**: Jean-Thierry Bloch (engineer), Roger Narboni (lighting), Jean-Claude Hardy (landscaping). **Photography**: Phillippe Ruault.

This project by Bruno Fortier and Italo Rota is the result of a contest announced by the Municipality of Nantes in 1991 for the renovation of an important area of public space in the center of Nantes. This was occupied by large stretches of parking lot and the remains of earlier commercial and even military activities, utilizing the two rivers, the Loire and the Indre, that form the basis of this urban wasteland.

The fact that this extensive area had previously been wide open, "a large emptiness," meant that this great expanse of space, much larger than one's normal idea of urban space, should be preserved, but at the same time properly cleaned up and organized according to the uses to which it was to be put. There had to be some way of directing the various kinds of traffic that would pass through it. Using street furniture and all kinds of urban accessory constructively the project managed to create an atmosphere totally opposite to the former disorder and desolation. The area was adapted to the functional needs of the contemporary city machine: traffic flow and transport requirements.

Overtown Pedestrial Mall

Wallace, Roberts & Todd: Gerald Marston

Location: Miami, USA. **Date of construction**: 1994. **Architects**: Wallace, Roberts & Todd: Gerald Marston. **Photography**: Gary Knight & Associates.

Overtown is the name used for the African-American district of Miami, where this pedestrian zone project is now located.

The Overtown pedestrian zone is part of a policy of revitalization, both economical and cultural, to stimulate both private investment and community pride in this historic district.

The project and its execution were carried out in the record time of four months, all the more commendable considering that the process involved public bodies, residents' associations, and such groups as landscape architects, civil engineers, and even a local artist,

Gary Moore. The latter, together with Gerald Marston, the landscape architect of the firm Wallace, Roberts & Todd, were the leading lights behind the genesis and coordination of the project's basic concept, in which special importance was given to historical and cultural references, the sense of African-American vibrancy, and the use of metaphoric meaning.

The project consists of two elements: one involving the closure of a section of the public highway to traffic; and the other, perpendicular to the first, running under the Dade County Railroad.

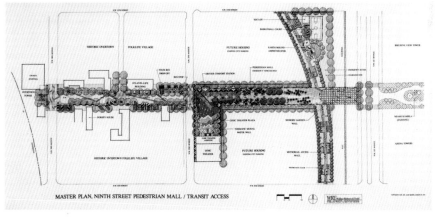

MASTER PLAN, NINTH STREET PEDESTRIAN MALL / TRANSIT ACCESS

Sea Front Promenade in La Barceloneta

J. Henrich, O. Tarrasó, J. Artigues, M. Roig, A. M. Castañeda

Location: Barcelona, Spain. **Date of construction**: 1996. **Architects**: J.Henrich, O. Tarrasó, J. Artigues, M. Roig, A.M. Castañeda. **Photography**: David Cardelús, Josep Gri, Jordi Henrich, Juli Espinás, David Manchón.

The Plaza del Mar and the new Paseo Marítimo occupy an area that until 1994 was full of public restrooms, snack bars, and sports clubs. These took up the entire front of La Barceloneta, the old fishing quarter, and cut off any relationship with the sea. Thanks to the Coastal Law it was possible to clear all areas of the coast that

came under public domain. Once the structures had been removed from the beach, the streets of La Barceloneta looked out to sea with no intervening obstacles; preserving these perspectives was the most important aim when it came to deciding the level of the new promenade. In order to integrate the two fully, it would be the same as that of the fishing quarter. With no need to worry about differences of level, the pedestrian can reach the large area of promenade from any street around.

The whole promenade is paved with gray-green quartz, which has textures and reflections very reminiscent of the sea; the stones are placed in lines of different widths which extend to the limits of the La Barceloneta area.

The irregular edge of the promenade on the built-up side, with little plazas looking out to sea, offers many more possibilities than a promenade with a uniform cross section. These variations in dimension by themselves define the diverse character of the spaces, which is underlined by the location of the street furniture.

Champs Élysées remodeling

Bernard Huet

Location: Paris, France. **Date of construction**: 1994. **Client**: Municipality of Paris. **Architect**: Bernard Huet. **Associates**: Olivier Bressac, Jean-Baptiste Suet (project designers); Omnium (engineering); Jean-Michel Wilmotte, Marc Dutoit (street furniture); GTM-DS (parking lot construction). **Photography**: Alessandro Gui, Alexandra Boulat.

Without doubt, the Arc de Triomphe is a memorable focal point from any perspective. But in regard to the architecture flanking the Champs Élysées it is above all the alignment and dimensional unity, rather than the somewhat modest quality of its façades when considered separately, which contribute to the coherence of this urban composition. As Bernard Huet says, the chief factors in this context are, for instance, the surface of the paving, the alignment of the trees, and the design of the street furniture.

The sidewalks, which are all at the same level, and therefore needed a proper drainage system designed, have been organized into two groups differentiated by the treatment of the paving. The pedestrian promenade, which is completely empty except for the exits from the subway and parking lots, has been designed with large light-gray granite slabs, punctuated by small blue-gray tiles. In the second group of sidewalks, between the new line of trees and the street furniture, the rhythm is marked by small light-colored tiles, cut by a series of darker double bands going across, in line with the trees. This system serves as a basis for the urban furniture. This

concept and the unity of aspect, color, and material sought by the project designers should reinforce the perception of space and the coherence of an urban plan to which contributions throughout the centuries have been the fruit of the same unique straight thinking in this regard.

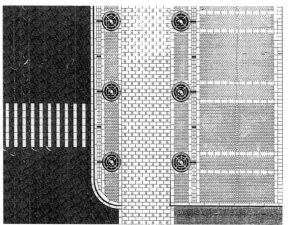

The Citadel

Martha Schwartz

Location: City of Commerce, California, USA. **Date of construction**: 1990–1991. **Architect**: Martha Schwartz. **Photography**: G. Leadmon.

Landscaping design is a doctrine, a way of perceiving the human being and our relationship with nature and the universe. Martha Schwartz starts with the idea that man, especially in North America, has used and abused Mother Earth; by becoming materialistic and losing contact with nature, we have lost a large part of our perception of ourselves. The apparent dislocation operating in the human environment does not, however, cancel out

our inspiration. Rather, it constitutes our starting point for working.
In the Citadel, the origin of the inspiration is in the form of the old factory of UniRoyal Tire and Rubber. On a piece of ground paved like a checkerboard in tones of gray, green, and ochre, lines of date palms planted in whitened tire like containers converge towards a plaza that takes us to another time and a different place.

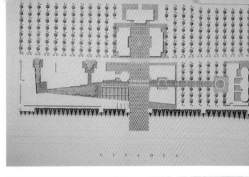

CITADEL

East Couplet Street urban improvement

Randall D. Beck, Carol F. Shuler, Kevin Berry

Location: Scottsdale, Arizona, USA. **Date of construction**: 1995. **Client**: Cities of Scottsdale and Phoenix. **Architects**: Randall D. Beck, Carol F. Shuler, Kevin Berry. **Associates**: Sandy Gonzales Conner (design and construction contracts administrator). **Photography**: Richard Maack, Carol Shuler.

The renovation undertaken in the East Couplet Street area comprised the development of a garden which winds along the paths, providing spaces of different sizes. The objective was to convert

this garden zone into a bird sanctuary. The planting was selected with the aim of providing cover and food for a wide variety of bird species. Trees and bushes were planted to act as windbreaks, deaden the noise of the traffic, and provide shade to people using the area. In the center of the Hummingbird Garden, five steel sculptures were installed, a little over 4.5 m (15 ft) high, which evoke the form of flower corollas. The configuration of the walks reproduces on the ground the shape of these flower sculptures. Low winding walls have been built along the walks and mini-plazas for people to sit, while the pavement has been painted red and ochre, the colors of the flowers alluded to by the sculptures. The effect achieved contributes to the transformation of an area previously not particularly pleasant for walking and leisure into a place of relaxation, with a highly original concept of modern aesthetics.

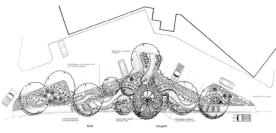

Cleveland Gateway

Sasaki Associates Inc.

Location: Cleveland, Ohio, USA. **Date of construction**: 1994. **Architect**: Sasaki Associates Inc. **Scheme**: Sports complex, baseball stadium, basketball stadium, and parking lot. **Photography**: Sasaki Associates.

The client was a foundation which contracted Sasaki Associates Inc. to design and construct an urban sports complex in the center of Cleveland. The project, which was located on an 11 ha (27 acre) plot of land below Public Square, included: an open-air baseball stadium for the Cleveland Indians, with a capacity of 45,000 spectators; a multi-use stadium for 20,000 spectators used by the Cleveland Cavaliers basketball team; a residential zone and a parking lot for 2100 vehicles next to it.

One important objective of the original project was the incorporation of this entertainment and sports area into the financial center of the city, at the same time obtaining a space that would allow the economic development of the zone to continue.

Sasaki Associates was responsible for the final design of the plan, the formal documentation, and the administration of the construction phase in all the locations, including plazas, streets, signage, and designs for traffic flow and control.

Schiedgraben and Hirschgraben in Schwäbisch Hall

Wilfried Brückner

Location: Schwäbisch Hall, Baden-Württemberg, Germany. **Date of construction**: 1990–1992. **Client**: Municipality of Schwäbisch Hall. **Architect**: Wilfried Brückner. **Associates**: Rolf Kronmüller (architect); Stiefel Engineering Office (surveying); Volker Ellsässer (landscaping); Edgar Gutbub and Michael Turzer (artistic collaboration). **Photography**: Wilfried Dechau.

The city's architecture is characterized by its ancient historical center: half-timbered houses and a city wall with bridges and turrets. Following ecological principles, materials from the project and from other demolition sites was collected, sorted, and used on the surfaces, materials which could both be reused and provide the basis for a diverse flora to flourish.

A flight of steps rising from the inner wall of the city joins two old defensive structures; steel structures that the sculptor Turzer designed together with the architect have been erected on these ruins. The weight and naturalness of the stone is dissolved in the transparency and technical perfection of the steel, so that the observer feels at the same time and in the same way both horizontal tranquillity and vertical growth. The continuity of the trench and the high walls of natural stone are interrupted by modern constructions: stairs, doorways, and roofs made of steel appear in spots that mark the ruined towers. The bases of these are made from the ashlars in the original walls, while the transitional layers to the foot of the steel construction are made of treated stones. A work made of steel bars forms a figure with an aeronautical air, partly covered by perforated sheets and a colored, varnished board. The bodies form rhythms in conjunction with the wall. The aesthetic effect complements the functionality of this architectural work which, conscious of its meaning, uses the historical substance and develops it from the original idea.

Christiania Quartalet urban remodeling

Niels Torp

Location: Oslo, Norway. **Date of completion**: 1994. **Client**: Aspelin Ramm AS. **Architect**: Niels Torp Arkitekter MNAL. **Associates**: Pal Ring Giske, Per S. Schjeldsoe, Trine Rosenberg, Lina Hyll; Selmer AS (contractor). **Area**: 20,000 m² (215,000 ft²). **Scheme**: Remodeling and construction of space for offices in a new development in the historic center of Oslo. **Photography**: Jiri Hayran, Hans Wrettling.

The urban area known as Christiania Quartalet forms part of a neighborhood in the ancient heart of Oslo dating from 1624. The colors, materials, and details used in the project reflect the historical importance of this part of the capital city.

Before starting the remodeling, the architects found themselves with a series of buildings with very little in common as far as size and height were concerned. It was aesthetically desirable to concentrate more on the façades facing the street than on the street itself. For this reason, the various walls on the block had to be dealt with differently depending on the surrounding environment. Obviously, one of the most important aspects of the project was the construction of a large new building opposite the Norges Bank (Royal Bank of Norway). In this case, the budget meant that prefabricated concrete elements had to be used in place of blocks of natural stone (as had been planned in the original project). Once again, in order not to be out of tune with the surroundings, the walls were painted the same color as the neighboring bank. Once more, the old was inspiring the new.

Indiana White River State Park Promenade

Angela Danadjieva & Koenig Associates

Location: Indianapolis, USA. **Date of completion**: 1988. **Client**: White River State Park Development Commission. **Architect**: Angela Danadjieva & Koenig Associates. **Scheme**: Recovery plan for the riverside. **Photography**: T. Hursley, J.F. Housel, A.Danadjieva

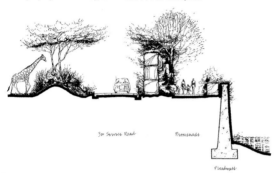

3m Service Road   Promenade

Floodwall

The promenade projected by Angela Danadjieva on the bank of the White River is part of a vast urban plan aimed at recovering the riverside as it passes through the center of Indianapolis. The specifications from the White River State Park Development Commission concentrated on accessibility for the public, by mixing leisure with the historical and cultural identity of the place and encouraging wider integration through the recurrent and symbolic use of Indiana limestone. The promenade is nearly 5 m (16 ft) wide and follows the gentle curve of the White River, flanked by 1272 irregular blocks of Indiana limestone, placed in such a way that they form an environment that is a combination of rustic naturalism and sculptural abstraction. The smoothly undulating outline allows different sequences to be created along the route, and the resulting variety of perspectives, textures, and sensations is one of the principal achievements of the project.

Different species of tree help to suggest the formal division of the promenade, articulated in four landscape variations: the amphitheater, the rose gallery, the bas-relief and one dedicated to the geological history of the limestone. These four sectors link the recreational purpose of the promenade with an educational impulse to the project.

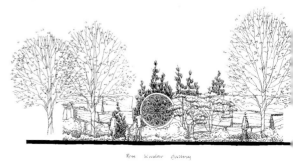

Rose Window Gallery

Voie Suisse

Georges Descombes

Location: Lake Uri, Switzerland. **Date of completion**: May 1991. **Client**: Municipality of Geneva. **Architect**: Georges Descombes. **Associates**: C. Chatelain, B. Spichiger (botanists), A. Coboz (urban development), H. Cauville (writer and critic), A. Leveille, R. Schaffert (architects and town planners), F-Y. Morin (art critic), M. Pianzola (art historian), B. Tottet (geographer), J.P. Cetre (civil engineer). **Scheme**: Routing and renovation of a footpath around a lake in Switzerland. **Photography**: Georges Descombes, Françoise Goria, Herve Laurent.

The Voie Suisse is a 35 km (56 mile) footpath around Lake Uri. The 26 cantons of the Swiss Confederation were involved in routing and building it. Each of them assumed responsibility for a section, without losing sight of the communal sense of the project. The extent of the stretches awarded to each canton was decided in terms of the number of inhabitants. Different types of action were suggested. The idea was to preserve the substance of the path while ensuring its accessibility to users; thus a great number of different levels were explored, with steps of wood and grass built into slopes so that people could feel and observe the landscape from high up. In other instances, there was a desire for reevaluation: introduced in this respect was the work of the musician Max Neuhaus, who installed a sound system with loudspeakers in a clearing in the woods which allowed one to listen to the life hidden within. In 1991, after the celebrations to mark 700 years of the

Swiss Confederation, many of the more ephemeral elements of this project disappeared; the site became overgrown, but a discreet trace remains, ready to be rediscovered on some future occasion.

Gavá Walk

Imma Jansana

Location: Gavá, Barcelona, Spain. **Date of completion**: 1992. **Client**: Municipality of Gavá and Biology Faculty of the University of Barcelona. **Architect**: Imma Jansana. **Associates**: S. Juan, J. Navarro (special planning), Bet Figueras (landscaping), F. Giro (botanical supervision), C. de la Villa. J. Lascurain, N. Abad, M. Jorba (works supervision). **Scheme**: Restoration of a 20 km (12 mile) stretch of coastline in Gavá. **Photography**: David Cardelús.

For many years, Barcelona has maintained a slender and marginal relationship with its natural coastline. One of the recent efforts undertaken to protect what remains of this delicate ecosystem was the new coastal walk at Gavá, an operation forming part of an ambitious plan which includes the restoration of 20 km (12 miles) of coastline. The contribution from the town has been centered on simply tidying up a number of footpaths that run along the beach and across a landscape of dunes held in place by vegetation. In an environment where we can also find younger dunes, built up by the wind, two winding paved paths were designed that, flirting with the shore line, run parallel to the sea. The ecological impact from the construction of the path was minimized by rescuing all those plants affected by the route of the new paved areas and transferring them to a nursery.

San Francisco tram stop

Sasaki Ass. Inc.

Location: San Francisco, USA. **Date of completion**: 1998. **Architects**: Sasaki Associates Inc. **Scheme**: Canopy for a tram stop, signage, and pavement. **Photography**: Sasaki Associates.

The electric tram line of the San Francisco Municipal Company represents an important link in this city's public transport system. At the same time, it constitutes an element in the redevelopment of the southern Embarcadero seafront promenade. The initial designs for this canopy, consisting of a series of curves on the roof, was strongly criticized by locals and some shopkeepers in the area, who thought that the construction would block their precious view of the bay. Sasaki Associates. Inc were contracted by the Municipality in 1994 as urban design consultants to lead the team responsible for designing the canopy and coordinate the different public and private groups involved in the project. Sasaki identified three principal objectives in the design, starting with the urban context of the project and the needs of the seafront promenade. The canopies had to contribute to the civic and commercial revitalization of the neighborhood and at the same time preserve the bay views, so they were finally made of transparent plate glass. Finally, a modular system had to be used to reduce the cost of construction. The curved shape of the roof is the work of the artist Anna Murch and alludes to the dynamism of the waves of the bay and the distant hills beyond.

Urban parks

The projects grouped together in this chapter are here because of a terminology that is as broad as it is ambiguous: the term urban park has a complex meaning derived from the disproportionate growth of cities as well as the typological confusion generated by this urbanization. This selection of contemporary projects is intended only to outline the semantic breadth of what should be understood as an urban park.

Le Jardin Atlantique

François Brun, Michel Pena

Location: Paris, France. **Date of construction**: 1994. **Architects**: François Brun, Michel Pena. **Photography**: J.C. Ballot, P. Marechaux, M. Pena.

Le Jardin Atlantique is located literally on top of the train stations of Montparnasse and Pasteur, adding a surface area of 3.5 ha (8.5 acres) to Paris, won back from the railroad. Totally removed from the traffic flows and surrounded by recently constructed buildings, there is nothing to link it to traditional Parisian city gardens.

The project had to solve particularly complex problems, both technical and environmental, such as the depth of the soil and the load limits, a 700 space parking lot located over the railroad but under the garden, the presence of a hundred openings for lighting the spaces underneath, the ventilation shafts, and the shadows cast by the surrounding tall buildings.

The distribution of the park on the ground was organized around a large central square surrounded by a strolling area that separates it from the other zones. The garden is built on strips of land around this central lawn area, on the edges of which, on one side, are areas planted with trees, featuring a linked series of smaller themed spaces and, on the other, sports installations.

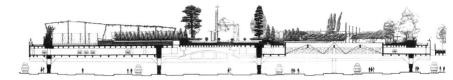

Vertical landscape: four projects in Manhattan

West 8

Location: New York, USA. **Date of construction**: 1996. **Architect**: West 8. **Scheme**: Design of four alternatives for urban revival in Manhattan. **Photography**: Jeroen Musch.

We had heard talk of this vertical city. We had seen pictures of its skyscrapers and looked forward, in its sublime expression of high rise construction, to finding striking pieces of vertical landscape, parks as ambitious as the Chrysler Building, the Empire State Building, the Rockefeller Center and others.

The first one we discovered was Central Park, the perfect empty space. A landscape sharply defined by 150 blocks, which enlivens the Manhattan skyline and satisfies the city's desire to expose itself to the sun. The remaining green spaces of Manhattan are in the form of Hanging Gardens of Babylon. The roof garden of the RCA building, the bamboo garden of the IBM building,

the interior cascades of Trump Tower, planting in the air and in the plazas: these can be considered genuine attempts to bring green inside and onto buildings and make it a part of the great spectacle that is Manhattan. However, this Babylonian ambition is revealed as

superficial and deceptive when it is examined more carefully. In order to awaken the potential of Manhattan, we explored the possibilities of using netting and the Manhattan principles of ambition and limitless verticality in landscaping projects.

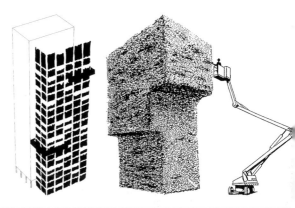

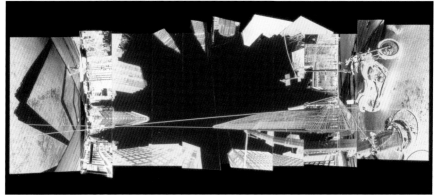

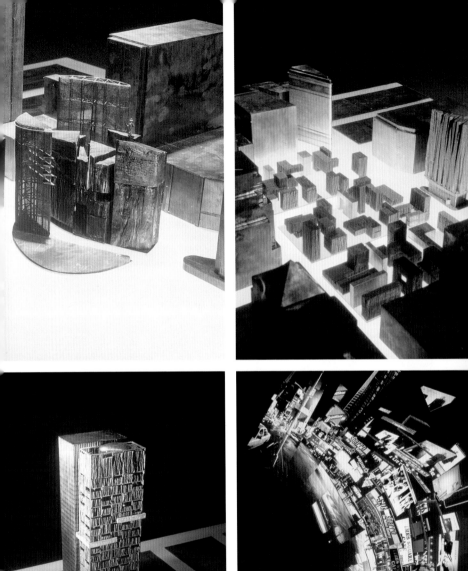

Santo Domingo de Bonaval Park

Alvaro Siza Vieira & Isabel Aguirre

Location: Rúa da Caramoniña, Santiago de Compostela, Spain. **Date of project**: 1990. **Client**: Consortium of the City of Santiago de Compostela. **Associates**: Alessandro D'Amico, Xorxe Nuno, Carlos Muro. **Photography**: Tino Martinez

The convent of Santo Domingo de Bonaval enjoys a fine situation on a hill to the north of the city of Santiago. De Bonaval Park, with a surface area of 3.5 ha (8.5 acres) occupies the same land as the convent, which dates from the 12th century, and is divided into three clearly differentiated areas. One is a terraced kitchen garden, the second an old oak grove, and the third an old cemetery. Working to transform such special surroundings into a public park meant respecting pre-existing features: remains of walls, ruins, old paths, tombs, and, above all, stone and water. Cleaning out the streams and fountains, the water was left to run where it wanted, this time to give life to the park itself.

In the lower part of the kitchen garden zone a small geometrically shaped garden used by the convent was restored. There were traces of old platforms at different levels, joined together by ramps. A sculpture by Eduardo Chillida, "The Door of Music," was placed on one of these platforms, against the walls of the enclosure, in a terraced area on the steep slope. The upper area, which is less populated, will house the Eugenio Granell Museum Foundation. Going through a door under an enormous lintel carved with the letter omega, one reaches the old cemetery, in the shape of an octagon.

The chosen materials and the way they were used bear witness to the extreme care with which the work has been done. These were the same materials that existed before–granite, grass, moss, water–even to the extent that the combinations of them are kept almost in the same plane as before.

Doosan Centenary Park

Sasaki Associates

Location: Seoul, Korea. **Date of construction**: 1993. **Architects**: Sasaki Associates. **Scheme**: Design and construction of a small urban park. **Photography**: Sasaki Associates.

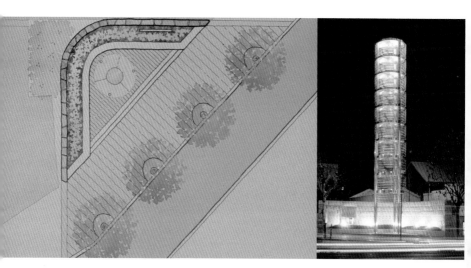

Sasaki Associates undertook the conceptual design of a small park in the historical center of Seoul. The park, situated on the site of the original Doosan store, was constructed on the occasion of the 100th anniversary of the Doosan Corporation, the oldest company in Korea. The idea behind the project was to use this historical place to create a memorable and lasting monument and to celebrate the past, present, and future successes of Doosan. The program for the project included a representation of the original store front, a time capsule, and a representation of the numbers 100 and 27, to indicate the number of years and the number of Doosan subsidiaries, respectively. The company wanted the park to be made from the best materials available and to be easily maintained.

The park, which measures some 94 m2 (1000 ft2), consists of a continuous parabolic wall of granite, a bed of flowers just in front of the wall, and a cylindrical tower 25 m (82 ft) high located in the center.

The wall provides a vertical space for the names of the 27 subsidiary companies, symbolizing unity (in a single wall) and at the same time the originality of each company. Parallel to the wall and the flower bed, there is a continuous bench on which to sit.

Story Garden

Doug Macy y Larry Kirkland

Location: Waterfront Park, Portland, Oregon, USA. **Date of construction**: 1993. **Clients**: City of Portland. **Architects**: Doug Macy, Larry Kirkland. **Associates**: David Oldfield (child psychologist).

Doug Macy and Larry Kirkland have created with their Story Garden a unique landscape for the Waterfront Park of Portland. Fables, myths, and reality are intertwined in a fantastic maze which is, in itself, an authentic metaphor for the journey of life. This is a surprising environment that entertains visitors by encouraging them to follow the route, posing them questions and offering them answers. The Story Garden is a two-dimensional maze measuring 18 m (60 ft) across, built on the luxuriant lawn of the Waterfront Park. Inside, the granite paths take a series of turns that never converge at a central point, but offer a huge variety of alternative routes. Dominating the area where the maze is situated is a small mound on which there is a throne of red granite, which looks down impassively on the tortuous paths of the monument. At the other end, there is a stone platform on which a door is built out of small geometrical stones, reminiscent of one of the construction kits in children's games. The perpendicular axis formed by these two figures is finished off by granite statues representing a tortoise and a hare, in a clear allusion to the fable. Thus, the four cardinal points of the maze are defined by the throne, the doorway, the tortoise, and the hare, and the whole perimeter is framed by a series of cubes similar to those used for the door. Macy and Kirkland interviewed child psychologists, parents, the police and people responsible for the maintenance of parks and gardens. The Story Garden is not simply a decorative element, a visual fancy; it could almost be thought of as a mental exercise, a simple hieroglyph full of symbolic elements and representations: a place that entices one in for leisure and reflection in equal measure.

Battery Park

Hanna & Olin, Paul Friedberg, Child Associates

Location: New York, USA. **Date of construction**: 1984–1995. **Architects**: Hanna & Olin, Paul Friedberg, Child Associates. **Client**: Municipality of New York and the Urban Development Corporation of the State of New York. **Associates**: Cooper Eckstut and Associates. **Photography**: Esto.

This park is an ambitious residential and commercial project on a 37 ha (92 acre) piece of land, located in Lower Manhattan alongside the World Trade Center and the Hudson river. The operation can be divided into two basic phases, and comprised the planning of an open public space that includes a mile long walk along the river and several miles of avenues and streets, as well as a considerable number of plazas and parks. The original space, which had no natural cohesion or urban identity, made the designers undertake a series of preliminary studies in order to find a way to connect this new public space with the urban and cultural idiosyncrasy of the city. In this way, it was proposed to integrate, for example, works of art in an everyday urban context.

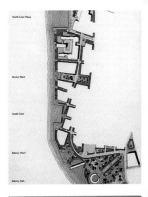

André Citroën Park

Jean Paul Viguier, Jean François Jodry, Alain Provost, Patrick Berger, Gilles Clément

Location: Paris. France. **Date of completion**: 1992. **Client**: Municipality of Paris, Department of Parks and Gardens. **Architects**: Jean Paul Viguier, Jean François Jodry, Alain Provost, Patrick Berger, Gilles Clément. **Scheme**: Restoration of a plot of land for the construction of a multifunctional park in the center of Paris. **Photography**: Alain Provost.

The Citroën Park is above all a conceptual garden of many parts: rejecting the idea of a multicultural forum or recreational use, it was built as a place for the contemplation of nature. Its current configuration dates back to the international competition to create gardens on the land spoiled by the Citroën car company. André Citroën Park, together with La Villette, is the most important green space created in Paris since the Second Empire. The central area, of 11 ha (27 acres), includes a wide esplanade on a gentle slope, closed off by two enormous hot-houses, a large rectangular parterre, and a series of levels that descend to the edge of the park. Flanking the end of the park furthest from the river, like two large ears, are the Black Garden and the White Garden. The first, thickly wooded, has an empty space in the middle; the second, very stony and light, with white flowering plum trees and plants with light-colored leaves, has no space in the middle.

To the northeast of the park, where the Black Garden ends, there is an area with many gardens, particularly the jardins sériels, poetic and intimate and laid out in a line. On the other side of the diagonal there is a more stony area, dotted about with towers and granite nymphs, and with a large canal feature.

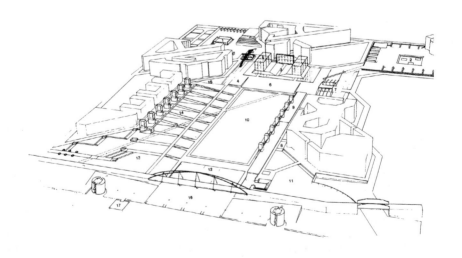

La Villette

Bernard Tschumi

Location: Paris, France. **Date of completion**: 1991. **Architect**: Bernard Tschumi. **Photography**: J.Y. Gregoire.

La Cité des Sciences, la Géode, le Grand Hall, le Parc de la Villette and la Cité de la Musique occupy the same area on the outskirts of Paris. This was one of the great urban debates of the 1980s and a much discussed subject in publications at the time. The construction of the monumental and scenic Cité de la Musique brought its architect, Christian de Portzamparc, the Pritzker Prize. The La Villette project was one of the star competitions of the 1980s yet, nevertheless, the celebrated scheme of the American Bernard Tschumi seems today a landscape in decline. This area is in competition with La Défense to be the least happy urban planning experience in Paris.

Place Stalingrad

Bernard Huet

Location: Paris, France. **Date of construction**: 1990. **Client**: Municipality of Paris. **Architect**: Bernard Huet. **Scheme**: Plaza for public use: landscaping, access bridge to the upper terrace, and street furniture. **Photography**: Francesc Tur.

The Place Stalingrad project was at first strictly related to the La Villette program, and was part of the Parisian plan for restoring the canals. Bernard Huet's strategy for this remodeling project can be summed up in five points, in order of priority: improving the image of the square as a public area, the only function of which is to be available for use by all; emphasize the spirit of the place, its essence and historical significance; carry out the great urban project formulated by Ledoux (and, especially, the later one by Girard) without resorting to strategies of continuity that make it appear totally finished; avoiding vulgar and direct pragmatic solutions, given that the role assigned to architecture is one of sublimating and emphasizing these aspects; and, finally, consciously refusing to give the same answer to every question, so that each part of the project can be dealt with in accordance with the stylistic language most appropriate to its nature.

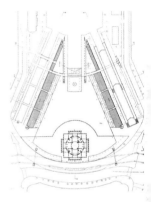

La Vall d'Hebrón Park

Eduard Bru

Location: Barcelona, Spain. **Date of completion**: 1992. **Architect**: Eduard Bru. **Clients**: Municipality of Barcelona. **Scheme**: Urban park for public use, sporting installations, changing rooms, office, and services. **Photography**: David Cardelús, Eduard Bru.

The 1992 Olympic Games in Barcelona gave the city a unique opportunity for urban renewal within the metropolitan area. The Olympic Ring provided the space that the sporting event so rightly deserved and bequeathed to the city a series of recreational areas. One of these is now the La Vall d'Hebrón Park: a complex of sports installations, equipment, and buildings that needed to be fitted in with neighboring development. This uncontrolled peripheral growth, which had been taking place for decades up to the limit of the Collserola hills, had to be rationalized.

Today this is a beautiful park for the public, in which all the sporting facilities left as a legacy of 1992 are used extensively.

Piccolo Giardino at Gibellina

Bruno Fortier & Italo Rota

Location: Gibellina, Trapani, Italy. **Date of construction**: 1985–1988. **Client**: Municipality of Gibellina. **Architect**: Francesco Venezia. **Associates**: Giuseppe Taibi (works assistant). **Scheme**: Remodeling a public plaza in a historical center. **Photography**: Mimmo Jodice.

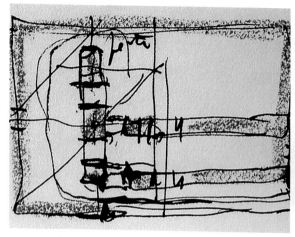

The city of Gibellina, destroyed in an earthquake in 1968, was the object of a series of plans which tried to reorganize its urban image. The Italian architect contributed to this reconstruction by means of a small public garden in which he has managed to reconcile concepts that are not usual in an urban setting. The small area is situated in a zone characterized by a slight slope up the hill dominating the location. Here has been located the central plaza, with the market, the library, houses, and the garden that closes off the island. The project was conceived as a difficult combination of a building and a park, as a public space, and, at the same time, a private one. This means architectural continuity of front elevations, creation of an accessible inner space that is in contact with the natural urban environment and that, finally, invites introspection and reflection, a dialog between the past and the present, carefully avoiding a clash of styles.

Peripheral parks

The only unifying parameter which the projects included here share is that of their location: the works chosen are situated halfway between urban area and nature, in an ambiguous no man's land. It is precisely this definition of location that distinguishes them from urban parks or squares. However, these projects also display a number of differences with respect to other aspects of landscaping, since peripheral parks do not insist on forced integration of green spaces into the city. The adjustment of the periphery aims to dignify marginal areas, create ecosystems that are fully valid both ecologically and aesthetically, and build a more intimate connection between the individual and nature.

El Besós Park

Viaplana & Piñón Arquitectes

Location: Barcelona, Spain. **Date of completion**: 1987. **Client**: Municipality of Barcelona. **Architect**: Viaplana & Piñón Architects. **Scheme**: Urban park for public use, sculptural trail. **Photography**: David Cardelús.

With the intention of returning lost space to the city, it was proposed to restructure this area according to a series of urban planning and landscaping criteria that have presided over the whole project: on the one hand, linking the park to the framework of the urban fabric, not only in a physical and material sense, but also in its most abstract and spiritual aspects, whether typological, tectonic, or landscaping; and, on the other hand, creating an area for collective enjoyment, emphasizing it as a place for dialog with the environment and one that is available to the people of the city.

In the planning stage, as well as considering physical factors, it was suggested there was a need to recover the identifying values of the place, both from the cultural point of view (typological tradition) and from the natural (selection of different species of vegetation in accordance with the climate and the landscape). At the same time, special emphasis was placed on the definition of spaces suitable for collective enjoyment, with a distribution of functional areas to be used for walking and for talking.

Culhuacán Historical Park

Grupo de Diseño Urbano

Location: Iztapalapa. Mexico. **Date of construction**: 1992. **Clients**: Culhuacán Community Center (National Institute of Anthropology and History). **Architect**: Grupo de Diseño Urbano. **Associates**: Elsa Hernandez (archeology), Juan Vanegas (history). **Scheme**: Design and construction of a historical theme park. **Photography**: Gabriel Figueroa

Recovering the history of a people is, sometimes, the prime objective of the landscape architect. The Culhuacán park uses historical and archeological remains as elements for organizing the space, where they are integrated into contemporary local culturural activities.

The basic objective consisted of recovering the historical character of the place and at the same time promoting the traditions of the local inhabitants. To achieve this, three thematic fields were established: the rescue of memory (the Aztec ruins), reevaluation of existing buildings (the former convent), and the creation of new areas. These three levels also had to re-create the type of environment of ancient Tenochtitlán's age of splendor. The overall compositional scheme adopted had to be orthogonal, in accordance with the urban outline and also with the orientation of the convent. As an element to generate interest in the site, a pool was proposed–a historical reference to the Aztec waterway–framed by the ruins of the ancient walls. An open air theater, with seating for 250, was built in the southeastern part of the park.

The special geometry of the different spaces and the use of local materials contribute to the way the park blends in with its surroundings. As an extension of buildings and historical remains that already existed, the Culhuacán park is a peaceful and tranquil spot which is also permanent, far from the vicissitudes of the present day.

Xochimilco Park

Grupo de Diseño Urbano

Location: Xochimilco, Mexico. **Date of construction**: 1992–1993. **Client**: Municipality of Xochimilco and Department of the Federal District. **Architects**: Grupo de Diseño Urbano. **Associate**: Jorge Calvillo. **Scheme**: Urban park for public use, sporting areas, greenhouses, information center, exhibition hall, shops, cafeteria, services, and offices. **Photography**: Jorge Sandoval.

The 280 ha (690 acres) of the park were used to create a natural bird sanctuary, a botanical garden with an area for gardening demonstrations, a recreational area with boating, a new lagoon, as well as a market selling plants and flowers, sports areas, greenhouses, and a visitors' information center. The information center is located in the access plaza, the heart of the park, a multifunctional building

which houses a small museum, an information post, a hall for temporary exhibitions, shops, cafeteria, services, and offices, in addition to a viewing point on the roof. The reddish concrete used is an allusion to tezontle, the local stone of the region, traditionally used for building. All the buildings are integrated into the landscape and are surrounded by paths, pergolas, vines, and brushwood fences, thus helping to preserve the natural character of the park's location.

Candlestick Point Cultural Park

Hargreaves Associates

Location: San Francisco, California, USA. **Date of construction**: 1985–1993. **Architecture**: Hargreaves Associates. **Associates**: Mack Architects, Doug Dollis. **Scheme**: Design and construction of an urban public park. **Photography**: Hargreaves Associates

The project arose in 1985 out of a joint initiative of the California Arts Council, the department of parks and the office of the architect for the state of California. Their objective was to integrate architecture, landscaping, and art in one location. The site is on the edge of the city of San Francisco, on some land reclaimed from the sea, in an industrial area buffeted by high winds. The plot, of 7.3 ha (18 acres), excluding an enormous area of open parking lot, is in the middle of a featureless urban landscape next to a sports stadium. There is a gentle grass-covered slope that extends directly down to the water. Depending on the direction of the wind, the conditions can be like a wind tunnel, and this intensifies the experience of visiting the cultural park.

Byxbee Park

Hargreaves Associates

Location: Palo Alto, California, USA. **Date of completion**: 1991. **Client**: City of Palo Alto. **Architect**: Hargreaves Associates. **Associates**: P. Richards, M. Oppenheimer (sculptures), Robert L. Davies (architect), Emcon (engineering). **Scheme**: Converting a garbage tip into a suburban park. **Photography**: Hargreaves Associates.

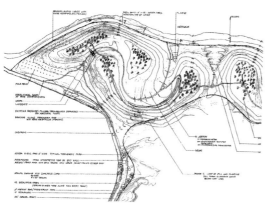

Byxbee Park is an interesting experiment in landscape recycling, inasmuch as it consists of the transformation of a 60.7 ha (150 acre) garbage tip into a coastal park on San Francisco Bay. Hargreaves's plan was to clean up the landscape and place sculptures to highlight the qualities of the location, such as the light and the breeze. The first step was to seal the garbage with a 60 cm (2 ft) layer of earth and 30 cm (1 ft) of clay. The upper layer of clay is shaped to produce mounds some 18 cm (7 in) high at the base of the slope to avoid erosion. To prevent this cover from cracking, and in view of the risk of toxic substances escaping due to the growth of large roots, it was decided not to plant trees. Instead, most of the park is covered by dense short grass, native to the area. The paths of crushed shells, some 1.8 m (6 ft) wide, wind along the contours of the park, and produce a special crunch when walked on. An earth wall, with a gap in it, marks the transition between the north part of the park, open and exposed, and the more sheltered areas, next to the marsh. Along the edge of the marsh, a series of tables and benches are sheltered from the wind and from here visitors can enjoy the view and watch the large population of migratory birds in this area of the park.

Papago Park

Steve Martino

Location: Phoenix. USA. **Date of completion**: 1992. **Architect**: Steve Martino. **Associate**: Jody Pinto. **Scheme**: Design and construction of a peripheral park and its irrigation system. **Photography**: R. Maack, S. Martino.

The progressive urbanization of the area and an uncontrolled demographic explosion of small mammals, together with a total lack of maintenance and protection in this natural park, were the reasons for the ecological disaster here. Having arrived at this situation it was necessary to take some sort of action that would serve as a catalyst for any future operations and give an indication that the park was going to change direction. The scheme included the elevation of a sculpture at the entrance to the park, a landmark in the immensity of the desert. The

highways, marking the limits of the park where they cross in one corner, only add harshness to the already arduous task of defining and giving content to the zone. Martino and Pinto's work makes a simple yet forceful contribution to the landscape: set against the speed of the highway, this is a static sculpture of sufficient dimensions to be seen and, set against the arid climate, it uses stone and native plant species as materials for expression. The structure consists of an aqueduct nearly 200 m (650 ft) long, with seven branches, small walls that spread sinuously across the adjacent terrain, irrigating the dry land.

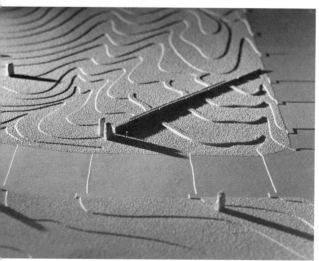

Princess Sofía Park

José Antonio Martínez Lapeña, Elías Torres Tur

Location: La Línea de la Concepción, Cadiz, Spain. **Date of construction**: 1990–1993. **Client**: General Directorate of Town Planning, Andalusia Board, Public Land Company. **Associates**: Iñaki Alday, Nuria Bordas, Arturo Frediani, Marisa García, Clara Jiménez, Eduard Mirallas, Joaquín Pérez, Inés Rodriguez, Quim Rosell. **Technical Architects**: José Maria Hervas. Carlos Sánchez. **Construction**: Fomento de Construcciones y Contratas. **Photography**: Fernando Alda.

In addition to one of the two zones projected for open air shows, these photographs show the general lighting system for the park: a number of masts, which are also used for irrigation, carry the lights that are suspended above the park.

The basic idea of the remodeling project is based on respecting and reevaluating the existing trees by means of a new area of park. There are four winding strips of land that follow the existing palm trees, planted between the lawn and edged by metal plates. In addition, new palm trees are planted to fill in the empty interstices to form continuous lines. These strips run the length of the park from north to south and, being separated, they define other similar strips that are paved with white gravel, in which the other, existing trees appear in haphazard order. Superimposed on these are two straight paths, also running north to south and paved with asphalt, that make the large area of the park more accessible to traffic. Another street, also asphalted and wider than the first, which is designed to be the axis for activities inside the park, crosses it from east to west. Eucalyptus trees are planted alongside this, taking advantage of the proximity of the water table, which makes the promenade a suitable area for the annual La Línea fair. To give better accessibility to the far reaches of the park there are a number of 3 m (10 ft) paths, parallel to the main promenade and crossing the strips of lawn. To the south of the promenade of eucalyptus there are two concrete buildings that are used for small open-air spectacles. There are also two large canopies, also made of concrete, to protect the temporary installation of kiosks or bars.

Le Domaine du Rayol

Atelier Acanthe & Gilles Clément

Location: Le Rayol Canade, France. **Date of project**: 1988–1997. **Landscape Architects**: Gilles Clément and Philipe Delian. **Associates**: François Macquert-Moulin (conservationist), Jean-Laurent Felizia, Jean-Michel Battin (gardeners), Albert Tourrotte (imports). **Client**: Conservatoire du Littoral. **Area**: 25 ha (62 acres). **Scheme**: Botanical garden. **Photography**: Alexandre Bailhache.

Le Domaine du Rayol occupies a particularly beautiful area of the Côte des Maures, on the French Mediterranean coast. Clément proposed to the Conservatoire the creation of an "austral garden," by which he meant, in his own words, "a complex for life's compatibility," where the real inhabitants are the flora planted in it, and which could also become a place for experimenting with the behavior of the different species when all are living together and in relationship with the climate. So, Clément divided the land into a small number of sectors, each one corresponding to a different area of the planet: Australia, New Zealand, Tasmania, South Africa, Chile, Mexico, California, and China. Many of the species planted over the six years of work were found in Europe, although a few were brought from their places of origin; others were planted by seed. The project was proposed as the creation of a garden for the improvement of plants: removing them from their natural habitats and replanting them in Le Domaine, the universal method of removing an organic element from its context and trying to maintain its vitality outside it, one of the best procedures. Clément calls La Domaine "a garden to understand," a place where the vitality and full growth of vegetation are the chief protagonists. He does not seek to create landscapes, but rather this is an operation of "ordered and planned reforestation," in the sense that the species recovered have clear autonomy with respect to man's colonizing experience in their area.

Le Jardin des Retours

Bernard Lassus

Location: Rochefort-sur-Mer, France. **Date of completion**: 1995. **Client**: Municipality of Rochefort-sur-Mer. **Landscape Architect**: Bernard Lassus. **Associates**: D. Anglesio, P. Aubry (landscaping), P. Donadieu (agricultural engineer). **Scheme**: Landscaping and historical restoration. **Photography**: Bernard Lassus, B. Poitevin

Starting with this landscaping operation, the architect tried to create a garden as a starting point for the cultural revitalization of this French city. Thus, Lassus proposed the idea of making a link between the city and the sea, giving a different scale to the connection between the town and the river Charente, without forgetting the important relationship with the historical past. With the planting of species of plant commonly considered to be from the interior, it has been possible to evoke the places of origin of those species and the historical period when they were introduced. Consequently Lassus calls them "plants for landscapes." A pedestrian link (357 m, 390 yds) was created between

the town and the Corderie building. There is a parallel access in the form of a ramp (140 m long by 21 m wide, 460 by 70 ft), which follows the ancient wall of Rochefort, parallel to the old industrial buildings. Nearby is the Maze of Battles, a landscape, a mediation between the river, the dikes, and the plants. This undulating garden can only be enjoyed from the inside and step by step. Finally, this garden also offers a simple walk by the river bank, in contact with the natural vegetation which borders it, principally comprising local woodland plants and trees.

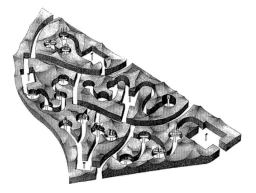

Poblenou Park

M. Ruisanchez and X. Vendrell

Location: Barcelona, Spain. **Date of completion**: 1992. **Client**: Municipality of Barcelona. **Architects**: M. Ruisanchez and X. Vendrell. **Associates**: S. Pieras, E. Prats (architects), M. Colominas, J. Consoia (agricultural engineering). **Scheme**: Recovery of an old industrial zone for the construction of an urban park. **Photography**: David Cardelús.

The old part of Poblenou forms part of the industrial expansion of the city of Barcelona that began at the end of the 19th century. The land consisted of waste material and was occupied by a number of industrial installations and a railroad station. Poblenou Park's configuration follows dunes running from the beach inland, through a break created between two walks. A Mediterranean woodland has been planted consisting of masses of bushes and groups of flowering trees.

The structure of the pedestrian walks in the park are in the form of a grid: longitudinally, a series of winding paths following the topography; across these, paths have been designed that are extensions towards the beach from the old streets of the neighborhood. These paths all have different surfaces, from colored concrete to impacted earth, depending on where they are and the directions they run. Each section of the grid has a different type of lighting: low beacons

beaming onto the pavement or standard lamps that project their light onto a small curved screen beyond.

The park has a system of water cannons that can provide irrigation in a way very much like the natural process of rain, while at the same time reducing the harmful effects of salinity brought by the wind from the Mediterranean.

Urban
monuments
and land art

It is difficult to judge the relationship
between art and nature from the
appearance of land art at the end of the
1960s. Now, nature is art. Now, not only
mountains, valleys, and atmospheric
phenomena but even open urban spaces
have become support, material, and
subject of new forms of artistic
intervention. Land art arose linked to the
minimalist idea that tried to break with the
decorative function of sculpture and was
nourished by the wish to dematerialize
works of art. The ephemeral nature of
works of land art (this is the principal
difference between the two types of works
included in this chapter) opened the doors
to the idea of art as an experience. The
examples that follow form a diverse
panorama which shows locations
dedicated to art in the search for new
connections between nature, art, and
urban life.

Mount Tindaya

Wrapped Reichstag

Tower of the Winds

Ice Walls

Boundary Split, Annual Rings, Formula Compound

Iceland Project

Fieldgate, Oak Tree, Elm Leaves, Red Pool

Bird's Nest, Empty Nest, Groups of Flowers

Toronto Project, Prefabrications, Frauenbad

Triangular Pavilion

La Grande Arche

Capsa de Mistos

Mount Tindaya

Eduardo Chillida Juantegui

Location: Fuerteventura, Spain. **Date of project**: 1996. **Architect**: Eduardo Chillida Juantegui. **Associates**: José A. Fernandez-Ordoñez, Lorenzo Fernandez-Ordoñez, Luis Ignacio Bartolomé Biot. **Photography**: Lorenzo Fernandez-Ordoñez, Daniel Diaz Font.

Making space in the bowels of Mount Tindaya means for Chillida creating a place between heaven and earth, from where to contemplate the horizon and deliver oneself up to light and the architecture that it creates.

The work on Mount Tindaya is on a world record scale for light in underground spaces, though these achievements are nearly always surpassed.

The space is located within the mountain in such a way that it is not affected by any of the currently known diaclases and dikes. Given the huge size of the hall excavated, an area of the mountain had to be found that would be unaffected by any sort of geological fracturing.

The opening for the sun was located on the south side of the mountain and that for the moon on the north, since a colder light was required. The opening that looks out to the horizon, to the infinity of the sea, has been hidden in a fold in the west side of the mountain, making use of a quarry and an existing road, which will serve as access. In order to preserve a clear vision of the horizon from the hall, the entrance tunnel has been located at a level a few meters lower than the hall.

In this way, visitors entering and leaving the monument will not appear in the line of sight to the horizon, out to sea from the space inside Mount Tindaya, but rather there will always be a neat horizon on view.

Wrapped Reichstag

Christo & Jeanne-Claude

Location: Berlin, Germany. **Date of realization**: 1995. **Architects**: Christo & Jeanne-Claude. **Associates**: Michael S. Cullen, Roland Specker Wolfgang Volz, Sylvia Volz. **Scheme**: Wrapping of the German Parliament building. **Photography**: Wolfgang S. Wewerka.

For 14 days, from 24 June to 7 July 1995, the German Parliament in Berlin, the Reichstag, was wrapped in a metallic fabric, tied down on all sides as if it were a parcel. Christo and Jeanne-Claude had been pursuing this idea since 1971. Twenty-four years of work and perseverance, involving the public and many institutions in the project, permitted them to realize their ambition with this emblematic new work. A contract was signed between the city of Berlin, government authorities in Bonn, and the artists whereby the artists had to provide:
– insurance for all the personnel and property involved with the city of Berlin and the federal government;
– complete and satisfactory removal of all the wrapping material;
– full cooperation with the Berlin community;
– personnel contracted from among the local inhabitants;
– communication with and access to the daily activities of the Reichstag during the process of the work.

The work was entirely financed by the artists, as on other occasions, when projects have been paid for by the sale of drawings, preliminary studies, collages, etc., thus dispensing with the need for sponsors, and guaranteeing the independence of the work. The artists used 10 ha (25 acres) of aluminized polypropylene material and more than of 16 km (10 miles) of cord of the same material, in order that, for a number of days, they could hide the Reichstag, the true symbol of German democracy, from public view.

Tower of the Winds

Toyo Ito & Associates

Location: Yokohama, Kanagawa, Japan. **Date of construction**: 1986. **Client**: Committee for the 30th Anniversary of Yokohama West Station. **Architect**: Toyo Ito & Associates. **Associates**: Gengo Matsui + O.R.S. (structure); TL Yamagiwa Inc. (lighting); Masami Usuki (programmer). **Photography**: Sinkenchiku-sha, Tomio Ohashi.

The Tower of the Winds is located on an urban center of accelerated energy typical of Japan's major cities, which are immersed in the vortex of the twin paradox about architecture that we are proposing.

The primitive ventilation and water tower that existed in the bus terminal square of Yokohama station has been re-covered, following its restoration, by an elliptical cylinder of perforated aluminum some 21 m (70 ft) high. When night falls, its surface loses all form. All that can be seen is a network that traps the essence of each moment, filters all the available environmental information, and interweaves it to produce the fabric that is the reality of the place.

The direction and speed of the wind as well as the intensity of the traffic noise are transformed into electrical impulses to become an ephemeral architecture of light. The tower is a mirror of its circumstances, and thus is not material. The tower is never the same, which makes it ephemeral, changing in essence.

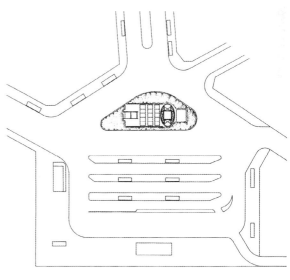

Ice Walls

Michael Van Valkenburgh Associates

Location: University of Harvard, Cambridge, Mass., USA. **Date of construction**: 1987. **Architect**: Michael Van Valkenburgh Associates. **Scheme**: Ephemeral installation in the form of a wall of ice. **Photography**: Hansen, C. Mayer, Michael Van Valkenburgh.

Michael Van Valkenburgh graduated as a landscape architect from the University of Illinois in 1977. He is professor and president of the department of landscaping of the Graduate School of Design of the University of Harvard (Massachusetts). In 1987, he undertook an experiment at Harvard which culminated in the installation, the following year, of a series of ice walls on the Radcliffe Yard of the campus. The design consisted of vertical panels, each 15.2 m long by 2.1 m high (50 ft by 7 ft). Made from a galvanized stainless steel mesh with a water channel along the top edge, the surface was sprayed to encourage the formation of small blocks of ice that finally finished up as a whole wall of ice. The extreme precariousness of the ice and the conditions of maintenance required certain techniques to be respected. So, with a view to the need to make repairs, the supply of water was located where it could be easily reached.

The channels were made of rubber, to make them less affected by the expansion of the water freezing inside and because, at lower temperatures, they were more flexible than plastic or metal. A heating cable, supplied by electricity or heat from the sun, controlled the freezing under extreme conditions. Both the increase in weight due to ice and the action of the wind introduced a factor of instability which was controlled by balancing the verticality using hydraulic jacks.

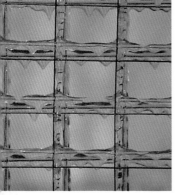

Boundary Split, Annual Rings, Formula Compound

Dennis Oppenheim

Location: St. John River. USA; US/Canada border; Potsdam, New York, USA. **Dates of realization**: 1968, 1968, 1982. **Artist**: Dennis Oppenheim. **Scheme**: Three ephemeral works of land art. **Photography**: Dennis Oppenheim.

Minimalism, land art, body art, conceptual art, installations, pieces, objects... Oppenheim has concentrated on the land art experience and so-called earthworks, especially during the periods between 1967 and 1969, and from 1973 onwards. In these, the works leave the galleries and museums and are transported to the great outdoors. The mountain, the sea, the countryside, even at times the city itself, will provide a new context for artistic creation. Land art, that in its time was considered as "the Anglo-Saxon variant of peasant art," originates from

suggestions similar to those of minimalism and endows the procedure and the material to be transformed by a value greater than the end result of the work. In accordance with this spirit, Oppenheim maintains that the important thing is not so much "what one does, but what drives one to do it," predicting moreover that "the movement of sensory pressures from the object to the place will be the greatest contribution of minimalist art." His interest in change urges him to experiment with deviations of course, transplants of material, transformations of energy, and the

breakdown of substances found in the natural world.

Iceland Project

Magdalena Jetelová

Location: Iceland. **Date of project**: 1992. **Architect**: Magdalena Jetelová. **Photography**: Werner Hannappel

A line traced by a laser separates the American and Eurasian continents. The Atlantic oceanic ridge is visible for more than 350 km (560 miles) in Icelandic territorial waters.

After a detailed study of the geography of Iceland, a concept was developed for a visualization of the intercontinental frontier that separates Eurasia from America. This island is the only place where it is possible to see, on the surface for more than 350 km (560 miles) the Atlantic mountain chain, which divides the two continental plates and runs more than 15,000 km (24,000 miles) under the ocean.

In the summer of 1992, Magdalena Jetelová went to Iceland with a small team of technicians to identify and represent the geological line between America and Europe.

Across the mountain range, from one end of the island to the other, this dividing line was redrawn using a laser beam. The photographs have become a document of the frontier, traced by laser across the rocky landscape, up and down the masses of lava or dissolving and disappearing into the steam from the geysers. But the artist's objectives did not stop there. She considers this work as part of a global process and not an end in itself: the division, the fracture into two, like the hope of renewal. The surprising act of cutting Iceland in two gives it a renewed beauty. The luminous line dividing the earth becomes part of the island; without it, the island could not exist in this way, and its power to fascinate resides in this total interdependence.

Fieldgate, Oak Tree, Elm Leaves, Red Pool

Andy Goldsworthy

Location: Poundridge, Dumfriesshire, Scotland. **Dates of realization**: 1993, 1994, 1994, 1995. **Artist**: Andy Goldsworthy. **Photography**: Andy Goldsworthy.

The work of Andy Goldsworthy (from Cheshire, UK, born 1956) is nourished by his immediate natural environment. The impact produced by direct contact with such elements as real as cold and rain, the weight of rocks, the vastness of sand, and the brightness and softness of other materials is nowadays restricted to the very limited worlds of children and artists, but, as Goldsworthy himself admits, "I need the effect of touch, the resistance of the place, the materials and the time..." Working directly with natural materials from the environment itself and without the artificial prosthesis of tools, he associates the triangular coordination of eye, hand, and mind with the world of the infantile state, with a child's admiration for minute things, their first attempts to handle small twigs and leaves. Goldsworthy weaves simple patterns and lines with colored leaves and thorns, superimposing them on the complex orders of slowly evolving nature. Lines drawn with leaves along the heavy branch of an oak are immediately recognized as human. The leaves of an elm extended the length of a rock remind one of the labors of a hardworking caterpillar on a summer's afternoon. But, he maintains, "I am not representing the primitive."

Bird's Nest, Empty Nest, Groups of Flowers

Nils-Udo

Location: Bavaria; Raimes Forest; Reunion Isles. **Dates of realization**: 1990, 1993, 1994. Artist: Nils-Udo.
Scheme: Various installations with reference to forms from nature. **Photography**: Nils-Udo.

"Nature interests me only so much!"
This defines the attitude of photographer and sculptor Nils-Udo, born in 1937 in the Bavarian town of Lauf. Since 1972 he has had exhibitions and installations in various places throughout the world and among the titles of his works is constant reference to forms from nature such as the sun, water, woods, valleys, bamboo, maize, or flowers. In some of his work notes, Nils-Udo expresses a series of ideas: "Draw with flowers. Paint with clouds. Write with water. Record the May wind, the fall of a leaf. Work for a storm. Anticipate a glacier. Bend the wind. Orient water and light..." There is, therefore, an evident desire to capture and record the currents of energy in the movements of nature, subject them to stress, and transform them into the power of expression.

 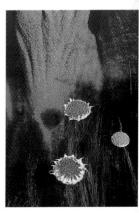

Toronto Project, Prefabrications, Frauenbad

Tadashi Kawamata

Location: Toronto, Canada; Tokyo, Japan; Zurich, Switzerland. **Dates of realization**: 1989, 1992, 1993.
Artist: Tadashi Kawamata. **Scheme**: Three constructions of ephemeral art. **Photography**: Tadashi Kawamata

Kawamata uses recycled wood as his raw material, and his work (social attitudes and shapes that transform the urban environment) speak to us of time, space, and the confrontation of rhythms. Four months of work were needed for the Toronto Project (1989), an open space between two neoclassical buildings located opposite a large shopping center. Following his usual method, Kawamata establishes a dialogue of contrast between static buildings and his own dynamic and ephemeral constructions of recycled wood. Prefabrications (Tokyo, 1992) is a good example of his work. This is an installation in the gardens of the Setagaya Museum of Art. Another of Kawamata's recent projects is Frauenbad (Zurich, 1993), in which the artist's work starts with the presence of some old bathing huts located on the river Limmat and the Helmhaus. In this case, his associates have been participants (alcoholics and drug addicts) in a rehabilitation program. His participation

consisted of building two new bathing huts, the symbolic purpose of which was to make an ironic statement on Protestant morality, which puts up walls so that the users cannot be seen: so, one of the bathing huts has been put into the river, far from the bank, so that it cannot be freely used; the other has been installed inside the museum, with the intention of showing the complex relationship between the inside and the outside. All of Kawamata's creations explore an ambiguous land of nothing, that seems to swing between urban land art and ephemeral architecture in form.

Triangular Pavilion

Dan Graham

Location: Museum of the Prefecture of Yamaguchi, Japan. **Date of realization**: 1990. **Architect**: Dan Graham. **Scheme**: Ephemeral work: triangular pavilion on a grid of wood and glass. **Photography**: Dan Graham.

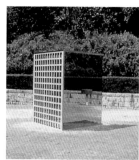

Along with many American artists who emerged in the 1970s, Dan Graham challenges any attempt to classify the dominant styles of that period. Neither pop art, nor minimalism, nor conceptual art offer a sufficiently flexible profile act as a label. The openings and multiplications that Graham has practiced on the prototype of the minimalist cube have been considered as a caricature of modernity and a criticism of the growing privatization of public spaces. Constant use of glass and two-way mirrors defines the interest that Graham places on the sociopsychological perception of individuals. In 1990 he was invited to undertake one of his projects in the Museum of the Prefecture of Yamaguchi (Japan), and he introduced a typical

wooden grille, so widely used as partitions in Japanese homes. This triangular pavilion with wooden panels had a two-way mirror that functioned as an optical frontier in opposition to the physical barrier represented by the latticework. Visual relationships can be affected when the viewer opens or closes the sliding doors of the mirror. In the

same way, their location parallel to a glass wall belonging to the museum provoked kaleidoscopic repetition and visual pleasure as an antidote to the alienating and monolithic effect of two-way mirrors in offices.

La Grande Arche

J.O. von Spreckelsen & Paul Andreu

Location: La Défense, Paris, France. **Date of construction**: 1989. **Architects**: Johan Otto von Spreckelsen (winner of the competition), Paul Andreu (Aéroports de Paris). **Consultants**: Coyne & Bellier (structural engineers), Peter Rice (design), Trouvin (air-conditioning), Serete (electrics), Commins (acoustics), CSTB Nantes (aerodynamic studies), Clair Roof (lighting), André Putman, and Jean-Michel Wilmotte (interior layout). **Scheme**: Viewing point, meeting and conference room, exhibition areas, offices, and services. **Photography**: Stockphotos, G. Fessy.

The major urban development of La Défense wanted to involve historical Paris, so the complex of skyscrapers and office buildings was organized around the same axis that joined the Louvre with the Arc de Triomphe.

In this way, the Champs Élysées were extended to the periphery. Within this strategy, the Grande Arche was built as a visual landmark that would allow La Défense to be identified from the center.

The design competition was won by Johan Otto von Spreckelsen, and the fundamental decisions concerning the project are his, but the premature death of Spreckelsen and the involvement of Aéroports de Paris in the construction of the building brought in Paul Andreu to be responsible for the final project.

Although the function of the Grande Arche is basically monumental, the building houses offices, conference and meeting rooms, and exhibition areas, downstairs, upstairs and in the sides, making full use of the structure.

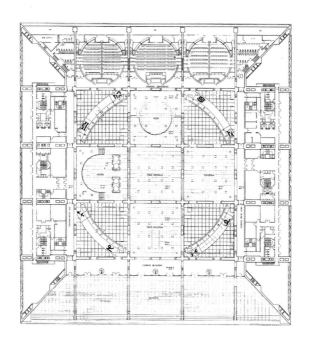

Capsa de Mistos

Claes Oldenburg and Coosje van Bruggen

Location: Barcelona, Spain. **Date of realization**: 1992. **Architect**: Claes Oldenburg and Coosje van Bruggen. **Scheme**: Sculpture in an urban plaza in commemoration of the Olympic Games. **Photography**: David Cardelús.

Claes Oldenburg and Coosje van Bruggen are two figures paradigmatic of the art of the second half of the 20th century who, starting with pop art, have brought a new vision of what they themselves call "private art in public spaces." One of the clearest examples is that of Capsa de Mistos. Since 1987, the idea of the matchbox presented itself in the artists' minds, as a result of a series of reflections on Spanish and Catalan culture. The formal composition of the box, with its profiles elevated, inclined, fallen, disseminated, and the palette of pure colors (red, blue, yellow, and black) make various symbolic references: the traumatic memory of the Spanish Civil War; the metaphor of Quixote; the colors of the Catalan and Spanish flags; or refer to the sculpture of Picasso for the Chicago Civic Center and the unfinished Sagrada Familia cathedral of Antonio Gaudí. But the clearest symbology is the commemoration of the Olympic Games of '92: the matches are like athletes and sportsmen, metaphors of triumph, power, strength, sacrifice, and, above all, the emblem of fire and the Olympic torch. The work has become one of the landmarks of post-Olympic Barcelona, a symbolic and commemorative element that, without resorting to traditional ideas of monuments, transforms the scale of landscape of the city, conferring on them a strange new dimension.

Cultural facilities

The 20th century has seen the development of architecture where new technologies have played a determining role, an architecture that, apart from cost, has no limits, succeeding in materializing the wildest desires of clients and designers, an architecture of ego. Architects who have enjoyed greatest recognition have become celebrities, idols, metaphors for the purest kind of creation. So, administrations have contracted such personalities to plan the cities of the future: in addition to providing a guarantee of quality, they lend prestige to the project. In this regard, the last few decades have seen many types of cultural facility flourish, the majority of which have become the symbol of the place they house, tourist attractions that are now generators of profit. The flow of visitors to museums, cultural centers, and art galleries has increased enormously thanks to the reworking of their image.

Previously, museums were repositories where works of art were held, and decontextualized. Nowadays, such buildings offer spaces with their own character, that appear like an extension of the works they exhibit. There is a double treat on offer here: contemplation of sculptures, pictures, and displays, plus the appreciation of quality architecture. Buildings both functional and unusual have been created that respond positively to client and user requirements and offer spaces that combine multiple sensations for the delight of the viewer. The four chapters included in this section hope to give an overall view of this species of building, presenting contemporary projects that have managed to become architectural standards: emblematic buildings, not only because of the unique works they contain, but also because of the quality of their construction, their singular aesthetics, and their perfect functionality.

Museums

Art galleries

Cultural centers and foundations

Schools and universities

Libraries

Religious buildings

Museums

If there is one idea that symbolizes modern thinking, it is that of the museum. The technological revolution brought about by computers and communications media has in the last few years meant a new transformation of our way of life and, likewise that of museums. Nowadays people are opening museums of every sort: of places, of wine, of coffee, or of art and, at the same time, traditional museums are being expanded out of all proportion, which makes it impossible to see all in a single day. On the other hand, they are being equipped with leisure in mind. They house shops and restaurants, they organize seminars and postgraduate courses, they are the monuments that identify and differentiate one city from another, they become tourist attractions, they act as market places for art, they promote some artists to the detriment of others, they anticipate fashions by organizing temporary exhibitions...and, in addition to all this, museums can now be visited not only physically, but also on the Internet or via the numerous documentary programs shown on television. The museum has without doubt become a temple to the turn of the century.

Nariwa Museum

Forest of Tombs Museum

Modern Art Museum of Fort Worth

Hyogo Prefectural Museum of Art – Kobe Waterfront Plaza

Nariwa Museum

Tadao Ando

Location: Nariwa, Okayama, Japan. **Date of construction**: 1993-1994. **Architect**: Tadao Ando. **Photography**: Mitsuo Matsuoka, Shigeo Ogawa.

Nariwa, in Okayama prefecture, in western Japan, is a financially prosperous place whose wealth comes from the copper mining industry. Culturally, also, it is rich because it is the site of many traditional houses, called "fukiya", buildings whose façades are colored in a distinctive reddish tone. This art museum is on the site of old residences, surrounded by a stone wall and limited on the south by a steep grade. The project is expressed in the form of a new perimeter wall containing a concrete edifice in which the different museum functions take place. Between the slanted plane and the building itself, a wide sheet of water reflects Ando's "fukiya" poem. Go up to this museum and you first find the old stone wall, a witness to the past. The next step is the ramp leading to the path that goes around the construction. It all becomes a place that fuses nature, culture, history. In its interior, vertical slabs of concrete merge with a large-scale glass cladding that fills the museum with diffused light and offers magnificent views of the surrounding landscape.

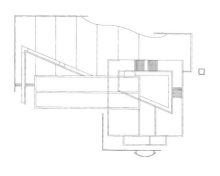

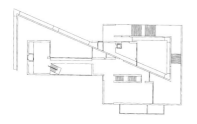

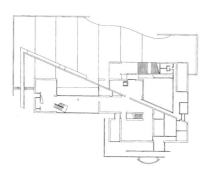

Forest of Tombs Museum

Tadao Ando

Location: Kamato, Kumamoto, Japan. **Design:** 1990. **Realized:** 1992. **Architect:** Tadao Ando. **Photography:** Hiroshi Ueda.

The region of Kyushu is steeped in ancestral Japanese history. In this mythical zone, in the northern part of the prefecture of Kumamoto, lies the tombs' historical museum of Kamoto. The nearby mortuary complex comprises the Futago-zuka keyhole shaped tumulos, surrounded by eight smaller burial mounds. Given its proportions, the slight incline of the hillsides and the elegance of its contours, Futago-zuka stands out as one of the most beautiful and important deposits in Japan. Conscious of the beauty and the significance of the place, Ando decided to subtly distance himself and not do any work with the tombs. He situated the museum some 250 meters from the tombs. The parking area, still farther away, lies below the natural plateau on which the complex was raised. This whole arrangement allows the visitor to come to the museum after having passed through a lush woodland. One is then in view of the sepulchers but without having reached the architect's contributions. The project's conception aims at transcending the mere spatial relationship between tombs and architectural volume: the museum sweeps up in evocation of the spirit of ancestral structures, a contemporary burial mound.

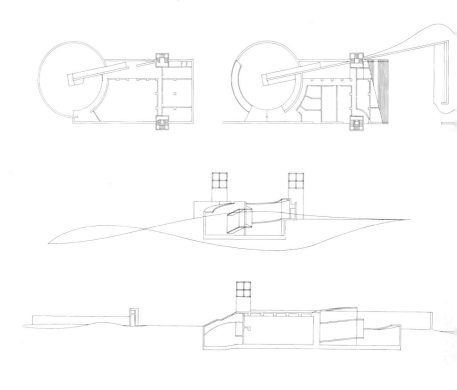

Modern Art Museum of Fort Worth

Tadao Ando

Location: Fort Worth, Texas, USA. **Date of design**: 1999. **Date of completion**: 2002. **Architect**: Tadao Ando
Photography: Mitsuo Matsuoka

This project is located on the outskirts of Fort Worth, Texas, in the center of a large park, adjacent to one of the masterworks of the 20th century, the Kimbell Art Museum by Louis Kahn. Naturally, the major challenge of the design was to provide a harmonious relationship between itself and Kimbell's. The strategy Ando used was one of generating a project diluting any strict border between interior and exterior and—importantly—to make the rooms appropriate for the display of art objects. A bucolic setting was drawn up containing a pond, a garden, and a wood that isolate the complex from the bustle of four-wheeled vehicles. The new museum comprises five rectangular concrete bays enclosed by glass façades. Two of these structures were to be used as public and administration areas, the remaining three as exhibition areas. The concrete, and its climatic and structural stability, contrasts with the glass its more fragile and intense relationship with the environment. Blending the two materials offers a great variety of settings, allowing many different types of transparencies and lightings.

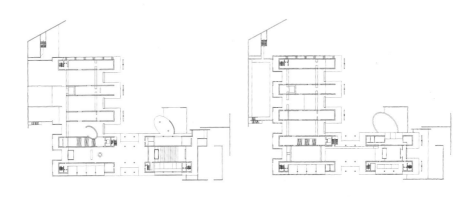

Hyogo Prefectural Museum of Art–Kobe Waterfront Plaza

Tadao Ando

Location: Kobe, Hyogo, Japan. **Date of design**: 1998. **Date of completion**: 2001. **Architect**: Tadao Ando. **Photography**: Mitsuo Matsuoka.

After the dramatic earthquake that took place in 1995, the authorities of Hyogo prefecture and those of the city of Kobe proposed the reconstruction of the oceanfront of the city as a symbol of the physical and moral recovery of the community. This symbol is located to the east of the city, at one end of the harbor where, earlier, important iron and steel industries stood. Tadao Ando was chosen to design two of the most noteworthy structures for the new neighborhood: a large municipal park on the ocean shore and the museum of fine art of the prefecture of Hyogo. While the fact that there were two clients did little to facilitate the articulation between the two proposals, it at least generated a negotiating challenge for the architectural office. The museum combines stone walls and three glass-enclosed volumes that receive the art display rooms. A passageway serves as functional interface between museum and park, the latter designed as refuge area in case of another earthquake. Its central zone can double as the scene of recreational-cultural activities. Camphor trees, the official tree of this prefecture, were planted and sculptures were placed.

Art galleries

The interest in systematically collecting works of art from all periods, including those more distant in time and space, is a recent phenomenon and one that is inseparable from modernity. No previous civilization has looked back to the past in such an analytical and structured way. The gallery and museum of art were born at the same time as the consolidation of scientific thought and the publication of the first treatises on history. The examples that have been included in this section are an attempt to show the evolution of the different ways of understanding architecture in relation to these cultural spaces which have proliferated.

Palais des Beaux-Arts de Lille

Guggenheim Museum

Stockholm Museum of Modern Art

Chicago Museum of Contemporary Art

Arken Museum of Modern Art

Hamburg Museum of Contemporary Art

San Francisco Museum of Modern Art

P.S.1 Museum

MACBA

The Lounge

Louvre Pyramid

Museum of Rock Art

Gagosian Gallery

Palais des Beaux-Arts de Lille

Jean Marc Ibos and Myrto Vitart

Location: Lille, France. **Dates**: March 1990 (competition); 1990–1992 (executive plans); 1992–1997 (construction). **Client**: Municipality of Lille. **Associates**: Pierre Cantacuzène (coordinator), Sophie Nguyen (façades and museography), Khephren Engineering (structure), Y.R.M. Antony Hunt & Ass. (façades), Alto Engineering (fittings). **Scheme**: Renovation and extension of the Palais des Beaux-Arts de Lille. **Surface area**: 28,000 m² (300,000 ft²) in total, of which the extension project is 11,000 m² (117,000ft²).

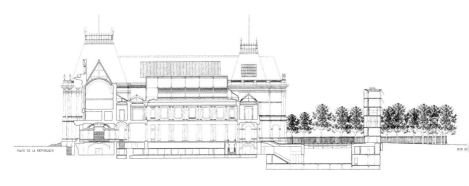

Ibos and Vitart have constructed a building/screen on whose glass façade the existing museum is reflected, thus duplicating its image and reviving the original project of 1895 that proposed a building double the size of the current one. The new temporary exhibition hall is buried in an artificial pool of glass, which is surrounded by one of water. On the southern façade, a system of probes measures the sunshine, temperature, and wind strength, and automatically activates external sun shades. The glass roof has a slope of 1%. Between the beams, an automatic system of blinds allows the amount of sunshine to be controlled and adjusts the level of natural lighting to the requirements of the work being exhibited.

Guggenheim Museum

Frank O. Gehry

Location: Bilbao, Spain. **Date of design**: 1990. **Date of completion**: 1997. **Architect**: Frank O. Gehry. **Associates**: Randy Jefferson, Vano Haritunians, Douglas Hanson, Edwin Chan. **Scheme**: Museum of contemporary art: exhibition halls, conservation rooms, auditorium, restaurant, shops, stores, and outdoor plaza for public use. **Photography**: Eugeni Pons.

The museum is on a bank of the river, beside a very much used suspension bridge that Gehry coopted as a further element of the museum project.

Due to the peculiar shape of the building, a great number of comparisons can be made but, according to the architect himself, his references were: the film Metropolis by Fritz Lang, the sculptures of Brancusi, the image of a quarry, and, above all, the contained force transmitted by the city of Bilbao. What most affected the final shape of the building was the actual modus operandi of Gehry, who started with sketches and free models, which were translated almost literally to the computer screen, then analyzed mathematically and any technical or structural matters resolved.

The museum consists of a large central atrium, with a height of 50 m (165 ft), crowned by a metal flower, and three wings facing east, south, and west. To the north, the museum borders on the river, and the virtual fourth wing is cut off, leaving in its place an enormous glass door.

The permanent collection is located in the southern wing, in a succession of square halls. The collection of living artists is in the west wing, in seven galleries of unusual shape and varying sizes. Finally, the temporary exhibitions are on show in an extended great hall (130 x 30 m, 426 x 98 ft) which stretches out to the east.

Stockholm Museum of Modern Art

Rafael Moneo

Location: Stockholm, Sweden. **Date of completion**: 1998. **Client**: Swedish National Board of Public Works. **Architect**: Rafel Moneo. **Associates**: Michael Bischoff, Robert Robinowitz, Lucho Marcial. **Scheme**: New museum of modern art: exhibition halls, cafeteria, offices, store, and services. **Photography**: Wenzel.

More than a designer, Rafael Moneo is an architectural scholar. Either because of his academic profile or his interest in history, each of his projects has a theme that reflects on the city, the topography, and classical typology. It is often said of his works that there are never two the same and this is precisely what

Moneo stands for: trying not to fall for the sensation one gets when looking at instances of contemporary architecture which have been destroyed and reconstructed with the sole intention of creating paradigms, while real problems are ignored. The Stockholm Museum of Modern Art is an example of Moneo's wish to integrate his work into its context, which he does in this case by adapting some of the architectural characteristics of the existing buildings that surround the museum. The project started with a typological study of the exhibition galleries inside. It was decided to design

four exhibition halls on a square plan, featuring pyramid roofs with a skylight in the middle to filter the sunlight. Another interesting aspect of the museum is the large glass roof over the area used for the cafeteria terrace.

Chicago Museum of Contemporary Art

Kleiues + Kleiues

Location: Chicago Illinois, USA. **Date of construction**: 1994–1996. **Architects**: Kleiues + Kleiues. **Associates**: Ove Arup (engineering), Claude R. Engle (lighting), Daniel Weinbach & Partners (landscaping). **Surface area**: 10,000 m (108,000 ft²). **Scheme**: Museum, services, parking lot, and exterior landscaping. **Photography**: Hélène Binet, Steven Holl, Hedrich Blessing.

The architects' attention concentrates, basically, on the modernist dialog with tradition and the relationship between their two aesthetic codes. With regard to design there was a wish to reflect the pragmatism that characterizes the city of Chicago and its architecture. At the same time, they tried to ensure that the building showed something of its "poetic rationalism." The characteristics that define the museum are simplicity, space, calm, silence, and the play between transparency and content.

One can reach the building from Michigan Avenue and see the lake from its central axis. Otherwise one can go in from the other side (the Sculpture Garden), in which case one will see the Water Tower and Michigan Avenue. In any case, when entering the exhibition halls visitors find themselves facing only art. They can enjoy the exhibits without having to be distracted by people moving up and down access ramps or stairs or by the cries of people lost and trying to find part of their group from a balcony.

Arken Museum of Modern Art

Soren Robert Lund

Location: Arken, Denmark. **Date of design**: 1993. **Date of construction**: 1996. **Architect**: Soren Robert Lund. **Associates**: Helgi Thoroddson, Jorgen Erichsen, Mette Adersen, Finn Bogsted. **Photography**: Friedrich Busam/Architekturphoto.

Robert Lund's project shows the influence of the "new empiricism" of Alvar Aalto: this architectural current is a reaction against the excessive schematism of 1930s architecture. On the other hand, the Arken Museum is also influenced by the "new formal abstraction." This trend generates an architecture that, paradoxically, is both abstract and figurative at the same time.

The proportions of the museum's entrance are squeezed down until they take on an almost domestic size. From this point there are two alternative routes, both on the same level: the art route leads the visitor through a sequence of exhibition galleries designed as differentiated spaces; from the foyer, a second route runs through areas where activities complementary to the exhibitions are held. Robert Lund is sensitive to the harshness of the environment and chooses concrete to give texture to the building. The rough surface contrasts with the façades and the metal skylights, giving a greater richness to the whole complex structure.

Hamburg Museum of Contemporary Art

Kleiues + Kleiues

Location: Hamburg, Germany. **Date of design**: 1990–1995. **Date of construction**: 1992–1996. **Architects**: Kleiues + Kleiues. **Associates**: Schon + hippelein (façade), Linder Ag. (construction), Scholz & Herzog (electrics), Max Sange (elevators), A. Kuhn Gmbh (locksmiths). **Surface area**: 104,822 m² (1.1 million ft²). **Scheme**: Restoration of the old train station as a museum; exterior landscaping. **Photography**: Kleiues + Kleiues.

There are three important aspects in the design of this project: firstly, the correct analysis (not nostalgic but rational) of the existing structure of the old Hamburg train station and remembering its importance to the architectural history of the city; secondly, the intention to create simple, transparent spaces; thirdly, the technology of museums high ceilings in the new galleries that combine natural with artificial light; integration of electrical systems into the older parts of the building using false ceilings; use of materials such as aluminum, granite, wood (particularly oak), and sandstone; walls painted in matte white so as not to affect color perception.

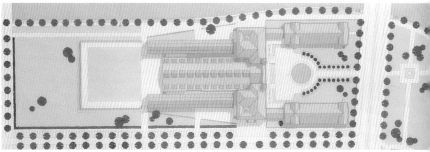

San Francisco Museum of Modern Art

Mario Botta

Location: San Francisco, California, USA. **Date of construction**: 1991–1995. **Architect**: Mario Botta **Associates**: Hellmuth, Obata & Kassabaum, Bechtel International Company. **Surface area**: 20,500 m² (2.2 million ft²). **Photography**: Robert Canfield.

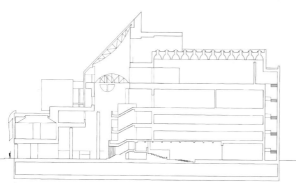

The central atrium connects all the rooms, which makes it easy to find one's bearings and select the rooms to be visited. Botta has achieved one of his original ideas: to illuminate the majority of the rooms with natural light, which he has implemented by using a stepped section design. On the first floor one finds all the independent activities: bookshop, cafeteria, auditorium, temporary exhibition halls, and main entrance hall. On the second floor are the exhibition halls proper. Botta uses the scaling of the building, from the main façade to the rear façade, to locate rooms only in areas that have no floor above, and he leaves the rest of the floor for offices or conservation rooms.

The main theme of all Mario Botta's work is the revival of monumentality. His projects try to invoke this quality in modern architecture: although it is often absent, it has been associated with this art for many centuries.

In the San Francisco Museum, Botta uses many of the architectural resources of this type of construction: simple, ascetic spaces, huge shapes lined with brick or stone, which provide no information about the look of the interior.
The lighting is provided through gaps or holes in the wall, since one cannot actually call them windows in any recognizable form.

P.S.1 Museum

Frederick Fisher

Location: Long Island, New York, USA. **Date of construction**: 1997. **Architects**: Frederick Fisher, David Ross, Joseph Coriaty. **Floor area**: 7800 m² (84,000 ft²), **Photography**: Michael Moran.

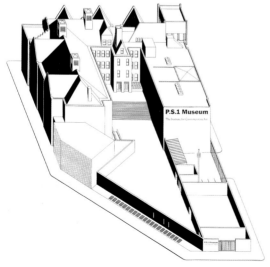

Fisher's method of tackling an art museum project is more akin to that of an artist or gallery owner who is occupying a space to keep and show his work, than that of an architect who has received one of the most juicy commissions of his career (a museum) and is trying to demonstrate his ability to create spaces and invent new images.

This is a former school, located in an industrial area near the Queens district of New York. The main value of the building lies in the wide variety of spaces available.

Therefore, the strategy of the project consisted of integrating the facilities into the existing structure of the building.

The second floor has kept the mythical galleries, to preserve the tradition of the P.S.1 as an alternative exhibition area. In the same way, the "art in residence" facility (several artists living and working in the museum) has importantly been retained.

MACBA

Richard Meier

Location: Barcelona, Spain. **Date of construction**: October 1990–March 1995. **Client**: Consorci del Museu d'Art Contemporani de Barcelona **Architect**: Richard Meier. **Associates**: Thomas Phifer (design team), Renn Logan, Alphonso Perez (architectural design), Fernando Ramos, Isabel Bachs (associate architects), Obio Brufau, Moya Arquitectos (structural engineers), F. Labastida (installations), Fischer, Marantz, Renfo & Ston (lighting technology), Secotec SL, Intecasa (quality control), Ibering, Estudis I Projectes SA, Gerard Esteba (consultancy), COMSA (construction) **Scheme**: Museum of Contemporary Art: exhibition halls, open air cour yard, offices, and services. **Photography**: Eugeni Pons.

The Barcelona Museum of Contemporary Art falls within the characteristic plastic idiom of Meier, based on clear rationalism in which straight and curved lines are combined to produce a harmonic dialog between the interior spaces and the exterior light through wide galleries and windows. Meier designed an elongated building measuring 120 x 35 m (394 x 115 ft), inside which he placed a circular room which crosses it vertically. He thus created a contrast which gives the whole a very particular appearance and acts as an axis around which the exhibition areas revolve. The virtually sculptural aesthetics of the building are conjugated with the provision of the latest technical innovations in terms of exhibition, convenience, and maintenance. Its bright, luminous appearance makes it one of the most attractive museums of the decade, paying off the deb that Barcelona owed to its famous, international contemporary art.

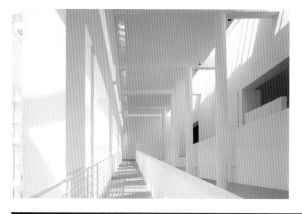

The Lounge

Zaha Hadid Architects

Location: Wolfsburg, Germany. **Date of completion**: 2001. **Architect**: Zaha Hadid Architects. **Collaborators**: Woody K T Yao and Djordje Stojanovic. **Gross floor area**: 700 m². **Photography**: Hélène Binet.

The Kunstmuseum and the town council of Wolfsburg, Germany, commissioned Zaha Hadid to reconvert a double space and one of the lobbies in this art museum. The team headed by Hadid is also building a center dedicated to science and new technologies in the same city, so the work on this building was to anticipate the architecture of the museum complex. At the time of construction, no specific function was assigned to two of the spaces created: a double-height gallery and a lobby on the first floor which adjoins the shop and café. Until recently, the former space had held photography exhibitions, small presentations of drawings, and an educational workshop. The lobby, in the form of a balcony, served for book consulting, video screenings, and as an extension of the bar. Initially, the gallery was to house an addition to a music library belonging to the Alvar Aalto cultural center, but when the administration rejected the proposal, the space was ceded to the museum. The institution sought to become a flexible, multifunctional, and dynamic center; it accordingly kept an entrance area independent from the gallery with the option of transforming it later into a space for experimentation with public functions and with a close connection to the outside environment. Zaha Hadid's intention was thus to create a link between the gallery, the lobby, and the exterior. She converted the remaining areas into a single space which accommodates different functions: it is at the same time an exhibition space for models, drawings, and paintings; a gathering point for the users of the complex; a waiting room; an auditorium; a bar; a concert hall and a discotheque. The project's name, the "English voice" lounge, refers to the combination of activities for which the new area is suited: talking, relaxing, listening, drinking, sitting, dreaming and eating. The continuity of the space was attained by covering the walls and floors in wood. The furnishings were designed by the architects themselves, who also inaugurated the space with an exhibition of selected drawings and models from their own projects.

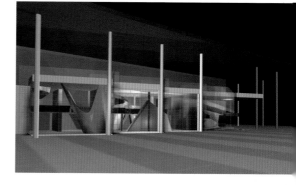

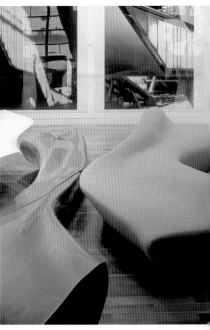

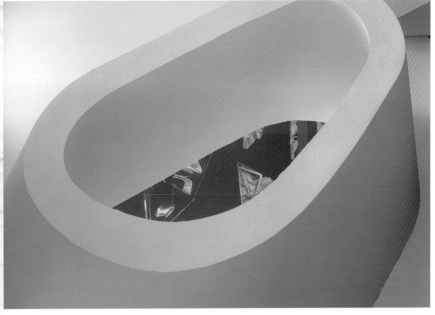

Louvre Pyramid

I.M.Pei

Location: Paris, France. **Date of completion**: 1987. **Architect**: I.M. Pei. **Scheme**: Construction of a glass pyramid as the new entrance to the Louvre Museum. **Photography**: Ana Quesada.

The project to modernize and extend the Louvre Museum, initiated by François Mitterand in 1981, envisaged a new underground building which would serve as a bridge between the three wings of the museum. The upper part of this building takes the shape of a huge glass pyramid, which rises up as the central feature of the huge courtyard, the center of gravity of the Louvre. The pyramid is now the new main entrance to the museum. Once inside, visitors find themselves in the Belvedere, shaped like a large triangular balcony, which overlooks the interior lobby and provides a view of the palace through the glass walls of the pyramid, providing a pleasing effect.

Museum of Rock Art

William P. Bruder

Location: Deer Valley, Phoenix, Arizona, USA. **Date of construction**: 1994–1995. **Architect**: William P. Bruder. **Associates**: Wendell Burnette, Bob Adams, Beau Dromiack, Rick Joy, Maryann Bloomfield. **Scheme**: Museum of Rock Art: reception, exhibition halls, archives, offices, lecture rooms and services. **Photography**: Bill Timmerman.

This museum was built over a watercourse: the building itself is designed as a funnel which channels visitor traffic from the parking lot to the mountain and the engravings of the Hohokam (native North Americans). The first floor is inserted in the angle formed by the mountain and a jetty, bringing civilization and nature into contact. The emotion produced by the architectural sweep helps to prepare one for contemplating the work of art. To make the space more cinema-like, there is a longitudinal area with two parallel stages at different heights: one continuous, for the public, where the museum itself is located, and the other more private, subdivided following the watercourse and housing the reception area, archives, offices, and lecture rooms. An opaque box was created with incisions which convert into light when any specific points or itineraries need to be emphasized. In this way the feeling of oppression is avoided, although the windows extend the gaze towards the rocks. The museum becomes a balcony over the jetty, and the visitor, as well as learning about the landscape, can enjoy it.

deer valley **rock art center**

Gagosian Gallery

Richard Gluckman

Location: Wooster Street, New York, USA. **Date of completion**: 1994. **Architect**: Richard Gluckman. **Scheme**: Conversion of an old garage into an art gallery. **Photography**: Paco Asensio.

The Gagosian is part of a New York trend for converting industrial premises into luxurious galleries. Designed by Richard Gluckman, it is the perfect venue for major exhibitions of contemporary sculpture. Conceived with the work of Richard Serra in mind, the building is a light, airy, and spacious design.

Gluckman believes that art should dominate the space, with the architect playing only a supporting role and merely creating a stage. Only the brick façade of the original garage remains intact although he added a new door in the original style as a historical tribute and a practical feature. This entrance remains open on summer afternoons, when the gallery glistens seductively, offering passers-by more than a glimpse of its contents. The interior was completely redesigned: the floor reinforced, the ceiling raised to its maximum height, and pillars built to increase the width. The smooth, polished floor contrasts with the brilliant white walls. Gluckman has left exposed beams, which match the original structure, visible in the new skylights, around which, in addition to natural light, industrial halogen lamps have been fixed.

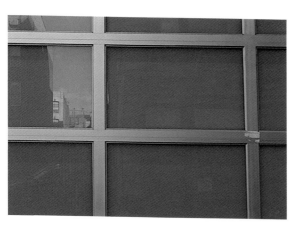

Cultural Centers and Foundations

There is no substantial difference, in fact, between the projects included in this chapter and the other structures under the general Cultural Facilities heading. This distinction has been adopted to throw into relief a number of buildings that fall halfway between museum and art gallery, between exhibition hall and show space. This Cultural Centers and Foundations category embraces institutions that are normally private, often bringing together works of one particular artist, movement, or country. These projects celebrate the history or tradition of a place, or act as a perpetual record of something significant.

Chinati Foundation

Donald Judd

Location: Marfa, Texas, USA. **Date of completion**: 1986. **Scheme**: Exhibition areas, offices, and services. **Photography**: Todd Eberle.

The Chinati Foundation is a museum of contemporary art founded and designed in 1986 by Donald Judd. It is located in Marfa, Texas, a small town of 2600 inhabitants in the southwest of the United States, near the Mexican border. The barren, arid countryside is part of the Chihuahua desert.
The Foundation is located on a former military base, Fort D.A. Russell.
The specific purpose of the Chinati Foundation is to exhibit large works by a few of the significant 20th-century artists.

Donald Judd himself was an architect who, when the military base was abandoned, renovated and adapted the buildings for their new purpose. Judd designed the windows, doors, and new access points, adding a new curved metal roof to the old warehouses and landscaping the grounds. He built new adobe walls and converted the barracks into exhibition halls.

Louis Jeantet Foundation

Domino Architects

Location: Geneva, Switzerland. **Date of construction**: 1996. **Architects**: Jean-Michel Landecy, Jean-Marc Anzévui and Nicolas Deville, Henri Bava, Michel Hoëssler and Olivier Philippe of Equipo Ter (landscape architects). **Scheme**: Garden and auditorium. **Photography**: Jean-Michel Landecy.

One of the issues the project team had to resolve was the imbalance in scale between the old neo-Renaissance building, with its grand front esplanade, the small space allowed for the project, and finally the extensive grounds surrounding the house. Another problem was the distance between the two buildings, the house and the auditorium, and how they could be linked.

The solution suggested by Domino was to optimize use of the garden area by breaking it down into two levels: a horizontal upper platform which occupied almost all the free space of the plot and which was on a level with the first floor of the house; and, cutting through the upper platform, a small patio garden acting as a common entrance to the house and auditorium.

The landscaping is inspired by Mogul gardens and the courtyards of Persian mosques, and, like them, uses natural elements to welcome visitors and prepare them for a new experience. The entrance walkway crosses the huge concrete wall which separates the courtyard from the street, and visitors suddenly find themselves in the small square courtyard on the inside.

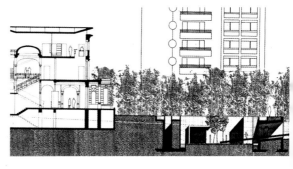

Cartier Foundation

Jean Nouvel

Location: Paris, France. **Date of construction**: 1991–1994. **Client**: Cartier S.A. **Architect**: Jean Nouvel. **Associates**: Didier Braoult (project architect); P.A. Bohnet, L. Ininguez, P. Mathieu, V. Morteau, G. Potel, S. Ray, S. Robert (associate architects), Ove Arup & Partners (structural engineers); Arnaud de Bussière et Associés (façade); Reidweg et Gendre (air-conditioning); Ingénieur et Paysage (landscaping). **Photography**: Christian Richters.

In the Cartier Foundation, the trees remain where they were, superimposing themselves on an architecture in which boundaries disappear and walls glide into space. The Chateaubriand cedar stands alone, between two enormous, unobstructed screens (only attached to the building by a few horizontal ties to counter wind pressure) which frame the entrance. Visitors walk under the cedar and enter an exhibition room in which the works of art intermingle with the trees and tall, stylized, evenly spaced pillars. As to materials, the whole expression of the building is given over to glass: a semireflective glass which avoids the emphasis and obstruction of completely transparent or totally reflective, mirror-like curtain walls. The vertical wall creates the impression of the Cartier Foundation as an ephemeral building on the verge of fading away. It belongs to an unspecified school of modern architecture.

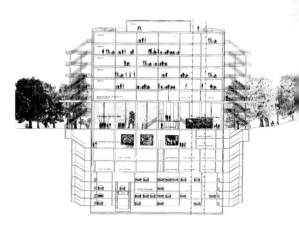

Galician Center for Contemporary Art

Alvaro Siza

Location: Santiago de Compostela, Spain. **Date of completion:** 1997. **Client:** Santiago City Hall. **Architect:** Alvaro Siza. **Scheme:** Exhibition halls, auditorium, library, documentation and administration centers, bookshop, cafeteria, service areas, administrative offices, management office, and viewing terrace. **Photography:** Tino Martínez.

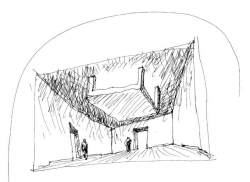

The main issue with this project was its insertion in an area surrounded by buildings of quite different scale and significance. It was up to the Center to overcome these difficulties by transforming an agglomeration of spaces and buildings into a coherent fabric. The preservation/transformation criteria involved included the selection of cladding materials, so granite was chosen for the exterior, with color variations. The building consists of two L-shaped wings each of three floors, which converge in a north–south direction at a point on the southern end. The west wing houses the main entrance, distribution and reception areas, and access to the auditorium, the second floor, the library, and the documentation and administration centers. The basement of the east wing contains the exhibition halls, the bookshop, the cafeteria, the temporary exhibition halls (709 m², 7630 ft²), and the auditorium (367 m², 3950 ft²) are on the first floor. The triangular space between the two buildings is an overhead-lit transition area housing the entrance to the exhibition halls. The third floor internal service areas cover 1908 m² (20,500 ft²); on the second floor are the administration and management offices. The terrace areas (957 m², 10,300 ft²) are open to the public and can accommodate sculpture exhibitions. The terrace walls are 3.2 m (10.5 ft) high with the floor raised at the southern end, producing a viewing platform overlooking the city of Santiago.

Cracow Center for Japanese Art and Technology

Arata Isozaki & Associates

Location: Cracow, Poland. **Date of completion**: 1994. **Client**: The Kyoto-Cracow Foundation. **Architect**: Arata Isozaki & Associates. **Associates**: Ghen Mizumo, Yusaku Imamura, Shigeru Hirabayashi, Dr. Jan Grabacki, EXIT engineers (structural engineers). **Plot area**: 0.49 ha (1.2 acres). **Net floor area**: 2120 m² (2280 ft²). **Gross floor area**: 3180 m² (3420 ft²). **Photography**: Yoshio Takase.

The building is on two floors: the main, upper floor to which direct access is provided; and the lower floor accommodating secondary offices and a large multipurpose room. With this layout, Isozaki is once again trying out a large undulating roof supported by a timber structure, designed by means of complex geometry. Thus, most of the perimeter of the building takes on a sinuous shape so that, at the intersection of the two planes, no part of the resulting arris has any straight lines. Moving down, floor by floor, towards the foundations, the building slowly acquires much more hybrid images: for example the bar terrace, or the access area, express idioms already tried and tested by modern tradition.

Stiklestad Cultural Center

Jens Petter Askim, Sven Hartvig

Location: Stiklestad, Norway. **Date project begun**: 1985. **Date of completion**: 1992. **Architects**: Jens Petter Askim, Sven Hartvig. **Scheme**: A museum to commemorate the Viking tradition. **Photography**: Bard Ginnes, Jens Petter Askim.

St. Olav is one of Scandinavia's most popular saints and Stiklestad is a place of pilgrimage. This museum therefore has a triple purpose: firstly, to commemorate the Battle of Stiklestad and St. Olav; secondly, to explain the significance and consequences of that historic event; and, thirdly, to demonstrate Viking culture prior to St. Olav, present scenes from and the remains of the battle, and provide information about the changes experienced by Norway since that date. Architecturally, the building is modern, carefully landscaped, and built with constant references to local architecture. The ridge roofs and the wall surrounding the courtyard on the southern side, the internal ridges, the slopes on which the building stands, and the structural design itself take their inspiration from simple, traditional elements. The architects had two intentions: that the building should harmonize with the landscape and that the architectural framework should visually prepare visitors for the archeological treasures and battle scenes they would find on the inside. Perhaps the main area of the museum is the courtyard, which is designed to accommodate all kinds of activities. The southern side is enclosed by a circular, concrete, windowless corridor, along which archeological items are displayed and scenes from the Battle of Stiklestad depicted.

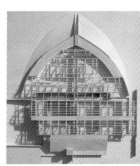

Institute of the Arab World

Jean Nouvel

Location: Paris, France. **Date of completion**: 1987. **Client**: Institut du Monde Arabe. **Architect**: Jean Nouvel. **Scheme**: Exhibition hall – Arab art and history museum. **Photography**: S.Couturier

The façade facing the Jussieu faculty at first sight looks like an ornament-decorated surface. Close up, however, we can see that this is not so, but a combination of the ancient art of controlling light and the use of the most modern technologies. Jean Nouvel himself explains: "This façade is not an imitation of ornamental decoration, but an interpretation of the tradition. More than that architectural form, what I wanted to reproduce is the play of light. To play with the system of its geometry, recover, and respect the principle of light filtration, of course adapted to the climate and the inconsistency of Parisian light. Because the most important thing about ornamental decoration is not its function per se but the way it adapts to the amount of light. It is a sensitive element. We could have achieved something similar with a venetian blind but, in line with tradition, I was able to use technology to instill the sensation rather than the function in this case."

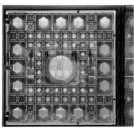

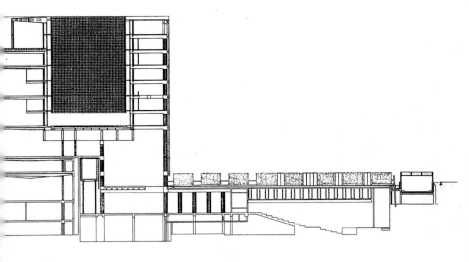

Yerba Buena Gardens Visual Arts Center

Maki & Associates

Location: San Francisco, California, USA. **Date of completion**: 1993. **Client**: San Francisco Redevelopment Agency. **Architect**: Maki & Associates. **Associates**: Fumikiho Maki & Maki & Associates; Robinson Mills + Williams; Structural Design Engineers (structural engineering); S.J. Engineers (mechanical engineering); F.W. Associates (electrical engineering); S. Leonard Auerbach & Ass. (lighting); Walsh & Norris (acoustics); Meachum O'Brien (landscaping). **Scheme**: Visual arts center, video projection room, exhibition rooms, and galleries; multipurpose forum; offices, and services. **Photography**: Paul Peck, Richard Barnes.

The San Francisco Visual Arts Center assumes a fundamental role in this cultural and commercial development, built in the city center, in the Market Street district. The building includes a video projection room seating 100 together with several exhibition galleries and a communal area in the form of a multifunctional forum. The internal and external areas have an informal flavor which contrasts with the usual serious and strict environments of museums and institutions. The projection room has a gallery, creating a more intimate area for small events, video screenings, and other related exhibitions. The rest of the areas are larger and can accommodate other activities. The forum accommodates avant-garde theater presentations as well as festivals, banquets, and concerts. Its L shape enables the building to be placed at a key point in this new urban development. The public square located at one of the corners of the complex acts as an open-air mall and an external extension of the internal facilities. Furthermore, some of the activities conducted in the building can be viewed from the outside through panels located in one of the two-floor facades. In this way, the building can be used as a single area to accommodate large-scale events where the public can move freely from one place to another.

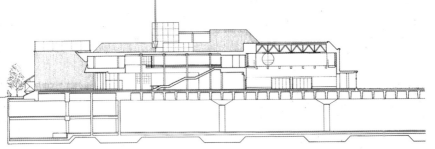

Yerba Buena Gardens Visual Arts Center 319

Schools and universities

Design, drama, theater, economics, law, journalism, technology, geological sciences, astronomy, architecture...these are the subjects being studied today. The students of the last decade of the 20th century have significantly changed the traditional trends. The lack of job opportunities has forced international institutions to create new opportunities to allow young people to integrate better into the job market. This has also meant that large numbers of architects have been responding to competitive tenders for commissions from schools and universities, in which, until now, they had not been interested as this was not previously a field for innovative design.

Utrecht School of Design and Fashion

Erick van Egeraat

Location: Utrecht, The Netherlands. **Date of construction**: 1994–1997. **Client**: Utrecht Local Authority. **Architect**: Erick van Egeraat. **Associates**: Maartje Lammers, Ard Buijsen, Boris Zeisser. **Structural engineering**: Strukton Engineering b.v., Maarsen. **Fittings**: Sweegers & de Bruijn b.v., Den Bosch. **Façade subcontractor**: Rollecate, Staphorst. **Scheme**: High school for graphic design and fashion. **Photography**: Christian Richters.

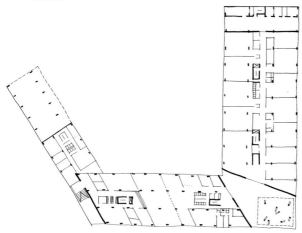

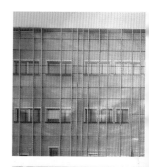

When Erick van Egeraat and his team were contracted for this project, the building had already been planned by another architect. In other words, they were not given a commission for a new building but were asked to take on an existing project in order to secure the approval of the regional Aesthetics Committee. The principal objective of the commission was to enliven the existing plans for the building and, as a secondary objective, to relocate the entrance hall. The architects decided to install a glass skin which would be superimposed completely independently on the existing façade. The building is thus enveloped by a kind of veil which reveals, and at the same time transforms, the perception of what lies behind it...

The redesigning of the entrance hall, located in one of the corners between two blocks, radically changed the whole concept of the space. Designed as a completely transparent building, the boundaries of which seem to disappear, the hall accommodates the lecture theater suspended on thin metal pillars, a reception area, and two connecting walkways between the two wings at the upper levels.

Glass is also used inside for the walkways, skylights, and façades, increasing the number of reflections from one surface to another.

School of Dramatic Art

TEN Architects

Location: Avenida Río Churubusco, Mexico City. **Date completed**: 1994 **Developer**: National Council for Culture and the Arts. **Cost**: $12 million. **Architects**: Enrique Norten, Bernardo Gómez-Pimienta. **Associates**: Gustavo Espitia, Héctor L. Gámiz, Miguel Angel González, Armando Hashimoto, Carlos Valdez, Óscar Vargas (design team), Alonso-García + Miranda (structural engineers), Jaffe, Scarborough & Holden (acoustics), Tecnoproyectos (mechanical engineering), Francisco de Pablo, Jesús Estiva (directors of works), Department of the Federal District (contractor). **Scheme**: Classrooms, theater (300 seats), administrative offices, dressing rooms, and services. **Photography**: Luis Gordoa.

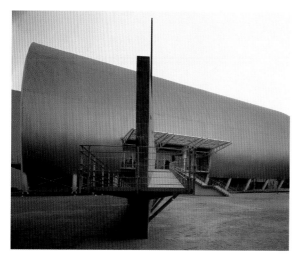

towards composition. The largest element is the large tubular metal roof. It is on an urban scale and is sufficiently abstract and monolithic that it can be recognized from a considerable distance and from a moving vehicle. Beneath the roof a collection of areas and planes contain and define the various facilities. All have their own expression according to their nature and particular conditions. They have been combined, apparently spontaneously and arbitrarily. But the virtual chaos nevertheless conceals a strict order derived from the specific function of each area and its complex inter-relationships, derived from the heterogeneity of the scheme as a whole.

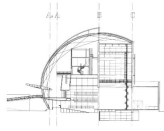

There are no clear boundaries, no complex topography (the plot is practically flat), nothing natural to be respected, no defined façades: reference points are broken up and dispersed. However, as Enrique Norten himself says: "The site is subject to frictional and tensile forces created by speed and the urban energies of the setting." Although not a concrete point of reference, these forces do suggest a way of setting out the architectural components and a certain attitude

The School of Dramatic Art is at the west end of an area containing the various buildings of the National Arts Center, between highways and connecting roads at various levels. It is a setting dominated by constant traffic and noise.

Vocational Training Center

Behnisch & Partner

Location: Bitburg, Germany. **Date of completion**: 2002. **Architects**: Behnisch & Partner. **Collaborators**: Stötzer & Neher (landscape), Christian Kandzia (color studies). **Gross floor area**: 27.550 m². **Photography**: Christian Kandzia.

The Vocational Training Center is a complex designed to accommodate young people from different countries, and includes dormitories, teaching facilities, and a recreation area. The primary objective of the commission was to create a dynamic and varied environment that at the same time would make the temporary residents feel at home. It was decided to eschew monumentality in the buildings, instead opting for a project that would fit in with the landscape, with low buildings scattered around the valley, and abundant vegetation.

A network of tree-lined paths and trails links the town, to the south of the site, with the recreational facilities at the north. The teaching units and workshops are located near the edge of the town and are arrayed around an expansive green yard. The rigid distribution of the rooms reflects a strict functional organization and a desire for all the spaces to offer views of the yard or countryside. Pitched roofs and wide eaves afford an ample variety of covered outdoor walkways and entries.

By playing with the elevations and planting trees, the architects were able to soften the impact of the complex on the area. The buildings that house the classrooms and the study areas appear to have two floors when seen from the town, while the façade that looks on to the valley reveals that they have three. The ground floor was erected in stone and the upper floors are clad in different-colored panels, creating an eclectic composition culminating in metal roofs.

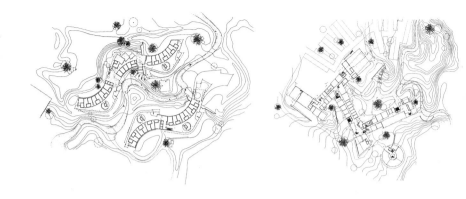

Faculty of Law, Cambridge

Sir Norman Foster & Partners

Location: University of Cambridge, UK. **Date of completion**: October 1995. **Client**: University of Cambridge. **Architect**: Norman Foster. **Structural engineers**: Anthony Hunt Associates. **Library capacity**: 120,000 volumes. **Gross floor area**: 9000 m² (97,000 ft²) **Scheme**: Auditoriums, classrooms, libraries, administrative offices, storerooms, and meeting rooms. **Photography**: Herman van Doorn.

The plot is in the middle of the Sidgwick campus, adjacent to the famous History Faculty building by James Stirling. It is surrounded by lawns and mature trees, which helps to minimize the impact of the buildings' size and retain as much as possible of the atmosphere of the garden in which it is located. The first floor contains various classrooms, and administrative and other staff offices. The underground floors consist of three large auditoriums, book stores, and student meeting rooms while, the top three floors are devoted to the library. The entrance opens onto a full height atrium providing access to all floors of the library building.

The library floors are terraced, tailored to the curved façade but not touching it.

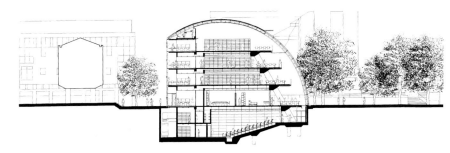

Faculty of Journalism

Ignacio Vicens/José Antonio Ramos

Location: Pamplona, Spain. **Date project begun**: 1994. **Date of completion**: 1996. **Architects**: Ignacio Vicens, José Antonio Ramos. **Associates**: Fernando Gil, Adam Blesnick. **Scheme**: Classrooms for theoretical and practical work, film studios, radio and television studios, conference rooms, offices, audio/video library, and services. **Photography**: Eugeni Pons.

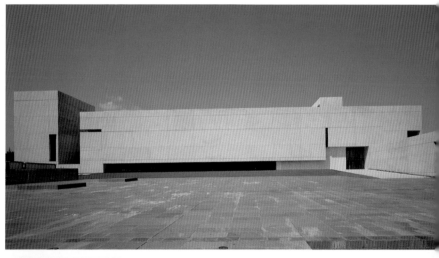

What gives the building its shape is the ratio between mass and space. The elements which stand out against the sky are just as important from the point of view of the skin, or image, as the spaces which penetrate the concrete to bring light to the interior. When the decision to adopt this shape, and not some other, was made, a dual strategy was at work. Firstly, the various functional areas are separated into different buildings. So, certain rooms, such as the main classroom on the first floor or the audio/video library block, with independent functions, tend to stand out as autonomous areas. Secondly, there is the desire to provide each area with a specific type of lighting and above all a special way of relating to the outside. Thus, regarding the building as a negative, looking down from above the exterior is built with holes and courtyard spaces.

Department of Geosciences, University of Aveiro

Eduardo Souto de Moura

Location: Aveiro, Portugal. **Date project begun**: 1991. **Date of completion**: 1995. **Architect**: Eduardo Souto de Moura. **Scheme**: Classrooms, laboratories, conference rooms, and services. **Photography**: Christian Richters.

The layout of the campus and conditions imposed by the university established clear guidelines: the gross floor area had to be 4314 m² (46,400 ft²); the maximum height three floors; the length of the building 80 m (260 ft); the width 20 m (66 ft); the floor area given over to traffic approximately 20%; the material for the wall finishes, red brick. With

such clear planning provisions, who needed an architect, Souto de Moura must have thought: "With the rules of the game so clearly defined, the building took shape almost without discussion: a box divided by a central corridor." All you had to do was glance at the other buildings on the campus: straight blocks of brick, all with three floors, parallel and equidistant, the only difference being whether the windows were oblong or square, or the blinds white or dark.

In contrast, Souto de Moura's building is very austere: an obvious rejection of all architectural decoration; enormous attention to detail with the intention of minimizing its

effect on the final appearance of the building; the determination, in order to make the rules of construction of the building patently obvious, not to clad the structural elements; and an effort to abstract geometrically the component parts of the building. The rooms are devoid of superfluities, containing only essential furniture in each case.

Expansion of the Architecture School

LWPAC

Location: Valparaíso, Chile. **Date of completion**: 1999. **Architect**: LWPAC, Lang Wilson Practice in Architecture Culture. **Collaborators**: Roberto Barria, Pol Taylor, Ricardo Luna SA (structures), Mainos SA (contractor) y Oscar Jalil (technical supervisor). **Gross floor area**: 19,300 sq. ft. **Photography**: Guy Winborne.

The commission was based on the requirements of the Universidad Técnica Federico Santa María for the expansion of the architecture school. In the first place, the project had to redefine the functional and spatial design of the expansion of the existing building.

Moreover, a period of only ten months was allowed from the initial sketches to the opening of the school, leaving three months for the design, one for calculating costs and awarding the building work. A further restriction was the limited budget for a 19,300 sq. ft. building. Finally, emphasis was placed on the relationship with the existing buildings, both at the structural level—given that this is an area of high seismic risk—and at the formal level, by which the result would have to respect the other buildings on the campus.

Once the requirements had been met, the architects' primary objective was to create a flexible space capable of evolving with the unpredictable design changes to which architecture schools are subject. To accommodate variable functions and future renovations, they proposed a building to a certain extent unfinished: a space which acts as an infrastructure for varied events rather than as a volume for fixed activities. The choice of materials was governed by environmental awareness and by the intention to create varied visual effects. The integration of this work with the existing buildings is achieved through the use of wavy perforated aluminum, a glass curtain wall, and translucent polycarbonate panels.

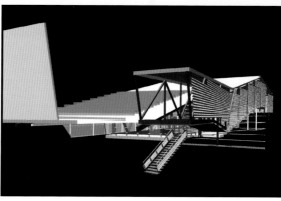

Libraries

Libraries, places of study and reference *par excellence,* have not escaped the architectural revolution of the last few years. From gloomy, poorly lit, cold, and neutral places, architects have turned them into welcoming environments conducive to reading and concentration. These new buildings combine general-purpose study rooms with other more specific ones. Thus, in this section, we find a series of libraries dedicated to the study of very specific topics such as poetry, the Catholic religion, world literature, and child education.

La Bibliothèque Nationale

Dominique Perrault

Location: Paris, France. **Date of completion**: 1997. **Developer**: French government **Architects**: Dominique Perrault, Aude Perrault, Gaëlle Lauriont-Prevost. **Associates**: Danielle Allaire, Gabrieel Choukroun, Guy Morriseau (director of studies), Pieffet-Corbin (economist), Séchaud & Bossuyt (structural engineers), Technip Serr Construction (fluids), Syseca (telecommunications and security), Sauveterre-Horizon (gardening), ACV (acoustics). **Photography**: Michel Denancé, George Fessy.

rectangular podium encompassing a central recreational park.

In this work, Perrault expresses two apparently opposed dimensions: monumentality, symbolized by the book towers, and the intimacy and calm of the garden next to the reading rooms. For its architect, the library embodies emotions based on the paradox between presence and absence, human scale and monumental, dark and light, opposing forces.

The Bibliothèque Nationale de France (French National Library) is located to the east of Paris, in Tolbiac, near the Seine, in accordance with the urban development plan of bringing more facilities and parks to this area. It is claimed that the city is expanding beyond its ring roads for the first time. This library was the last major commission of former president, the late François Mitterrand.

The new building, which has a capacity of more than three million visitors a year, has 3600 reading places, an exhibition center, an auditorium, conference rooms, and restaurants. It will also act as the hub of a computerized network of French libraries.

Four glass towers, lined with bookshelves, stand at the corners of a huge

La Mesa Public Library

Antoine Predock

Location: Los Alamos, New Mexico, USA. **Date of completion**: 1994. **Cost**: $5.1 million. **Architect**: Anto ne Predock. **Associates**: Geoffrey Beebe (managing partner), Paul Gonzales, Breatt Oaks (design directors Rebecca Ingram, George Newlands, Deborah Waldrip, Linda Christenson, John Brittingem, Cameron Erc mann, Geoff Adams, Mark Donahue (design team), Randy Holt & Associates (structural engineers), P2R Group (mechanical engineers), Telcon Engineering (electricity), High-Point Schaer (construction manage ment), Bradbury & Stamm Construction (construction). **Scheme**: Reading rooms, storage, administration, an services. **Photography**: Timothy Hursley.

The new library is halfway between abstract sculpture and integration into the natural surroundings. The library is a low, two-floor building. It is curved to enjoy the magnificent views to the north. A taller, pyramid-shaped tower cuts the library in two. This feature is reminiscent of the edges of the rock walls near Turfa close to Los Alamos. Where the tower intersects with the building, Antoine Predock has designed a courtyard over which access to the building is gained.

As with many of Antoine Predock's works, the main material used is concrete, both blocks and in situ shuttered concrete. Predock works with this material in a certain way, with the intention of achieving an image similar to that of the monumental constructions found in primitive villages.

Denver Central Library

Michael Graves

Location: Denver, Colorado, USA. **Date of completion**: January 1996. **Developer**: Denver City Council. **Cost**: $46.5 million. **Architect**: Michael Graves. **Associates**: Klipp Colussy Jenks DuBois Architects (managing), Hyman/Etkin Construction (management), S.A. Miro (structural engineers), The Ballard Group (mechanical engineers), Gambrell Engineering (electricity), Clanton Engineering (lighting), Engel/Kieding Design Associates (interior design), Badgett and Cover-Clark (landscaping), David L. Adams (acoustics). **Scheme**: Thematic reading rooms. **Photography**: Timothy Hursley.

Michael Graves built this extension to Denver's Central Library. The original building, designed by Burnham Hoyt in 1956, is listed in the National Register of Historic Places. The old library retains its institutional presence in the Civic Center Park, to the north, and its own identity as one element of a larger composition. The extension is to the south, at the back, with a strong, new public image. With its signature round, south-facing façade, it is destined to become a focal point of Thirteenth Avenue.

Scale, color, and variety of shape synthesize with the surroundings. The downtown image is an authentic geometric composition of prisms of different sizes and colors which overlap in a horizontal plane. Michael Graves in turn works with absolute, known shapes: cylinders, prisms, cones, pyramids, etc.

Graves in some way applies to an individual design the ratios which the buildings establish with each other within the overall cityscape.

However, the Indianapolis architect is not only seeking to integrate the design into the city but also for it to carry a symbolic and meaningful charge. In other words, Graves is trying to give architecture a quality which is absent from the modern movement: monumentality. Especially in the case of public buildings, Graves believes that architects have an obligation to translate into their work the significance of every institution in society.

Peckham Library

Alsop & Stormer

Location: London, United Kingdom. **Date of completion**: 1999. **Architects**: Alsop & Stormer. **Collaborators**: Adams Kara Taylor (structures), Concord Lighting Design (lighting), Battle McCarthy (environmental engineering). **Gross floor area**: 4.500 m². **Photography**: Roderick Coyne.

This project is part of a major urban renewal program for the Peckham area in southeast London. In conjunction with other proj-ects, such as the construction of a modern sports center in 1998 or the refurbishing of the urban furnishings, the library creates a new landscape. The local authorities who commissioned the work were very clear about their requirements: the building was to bring prestige to the neighborhood with a design that was ahead of its time while eschewing an elitist appearance that might inhibit users–the public should be able to identify with the building. The goal was also to create

a flexible facility, adaptable to the needs of future generations.

The library designed by the architects Alsop & Stormer takes the shape of an inverted L, with a horizontal block raised twelve meters above street level and supported partially on columns and partially on a vertical block. This design creates a covered space for outdoor activities. In addition, the cantilevered volume shades the south façade, such that neither blinds nor any other sort of sun protection were needed. Enormous stainless-steel lettering two meters tall contributes to the building's peculiar

silhouette.

The horizontal block consists of a double-height space that houses the main desk, the book area, and, at the north, the children's library. Three ovoid volumes on columns that house a center for Afro-Caribbean literature, a children's activities area, and a conference hall inhabit this large area. Capping the largest space is a large orange skylight-roof that can be seen from the street.

The main façade is covered by metal mesh, while the south, east, and west enclosures are clad in copper panels. The windows of the vertical block are of colored glass fixed with silicone to aluminium frames, forming a peculiar curtain wall.

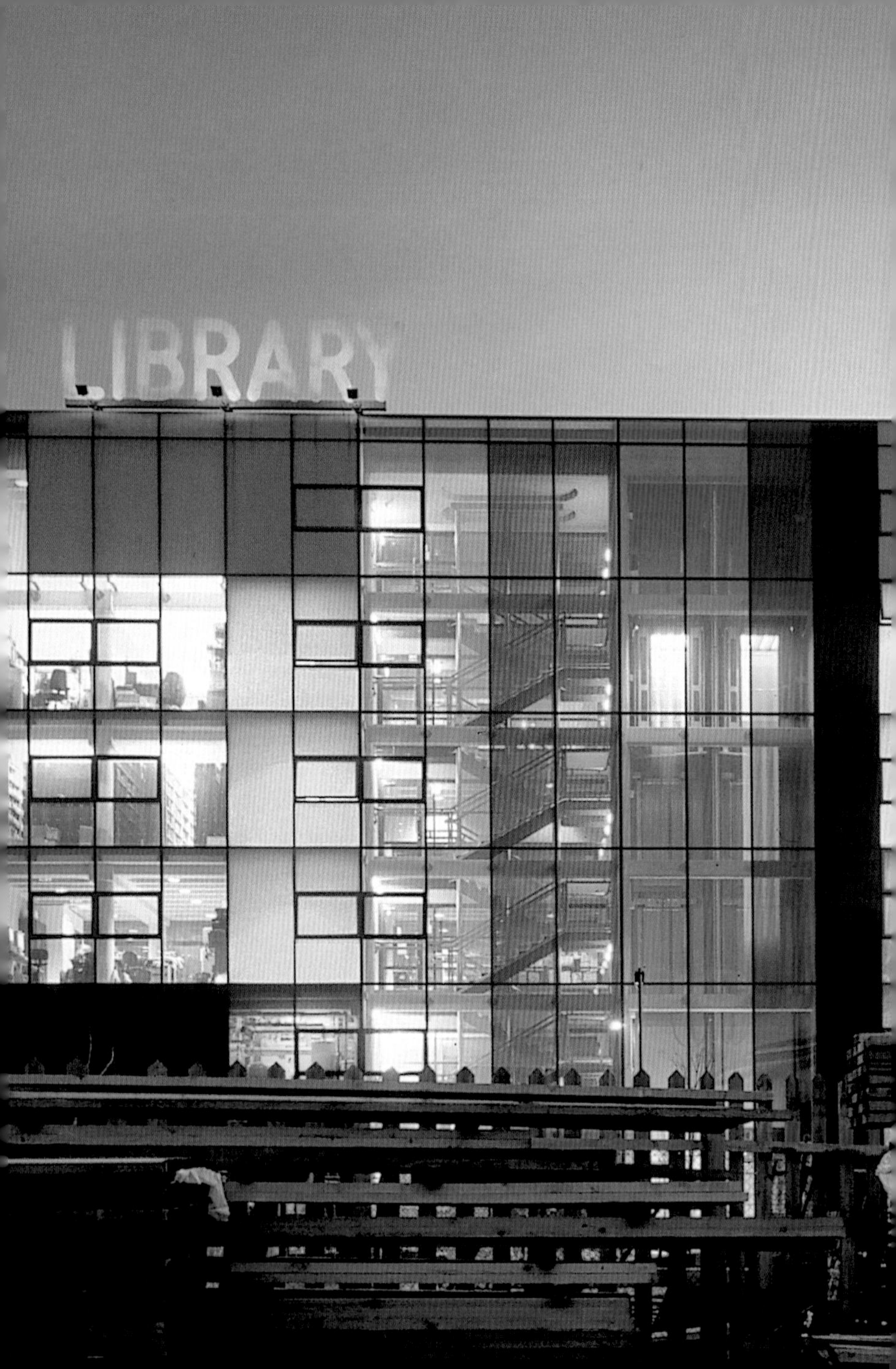
LIBRARY

Monterrey Central Library

Legorreta Architects

Location: San Nicolás de los Ganza, Nuevo León, Mexico. **Date of completion**: 1994. **Client**: Universidad Autónoma de Nuevo León. **Architect**: Legorreta Arquitectos. **Associates**: Armando Chávez, José Vigil. **Interior design**: Legorreta Arquitectos, Chávez Vigil Arquitectos Asociados. **Photography**: Lourdes Legorreta.

traditional Mexican architecture appear in a totally contemporary form. The focal points of intense color and light filtered through courtyards and latticework remind us of the country's popular architecture, which the library incorporates in its essence, referring to the context through its reworking, but not quoting the forms literally.

The main section of the library consists of two large structures: a central cube within an embracing cylinder. The cylindrical corona opens towards the lake, terminating in triangular buttresses, the largest of which spills directly into the water. The central cube, hidden from the rest of the perimeter by the cylinder, can be seen through these two wedges. The reading areas are located in the cylindrical corona, offering panoramic views over the park.

Externally, the building impresses by the roundness and simplicity of the geometric twins, which, despite their size, harmoniously integrate themselves into the surrounding park. Only two materials are used for the walls: the brick of the imposing cylinder, in perfect harmony with the visible concrete of the rest of the buildings, with the exception of the tower and access corridor, which are also made of open brickwork. Elements of

Monterrey Central Library 363

Children's library

Paula Santos

Location: Oporto, Portugal. **Date of completion**: 1996. **Architect**: Paula Santos. **Associates**: Rui Ramos, Joaquin Santana. **Photography**: Luis Ferreira Alves, Paula Santos.

The little pavilion located among the trees in the garden has a dual height lobby and two floors intercommunicating via a wooden staircase. The library has the appearance of an *objet trouvé* in the wild, part of the hazardous nature of the countryside. The light, welcoming building looks like a railroad car slightly raised off the ground. It gives the impression that it has been carefully placed there without damaging or altering the surroundings. The materials used in its construction respect and adapt to the countryside following the textures and colors of nature.

The structure and wall panels are of timber and the windows are strips of transparent polycarbonate, located at a child's height, with excellent views over the garden. The idea of a toy box met with such approval that the local authority decided to build another pavilion in Oporto City Park, now in use, to serve as a children's library and toy library.

A few modifications have been introduced in this second building to make the walls able to withstand the cold of an Oporto winter. Wood has been used as it is a versatile material which is suitable for various building systems and because it is very expressive. Wood is also perfect for parks.

Religious buildings

Of all the sections of *The World of Architecture*, this one features projects that have probably recently undergone the greatest change in concept and design. This is the main reason that we decided to allocate these buildings a separate section. Edifices dedicated to keeping the faith and developing the spirit always used to be very old structures which had endured up to the present. Many of the projects presented here are, of course, from countries with strong religious traditions. However, there are many major international architects who have decided to take the risk involved in merging architecture and spirituality in a building. We have included the most recent works by Siza, Maki, Holl, Fuksas and others.

Mänistön Church and Parochial Center

Juka Leiviskä

Location: Kuopio, Finland. **Date of completion**: 1993. **Client**: Kuopio Lutheran Evangelical Parish. **Architect**: Juka Leiviskä. **Associates**: Pekka Kivisalo (urban development), Parkku Pääkkönen, Mirja Arias (plastic arts), Harry Dunkel (structural engineer), Markkanen & Tiirikainen (mechanical engineering), E. Pitkänen & K (electricity). **Photography**: Arno de la Chapelle, Jussi Tiainen.

The church, parochial center, and local authority social center are located on a slope, on a strip of land between tall 1960s apartment blocks and a recreational park.
The entrance is on the lower level. The church has an undefined profile: light enters through its many folds. The inner spaces are built around the natural lighting of the building.

"I have tried to ensure that all the component parts, the walls (with their respective works of art), the ceiling, the first floor amphitheatre, the organ… form a whole. My intention is to provide vital interaction between the large and the small, the open and the closed, the high and the low, spaces as instruments to interpret the light, the veil woven by the reflections and their continual changes." Its proximity to the baroque world (Lutheran asceticism, but not the suffering and punishment of the Counter-reformation) is not so much aesthetic as epistemological.
Leiviskä identifies artistic experience with religion and mysticism. Therefore, it is acceptable to say that his work transcends architecture, because space is not the end-purpose of the work but rather seeing reality as a revelation.

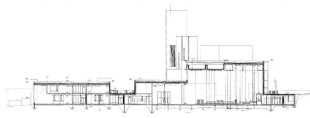

Kol Ami Temple

William P. Bruder

Location: Scottsdale, Arizona, USA. **Date of completion**: 1994. **Client**: Temple Kol Ami. **Architect**: William P. Bruder. **Associates**: Wendell Burnette, Eric Robinson, Beau Dromiack, Maryann Bloomfield, Tim Wert (design team). **Photography**: Bill Timmerman.

The architecture of the Kol Ami Temple provides Spartan spaces which acquire their definitive value from the precise entry of the light. William P. Bruder summons all the significance of natural lighting: its physical reality, its spiritual feeling, and its emotive capacity. At the same time, he juxtaposes that which is rightfully the opposite of light: matter (texture, earth, and place). The project provides a center of religion and of learning in the form of an archaic settlement, in the image of the ancient communities of Masada and Jerusalem. The Jewish temple and school are like a fortified village which continues the tradition of those desert communities, 2000 years later, on another continent and in another desert.

With the restrictions imposed by an extraordinarily small budget and the aspiration to encompass a strong symbolic presence, the emphasis of this center's design lies in the employment of concrete blocks as an essential building material. They have been used as a finish, both internally and externally; they have not been covered and the expressive possibilities of their texture have been carefully studied. This has created a special impression, with dry, irregular surfaces, deliberately weathered by sandblasting, conjuring up an image of thousand-year-old stone walls and forming a strong link to the ground underneath them.

Kaze-no-Oka Crematorium

Fumihiko Maki & Associates

Location: Nakatsu, Japan. **Date of design**: 1993–1994. **Date of construction**: 1995–1997. **Client**: Nakatsu Local Authority. **Architect**: Fumihiko Maki. **Associates**: Sasaki Environment Design Office. **Scheme**: Park, parking, crematorium, private chapel, chapel, and offices. **Total area of the park**: 3.3 ha (8.2 acres). **Photography**: Nacasa & Partners Inc.

The crematorium is built on a single floor, on an obviously large scale, so that its outline, visible from the park, is one of the outstanding features of the area. The building is basically in three sections: the sloping chapel (the tallest of the buildings), a blank, sloping, crowning wall which encloses some of the functional areas, and a gateway opening onto the park which links the other two sections.

Behind this screen lie the facilities of the crematorium, which are generous in terms of size and scrupulously arranged according to the functional requirements of the cremation service.

The interior, however, is in itself a precise form of landscaping: by painstaking control of the entry of light, the layout of courtyards, openings, pools, screens, etc. Proceeding through the interior has all the qualities of a walk in the countryside areas of Japan.

1. Parking lot
2. Court yard
3. Porch at the entrance
4. Oratory
5. Crematorium
6. Mortuary
7. Court yard
8. Waiting hall
9. Offices
10. Chapel
11. Park

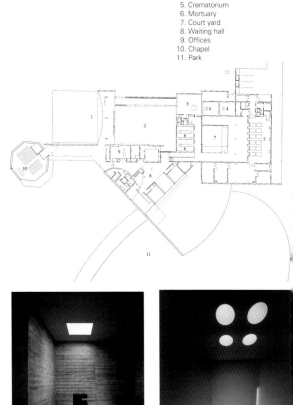

Cemetery and place of worship

Bernard Desmoulin

Location: Fréjus, France. **Date of construction**: 1997. **Architect**: Bernard Desmoulin. **Scheme**: Cemetery, museum, and place of prayer. **Photography**: Michel Denancé, Hervé Abbadie.

On the site of the former encampment from where French soldiers set sail for Indo-China, Bernard Desmoulin has created a cemetery, a garden, a small museum, and a place of quiet meditation for Christians, Buddhists, Jews, and Muslims. Desmoulin's intention is for Mediterranean plants (mimosa, olives, lavender) to cover entirely the concrete walls surrounding the circular garden and the cemetery itself, located along its center line. On one side, set slightly away from the cemetery, a small copper pergola encloses the four prayer houses, one for each religion. The museum is at the entrance to the precinct.

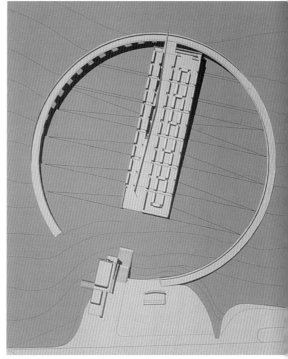

Church of Christ, Tokyo

Maki Associates

Location: 1-30-17 Tomigaya, Shibuya-ku, Tokyo, Japan. **Date of completion**: 1995. **Architect**: Maki Associates. **Associates**: Kimura Structural Engineers; Sogo Consultants (furniture, lighting, etc.), Takenaka Corporation (contractor). **Photography**: Toshiharu Kitajima.

The building is divided vertically: the first level, a dense and complex layer, houses all the ancillary facilities of the church (offices, dining room, kitchen etc.). Above this is the main area, designed as an extensive, diaphanous space, which occupies the whole of the second floor of the building, where the community meets to worship. The shape of the building expresses the idea of placing on a complex base a single area which is open to the sky and the light. The side walls are slightly inclined so that the building expands as it rises; and the roof is designed like a thin, plain dome, imitating the dome of the heavens. The front wall is designed as a huge screen of light to flood the inside of the church with diffused, filtered, magical, intense light.

The curtain wall consists of two layers of glass with an 80 cm (30 in) gap which provides excellent soundproofing, as well as a current of air between the two layers, which reduces overheating due to the rays of the sun.

Chapel of St. Ignatius

Steven Holl

Location: University of Seattle, Washington, USA. **Date of construction**: 1997. **Client**: University of Seattle. **Architect**: Steven Holl. **Associates**: Olson/Sundber Architects (associate architects), Baugh Construction (general contractor). **Area**: 790 m² (8500 ft²). **Photography**: Paul Warchol.

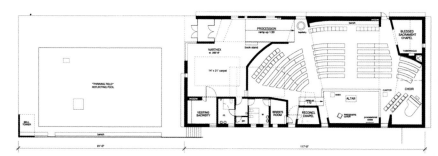

The Chapel of St. Ignatius serves the Catholic Jesuit community of the University of Seattle and is therefore designed to meet their religious requirements.

It has a rectangular floor plan, whose first roof (from which all the others start) is a basic horizontal plane which gives rise to a prism whose subsequent changes define each of the dimensions of the chapel. Insofar as the bell tower, the highest structure, is located on the opposite side of the pool, the whole of the religious area strictly speaking is confined within the larger rectangle which runs from the bell tower to the opposite end, including the location of the pool.

For the interior, Holl uses very deliberate devices for lighting purposes. Each area has its own skylight. In defining the quality and significance of the light for each area, Holl talks about a "field," which is where the internal dividing walls of each area are located, and "lenses," which specify the color of the light filter of each opening. Thus, the code can be defined as follows:

– Processional entrance and narthex: natural daylight
– Nave: yellow field with blue lenses (east); blue field with yellow lenses (west)
– Holy Sacrament: orange field with purple lenses
– Choir: green field with red lenses
– Reconciliation : purple field with orange lenses
– Bell tower and pool: projected and reflected nocturnal light.

Catholic Church of Paks

Imre Markovecz

Location: Paks, Hungary. **Date of completion**: 1988. **Architect**: Imre Markovecz. **Scheme**: Design and construction of a Catholic church in pine. **Photography**: Miklos Csak.

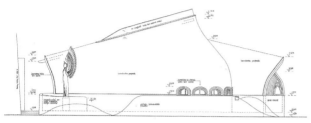

The design consists of a building with an ogee arch over which rises a sleek tower capped off by three pinnacles each about 25 m (80 ft) tall. The church also has a noticeable dimorphic character, both in the configuration of the floor plan and the layout of the various elements it contains. The central nave is vaguely triangular and is accessed from the southwest. The structure of the church has been made entirely of pine, which is a very soft and highly malleable material. The role played by light is highly symbolic: a dark area, the lower part of the nave, represents the mundane; the middle section, halfway between heaven and earth; and the highest part of the church, a celestial canopy with an almost supernatural quality to its design.

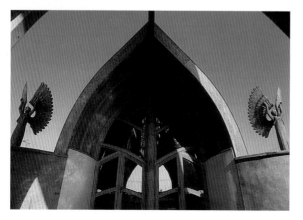

Città Castellana Cemetery

Massimiliano Fuksas, Anna Maria Sacconi

Location: Città Castellana, Viterbo, Italy. **Date of completion**: 1987. **Architects**: Massimiliano Fuksas, Anna Maria Sacconi. **Area**: 1.6 ha (4 acres). **Photography**: Doriana O. Mandrelli.

with a common formal line all of them have been built several meters off the ground and, like the house outside, are raised on pillars as if in an attempt to get spiritually closer to the life after death.

The circular shape seems to encompass the whole atmosphere of the surroundings. Only the railway track breaks this continuity by breaching the wall and, after crossing the whole of the cemetery, it exits through the second opening to finish its run in a tunnel outside. Those who wish to access the cemetery can only do so across this track.

What at first sight seems to be a warehouse is the chapel, and the water tank has been converted into an ossuary. The niches inside the wall which runs round the site have been disguised so that it is impossible to identify them from the outside. The track runs into the consecrated ground as far as the covered square, the church, and finally the ossuary. Three completely different structures, but

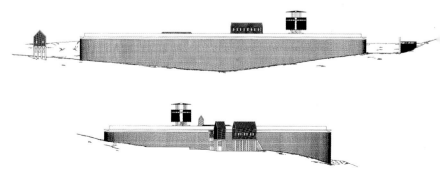

Church of Santa Maria-Marco de Canaveses

Alvaro Siza

Location: Marco de Canaveses, Portugal. **Date completed**: 1999. **Architect**: Alvaro Siza. **Scheme**: New Church of Santa Maria: entrance door, font, embrasure, presbytery, altar, pulpit, sacristy, and furniture. **Photography**: Luis Ferreira Alves, Rosina Ramirez.

On entering the town, the first aspect of the church you see is its northeast façade, less stark and more airy than the main façade due to its curvilinear shape and the different heights of its various sections. The main façade opens onto a pedestrian area, houses, a school, a nursery school, and a nearby parochial center. The building is completed by two further façades: to the southeast, a huge rectangular white wall with a narrow horizontal opening at the bottom; and, to the northwest, another wall, with five enormous upper windows through which sunlight enters at the top. It is controlled illumination, filtered by its direction to prevent the nave being flooded with too much light. Before entering the church we find ourselves before the tall, dignified, extremely heavy main entrance door in the façade of the building. Once inside, the interior seems like an "empty box" full of order and light, in which a curvilinear wall with a huge visual impact stands out. This wall gives depth to the three large windows. The presbytery stands on an area slightly raised above the nave by means of three steps. The light, transparent design of the nave requires complementary furniture. The seats are light, simple, functional and safe. Their shape discreetly imitates kneeling to pray.

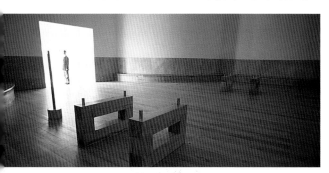

Leisure facilities

All the buildings presented here are the result of both the application of the particular style of each architect and their attention to the specific requirements of the projects. In fact, a leisure facility is an example of the ability to combine creative freedom (expressed in the morphology of the building, construction techniques, and finishes) with existing regulations (which determine dimensions, public access, safety, and the functioning of facilities). On the other hand, holding sports events unfailingly goes hand in hand with significant quantitative and qualitative changes in the urban scene, from which the city and its inhabitants benefit. The analysis of the projects in this section covers these favorable repercussions and other design-related issues resulting from the desire for integration. This philosophy rejects the concept of the architectural design as an independent and self-sufficient entity. Even in the most isolated situation, there are still factors conditioning the shape of the building in relation to the countryside and the configuration of the site. The location also, to a large extent, determines the design decisions: the selection of materials, specific matters of form, and access systems, which differ according to the degree of integration of the building into the urban framework. Finally, a review of the projects included here reveals the importance of certain aspects of construction such as lighting technology, paving, and roofs.

Auditoriums

The design of auditoriums is undoubtedly
conditioned by their functional
requirements. Acoustic demands
determine the final shape of the concert
hall. Materials and finishes have specific
sound reverberation qualities and thus also
influence the acous-tic behavior of the hall.
Architects, assisted by specialists, must
ensure that the building works correctly
from both the technical point of view and
in relation to its patrons: travel
connections, auxiliary services,
external connections, etc. The examples
given here achieve a perfect balance
between functionality and aesthetic
harmony; they are emblematic buildings
which are regarded as unique, virtually
essential to the city which houses them.

Auditorium Niccolà Paganini

Barcelona Auditorium

Parco della Musica Auditorium

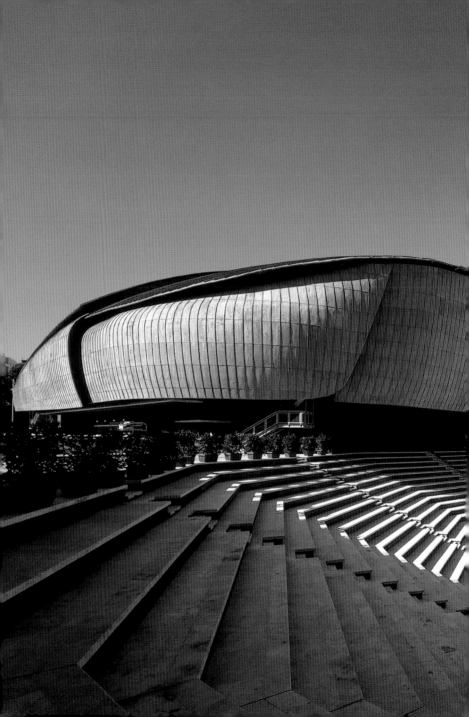

Niccolò Paganini Auditorium

Renzo Piano

Location: Viale Barilla, Parma, Italia. **Date of construction**: 1997-2002. **Architect**: Renzo Piano. **Photography**: Enrico Cano.

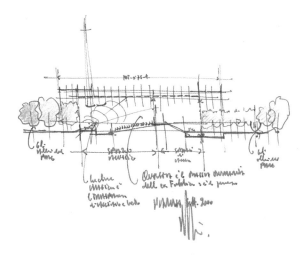

with acoustic insulating material suspended from the beams provides the finishing touches to the interior spatial organization. The audience enters the complex from the southernmost point and crosses a covered courtyard to arrive at the double-height foyer that leads on to the large concert hall. The 2,700-square foot stage to the north can hold big orchestras and choirs.

The Niccolò Paganini Auditorium was built inside the old Eridania sugar factory, an industrial complex made up of several buildings in a variety of styles. These manufacturing premises are located near Parma's historic center, in a park studded with indigenous trees and shrubs. The factory's conversion into an auditorium was made possible by the original layout–which enabled all the installations to be fitted in with ease–as well as its privileged position in the middle of the park, which made it easier to soundproof the auditorium.

The original façades were replaced by large glass walls, which endow the entire building with light and views–wonderful views of the surroundings can even be enjoyed from the seats inside the hall. A series of panels covered

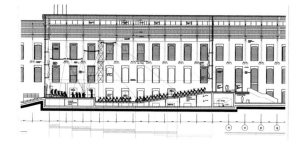

Barcelona Auditorium

Rafael Moneo

Location: Barcelona, Spain. **Date of construction:** 1999 **Architect:** Rafael Moneo. **Client:** Barcelona Local Authority. **Scheme:** Two concert halls, practice rooms, museum of music, library, recording rooms, restaurant, offices, and services. **Photography:** Ana Quesada.

The Barcelona Auditorium is located on an unattractive plot which did not offer the architect any inspiration. The compelling, forceful autonomy of the building can be seen in the contained and compact architecture, which must nevertheless accommodate and house highly complex and extensive facilities: two concert halls, one with seating for an audience of 2500 and the other for 700, with all the services that accompany such halls; practice rooms for orchestras and soloists, a museum of music, library, recording rooms, restaurants, store rooms, and other facilities.

Faced with such elaborate demands, the design opted for compactness, imposed by the strict size dictates of the structure. The fabric of the building is a network of reinforced concrete complemented by stainless steel panels on the outside and oak panels on the inside. Compactness also requires empty spaces which establish distances and define contiguities.

Parco della Mùsica Auditorium

Renzo Piano

Location: Roma, Italia. **Date of construction**: 1994-2002. **Architect**: Renzo Piano. **Photography**: Gianni Berengo Gardin, Moreno Maggi.

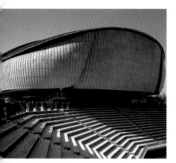

intensely devoted to music, with three concert halls surrounded by dense vegetation and laid out in such a way that they create an amphitheater for open-air performances. Each auditorium was planned to put on a certain type of performance. So, the 700-seater is intended for Baroque and chamber music; the 1,200-seater is characterized by its great flexibility, enabling it to accommodate large orchestras and ballets; while the largest, with 2,800 seats–the maximum capacity guaranteeing good acoustics–is designed for symphonic concerts. The project placed a

special emphasis on the acoustics in all the spaces, including the rehearsal rooms, the dressing rooms, and the amphitheater. Flexibility was another top priority in the brief as the complex had to be able to absorb different groups of spectators. The remains of a villa dating from the fourth century BC were found during the building works, and so the main foyer had to be adapted to this site and make room for a small archeological museum.

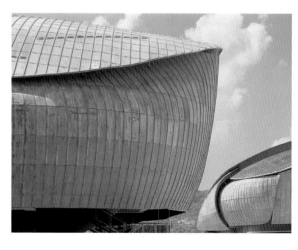

This superb auditorium is a further addition to the Italian capital's already long list of cultural venues. It is a multipurpose center

Theaters and cinemas

The theater can be a sacred ceremony or simply entertainment, a show of three acts or a spontaneous production, the actors can declaim from the stage or mix with the audience... Although they may come in many shapes, theaters do not vary much because in the end the problem to be solved is always the same: lots of spectators looking at a few actors. But what has changed, and it is different in every project, is the way in which this isolated space relates to the rest of the world, both inside and out.

The external appearance of the building, the method of access to the reception area, the stairs, the lobbies... as well as the finishes, colors, materials, fabrics, and decorations. In other words, everything which exists before the actors start to speak, before the lights go down, before the band begins to play.

Pathé Cinemas

Kosmos UFA-Palast

City of Arts Cinema-Planetarium

La Géode

American Conservatory Theater

Chassé Theater

Cultural center in Tapiola

Theater Arts Center

The Hague Dance Theater

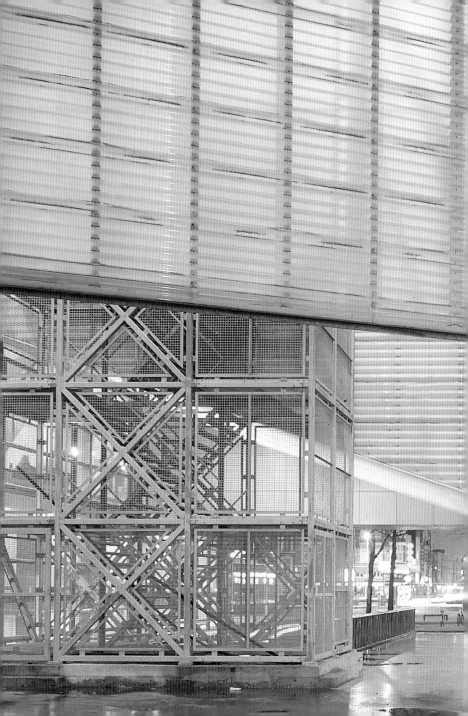

Pathe Multiplex Cinema

Koen van Velsen

Location: Rotterdam, The Netherlands. **Construction dates:** July 1994 - December 1995. **Client:** Pathé Cinemas. **Architect:** Koen van Velsen. **Collaborators:** Gero Rutten, Marcel Steeghs, Lars Zwant, Okko van der Kam. **Acoustical engineering:** van Dorsser. **Scheme:** A seven-screen cinema center, a restaurant and a café. **Gross floor surface:** 8473 m². **Photography:** Kim Zwartz.

Pathé Cinema's new cinema center adds to the variety of cultural activities offered in Rotterdam's central Schouwburgplein (Shouwburg Square). The complex contains seven screens with a total seating capacity of 2700.

Much of the project has been conditioned by technical factors. The building rests on a preexisting underground parking garage, part of which has been removed to allow space for the restaurant, or Grand Café. A metallic structure is wrapped in a thin translucent skin, lightening the building both in physical weight and in visual presence.

Each cinema hall is an isolated box separated from the other halls by corridors and restrooms. The façade of undulating polycarbonate cladding has a structure independent from the rest of the building but which wraps around it in free form. The translucent polycarbonate cladding covers both the inside and outside of the surrounding independent wall so that air pipes and fire escapes are partially hidden. The undulating sheets lend the construction an industrial appearance during the day, and at night transform it into a softly glowing light bulb, becoming the center of attention on the plaza.

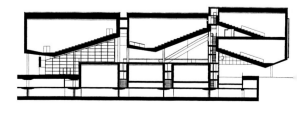

Kosmos UFA–Palast

Rhode Kellermann Wawrowsky

Location: Berlin, Germany. **Date of construction**: 1997. **Design team**: Andrew Barley, Stefanie Bode, Daniel Bush, Hans Feyerabend, Kathleen King, Matthius Pfeiffer, Katharina Riedel, Willi Robens, Michael Ross, Brigitte Treutner, Marc Ulrich, Walter Wernecke. **Floor area**: 9000 m² (97,000 ft²). **Photography**: Christian Gahl, Florian Protitlich.

The Kosmos cinema was built in 1962 by Josef Kaiser as part of the monumental Karl-Marx-Allee in the Friedrichschain district of East Berlin. It was a detached building surrounded by enormous apartment blocks, set back from the road behind a parking lot.

After reunification, it was purchased by a private company which decided to modernize and extend it. As it was a listed building, RKW decided to restrict themselves to restoring the original building and to place the new buildings around it. The old and new sections are connected by

an elliptical corridor lit from above in the daytime by means of a skylight. The surface parking lot has been replaced by an underground one and a square created in front of the cinema.

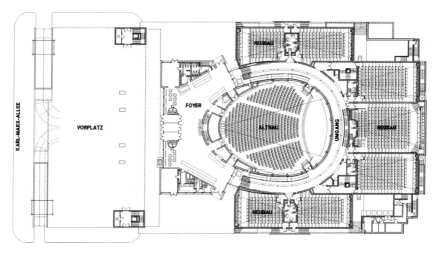

City of Arts Cinema-Planetarium

Santiago Calatrava

Location: Valencia, Spain. **Date of construction**: 1999. **Architect**: Santiago Calatrava **Scheme**: Cinema-planetarium, exhibition hall, bar, offices, and services. **Photography**: Paco Asensio.

The City of Arts & Sciences is the beacon project of a culture/leisure complex built on the dry bed of the river Turia in the city of Valencia which includes, in addition to the cinema-

planetarium, an art gallery, science museum and oceanographic center. Virtually all the buildings were designed by the Valencia-based engineer and architect Santiago

Calatrava.
The cinema-planetarium is designed for showing Omnimax films as well as regular flat projections in a planetarium. The cinema itself is a white sphere. However, Santiago Calatrava built a second roof on it which protects the lobby and access areas. A system of telescopic arms on the sides enables a huge area of glass to be closed or made into a protective canopy.

La Géode

Adrien Fainsilber

Location: La Villete, Paris, France. **Date of completion**: 1988. **Client**: Paris Municipality. **Architect**: Adrien Fainsilber. **Scheme**: Museum of science and technology, cinema. **Photography**: Charlie Abad.

La Géode is the result of an urban development project by the Parisian authorities to reconstruct some old buildings, previously used as abattoirs, and convert them into a major science museum known as the City of Science and Industry. The whole of the museum is designed as a surprise for the visitor, who enters an unknown world where the latest advances in scientific and technological innovation are revealed. One of the main attractions of the complex is the Géode, a huge steel sphere, somewhere between a building and a monument, which houses a high-tech cinema whose audiences are bombarded with spectacular images. Like a crystal ball, the circular geometry of La Géode makes a striking visual contrast to the straight lines of the museum's main building. From a distance, this compact steel ball seems to float gently on a platform of water, giving a surreal impression.

American Conservatory Theater

Gensler & Associates

Location: San Francisco. USA. **Date of completion:** 1997. **Client:** City of San Francisco. **Architects:** Gensler & Associates. **Scheme:** Refurbishment of the old City Hall, new annex. **Photography:** M. Lorenzetti.

increased. New elevators to all floors have been installed and disabled access improved. New dressing rooms, offices, and costume maintenance workshops have been built in an annex to the main building.

After the damage suffered by the 82-year-old building from an earthquake in 1989, the authorities decided to appoint Esherick Hornsey & Davis to produce an initial scheme for its refurbishment. Gensler was later commissioned to revise the design and take it through to the construction stage. Appropriate permits were obtained from local and national institutions to work on the remains of a protected building of historical importance.
The Geary Theater, as it is currently called, now has a larger reception area after the removal of several walls located at the rear of the auditorium. The acoustics, which previously suffered from outside traffic noise, have been improved. Space on the

upper floors has also been expanded and used to build additional boxes, areas for use during intermissions, and new restrooms. Although the seating capacity has been reduced by 400 seats, the size of the remaining 1035 seats and the distance between rows has been

American Conservatory Theater

Gensler & Associates

Location: San Francisco. USA. **Date of completion**: 1997. **Client**: City of San Francisco. **Architects**: Gensler & Associates. **Scheme**: Refurbishment of the old City Hall, new annex. **Photography**: M. Lorenzetti.

increased. New elevators to all floors have been installed and disabled access improved. New dressing rooms, offices, and costume maintenance workshops have been built in an annex to the main building.

After the damage suffered by the 82-year-old building from an earthquake in 1989, the authorities decided to appoint Esherick Hornsey & Davis to produce an initial scheme for its refurbishment. Gensler was later commissioned to revise the design and take it through to the construction stage. Appropriate permits were obtained from local and national institutions to work on the remains of a protected building of historical importance.

The Geary Theater, as it is currently called, now has a larger reception area after the removal of several walls located at the rear of the auditorium. The acoustics, which previously suffered from outside traffic noise, have been improved. Space on the upper floors has also been expanded and used to build additional boxes, areas for use during intermissions, and new restrooms. Although the seating capacity has been reduced by 400 seats, the size of the remaining 1035 seats and the distance between rows has been

Chassé Theater

Herman Hertzberger

Location: Breda, The Netherlands. **Date of construction**: 1992–1995. **Client**: Breda Local Authority. **Architect**: Herman Hertzberger. **Associates**: Willem van Winsen, Folkert Stropsma, Ariënne Matser, Patrick Fransen, Marijke Teijsse-Braat. **Scheme**: Main auditorium for 1200 spectators, hall for 500 spectators, two cinemas, small multipurpose room, offices, and ancillary facilities.

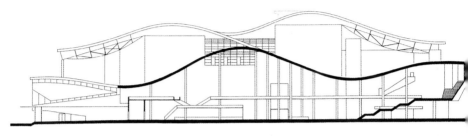

The exterior of the building is notable for its undulating roof, which adapts to the varying size requirements of its component parts and unifies the complex.

The layout of the main auditorium follows the traditional stage/audience pattern but not as far as the seating layout is concerned, where asymmetry follows the visual and acoustic asymmetry of the presentation itself, appearing in the design as a result of the linear structure of the foyer.

Access to each level is by various staircases running along the rear walls and enjoying panoramic views of the outside.

The medium-sized auditorium is designed like a "black box," a theater with retractable seats offering immense versatility for shows.

Between the two large stages, raised above the level of the foyer lies the third theater, a small area also suitable for various uses, above which is the complex's office suite. Structurally, the theaters are three concrete boxes 30 cm (1 ft) thick, which provide sound insulation; in the roof, prefabricated concrete profiles support all the machinery and equipment located in the spaces created by the undulations in the design of the roof.

Tapiola Cultural Center

Arto Sipinen

Location: Tapiola, Finland. **Date of completion**: 1991. **Client**: Tapiola Local Authority. **Architect**: Arto Sipinen. **Facilities**: Public cultural center: auditorium, exhibition halls, café-restaurant, library, workers' music institute. **Photography**: Arto Kiviennemi.

The factors which the design had to consider can be summarized as: a large building which faces the presence and complexity of an artificial lake and a hotel, at the same time that it has to take on a horizontal layout that enhances the verticality of the neighboring office complex. The large central buildings of the Center accommodate the two auditoriums, while behind the glass façades lie the cloakrooms, reception area, exhibition halls, and the café-restaurant.

The south wing of the complex is a more layered structure which houses various cultural activities: the library and the workers' music institute.

The external finishes consist of large blocks of quartz sandstone, tiled floors, and glass. Inside, the building is characterized by the use of see-through partitions, birch cladding, and decorative plants.

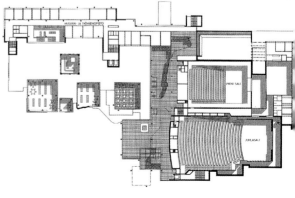

Theatre Arts Center

James Stirling & Michael Wilford Ass.

Location: London, UK. **Date of completion:** 1990. **Architects:** James Stirling & Michael Wilford Ass. **Scheme:** Theater and visual arts center: dance studios, mini-theaters, and outside courtyard. **Photography:** Richard Bryant/Arcaid.

The PAC module consists of an 80 m² (860 ft²) octagonal pavilion which acts as an information center and a shelter for the nearby bus stop. The unit consists of an upper floor with premises belonging to the Theatre Arts Department which can be adapted for touring companies. A smooth cylindrical body, arranged on the roof of the prism, exercises an expressive counterpoint of geometry and color.

On the faces of the basic building there are various openings complemented on their upper section by a series of circular windows. Next to the pavilion is an open space which can be accessed from College Avenue. This area is designed as a meeting and recreational area for students, and various items of street furniture, such as seats and a pergola, have been installed. The pergola is made of five visually strong prism-shaped pillars on which sit wooden structures supported by two back-to-back triangles. The most expressive elements which make up the image of the façade are a large circular opening, located asymmetrically at one end, and a large central arch from which emerges a glass prism, which is the main dance studio in the complex.

The Hague Dance Theater

Rem Koolhaas

Location: The Hague, The Netherlands. **Date of completion**: 1984. **Architect**: Rem Koolhaas. **Associates**: Jeroen Thomas, Willem-Jan Neutelings, Frank Roodbeen, Jaap van Heest, Ron Steiner, Dirk Hendriks, Frans Vogelaar, Wim Kloosterboer, Hans Werlemann, BOA, Petra Blaisse. **Scheme**: The Hague Dance Theater: auditorium, box office, cafeteria, offices, and services. **Photography**: Peter Aaron, Esto Photographics.

The site intended for the Koolhaas project leads into a pedestrian area which shares space with other new buildings: a hotel, a concert hall and the town hall and its offices. This physical proximity issue was resolved by instituting a shared area, located in the tinted glass lobby, where the access doors to the respective buildings are placed side by side. The building looks more like a "nave," in industrial terminology, than a compact, monumental theater complex.

The structure is designed in three individual yet integrated components: an inverted conical building, glazed at the top with a golden finish, which houses the box office and cafeteria; the sinuous, undulating profile of the auditorium roof; and finally the vast cube of the gridiron tower, presided over by a magnificent mural by Madelon Vriesendorp (Koolhaas' wife), which suggests pictorially what happens inside the theater. The sobriety of the background and minimalist rationality of the interior design turns the Dutch dance theater into a lucid example of a new way of understanding architecture in the 20th century.

Sports facilities

Designing sports facilities is a fascinating
challenge, from which have emerged
magnificent buildings that successfully
resolve aesthetic and pragmatic issues,
at the same time balancing the individual
style of the architect with the various
demands of the natural environment,
the regulations of the sport in question,
or the requirements of the developer.
This chapter aims to summarize trends in
international architecture in recent years.
The projects included clearly demonstrate
wide diversity, a direct consequence of
evolution in sporting practice.

Tobu Golf Club

Fuji Chuo Golf Club

Le Stadium

Spa Bad Elste

Utopia Pavilion

Palau Sant Jordi

Tokyo Metropolitan Gymnasium

Hamar Olympic Hall

Olympic Archery Stadium

Tobu Golf Club

Masayuki Kurokawa

Location: Yubari-gun, Hokkaido, Japan. **Date of completion**: July 1983. **Architect**: Masayuki Kurokawa Architect & Associates. **Associates**: Sasaki Structural Consultants and Nishida Engineering Equipment, Kankyo Engineering Inc. (structural engineers), Matsushita Electric Works Ltd. **Scheme**: Club room, restaurants, cloakrooms, gymnasium, meeting rooms, administration, and services. **Photography**: Nacasa & Partners Inc.

The club consists of a main building and an annex. The main building is rectangular in shape with another rectangular open space at the center. The annex roof continues the slope of the main building so that they seem to be joined. The building attempts to blend into the scenery. However, when the door is opened and the lobby is accessed, the building's image changes completely. The central courtyard contains a large pond; the areas around the pond, the lounge and a corridor, take light from the courtyard. In other words, the empty space becomes the heart of the building. It works like a trap which ensnares nature, to the benefit of the members.

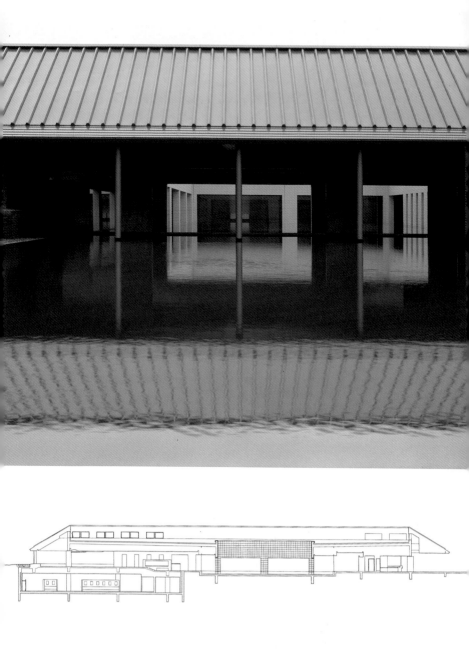

Fuji Chuo Golf Club

Desmond Muirhead

Location: Mount Fuji, Japan. **Date of construction:** 1995. **Architect:** Desmond Muirhead.

Muirhead based the layout of the 18 holes on the wood engravings of the Japanese artist Hokusai. They are laid out exactly like a hundred different readings of Mount Fuji, the most famous of which is "The Great Wave," which is the 17th hole. Thus from a list in which each of the 18 holes was assigned an engraving by Hokusai, with its own title and theme, Muirhead independently designed each of the holes, giving the theme shape through the very design instruments of golf courses themselves: bunkers, lakes, wooded areas, slopes, etc.

The various changes that the landscape undergoes during the day and the seasons (changes in light, presence or absence of snow, fog or other elements which alter the appearance of the mountain) are taken into account in Muirhead's project as factors of a landscape in constant metamorphosis, reflecting the passage of time and the special feeling of every hour of the day or time of the year.

Le Stadium

Rudy Ricciotti

Location: Vitrolles, France. **Date of completion**: 1995. **Architect**: Rudy Ricciotti. **Scheme**: Sports track, bleachers, ticket offices, offices, bar, foyer, and services. **Photography**: Philippe Ruault.

Le Stadium is a kind of enormous monolith that breaks up the countryside, a completely hermetically sealed building, such that its purpose cannot be distinguished from the outside. The inside of the building has a much clearer layout. Bleachers are laid out on one side only because the stadium is primarily for rock concerts and to a lesser extent for sports meetings. The ground plan is almost a perfect square: 58 x 56 m (190 x 184 ft). The foyer is just underneath the bleachers.

The restrooms are located on both sides, with the stages just opposite them.

Spa Bad Elste

Behnisch & Partner

Location: Bad Elster, Germany. **Date of completion:** 1999. **Architects:** Behnisch & Partner. **Collaborators:** Luz & Partner (landscaping), Erich Wiesner (color study). **Grossfloor area:** 17.320 m². **Photography:** Christian Kandzia & Martin Schodder.

The Spa Bad Elster is one of the oldest peat moss spas in Germany. Through the years it has undergone numerous modifications to improve and enlarge its installations, and thus reflects diverse architectural styles. After winning the competition for the new work, the Behnisch & Partner studio faced the challenge of restructuring the complex, including the demolition of a number of obsolete buildings, the construction of a new bathhouse and an information center, as well as the rearrangement of the existing spaces.

The original buildings are grouped around a large rectangular courtyard, on to which face in a somewhat helter-skelter manner the rear façades. The main façades, of which some in baroque style stand out, open outwards, with views of the town and the nearby woodlands. The architects' primary objective was to instill the complex with a new life: redesigning the central area and attempting to harmonize the new buildings with the existing ones.

With this project, the courtyard, formerly used as a storage area and to prepare the mud, became the heart of the complex, with the new bathhouse as its most outstanding structure. The design of the bathhouse was governed by extreme sensitivity: it was endowed with a peaceful and gratifying atmosphere which, along with its therapeutic virtues, make the building an ideal place to relax.

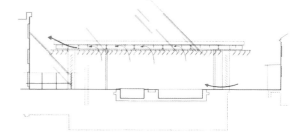

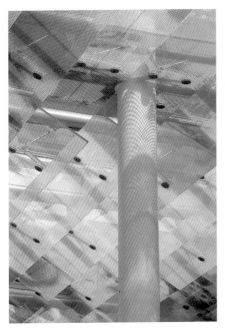

442 Leisure facilities

Utopia Pavilion

S.O.M.

Location: Lisbon, Portugal. **Date of completion:** 1998. **Client:** Lisbon Municipality. **Architect:** S.O.M. **Scheme** Multifunction stadium. **Photography:** Paco Asensio.

The Utopia Pavilion is the result of collaboration between the US team S.O.M. and Regino Cruz. Beneath the metal roof with sawtooth skylights, the huge laminated timber beams which support an opening of 114 m (375 ft), make the inside of the pavilion seem like the hull of a ship. Externally, the building consists of a metal casing, something like a seashell, which provides access for the public via a glazed façade. The texture of the casing is broken only where ventilation shafts or projections housing services appear. The appearance of the pavilion is the result of a complex paradox: though the external shape is very organic, very natural, the metal and glass finish gives it a markedly futuristic appearance. This unusual combination, and the fact that it stands free and clear on the plot, distinguishes the building and makes it one of the flagships of the architectural and urban development work carried out for Expo '98.

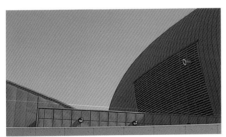

Palau Sant Jordi

Arata Isozaki & Associates

Location: Montjuïc, Barcelona, Spain. **Date of construction:** August 1985–1990. **Clients:** Barcelona Municipality, COOB'92, Institute for Energy Saving and Diversification (IDEA), and HOLSA. **Architect:** Arata Isozaki & Associates. **Scheme:** Multisports pavilion for the 1992 Olympic Games. **Photography:** Fransesc Tur.

The invitation to tender specified a sports arena which would comply with the requirements of senior competition and at the same time meet the requirements of Barcelona, which needed a covered area also able to accommodate major non-sporting cultural events. The construction design was based on three factors: firstly, formal integration with the contours of the mountain, resulting in the Palau being built as a set of low buildings covered by a vast roof whose undulations were suggestive of the curves of the landscape. Size,

smoothness, and balance were the essential guidelines followed by the Japanese architect. The second factor was the use of the most advanced building techniques, especially for the roof, a spatial mesh which combines architecture and technological processes. Finally, the new building had to be integrated into its cultural environment, using traditional materials and those most closely related to the architecture of Barcelona.

The most interesting construction feature is undoubtedly the impressive cupola which

covers the main arena. In a structure of such vast dimensions (128 x 106 m, 420 x 350 ft), the design and its implementation must be the result of a deep dialectic process in which very diverse factors are at work. Furthermore, despite its irregular shape, the cupola must act as a roof to an approximately rectangular floor. All these features place the Palau Sant Jordi in a well-deserved position among the major works of current world architecture.

Tokyo Municipal Gymnasium

Fumihiko Maki

Location: Tokyo, Japan. **Date of completion**: 1988. **Client**: Tokyo Municipality. **Architect**: Fumihiko Maki
Scheme: Public gymnasium/sports center: gymnasium, swimming pool, tennis courts, changing rooms, cafeteria, equipment store. **Photography**: Toshiaru Kitajima.

The importance of the Tokyo Gymnasium lies in the relationship between the structure and the location. The most outstanding feature is a roof which rests on a pair of parallel arches; these form a triangular structure which covers a distance of about 80 m (260 ft) on the north-south axis and reaches a maximum height of 23 m (75 ft) at the apex. The extensions of these arches are made of reinforced concrete. The basic framework of the roof runs over both arches in a transverse direction. By contrast, the side structures, which copy the same spatial design, describe a slope which starts at the arches and terminates at the pillars of the bleachers, and are made of pre-stressed concrete. In an effort to make the volatile quality of the roof apparent, it is separated from the base of the structure. In this way the roof is erected as a structure capable of determining the layout of the inner space and also contributing to the creation of the productive tension between the various areas. Another of the features which makes the Gymnasium an outstanding architectural structure is its asymmetry. Fumihiko Maki decided to encircle the multiple apparent symmetries by rotating the axis of the secondary area, the oblique structure of the stairs and the extensions emanating from the main hall area.

Hamar Olympic Hall

Niels Torp AS Arkitekter Mnal

Location: 2300 Hamar, Norway. **Date of completion**: 1992. **Client**: Hamar Olympiske Anlegg AS (HOA). **Architect**: Niels Torp AS Arkitekter Mnal. **Associates**: Biong & Biong Arkitektfirma AS; Bjorbekk & Lindhem AS (landscaping). **Gross floor area**: 25,000 m² (270,000 ft²). **Cost**: NKr 230 million. **Scheme**: Olympic ice stadium. **Photography**: Jiri Havran.

The concept for the special design of this Olympic complex started with the team of architects coming up with an idea for the roof, which is undoubtedly the building's most outstanding feature. The architects managed to give it essential flexibility and luminosity by releasing it from the unattractive structure of the rest of the building. Its vastness and design made the selection of materials and colors a secondary issue.

With regard to the general layout, it was difficult to get away from the traditional dull lines of this type of sports facility, and so the team concentrated on producing this attractive roof completely separate from the rest of the building proper.

The team thus decided to adopt the structure of 1000-year-old Norwegian ships, which still retain the beauty of the original designs. They were careful to show the detail of the old wooden arches and joints where steel is now joined to concrete. In this way they managed to make the finishes look both simple and attractive.

Another important factor that had to be taken into consideration was how to bring natural light inside the building. This was achieved with self-illuminating glass.

All details were simplified as far as possible, which enabled the traditionally low budget for this type of construction to be met.

Olympic Archery Stadium

Enric Miralles, Carme Pinós

Location: Hebron Valley Olympic Park, Barcelona, Spain. **Implementation phase**: 1990–1992. **Client**: Olympic Committee. **Architect**: Enric Miralles, Carme Pin(s. **Associates**: A. Ferr(, E. Prats, R Prats S. Mart(nez, A. Obiols, R. Brufau (structures). **Scheme**: Archery training and competition stadium, changing rooms, and storage facilities. **Photography**: David Cardel(s.

The scheme, situated at the foot of the Collserola massif, is divided into two areas – one for training, the other for competition. Each has its own archery fields, as well as athletes' buildings, including toilets and changing rooms. The gradient of the site and its terracing have been turned into the principal feature of the buildings. The structures seem to vanish into the ground and support the soil of the terrace immediately above. They therefore have only one façade connected with the shooting, over which they display an unobtrusive dominance. In the training enclosure, it is the movement of the containing wall that defines the limits of the building. The tectonic dynamism of its concave lines generates a series of curved, flat, vertical and horizontal surfaces with an array of pitches serving to close off, cover, separate, and protect. By contrast, the competition enclosure was designed with accessibility in mind. Here, the movements of the earth form traverses, including the spectator in the landscape. The building emerges from the repetition of changing room and shower units, each of which is a block closed off at the front by concrete screens. In the words of the architects themselves, they built a tectonic fault and a hole, with concavities in the containing wall.

Theme parks and attractions

In an era in which virtuality and fiction are gaining an increasing presence in our daily lives, reality is continually breaking down. It is no surprise that the places where adventures and fantasies are lived out have ended up by surpassing even the wildest dreams and have crystallized into actual cities. The sites are being used to weave a network of venues whose sole function is recreation and entertainment. These leisure and theme parks are characterized by the way in which they take on the form of isolated "cities" surrounded by nature, with a landscape completely at odds with the traditional. Alongside these have appeared another type of center within an enclosed domain. Here, adventures are no longer played out in real space but, for example, behind a computer screen.

Sydney International Aquatic Centre

Philip Cox

Location: Sydney, Australia. **Year of opening**: 1994. **Client**: Kaiser Bautechnik. **Associates**: Reinhold Meye (structural engineering), Kaiser Bautechnik (works supervision), Roger Preston (mechanical and electrica engineering). **Photography**: Ralph Richter (Architekturphoto).

The Sydney International Aquatic Centre was one of the key elements in the success of Australia's bid to host the Olympic Games in the year 2000. This complex will house the main water sports events, but is also intended as a major leisure center. It combines the functions of a specialized facility capable of staging top class sporting events and a recreational center.

The huge arch supporting the roof has the greatest visual impact and can be seen for miles around. A talus, like a fold in the landscape next to the building, reduces the architectural impact. Access is at intermediate level. Passing through the entrance, the visitor reaches one of the walkways beneath the rows of seats. A bridge crosses to connect the side tiers, separating the competition side from the recreation and entertainment area. This is an elevated walkway for the public with views to both sides, which breaks up the area's continuity without separating the two zones completely. It also has a false corrugated ceiling, which helps the transition to be made between the different roof heights from one zone to the following one.

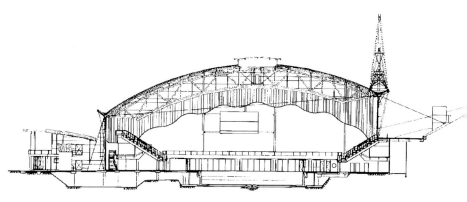

Duisburg-North Park

Latz & Partner

Location: Duisburg, North Rhine-Westphalia, Germany. **Date of project**: 1990 (competitive tender). **Date of construction**: 1991–2000. **Client**: Development Company of North Rhine-Westphalia and the City of Duisburg. **Architects**: Latz & Partner. **Associates**: IBA (Internationale Bauausstellung), IG Nordpark, Society for Industrial Culture and Duisburg City Gardens Department. **Scheme**: Recreational, sporting, and cultural park. **Area**: 230 ha (570 acres). **Photography**: Latz & Partner, Christa Panick, Peter Wilde, Michael Latz, Angus Parker.

The Duisburg-North Park project is part of an enormous green belt area in the Emscher region. The German state of North Rhine-Westphalia, along with cities in the Emscher region, have implemented several projects aimed at regenerating former industrial areas in the Ruhr river basin. Duisburg-North Park is located in an area of heavy industry centered on coal and steel between the urban districts of Duisburg and Oberhausen. Disused plant is still to be found on the site of the former Thyssen foundry–boilers, storage sheds, furnaces, and railway installations. An international competition, won by the Latz & Partner team, planned to regenerate the area completely. The aim was to provide the region's dense population with recreational, sporting, and cultural venues in the context of the regeneration of old industrial plant, exhibiting an awareness of its enormous value, not only as a memorial to the site, but also as a genuine act of research into industrial archeology. Wherever possible, materials found in the area have been used, either directly or as recycled products, such as the iron for the walkways, platforms, or gates.

Port Aventura

Peckham, Guytin Albers & Viets, Inc.

Location: Salou, Tarragona, Spain. **Date of completion:** 1995. **Architect:** Peckham, Guyton Albers & Viets, Inc. **Scheme:** Theme park. **Photography:** David Cardelús.

To visit Port Aventura is to become immersed in the seductive charms of the far-off and the unknown. Visitors become the main protagonists in five fascinating adventures:

they are moved by the quiet, unobtrusive charm of the Mediterranean coast, discover the exuberance of tropical Polynesian vegetation, move on to China ruled by mandarins and emperors, get to know Mexico, both in its pre-Columbian days and during the heights of its colonial era, and even play the boldest cowboy in the Wild West. The single element that unifies the park and, at the same time, allows such distinct landscapes to coexist within a limited space, is water. The construction of a giant artificial lake in the middle of the site affects the project in a variety of ways and is of fundamental importance to its internal organization. The fact that the center is inaccessible creates a circular sequence between spaces, making it easier for each sector to

become an isolated unit. A perspective view emerges of each setting, from one side of the lake to the other, giving visitors a general view of each area and of the park as a whole, which enables them to control the pace of their visit and decide on their priorities. Crossings from one zone to another can be made by boat or steam train. Water is also the main ingredient of some of the park's most exciting rides, such as the Rapids, the Wild River Ride or the Tutuki Splash. The park's vegetation has been another of its major successes, with the importation of native species and the use of other indigenous varieties similar to those found in the countries represented on the site.

Disneyland Paris

Derek Lovejoy Partnership

Location: Marne-La-Valle, France. **Date of completion:** 1990. **Client/Developer:** Disney Corporation. **Architect:** Derek Lovejoy Partnership. **Associate:** Imagineering. **Scheme:** Leisure and theme park. **Photography:** David Blackwood Murray, Clive McDonnell.

This park, situated in Marne-La-Valle, 32 km (20 miles) from Paris, marks Europe's introduction to the concept of the theme park and recreational center created by the Walt Disney Corporation, which has already enjoyed 40 years of success in the United States and Japan. The project involved the commissioning of the Derek Lovejoy Partnership to complete the general background scenery and landscape design in the five zones and service areas. The generous dimensions of the site of this magical kingdom (2000 ha, 4800 acres) are bounded by a bank rising to a height of 20 m (65 ft), which transforms the park into a landmark, standing out against the plane of this French plateau. This acreage is in turn subdivided into the five main attractions or "worlds." The elements used to create this subdivision are secondary banks planted with vegetation – trees and shrubs, which are strategically placed to create an individual backdrop for each of the five zones.

The use of the company's CAD system in the final design phase also helped to achieve the theoretical objectives and demonstrate that landscape design, like art, can be skillfully used to combine reality and fantasy in such a park.

Nasu Highland Park

Swa Group

Location: Naju, Japan. **Date of completion:** 1996. **Client:** Towa Real Estate Development Company. **Architect:** SWA Group. **Photography:** Tom Fox.

This project has been developed over successive phases, in view of its magnitude and the nature of each of its attractions. The first of these is the rock 'n' roll neighborhood, where the main street has a distinctly '50s feel, with its neon signs and parked-up Cadillacs: music is the main theme of this area. The second phase is the 38 m (120 ft) high carousel. The third phase consists of the House of Cards and Toyland. The inspiration here is the world of toys, making visitors feel as though they are walking through a child's playroom, strewn with toys and brimming with imagination. Another of the zones has a galaxy theme: an area with three roundabouts and blue paving, situated alongside one of the park's most impressive Russian mountains. Waterplay, where the paving is in the form of indigo-colored metal palm trees and waves, is one of the latest of the many new projects under way in this park. Apart from the rides and attractions found at Fantasy Point, Nasu Highland Park also includes hotels, tennis courts, and golf clubs.

Asahikawa Shunkodai Park

Mitsuro Man Senda

Location: Asahikawa, Japan. **Date of completion:** 1994. **Architect:** Mitsuro Man Senda. **Scheme:** Children's adventure park in an urban setting. **Photography:** Fujitsuka Mitsumara.

Touch and smell are in no way alien to the games played out by children in the park. Touching, jumping, chasing, feeling their way, climbing, and sliding. Using all their senses. Adapting their bodies to each of the different situations as they emerge, one after the other, along the length of the course, which is constructed using wood, rope, netting, mesh, sheet metal, lights, shade, and ramps.

There is no single path, but a whole complex of to's and fro's, crossroads, discoveries and encounters. Play is intermingled with nature, creating a sort of partnership. It is no coincidence that the park in

this project is located on a site affording the maximum contact with nature.

In the words of the architect, Mitsuro Man Senda, play can involve nature as its friend. In an attraction aimed at children, it is their height and, more particularly, their height of vision, that must be the determining factor when considering the project and its design. The details must also be studied meticulously, as must the materials, to ensure they are both harmless and suitable, no matter how the children choose to use the play area and whatever whim overtakes them at any given moment.

Ski Dome

Kajima Design

Location: Funabashi-Shi, Japan. **Date of completion:** 1993. **Architect:** Kajima Design. **Construction area** 87,300 m² (940,000 ft²). **Scheme:** Ski dome with restaurants, equipment hire shops, shopping center, changing rooms, gymnasium, sauna, and swimming pool. **Photography:** Satshi Asakawa.

The main Ski Dome building is a steel structure supporting a sloping concrete slab foundation which is 500 m (1640 ft) long and has a maximum height of 100 m (325 ft). There are three different grades of piste – beginners, intermediates and advanced, with gradients of between 7 and 20. The chair lift takes a minute and a half to travel from the bottom of the piste to the top. Connected to the main complex via its lower level, another four-story building houses the ski-related services and leisure facilities (restaurants, shops, equipment hire, ticket offices, gymnasium, sauna, and swimming pool). The inside temperature varies between 2 and 6°C and is primarily maintained thanks to an efficient insulation system that prevents any air from escaping outside. The shape of the structure is dictated by the building's response to earthquakes, which are commonplace in Japan. A variable height structure may be affected by different vibrational frequencies during the same seismic movement, which can prove extremely dangerous. In order to alleviate this situation, the architects decided to divide the building into six parts separated by joints, each with an independent structure, so giving scope for movement.

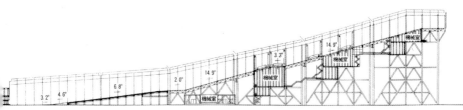

Florida Aquarium

Hellmut, Obata, Kassabaum, Inc.

Location: Tampa, Florida, USA. **Date of completion**: 1995. **Architect**: Helmut, Obata, Kassabaum, Inc. **Associates**: Joseph Wetzel, Gyo Obata. **Photography**: George Cott.

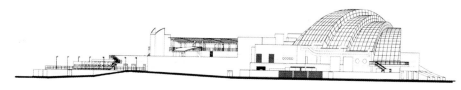

The aim of this project is to give visitors the sensation of being submerged in a marine environment. The immersion begins in a sort of cavern next to the stairs. Here, visitors can learn about the origins of Florida's water, while walking under a course of fresh water flowing above their heads. A winding path then takes them through the various habitats of the swamplands, a journey of light, passing between vegetation beneath a magnificent glass roof shaped like a seashell and designed by Gyo Obata. The last stage of the journey marks the start of Florida's bays and beaches, moving from a sunny environment to shade and grottoes, where visitors can see the fish moving about on the same level. The second section of the aquarium is devoted to an extraordinary habitat found off the Florida coast–the coral reef. The final stage is an enormous window opening onto the seabed for viewing the reef.

Oceanarium

Peter Chermayeff

Location: Lisbon, Portugal. **Date of completion:** 1998. **Client:** Expo '98 Lisbon. **Architect:** Peter Chermayeff. **Scheme:** Oceanarium. **Photography:** Paco Asensio.

One of the most symbolic elements of Expo '98 is the Oceanarium, designed by Peter Chermayeff, which proved the greatest daytime attraction.

This huge nautical-style structure anchored in the harbor waters consists of a main tank housing marine species, around which the other exhibition areas are carefully arranged.

Access to the Oceanarium is by way of a metal grid ramp, which leads the visitor to the upper level. The building, which takes the form of a sophisticated oil production platform, is made up of a solid base of rocky materials and a glass covered upper section with views of the sea and Expo. The awnings create wings and afford protection from direct sunlight. They are hung from cables suspended from metal pillars standing at the edges of a cross on the floor, which delineates the structural rhythm.

This pavilion was one of the most remarkable buildings at the Lisbon Expo in 1998.

Itäkeskus

Hyvämäki, Karhunen & Parkkinen

Location: Helsinki, Finland. **Date of completion:** 1993. **Architect:** Hyvämäki, Karhunen & Parkkinen. **Scheme:** Public baths and swimming pool complex. **Photography:** Jussi Tiainen.

In the years leading up to the disintegration of the Soviet Union, Helsinki's eastern suburbs needed an emergency shelter while at the same time planners were looking at the possibility of building a public baths and swimming pool complex within the environs of a central park area. By making use of an easily excavated rocky hill situated in the forest, developers were able to fuse the two ideas into a single project. This enabled them to save on the cost of two independent projects and, at the same time, prevent the park from being developed.

The only area not underground is the entrance, designed as a semicircular glass arch, which seems to emerge from inside the earth, like a transparent phalanx proclaiming a crystalline secret within.

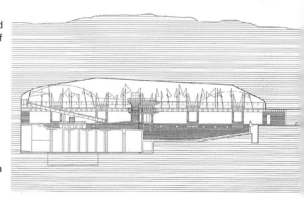

Beneath an enormous white dome, a wide ranging program of functions includes an Olympic swimming pool with a separate diving area, fun, leisure, and children's pools, plunge pools, Turkish baths and steam rooms, saunas, solariums, a gymnasium, treatment rooms, and two cafeterias. Accompanying all this is a series of individual tableaux, linked by music and brought together by sound screens, which enable visitors to remember each area and find their way around an originally mystifying enclosed environment.

Mad River Trips

William P. Bruder

Location: Jackson, Wyoming, USA. **Date of completion:** 1997. **Architect:** William P. Bruder. **Associates** Wendell Burnette, Tim Christ, Jack De Bartolo III, Leah Schneider (design team). **Photography:** Bil Timmerman.

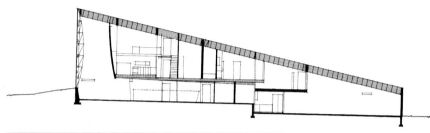

The Arizona desert is one of the few places where architecture retains both an artistic and a symbolic function. This is where William Bruder has been designing structures since the end of the 1970s. His work creates a continuous dialog with the landscape – the mountains, water, dryness, color, and also the indigenous architecture of Arizona – old rural buildings, mines, barns, etc... His buildings try to evoke lyrical images of Arizona and, at the same time, endeavor to salvage the simplest building materials, reusing them exquisitely. The Mad River Trips building houses both the offices and storeroom and the home of the owners of this small company, which organizes river-rafting trips.

Shonandai Cultural Center

Itsuko Hasegawa

Location: Fujisawa, Kanawaga, Japan. **Date of completion:** 1990. **Client:** Kanawaga City Hall. **Architect:** Itsuko Hasegawa. **Associate:** Architectural Design Studio. **Scheme:** Cultural center, public square and theater, panoramic cinema, children's museum, and services. **Photography:** Shuji Yamada.

This is a Cultural Center with ambitious pretensions. It includes a public theater, a panoramic cinema, a children's museum, and a division of the city hall's administrative services. All the Center's units embody the design philosophy of the Japanese architect, as is reflected in the formal diversity of the pavilions and the way in which sunlight penetrates the offices at midday. However, the feature that most accurately embraces Hasegawa's creative doctrine is the square, whose proportions determine those of the structures rising so majestically from around its surface. The square was conceived as a backdrop for a multiplicity of events, a vessel for the entire universe, with spherical objects dotted within its boundaries to represent the cosmos, the earth, and the moon. These, on the other hand, act as the architectural hallmark of this magnificent Cultural Center, with all its attractive buildings.

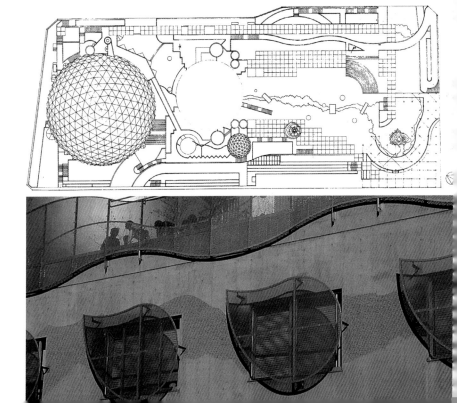

Planetarium of the Northern Lights

John Kristoffersen

Location: Tromso, Norway. **Date of completion:** 1988. **Architect:** John Kristoffersen. **Scheme:** Construction of a planetarium, telescope, tower, laboratory, and spectators' module. **Photography:** John Kristoffersen.

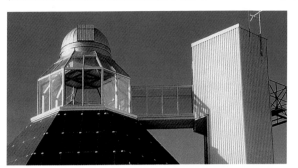

One of the principal attractions of this planetarium is the way it recreates for the visitor the marvelous spectacle of the Northern Lights, projected onto the immense semispherical screen erected inside the building. At the same time, in the knowledge that the re-created phenomenon is a long way from reality, the building has been clad in gray glass, which acts as a mirror, reflecting the surrounding countryside. A telescope positioned in the equatorial cupola, which crowns the structure, evokes the investigative aspect, albeit intended for teaching purposes. The complex is made up of a tower in which elevators travel to the laboratory above, the bridge linking up to this, and the large octagonal building where spectators are welcomed beneath the 12 m (39 ft) diameter screen. The structure is made from reinforced concrete, chosen principally to insulate against the aircraft noise from outside. The outside of the octagonal building is clad in 8 mm (1/4 inch) thick gray glass, the tower in gray steel panels, which provide protection from the elements.

Bars, disco-theques, and games rooms

The projects presented here serve a surprising variety of different functions. This collection of interior public spaces constitutes a broad and at the same time ambiguous category. However, all these restaurants, bars, discotheques, and night clubs are part of the leisure culture, a concept that is both frivolous and vital to human existence, and, like all activities, subject to constant change. Nevertheless, the individuals responsible for these projects have met these challenges energetically, their work combining their own creative experience with the demands of the consumer.

Pachinko Parlor

Kazuyo Sejima

Location: Hitachiohta, Ibaraki, Japan. **Date of completion**: 1996. **Architect**: Kazuyo Sejima. **Structural engineers**: Matsui Gengo & O.R.S. **Scheme**: Games room, rest area, and office. **Gross floor area**: 800 m² (8600 ft²). **Photography**: Nacasa & Partners Inc.

Pachinko Parlor is a very popular game in Japan, combining recreation and skill. Games rooms are to be found across the length and breadth of the country, each offering similar facilities–simply rows of individual pachinko games machines.

Situated in the provincial city of Hitachiohta, Pachinko Parlor occupies a large site overlooking a busy freeway.

The curve of the façade and the use of light and materials are a sufficient advertisement in themselves, with only a modest sign being required to indicate the name of the establishment. On the façade, shiny black strips frame apertures of colored glass. While during the day it is the black that softly reflects the light, at night the interior light makes these strips disappear, giving the façade a disjointed air.

On the ground floor there is a typical pachinko room with rows of games machines, a prize collection corner, as well as a rest area. The office is separate from the rest of the facilities in the design.

Stop Line

Studio Archea

Location: Curno, Bergamo, Italy. **Date of completion**: 1996. **Architects**: Laura Andreini, Marco Casamonti, Giovanni Polazzi (Studio Archea). **Associates**: Antonella Dini, Paolo Frongia, Michael Heffernan, Claudia Sandoval, Andrea Sensoli (architects), Silvia Fabi, Nicola Santini, Giuseppe Fioroni, Pier Paolo Taddei (design team), Studio Myallonnier (structural engineers), Studio Armondi (layout), Kreon (lighting), Martin (scenic lighting), Outline (audio), Alessandro Trezzi, Antonio Falduto (video). **Scheme**: Discotheque, bowling alley, ice rink, billiards, games rooms, and restaurants. **Photography**: Pietro Savorelli, Saverio Lombardi Vallauri.

Stop Line is located on the outskirts of the city of Bergamo, in an industrial landscape where it coexists with large factory buildings, traffic signals, and billboards. The building is actually an old warehouse with a total area of 5400 m2 (58,000 ft2).This is perhaps why during the day the building, with its façade measuring almost 60 m (200 ft) overlooking the freeway, is a plain yet impressive giant of a structure. A single,

hermetically sealed wall clad in Corten steel gives no clue as to the activities within the building.
At night, a series of holes drilled in the steel plate turn into an array of points of light, creating an intangible wall in the darkness. The lights are reflected in the pond at the foot of the façade.
Stop Line houses a discotheque, ice rink, billiard tables, restaurants, video screenings, computer games rooms, and more... It is a huge center created

for entertainment, but at the same time capable of being turned into a venue for fashion shows, conferences, and business presentations. The main corridor, running parallel to the main façade, consists of a module on three levels, one of which is underground. The rest of the building is a single space, an enormous hall with free-standing structures here and there, which are reached by stairs or ramps.

Café Charbon/Nouveau Casino

Louis Paillard & Anne Françoise Jumeau, de Périphériques

Location: Paris, France. **Date of completion**: 2001. **Architects**: Louis Paillard & Anne Françoise Jumeau, de Périphériques. **Collaborators**: Paris Comptoirs (building), Christophe Valtin and Shirin Raissi (synthesis images). **Gross floor area**: 5,376 sq. ft. **Photography**: Luc Boegly/Archipress .

The project developed by the Périphériques group occupies the back of a beautiful early 20th century Parisian café, the Café Charbon. The architects' brief called for the design of a new dance club, to be called Nouveau Casino, which would include a concert hall for 300 people, a bar, and a restaurant. One of the primary objectives was to avoid interfering with the activity on the original premises, and accordingly the design included an independent entrance and a perfect soundproofing system. The entrance to the original café is through a glass façade with doors and windows that open on to the street, while access to the concert hall is through a small metal door at one end of the enclosure. A corridor runs the length of the site to the club, where it disappears in a diaphanous space with no partitions. This corridor is lit with small red spotlamps recessed in a ceiling of perforated panels. The architects took advantage of the space's considerable height to create, at one end, a mezzanine with tables and sofas, under which are located the toilets, and, at the other end, to raise the stage and backstage storage area. The bar follows the contours of the dividing walls, leaving a large area free for dancing or simply listening to the music in comfort.

From the outset the designers' intention was to create a changing and flexible space capable of accommodating simultaneously different ambiences. Clubs are subject to the whims of fashion, and thus it is not surprising that they should fall from favor as club-goers hunger for new sensations and settings in which to interact with music. With that in mind, the architects came up with a system that allows the setting to be changed in a matter of seconds and generates an infinite range of ambiences. A system of projectors was installed to cast images on the walls and ceiling, both covered with triangular steel-plated panels arrayed in varying orientations so that they scatter the reflected light.

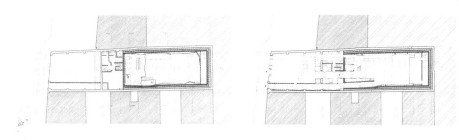

Iridium Restaurant

Jordan Mozer

Location: New York, USA. **Date of completion**: 1994. **Architect**: Jordan Mozer. **Photography**: Mihail Moldoveanu.

The Iridium is situated between Columbus Avenue and Broadway, right next to New York's Lincoln Center Complex.
Jordan Mozer conceived a place where the furniture and the columns, the doors and the roof, all the elements, had to dance. Although the forms used in the Iridium may appear random, almost all of them transform into architecture images from the world of music and dance. Each architectural detail, each piece of furniture, each lamp, has been individually designed. The sequence of the work is extraordinarily direct and specific. Otherwise, it would have been almost impossible to complete such an outstanding and personal project and bring it to fruition successfully.

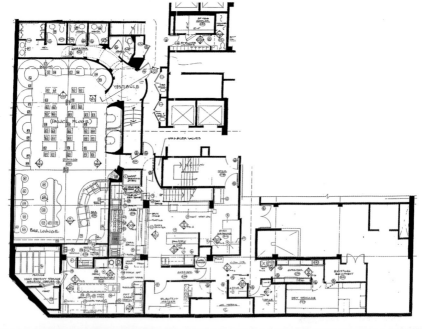

Caroline's Theater and Comedy Club

Paul Haigh, Barbara H. Haigh

Location: Manhattan, New York, USA. **Date of completion**: 1993. **Client**: Caroline Hirsch. **Architects**: Paul Haigh, Barbara H. Haigh. **Associates**: Nicholas Macri, Miriana Donaya, Justin Bologna, Karla Kuperc; CMA Enterprises (construction). **Scheme**: Club for staging theater and comedy performances. **Photography**: Elliot Kaufman.

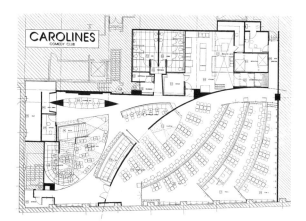

In this theater especially designed for comedy performances, the architects tried to create a closeness between audience and performers.

Inside the club, the visitor encounters a neomedieval world of harlequins, pantomime, and jokers. This iconography extends throughout the club, in different colors, forms, and scales. Paul Haigh has used velvet wall coverings, varnished woods, terrazzo flooring, and moquette for the finishes. The basement is divided into two by a curved wall. On one side is the theater, with three rows of continuous, curved seats at different levels. On the other is the restaurant/bar, which also acts as a foyer and a venue for occasional performances; it is made up of a series of small separate areas, with wide corridors running between them, providing easy access.

Obslomova

Shiro Kuramata

Location: Hotel Il Palazzo, Fukuoka, Japan. **Date of completion**: 1991. **Architect**: Shiro Kuramata. **Scheme**: Design of a restaurant/bar within the Hotel Il Palazzo. **Photography**: Nacasa & Partner.

Within the Hotel Il Palazzo complex there are four venues situated in the two parallel modules making up the central building. These are restaurant/bars, each of them designed by a great name of international repute: four bars commissioned for a genuinely international project, endorsed by the creativity of top class designers. Each bar has a totally different ambience. The Obslomova is a bar with an intimate atmosphere where soft colors and light forms suffuse both the furnishings and the actual structure of the space.

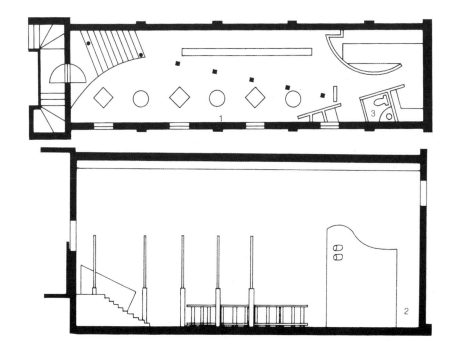

Circus Theater

Sjoerd Saeters

Location: Zandvoort, The Netherlands. **Date of construction**: 1996. **Architect**: Sjoerd Saeters. **Scheme**: Amusement arcade in the old town of Zandvoort. **Photography**: Koo Boji.

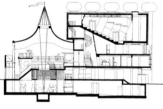

Sjoerd Soeters was commissioned to construct an amusement arcade and cinema in the old town of Zandvoort. The building had to be both attractive and colorful.

The result is a showy structure of stimulating façades, with giant banners in every color imaginable, enormous orange painted pillars, and a curved roof like a circus tent, supported by three posts. Soeters designed the games room as a genuine labyrinth, with numerous islands at different levels and ramps connecting them, mirrors that doubled the space, and every conceivable type of staircase – all painted in striking, vivid colors. The site is roughly L-shaped. The longest leg is divided into three circles corresponding to three imaginary circus rings; this strip leads onto a pedestrian walkway that joins a busy shopping street. The short leg of the L leads off to a quiet square. On the first floor there is a bar and the cinema foyer. Above this are the offices and services necessary to manage the establishment, and on the top floor is the cinema. The building is clearly divided into two wings, in terms of both space and form. On the one side is the games area located within a large, double-sized continuous space and, on the other, are the quieter areas, separated by different floor levels.

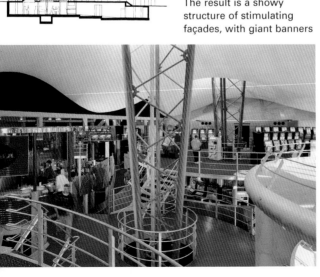

Shopping malls

The importance acquired by large
shopping malls is due to a number of
sociocultural and economic factors that
can be broadly divided into two main
groups for analytical purposes. Firstly,
there is the supremacy of the concepts of
commerce and the marketplace as pillars
of the macroeconomic structure that
governs today's society and, secondly, the
profound interrelationship established
between leisure and consumerism.
Due to the vast number of shopping mall
projects, it is impossible to make
generalizations about them.
Consequently, this section aims to reflect
the great variety of shopping mall schemes
that can be found today within the field of
commercial architecture.

Emmen Shopping Mall

Galeries Lafayette

Triangle des Gares, Euralille

L'Illa Diagonal

Bercy 2 Shopping Mall

Nordwest-Zentrum

Stockmann

Haas Haus

Saar Galerie

Rio Shopping Center

Centro Torri

Emmen Shopping Mall

Ben van Berkel

Location: Emmen, The Netherlands. **Date of construction**: 1994–1996. **Client**: Multi Vastgoed bv, Gouda **Architect**: Ben van Berkel. **Construction**: IHN Noord bv, Groningen. **Project coordinator**: René Bouman, Harrie Pappot. **Project manager**: Wilbert Swinkels. **Glass**: HuMa-glas bv. **Scheme**: Shopping center and apartments **Photography**: Christian Richters.

The building housing the new Vroom & Dreesmann stores is the result of a large-scale remodeling of an old building dating back to the 1960s, which was used for the same purpose then. Van Berkel's project adds an apartment building, reorganizes the entire complex, and completely changes the façade, replacing it with an all-enveloping skin. The project intelligently recognizes the impossibility of achieving a strict style for the building's remodeling. The shopping mall complex consists, from the point of view of space, of a large number of elements, forming a system. There is the base on the first floor, some of its stores with direct access from the street; the sheer size of the second floor, which van Berkel has converted into an enormous, squat, glass-covered unit; a five-story tower situated in one of the corners, which will house the apartments; a three-floor prism, which has received special treatment in terms of its strictly cubic nature; and an intermediate structure that projects above the large, glass-covered element.

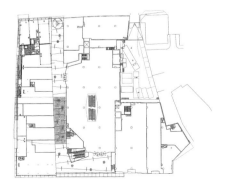

Galeries Lafayette

Jean Nouvel

Location: Friedrichstadt Passagen Block 207, Friedrichstrasse-Französischestrasse, Berlin, Germany. **Competitive tender**: March 1991. **Date works commenced**: September 1992. **Date of completion**: March 1996. **Client**: Euro-Projekt Entwicklungs GmbH. **Architect**: Jean Nouvel. **Project managers**: Barbara Salin (tender phase), Laurence Daude (execution phase), Judith Simon, Viviane Morteau (works management). **Net floor area**: 39,585 m² (426,000 ft²). **Scheme**: Shopping mall, offices, apartments, and parking. **Photography**: Philippe Ruault.

This is a building with a fairly diverse composition, including store space for Galeries Lafayette, as well as offices, shops,

apartments, and parking. As shown in the photograph, the chosen site occupies a little over half a block in Berlin, next to the Schinkel Schauspielhaus.

The size of the block will enable up to seven floors to be constructed, as well as four underground levels. Nouvel plans to have the four sides of the building (including the roof) completely covered with glass, so that the play between the natural light

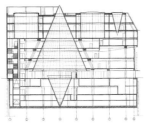

penetrating from outside, the artificial light produced by the building itself, and, finally, the various reflections generated by all these creates an atmosphere that is both spectacular and at the same time clearly has a functional element.

In order to achieve these objectives, and given the dimensional characteristics of the building, Nouvel resorted to the strategy of drilling holes from the roof through the entire glass structure, so that the light penetrates at numerous points, all of them different and organized in hierarchical fashion.

Triangle des Gares. Euralille

Jean Nouvel

Location: Lille, France. **Date of completion**: September 1994. **Client**: Shopping mall: SNC (Société du Centre Commercial du Centre Euralille). **Architects**: Jean Nouvel, Emmanuel Cattani & Associés. **Associates**: Patrick Cosmao, Cyril Ruiz (planning team), OTH NORD PROJETUD (engineering), Sophie Berthelier, Isabelle Guillauic (project managers). **Scheme**: Shopping mall, offices, hotel, apartments, and parking. **Photography**: Philippe Ruault, Ralph Richter.

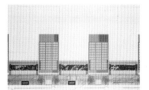

Situated at the junction between the Paris-London high speed rail (TGV) link and the future Paris–Brussels–Amsterdam–Cologne line, Lille is the city that has experienced the greatest transformation due to the opening of the Channel Tunnel. It was a major protagonist in this enormously ambitious project, aiming to become a major center in a new "borderless" Europe.

As part of the remodeling of Euralille, Nouvel was entrusted with the Triangle des Gares project, an extensive shopping mall crowned by a row of office blocks to the south, and flanked by a line of apartments and a hotel on the west side.

The project has been planned as a single unit, with simple, understated forms; yet the treatment of materials and colors, and the incorporation of symbols and images as elements of the architectural composition succeed in transmitting, with subtlety, the building's overall complexity.

L'Illa Diagonal

Rafael Moneo/Manuel de Solà-Morales

Location: Barcelona, Spain. **Date of construction**: 1994–1997. **Developer**: Winterthur. **Architects**: Rafael Moneo Vallés, Manuel de Solà-Morales i Rubió. **Associates**: Lluís Tobella, Antón María Pàmies, Andrea Casiraghi, Francesc Santacana, Lucho Marcial, Félix Wettstein, Román Cisneros, Isabel Pericas, René Hochuli, Kate Webb, Toni Casamor, Oriol Mateu (design), Mariano Moreno (structural engineer), Sereland (mechanical), SECOTEC (supervision), AGROMAN (construction). **Scheme**: Offices, shopping mall, auditorium, discotheque, parking, and services. **Photography**: Ramón Camprubí, Ivan Bercedo.

L'Illa Diagonal is not strictly speaking a building, but a chunk of city designed on the basis of a single project. The complex includes offices, a hotel, various shopping malls, small shops, squares and pedestrian precincts, a public park, parking levels, a discotheque, and an auditorium. Now, when we talk about L'Illa Diagonal being a chunk of city, we are not referring to its size, nor to the concentration of activities, nor to the fact that it is a complex of different buildings. On the contrary, L'Illa Diagonal is a single building which, nevertheless, is not designed as such, but as a segment of a major thoroughfare or part of a neighborhood that includes alleys, a square, a small park – that is what makes it a chunk of city. In other words, the play of forms conceived by Manuel de Solà Morales and Rafael Moneo is not designed to produce an architectural image, but rather a specifically urban one.

Bercy 2 Shopping Mall

Renzo Piano

Location: Charenton-le-Pont, Paris, France. **Date of construction**: 1987–1990. **Client**: Emin, J. Renault. **Architect**: Renzo Piano. **Associates**: Noriaki Okalie. **Gross floor area**: 100,000 m² (1.08 million ft²). **Photography**: Anne Fauret, Archipress.

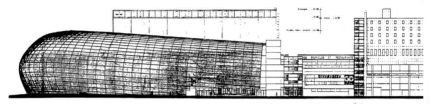

Growing from within, the building's ovoid form is repeated with different radii until it merges with the outer shell, ceiling and façade, since the roof presents no break in continuity along its curvilinear course.

The monumental roof was designed by superimposing three circular matrices with varying radii and cladding them in a vast metal skin. As to the building's internal articulation, the height of 25 m (81 ft) is distributed between six floors, with the three lower ones–two of which are underground –being devoted to the creation of 2118 parking spaces, occupying an area of some 50,000 m2 (538,000 ft). The three remaining levels, each of which is 10 m (33 ft) wide and 100 m (325 ft) long, accommodate the sales areas, covering an actual space of 34,000 m2 (366,000 ft).

Renzo Piano imagined the internal space as a valley. In the center, from the first underground parking level to the second shopping mall floor, is a 1000 m2 (10,100 ft) garden area, with trees growing to heights of up to 12 m (39

ft). A waterfall cascading down from above through an inclined plane introduces the symbol of a watercourse flanked by two banks. The entire site is fragmented by long, gently sloping moving walkways, which link the different floor levels.

Nordwest-Zentrum

Estudio RKW

Location: Frankfurt, Germany. **Date of conversion**: 1990. **Architect**: Estudio RKW (Rhode, Kellerman, Wawrowsky & Partner). **Scheme**: Conversion of a former shopping mall: stores, pedestrian area, kindergarten, social center, library, banks, police station, fire station, and census center.

This shopping mall and leisure center is the result of the renovation and redesign of a multifunctional center opened in 1968, whose structure had become outdated. The main aspects of the conversion involved covering over the pedestrian walkways, reorganizing the shopping and leisure facilities, improving internal communications and accessibility, and creating a new, more attractive, and up-to-date overall design. Some 10,000 m2 (108,000 ft) of glass were used to cover the two existing shopping streets and the different interconnecting sections. A total of 5200 glass panels rise to a height of over 17 m (55 ft), spread across a pedestrian area of 9200 m2 (100,000 ft). Another feature has been the planned combination of types of activity, with the addition of 18 medical practices, a veterinary surgeon, a pharmacy, and various auxiliary facilities. All this is rounded off by the municipal infrastructure–a children's park, centers for the young and old, a library, post office, banks, a police station, fire station, and census center.

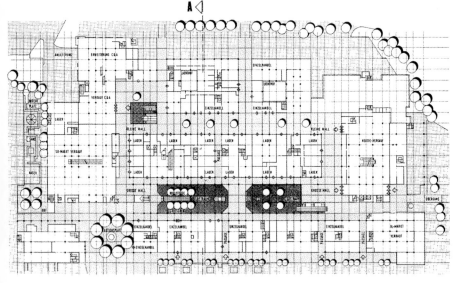

Stockmann

Gullichsen, Kairamo & Vormala

Location: Helsinki, Finland. **Date of completion**: 1989. **Architect**: Gullichsen, Kairamo & Vormala. **Scheme**: Shopping mall, warehouse area, parking, offices, beauty salon, and cafeteria.

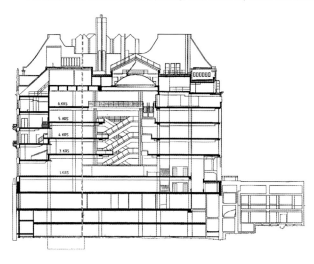

The functional scheme adopted for the project is characterized by its schematic simplicity, as well as its spatial clarity. The building is on various levels, starting with the underground, basement level, where there is parking, storage, and one of the sales floors. The four floors above this function as shopping areas.
On the fifth floor is an extensive exhibition room, from which there is an escalator giving access to the restaurant on the floor above.
A small offices area and all the technical equipment are housed at the top of the building. There is also a beauty salon and a cafeteria on this floor.
The highest point of the structure is crowned by a large dome, which is completely covered in glass. This has a dual function, creating a system of natural lighting from outside and adding great aesthetic value, encouraging visitors to keep going until they reach the upper floor levels of the building.

Haas Haus

Hans Hollein

Location: Vienna, Austria. **Date of completion**: 1989. **Architect**: Hans Hollein. **Scheme**: Design and construction of a new shopping mall with parking. **Photography**: Albert Worm.

The new building presents itself as a series of adjacent, superimposed cylindrical shapes–a sort of visual collage, whose variety is one of its most important characteristics. The structure appears to be dominated by curved lines, forming an undulating outline, which increasingly gains space towards the outside walls.

The significance of the exterior lies essentially in the plurality and expressiveness of the complex, contrasting radically with the surrounding environment, but coexisting in complete harmony. Inside, the need to introduce a broad, varied scheme called for considered planning, distinguishing between functional spaces, and strategic location of the communication systems. To ensure optimum selling space, the technical installations were located on two underground levels; on the first of these levels is a cafeteria, visually linked to the shopping area as a whole.

The method used to make this connection involved organizing the four public access areas around an enormous central atrium, in the form of an inverted cone, in which the stairs connecting the different levels were arranged.

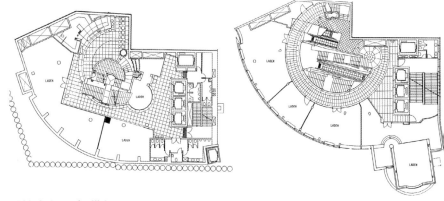

Saar Galerie

Volkwin Marg

Location: Saarbrücken, Germany. Date of completion: 1991. Architect: Volkwin Marg. Scheme: Shopping galleria with store and parking. Photography: W. Giencke.

The galleria, over 100 m (325 ft) long and 12 m (39 ft) wide, and divided into six floors, is surmounted by a 38 m (125 ft) high octagon, which is clearly visible and is now a famous landmark on the Saarbrücken skyline. The main entrance, in the form of a wide, open portal, looks onto the busy Reichstrasse. The body of

the building, which houses local stores and offices, is connected to a four-story parking lot by a series of panoramic elevators, serving all the floors and supported by an independent steel structure. Inside the galleria, the stores are spread over two levels and the appropriate arrangement of entrances and stores ensures optimum circulation of customers between them. The external perspective of the Saar Galerie is articulated by caesuras in the structure, designed in the form of recesses housing the lightweight steel emergency exit staircases. As it approaches the Reichstrasse, the galleria reverts to the classical motif of its porticoes.

Above, the external walls are clad between pillar axes in light-permeable concrete elements, in the form of a huge lattice in square modules with staggered relief. To achieve the façade's vertical structure, the galleria's mezzanine level is framed with laminated steel profiles.

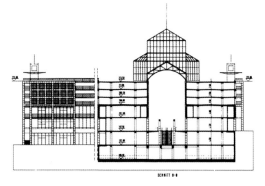

SCHNITT B-B

Rio Shopping Center

Martha Schwartz

Location: Atlanta, Georgia, USA. **Date of completion**: 1988. **Client**: Ackerman and Co. **Architect**: Martha Schwartz. **Associates**: Arquitectonica Architects. **Scheme**: Incorporation of landscaping in a shopping mall. **Photography**: Rion Rizzo.

The artificial hedges of the Whitehead Institute are perhaps the best example of visual interest done economically, as demonstrated by Martha Schwartz. These features have pop connotations, with the use of synthetic accessories, the sort of everyday objects found in the popular landscape, a theme also undeniably represented in the golden frogs that stake out the black fishpond of the Rio Shopping Center, symbols of the purest suburban American kitsch.

The Rio Shopping Center, with its relatively modest dimensions, was designed to accommodate specialist stores. Visualized as a small urban nucleus, with separate, defined structures, the complex planned by the Arquitectonica International Corporation enables the visitor to stroll from the interior patio to the parking area outside. The objectives of the landscaping project were to create a highly visible space that would encourage a high level of activity, to make the transition from the road running about 3 m (10 ft) above the first level of stores, and to create an image in the adjacent crossroads, jammed with traffic, an image that would be at once striking and memorable, and would incorporate the energy of the nearby intersection as a further element of the shopping mall.

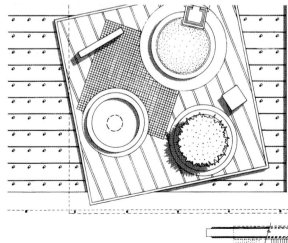

Centro Torri

Aldo Rossi

Location: Parma, Italy. **Date of completion**: 1988. **Architect**: Aldo Rossi. **Associates**: G. Braghieri, M. Baracco, P. Digiuni. **Scheme**: Shopping mall: home improvement center, supermarket, specialist stores, parking, and community and support services. **Photography**: Federico Brunetti.

The new Torri Center is made up of three units, which combine to create the shopping galleria. The most characteristic features of the complex are the ten brick towers, rising up to indicate the entrance door and main foyer. Inside the building are a home improvement center, the IPERCOOP supermarket, and a further 31 specialist stores. Community and support services are also included. The structure is built almost entirely on the same level, except for the towers, the central section housing the home improvement center offices, and an elevated room within the supermarket. The towers have exposed brickwork and are finished with a profiled cornice and copper plate. Just under the cornice, the bricks are clad in ceramic tiles, a decorative motif repeated on all the towers. The shopping galleria is clad in copper plate and underpinned by a supporting green iron structure.

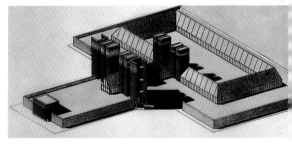

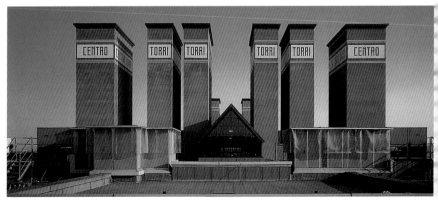

Stores and showrooms

The design of the setting in which any sort of sale takes place is of prime importance. Aesthetic considerations are not the sole preserve of garment or perfume bottle design, but extend to the architecture of chain and flagship stores. This chapter aims to bring together a selection of recent projects that have proved internationally outstanding, due to both their interior and exterior architecture–Calvin Klein, Christian Lacroix, Carita... the big brands are investing increasingly in the designs and architecture of famous names (John Pawson, Shigeru Uchida, Renzo Piano, Andrée Putman...) when opening stores and showrooms in the world's major cities.

Calvin Klein Madison Avenue

Maison Hermès

Dr Baeltz

Boutique Christian Lacroix

Carita

Calvin Klein Madison Avenue

John Pawson

Location: New York, USA. **Date project begun**: 1995. **Date of completion**: 1996. **Architect**: John Pawson. **Scheme**: Men's and women's fashion and accessories store. **Photography**: Kristoph Kicherer.

The similarity between this store and an art gallery is no accident–it is both intentional and merited. The interior uses none of the usual sales strategies, instead inviting the shopper to stroll through an environment expressing a personal idea of elegance and luxury.

The store is situated within four floors of a building with classical façades, which once housed the J.P. Morgan bank.

Inside, the defining features are the stone floor, white walls, and, above all, the careful placement of objects. No attempt is made to guide, lead, or direct the customer, as is the case in most stores. On the contrary, visitors are intended to move serenely, unhurriedly, with a sense of privilege, soaking up the atmosphere. The arrangement of the establishment itself provides them with their reference point.

The store has a total floor space of 1860 m2 (20,000 ft), with ceilings up to 6 m (19 ft) high. The first floor is devoted to women's accessories, the next two floors to women's and men's fashion, respectively. In the basement, household items are exhibited room by room, with accessories for the bathroom, kitchen, and dining room.

Maison Hermès

Renzo Piano

Location: Ginza Chuo-ku, Tokyo, Japan. **Date of construction**: 1998-2001. **Architect**: Renzo Piano. **Photography**: Michel Denancé.

The French Hermès group chose Tokyo's central Ginza district as the site for its Japanese headquarters, which comprise commercial outlets, workshops, offices, and showrooms spread over 64,500 square feet and crowned by a French-style roof garden. The project represented an aesthetic and technical challenge as it had to blend into the surrounding urban setting while also guaranteeing stability in the face of possible earthquakes. The building's façades, spanning 15 floors and a rectangular perimeter, are entirely made up of prefabricated glass blocks measuring 9 x 9 inches. These elements were specially designed and built for the project, in order to form a luminous and uninterrupted barrier between the peacefulness of the interior and the hubbub of the city, as well as providing a traditional yet technological touch. In order to prevent any damage in the event of an earthquake, an innovative structural system was designed; this consists of a flexible steel truss, articulated at strategic points by buffers that absorb any possible movements made by the structure and also strengthen the building's floors.

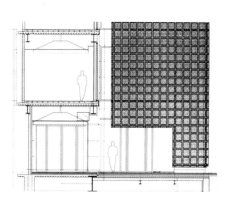

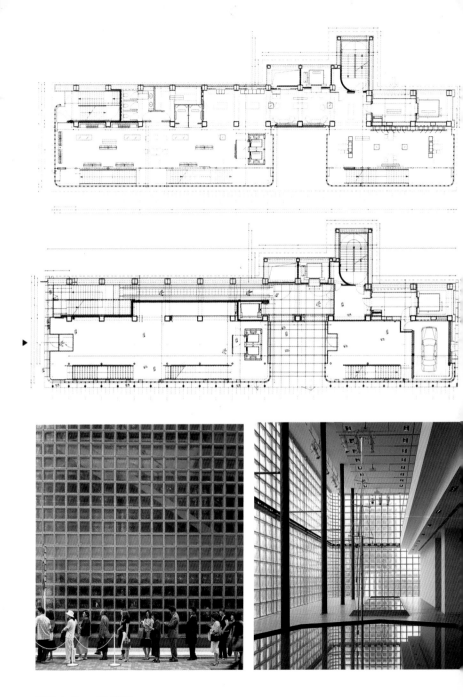

542 Leisure facilities

Dr. Baeltz

Shigeru Uchida

Location: Kitazawa y Hiroo, Tokyo, Japan. **Date of construction**: 1995. **Architect**: Shigeru Uchida. **Scheme** Small cosmetics store; warehouse/office. **Photography**: Nácasa & Partners.

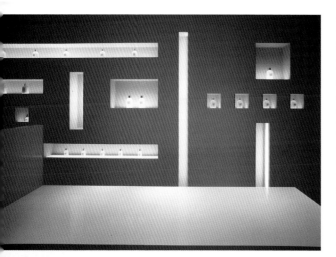

The cosmetics store designed by Shigeru Uchida for Dr. Baeltz represents the adaptation of an atypical functional scheme to small-scale commercial premises. This has involved the components being minimized right down to their fundamental characteristics, as part of an analytical process resulting in their complete integration in a unitary design combining aesthetic and functional features. The premises are limited in size (29.80 m2 and 38 m2, 320 ft and 409 ft) and rectangular in shape, with the entrance incorporated in a continuous glass wall, which forms part of the façade towards the shopping mall and gives a complete view of the interior. The area is divided into three sections: the store, a client consultation counter, and facial treatment area at the back. The counter, running along the length of the store, with steel chairs upholstered in blue, is the only element to invade the empty space. The merchandise has been positioned close to the peripheral walls and the facial treatment area is separated from the rest by a panel stopping short of the ceiling and permitting the physical and visual continuity of the space. The composition of openings in the walls is reinforced by their own individual lighting, which provides a dramatic backdrop for the products being displayed in a small number of packaging combinations. The use of beige as the predominant color is aimed at giving the premises a more spacious feel.

Boutique Christian Lacroix

Caps Architects

Location: Tokio, Japan. **Date of completion**: 2001. **Architects**: Caps Architects. **Colaborators**: Ueno Glass (furniture production), Obayashi Construction (building), Axe design (local architects), Ansorg GmbH (lighting), Glace Controle (holographic films). **Gross floor area**: 2,688 sq. ft. **Photography**: Nácasa & Partners.

The Swiss studio Caps Architects, led by Christophe Carpente, was commissioned to design the new Christian Lacroix clothing shop in Tokyo. From the outset Carpente sought a project which oozes temporality, which evokes the nomadism of travellers, is capable of change, and will adapt itself to the specific needs of each space.
The shop is distributed on two floors and enclosed within a totally transparent façade overprinted with a calligraphy text by Lacroix himself. The between-floors slab does not meet

the façade, thus the enclosure appears continuous, broken up only by a subtle aluminium-work framing.
The layout of both floors is governed by the deployment of the displays. The customer's itinerary is marked out by these furnishings, which are moveable to make the shop easily transformable. The displays were conceived as transparent colored-glass modules offering the public varied perspectives of different hues. The right angles of these furnishings contrast with the curvy chairs by

designer Pierre Paulin, as well as with the fitting rooms, shells of organic contours lined with silky, golden velvety fabrics. The existing structure of the premises remained unchanged and only the distribution was altered, tearing out all the partitions while the preserved outer walls were painted completely white with a subtle coat of nacre.

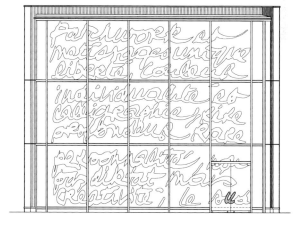

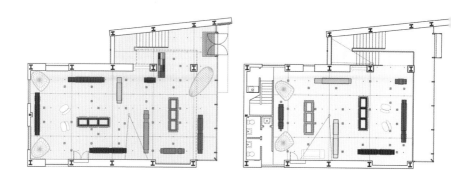

Carita

Andrée Putman

Location: Paris, France. **Date of completion**: 1986. **Architect**: Andrée Putman. **Associate**: Bruno Moinard. **Photography**: Archipress.

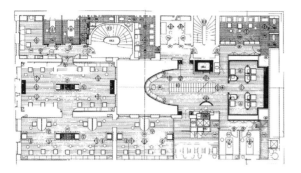

In Carita, the display cases where the establishment's exclusive products are exhibited are to be found, eventually, in the corridor leading to the lounge. They occupy a single narrow strip running at eye level in a linear showcase built in between neutral gray panels. Carita has a first floor and three further floors arranged by theme. The first floor houses the reception, a skin diagnosis cubicle, Christophe Carita's studio, the point of sale for the products on offer, a video room, the cloakroom, and a cash desk.

The first floor focuses on hair treatments, while the hair salon, with all the usual associated services, is located on the second floor. The third floor is divided into one area for women's beauty treatments and one for men's. The staircase is the heart of the establishment. The designers preferred to opt for neutral finishes, offering tranquillity and elegance, rather than excessively innovative elements that would have a jarring effect on the clients or could become outmoded.

Restaurants

Restaurants, perhaps more than any other business establishments, are places most closely connected to our personal experience. They are intimately linked to the memory of a date, a celebration, a journey, a city where we used to live, or an era. Not all restaurants, however, seek this complicity with the user. There are others with a more pragmatic spirit that try simply to fulfill their essential function; they are perhaps integrated, as in a museum, concert hall, or station. The selection described here is intended to illustrate a range of very different restaurant concepts: intimate spaces and mass purveyors, establishments situated within a company, a government body, a viewing tower... none of these projects remotely resembles any other. On the contrary, the aim is to demonstrate the various ways of approaching an architectural project: with different sensibilities, but with equally valid results.

Oxo Tower

One Happy Cloud

Brindley Place Café

Restaurante Théatron

Río Florida

Wagamama

Gagnaire

Restaurant at the Department of Foreign Affairs

Petrofina Restaurant

Televisa Restaurant

Oxo Tower

Lifschutz Davidson

Location: London, UK. **Date of completion**: 1997. **Client**: Harvey Nichols. **Architect**: Lifschutz Davidson. **Scheme**: Lifschutz Davidson. **Associates**: John Sisk & Sons (construction), Buro Happold/WSP (structural engineers), Mecserve/How Engineering (construction services), Equation Lighting Design (lighting), ECHarris and Partners (quality control). **Photography**: Chris Gascoigne/VIEW.

Since 1930 the Oxo Tower has been one of the landmarks on the banks of the Thames. In recent years the building has been renovated to house a diverse range of activities.

The first three levels are used for commercial purposes, the five intermediate floors are occupied by 78 apartments, and, finally, on the ninth floor there are two places to eat (a restaurant and a brasserie) and the Harvey Nichols bar. Aware of the exceptional panoramic view offered by the restaurant, the architects have constructed a light ceiling supported by a latticework of beams in the form of a bobbin, which rests on two pillars situated in the center of the building. The glass skin has virtually no uprights or carpentry. A few ties attached to the ceiling support the intermediate anchors of the plate glass. The first 3 m (10 ft) of the façade are therefore completely transparent.

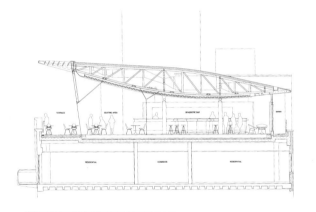

One Happy Cloud

Marten Claesson, Eero Koivisto, Ola Rune

Location: Karlavägen 15, Stockholm, Sweden. **Date of completion**: 1997. **Client**: Masao Mochizuki. **Architects**: Marten Claesson, Eero Koivisto, Ola Rune. **Associates**: Christiane Bosse, Mattias Stahlbom (assistants), New World Inredning AB (construction), Ralambshovs Snikerier AB (carpentry), Nybergs Glas AB (glass). **Photography**: Patrick Engquist.

The developer of One Happy Cloud, a Japanese restaurant situated in Stockholm, wanted to convert his establishment into a point of integration between the Japanese and Scandinavian cultures, both from a gastronomic and an aesthetic point of view. The result is a space of extraordinary simplicity and elegance, without direct references to Japanese culture, but with subtle allusions to the atmosphere and tranquillity found in that country's traditional architecture.

The restaurant takes up an area of approximately 150 m2 (1600 ft), with an almost square floor plan. The eating area is organized into two narrow rooms, which form an L shape. The rest of the space is occupied by the rest rooms and kitchen. All the walls are plastered and painted white, except for the one behind the bar, where there are drawings by graphic designer Nill Svensson.

Brindley Place Café

CZWG Architects

Location: Brindley Place, Birmingham, UK. **Date of completion**: 1997. **Client**: Argent Development Consortium. **Architect**: CZWG Architects. **Associates**: Adams Kara Taylor (structural engineers), Townsend Landscape Architects (landscape design), Silk & Frazier (monitoring), Kyle Stewart (contractor). **Photography**: Chris Gascoigne.

The Rouge restaurant-bar, now the Brindley Place Café, is a small eatery on a square in the city of Birmingham; it re-creates the spirit of old pavilions–minimal buildings falling halfway between urban fixtures and sculpture. CZWG Architects felt that the project should not only satisfy the scheme's functional requirements and the relationship with the urban environment, but it should, above all, constitute a significant piece of work in itself.

In this sense, it is far removed from the typical hermetically sealed structures that normally occupy the streets, and both the façade looking onto the square and the roof are constructed using glass and steel. This means that, although the pavilion is an element of the square, from the inside it seems that the relationship of dependence is reversed, with the square becoming the bar's terrace.

Restaurante Thèatron

Philippe Starck

Location: Mexico. **Date of completion**: 1996. **Architect**: Philippe Starck. **Associates**: Baltasar Vez (project management), Cardona y Asociados (electricity), Electro Media (special installations). **Photography**: Alfredo Jacob Vilalta.

Beyond its immediate function, the restaurant Théatron has a scenographic side, in which customers become leading characters in their own plays.

One room is lit by an antique chandelier, the next by a bare bulb hanging from the ceiling by a flex. Guests ascend a disproportionate, monumental staircase and then pass through a dark, narrow corridor. The restaurant itself is submerged in a misty atmosphere. Light, airy curtains adorn the room, meandering their way down from the ceiling to chair height, so that they only half divide the space. Although it covers an area of over 300 m2 (3200 ft2), the lobby displays only three decorative elements: a huge picture frame approximately 10 m (32 ft) high by 6 m (19 ft) wide, containing a photograph by Richard Avedon, a large staircase, and a gray velvet curtain backed with scarlet silk, which is over 12 m (39 ft) high by 16 m (52 ft) wide, and very striking.

Río Florida

Roberto Ercilla, Miguel Ángel Campo

Location: Florida Park, Vitoria, Spain. **Date of completion**: 1995. **Client**: Pablo Calvo Aguriano. **Architects**: Roberto Ercilla, Miguel Angel Campo. **Associates**: Javier Valdivieso (foreman), Eduardo Martín (structure), Javier Bárcena. **Photography**: César San Millán.

There is not much of a modern tradition for the building of stalls and kiosks in the middle of large parks or public spaces. The difficulty involved in positioning this structure here led the designers to split the building into three interconnected pavilions. Each of these has an associated function: restaurant, bar, and terrace. The whole building was envisaged as a complex of prefabricated units, subsequently assembled on site. The sectional structure of the three elements is made entirely from Oregon pine, assembled using galvanized steel parts. The flooring, wall facing, and furniture are of the same material. Glass envelops the two closed, transparent units. The aim of the project is to create for guests the sustained illusion that they are eating in the middle of a forest. Architectural expression is minimized in favor of the landscape, so as not to dominate it.

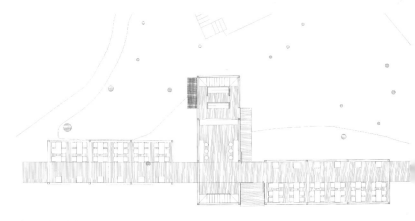

Wagamama

David Chipperfield, Victoria Pike, Pablo Gallego-Picard

Location: 10 Lexington Street, London, UK. **Date of completion**: 1996. **Architects**: David Chipperfield, Victoria Pike, Pablo Gallego-Picard. **Associates**. Overbury Interiors Ltd. (contractor), Chan Associates (structural engineers), BSC Consulting Engineers (service engineers), Tim Gatehouse Associates (section supervisor). **Photography**: Richard Davies.

Wagamama, a Japanese restaurant in London's Soho district, occupies the first floor and basement of a low yet wide-fronted building. The dining room is situated in the basement, while the kitchen is on the first floor. Inside, diners wait to be seated in a long corridor from which they can see into the kitchen and therefore follow the preparation of the different dishes. On the other side of the corridor, an acid etched glass screen separates the customers from the double space and the street. At night, diners waiting for their tables can be seen from outside silhouetted against the glass of the screen. Dishes prepared in the kitchen are delivered to the basement by a system of anodized aluminum service lifts, from where they are distributed to the tables. A series of counters lined up against the back wall of the basement display the desserts, juices, and drinks on offer to diners. There is also another counter just below the staircase, with items for sale to the restaurant's customers.

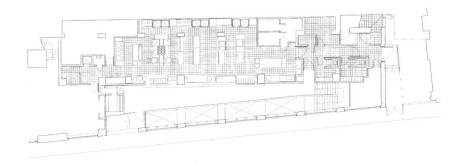

Gagnaire

Studio Naço

Location: Saint Etienne, France. **Year of opening**: 1992. **Client**: Pierre Gagnaire. **Architect**: Studio Naço (Alain Renk, Marcelo Joulia). **Associates**: Jean-François Pasqualini, Allard Kuyken, Beatrice Berin (architects), Muriel Quintanilla (designer), Olivier Dubos (graphic designer). **Scheme**: Conversion of a former country house into a restaurant. **Photography**: Mario Pignata-Monti.

Pierre Gagnaire is one of the world's best-known chefs. He chose a country house built in the 1930s as the place to start up his own business as an independent restaurateur. The conversion project bestows equal importance on the cooking areas and cellars and the rooms reserved for guests.
Each of the former rooms has been turned into a dining room.
Studio Naço uses systems of sliding doors, engraved glass screens, and large wall hangings painted in different colors to establish a relationship of variation, repetition, continuity, and isolation between the different rooms in the building.

Restaurant at the Department of Foreign Affairs

Bernard Desmoulin

Location: Paris, France. **Date of completion**: 1995. **Client**: Department of Foreign Affairs. **Architect**: Bernard Desmoulin. **Associates**: MAE (master of works), Serete Constructions, Novorest (studies), Bouygues TEP, La Felletinoise (construction), Christian Granvelle (basement fresco). **Photography**: Hervé Abbadie.

The project endeavors to explore the potential of a privileged space by re-creating the conditions that turn these small and often concealed courtyards into almost magical places. Only a partially underground structure (see section diagram) could satisfy all the scheme's requirements and, at the same time, restore the garden. The first floor's glass façade is continued by the ground surface in the garden and becomes the roof/skylight of the restaurant's basement. It is, therefore, a glass square through which natural light enters the two dining room levels. A bridge made from wooden planks crosses the bed of a stream, leading to the orchard with its rows of

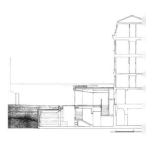

apple and pear trees. Metal guides have been fitted to the dining room roof, enabling an awning to be released on very sunny days if required.

Petrofina Restaurant

Samyn et Associés

Location: Brussels, Belgium. **Date of construction**: 1994-1995. **Client**: Petrofina S.A. **Architect**: Samyn et Associés. **Scheme**: Construction of a restaurant in the head offices of an oil company. **Approximate area**: 2086 m² (22,450 ft²). **Photography**: J. Bauters, Ch. Bastin, J. Evrard.

The building, constructed in 1851, is typical of the mansions of this period still remaining in the district. The scheme expresses the oil company's objectives for its image–transparency, openness, and humanity. The space at the back of the building has been replaced by a large glass canopy suspended between the back of the mansion and the small office building. This canopy covers the staff dining room, creating a garden-like atmosphere. A second restaurant is to be found on a second floor terrace, running along the mansion's rear, north facing façade, above the food service area of the first floor restaurant. A large lobby unites the curved ceiling area with the main office infrastructure, which houses the restaurant's cleaning and storage facilities.

Televisa Restaurant

Ten Arquitectos

Location: Mexico City. **Date of completion**: 1993. **Client**: Televisa S.A. **Architects**: Enrique Norten, Bernardo Gómez-Pimienta (TEN Arquitectos). **Associates**: Roberto Scheimberg (project manager), Gustavo Espitia, Rebeca Golden, Héctor Gámiz, Javier Presas, Leonardo Saldívar (design team), Ove Arup + Partners NY, Salvador Aguilar (structural engineering), Electroinstalaciones Industriales (electromechanical engineering), Inrasa (drainage), Eclisa (air-conditioning), Guma Gas (gas), Inseurban, David Serur (works management). **Photography**: Luis Gordoa.

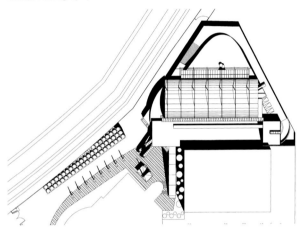

This project has two essential characteristics. Firstly, it is a space designed on the basis of an existing structure and, secondly, it is a building that is difficult to see, since it is concealed by another construction and, above all, the adjacent street layout means it is only possible to catch partial glimpses of it. Perhaps the most important decision was the choice of a light roof for the restaurant itself, since the existing structure could not support a greater load. Yet this solution, of purely technical origins, became the most important formal proposal of the entire project. The roof and façade constitute a unit and are defined by a single outline. The project is made up of three independent roofing sections, of which only the largest (and central one) is curved. The other two, the one covering the kitchen and the canopy above the square, are slightly inclined, adapting to the dynamism of the curved roof. This discontinuity also enables natural light to enter, through skylights located at the junctions between the three sections.

Public buildings, institutions, and offices

Among the virtues of contemporary architecture it is worth highlighting the notable efforts made to reconcile the urban and natural environments. This issue occupies a place of special importance for the subjects under analysis in this chapter – public buildings, institutions, and offices. These constitute one of the most interesting areas of architecture, combining fundamental elements of design, construction, and landscaping. The principal characteristic of the projects included here, apart from their indispensable aesthetic and pragmatic values, is their relationship to the world of work. The major corporations and multinationals have finally recognized the need to harmonize architecture with the landscape, not only as a sign of respect for environmental conditions, but also as a means of achieving an attractive corporate image and a suitable working environment. As a result, the design of all these recent buildings has been based on two fundamental parameters – the construction of a meaningful, identifying image and the creation of a working environment that is pleasant, harmonious, and, above all, respectful of the all-important human dimension.

In fact, the importance today's society attaches to image is reflected in the headquarters of the major corporations and in many public buildings, where top class architectural design has become the best way of expressing a philosophy, whether corporate or governmental.

In some cases, the emphasis has been placed on tradition and perpetuity; in others, on innovation and creativity. The common thread running through all the projects, however, is their attempt to present an image that accords with a philosophy of work.

Public bodies

Public institutions at international level have been caught up in the general trend for updating and reviewing the architectural principles of their buildings. There is a clear desire to dispel the myths surrounding the role of public bodies in the personal life of the individual and what better than a change of image and structure to try to create a friendlier face? But this is not simply a question of redesign. The idea goes much further than this. It also involves the inclusion of environmental considerations in the construction of these buildings, which house anything from the parliaments of major countries to city halls, law courts, embassies, and courts of human rights. In following this new direction, landscaping and environmental activities place these new buildings on the threshold of a fresh, intensely ecological millennium.

Court of Human Rights

Richard Rogers

Location: Strasbourg, France. **Date of completion**: December 1995. **Client**: Council of Europe. **Cost**: FFr 455 million. **Architects**: Sir Richard Rogers (Rogers Partnership Ltd.), Claude Bucher. **Associates**: Ove Arup, Ominium Technique Européen (engineering and structures), Thorne Wheatley Associates (work sections supervision), David Jarvis Associates, Dan Kiley (landscape design), Lighting Design Partnership (lighting), Sound Research Laboratories, Commins Ingemansson (acoustics). **Scheme**: Court and Commission rooms and administrative services. **Photography**: F. Busam/Architekturphoto.

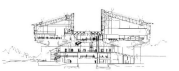

The building claims to be the symbolic and mechanical representation of the tasks undertaken by the internal organs of the Court of Human Rights: it is an open, transparent structure. According to Richard Rogers, it is an articulated complex of head and body: the two parts are linked by a vertical communications nucleus. The head is the public part, where the working rooms used by the Court and Commission are to be found; the lower section or body, by contrast, contains the administrative divisions. As in almost all of Richard Rogers' buildings, there is an extraordinary precision in the expression of details. His architecture always exhibits the desire for transparency and lightness. Rogers does not try to conceal the structure, but elevates it through the use of high tech.

Deutscher Bundestag

Günter Behnisch

Location: Bonn, Germany. **Date of completion**: 1993. **Developer**: Bundestag (German Parliament). **Architects**: Günter Behnisch, Winfried Büxel, Manfred Sabatke, Erhard Tränkner. **Associates**: Gerald Staib, Hubert Burkart, Eberhard Pritzer, Alexander von Salmuth, Ernst Tillmanns (project architects), Ulrich Liebert, Heinz Schröder, Bernd Troske (contract architects), Schlaich, Bergermann and Partner (structural engineers), S.H. Keppler (air-conditioning and installations), Zimmermann + Schrage (electricity), Graner + Partner (acoustics), Lichtdesign Ingenieurgesellschaft, Lichtplanung Bartenbach (lighting), Berthold Mack (façade consultants), Hans Luz + Partner (landscape design). **Scheme**: Parliament, presidential offices, administrative offices, lobbies, restaurant, visitors' area, and services. **Photography**: Christian Kandzia.

The Bundestag (German Parliament) occupies a privileged position–close to the Rhine and next to a long riverside avenue. In view of its considerable size, it was felt necessary to make doubly sure that it did not distort the landscape. The roof is virtually transparent. Beneath the skylight, the hall is transformed into a miniature valley in the midst of a forest, into which the light filters through the branches of the trees. Day and night, sunsets, seasons, snow in winter, the leaden skies of fall, the color of flowers in spring–they all penetrate the building. This metaphor naturally demands great technological application, not only in matters of climate control, but also problems of security. Nevertheless, the transparency motif has endured: it is always possible to see through the building. From the chamber floor, trees can be seen, from the lobby the chamber of deputies, and from the staircases the river Rhine...

Finnish Embassy in Washington D.C.

Mikko Heikkinen and Markku Komonen

Location: Washington D.C, USA. **Architects**: Mikko Heikkinen and Markku Komonen. **Date of completion**: 1994. **Associates**: Sarlotta Narjus, Angelous Demetriou & Associates, Eric Morrison (architects); Lee & Liu Associates (landscape design); Chas. H. Tompkins Co. (contractor). **Scheme**: Offices, conference rooms, meeting rooms, and services. **Photography**: Jussi Tiainen.

The Finnish Embassy in the United States is situated on Massachusetts Avenue, in the heart of embassy land. It is an area of low density, populated by noble buildings, isolated from one another by hundreds of different types of trees. The building combines the rational, coherent distribution of its office areas and studies in two parallel rectangular blocks, with a Piranesian central space four stories high, in which walkways interrupted above the void, sections of circular staircases, and volumes suspended in the air are interwoven.

By contrast to such innate exuberance, the outside of the building seems to reject the introduction of bold forms. On the side façades, the green granite reflects the branches and foliage of the trees. The front façades are constructed using blocks of translucent glass with a soft, greenish hue, echoing the structural elements and metal panels, which have been painted with a patina of the same color.

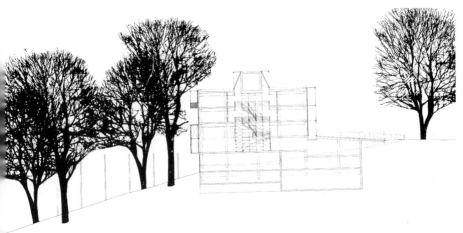

Finnish Embassy in Washington D.C. 591

European Free Trade Association

Samyn and Partners

Location: Brussels, Belgium. **Date of construction**: 1993. **Architects**: Y. Azizollahof, W. Azou, J. Ceyssens, A. Charon, P. de Neyer, H. Dossin, L. Finet, S. Finet, D. Gelhausen, T. Hac, T. Khayati, P. Mandel, P. Mayeur, A. Mestiri, N. Milo, Ph. Samyn, B. Selfslagh, V. Van Dijk, D. Verboven, B. Bleurick. **Scheme**: Offices, meeting rooms, parking, and services. **Area**: 11,000 m² (118,000 ft²). **Photography**: Ch. Bastin & J. Evrard, J.M. Byl.

The European Free Trade Association (EFTA) building is in the heart of the Léopold district, Brussels' financial quarter. The building can accommodate any sort of office, from individual rooms to full floor, open plan designs.

The structure is divided up by two rows of separate pillars measuring 10.8 m (35 ft), which provides a great deal of flexibility in the arrangement of desks. The façade consists of a double glass skin with a perimeter corridor.

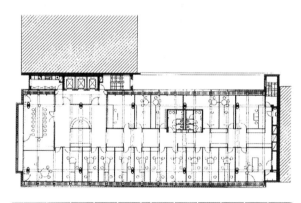

Reichstag

Foster & Partners

Location: Berlin, Germany. **Date of construction**: 1999. **Client**: Federal Republic of Germany. **Architects**: Foster & Partners. **Associates**: David Nelson, Mark Braun, Dieter Muller, Ingo Pott. **Photography**: Dennis Gilbert, Nigel Young.

This project emerged from the initiative to transfer the German Parliament from Bonn to Berlin and rehouse it in the Reichstag building. In 1992 a competitive tender was issued for the construction of an area measuring 33,000 m2 (355,000 ft2), almost double the size that could be contained by the Reichstag building. The total area was later reduced to a realistic 9000 m2 (97,000 ft2).

The scheme involved reopening a chamber within the Reichstag building–a structure that had been opened in 1894, set on fire in 1933, partially destroyed in 1945, restored during the 1960s and "wrapped up" in 1995. The complexity of the architectural planning was heightened by the desire to review the building's design from an environmental viewpoint. This involved designing an energy efficient structure, with ambient heating inside and, associated with this, self-generation of heat and energy production and a reduction in waste emissions from it.

The new glass dome is the point of departure for the interior work and enables the building to be opened up to natural light and views. It acts as an essential component in energy saving and natural lighting strategies. The dome was envisaged as a "lantern," with the broad interpretations implied by this description.

Federal building on Foley Square

Hellmuth, Obata & Kassabaum

Location: New York, USA. **Date of construction**: 1995. **Architects**: Hellmuth, Obata & Kassabaum. **Associates**: Tishman Foley Partners (contractor), Linpro NY Realty (developer), Israel A. Seinuk (engineer). **Area**: 87,300 m² (939,000) ft². **Cost**: $276 million. **Scheme**: US Federal Government office building. **Photography**: Paco Asensio.

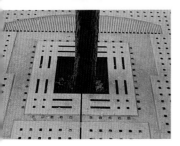

This building's steel structure began to emerge even before the final contract designs had been completed. The architects were responsible for each of the design details on every floor and for making the most cost effective use of the space available. The result is a high rise, but not aggressive, building which combines authoritarian architecture with some softer finishes. These create an extremely dignified structure, highlighted by the circular section towards the top of the building, which was inspired by skyscraper designs from the 1920s. Decorative elements in the form of cornices and pilasters give form to the façade. Building work on the entrance hall had to be suspended following the discovery of Afro-American remains during the excavation work. This building is currently protected as an area of historical interest.

Court building on Foley Square

Kohn Pedersen Fox Associates

Location: New York, USA. **Date of construction**: 1995. **Architects**: Kohn Pedersen Fox Associates.
Associates: Lehrer McGovern Bovis (contractor), Structure Tone (interiors), BPT Properties (developer).
Photography: Paco Asensio.

This is one of the greatest Federal buildings in the United States, situated in an area of large-scale urban development. The designers had difficulties with the scale of the project during the initial phase, due to the problems involved in incorporating this skyscraper in a district in which civic centers and residential buildings coexist. A square at the front of the building minimizes the visual and spatial impact of a structure of this height.

The building's west wing includes a first floor gallery, which creates a sensation of continuity and connection between the different public buildings. Neoclassical in style, it takes its design reference from the earlier 1936 court building here.

Inside, an effort has been made to situate the large courtrooms and the judges' chambers in the most accessible areas. This has been achieved by situating these rooms within an oval space connected to the main tower. The judges have their own access route and move around within an independent domain, which includes private elevators, enabling them to be completely isolated from the defendants, who enter and leave the building through specially constructed tunnels. The public access area includes a reception area and the gallery connected to the square at the front.

Government offices for the Department of Bouches-du-Rhône

Alsop & Störmer

Location: Marseilles, France. **Date of construction**: 1994. Architect: Alsop & Störmer. **Associates**: Ove Arup (structural engineering and fittings), Hanscomb (sectional supervision). **Scheme**: Offices, meeting and conference rooms, cafeteria, and services. **Area**: 44,500 m² (479,00 ft²). **Photography**: Roderick Coyne.

After Alsop & Störmer were awarded this contract, the construction of the building in Marseilles marked a point of departure in their career. The importance of the structure in the building's image and its intense blue color make it a highly unusual piece of work. It is a powerful, futuristic construction reminiscent of Archigram images in its overall effect.

The scheme is divided between two parallel rectangular blocks containing the offices and a cigarette-shaped structure housing the assembly and conference rooms. Between these is an atrium with a network of suspended passageways and bridges.

Tokyo City Hall

Kenzo Tange

Location: Tokyo, Japan. **Date of construction**: 1986–1991. **Client**: Tokyo Municipality. **Architect**: Kenzo Tange. **Photography**: Osamu Murai, Shinkenchiku Shashinien.

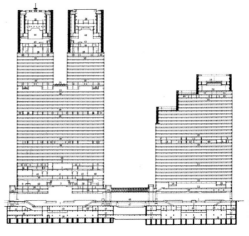

Two aligned towers face the central park of Shinjuku, forming a complex together with the Assembly Building and the square lying between them. Tower I, located between the square and the park, contains the office of the governor, the most important of the administrative departments, conference rooms, and a disaster control center. From floor 33 the building divides into two twin towers, reaching a height of 243 m (800 ft). Tower II, 163 m (535 ft high), accommodates a number of agencies, public corporations, and other departments. The upper part progressively decreases in size, in a stepped arrangement in relation to Tower I, to form a combined profile at the summit of the buildings. The floors develop from a reticular network of 6.4 m (21 ft). In order to achieve flexibility and free space for the working areas, a superstructure was conceived for each tower, formed by eight large nuclei of 6.4 x 6.4 m (21 x 21 ft), supported on some floors to form "superbeams." The result, with lights of 19.2 m (63 ft), is a spatial distribution which opens to the outside with a sense of total freedom, exceeding the virtual perimeter defined by the nuclei. The façade, in modular design with panels measuring 3.2 x 4 m (10.5 x 13), reflects the superstructure and acquires a certain traditional character in its latticework design element.

City Hall, The Hague

Richard Meier

Location: The Hague, The Netherlands. **Date of completion**: 1998. **Client**: City of The Hague. **Architect**: Richard Meier. **Scheme**: Construction of the City Hall of The Hague, Central Library for public use, administrative rooms, and services. **Photography**: Anna Tiessler.

In one single project, the City Hall harmonizes with the spatial complexity of the centre of the city in which it is located. This is a theme which is encountered in many of Richard Meier's buildings: urban and rural situations are expressed in the same buildings, which in this way are converted into the natural epicentre of their location. The spatial composition of the axes of perspective, lines, and throughways creates an image of the building and its surroundings which is complex yet balanced. At street level, the building is open on all sides; the interior and exterior have a natural flow, and at each corner subtle relationships are created between open and enclosed spaces, access routes, and lines of perspective. This is clearly seen on the two glazed sides of the entrance atrium, a space of intense use and direct access, and the focus of attention from the working areas. Essentially, the project is a large, empty, covered square, which the population of The Hague must take it upon themselves to fill.

Rezé-le-Nantes City Hall

Alessandro Anselmi

Location: Rezé-le-Nantes, France. **Date of completion**: 1988. **Architect**: Alessandro Anselmi. **Scheme** Construction of a new City Hall which encompasses the two existing old buildings. **Photography**: Philippe Ruault.

The task was to construct a modern City Hall which would function as a means of rejuvenating the municipal administration and act as a dynamic source of development for Rezé. Anselmi designed the new project by concentrating the structures on the east and west of the site, leaving a vast amount of free space. The result is that this area, treated as a garden amenity, provides the image of the whole of the architectural complex, in the form of a thoroughfare running north to south, which surmounts the hill and extends into the extraordinary residential estate of Le Corbusier. The municipal technical services are accommodated in the west part of the building, and are connected at the entrance level by means of a vertical traverse in the form of stairways and elevators. Finally, the politico-administrative functions, the municipal council chamber, the offices of the mayor, the secretariat, the finance department, and the information center are all located in the eastern part.

Portugal Pavilion

Álvaro Siza

Location: Lisbon, Portugal. **Date of completion**: 1997. **Client**: Expo '98. **Architects**: Alvaro Siza. **Scheme** Pavilion for the celebration of Portuguese culture at Expo '98. **Photography**: Paco Asensio.

The Portugal Pavilion at Expo '98 is located next to the northwest corner of the Muelle de los Olivares. The border between the building and the adjacent area is covered by an awning supported on slender columns, forming an enormous, lateral covered walk along the eastern side of the building. This structure, made of reinforced concrete, has not had a specific use since the event: Expo '98 called for a great deal of flexibility and versatility in the use of space, but its representative function nevertheless required a clear and powerful image. The building, which was developed along a longitudinal north–south axis, consists of two units separated by a composite structural unit. The first of these is in fact a grand ceremonial square flanked to the north and south by two great porticoes, clad in glazed tiles of different colors, between which runs a very fine strip of concrete describing a curve, in the manner of a gigantic sail. The second unit consists of a rectangular-based structure with a basement and two surface stories. These three levels are developed around a courtyard covering the ground as far as the lower story, to allow for the planting of trees. From one corner of the building a two-story annex projects, which is separated from the main building in the complex by a gallery.

Public service buildings

The focus of attention in this section will
be on those small urban buildings which
for practical purposes form part of the
urban furniture of every large town and
city. These might be small medical
facilities, weather centres, water circulation
control centres, or shipping navigation
beacons and lighthouses, the proper use
of which enhances the quality of life for
the local population. They have been
chosen for inclusion in this selection of
contemporary architecture because of the
innovation of their design; they have given
added value to the landscape of each
individual city.

Manliu mountain area

Signal box

Montfort Werbung GmbH

Pincelli

Manliu mountain area

Enric Batlle and Joan Roig

Location: Manliu, Meranges, La Cerdaña, Spain. **Date of construction**: 1994. **Architects**: Enric Batlle, Joan Roig. **Associate**: David Closas. **Photography**: David Closas, Gregori Civera, Enric Batlle.

The project was developed around an already extant mountain refuge, in an area of the Catalan Pyrenees; it is at an altitude of 2000 m (6500 ft), next to a lake occupying the site of an ancient glacier, at the boundary between sub-alpine woodlands and alpine vegetation areas. The task was to construct an arrangement for the end of a mountain track leading to the refuge so as to provide information and channel visitors onwards. The biggest problem was to harmonize the existing uses, for open air stock rearing, with the increasing presence of the public enjoying the natural surroundings. The basic operations involved limiting vehicular traffic so as not to intrude on the surrounding meadowland, yet still provide minimum amenities for visitors, such as restrooms, litter collection points, drinking fountains, tables, and barbecue sites, which were nevertheless required to have a spontaneous, natural appearance.

Given the location and the project, there was only one material – stone – which could be used to construct virtually all the elements of the site without excessive handling and transport. Stone was, furthermore, the material used for the few buildings in the area and was also the most readily available. Consequently stone was used to construct the boundary walls, tables, barbecue sites, water fountains, traffic tracks, signage, and restrooms.

Signal box

Herzog & De Meuron

Location: Basle, Switzerland. **Date project begun**: 1989. **Date of completion**: 1995. **Architects**: Jaques Herzog, Pierre de Meuron, Harry Gugger. **Associates**: Hansueli Suter, Philippe Fürstenberger. **Photography**: Margherita Spiluttini.

Adjacent to the 18th- and 19th-century walls of the Wolf-Gottesacker cemetery is a substantial volume of copper: a railroad signal box and control center. It stands beside the railroad tracks, close to the new locomotive sheds. Distributed over its six floors are sophisticated control instruments and electronic equipment for managing switch points and coordinating the signals along the tracks. The concrete structure of the building is provided with external insulation, and is clad in copper panels approximately 20 cm (8 in) in thickness. These panels are open at a number of points to allow ingress of natural light. The orientation of the panels, opening out, casts lines of shadow on the façades, resembling the scales of a fish. This introduces a variation in the texture of the skin of the building, while at the same time emphasizing the dramatic character of its isolation. The building is, by definition, a striking point in the landscape which does not evoke any echoes of known forms or images, codified in terms of culture. It is a unique feature of its kind.

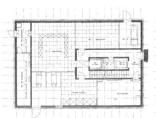

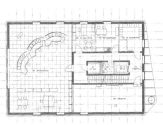

Montfort Werbung GmbH

Oskar Leo Kaufmann

Location: Klaus, Austria. **Construction Date**: 2001. **Architect**: Oskar Leo Kaufmann Architects **Client**: Montfort Werbung GmbH **Photography**: Adolf Bereuter

The construction, conceived as a large transparent rectangle, is an ingenious and rational design. The light, the glass, the polished surfaces, the fluidity, and the spatial continuity are the protagonists. The only element that breaks up the straightness of the lines is the evocative entrance, symbolically designed in the shape of a gentle wave penetrating the interior of the building.

The structure, which consists of different levels, was built of steel and glass. Replacing solid walls with transparent ones allows a clear view of the various areas and establishes an interesting dialog between the interior and exterior while letting in plenty of natural light. The metaphorical wave that becomes the entrance is made of concrete with an insulated covering. Inside, the arrangement of the spaces is defined through the use of the different materials that cover the floors.

The work areas have been placed on the upper floors and are connected to the lobby and reception through evocative carpeted stairs, a material that is also used on the floor in the workspaces. The use of materials, textures, and colors, such as steel, glass, chrome, and the whites, greens, or grays, contribute to an overall feeling of industrial starkness, luxury, and serenity..

Pincelli

Domenico Biondi/Progettisti Associati

Location: Sassuolo, Italy. **Date of completion**: 1999. **Client**: Pincelli & Associati. **Architect**: Domenico Biondi/Progettisti Associati. **Photography**: Matteo Piazza.

significant phase of the project was the restoration of the colors of the exterior walls, which were covered with graffiti.

The project designated the first floor of the building, which has different levels, as the headquarters of an important commercial consulting firm that needed its own modern and comfortable space. This requirement determined the treatment of the site as a modern and rational volume of iron and glass, whose rooms were organized based on their function. This solution allowed the original spaces to be preserved while adapting them using reversible methods. This complex undertaking achieved a balance between past and present. Stone, wood, iron, and glass bring to life this suggestive and successful combination of styles and periods. The stone and the wood are reminders of the building's past, while the iron evokes the present.

The first phase of the remodeling consisted of saving the structure while preserving, whenever possible, the least-damaged original features. Therefore, the original cross beams and roof were put back into place, and the structural walls and the profiles of some of the vaulted arches were repaired. Another

Offices

Dynamic action, flexibility, communications, and flow—all terms used to define the designs for the offices included in this section. Technology now comes to the aid of those working at tasks which were hitherto monotonous and solitary, and offices are no longer the exclusive domain of the bosses. Instead, the areas destined for office use have become the venue in which both ideas and products are created. The image created by the office is studied in minute detail, with the same care that goes into designing a logo or planning a publicity campaign. Taken all in all, the exterior and interior of an office reflect equally the true spirit of the company.

Riddell's

Loop Telecom

Elisabeth Alford

Riddell's

William P. Bruder

Location: Jackson Hole, Wyoming, USA. **Date of completion**: 1995. **Client**: Riddell's advertising and design agency. **Architect**: William P. Bruder. **Associates**: Ed Ewers, Dewayne Smyth, Maryann Bloomfield (design team). **Scheme**: Offices, meeting and conference rooms, library, and services. **Photography**: Bill Timmerman.

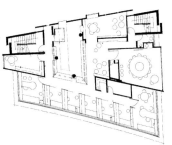

This is a three-floor office block, constructed for an advertising agency in Jackson Hole, located in the city's new commercial district, an area where the human imprint has not changed the attractive natural conditions of the surrounding landscape. It features an atrium to the full height of the three floors, a vertical space lit by a rising casement window, long and narrow, which, on reaching the roof, unfolds and is transformed into a light well. This open space is the nucleus of the whole structure, with the offices arranged around it. Riddell's advertising agency is located fronting onto a bend in the highway, and the façade reflects this shape. The remaining lines which delineate the building are determined by nonorthogonal geometry, a feature often encountered in Bruder's designs. The walls are placed in perspective, and jointed, which incurs a number of inevitable implications as far as spatial relationships are concerned: the space is rendered more dynamic, and its perception is distorted. Immediate comprehension is altered, and the space is expanded or reduced, depending on whether the walls are opening out or closing in; all these are changes which play with depth perception. The building echoes the architecture of the farms, ranches, and hay barns which proliferate in the region and are such a characteristic feature of the countryside. We can therefore speak of contextualization, in this case being understood as an imitation of a given situation, specific to the location in which the project has been created. But, in turn, this is also an image which is decontextualized, in that Riddell's is plainly not a hay barn, even though the façade overlooking the road takes its shape from that prototype.

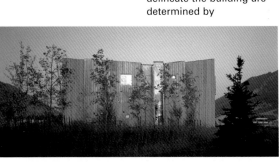

Loop Telecom

Roger Bellera

Location: Barcelona, Spain. **Date of Completion**: 2000. **Interior Designer**: Roger Bellera. **Client**: Loop Telecom. **Photography**: Jordi Miralles.

piece of auxiliary furniture has been placed behind. Display units have been placed at each end of the counter, and access to the offices and work areas is located on the right, through columns painted green in order to emphasize the entryway. At the far end of this reception space lie two meeting rooms and the public area, separated by open glass panels.

Loop Telecom is a telecommunications company that specializes in corporate services. Their offices should reflect a true image of the company. In order to emphasize its graphic and corporate image, it was decided to combine materials and colors while distributing spaces into clearly distinctive areas. Blue and green, the colors in its logo, are the predominant tones, which bring a freshness and vitality to the carpet as well as to some of the furniture pieces and display units.

The access to the lobby is located at one end of the rectangular floor, which echoes the shape of the building. Two areas framed by the outlines of two intersecting ellipses divide the main space. The floor treatment—blue or green carpet, depending on the surroundings—defines each area visually as well as physically.

The reception counter, located directly across from the entrance, was constructed of wood with aluminum and corporate blue laminates. The carpet in front of the counter displays the logo of the company, while an original

Elisabeth Alford

Elisabeth Alford

Location: New York, USA. **Date of completion**: 2001. **Client**: Elisabeth Alford. **Architect**: Elisabeth Alford. **Photography**: Jordi Miralles.

The plan was designed in such a way that both spaces are physically separated. This division is defined by a long fluorescent tube that runs through them and by the placement of furniture

pieces. A shelf unit, full of jars of sand that the artist uses for her work, functions as the visual partition between both spaces. It is an industrial steel structure that serves as an organizer, yet at the same time, it is a decorative element of great visual power in the space. The steel used for the organizer is repeated in the long desk and shelves in the area devoted to the office. Wood paneling ties the ceiling and floors together. The use of noble materials, such as wood, and the evocative color palette give the space the exquisite warmth that

characterizes it.

The project, designed by Elizabeth Alford herself, pays as much attention to the decoration of the interiors as to the environment created. It relies on functional design, straight lines softened by touches of color (nothing loud and all within the same range) that are distributed through the space, and a close relationship between materials. These textures and a sound aesthetic sense have created a pleasant and contemporary place where work can be carried out freely and in harmoniously.

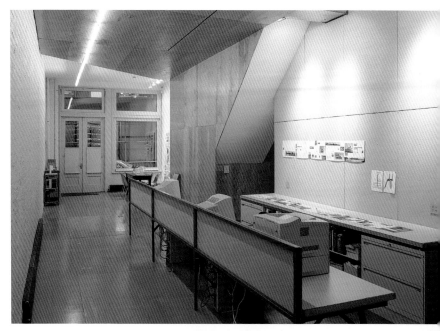

644 Public buildings, institutions, and offices

Banks

Money has not always been associated
with good taste, and the same is true of
architecture. Traditionally, the biggest
budgets have not always translated into
the best designs, still less into the greatest
innovations in the field of architecture. In
any event, it is certain that banks, deeply
involved in their mergers and acquisitions,
still need somewhere to carry out and
centralize their operations. Moving on
from the names traditionally associated
with bank buildings (Rocco Sen-Kee Yim,
Nikken Sekkei, Kohn, Pederson & Fox, for
example), there has been a succession of
new figures winning commissions for
constructing headquarters for some of the
big banks.

Commerzbank

Hypo Alpe Adria Bank

Nord LB. North German State Clearing Bank Building

Commerzbank

Norman Foster and Partners

Location: Frankfurt, Germany. **Date project begun**: 1992. **Date of completion**: 1997. **Client**: Commerzbank. **Architect**: Sir Norman Foster and Partners. **Scheme**: Ecological office building.

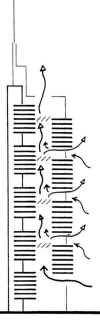

This project is the largest commissioned by the city of Frankfurt in recent decades, and represents a prime example of a skyscraper designed in line with ecological criteria. Each office is designed to provide natural ventilation through practically designed windows, which also serve to provide fine views of the city and of the landscaped courtyards in the form of cloisters located on every floor of the building. The relationship with the other buildings in the area is of great importance: the perimeter of the block has been rebuilt in the form of a low block which accommodates parking facilities and apartments, levelling up the height of the street and restoring the scale of the whole district. The tower itself, which is triangular in section, merges neatly with the existing buildings as well as with the new residential block, to smooth its passage into the urban context in such a way that it is only from the main access, on the north side, that we appreciate the tower in its full height from ground level. From Grosse Gallusstrasse, with its heavy flow of traffic, a grand stairway rises up, opening into a new public space dedicated to the city.

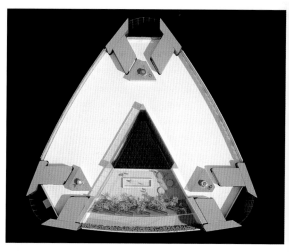

Hypo Alpe Adria Bank

Morphosis

Location: Klagenfurt, Austria. **Date of completion**: 2001. **Architect**: Morphosis. **Collaborators**: Dipl. Ing. Klaus Gelbmann, Richard Kuglitsch (structures), Robert Sorz, Fritz Aufschlager (mechanical engineering). **Gross floor area**: 1,156,193 sq. ft. **Photography**: Ferdinand Neumüller and Ernst Peter Prokop.

The design for the new Hypo Alpe Adria Bank headquarters, developed over three stages, had to accommodate firstly the company's head offices and a convention center, then commercial spaces and underground parking, and finally residences and a day-care center.

The site is located about 3,1 miles from the center of the town of Klagenfurt, Austria, in an area where the urban fabric melds with farmland. The nearby constructions consist of isolated buildings surrounded by parking garages, a situation that is aggravated by the flat blocks that dot the poor, fragmented suburban landscape.

Morphosis's goal was to improve the conditions in these areas, thus they focused on integrating rural qualities with urban typologies: they designed a large vaulted roof which imitates the undulating contours of the landscape. While the pedestrian spaces were created by making incisions in this large constructed mass, the parking garage was relegated to the underground levels. The planning located the denser part of the project to the south, near the busier street, while the residential area is at the north, mixing with the suburban environment. Users enter the complex under a large projecting roof which leads to a plaza. This space, reminiscent of a Roman forum, provides access to the banking institution, to the convention center, and to an indoor network of pedestrian walkways. The offices, which face on to the street, occupy a five-storey building which seems to emerge from a collision between the mass of the building and the site. The different departments are arrayed around a sunlit courtyard.

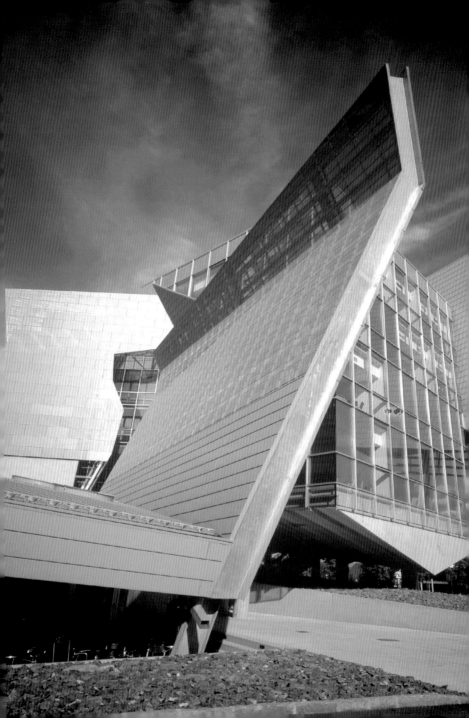

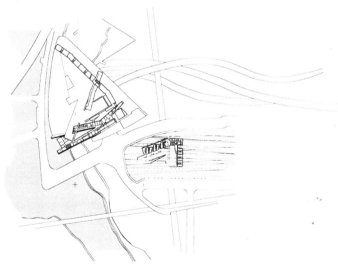

Nord LB. North German State Clearing Bank Building

Behnisch, Behnisch & Partners

Location: Hannover, Germany. **Date of completion**: 2002. **Client**: Demuro Grundstücksverwaltung mbH & Co KG. **Architect**: Behnisch, Behnisch & Partners. **Photography**: Christian Kandzia / B, B&P.

priority for creating natural ventilation and providing fresh air to most of the rooms. The double outer shell helps create ventilation and, at the same time, reduces noise pollution. Also, the use of glass on the entire surface of the building makes it possible to easily control the natural light that filters through to the interiors.

At first glance, the construction begins as an integral part of the surroundings and extends out from the perimeter of the central body, taking the form of a 180-foot-tall tower. It is a complex puzzle in which each piece fits perfectly. The enigmatic and unique multilevel tower, a spiral of provocative and acute angles that can be seen from a distance, is the main feature of the building. In addition to the offices, the complex includes commercial, residential, cultural, dining, and sports facilities. The objective was to create a space that was open to and accessible by the public.

The architects have designed a building that emerges from the landscape and forms an integral part of it, while the highest portion resembles an independent entity connected to the whole but perceived as a remote figure, as if it were part of the distant city. One of the main goals was to create a smart and environmentally friendly building. The architects used natural resources in the construction process, requiring energy consumption and the reduction of carbon dioxide emissions to play a part in the planning of the modern and spectacular body. Windows were given

Corporate buildings

The corporate buildings described in this section consist of offices and their ancillary services, such as restaurants, conference rooms, bars, and so on, as well as the areas around them, in the form of parks or squares. This type of architectural combination provides accommodation for companies, and, apart from fulfilling a variety of different functions, these buildings also serve as publicity generators in their own right: in other words, they put across a specific image which represents the interests and the distinctive features of the company. In this context, the work of the architect is based on a clear understanding with the client, and the design will be the materialization of ideas born of the dialog between them. There are two clear objectives: first, to construct a complex which will incorporate concepts of functional performance and comfort, and, second, to create an exclusive and communicative symbol to elicit recognition on the formal level.

Jean-Baptiste Berlier Industrial Hotel

Dominique Perrault

Location: Paris, France. **Date of planning**: 1986–1988. **Date of construction**: 1988–1990. **Client**: Société Anonyme de Gestion Immobilière. **Architect**: Dominique Perrault. **Scheme**: Industrial premises, restaurants, and parking lots. **Gross floor area**: 21,000 m² (226,000 ft²). **Photography**: Michael Denancé.

In 1986 the Paris City Council and the Société Anonyme de Gestion Immobilière issued an invitation to tender for a new building: an industrial hotel. Intended neither as an office block nor as an industrial building, it was to be simply a space, intelligently used and capable of accommodating a wide variety of activities. This not only involved providing a design for a new building, but the actual choice of site called for a specific solution in a difficult area between the ring road encircling Paris and the railroad tracks running from the Gare d'Austerlitz station. Given the apparent chaos of this situation, the clarity of Dominique Perrault's vision lends the area a whole new identity. The building provides 17,000 m2 (183,000 ft2) of space for industrial operations of various sizes. What is provided is simply a space between wrought iron partitions, connected to the utilities. No other conditions are imposed other than the actual limitations of the block and the communications systems.

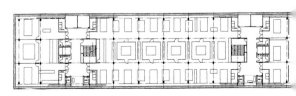

Centraal Beheer extension

Herman Hertzberger

Location: Apeldoorn, The Netherlands. **Date of completion**: 1995. **Client**: Centraal Beheer. **Architect**: Hermann Hertzberger. **Associates**: Dolf Floors, Dickens van der Werff, Jan van den Berg, Arienne Matser. **Scheme**: Reception area, visitors' area, function rooms, conference rooms, and services. **Photography**: Lock Images.

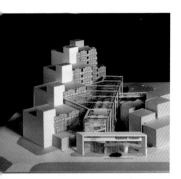

During the 1960s and 1970s, Hertzberger, through the medium of the journal Forum (edited jointly by Bakema and Van Eyck), studied the application to architecture of structuralist philosophy. He was seeking to create objective spatial structures which would respond to a previous and underlying arrangement of structures, before actually defining any specific elements. In other words, the first phase of the project, and the most important, consists of defining the fundamental structures of the architectural language, and establishing a syntax. Based on this, the building then develops in much the same way as a written text. Phrases are constructed on the site, based on the combination of the basic elements: windows, doors, furnishings, walls, rooms, stairways, office blocks, etc. The building which houses the headquarters of the Centraal Beheer in Apeldoorn is a clear example of structural architecture: its small, polyvalent units, subject to different interpretations depending on the functional needs, are arranged on an orthogonal latticework, which makes the provision of subsequent extensions an easy task. The extension completed in 1995, however, represents a revision of all these theories. The structural techniques, the aesthetics, and, above all, the latent philosophy running through all these projects, spanning 25 years, is absolutely distinct. Hertzberger's project involves the construction of a central building and an entrance area; being specifically areas which do not exist in structuralist architecture, they seem to grow like a woven fabric or a net.

One of the most arresting features is the design of the stairwells: they are all different, designed as unique, almost sculptural objects.

German Federal Railways Customer Service Building

Rhode Kellermann Wawrowsky

Location: Duisburg, Germany. **Date of construction**: 1998. **Consultants**: Arup GmbH (structural engineers), EGL (landscaping). **Design team**: Rhode Kellermann Wawrowsky. **Area**: 32,500 m² (350,000 ft²). **Scheme**: Offices and services. **Photography**: Holger Knauf.

Built on the site of a former locomotive repair workshop, this office building is arranged along a curved axis 220 m (720 ft) long. Opening off this central three-story corridor are 11 separate structures, creating a zig-zag line. This helps create a larger façade area, allowing all the offices to have windows and a view outside. This backbone structure also allows for the building to be extended at its ends. In addition, each of the peninsular buildings is organized around a central atrium. At the time of its construction, this building represented one of the most technologically advanced and best equipped centers of its kind, in operation 24 hours a day, providing important customer service.

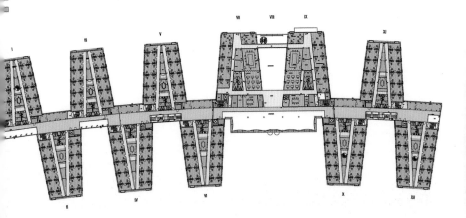

German Federal Railways Customer Service Building 675

Oracle

Gensler

Location: Redwood Shores, California, USA. **Date of construction**: 1989–1998. **Client**: Oracle Corporation. **Architect**: Gensler. **Associates**: William Wilson & Ass. (contractors), Seccombe Design International (interiors). **Scheme**: Campus for the facilities of a leading software company: office buildings, conference and press center, gymnasium, parking lots, and exterior landscaping. **Photography**: Gensler.

In the mid-1980s a Canadian entrepreneur purchased this site in the popular tourist area of Redwood Shores, California. Gensler became involved with the project for reorganizing the area and converting it into the Centrum Business Park. Today, 11 years later, the final phase of the project is being brought to a conclusion. With six office buildings, covering a total area of 1.6 million m2 (17.2 million ft2), a conference and press center, gymnasium, and four parking lots, the site has recently been converted into the headquarters of the Oracle Corporation, a leading software producer. The first building to be developed on the campus was the "access" structure, which now accommodates the Oracle executive offices. Architecturally speaking, the design is based on simple geometrical forms: a rectangular block supported by two cylinders, projecting an image which is both striking and strong. This building faces the lake, with which it interacts by way of its blue-green glass panels. With one single exception, the remaining office buildings are designed on the basis of a simple cylinder, 3.5 m (11.5 ft) in diameter, which intersects with a rectangular block, forming a 45° angle. This sole exception is an office block which retains the cylindrical element of its neighbors but has a completely different curved shape, giving contrast in the layout.

Grain treatment plant

Samyn and Partners

Location: Marche-en-Famenne, Belgium. **Date of construction:** 1995. **Architects:** Gh. André J.L. Chapron, A. Charon, R. Delaunoit, Ch. Fontaine, D. Mélotte, S. Peeters, Ph. Samyn, D. Singh, B. Vleurick; Boun Construction sprl (construction), Menuiserie Fréson sc (structure and carpentry). **Scheme:** Workshop, store, offices, laboratories, and services. **Floor area:** 1400 m² (15,000 ft²). **Photography:** Ch. Bastin & J. Evrard.

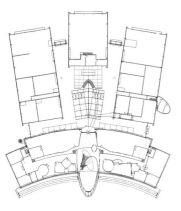

Located in the forest of Ardennes, this building consists basically of a grain treatment workshop, cold storage, and a number of offices and laboratories. The plot is an irregular space surrounded by splendid oaks; which prompted Philippe Samyn to design a simple and striking shape. This is an oval glass dome formed by a structure of wooden arches. In fact, this is one of the simplest of structure in architecture, which relates this building to the Mongolian yurt and the Zulu hut. Philippe Samyn takes advantage of the research done into these types of structure by Mutschler and Otto in Mannheim (1975), Kikutake in Nara (1987), and the experimental buildings erected in Dorset, UK, in 1982 by Edmund Happold and the architects Ahrends, Burton & Koralec. Inside the dome two auxiliary buildings have been put up alongside the central workshop to house the cold rooms and offices.

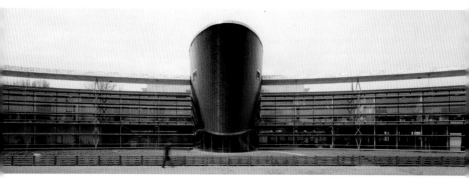

NTT Office Center

César Pelli & Partners, Fred W. Clarke

Location: Tokyo, Japan. **Date of construction**: 1990–1995. **Architects**: César Pelli & Partners, Fred W. Clarke. **Scheme**: Office for NTT, conference hall, telecommunications center, restaurant, and garden landscaping. **Photography**: Misuo Matsuoka, Kanedi Monma, César Pelli.

the conference hall, and, above these, the employees' restaurant. The building is divided into two clearly distinct parts: a strip section curving above the interior garden, intended for office use, and a triangular area with its façade facing outwards, grouping the services and communications nuclei.

On top of the initial rectangular shape, the architects set about enveloping the building to the greatest possible extent, pulling back from the borders of the site and with the edges rounded symmetrically on the side facing the highway. The scheme is divided into two buildings, presenting their exterior façades on this line. One tower is a slender entity merging with its plinth in the parking area, with a low body element in the rounded area of the elevated highway. A break in the construction of the perimeter allows a glimpse from the road of the interior; this interior is formed by an intermediate space providing a public garden that opens in a fan shape from the entrance in the lower part of the façade, moving into the area delimited by the enveloping structure until the opposite face is reached, above the residential area. The lower body element is supported on the rounded façade, and accommodates a commercial center three stories in height, faced in Minnesota stone in a delicate warm pink color; this extends along the entire plinth of the building, seeking to provide continuity for the envelope. The tower rises 30 stories above ground level for use as offices, and six floors below ground to accommodate, at the deepest levels, the telecommunications center,

Morgan Stanley Dean Witter

Gabriel Allende

Location: Madrid, Spain. **Date of completion**: 2000. **Architect**: Gabriel Allende. **Client**: Morgan Stanley Dean Witter. **Photography**: Jordi Miralles.

The location of the building, between two other buildings and situated on a main street in Madrid, was undoubtedly an influence at the time of its conception and planning, but that was not the only determining factor. The principal activities of the company, which specializes in financial services, also needed specific spaces that had to fulfill a series of requirements. For example, a publicity area (a storefront designed to attract clients) was provided to display the company services offered to the public, and interiors were made available in which it would be possible to work under optimum conditions.

From the outside, three clearly differentiated zones can be seen: one for pedestrian access, one for vehicles, and one for information. The interior space becomes the communication hub between the inside and the outside. This solution makes it possible to have two reception areas: one for the exterior of the building and another one for the internal flow. The building is divided into different levels: the basement or lower one at street level; a middle zone, where a hierarchy of vertical spaces can be seen; and a top floor, which finishes the building with an attic. The interior spaces have been arranged with effectiveness and intuition. The lack of natural light, a main concern of those responsible for the project, was resolved with an interior courtyard located along the side of the building. This provision allows light to enter through a skylight that extends the length of the space from east to west.

TRW Central Office

Sasaki Associates

Location: Lyndhurst, Ohio, USA. **Date of construction**: 1989. **Architect**: Sasaki Ass. Inc. **Scheme**: Garden and landscaping design for a corporate center. **Photography**: Sasaki Associates.

Sasaki Associates were entrusted with landscaping the new TRW headquarters in a rural setting in Lyndhurst, Ohio. With an area of 49 ha (120 acres), the site was an old ranch with an extremely diverse topography. The design of the facilities has preserved and enhanced this landscape, integrating the roadways, buildings, services, and characteristics of the existing environment in a compatible and sensitive way, with minimal effect on the nearby residential areas.

The greater part of the land consists of meadows surrounded by ancient woodlands. One striking natural feature is the Euclid river, which crosses the site; the seasonal floods have produced a range of gullies and ravines across the width of the area, creating a variety of natural landscapes. In order to preserve the existing qualities and character, Sasaki Associates and Urban Forest Management (Prairie View, Illinois) have established a register of more than 2500 trees on the site.

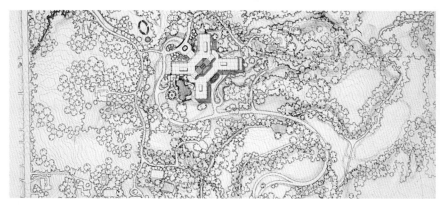

British Airways offices ("Waterside")

Niels A. Torp

Location: Heathrow, London, UK. **Date of construction**: 1992–1998. **Client**: British Airways. **Architect**: Niels A. Torp. **Associates**: Land USE Consultants (landscaping). **Area**: 105,000 m² (1.2 million ft²). **Scheme**: Office center for British Airways, restaurant, cafeteria, small commercial center, gymnasium, bank, and conference hall.

To obtain the most rational layout possible for its operations, British Airways decided to construct its office center, with capacity for 2800 employees, immediately adjacent to Heathrow Airport. Because the area is anything but "human" in terms of environment, it was felt that this large number of people would need to have confidence in themselves and in the environment surrounding them in order to work properly both inside and outside the complex. The only inhabited area anywhere around is the village of Harmondsworth, with an entertaining pub and a small church dating from the 13th century. The village itself needed to be protected from an "invasion" of 2800 new employees. The first decision was to convert one of the areas which had not been built on into a small park with a social center for use jointly by employees and the villagers. There was still the problem, however, of how to keep so many people motivated in such an inhospitable environment, surrounded by one of the biggest airports in the world. The architects decided to give the buildings the character of a "town," and to provide the large number of users with a sense of "community." The 55,000 m2 (590,000 ft2) of the office complex was accordingly divided into six buildings set out in the shape of a U, inside which was sited a free-standing pavilion; this accommodates a school, linked to a leisure area, a restaurant, and the computer center. Between this pavilion and the office facilities an elegant park is provided for the use and enjoyment of staff from the six buildings.

Convention and
exhibition centers

Convention and exhibition centers and trade
fair sites are characterized by the temporary
nature of the events to which they play host.
This means that there is a very intense flow
of visitors and exhibitors passing through in
specified periods of time, with the venue
being cleared again before the next event
begins. Added to this is the fact that, born of
the desire to provide an air of exclusivity, the
associated buildings seek to be aesthetically
striking, while not overlooking their
functional purpose. Trade fair complexes in
turn are national flag bearers: they are
structures which represent a country or a
region; they are buildings which are
intended for publicity, and their architecture
must be capable of reflecting the most
significant features of the geographical area
which they represent. Over the past few
years, exhibition pavilions have proved, for
architects, to be the perfect area for
experimentation, giving them the
opportunity to test out structural solutions
and new materials alike; in short, the chance
to speak their own architectural language.

New Leipzig Trade Fair Building

Von Gerkan, Marg & Partner

Location: Leipzig, Germany. **Date of competition**: 1992. **Date of construction**: 1993–1996. **Client**: Leipziger Messegesellschaft. **Architect**: Von Gerkan, Marg & Partner. **Associates**: PBI, Klaus Glass, Büro Wronn (consultants on façade); Ian Ritchie Architects, London (structural engineers); Wehnberg, Eppinger, Schmidtke (landscaping). **Scheme**: Exhibition areas, congress center, administration area, storage facilities, and parking lot. **Photography**: Architekturphoto.

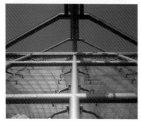

This enormous trade fair project for Leipzig continues the city's long tradition of fairs and exhibitions, and represents part of a new initiative by unified Germany to revitalize the former German Democratic Republic, East Germany, by making this fair one of the most important focal points for meetings and commercial interchange between Eastern and Western Europe.

The new fair facilities are located on the northern periphery of Leipzig, with good communications both to the main highways leading out of the city as well as to the airport. In addition to the traditional exhibition areas, the scheme also includes facilities for organizing congresses and gatherings in parallel with the fair. The central vaulted area accommodates the ticket sales counters, location boards, information points, and access to the upper area. More than 250 m (820 ft) long and 80 m (260 ft) wide, this great glazed hall is the biggest of its type ever constructed and is an impressive sight.

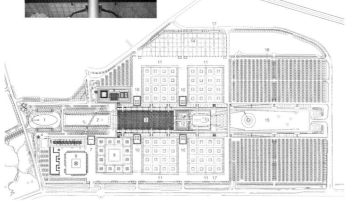

2

Tokyo International Forum

Rafael Viñoly

Location: 3-5-1 Marunouchi, Chiyoda-ku, Tokyo, Japan. **Date of competition**: November 1989. **Date of completion**: June 1997. **Client**: Metropolitan Government of Tokyo. **Architect**: Rafael Viñoly. **Associates**: Masao Shima Architects; Kunio Watanabe (Structural Design Group). **Scheme**: Four halls for theater, concerts, conferences (largest with capacity for 5000, smallest for 1500), fair site, exhibition halls, congress center, offices, commercial facilities, restaurants, and parking lot. **Total floor area**: 145,000 m² (1.56 million ft²). **Photography**: Nacasa & Partners, Tim Hursley.

In the central district of Marunouchi, in the business area and close to the commercial district of the Ginza, the site is strategically connected to the city's subway network, as well as to the railway stations of Tokyo and Yurakucho.

Right from the outset, the plan was to treat the most important sections of the scheme as separate entities. One element, on the western side, consists of the four large halls for concerts, exhibitions, and congresses, harmonizing with the surrounding urban landscape in size and linked by a common façade facing the city. The great hall, on the other side of the site next to the railroad tracks skirting the area, has an extended cylindrical shape that harmonizes perfectly with the plot perimeter. Running between the great hall and the other halls is a thoroughfare sufficiently wide to be turned into a plaza, providing a link not only between the different parts of the project but also with the rest of Tokyo, and creating a valuable space for public use in a city in which such facilities are a rare feature.

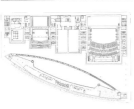

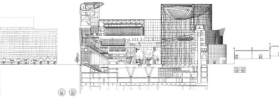

Kunibiki Trade Fair Building

Shin Takamatsu

Location: Matsue, Shimane Prefecture, Japan. **Date of construction**: 1993. **Architect**: Shin Takamatsu. **Associates**: Yamamoto-Toshibana A & E (structural engineers), Architectural Environmental Laboratory (fittings). **Floor area**: 8733 m² (94,000 ft²). **Scheme**: Exhibition hall, conference and meeting rooms, offices, and services. **Photography**: Nacasa & Partners.

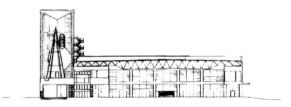

This building is used for major fairs and congresses, for the everyday commercial needs of the Shimane prefectural authorities, as well as for small-scale congress events. The name Kunibiki literally means "meeting of lands," and refers to the legend of the gods of Izumo who brought the Japanese islands together to create the country. The basic thinking behind the project was to separate the different elements of the scheme and to transform them into independent structures. Accordingly, in front of the great exhibition hall there is a linear office block, at the front of which are positioned the cylindrical bodies of the conference rooms. The most outstanding feature of the trade fair building, however, is a lobby 24 m (80 ft) high, located at the front, featuring geometrical shapes suspended in the air (three cones, a sphere, a glass cube, and a cylinder), which contain the lighting elements and a tearoom providing refreshments for visitors to the building.

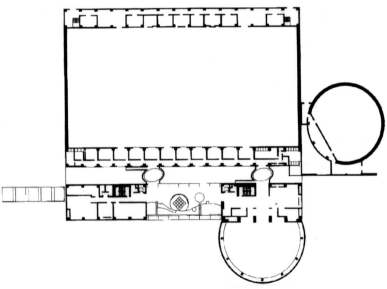

Lille Congress Center

Rem Koolhaas

Location: Lille, France. **Date of construction**: 1994. **Architect**: Rem Koolhaas. **Scheme**: Congress halls, concert hall, and exhibition area. **Photography**: R. Richter.

The Grand Palais congress center was essentially an OMA development. In principle it consists of a large bridge structure which links the two earlier areas, but it has evolved in such a way that it presents an ovoid form incorporating three functions: Zenith (concert hall), Congrès (congress hall) and Expo (exhibition area). The building can be adapted to different uses, with the structure becoming virtually invisible in the concert hall, yet with the exhibition area displaying a forest of columns in different sections. The roof becomes a technological landscape, which accommodates equipment, the façade itself changes depending on the internal requirements, combining metal (opaque) for the service and loading areas, plastic (semitransparent) in the section which looks out onto the city, and concrete (fire resistant).

EXPO Lisboa '98

Location: Lisbon, Portugal. **Date of construction**: 1995–1998. **Scheme**: Complex for the Universal Exhibition at Lisbon, EXPO '98. International and multitheme pavilions and commercial areas, with recreation and leisure facilities, parking lot. **Photography**: Paco Asensio.

Lisbon regarded Expo '98 as its starting point for the launch into the next millennium, and the project was planned to provide the definitive metropolitan take-off point for this Atlantic capital. Concentrated on 50 of the 300 ha (125 of the 740 acres) assigned for urban development, the Portuguese Expo involved the construction of one or two dozen self-contained units, of differing dimensions and for different uses, of which only some were demolished at the end of the event. It was then that the site took on a second lease of life, with the new infrastructure and access created for the original event being adopted to support continued use of part of the site for the functions already assigned to it: residential use, tertiary educational purposes, or recreational facilities. Most of the theme pavilions which had been intended as permanent structures were planned with an eye to the future, which has meant that excellent results have been achieved in bringing them back to life. Portugal is the only country with its

own individual location; the other countries taking part erected their pavilions beneath the undulating covering of the new Lisbon fair site. The Expo includes, among others, the Portugal Pavilion by Alvaro Siza, the Knowledge of the Sea Pavilion by Joao Luis Carrilho da Graça, and the Oceanarium designed by Peter Chermayeff.

Cartuja 93

Corporativo

Location: Seville, Spain. **Date of construction**: 1993. **Client**: Cartuja 93. **Architects**: Corporativo. **Scheme**: Leisure and cultural area. **Photography**: Expo 92 Photographic Archive and Cartuja 93, David Cardelús.

In the case of Seville, the urban development project which provided the physical support for Expo 92 was extended into the Cartuja 93 project, with the aim of optimizing the "assets" created during the event. There were two basic objectives on which the project was focused: development of the center by way of scientific and technological innovation, and development in the metropolitan area in terms of cultural and leisure resources. The first of these involved the provision of facilities such as the science and technology park, the university campus, and the tertiary educational resource center, while the second allowed for the creation of the cultural area, linked to the monumental La Cartuja complex, a theme park, the Alamillo urban park, and other leisure and sports facilities. The construction of the island provided a miniature encapsulation of all these aims, inasmuch as it involved civil engineering works, the release of land for urban growth, and provided enrichment for the urban landscape, while at the same time keeping the natural surroundings.

Millennium Experience

Richard Rogers Partnership

Location: Greenwich, London, UK. **Date of construction**: 1996–1999. **Client**: The New Millennium Experience Company Limited. **Architect**: Richard Rogers Partnership. **Associates**: Ove Arup & Partners (supervision), Buro Happold (structural engineers and services), Fedra (fire resistance engineering), McAlpine (building contractors), Bird Air (roof), Bernard Ede (landscaping). **Scheme**: Design and construction of the site, the structure of the complex itself, and the outside installations: catering, reception area, parks, pier, exhibition areas, services. **Photography**: Grant Smith.

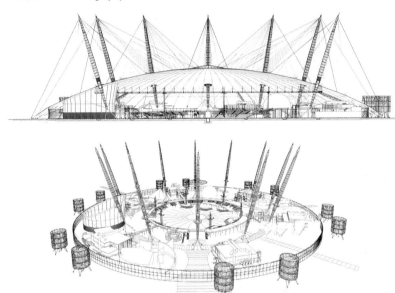

This complex for celebrating the entry into the Millennium will be inaugurated on 31 December 1999, and will play host to exhibitions and festivities marking the start of the new century. The "Millennium Dome" measures 1 km (0.6 mile) in circumference, with a diameter of 365 m (1200 ft), and maximum height of 50 m (165 ft). Its roof is suspended on a series of steel masts, 106 m (348 ft) high, and is secured by more than 70 km (42 miles) of cable. The roof is made of Teflon fibreglass, with an open space in the interior well suited for the various celebratory events. Work began in June 1997, with the construction of the main body of the complex, next to the "Millennium Pier," an artificial island, a leisure area designed in an undulating shape, with lighting and music to aid relaxation, and, finally, the Greenwich Dome, which will incorporate exhibition areas and a cafeteria. The pier (costing £2 million) is the longest of a series of state-sponsored construction projects of this type, aimed at improving river traffic through London. The artificial island (the "Living Island") has been landscaped with a number of native plant species, and is scheduled for completion in the summer of 1999, before the dome itself.

Brussels Exhibition Center. Pedestrian Route

Samyn et Associés

Location: Chaussée Romaine, Brussels, Belgium. **Date of construction**: 1995–2000. **Client**: Parc des Expositions de Bruxelles. **Architect**: Samyn et Associés. **Associates**: Setesco (stabilization), Atenco (basic engineering), Gh. André, Y. Avoiron, F. Berleur, B. de Man, J.P. Dequenne, A. d'Udekem, F. el Sayed, Th. Henrard, L. Kaisin, D. Mélotte, N. Milo, J.Y. Naimi, N. Neuckermans, T. Provoost, J.P. Rodriguez, O. Steyaert, Ph. Samyn, B. Thimister, G. van Breedan, M. Vandeput, S. Verhulst. **Area**: 14 ha (35 acres). **Scheme**: Exhibition center, pedestrian route providing a link between halls, parking lot, business center, post office, press center, garden landscaping, crèche. **Photography**: Ch. Bastin, J. Evrard, Andrés Fernández, Bauters Sprl.

To give an idea of the enormous numbers of visitors who arrive at the complex through the North Gate (Porte Nord), the parking lot, for example, provides 12,000 spaces; more than 70% of the visitors gain access to the area through this entrance, which means one million people a year, not counting delivery trucks and vans, to visit an exhibition area of 14 ha (35 acres). Obviously, this means there is an urgent need for a large area to be created to provide reception facilities, capable of handling the massive number of people arriving through the North Gate. Those using public transport continue to enter through the gentle landscaping of the south access route.

The entrance hall of the Brussels Exhibition Center consists mainly of an enormous parabola roof in wood and glass, a structure covering a total area of approximately 26,000 m2 (280,000 ft2)in latticework measuring
15 x 16.2 m (49 x 53 ft).

A thoroughfare 10 m (32 ft) wide and 90 m (292 ft) long, constructed in three sections, provides a direct link between parking lot C and the reception area. Located beneath the glazed canopy of the roof and 6 m (20 ft) above ground level is the covered area for commercial vehicles accessing the halls. Functioning literally as an axis, this also provides the way into a network of aisles between the existing halls, allowing the public independent access to the different facilities.

Valencia Congress Center

Sir Norman Foster

Location: Valencia, Spain. **Date of construction**: 1996–1997. **Architect**: Norman Foster. **Scheme**: Congress halls, auditorium, landscaped garden area, lobby, facilities for equipment, offices, cafeteria, restaurant, press centers, and exhibition areas. **Photography**: Paco Asensio.

This new congress center provides the focal point of an area of heavy urban development on the outskirts of Valencia. The building has a gentle convex shape, with two curved façades of different lengths. The scheme includes three auditoria of various sizes and capacities, each of them equipped with simultaneous interpreting cabins and the smallest able to be divided into two areas. The large glass façades are protected by external slatted blinds, based on movable sheets of translucent glass, which help save energy and provide a very pleasant light. In front of these vertical blind elements are a number of curved pools, which help reflect the natural light into the interior. The roof, which covers the whole of the structure, is of zinc-coated aluminum, and, thanks to the subtlety of its design, appears to float above the body of the building while in fact being supported on a number of large concrete porticoes. The whole complex resembles the prow of a great ship in the open sea.

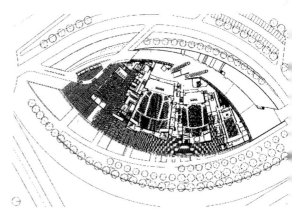

Brisbane Convention and Exhibition Center

Philip Cox

Location: Southbank, Brisbane, Australia. **Date of completion**: June 1995. **Client**: Government of Queensland. **Architect**: Philip Cox. **Associates**: Cox Rayney, Ove Arup (structures and engineering). **Scheme**: Convention and exhibition center; five exhibition halls, a further hall, and 20 meeting rooms. **Photography**: Cox Group Brisbane.

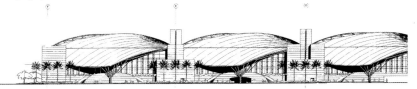

The Center contains five exhibition halls, one of which contains a mechanical system for raising or lowering the seats to allow for gatherings with more than 4000 participants. Other facilities include a hall with capacity for 2000 people and 20 meeting halls varying from 15 to 1000 m2 (160 to 10,750 ft2). The halls are contiguous along the building, and can be extended to provide an exhibition area of more than 25,000 m2 (270,000 ft2) in total area.

The Center is designed to create the impression of waves when viewed from the gardens, using a series of shell-shaped forms based on the geometry of the parabola. The main idea behind the design was to develop a structure which descends as far as possible down the façades so as to endow it with a human scale.

The Brisbane Convention and Exhibition Center has won five national architectural awards, as well as the Royal Institute of British Architects Engineering Award for the year 1996.

Torhaus

O.M. Ungers

Location: Frankfurt, Germany. **Date of construction**: 1991. **Client**: Frankfurt Fair. **Architect**: O.M. Ungers. **Scheme**: Gallery and high rise building for the fair's administrative offices. **Photography**: Francesc Tur.

The Torhaus is located in the center of Frankfurt, next to the freeway access road. There are also two railroad tracks crossing the site on overpasses, resulting in a triangular open space which was causing some problems in the fair's activities. The solution was this glass and stone building, which made communications possible between both parts of the site. Its name ("Tor" means "gate" in German) is a reference to this converted complex providing a symbolic gateway to the city. The structure consists of a horizontal strip element and a tower set on an irregular base. The service facilities are located in the first element, and are spread over four floors: nursery school, hairdressers, food shopping outlets, offices for consultants and interpreters, press offices, and a business center are located in this module, the southeast face of which accommodates the heating and air-conditioning systems. A pedestrian throughway passes onto the third floor in the form of a moving pavement, and around this element the towers rise up, providing an additional 24 floors to house the administrative offices of the Fair. The main body consists of two integrated elements: the interior element in glass, and the outer element in stone, protecting the interior element and forming a backdrop for it. The structure totals 29 floors, and reaches a height of 117 m (385 ft). The fact that the building still inspires admiration today is the best tribute that can be paid to this spectacular skyscraper.

Research Centers

The specific nature of some architectural categories means that additional strengths are required; this is the case with buildings intended for research, which call for a specialized process of design. Architects must be prepared to confront the technical challenges which the researchers pose for them. Accordingly, the structures in this section are the result of teamwork, providing an answer to all the problems which arise in the course of development of the project. The main challenge is to support the technical research work by creating properly functional areas which at the same time will provide a pleasant working environment, i.e. paying particular attention to the use to which the building is to be put, but likewise to the people who are going to work in it.

Seibersdorf Research Center and Offices

University of Cincinnati Research Center

OCAS

M & G Research

Design Cube

Institute of Neurology

IMPIVA

Skirball Institute of Biomolecular Medicine

Wexner Visual Arts Center

Social Science Studies Center

Heureka

Pacific Design Center

Hysolar Institute

Lucille Halsell Botanical Garden

Graz Botanical Garden

ESTEC

Seibersdorf Research Center and Offices

Coop Himmelb(l)au

Location: Seibersdorf, Austria. **Date of construction**: 1995. **Client**: Austrian Research Center. **Architects**: Wolf D. Prix, Helmut Swiczinsky. **Associates**: Sam, Hopfner, Hornung, Mündl, Pillhofer, Spiess, Péan, Postl (design team). **Scheme**: Offices and laboratories. **Photography**: Hélène Bisnet.

The task was to refurbish and extend an existing warehouse on the Seibersdorf Research Center site. The building was to be modified and enlarged in such a way that it could accommodate the Center's offices. The research group had the peculiarity of involving professions from a variety of disciplines, and the planning required that the building should reflect this style of work. The presence of different systems at the same time was to be represented not only in the method of working, but also in the structure itself. Sections of the building which were broadly differentiated were overlapped, with different structural systems existing side by side, the old and the new manifested simultaneously on the same level. This can be seen in the dimensions of the building, the structure, and the surfaces; there is no façade as such.

The element added to the original warehouse takes the form of a two-story beam structure, supported on a series of inclined pillars, some of them arranged in the shape of a cross, depending on the structural requirements. This is in effect a framework from which are suspended the slabs of concrete which form the floors. The direction of this framework structure does not follow that of the previous building, but is situated perpendicular to it, and, at one end, passes above the roadway. This accordingly creates a bridge effect, which then in turn launches out into a number of different directions.

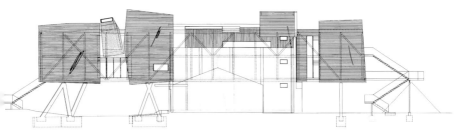

Seibersdorf Research Center and Offices 723

University of Cincinnati Research Center

Michael Graves

Location: Cincinnati, Ohio, USA. **Date of construction**: May 1995. **Client**: University of Cincinnatti. **Cost**: $32 million. **Architect**: Michael Graves. **Associates**: KZF Inc. (associate architects), Smith, Hinchman & Grylls Assocs. (design), Hargreaves Associates (landscaping), Monarch Construction (building contractors). **Scheme**: Research institute. **Photography**: Timothy Hursley.

Since embarking on his architectural career in 1964, Michael Graves has developed from the neo-avant-garde abstraction of his origins to the language of the postmodern, which characterizes his most recent work. It was in the realization of a number of extension and enlargement projects that he was brought into direct contact with history, so classical and vernacular allusions began to appear in his work, together with abstract forms in a linguistic combination which defines his architectural style. Color, defeating one of the prejudices of modern architecture, and the use of the façade as a pictorial and scenic element have acquired great importance. Likewise, the system of axes used to create the layout and the free combination of elements hark back inevitably to the classical tradition.

In May 1995 work was completed on the Engineering Research Center for the University of Cincinnati, Ohio. In terms of structure, the building can be seen as a mixture of a grand longitudinal pavilion design, and four other transverse elements, with the entrance extending from between them. Despite the variety of materials (ochre and terracotta masonry), or the shape of the windows (round or square), the façades present a sense of ordered uniformity. Similarly, in the copper-clad roof, the suggestion of industrial shapes appears beneath a large longitudinal vault.

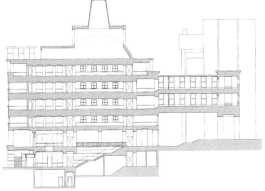

OCAS

Samyn and Partners

Location: Ghent, Belgium. **Date of construction**: 1991. **Architects**: W. Azou, M. Bouzahzah, K. Delafonteyne, H. Dossin, T. Hac, C. Hein, T. Khayati, A. Mestiri, Ph. Samyn, B. Selfslagh, D. Spantouris, J. van Rompaey, L. van Rhijn. **Consultants**: Samyn and Partner, NV Sidmar (structure), Heacon (hydraulics). **Scheme**: Offices, laboratories, test workshops, and parking lot. **Area**: 9000 m² (97,000 ft²). **Photography**: Ch. Bastin & J. Evrard, G. Coolen nv.

The Research Center for the Applications of Steel (OCAS) is located at the intersection of a freeway and a highway, bordering the facilities of the steel company Sidmar. OCAS consists of office buildings, laboratories, and experimental workshops. The greatest possible degree of spatial flexibility was specified, in order to be able to incorporate new machinery and technical resources without interfering in day-to-day Center operations.

The project was designed in a circular bank structure 180 m (590 ft) in diameter. Access to all the sections of OCAS is provided through a gate, located in its geometrical center. The different functions are arranged along two orthogonal axes. The laboratories are located on the first floor, in a bridge structure 162 m (530 ft) in length and 19.5 m (64 ft) wide. The two major experimental workshops are perpendicular, with a parabolic roof allowing light to enter over a length of 42 m (138 ft), and rise to a height of 16.5 m (54 ft). Direct access to the workshops is provided by means of an interior throughway, for moving heavy loads.

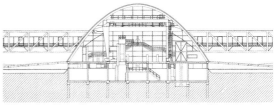

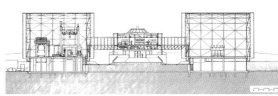

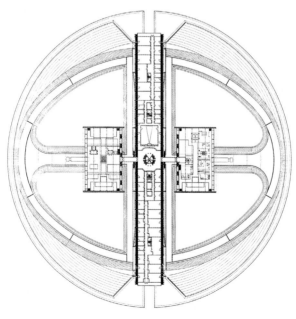

M & G Research

Samyn & Partners

Location: Venafro, Italy. **Date of construction**: 1992. **Architects**: Ph. Samyn, A. Cermelli, A. Charon, M.D. Ramos, M. Van Raemdonck, B. Vleurick, Studio H. **Consultants**: SETESCO (structure), CANOBBIO (roof structure). **Area**: 2700 m² (8900 ft²). **Photography**: Matteo Piazza.

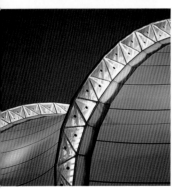

These chemical laboratories are in Venafro, a township in the south of Italy located in a long valley surrounded by hills, fields of crops, and traditional buildings. Right from the initial sketches, the idea was to create a roof which would form a single volume, of an awning type, oval in shape, with dimensions of about 85 x 32 m (280 x 105 ft) and a height of 15 m (49 ft), supported by transverse arches and longitudinal cables. The whole structure is located in the center of a pool, likewise oval in shape, which not only has a landscaping function but also provides a means of regulating the heat of the laboratory facilities.

The interior space is lit by the inherent transparency of the membrane, and by a series of perimeter arches, adapted to serve as windows. The membrane is made of PVC-coated polyester. Inside, research programs are carried out which call simultaneously for heavy machinery and delicate experimentation. Located beneath the awning are the equipment and a second two-story structure which accommodates offices and services, these being accessed by a system of linking passageways.

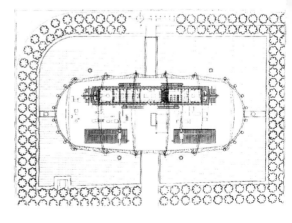

Design Cube

Ortner & Ortner

Location: Klagenfurt, Austria. **Date of construction**: 1992–1995. **Client**: EDD-Designentwicklungs. **Architects**: Ortner & Ortner. **Associates**: Sabien Krischan; Reinhold Svetina (structure). **Photography**: Ralph Richter/Architecturphoto, Lang & Lang.

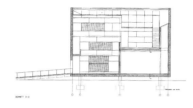

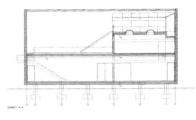

Ortner & Ortner have certainly made their presence felt. A gigantic box shape (18 x 26 m, 59 x 85 ft, in plan and 12 m, 39 ft, in height), indigo blue in colour, raised above a white gravel surface on 18 concrete pylons, secured at the four cardinal points as a reference to a higher order of things: a pure structure. Visitors use the metal access ramp, ascending from ground level and emerging in the interior of the box. Once inside, natural light filtering through an awning canopy illuminates a patio of façades in red and a gray floor, the same rough gray as the concrete blocks which compose the outer casing. The façades are clad in panels of vitrified plywood. Opposite the entrance, above the longitudinal axis, is the façade of the exhibition and conference hall, of a height and width such as to occupy the northern half of the structure; on the left, following the transverse axis, the façade extends over three stories of the administration section, then at half height above the terrace which extends over the hall. On the right, a stairway leads to the balcony, the only element to reach beyond the limits of the box shape, and providing a view of the outside world.

This structure is separated from the box by a narrow perimeter strip, defined by the passageway above the entrance, the inclined ramp from the balcony to the terrace, the admission of light into the hall, and the new light source and stairway on the way from the entrance to the elements of the building.

Institute of Neurology

Burton Associates, Tod Williams, Billie Tsien

Location: La Jolla, California, USA. **Date of completion**: 1996. **Architects**: Burton Associates, Tod Williams, Billie Tsien. **Scheme**: Multidisciplinary center for neurological research. **Photography**: Pablo Mason.

The project was to create a multidisciplinary center for neurological research, with an environment which would favour both practical experimentation as well as theoretical research, in a major complex which would attract specialists from all over the world. The site is surrounded by land used by the Scrippscampus , with a view of the eastern hills of the Pacific Ocean. Located on a hilltop, the center, occupying some 5000 m2 (54,000 ft2), consists of three main buildings arranged across a plaza. This semicloistered arrangement allows for the unfolding of an interior landscape, where the discovery of the different spaces seems to be of more importance than the actual shape of the

buildings. The three structures involved are: a three-story center for theoretical work; a U-shaped laboratory wing surrounding the plaza; and an auditorium. A series of passages and stairways extends around the perimeter, passing between the different levels of the complex and providing a range of different views over the plaza and the hills of the surrounding countryside. The truly

outstanding feature of this project was the very close cooperation between the teams of architects and of landscaping specialists. Far from imposing themselves on one another, these professionals worked together in the same direction, constantly adding new details which enrich the final result.

IMPIVA

Ferrater, Bento and Sanahuja

Location: Castellón, Spain. **Date of construction**: 1996. **Architects**: Carles Ferrater, Carlos Bento, Jaime Sanahuja. **Associates**: Carlos Martín, Carlos Escura. **Scheme**: Offices and services. **Photography**: Paco Asensio.

The Institute of Small and Medium-sized Businesses (IMPIVA) on the outskirts of Castellón is among the last of the town's buildings before one enters the orange groves which proliferate throughout this part of the Mediterranean, and is located in a technology park. This is a somewhat chaotic area in architectural terms, in which various styles compete. In the midst of this, the architects of IMPIVA opted for a building based on a rigorous geometrical composition, in the manner of the abstract artists of the avant-garde. The focus of the project is to provide leased offices and facilities for companies in their first few years of existence, at a time when they need the greatest possible flexibility.

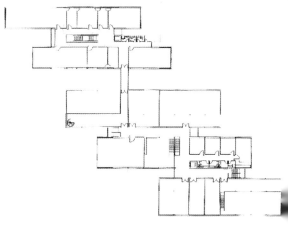

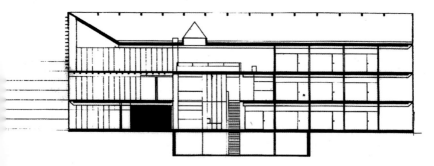

Skirball Institute of Biomolecular Medicine

James Stewart Polshek and Partners Architects

Location: New York, USA. **Date of construction**: 1992. **Architects**: James Stewart Polshek and Partners, Architects. **Scheme**: Annex to Tisch Hospital, for biomolecular research. **Area**: 51,000 m² (549,000 ft²). **Photography**: Paco Asensio.

The layout of this project aimed to meet a variety of needs simultaneously: a main entrance, a connecting nucleus, and an internal garden acting as a structural delimitation. The principal lobby area measures 1560 m2 (16,800 ft2), and is covered by an aerodynamically shaped aluminum and glass canopy. Its double height makes the entrance to the hospital and medical school a comfortable space of generous dimensions. In formal terms, the linking element with the north wing is the most freed up: a curved glazed structure and an anthropomorphic appearance provide a welcoming atmosphere for the admissions and waiting room section of the hospital. The use of different materials on the façade provides a hint of the different functions inside: the laboratory floors are clad in granite, the wards in brick.

Movement between the laboratories is facilitated by a double passageway. Each module is divided into a working area, with tables mounted on the outside wall, and a rest and recreation area facing the passage, creating a circular corridor around the nucleus. The height of the floors intended for the laboratories has been restricted so as to allow maximum sunlight to enter. This principle is also applied to the medical areas; there are four suites arranged on each floor, with the greatest possible number of windows.

Wexner Visual Arts Center

Peter Eisenman

Location: Minneapolis, Minnesota, USA. **Date of completion**: 1991. **Architect**: Peter Eisenman. **Scheme**: Lecture theaters, laboratories, library, workshops, exterior public plaza, teaching staff accommodation, and exhibition hall. **Photography**: Leff Golberg/Esto Photographics.

From the outside, this appears a compact building divided into two parts: a solid structure as the plinth, with large rectangular openings on one side and arcades on the other; and a much lighter timber and glass upper element. A secondary structure supports an awning which provides protection from the sun and serves as the horizontal termination of the building. The apse element is a solid body with very narrow, high vertical openings accommodating the windows in a Romanesque apsidal structure.

Social Science Studies Center

James Stirling, Michael James Wilford

Location: Berlin, Germany. **Date of completion**: 1990. **Client**: Social Science Studies Center of Germany. **Architects**: James Stirling, Michael James Wilford. **Scheme**: Building to accommodate a science and study center. **Photography**: Richard Bryant-Arcaid.

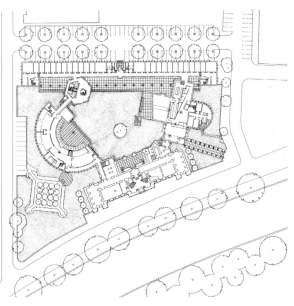

The arrangement of the different structures around the large central patio, and the colorful, bright finish, are the key features of this academic center in Berlin. The new facility incorporates a majestic façade which miraculously survived the war; that of the old School of Fine Arts. The variety of the elements, in their design, form, and shape, was one of the basic criteria for the project. Its location with respect to the original building meant that a highly involved technique had to be adopted using the composition of fragments method: each specific function is introduced in an individual architectural module, the location of which accords with the development of the project as a whole.

Heureka

Mikko Heikkinen and Markku Komonen

Location: Tikkurila, Vantaa, Helsinki, Finland. **Date of construction**: 1987–1988. **Client**: The Science Center Foundation. **Architects**: Mikko Heikkinen and Markku Komonen. **Associates**: Juva Oy, Matti Alho (project management), Kimmo Friman (associate architect), Paloheimo & Ollila Engineers, Matti Alho (basic engineering), Ernst Palmen, Finnish State, Municipality of Vantaa, and a number of private companies. **Scheme**: Central hall, exhibition hall, theater, auditorium, access bridge, cafeteria, offices, and services. **Photography**: Jussi Tiainen.

Designed for the demonstration of the scientific foundations of the universe, this center's appearance has the characteristics of an exhibition facility, a complex which is homogeneous in terms of structure, but compact in its expressive content. The Heureka center is located on a site bounded by the intersection of a railroad line and the course of the river Keravanjoki. The structure was designed as a series of pure geometrical shapes and planes: a cylindrical central hall, a curved hall, a spherical theater, and an auditorium in the shape of a fan, all leading from a basic prism element. The structure also comprises a bridge which marks the presence of the river. Its access area features a metal fascia and a system of highly stylized tensioning elements, while another characteristic space is provided before entering the building proper, the stone garden, which dominates the way in. This accommodates a geological map of Finland, the aim of which is to impress the visitor, right from the outset, with the message of the building. The exterior and the supplementary structures harmonize with these informational elements, in a mixture of content and form or style.

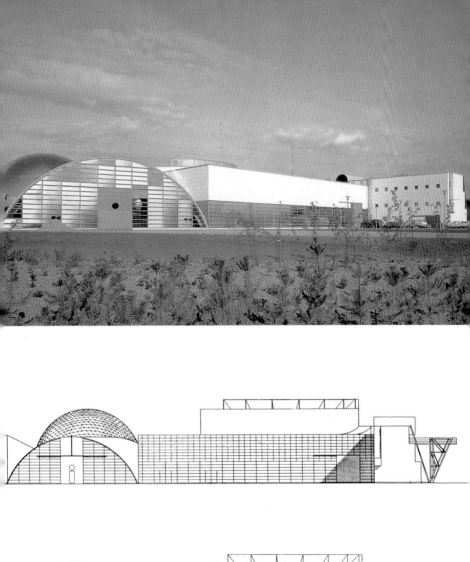

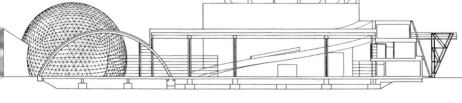

Pacific Design Center

Cesar Pelli & Associates

Location: Los Angeles, California, USA. **Date of completion**: 1998. **Client**: Municipality of Los Angeles. **Architect**: Cesar Pelli & Associates. **Scheme**: Exhibition center for furniture and design (furniture, carpets, drapes, decorative items, and accessories): exhibition halls; parking lot; terrace; patio and public plaza, with ampitheater and exhibition gallery (Murray Feldman Gallery). **Photography**: Marvin Rand.

The project is an extension of the original Pacific Design Center site, the Blue Whale, with six levels, to which in 1988 Cesar Pelli made an addition of 76,000 m2 (818,000 ft2), approximately double what was there originally. The reason for this expansion was the increased demand for exhibition space, which was what then prompted the construction of two additional buildings. To provide a sense of continuity for the new structures, some elements of the earlier buildings are included in the new ones: the base includes a plinth clad in the same blue tinted glass that is in the original structure's base. It was decided to implement the construction of the new modules in two phases: first, a steel structure, with panels of green glass in the base; and the second, a structure likewise of steel, but clad with panels of red glass. The green section is a structure of 40,000 m2 (430,000 ft2), with eight floors, crowned by a cupola or lightwell, again of glass, in the form of a hexagonal pyramid, following the form adopted by the floor plan of the container element. The Pacific Design Center has become a distinctive symbol of the area, thanks to the colors, which are such a striking contrast to the harmonized shades of the surrounding buildings.

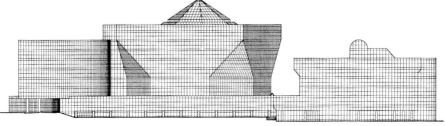

Hysolar Institute

Richard Rogers

Location: Stuttgart, Germany. **Date of completion**: 1987. **Client**: IPE, DFLUR. **Architects**: Behnisch and Partner. **Scheme**: Accommodation for offices, laboratories, storage facility, and ancillary areas. **Photography**: Behnisch and Partner.

There are two institutions housed in the Hysolar Institute: the Institute of Physical Electrotechnology, and the German Research Center for Aerospace Navigation. The first of these carries out basic research into semiconductor electrodes which make use of the energy provided by light; the second is engaged in exploring ways of optimizing the yield from this energy.

This commission was essentially straightforward: accommodation for offices, a certain amount of laboratory space, a storage facility, and ancillary areas. This offered sufficient margin for some stylistic experimentation but there was limited time for the design and construction, which prevented Behnisch from pursuing the project in its usual manner.

As a result, at first sight it seems surprising that this project comes from the studios of Behnisch and Partner. The materials, the coloring, the unrestricted layout, and what in the firm's other works would appear discordant, on closer observation becomes recognizable, however. It is precisely this quality which is one of the decisive characteristics of the Hysolar Institute in the city of Stuttgart.

Lucille Halsell Botanical Garden

Emilio Ambasz

Location: San Antonio, Texas, USA. **Date of completion**: 1987. **Architect**: Emilio Ambasz. **Scheme**: Botanical garden consisting of a complex of greenhouses.

The San Antonio Botanical Garden is a complex of different greenhouses on a large area of land with an irregular surface. Though, in other zones with cooler climates or fewer hours of sun, glass greenhouses are usually employed to make better use of the sun's rays, in this area of Texas, where the weather is very hot, this practice would be counterproductive.

The complex consists of a number of circular buildings, partially visible – all of them in whitish concrete to achieve a greater identification with the dry landscape – on which rest the spectacular glass structures, which remind one vaguely of old architectural forms: pyramids and truncated cones. A kind of sunken street, the main axis, joins the different parts of this greenhouse complex. One reaches it via a semicircular set of steps built into a wall that takes us into the bowels of the earth. From here, a narrow gallery leads to a more open space presided over by a solitary palm tree. Carrying on, one arrives at another, larger area flooded by a strange light from the roof, which projects pyramidal and hemispherical shapes. This filtered light has allowed a varied flora to grow. From here, some revolving doors lead to a porch and a patio, a central space where there are other buildings (square on the right and long and circular on the left).

This is without doubt a project in which intelligent action has been used to synthesize different growing environments.

Botanical garden in Graz

Volker Giencke

Location: Graz, Austria. **Dates of construction**: 1989–1990, 1993–1994. **Client**: University of Graz.
Architect: Volker Giencke. **Associates**: Ove Arup & Partners, Szyskowitz & Graber (engineering).
Photography: Ralph Richter/Architecturphoto, Peter Eder, Atelier Gienoke, Hans-Georg Tropper.

In each of the three cylinders a different climate has been created: subtropical, arid, and temperate. Under a flat and inclined roof, which rises out of the ground, there is the cultivation zone. Designed by computer, the main structure takes the shape of the cylinder sections using parabolic ribs, while the secondary one follows generatrix lines. The sections are made of an aluminum alloy for lightness, and are as small as possible, allowing 98% of natural light to enter the building.

The water heating system uses pipes with a parabolic structure that give a constant temperature throughout the inside. Cooling is done by a new propulsion system that mixes water and air to generate steam, instantly dropping the temperature to 5°C (41° F).

The exterior enclosure is formed by a double layer of transparent acrylic elements that cover the structure like a skin. The growing area is ventilated by units in the roof that open hydraulically.

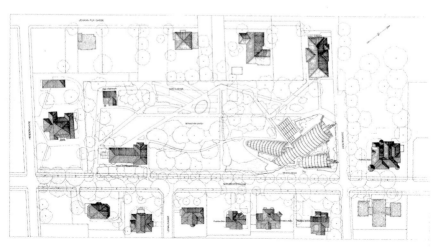

ESTEC

Aldo van Eyck, Hannie van Eyck

Location: Noordwijk, Netherlands. **Date of completion**: 1989. **Client**: ESTEC. **Architects**: Aldo van Eyck, Hannie van Eyck. **Scheme**: Building to house the European Center for Space Research and Technology: conference and audiovisual rooms, restaurant, conservatory, stores, offices, kitchen, and services. **Photography**: Alexander van Berge.

The plan for the new complex is dominated by a classical scheme that subdivides the building into a tripartite octagon. In essence the project has been described as an atrium inscribed in a large square.

The atrium was given a circular treatment, while the sides of the square are like arches. The building would need to be highly flexible, so the architects employed hendecagonal columns to form a sinuous and flowing arrangement, combining both curved and straight lines. This method is very successful in yielding simple and natural juxtapositions, matching polygons that can freely assume the curved line. Thanks to this system, the building could be divided up into various geometric shapes of great purity, but with fluid and undulating forms, in accordance with the topographical characteristics of the ground. The complex has been endowed with a range of color tones that runs the whole range of the spectrum, in order to define the different functional areas. In the same way, the slope of the roof allows the whole space to be reorganized, playing the game of volumes and vacuums, presences and absences, that contribute to the visual morphology of the complex.

ESTEC 753

Factories

Industrial activity has become an indicator of the extent of a country's development. The idea that people are a further factor in production has evolved thanks to a greater social conscience, so a new concept of "factory" has developed, according to which it has become quite a challenge to ensure that the worker feels like a human being within its walls. The architectural projects included in this chapter reveal a range of idiosyncratic industrial activities related to the products being made, which might be described as unusual.

In spite of their obvious diversity, there are several constants that all of these buildings must adhere to, in order to be able to achieve optimum functionality. These include: setting the plant up properly for the production process, elimination of superfluous elements that will increase costs, and installing the right equipment to ensure that the workers are operating under the most favorable conditions.

Ricola warehouse

Herzog & de Meuron

Location: Mulhouse, France. **Date of design**: 1992. **Date of completion**: 1993. **Clients**: H.P. Richterich, Ricola AG, Laufen/CH. **Architect**: Herzog & de Meuron. **Associates**: André Maeder (project leader), Dieter Kienast (landscape architect), Marc Weidmann (polycarbonate panels). **Scheme**: Storage and production facility. **Floor area**: 2760 m² (29,000 ft²). **Photography**: Margherita Spiluttini

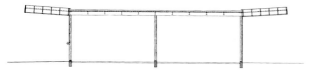

The new warehouse for the company Ricola-Europe S.A. is located to the south of the city of Mulhouse, in an industrial zone in the middle of the forests of Alsace. The plot, which was quite large, is almost flat, and the new warehouse was to be for both storage and production. Herzog and de Meuron proposed a rectangular building on one level, totally transparent inside.

The longer sides are dominated by two large canopies, which give protection from both sun and rain. These are two large sets of translucent polycarbonate panels on which plant outlines are screen printed. These reflect the landscaping outside and the luminous atmosphere inside.

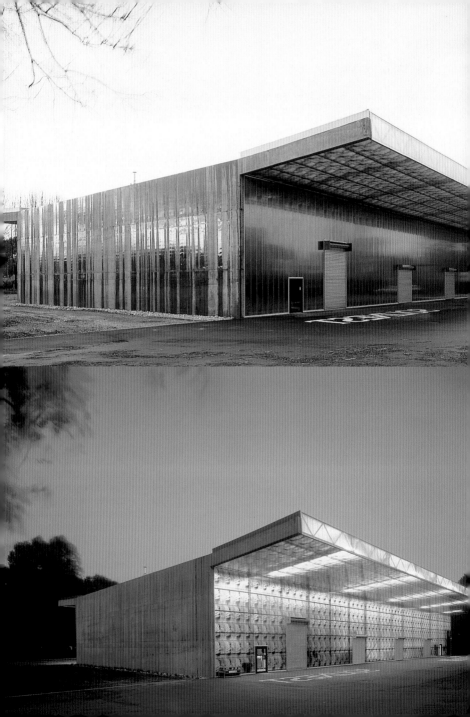

The Box

Eric Owen Moss

Location: Culver City, California, USA. **Date of construction**: 1994. **Client**: Frederick Norton Smith. **Architect**: Eric Owen Moss. **Associates**: Lucas Ríos. Scott Nakao, Scott Hunter, Eric Stultz, Todd Conversano, Sheng-yuan Hwang, Paul Groh, Thomas Ahn (design team), Joe Kurily (structure), John Snyder (electrics), Peter Brown-Samitaur (construction). **Scheme**: Reception and meeting room. **Photography**: Tom Bonner

The Box is not an item of new plant, but rather an annex to an old industrial building which is in tune with this type of space. The plan is rectangular and the structure is of wooden struts with a central pillar and a longitudinal lantern. The Box is a very small structure, about the size of a family house, not counting the surface area of the existing building. Its functions are minimal: it houses a reception on the ground floor and a meeting/conference room upstairs. Conceptually, it is a box (hence its name) but a box where things start to happen (and that is Moss's ingenious game).

In spite of their spectacular appearance, Eric Owen Moss's buildings are hard to understand without visiting them and, despite their extravagant look, they are made with very few materials and with a uniform finish. Their strength comes from their plasticity, from the flow of forms, and from the implicit movement. They are full of games, puzzles, and spatial riddles. Moss does not build spaces, he presents sensations and experiments with sequences of images that have to be re-elaborated in the mind of the observer. The forms of his architecture are improbable because they are geometrical wagers and great adventures.

Toto

Naoyuki Shirakawa Atelier

Location: Kitakyushu City, Japan. **Date of construction**: 1994. **Client**: Sun-Aqua Toto Ltd. **Architect**: Naoyuki Shirakewa Atelier. **Associates**: Sankyu Inc. (construction). **Photography**: Nobuaki Nakagawa.

By night one can see TOTOTOTOTO written on a black background. The letters consist of points of light floating in the air. By day, one can read the same on a blue plane. This sign is designed to be seen in motion, at the speed that the automobiles travel on the highway.

Shirakawa's architecture derives in general from clear geometrical principles and simple spaces. This is an architecture that employs geometry as a major source and tool of the project. Its apparent complexity derives from the play instituted throughout development, in terms of its own properties and the specific requirements of each case.

Shirakawa's buildings normally feature patios, which are a fragment of privatized nature, and which provide light. The TOTO project, however, is not a building of explicitly opened up interiors. Its structure is based on an axis which runs parallel to the axis of entry. The structure and function of the factory are dependent on this passage, which is open at both ends. The rest of the building consists of spaces attached to this.

Holz Altenried warehouse and showroom

Carlo Baumschlager, Dietmar Eberle

Location: Hergatz, Germany. **Date of construction**: 1995. **Client**: Altenried Bernd. **Architects**: Carlo Baumschlager, Dietmar Eberle. **Associates**: Michael Ohneberg (design), Oliver Baldauf (supervisor), Büro Plankel (structure). **Scheme**: Warehouse, showroom, and offices. **Photography**: Ed Hueber.

The project consisted of creating a storage area and a showroom, with a small space for offices and administration area.

It is divided between an unlit warehouse on the first floor, a light upper floor housing a well-illuminated area for samples, and a complex of offices and auxiliary services, located at the west end of the building. The façades that compose the greater part of the structure, as well as the roof, are slightly bowed outward, as if the building were swollen. The skin has been molded over wooden battens to the shape determined by the changing profile of a succession of wooden laminated and glued ribs that is, in fact, the structure of this box of curved walls. These ribs are prefabricated spruce arches; each has a different profile. The larch covering is homogeneous: there is no difference between the surface of the façades and that of the roof.

The project, through its geometry and its method of construction, suggests the work of artisans, as though it were a handmade object. It is quite clear that the objective of the construction of this building is an advertisement for the Holz-Altenried company and its work with wood.

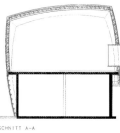

SCHNITT A—A

Technical Center for Books, Marne la Vallée

Dominique Perrault

Location: Bussy-Saint-Georges, France. **Date of design**: 1992. **Date of construction**: 1995. **Architect**: Dominique Perrault. **Associates**: Maxime Gasperini, Jérôme Besse (assistants), Daniel Allaire (engineer), Pieffet-Corbin (economist). **Scheme**: Book store, workshops, offices, meeting rooms, and services. **Photography**: Georges Fessy.

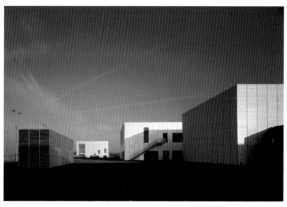

The basic functions of the technical center are, firstly, the storage in good condition of individual books or collections that are rarely consulted, with special emphasis on temperature and relative humidity. Secondly, in order to ensure efficient

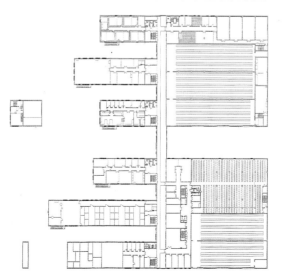

functioning and the ability to respond to the demands of users, it must be possible to transmit or transport documents flexibly, rapidly, and easily, within 24 hours of an order having been placed.
A technical image, homogeneous surfaces bearing simple, clearly conceptual symbols: this is an extremely organized, pure, and beautiful structure, thanks to the clear absence of anything superfluous. A silent building, certainly, despite the fact that it houses an infinite number of texts.

Grain treatment plant

Samyn and Partners

Location: Marche-en-Famenne, Belgium. **Date of construction**: 1995. **Architects**: Gh. André, J.L. Chapron, A. Charon, R. Delaunoit, Ch. Fontaine, D. Mélotte, S Peeters, Ph. Samyn, D. Singh, B. Vleurick; Bouny Construction sprl (construction), Menuiserie Fréson sc (structure and carpentry). **Scheme**: Workshop, store, offices, laboratories, and services. **Floor area**: 1400 m² (15,000 ft²). **Photography**: Ch. Bastin & J Evrard.

Located in the forest of Ardennes, this building consists basically of a grain treatment workshop, cold storage, and a number of offices and laboratories. The plot is an irregular space surrounded by splendid oaks; which prompted Philippe Samyn to design the building with a simple and striking shape. This is an oval glass dome formed by a structure of wooden arches. In fact, this is one of the simplest of structures in architecture, which relates this building to the Mongolian yurt and the Zulu hut. Philippe Samyn takes advantage of the research done into these types of structure by Mutschler and Otto in Mannheim (1975), Kikutake in Nara (1987), and the experimental buildings erected in Dorset, UK, in 1982 by Edmund Happold and the architects Ahrends, Burton & Koralec. Inside the dome two auxiliary buildings have been put up alongside the central workshop to house the cold rooms and offices.

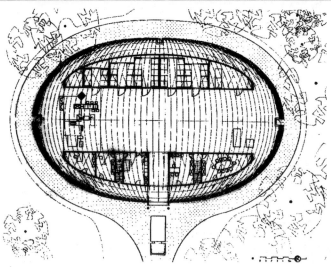

Grain treatment plant 769

Phosphate plant

Gustav Peichl

Location: Nordgraben, Berlin-Tegel, Germany. **Date of construction**: 1985–1987. **Architect**: Gustav Peichl. **Scheme**: Installation of a purifier, outdoor landscaping. **Photography**: Uwe Rau.

This purifier installation, made between 1985 and 1987, forms part of a residential area plan for the neighborhood of Nordgraben, in Berlin-Tegel (Germany), a traditionally industrial zone. The proposal was to construct a space that would constitute a major advance, in the form of a qualitative improvement in all senses (technological, aesthetic, environmental, and in urban planning).

One of the motifs repeated almost constantly in the design is the creation of as much open space as possible, with the proliferation of lawn-covered slopes complemented by trees, alongside adjacent avenues or inside the plant. The northern part of this complex must be open to the general public as an urban park, while the western sector remains as part of an area including the adjacent residential housing zone.

The individual functional units are shared radials in the center of the plant, tracing the form of a star that is formed by the mixing tower and the central block, the three waste removal tanks with their respective filtering systems. The three tanks are covered by a layer of earth, in such a way that a triangular green-colored embankment can be created by the slopes of the lawn. For the roof, metal sheets have been used incorporating channels to prevent the accumulation of water.

Herman Miller furniture factory

Frank O. Gehry

Location: Rocklin, California, USA. **Date of construction**: 1989. **Client**: Herman Miller Furniture Manufacture and Distribution. **Architecture**: Frank O Gehry. **Associates**: Stanley Tigerman. **Scheme**: Construction of the production and distribution units of a furniture factory. **Photography**: Hedrich-Blessing.

The building is located on an inhospitable plot on the edge of a lightly undulating piece of land. Natural vegetation is scarce and the climate is very dry. The plan adopted to counteract the sterility of the environment was the architectural creation of a species of plaza, crowded and warm, as if it were a small town of about 300 people. Frank O. Gehry also used planting as an important element conferring spatial order. The most dramatic feature of this ambitious project is the curious hemispherical dome in the oriental manner, designed by Stanley Tigerman, which is located on a small neoclassical-style building housing a conference and meeting room.

Vitra Conference Pavilion

Tadao Ando

Location: Weil am Rhein, Germany. **Date of construction**: 1993. **Client**: Vitra Gmbh. **Architect**: Tadao Ando. **Scheme**: Conference pavilion for design production company Vitra: lobby, conference room, personnel training rooms, offices, library, outside gardens with patio and services. **Photography**: Friedrich Busam/Architekturphoto.

The firm Vitra produces high-quality designs for furniture, whether in the classical style or by contemporary designers such as Bellini or Philippe Starck, among others. This conference pavilion is situated close to the company's factory in southern Germany and various activities take place there, from training of personnel to conferences on all kinds of matters. Tadao Ando decided, because of the extraordinarily flat site, not to give the building any height, so as not to disturb the tranquillity of the area. The building has been sunk into the ground: parts of it are buried underground and part of the plot is taken up with a patio. The building is made up of three elements: a rectangular block parallel to the walls that delimit the sunken patio, another rectangular block that penetrates into this patio at an angle of 60° and a cylindrical block that creates a space cutting the two rectangular ones. The pavilion building has two levels, conference rooms, a library, private offices, and a lobby. All these spaces open onto the sunken patio, which functions as a device to attract and retain those elements of nature, light and wind, between the spaces of the building. This patio reinforces the austere silence of the architecture around it.

Funder Werk 3 factory

Coop Himmelb(l)au

Location: St. Veit/Glan, Carinthia, Austria. **Date of construction**: 1988–1989. **Architect**: Coop Himmelb(l)au. **Associates**: Wolf D. Prix, Helmut Swiczinsky. **Scheme**: Woodworking factory: power plant, production workshop, and bridge connecting two workshops. **Photography**: Gerald Zugmann

The project was to build a woodworking factory which was to be emblematic of a new industrial architecture. The primary concept is that of dismembering the workshop, dividing it into a number of autonomous elements, like the different pieces of a Cubist still life. The building consists of two parts, the power plant and the production workshop, which is much larger. These two areas are connected by a covered bridge between them. In the production warehouse the roof has been constructed of steel and concrete, with three small gables and a large slab measuring 650 m² (7000 ft²). The walls consist of prefabricated sections of concrete and steel at the bottom, on which are placed brass fillets. The southeast façade is divided by an inverted corner, made of steel and glass, in which one can see a framework of beams and crosspieces placed on the diagonal.

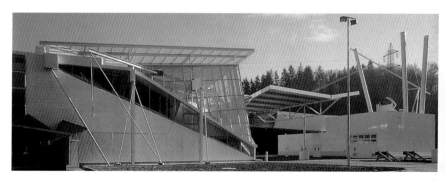

Financial Times

Nicholas Grimshaw & Partners

Location: London, UK. **Date of completion**: 1988. **Architect**: Nicholas Grimshaw & Partners. **Floor area**: 14,000 m² (150,000 ft²). **Photography**: Jo Reid.

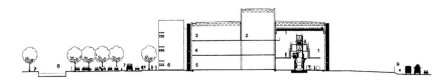

The main task was to design new premises for two printing presses. The structure is noted for its simplicity and symmetry. With a rectangular plan, it has two lateral sections of 18 m (59 ft), with a backbone or axis of 12 m (39 ft). These sections face north (where the presses are) and south (where the administration and auxiliary services are). One of the most outstanding aspects of the complex is the transparent glass roof of the printing press area, so the presses can be seen from outside.

This roof is an enormous window measuring 96 x 16 m (315 x 52 ft), and consisting of square panes screwed into each corner and sealed with silicone. Six columns positioned in the centers hold two semicircular steel sections of differing diameters, linked by flat plates. Each face of the column has steel projections for protection purposes. The façades of the long sides are also made of glass; in contrast, the dispatch end of the building and the stairwells in the entrance are solid.

The entrance façade, which is located on the south side, is guarded by separate, curved stairwells lined with aluminum.

West 8 MTR Terminal

Koen van Velsen

Location: Stonecutters Island, Kwai Chung, Hong Kong. **Date of completion**: November 1996. **Architect**: Koen van Velsen. **Client**: Modern Terminals Ltd. **Scheme**: Offices, ticket offices, and technical workshop.

This 15,000 m² (160,000 ft²) complex consists of a six-story building for administrative offices, entry and exit ticket offices, and a technical workshop which provides operational support for the fleet. The buildings are located on a piece of reclaimed land next to Stonecutters Island, with views towards the jetty to the south and the cargo terminal to the north. Within the context of the cargo terminal, with its heavy, aggressive landscape of cranes and steel containers, it was essential to create an architecture style that was not suppressed by its surroundings. It was also imperative that the buildings should be appropriate to the utilitarian nature of their functions and be constructed of materials that are simple and efficient. The administration building responds to this premise by having basic functional elements, such as the staircase and high towers, that appear like sculptured objects separated from the framework, which is covered with ceramic tiles like the office installations. This separation is emphasized by the use of brightly colored ceramic tiles in the elevator and on the elliptical staircase, later covered by a block of glass with a light inside to project the client's logo.

The ticket offices, used to check the state of the containers when they enter or leave the terminal, are long steel structures, 45 m (150 ft) across, to give maximum flexibility to the operations at ground level. The metal floor between the ticket offices and the workshop equipment also accentuates the architectural response to the context. The total cost of the project was approximately 150 million Hong Kong dollars.

Skyscrapers

Skyscrapers are undoubtedly a celebration of technological progress, a grand gesture to man's capacity to construct ever higher in his attempts to reach the heavens. But they are also a product of territoriality, of the property market, of speculation. The basic questions to be answered by today's architects are the same as those faced by those who designed the first skyscrapers in Chicago at the end of the 19th century. How to relate the skyscraper to an environment alien to its scale? How to get to and from the ground? How to build the structure? How to dress the skeleton? Those erecting skyscrapers now are at least aware of urban problems and try to confront them by responding to the environment in which their giant projects are situated.

Petronas Towers

Cesar Pelli & Associates

Location: Kuala Lumpur, Malaysia. **Date of construction**: 1997. **Client**: Kuala Lumpur City Center. **Architect**: Cesar Pelli & Associates. **Associates**: Adamson Associates (associate architect), KLCC Berhad Architectural Division (surveying), Thornton-Tomasetti Engineers, Ranhilt Bersekutu (structural engineers), Flack + Kurtz, KTA Tenaga (mechanical engineering), Lehrer McGovern (management), STUDIOS (interior), Balmori Associates (landscaping). **Photography**: J Apicella, P Follet/C.P. & A

The most important design decision in this project was to make the towers symmetrical: this characteristic carries all the figurative and symbolic charge. Between them lies the key element of this structure's composition: empty space, an essential concept in all Asiatic cultures.

Although each tower has its own vertical axis, the axis of the whole complex is between them, in the empty space. The force of the void is empowered by the pedestrian bridge that connects the two towers (of 88 stories) at levels 41 and 42, where there are public observation platforms looking over the sprawling city. The bridge, with its support structure, creates a door to the sky, a door 170 m (560 ft) high, a door to the infinite. The towers diminish six times in plan section as they get higher and, in the last setbacks, the façades lean slightly inwards, completing the form and reinforcing the vertical axis of the towers, which is emphasized by the needles on the summits of these towers. Every attempt has been made to reduce the effects of excess sunlight on the interior of Petronas Towers. For this reason the continuous strips of window are of reduced height and are protected by sunshades that, together with the multiple setbacks in the façade plane, create a constant set of shadows that together form a three-dimensional façade. The cladding material is stainless steel, which amplifies the multiple reflections of Malaysia's light conditions.

Osaka World Trade Center

Nikken Sekkei

Location: Osaka, Japan. **Date of completion**: 1995. **Architect**: Nikken Sekkei. **Scheme**: Building containing offices and spaces for public use: shops, restaurants, cafeterias, and auditorium. **Photography**: Kouji Okamoto.

The World Trade Center Osaka (WTCO) is the identifying landmark of the district of Nenko, on the artificial island of Sakishima. With its height of 256 m (840 ft) distributed over 55 stories and a total floor area of more than 150,000 m² (1.6 million ft²), the highest building in the west of Japan has quickly become a visual reference for the whole bay and the Kansai region. Its distinctiveness, impossible in the center of a city, is achieved not only through its sheer size, but also through the various public spaces inside, which make it accessible to the general public not necessarily visiting any of its office suites. A large atrium, 3000 m² (32,000 ft²) and 21 m (70 ft) high, known as the Fespa, forms a lively yet relaxing public area. It serves as access to both the tower's main nucleus of vertical communications, and to the different public facilities, such as shops, restaurants, cafeterias, and an auditorium for 380 people, in a global design thought of as a large indoor park. This large atrium not only serves the building but integrates the complex into its urban environment, both in function and in scale, serving as the main access route to Cosmo Square.

Suntec City

Tsao & McKown

Location: Singapore. **Date of completion**: 1997. **Architect**: Tsao & McKown. **Scheme**: Building containing offices, convention center, shops, cafeteria, restaurants, and various leisure areas. **Photography**: Richard Bryant/Arcaid.

The scale of recent development in Singapore is matched only by the speed at which it has been carried out. In this context the Suntec City operation is remarkable. The team of Tsao & McKown has made a real effort to create a civic space, where there is still room for the pedestrian in a high-rise environment. Located at the confluence of the city's main traffic arteries, there have been a number of modifications to the road system at the site in order to provide better communications with the historic part of the city. Between this and Suntec City, a public pathway is being constructed along a green strip of land running parallel to the water, with which it will later be joined. An operation of this magnitude, which at present is the largest private complex in the country, addresses itself to the urban context of the towers, but also pays special attention to pedestrians, bringing its vastness down to a more human scale.

Puerta de Europa Towers

Burgee & Johnson, Domínguez y Martín

Location: Madrid, Spain. **Date of completion**: 1996. **Architects**: Burgee & Johnson, Dominguez and Martin. **Scheme**: Office building, underground parking lot, first floor, mezzanine, 24 stories of offices, and heliport. **Photography**: Robert Royal.

Why are there two glass towers bowing to each other at the entrance to Madrid? What is the reason for constructing two buildings that seem to contradict traditional structures, which generally demand vertical transmission of loads? There are no immediate answers. These have to be sought in the origin of the project and the preconditions imposed on it, as well as in the wish of its developers to construct something original. This area of expansion to the north of Madrid has been the object of numerous remodeling projects lately. The two blocks had to be separated by a sufficiently wide strip of land to avoid three existing subway stations, the corresponding walkways below for pedestrians, and the rights of access to and from an unbuilt-up street. Later there was a need to build a road under the plaza to relieve traffic congestion. Starting with these requirements the New York architect John Burgee proposed the construction of two towers leaning at 15°, meeting at a common point on the axis of the Paseo de la Castellana.

This scheme filled the role that the municipal planners had assigned to the towers as part of an array of tall buildings aligned along the street. It also managed to emphasize the image of these two unusual structures, in addition to resolving the excessive separation between the two that lessened their impact on the city's skyline.

Umeda Sky Building

Hiroshi Hara

Location: Osaka, Japan. **Date of completion**: 1993. **Architect**: Hiroshi Hara. **Scheme**: Office building: two towers of 40 stories joined by a platform, and gardens. **Photography**: Tomio Ohashi.

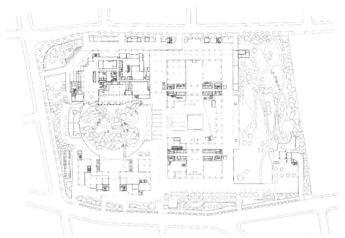

Located to the south of Tokyo, Osaka is one of the Japanese cities where Asian economic activity has been concentrated in an attempt to decentralize the country's business. Until a few years ago, the area where this project is located, Umeda City, was a vacant plot in the north of the city, very close to the Kanjo railroad track, which connects Osaka peripherally. As in any other project of this type, the developers needed a symbol capable of representing the newly created area: in the modern city this translates unfailingly into an imposing skyscraper. Skyscrapers have been erected as symbols not only of the modern city, but also of technological progress. According to the board of Japanese architects, it was not a case of building the highest skyscraper, but of conceiving a new type, in the form of two towers connected at their summits. For Hiroshi Hera this was a structure that could be the image of the city of the future.

Melbourne Central

Kisho Kurokawa

Location: Melbourne, Australia. **Date of completion**: 1991. **Architect**: Kisho Kurokawa. **Scheme**: Offices, commercial and leisure spaces, underground access to a subway station. **Photography**: Tomio Ohashi.

This complicated structure by the Japanese architect Kisho Kurokawa is located in the financial district of Melbourne. In its more than 260,000 m² (2.8 million ft²) there are offices, spaces for shops and leisure pursuits, together with underground access to a subway station. By the juxtaposition of various activities in a single building complex it is

hoped to revitalize a part of the city that had lost all its urban dynamism. The 2.6 hectare (6.4 acre) plot does not take up the whole area of the block where it is located, and coexistence with the adjacent buildings was a clear objective of the project. The lower part of the building, over which the glass tower juts out, in contact with the immediate urban environment, attempts by the composition of its space to testify to the complexity of the city. Under the huge glass cone a large central space opens out like a giant atrium, and this is the heart of the shopping center. A number of balconies on different levels look out over the space, and vertical movements are made architecturally to communicate between them. The building is presented, there is no doubt, as an attempt to combine all the convolutions of a city into a heterogeneous mix of uses, materials, and forms.

750 Seventh Avenue

Kevin Roche, John Dinkeloo and Associates

Location: 750 Seventh Avenue, New York, USA. **Date of completion**: 1991. **Architect**: Kevin Roche, John Dinkeloo and Associates. **Associates**: Weiskopf & Pickworth (structural engineering). **Scheme**: Skyscraper for company use. **Photography**: Paco Asensio

This surreal sight, on the edge of the theater district next to Times Square, is a steel tower with a short, thick antenna on top, which makes it appear like an enormous mobile telephone. It is customary in this area to present a progressively stepped envelope, and so Roche decided on a spiral shape in order to achieve a more dynamic design than the traditional set of boxes piled one on top of another. The final result has been harshly criticized by some of the most important architects of the AIA (American Institute of Architects). What does provoke a certain amount of admiration and surprise is the cladding based on satined glass. This is a kind of glass wickerwork with a horizontal line of ceramic and a vertical line of dark gray reflective glass. These two components give the building a really strange and dramatic texture.

Carnegie Hall Tower

Cesar Pelli & Associates

Location: W. 57th Street, New York, USA. **Date of completion**: 1999. **Client**: Rockrose Development Corporation. **Architect**: Cesar Pelli & Associates. **Associates**: R. Rosenwasser Associates (engineering). **Floor area**: 49,000 m² (527,000 ft²). **Photography**: Paco Asensio.

On W. 57th Street, between Sixth and Seventh Avenues, there is a curious quartet of buildings. Carnegie Hall Tower, light and golden, is practically stuck onto the edge of the brilliant, dark Metropolitan Tower, often referred to as the "Darth Vader Building," a symbol of the 1980s' shiny confidence.
The second highest building in New York, Carnegie Hall Tower is a commercial development that utilizes the space of the adjacent Carnegie Hall. Pelli has managed to relate his new building to the iconic concert hall. The tower, which has 60 floors, extends its illustrious neighbor's range of shades and shapes, reinterpreting the size, color, and ornamentation of the concert hall. Pelli compares his position as architect working inside the framework of the city to that of the assistant to a great painter like Raphael. The Tower comprises two interlinked soffits, of different sizes. It is raised 10 m (33 ft) above the level of the street in order to complement the five-story Russian Tea Room.

Shanghai World Financial Center

Kohn, Pedersen & Fox

Location: Pudong, Shanghai, China. **Date of construction**: 1997–2001. **Architect**: Kohn, Pederson & Fox. **Scheme**: Tower and base: hotel, observatory, commercial area, and underground parking lot. **Photography**: Edge Media NYC.

Located in the financial and commercial center of Lujiazui, the building is being erected as a distinctive landmark of the Pudong district. Within Shanghai's economic resurgence, Pudong is the most favored area of expansion, and the large majority of the skyscrapers planned for the 21st century are to be built there. The Shanghai World Financial Center was started in 1997 and is due to be completed in 2001. The plan for this 460 m (1510 ft) high, 95-story skyscraper, which will have 300,000 m² (3.2.million ft²) gross floor area, includes a hotel, a viewing zone, commercial premises, and underground parking, within the two elements of the project, the tower and the base. The tower will contain the hotel and, on the top floors, the viewing zone, while the remainder will be distributed in the base. Its aerodynamic shape, the enormous hole in the top, the sharp edges, a smooth skin that will reflect the changes of light throughout the day, are the tools being used to make this building the reference point for the urban landscape of Shanghai.

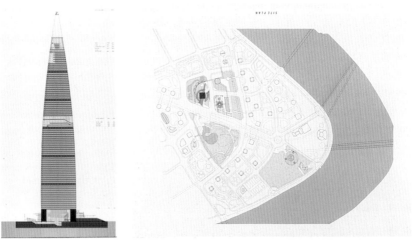

Shangai World Financial Center 803

Jin Mao Building

Adrian D. Smith (SOM)

Location: Shanghai, China. **Date of completion**: 1998. **Architect**: Adrian D. Smith (SOM). **Scheme**: Building containing offices, hotel, shopping center, cinema, convention center, landscaped exterior public space, and underground parking lot. **Photography**: Steinkamp/Ballog Chicago

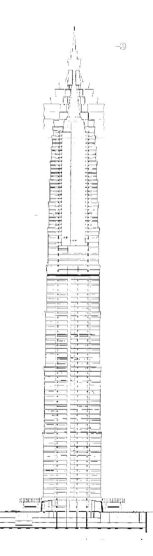

Recently completed, this 88-story building, with its stepped sections at the highest levels and, above all, the style of its pinnacle, is reminiscent of the shape of Chinese pagodas. Integration into the urban environment, which is one of the project's objectives, has been entrusted to an image already well absorbed into the country's collective consciousness. The first 50 stories of the tower are to be used for offices, while the rest will contain a luxury hotel with outstanding views of the city. An accompanying building is designed to house a shopping center, cinema, convention center, and services for the hotel. There are independent entrances to the skyscraper on each of the four sides of this building, which is surrounded by a landscaped public area which acts as an intermediate zone between this structure and the surrounding streets, reinforcing a symmetry that we also find in the layout of the elevator wells. Three underground levels for parking cars and bicycles complete the project's design.

Millennium Tower

Foster and Partners

Location: London, UK. **Date of completion**: At planning stage. **Architect**: Foster and Partners. **Scheme**: Tower for commercial and residential use. **Photography**: Richard Davies.

London's Millennium Tower, designed by Norman Foster, has been the object of debate for a long time. The feasibility and necessity for a building with these specifications in this particular area, plus financing problems, have caused protracted disputes between the architects and the local city planners, leading to constant delays in proceeding with construction: the tower has still not been built.

The building consists of a tower 385 m (1260 ft) in height, to which has been added a mast measuring another 60 m (197 ft) Within its 91 stories, the tower will house a communications zone at the top and, below this, 12 stories of apartments. The rest of the complex will consist of offices (60 stories), three restaurants, a viewing area, a shopping center in reception, and various levels for parking and storage. With its clearly futuristic design, the tower is intended to become an emblem of the new millennium in London.

Homes

Residential architecture is of fundamental significance inasmuch as it refers to the evolution of our way of life. This field has the privilege to examine at close quarters today's domestic dreams, to investigate new lifestyles, and to speculate on changes in the family, social, and even work environments. In fact, the house is the concrete manifestation of the interests, wishes, and whims of both purchaser and architect. This section includes a selection of homes built just before the year 2000. The choice has not been based on economic, aesthetic, or fashion criteria; we wanted to go beyond these dictates and include homes that mark a schism, that are today's innovations and tomorrow's classics. Nor are they intended to be prototypes, or examples to be followed. They are included because they are characteristic of their time, their location, and their owners. These projects have been grouped into different chapters, although all have features in common. First, respect for the environment, not specifically at an ecological level but in the way in which the buildings relate to the landscape. Second, respect between client and architect, so that the wishes of the former are an inspiration for the latter. Third, proper choice of materials used in the construction as, apart from determining tonality, light reflection, and surface textures, the materials complete the final image of the house, influencing this on many levels. Finally, the exclusivity that is implicit in this type of project, since they are usually born out of very personalized commissions. The tastes and resources of each owner vary, so each project is unique. Moreover, the architects have the opportunity to immerse themselves in their creative work, suggest fresh ideas, and try out new functional or structural concepts.

Multifamily urban homes

Although throughout the Modern Movement era the design of multifamily housing was the central question and exemplified the architectural situation of the moment, at the present day it would be questionable to view the status of multifamily homes in the same terms. The reason is not that architects have lost interest in such an important subject, but that it is difficult to offer concrete and realistic solutions to a problem that includes ever more parameters. City planning, regulation, and economic speculation are responsible for many of the horrors produced in this field. Those responsible for the examples included here have been able to avoid these pitfalls, however, by investigating this area in depth. These are not mere exercises in how to prettify façades, but projects that contribute to a social, urban planning, and architectural debate.

Homes in Haarlemmerbuurt

Claus en Kaan Architekten

Location: Binnenwieringerstraat 8, Amsterdam, Netherlands. **Date of completion**: April 1995. **Promoter**: Lievan de Key. **Architects**: Felix Claus, Kees Kaan. **Associates**: Floor Arons, Roland Rens, Michael van Pelt (design), Stracke (construction) **Scheme**: Apartments. **Photography**: Ger van der Vlugt

The Haarlemmerbuurt area is between the port of Amsterdam and the canals. This is a very lively area; its atmosphere is a mixture of the bourgeois environment of the canals and the landscape along the banks of the river Ij. The history of this part of Amsterdam is reflected in the façades of the houses: like a film set, the streets are a string of architectural styles from all periods, tied one to another at random.

In the case of Binnenwieringerstraat 8, the work was to an existing building: it was very small, only 3.5 m (11.5 ft) wide by 8 m (26 ft) deep. For that reason, the architects decided to use an adjacent space to locate all the services and installations needed so that the old structure could house comfortable apartments. Indeed, after the remodeling, the old house contains only three rooms. The project allowed the old building to be preserved, including its typical constructional details done by artisans (which would be impossible to reproduce today), without having to cause any damage when installing staircases, pipework and so on. Everything necessary to comply with current regulations and requirements is built into the annex. The old house, instead of becoming a museum to 19th-century living, has been turned into an open space measuring 7 x 3 m (23 x 10 ft), a well-appointed example of social housing.

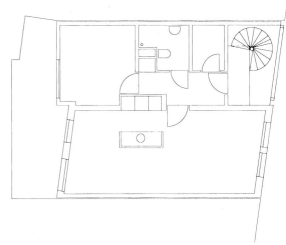

Gasometer B

Coop Himmelb(l)au

Location: Vienna, Austria. **Date of completion**: 2000. **Architect**: Coop Himmelb(l)au. **Collaborators**: Fritsch-Chiari (structures), Kress & Adams (lighting). **Gross floor area**: 376,344 sq. ft. **Photography**: Gerald Zugmann.

The four gasometers comprise an old gas storage facility that once supplied Vienna. After being closed down, the facility was demolished, with only the striking brick façades left standing. The particular location of these buildings in an industrial area, along with the unusual character of the resulting spaces, led to their being used for years as cultural centers for numerous activities.

The location of the project presented a magnificent opportunity to develop the urban fabric on the outskirts of Vienna, given that the renovation went hand in hand with improvements in the transport system, including the extension of a metro line and the construction of a new motorway. Apart from Coop Himmelb(l)au, three other architecture studios participated in the project, de-signing new housing concepts, a shopping center, and a leisure complex, converting the site into a new focal point for the city.

The project developed by Coop Himmelb(l)au for Gasometer B entailed the addition of three new volumes: a large cylinder inside the gasometer, a striking shield-shaped flat block just beside the latter, and a multifunctional space for holding different sorts of events at the base. Flats and offices were lo-cated inside the cylinder and in the new building. A conical courtyard was designed to provide natural light for the indoor spaces of the cylinder, while north-facing balconies serve the same function for the flats in the new building. The 360 residences range in type from spacious homes with terraces to small studios for students. The combination of office and residential uses is intended to generate new ways of living and working in a single environment.

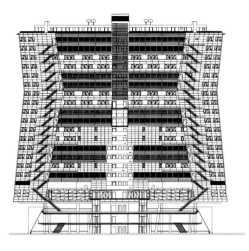

0 2 4

Apartment building in La Croix Rousse

Jourda & Perraudin Architectes

Location: Rue Grataloup, Lyon, France. **Date of design**: 1990. **Date of construction**: 1995. **Client**: OPAC, Lyon. **Architects**: Jourda & Perraudin Architectes. **Associates**: Gavin Arnold, EZCA, Claude Brenier, Catherine Vardanégo. **Photography**: Georges Fessy.

This apartment block is located in the La Croix Rousse district in Lyon. This is a neighborhood which has long been inhabited by craftsmen, so most of the houses here have craft workshops, with a large amount of work space, and are served by a few local businesses providing essential services. This new structure aims to have some continuity with the existing building types.

The key decision consisted of concentrating all the available space into the apartments themselves, by making the stairs a completely separate element, attached to the rear of the property. This structure consists of the stairs to the different floors, but it is much more substantial than would be required just for that function. This feature is used for going up and down, getting to the elevators, or moving between apartments, so it is a real communal space for the whole block.

The six floors of the building contain two small single apartments on the first and second floors, and two duplex apartments on the four upper floors. The mansards house small studio/workshops.

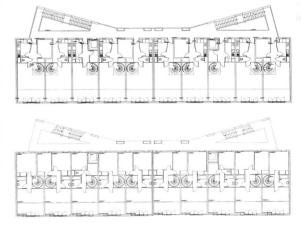

Apartment building in Oporto

Eduardo Souto de Moura

Location: Rua do Teatro, Oporto, Portugal. **Date of design**: 1992. **Date of construction**: 1995. **Architect**: Eduardo Souto de Moura. **Client**: Eng. Miguel Cerquinho. **Associates**: Graça Correia, Pedro Mendes, Silvia Alves, Francisco Cunha, Manuela Lara; Soares da Costa/San José (construction). **Photography**: Luis Ferreira Alves.

The Rua do Teatro is in an area of Oporto outside the medieval walls. This new apartment building is located on a plot that is much wider than the others around it. Given that the neighboring houses are quite small, Souto de Moura designed this project to effect continuity with them. The two neighboring houses are on a different alignment: the one on the left is taller and not set back very far; and that on the right is smaller and set back much further. Consequently Souto de Moura's design strictly respects the different alignments of the neighboring houses: his own building compromises between the two.

Kop van Zuid residential complex

Frits van Dongen

Location: Landtong, Rotterdam, Netherlands. **Date of construction**: 1998. **Architect**: Frits van Dongen. **Associates**: A.J. Mout, R. Puljiz, A.J. de Haas, M. Heesterbeek, F. Veerman, J. van Hettema, J. Molenaar. **Scheme**: 625 homes in a cooperative, sports club, six tennis courts, children's play area, 1000 m² (10,100 ft²) of commercial premises, 200-place parking lot. **Photography**: Daria Scagliola and Stijn Brakkee.

This complex, which alone contains 623 homes, is located on an ex-docklands plot with three sides facing the river: the two longer ones on both flanks, and the third at the end. Located on the lengthened wharves, the complex consists of a system of linear blocks that form three semi-enclosed courtyards. The blocks running across, with high density housing, are higher, while the land parallel to the wharves is closed in by smaller blocks, separated by the ends of the others; these are single family homes set out in rows. There are five large, equidistant blocks, although they are all different from each other. In addition to the three courtyards, there is a large open space in the middle of the complex, on top of the parking block: this is to be developed as a public garden area.

The initial design more or less guarantees that the complex will avoid seeming too regular. In each stepped block, the access corridors, located on its spine, are joined two by two, forming a double space, so that the entrance to the higher apartments is via a raised passageway. In addition to this, halfway along the block there is a large glazed courtyard that allows maximum light to enter the common areas of this interior spine, where there are restrooms, kitchens, and, in many cases, cupboards and storerooms. The single family homes, which face the wharves on the side, are of particular interest: here regularity is firmly restored in the minute details of each dwelling unit.

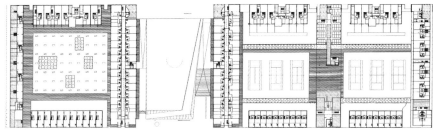

Apartments in Tilburg

Wiel Arets S.L.

Location: Timmermanspad Street and the corner with Kuiper Street, Tilburg, The Netherlands. **Date of construction**: 1993–1995. **Architect**: Viel Arets S.L. **Client**.: Stichting Verenigde Woningcorporaties SVW. **Associates**: Michel Melenhorts (coordinator), Tina Brandt, Reina Bos, Andrea Wallrath; DVHV Amersfoort (budget). **Scheme**: 67 three-room apartments divided into three blocks of 37, 14, and 16 units. **Photography**: Kim Zwarts.

An old industrial zone in the center of Tilburg is being transformed. It has been decided, for example, to house the De Pond Museum, which has an important collection of contemporary art, in one of the old factories in the once run-down area. The apartments that Arets designed are distributed between three blocks on Timmermanspad Street, where the museum is to be. Two blocks are located in a U shape at one end of the museum, making room for an interior garden alongside one of the façades; the third, a long block, with views over the De Pond Museum garden, is just inside the plot, opposite its main entrance. Each apartment has 77 m² (830 ft²) of floor area;

access to each is via a common corridor, some 3 m (10 ft) wide. The external treatment of the blocks' façades differs according to whether the block is a main one, facing the street, or a rear one, protecting the corridor from which there is access to each unit. The first type is of rough stucco, called "putz," with interior balconies from which one can watch movement in the street. The second type, which looks over the garden areas, is made of open brickwork containing relatively large windows, which light the access corridor of the building.

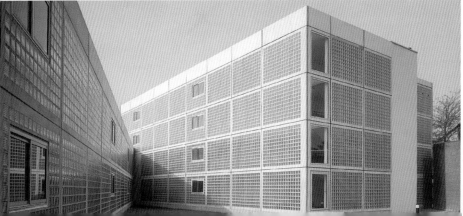

Résidence Les Chartrons

François Marzelle, Isabelle Manescau, Edouard Steeg

Location: Rue Poyenne, Bordeaux, France. **Date of design**: 1991. **Date of construction**: 1994. **Client**: Sonacotra. **Architect**: François Marzelle, Isabelle Manescau, Edouard Steeg. **Associate**: Edouard Steeg. **Scheme**: 102-room residential complex. **Photography**: Vicent Monthiers Schlomoff.

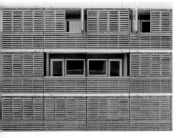

Résidence Les Chartrons, in the center of Bordeaux, is an experimental attempt to find quantitative, functional, and aesthetic parameters that will ensure an acceptable quality of life in this type of residential complex. A starting point is the fact that all the rooms have their own bathroom, consisting of a basic module repeated and varied throughout the complex. This module, repeated five times, forms part of a larger unit comprising five bedrooms, which share a common living room and kitchen. The layout of this unit is very simple: organized as a duplex, there are two bedrooms and the communal areas on the lower floor, while the three remaining bedrooms are upstairs. Although an interior staircase joins the two floors, making the unit rather like a conventional house, there are independent entrances to the five bedrooms, making the system of staircases for the whole complex relatively complicated and significant in style.

The layout consists of two blocks of four floors in parallel, with a fairly small interior courtyard. The use made of the courtyard, which contains some communal services, is determined by the fact that all the staircases and passages leading to the various rooms leave from this point.

113, rue Oberkampf

Frederic Borel

Location: 113, rue Oberkampf, Paris, France. **Date of completion**: November 1993. **Clients**: Ministry of Telecommunications and Post. **Architect**: Frédéric Borel. **Associates**: Joel Gallouedec, Carola Brammen, Massimo Mattiussi; SCGPM (contractor); G.I.I. (engineering). **Scheme**: 80 apartments, building for a post office, and a small shopping center. **Floor Area**: 7000 m² (75,000 sq. ft). **Photography**: F. Borel.

The site for this project is a narrow urban plot, measuring 20 m (66 ft) on the street and 87 m (285 ft) long. One added difficulty on the plot was the presence of shared walls, to a height of 23 m (75 ft). Contained within natural limits, similar to the walls of a fortification, the project became a microterritory, an urban microcosm. The particular requirements of the scheme, a post office, small shopping center, and a building of small apartments (studios and floors with two rooms) for young people, became the active parameters of the overall project.

The post office, the stores, and the entrance to the apartments are organized around transparent elements through which one can see a small fraction of the infinite: "presence and absence of distance." A small bit of landscaping, in the form of a garden visible from the street, is laid out in the central area. The apartments are spaced around the periphery and have views of the garden: the fragment of ground that breathes, the last façade, looking to the sky.

The final block, deep into the plot, has three levels of apartments, each with a terrace, facing south. The floor layout, designed to attract young couples, suggests somewhere that can be adapted for a family: the service room situated in the middle of the domestic space can become a nursery, a bedroom for the parents, a library/studio or even the living room.

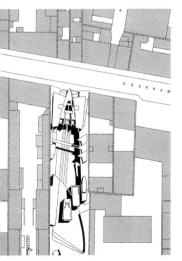

Apartments in the historic center of Maastricht

Mecanoo

Location: Herdenkingsplein "Memorial Plaza", Maastricht, The Netherlands. **Date of design**: 1990–1992. **Date of construction**: 1994. **Client**: Municipality of Maastricht (plaza), Stichting Pensioenfonds Rabobank (apartments). **Architect**: Mecanoo. **Associates**: Technical consultants ABT, Delft. **Scheme**: 52 apartments. **Photography**: Christian Richter.

The apartments are located behind a screen of varnished cedar that hides the living rooms. The balconies and galleries, by which one reaches each of the apartments from the stairwell, are in line with the outer portico, which is paved in marble. This connects the two blocks containing the apartments, creating the illusion of a single façade when in reality they are independent buildings. The interior distribution of the block that faces the plaza is reminiscent of traditional Dutch houses, with each apartment occupying the whole of the corridor. The block that is set further back is occupied by a duplex, also stretching from façade to façade, and apartments in the corner, facing the plaza. The side wall is painted white, to differentiate it from the living room window side.

In the indoor courtyards there are gardens for the ground floor apartments and some small storage cubicles made of a special local stone, rescued from a nearby demolition site. The same stone is used to line the stairwells and in the reconstruction of the wall around the plot.

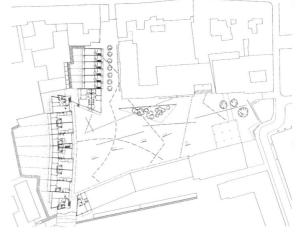

Grand Union Walk

Nicholas Grimshaw & Partners Ltd

Location: Grand Union Walk, Camden, London, UK. **Date of completion**: 1986--1989. **Client**: J. Sainsbury plc. **Architect**: Nicholas Grimshaw & Partners Ltd. **Associates**: Neven Sidor, Mark Fisher, Hin Tan, Ingrid Bille, Sally Draper, James Finestone, Thomas Fink, Rowena Fuller, Andrew Hall, Christine Humphrey, Gunther Schnell, Ulrike Seifritz, Simon Templeton. **Scheme**: Commercial and residential complex: major store, workshops, and attached apartments. **Photography**: John Peck.

The principal objective of this commercial and residential complex was to try to reconcile the potential of high-tech architecture with the needs of municipal planners. It was decided to construct a complex comprising a major store, a series of workshops, and a group of attached apartments on a triangular plot. The shape of the land made viable a functional separation into modules, due to the different directions of the sides of the plot, one of which faces the Grand Union Canal. The commercial and workshop schemes were allocated two modules, while the northerly side, on the canal, was reserved for the nucleus of the apartments, thus offering an interactive combination of architecture and nature. The important role given to the physical presence of the water in its relation to the building means that consideration also had to be given to the security of future inhabitants and the environmental protection of the canal. Use of the unusual bowed structures reduces the problems of an oblique frontage, reinforces the private nature of each of the balconies, and gives a better view over the water. The architects based their plans on some essential points: the almost industrial process for installing the structures; the alternation of surfaces straight and curved, transparent and opaque; and, lastly, an effective ratio of external and internal space.

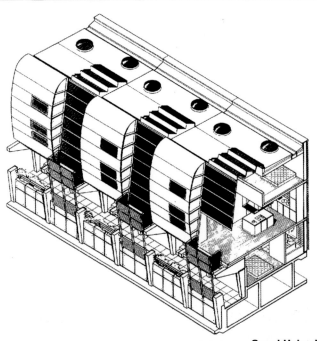

Multifamily suburban homes

The demographic and migratory explosion has called for the urgent construction of residential complexes in the suburbs. These blocks, only planned in economic terms, have temporarily solved the problem of housing provision for a considerable increase in the urban population. These box-like buildings have involved no advances either socially or structurally. Currently the suburbs, where the city gradually turns to country, are colonized by multifamily residential architecture more attentive to durability and comfort. There are, however, projects that seek a balance between functionality and aesthetics: on the one hand, investigating the nature of residential architecture, assimilating new concepts of the family; and, on the other, adapting to an ambiguous environment which is being defined at the rate that buildings are erected on the land, establishing its character and appearance.

Homes in Fukuoka

Steven Holl

Location: Fukuoka, Japan. **Date of construction**: 1989–1991. **Architect**: Steven Holl. **Project supervisor**: Hideaki Arizumi. **Associates**: Peter Lynch, Thomas Jenkinson, Pier Copat; Shimizu Corporation (structural engineering); Schwartz-Smith-Meyer/Martha Schwartz (landscaping). **Photography**: Richard Barnes.

surface and the pavement of the porticoes. These are the fundamental elements of a system of public spaces and walks that articulates the whole block.

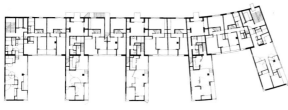

This is a complex of 28 apartments located in a suburban area of Fukuoka, comprising what is basically a single block, although there are two concepts involved: "articulated space" and "empty space," a container of silence.

The block encloses four large south-facing courtyards, that on the lowest level featuring a pond. These are designed as spaces for meditation, away from the everyday life of the home. These four spaces, which are higher than street level, are articulated with the rest of the complex by being connected to a number of porticoed areas which face inwards towards the block: these double-height spaces are linked to the stores, the café terraces, and the children's play area. The silent spaces facing south and the activity-packed porticoes facing north are separated by only one story. In addition, a single flight of stairs connects one type of space to the other, bridging the difference between the pond's flat

Homes in Makuhari

Steven Holl

Location: Makuhari New Town, Chiba, Japan. **Date of construction**: 1996. **Client**: Mitsui Fudosan Group. **Architect**: Steven Holl. **Project supervisor**: Tomoaki Tanaka. **Gross floor area**: 8415 m² (90,500 ft²). **Scheme**: 190 apartments and small stores. **Photography**: Paul Warchol.

The objective of the project was to design a complete block of the city of Makuhari, on the Bay of Tokyo. The main operations involved:
1– Opening the original ring of buildings at the four corners, by what Holl calls "gates," each one related to a cardinal point: north, south, east, and west gates.
2– Turning and changing the spaces in the blocks as appropriate to favor the best sunlight.
3– Locating a central block to divide the original courtyard into two parts, thus generating two smaller courtyards, called the north courtyard and the south courtyard. These basic areas form what Holl defines as weighty and silent space that witnesses the ordinary and most prosaic events of life.

Some unusual work is included in the scheme, for the most part in the form of single family homes, of which there are six, one for each of the gates and the two courtyards.
The houses that correspond to the four gates are usually suspended or half-suspended over the large gaps between the blocks which form the gates themselves, while those related to the courtyards, which incorporate ponds, tend to be built in a seemingly unstable situation, tipped towards the surface of the water.

M-30

Francisco Javier Sáenz de Oíza

Location: Polígono 38, La Paz, Madrid, Spain. **Date of completion**: 1991. **Client**: Land, Environment, and Housing Council, Community of Madrid. **Architect**: Francisco Javier Sáenz de Oíza. **Scheme**: Construction of 400 homes over 8 floors. **Photography**: Francesc Tur.

A review of the architectural scene over the last few decades shows that the restructuring by planners of suburban areas tends to involve the construction of social housing, a structured element in the often sprawling periphery.

The building was planned as one continuous block, in a spiral shape, that runs along the contour as far as the road junction, where it turns back inside, to form an open ring. Sáenz de Oíza decided to adjust the route of this side road, so that, on the northeastern slope of the land, the building is facing inwards, to give better definition to the complex's access zone and the underground parking lots serving the building.

The sinuosity of the structure is another of the keys to the project, since from it are derived two architectural realities: the building itself and the space it encloses, the lung to help it breathe and the communal facilities on view. The selection of solid brick 15 cm (6 in) thick as the principal building material contributes to the homes' insulation from the annoyance of traffic noise.

Nemausus I

Jean Nouvel and Jean-Marc Ibos

Location: Nîmes, France. **Date of completion**: 1987. **Architect**: Jean Nouvel and Jean-Marc Ibos. **Scheme**: 114 homes, 146 parking places, garden area. **Photography**: Pierre Berenger.

The architects have tried to distance themselves from the typical compact, solid image of social housing, and have opted for an apartment complex where the accent is on those features underlining the sensation of mobility and dynamism. The design of these homes has been inspired directly by cultural and aesthetic references to the "loft." The need to keep to a budget, as well as maintain the industrial nature of the area, have meant basing the project on the use of industrial materials and raw materials, achieving a curious combination that re-creates in a personal space the kind of decoration more often found in a manufacturing space. With this experimental project a number of objectives have been achieved: creating homes that are larger than usual; gaining the extra space within the budget for smaller homes; and, finally, using part of the terrace area to extend the living area, thereby taking advantage of the site's superb climatic conditions to the full.

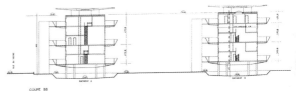

COUPE BB

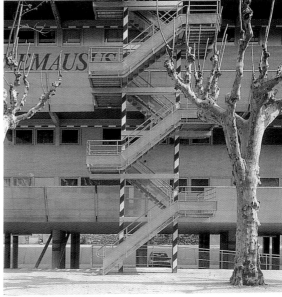

Wozocos

MVRDV

Location: Woonzorgcomplex Joh. De Deo, Reimerswaalstraat, Amsterdam-Osdorp, The Netherlands. **Date of construction**: 1994–1997. **Client**: Woningbouwvereniging Het Oosten, Amsterdam. **Architect**: MVRDV. **Associates**: Willem Timmar, Arjan Mulder, Frans de Witte; Bureau Bouwkunde; Pieters Bouw Techniek, Haarlem (structural engineering). **Scheme**: 100 homes for elderly people in the west of Amsterdam. **Photography**: Hans Werlemann.

MVRDV was contracted to design a block of 100 apartments for elderly people in an area to the west of the center of Amsterdam. After analyzing the town planning regulations drawn up by Van Eesteren for this area, they reached the conclusion that only 87 of the 100 homes planned could be built without blocking the sunlight to the neighboring buildings. Where could the other 13 be located? They decided to hang them from the northern façade, literally suspending them in the air. In the building there is a corridor along the north façade that is reached by the only stair and elevator well, and in which are situated the entrances to each of the homes, including those that

overhang; and a south façade, onto which the apartments give directly. The homes consist of three smaller rooms opening from a peripheral room that contains the kitchen and a sitting room/dining room/bedroom with a balcony. The size of the balconies varies, as does the color of their covering material, and, like the windows, their placement seems to be independent of the internal layout, some of them coinciding with the dividing wall between each of the homes.

Wozocos 851

La Venerie residential complex

Dubosc & Landowski

Location: Montargis, Loiret, France. **Date of construction**: 1994. **Client**: OPAC du Loiret. **Architect**: Dubosc & Landowski. **Associates**: Andrea Mueller, Monica Alexandrescu. **Scheme**: 48 homes. **Photography**: J.M. Monthiers.

In this complex of homes two symmetrical blocks face each other to create a more controlled inner space, protected and integrated into the urban framework of Montargis. In this case maximum use is made of the useful surface that this construction can offer. This is achieved by placing the staircases outside the building, thus reducing the communal areas, which are usually dead space. The homes are placed transversally to the blocks, which allows them to have a double orientation. On the ground floor, where the layout is vertical, there are duplex homes for four or five people with their own access and garden. The second level is formed by units for one or two people; these are laid out longitudinally and are reached via a staircase and corridor outside. The top two levels are occupied by homes for two or three people and have recently been reorganized as duplex apartments.

The materials used are of industrial origin, which allows greater ease of installation and a minimum of maintenance in subsequent years.

The La Venerie residential complex has a new architectural plan which tries to make the social dimension of collective housing compatible with the autonomy of individual living in the 20th century in France.

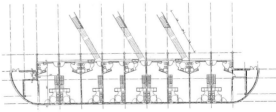

Social housing in Alcobendas

Manuel de las Casas

Location: Alcobendas, Madrid, Spain. **Date of design**: 1993. **Date of construction**: 1996. **Client**: Ivima. **Architect**: Manuel de las Casas. **Associates**: José Luis Cano, Indagsa (structural engineering), Ortiz & Cia (construction, fittings), Felicidad Rodríguez (model), Iciar de las Casas (gardens and landscaping). **Scheme**: 198 social housing units and garages: 183 three-bedroom homes (70 m², 750 ft²), 15 two-bedroom homes (60 m², 650 ft²), 84 parking spaces. **Photography**: Ángel Luis Baltanás, Eduardo Sanchez.

The complex consists of a series of blocks perpendicular to the road, and others parallel to the edge of the plot, which visually shut in the complex. The layout of the blocks is determined by the curve of the street, creating a façade and closing off the noise and sight of the traffic. The complex is treated as one single residential unit, in other words, the plot is enclosed in such a way that the spaces between the blocks are for private pedestrian use. The blocks are five floors high and are of high density – four apartments per floor. Inside, the homes are planned as linear units with the service rooms and storage spaces grouped around a central nucleus, the majority of them having two façades for better ventilation.

The structure and the outer enclosure are dealt with by means of a system based on large, 12 cm (4.5 in) thick panels of reinforced concrete, which act as load bearing walls. These panels are used both for the façades and for the inside walls, which gives great strength to the building.

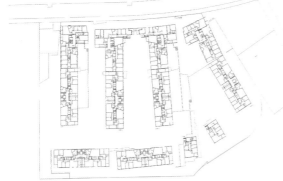

Residential block in Graz

Riegler & Riewe

Location: Bahnhofstrasse, Graz, Austria. **Date of design**: 1991. **Date of construction**: 1994. **Architect**: Riegler & Riewe. **Associates**: Margarethe Müller, Brigitte Theissl. **Scheme**: 27 homes. **Photography**: Margherita Spiluttini, Paul Ott.

There are two different types of home in this block: some of 50 m² (540 ft²) with two and a half rooms, and others of 78 m² (840 ft²) with four and a half.

The whole building, which is three floors high and 75 m (250 ft) long, is designed, so that, with its outer skin, it looks less bulky. A number of sliding doors run the whole length of the façades. The façade which gives access to the homes is broken by the stairwells. Sections of metal grating have been used to cover this façade, fixed on the stairs and movable on the apartments; on the side that gives onto the garden, however, nylon has been used. The continuous movement of these panels, which provide both privacy and protection from the sun, gives an ever-changing appearance to the home. The façade closest to the street looks out onto the pavement of the access approach to the entrances, up stepped ramps. On the other side, a garden provides more direct contact with the exterior, on the side of the building where each home has a longer façade and where there are two rooms.

Apartments in Graz

Ernst Giselbrecht

Location: Graz, Austria. **Date of construction**: 1998. **Architect**: Ernst Giselbrecht. **Photography**: Paul Ott.

The building is aligned north to south and has four floors, with duplex homes grouped two and two. Those upstairs have balconies and views of the surroundings, while those on the ground floor have direct access to the garden. The entrances, stairs, and balconies are not placed symmetrically and, while forming part of the building, appear like independent elements that vary in form according to their use or function. The dividing walls of the apartments stretch across the whole width of the building and constitute the dominant rhythm of the interior structure. Each pair of homes is joined by a linking gallery.

This layout of walls and apertures allows the apartments to be subdivided freely, thus providing a structural system governed by the spirit of classic modernism.

Thanks to the generous amount of glass, the whole building can be seen from the entrance.

The staircase looks like one continuous element that runs up through the building as far as the roof. The transparency of the tops of the internal divisions allows the different rooms to be imagined as independent bodies in a common space. The place is perceived to be larger, there is an overall view of the apartment, and the walls are dissolved in the home's large, multifunctional interior space.

Hotels and residences

The projects included in this section differ from the other residential categories in just one speciific respect: they are temporary residences. The buildings that house them must provide hospitable spaces that can tolerate considerable turnover of users. So, apart from addressing the particular functional requirements of each project, the design will need to make flexible use of space to meet the needs of many different clients.This chapter includes, among others, hotels in different parts of the world, student residences, and guest houses for visitors. Although they vary regarding location and use, all the examples have something in common: they succeed in creating pleasant surroundings in robust buildings, despite the wear and tear they might undergo.

Visitors' center in Yusuhara

Kengo Kuma

Location: Takaoka, Kochi Prefecture, Japan. **Date of completion**: March 1994. **Architects**: Kengo Kuma & Associates, Todahiro Odani & Associates, Plaza Design Consultant. **Associates**: K. Nakata & Assoc. (structural engineers). **Scheme**: Restaurant and hotel (eight Western-style and eight Oriental-style bedrooms). **Photography**: Fujitsuka Mitsumasa

Yusuhara-cho is at the source of the Shimanto, a river whose waters are maybe the clearest in Japan. The place is extraordinarily beautiful: the river, the valley, the cedar-covered slopes, the terraced banks where rice is grown... all this makes the park a special place which is sought out by many visitors.

Kengo Kuma is aware that the place is the reason for building the center.

In fact, this building is for housing visitors and, theréfore, its occupants are there precisely to appreciate the beauty of the environment. For that reason, the architecture must be in keeping with the landscape and must open a dialogue with the natural world.

The building has two floors and a markedly linear shape running north to south. The gross floor area is approximately 1300 m^2 (14,000 ft^2). It is clearly divided into three modules with different functions: in the first are the restaurant, kitchen and services; in the second, the bedrooms (Oriental-style downstairs and Western-style upstairs); and, finally, there is a building for machinery and equipment.

The restaurant module is the most interesting and complex. It is based on an opposition between two planes: that of the roof and that of an artificial pool. These two planes define an interior space with no precise limits, which varies continuously with the light.

Hotel Kempinski

Helmut Jahn

Location: Munich, Germany. **Date of construction**: 1996. **Architect**: Helmut Jahn. **Associates**: Peter Walker (landscaping). **Floor Area**: 38,300 m² (412,000 ft²). **Photography**: Helmut Jahn.

The Hotel Kempinski is the first building of the neutral zone at Munich airport, dedicated to commercial and business activities, and promoted as a city within the airport itself. In this spirit, it is modular in style, forming part of a series of buildings being planned.

The organization of the hotel corresponds to the airport's system of different levels. The rooms, a total of 400, surround a central covered garden.

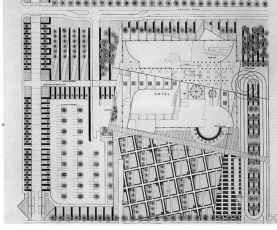

Hotel Martinspark

Dietmar Eberle & Karl Baumschlager

Location: Dornbirn Vorarlberg, Austria. **Date of completion**: 1995. **Architects**: Dietmar Eberle & Karl Baumschlager. **Scheme**: Design and construction of a hotel, and its restaurant as an annex. **Photography**: Eduard Hueber

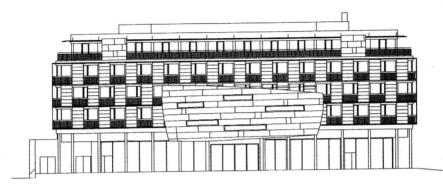

The rooms of this small, rectangular shaped hotel are distributed around a central patio. The appearance of the hotel is characterized by the façade, based on sliding blinds made of blue panels. The blue panels slide over glass windows, on all of the floors, creating a moving mosaic.

On the western façade of this sober building, there is a large structure of oxidized copper: this is the restaurant. It is supported on very fine metal pillars and its windows are long narrow slits opened at different heights, which coincide with the longitudinal lines of the joints of the copper sheet.

The inside of the restaurant is simplicity itself. There are no decorative elements, so that diners can appreciate the singular form of the space without any kind of distortion.

Hotel Paramount

Philippe Starck

Location: New York, USA. **Date of completion**: 1990. **Client**: Ian Schrager, Philil Pilevsky, Arthur Cohen, Morgans Hotel Group. **Architect**: Philippe Starck. **Associates**: Anda Andrei (associate architect), Michael Overington (works director). **Photography**: Peter Mauss/ESTO Photographics.

The plan for the hotel included 610 rooms, two restaurants, an elegant club, a gymnasium, a crèche space, areas for shops and exhibitions, and even a small cinema. The hotel aspires to offer functional comfort in the context of almost poetic design. The emblematic façade of the building has made respectful use of its original structure. The first floor is defined by a series of 12 pointed arches over a glass surface with no visible frame or joins. The central interior courtyard is a rectangular space of double height. The whole area becomes a stage set, an idea that is reinforced by the checkerboard carpet reminiscent of the game of life itself.
The intermediate floor, occupied by one of the hotel restaurants, is in the form of a gallery that is open to the interior courtyard. A glass screen reveals the ambiguous function of these balconies, which act both as viewing points and display cabinets at the same time.
The architectural forms used in the hotel are based on chromatic and structural neutrality. Their severity and rigidity are transferred outside by the use of the color gray on stucco or plaster ornaments, roofs, and paving. The hotel's interior color scheme looks energetic and sensual, lending vitality to the activities taking place. The color motifs are repeated in the bathrooms. The polished surfaces and the mirrors multiply the visual perspectives and the sensation of size. The recurring rose red theme evokes lyrical references. The interior of the rooms has been designed personally by Starck himself with the very clear intention of creating a comfortable atmosphere that is like a second home.

Sea Hawk Hotel

César Pelli & Associates

Location: Fukuoka, Japan. **Date of completion**: 1995. **Architect**: César Pelli & Associates. **Scheme**: Hotel/resort, exterior gardening. **Photography**: Taizo Furukowa, Osamu Murai, César Pelli, Yukio Yoshimura.

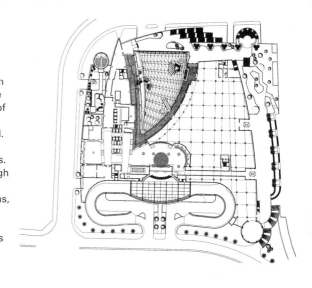

Built on the edge of the sea, visible from the city and constructed like a lighthouse, the hotel's design creates a collection of sculptural forms on the bay. The curves of the roof and walls relate to the elements: water and wind. The complex consists of buildings of different sizes. On the 34 floors of the high tower (in the shape of a boat) there are 1052 rooms, all with a view of the sea. The composition of fragmented curves echoes the profiles of a baseball stadium's monumental roofs. This tall tower contrasts with the round shapes of the lower building's glass cupolas. The walls are finished in ceramic tiles that form a rich texture of different colors and designs. The foyer is an elegant and quiet entrance for hotel guests, as opposed to the high, luminous and lively space of the glass atrium. In the form of a glass horn and open to the sea, the atrium is designed as an urban plaza with fountains and trees that invite both private conversations and public performances.

Cooper Union Residence

Prentice & Chan, Olhausen

Location: New York, USA. **Date of completion**: 1992. **Architect**: Prentice & Chan, Olhausen. **Scheme**: Student residence: dormitories, meeting room, communal service area, campus. **Photography**: Paco Asensio.

The design for this project managed a synthesis of both 19th- and 20th-century styles, in accordance with existing codes for the area, and the inclusion of a campus. One of the most significant elements is the sequence of grilles superimposed on the façade, that emphasize the square and rectangular shapes of the building. There are three separate structures and the proportions of the complex are very rational. The expression of the old and the new is achieved by the different widths of the layers of the façade: the narrow bands conserve the character of the neighborhood, while the wide outer wall of the tower has a more contemporary look.

Inside there is a campus with private spaces. The design offers two bedroom apartments reminiscent of the "loft" concept, together with meeting rooms and communal areas. Large windows create a light and well-ventilated interior.

S. María de Bouro Hotel

Eduardo Souto de Moura, Humberto Vieira

Location: Braga, Portugal. **Date of design**: 1989. **Date of construction**: 1997. **Client**: Enatur. **Architects**: Eduardo Souto de Moura, Humberto Vieira. **Associates**: Manuela Lara, Antonio Loussa, Marie Clement, Ana Fortuna, Pedro Valente. **Photography**: Luis Ferreira Alves.

The purpose of this project was to make use of the stones available from a ruin to construct a new building, which involves various different aspects and functions (some already decided, others still pending). The scheme does not involve reconstruction of the building in its original form or plan.

In this case, the ruins are more important than the "convent," since it is the ruins that are open and manipulable, just as the building was in its time. The layout does not claim to express or represent any particular house by reproducing some original plan, but it does rely on a type of architecture that has remained more or less unchanged over the years. During the design process, we looked for clarity between the form and the scheme as a whole. Faced with two possible courses, we rejected pure and simple consolidation of the ruins to aid contemplation, choosing to introduce new materials, uses, forms, and functions "between things," as Le Corbusier said. "Picturesque" is a question of destiny, not part of a project or program.

Hotel Il Palazzo

Aldo Rossi

Location: Fukuoka, Japan. **Date of design**: 1986. **Client**: Mitsuhiro Kuzawa. **Architect**: Aldo Rossi. **Associates**: Shigeru Uchida (artistic direction). **Photography**: Nacása & Partners Inc.

The project began at the end of 1986, when Mitsuhiro Kuzawa, owner of the hotel, commissioned the architectural design from the Italian Aldo Rossi and the artistic direction from Shigeru Uchide. He also requested the assistance of an excellent group of creative people to develop particular aspects of the scheme. The objective was to change the perception of the hotel, to have it thought of as socially, culturally, and intellectually functional rather than merely providing accommodation. The structure was to influence the urban landscape of the city (Fukuoka, Japan) by its visual significance, so that the hotel could make an impact on an already varied landscape. Those in charge of the project, Aldo Rossi and Shigeru Uchida, have been leading names in architecture and interior design for many years.

Sapporo Beer

Toyo Ito

Location: Sapporo, Japan. **Date of construction**: 1989. **Floor Area**: 300,000 m² (3.2 million ft²). **Architect**: Toyo Ito. **Photography**: Nacása & Partners.

The Sapporo Beer Company is one of the many industries located between Chitosa airport and the city of Sapporo. The project was a collaboration between the client, the Sapporo brewery, Y. Uede (of Uede Cultural Projects), S. Fukukawe (landscaper), and Y. Kanno (composer).

The Guest House, which is designed to accommodate visitors to the brewery, was built in a garden which occupies a third of the plot and comprises the Odin Pool, the Hill of Elms, the Forest of Fairies, the Plaza of the Fire and the Marshland, in representation of a Scandinavian landscape. The Guest House was designed to blend into the existing topography, so it is entirely buried, except for the façade, which looks out onto the garden. This made the whole complex more an earth-moving job than an architectural construction. The bar, the restaurant, and a rest area are located in polygonal spaces lit by skylights and decorated with painted ceilings and textiles. The ventilation towers, the skylights, and the awnings at the entrance appear above ground level; they are designed to simulate the wings of an aircraft, thus reflecting the nearby airport.

The project is a welcome resting place for visitors to the factory. They arrive at the Guest House, and descend into the earth, where they find a warm and bright atmosphere.

House of Water and Glass

Kengo Kuma

Location: Shizuoka, Japan. **Date of completion**: 1996. **Architect**: Kenzo Kuma. **Scheme**: House for guests of a Japanese company. **Floor Area**: 1125 m² (12,100 ft²). **Photography**: Futjitsuka Mitsumasa,

The House of Water and Glass is located on the edge of a cliff, on the coast of Ataml, looking out over the Pacific Ocean.

The materials used are all light, such as glass, steel, or wood; these, according to Kengo Kuma, are materials of the present. The floor of the top level is covered by a sheet of water 15 cm (6 in) deep. Three glass structures, two square and one oval, have been placed over this and are reflected on the water. These are covered by a roof of metal sheets.

Access is from the parking lot through an open door in a granite wall, which leads directly to a bridge of concrete and steel. On the floor below there is a bedroom in the Japanese style, a room for administration, a meeting room, and a gymnasium.

On the access level floor is the dining room, to the right the kitchen and the sushi bar, and to the left visitors' rooms. On the top floor, the two rectangular structures contain guest rooms, and in the oval one there is a dining room.

The central idea of the House of Water and Glass is the study of different ways of seeing, in this case, nature: all in a general atmosphere of calm and equilibrium and with a rational use of materials.

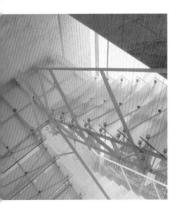

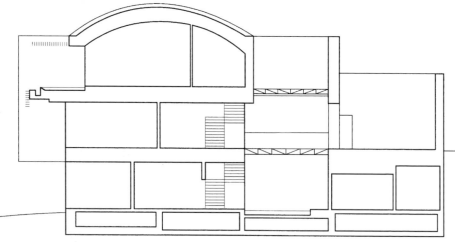

Timanfaya National Park Visitors' Center

Alfonso Cano Pintos

Location: Lanzarote, Canary Islands, Spain. **Date of construction**: 1993. **Client**: National Institute for the Conservation of Nature. **Architect**: Alfonso Cano Pintos. **Scheme**: Visitors' center for Timanfaya National Park, with staff accommodation. **Photography**: Alfonso Cano Pintos, Steve Chasen.

Alfonso Cano Pintos thought it right that the building should have a certain presence: he rejected the idea that the architecture could visually "contaminate" such an extreme landscape.

The scheme for the building had various functions. Firstly, the principal task of the complex is that of collecting and disseminating information on what the visitor is going to see in the National Park. For this there has to be a space for an explanatory exhibition and a projection room, as well as a small shop for selling books and objects related to the park, a multipurpose room, a library, administrative offices for the center, and other complementary facilities. In addition, another building meets the requirements of the park's personnel: two homes for the 'rangers', changing rooms, first aid station, stores, and parking lot for all-terrain vehicles.

The quality of the materials used, the white of the lime-wash on the outside, the scrubbed concrete and the steel plate emphasize the contrasts between artificial, man-made creation and the natural world.

Hotel Arts

SOM (Skidmore, Owings & Merrill), Bruce J. Graham

Location: Barcelona, Spain. **Date of completion**: 1992. **Client**: Hotel Arts. **Architects**: SOM (Skidmore, Owings & Merrill), Bruce J. Graham. **Scheme**: Building for the Hotel Arts: restaurants, convention rooms, and shopping center. **Photography**: David Cardelús.

As a kind of gateway to the waves, the towers, which are visible from all over the city, have become a symbol of the new efforts to open Barcelona to the sea, an issue which has been ignored for too long. The hotel makes a striking impression: a metal structure that can be seen all down the length of its 43 floors. It is the skeleton itself that provides the overall image of the project from any viewpoint. Behind this structure, an aluminum curtain wall encloses the building within, and gives depth to the façade, providing a rich pattern of light and shadow across it.

At the foot of the tower, to smooth the transition to ground level, there are 16,000 m² (172,000 ft²) of shops, restaurants, cafés, and a major store, built around a large pool open to the sea. Over this, as if floating on the water, is positioned an enormous fish covered in anodized aluminum. Frank O. Gehry collaborated in the project to install this, which, in addition to giving shade to the courtyard/pool, is a distinctive symbol for the shopping area and the whole stretch of beach.

Vantaa Home for the Elderly

Heikkinen & Komonen

Location: Vantaa, Finland. **Date of completion**: 1993. **Client**: Foibe Foundation. **Architect**: Heikkinen & Komonen. **Associate**: Janne Kentala. **Scheme**: Home for the elderly: residential blocks and communal service block. **Photography**: Jussi Tiainen.

This residence for the elderly is a new example of an architectural style that in the last few years has again caught the eye of international critics. Although all the buildings belong to the same complex, the plan was to keep the different sections away from each other and to separate the buildings, to ensure that the residents do not feel as if they are in a hospital, but in their own home. The architect has divided the residents' apartments into a number of blocks and concentrated the communal areas in an independent building. The service block divides the plot longitudinally, following the topological line of the terrain. On one side is the hospital and the old buildings of the Villa Rekola, on the other the apartments. The central building contains a restaurant, a library, rooms for residents' activities, a gymnasium, a swimming pool, a sauna, the specific facilities for residents with senile dementia, and various other services such as the hairdresser's and chiropodist's premises.

Group of homes for the Cheesecake Consortium

Fernau & Hartman

Location: Mendocino, San Francisco, USA. **Date of completion:** 1994. **Architect:** Fernau & Hartman. **Associates:** T. Gray, K. Moses, E. Stussi. **Gross floor area:** 8000 m² (86,000 ft²). **Scheme:** Complex of single family homes, verandahs, pergolas, platform for visitors' tents, laundry, library, and workshop. **Photography:** Richard Barnes.

The project consists of the construction of a complex of homes in a forest area in Mendocino County, to the north of San Francisco, for a group of friends. The scheme was finally built in three groups, each with various components: a building of two floors with communal services on the first floor and an apartment on the second floor, a residential wing with five apartments, a laundry and a library, and finally a workshop for repairing cars, developing photos, making furniture, or playing ping pong.

In total, there is a floor area of 5000 m² (54,000 ft²) of construction and 3000 m² (32,000 ft²) of covered areas: verandahs, pergolas, platforms for occasional visitors' tents, and terraces that connect the different buildings and encourage life in the open air.

At the same time, it has been ensured that all the rooms are easily accessible to elderly people, with ramps and elevators suitable for wheelchairs.

Semidetached and row houses

Homes with shared walls presuppose an obligation for neighboring buildings to have respect for each other. There are two strategies for approaching this situation: the first is based on a study of the surroundings, adapting to the parameters of proportion and style, and making use of existing architectural features. The other strategy is to start with a real building and use its originality to highlight its qualities and those of the neighboring buildings. Both approaches result in contemporary homes that have regard for the place they occupy, whether in cities or in small towns and villages. All the projects presented here pay special attention to how to make the best use of space, which is smaller than in the case of free-standing buildings. The architects' efforts are concentrated on their wish to create environments that give the impression of size.

Home/studio in Islington

Caruso/St. John

Location: London, UK. **Date of completion**: 1994. **Architects**: Adam Caruso, Peter St. John. **Associates**: Alan Baxter and Associates (structural engineers). **Scheme**: Home and studio. **Photography**: Hélène Bisnet.

Adam Caruso and Peter St. John were involved in the conversion of an old store on two floors in Islington, North London, into a home and studio. The store, rectangular in shape and measuring 4.7 m (15 ft) wide by 9.8 m (32 ft) deep, provided a useful area of approximately 45 m² (484 ft²) per story. The floors were completely open, with no walls or even a pillar intruding on them. Caruso and St. John decided to replace the old façade with a glass wall. This consists of double glazed Climalit glass (8+24+6) with both insulation and acoustic properties. The panes are translucent but, although they let light through, they visually insulate the inside from the outside. They act like a silk screen or China paper. During the day the façade is hermetically sealed, as if it were made of a metal sheet. At night it becomes a light that illuminates the street.

Price/O'Reilly House

Tina Engelen, Ian Moore

Location: Redfern, Sydney, Australia. **Date of construction**: 1996. **Architects**: Tina Engelen, Ian Moore. **Photography**: Ross Honeysett.

This two-story house is built on a piece of land that was formerly occupied by two traditional flat-roofed houses. The local authorities insisted that the new house should look like a traditional house and not like a store.

The main façade is divided into two vertical sections; both the horizontal elements and the proportions of the sections are designed to be in keeping with the neighbouring houses. In contrast, the rear façade consists of one opening 6 m x 6 m (20 x 20 ft). The layout inside has been adjusted accordingly. Behind the main façade are the small rooms of the home, divided into two levels: garage, storage area, and services (first floor); bedrooms and bathroom (second floor). Meanwhile, next to the garden, a single, double-height space has been constructed, which functions as sitting room, dining room, kitchen, and, eventually, photographic studio facilities.

Home/studio (for an Ikebana artist)

Hiroshi Nakao

Location: Tokorawa, Japan. **Date of completion** 1996. **Architect**: Hiroshi Nakao. **Associates**: Hiroko Serizawa. **Scheme**: Workshop and home with three bedrooms. **Photography**: Nacása & Partners.

The house is a tomb. It is an exterior injected into the world, converted into an interior, and closed. This is definitely an inverted tomb. The outer walls are clad with a steel which changes dramatically from black to red as it rusts. And later, it subtly and bit by bit changes back to black. The house is submerged in the occurrence and recurrence of black. The inside is painted black. Like a flat image sliding over the world, the black temporarily takes over and silences all substance. And it requires one only to feel and wait. Wait for whatever manages to recover its deep memory and make it talk: light. An interminable cycle of reflections that appear and spread to illuminate the contours of the material (or the flesh) or to mute them, in a continuous process of renovation. The house organizes the dynamics of memory and forgetfulness. Space, its center, is in turn compressed and stretched. Depth is unfolded horizontally and vertically. In this space, our bodies, unstable and withdrawn, acquire a new rhythm and another gravity. The house organizes the movement, we throw ourselves down and we stand up. Memory and forgetfulness, standing and lying down. The house is definitely a tomb. A tomb that claims thought, life. A black box that tries to create life.

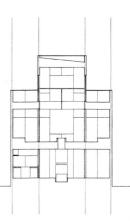

Offices and home of architect Stanley Saitowitz

Stanley Saitowitz

Location: Redfern, Sydney, Australia. **Date of construction**: 1993. **Architect**: Stanley Saitowitz.
Photography: Richard Barnes.

The location, to the south of Market Street, consists of a typical 7.5 x 24.5 m (25 x 80 ft) urban plot. The fact that the client and architect were one and the same person, added to the prototypical characteristics of the plot, meant that the project would be a research exercise.

The aluminum sheet façade and full-width windows contrast with neighboring Victorian buildings, revealing interiors of a different scale and architectural design. The building is split into three units, each with ample double height space. The top section is occupied by Stanley Saitowitz's office, lit by a large central skylight. The middle section is the architect's home, and the first floor has the garage.

The framework consists of two rows of pillars located 1.5 m (5 ft) from the neighboring properties. These two projections contain all the building's services and stairs. In this way the central bay is left completely clear.

The construction system itself and the fittings create the architectural image. The strategy was to select materials, like chromium plating or wood veneer, which did not need to be finished: they could be covered eventually but could safely remain.

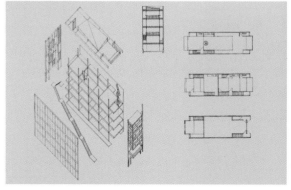

Zorn Residence

Krueck & Sexton

Location: Chicago, USA. **Date of completion**: 1995. **Architect**: Krueck & Sexton. **Photography**: Korale Hedrich Blessing.

The Zorn house is located in a residential area of north Chicago. It is positioned on its plot in such a way that it breaks the symmetry of the adjacent façades and enjoys views to the south. The house was designed as a simple brick and glass building, the interior of which revolves around a double height communal area. The south facing wall is the most transparent and is designed to receive the maximum light.

A long, narrow, vertical window opens to the west, projecting slightly from the plane of the façade, and offers views of the street at the same time as it extends along the roof in order to provide overhead diffused lighting for the central area of the second floor.

The starting point of Krueck & Sexton's architecture is the concept of a rectangle. Initially designed as a pure rectangle, the house has been transformed, slightly broken up, moved around a bit, and had parts added. Some of the additions were in height and some in width. In this way the various areas have been given expression and the building finally becomes a unified composition with all its features.

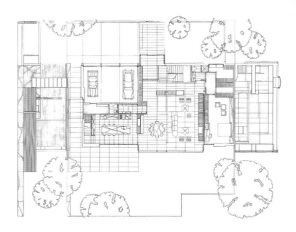

Duffy House

Bercedo + Mestre

Location: Sitges, Barcelona, Spain. **Date of completion**: 1998. **Architect**: Bercedo + Mestre. **Associates**: D. Schleipen (design), J.M. Ambros (technical architect). J. Marín (construction), R. Mayne (carpentry), Islathermic (aluminum) **Scheme**: Single family home. **Photography**: Jordi Miralles, Dominik Schleipen

The project consisted of the refurbishment and extension of an old, self-built house which was very run-down and damp, on a single floor, with a central corridor and small rooms on both sides. The house stands on an urban plot nearly 7 m (23 ft) wide between a four-floor and a three-floor building. What was created is an intimate setting, a private space which brings together different scenes and atmospheres. Shapes are therefore simple and stark. Part of the framework of the existing house has been demolished in order to insert an inner courtyard just beyond the entrance. In contrast to the reticence of the façade which overlooks the street, walking through the entrance the visitor encounters something quite unexpected. From this initial paradox, interior and exterior spaces constantly overlap, providing unaccustomed visual relationships and complex situations. This is a house which one constantly exits and enters. The architects have managed to develop a private exterior space in which the owners can live life in the open air.

Single family homes in Montagnola

Mario Campi, Franco Pessina

Location: Lugano, Switzerland. **Date of construction**: 1988. **Client**: Mr. Corecco. **Architects**: Mario Campi, Franco Pessina. **Associates**: Benedikt Graf, Gianmarco Ciocca, Enzo Vanetta. **Scheme**: Three single family homes. **Photography**: Eduard Huelver.

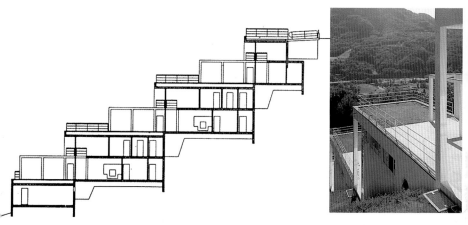

The project consists of three single family homes. The architects present these in a single block which blends naturally with the topographical relief, sloping down from west to east. In the southern area, chosen to accommodate the access staircase backing onto the various dwellings, the style of the façade looks more closed and compact, with six stepped floors which translate the concepts of duplex and double height, and provide alternative access doors. The opposite elevation is more open. On this northern face, the basic geometry of the building is organized into the three dwellings.

Inside, Campo and Pessina make space and light the focal point of their work, arranging the various rooms according to the panoramic views. The three units have been treated in the same way, although the highest one is smaller. All in all, the complex presents seven horizontal planes which, over the living room, develop more vertically due to a gap in the floor separation framework which causes the double height. One of the most effective strategies of the complex is the use of space: the roof of each unit functions as a terrace.

Homes with panoramic views over Lake Gooi

Neutelings & Riedijk

Location: Fourth quadrant of the shore of Lake Gooi, Huizen, The Netherlands. **Date of construction**: 1994–1996. **Client**: Bouwfonds Woningbouw SL Haarlem. **Architect**: Neutelings & Riedijk. **Associates**: Willem Bruijn, Gerrit Schilder; Juurlink & Geluk, Rotterdam (landscaping). **Scheme**: 32 single family homes with integral garages. **Photography**: Stijn Brakkee.

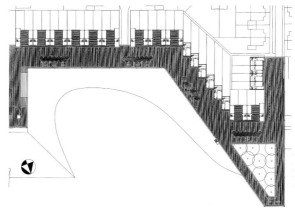

The project forms part of a larger plan consisting of 152 homes, the first phase of which comprises these 32 homes with panoramic views. Their internal layout is designed to make the most of their special position: water on one side, a great deal of light on the opposite side.

There are two types of home in this new project by Neutelings & Riedijk; both are designed within a 6 m (20 ft) bay and both exploit the visual perspectives of the lake to the maximum. Those which face the lake directly are built in pairs with the living room of one resting on the living room of the other, occupying the full width of both homes, 12 m (39 ft).

Those which are at an angle to the lake are built back to back, with one set back from the other, producing an indented façade for the development.

All the houses have gardens, their own integral garage, and either a generous roof terrace (homes facing the lake) or a terrace suspended over the back garden (homes at an angle to the lake).

The promenade between the edge of the lake and the homes has been designed to blend with them.

Double house

Thomas Herzog and Michael Volz

Location: Pullach, Munich, Germany. **Date of completion**: 1989. **Architects**: Thomas Herzog and Michael Volz. **Associates**: Michael Streib, Julius Natterre, Bois Consult, Lausana (statics), Rainer Wittenborn (color design). **Scheme**: Single family home, exterior landscaping. **Photography**: Dieter Leistner.

This home is configured as a combination of traditional materials and techniques together with other more innovative materials and techniques for additional quality. The outcome is a house which synthesizes aesthetic simplicity with more intelligent pragmatism and becomes a kind of prototype or model which can be used with a moderate degree of naturalness in different kinds of environment. The initial theme of the project was to build a residential building, with two apartments, on a flat, vacant plot in Pullach, on the outskirts of Munich, an area of traditional styles of rural architecture. The requirements of the client, who wanted a wooden building, with particular attention paid to the problems of energy saving, and yet with a fairly limited budget, had to be addressed. This whole set of factors had a decisive influence on the design of the future home, finally dictated by the technical aspects of solar energy, on which subject Herzog's team (with Michael Volz and Michael Streib) were constantly advised by the Freiburg Solar Energy Institute.

Patio Villas

Rem Koolhaas (OMA)

Location: Rotterdam, Netherlands. **Date of construction**: 1984–1988. **Architect**: Rem Koolhaas (OMA). **Associates**: George Heintz, Götz Keller, Jeraen Thomas, Thÿs de Haan, Jo Schippers, Petra Blaisse, Yves Brunier (landscaping). **Scheme**: Single family home on two floors, garden, and garage. **Photography**: Peter Aaron/ESTO.

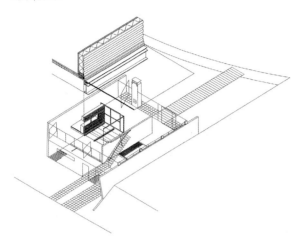

The two floors have different floor areas due to the slope. The glazed patio is the central organizational feature. With its off-center layout, four different areas become apparent: to the north, the dining room; to the south, the garden and living room; the Oriental metal wall of the prism houses the kitchen; on the other side, between the cube and the unobstructed wall, lies the rectangular stairwell flanked by its sinuous protective structure.

This villa is a virtually philosophical reflection on the architectural possibilities of designing a home today.

The whole of the interior has been laid out around a prism of light which not only acts as a central area but also affects the question of transparency and clarity. There is an almost total absence of physical barriers between rooms in the home.

On the outside the building has been designed with a desire to parody the traditional style of local villas, with the use of chromatics and glass borders as expressive motifs. The simplicity of all the details and components, the lightness of the dividing walls, and the lack of furniture give the lifestyle of its inhabitants a feeling of sober yet elegant luxury.

Silver House

Thom Mayne and Michael Rotondi, Morphosis

Location: Los Angeles, USA. **Date of completion**: 1987. **Architect**: Thom Mayne and Michael Rotondi, Morphosis. **Scheme**: Family home on the outskirts of Los Angeles. **Photography**: Morphosis.

This home, consisting of three floors built in a most unusual way on a completely irregular plot, has the living area on the top floor and the bedrooms and bathrooms on the lower floors. In this way, the inhabitants can see the Pacific Ocean, which would otherwise have been concealed by the row of houses on the other side of the coastal highway. The plans also clearly show the intersection of two separate units: a central block which contains the bathrooms, kitchen, and elevator, and a second diagonal unit which contains the remaining rooms. Special attention has been given to the circular entrance located on one side of the building's central unit. This leads to a lobby which provides access to a courtyard to the left and a guest area to the right, opposite the bathroom and sauna. The top floor contains the study and living room, located between the kitchen and dining room. Finally there is also a basement, which is used as a garage and storeroom with its own service area.

Single family suburban homes

The suburbs have in the past often been
associated with entropy, ambiguity, and
even indifference. Their appearance may
be uncared for as a result of precarious
and speculative property deals. The last
few decades of the 20th century, however,
have seen an upsurge of interest in
renovating these areas. Firstly, at a town
planning level, there have been efforts to
improve the infrastructure and give
districts on the periphery the advantages
of both city and country. Secondly, on an
architectural level, in-depth studies have
been carried out on the type of houses
required in suburban areas, and their
functional requirements. Over recent
years suburban homes have become
highly sought after. The examples shown
here demonstrate the special nature of the
location and the ideas of clients and
designers for them.

Burnette House

Wendell Burnette

Location: Sunnyslope. Arizona. USA. **Date of construction**: 1995. **Scheme**: Single family home, garden, and garage. **Photography**: Bill Timmerman.

The Burnette House is in the Sonora desert in the city of Sunnyslope. It is located at the end of an old abandoned route which led into the desert, cutting its way across the territory. In its center, the house is cut in two by an interior courtyard, which is the access from both the garden and garage. It is an ambiguous place where all levels of the house meet and where light penetrates at irregular angles, producing a strong contrast between light and shade. A staircase, consisting of squares of steel plate of different sizes, apparently suspended in the air, terminates at a small pool which reflects the staircase and makes the floor seem to disappear.

The side walls of the Burnette House have even, vertical slits every 2.5 m (8 ft) on the south wall and every 1.25 m (4 ft) on the north wall, which act like a sundial. Depending on the time of day and the season of the year, the shafts of light passing through the slits trace a specifically slanted line on the floor.

Wildbrink Villa

Ben van Berkel

Location: Ameersfoort, The Netherlands. **Date of project**: 1994. **Architect**: Ben van Berkel. **Associates**: A. Krom, P. van der Evre, B. Medic BV, ABM **Description**: Single family home, courtyard, and garden. **Photography**: Hélène Bisnet, Kim Zwarts.

From the street, the house looks like a single slope covered with gravel: the main façade appears to have sunk below ground level. The slope is divided by a ramp running down to the garage and a pedestrian walkway leading to the central courtyard. So the house does not have a specific, recognizable entrance but a gradual one.

The shape of the central courtyard is irregular. It is open to the west but is reached from the pedestrian walkway. The garage cuts it off from the road, which enables it to become the living heart of the house. It receives sun from the south and all rooms open onto it via large glass doors.

The interior of the house is L-shaped, with the living room right in the corner. The short wing houses the services (kitchen, pantry, laundry) and the long wing the bedrooms. The bathroom is an extra building added to the house, with wood clad external walls. It juts out from the main structure and helps to close off the courtyard area.

Rotterdam house/studio

Mecanoo Architekten

Location: Rotterdam, Netherlands. **Date of construction**: 1989–91. **Client**: Erick van Egeraat and Francine Houben. **Architect**: Mecanoo Architekten b.v. **Associates**: Erick van Egeraat, Francine Houben (design), Theo Kupers, Bjarne Mastenbroek, Cock Peterse, Inma Fernandez, Birgit Jurgenhake, Marjolin Adriaansche, Van Omme & De Grooth (contractor). **Scheme**: Single family home with studio, garden, swimming pool, and garage. **Photography**: Scagliola, Brakee, Francine Houben.

The building is located at the end of a row of houses built in the 19th century and surrounded by single family homes and apartment blocks built by some of the Netherlands' current top architects. The first floor houses the lobby, garage, and the architects'/owners' studio. The studio leads through glass doors to a Japanese garden. The pool is separated from the house by a wooden platform. The living room is on the second floor, with excellent views over the river. This is a large floor which, in addition to the living room, accommodates the kitchen and dining room. There is a terrace adjoining the south wall, with views over the canal. The north façade, made of glass, continues to the top floor, where a library serves as an anteroom to the three bedrooms situated here.

Lawson-Western House

Eric Owen Moss

Location: Los Angeles, USA. **Date of completion**: 1994. **Architect**: Eric Owen Moss. **Photography**: Tom Bonner.

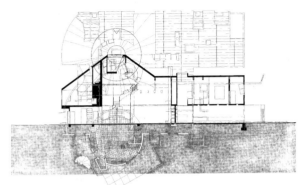

The functional, spatial, and formal ideas of the clients were garnered and interpreted by the architect and became the true starting points of the project's design.

The house is in one of the most prosperous parts of the city of Los Angeles. Its position, along the northern boundary of the plot, meant that a garden could be located in front of the south façade. Automobile and pedestrian access is from one end of the building, creating a sequential interior pathway which leads to the kitchen, the true functional and spatial nucleus of the home. The first floor accommodates the interconnected communal areas; the kitchen has a perimeter ring, for service and storage areas and from where the main staircase of the house starts. The large living room is a very high, vaulted room containing a metal fireplace; adjacent to both of these is the dining room, a room of more domestic proportions. The floor is completed by a playroom adjoining the kitchen on the west side, plus the garage and guest area on the east side. The central position of the staircase means that the second floor is divided into two main areas linked by a bridge over the living room. In the west wing is the master bedroom with its ancillary rooms, with direct access to an outside terrace, with a Jacuzzi, leading to the garden via an outside spiral staircase. The east wing has two bedrooms and the bathroom, over which a corner window makes an interesting feature on the access façade.

Koechlin House

Herzog & de Meuron

Location: Basle, Switzerland. **Date of construction**: 1994. **Architect**: Herzog & de Meuron. **Scheme**: Home, garden, and garage. **Photography**: Margheritta Spilutini.

The Koechlin House is built from the inside out. The courtyard can be open or enclosed and at certain times of the year can be turned into a conservatory. The upper floor can be closed off with a long wall of glass. This dual purpose has direct consequences for the design of the other parts of the house. The courtyard has no clear boundary and can become part of the first floor living room, with a window in the façade, or take over a section of the second floor framework to create a terrace. According to the architects themselves, this means that the rooms overlap, flow together, and enfold each other.

Another of the major ideas of the design is the intention that the outside forms a constant part of the inside, that the house is part of its surroundings, the garden, and views of the city in the distance. The outside walls are finished in cement gray rendering, which gives the house a sober appearance.

Hakuei House

Akira Sakamoto

Location: Tokyo, Japan. **Date of completion**: 1996. **Client**: Hakuei family. **Associates**: Reinhold Meyer (structural engineer), Kaiser Bautechnik (works supervision), Roger Preston (mechanical and electrical engineer). **Photography**: Nacasa & Partners.

The Hakuei residence is located on a relatively small and narrow suburban plot. For Sakamoto the decision to build a simple building with white walls signifies creating visual silence in the city where passers-by can rest their eyes. In this project, more important even than the composition of the rooms was to define the courtyard as an exterior, but at the same time private, area, around which to organize the day-to-day life of the occupants of the house. Akira Sakamoto built a side wall which runs across the plot from the entrance to the rear boundary and acts as a screen. The wall is located on the east side and the afternoon sun reflects off it into all areas of the house. Opposite this wall, Sakamoto built three white boxes, two of them exactly alike.

The radical simplicity of this house seems to strip any notion of the superfluous, to slow down sounds which cross the room from one window to the other, and to project the movement of people crossing the rooms onto the white walls.

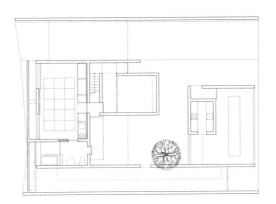

Kidosaki House

Tadao Ando

Location: Osaka, Japan. **Date of construction**: 1990. **Architect**: Tadao Ando. **Scheme**: Single family home.
Photography: Richard Bryant/Arcaid.

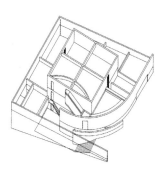

This building stands on an irregularly shaped plot. The main building consists of a perfect cube with 12 m (39 ft) sides, around which is arranged the rest of the house. This cube is located almost in the center of the plot, leaving open space both to the north and south. The area to the north consists of the entrance. This area has the peculiarity of cutting the straight line of the elevations which border the plot. Thus, one of the side walls, that facing west, begins to curve in towards the center, coming out on the north side, producing an open space which becomes the entrance. The interior has clean lines, providing an austere space devoid of embellishments, faithful to Japanese tradition. The rooms are open plan, very large, and empty. You could say this is an amorphous building which is integrated with nature, producing an almost floating space.

House in Yokohama

Kazuo Shinohara

Location: Yokohama, Japan. **Date of construction**: 1987. **Architect**: Kazuo Shinohara. **Scheme**: Construction of a single family home as an annex to an old house. **Photography**: Richard Bryant/Arcaid.

This house was designed as an extension to an old wooden house with the intention of preserving as many trees as possible on the site it was to occupy. The new building takes up only a small part of the original garden.

The house is located in Yokohama, Japan, at the top of a very steep slope on an extensive, quiet plot. The site is covered with a large number of enormous trees, which is why this green belt area was treated with great respect. The new structure, an L-shaped section on two floors, was added to one side of the existing building, a rectangular bungalow, totally regular and uniform. The first floor of the new extension contains the entrance (which is located between the two buildings), the master bedroom, and a bathroom with a *tatami*. The second floor is accessed by a staircase near the entrance and accommodates the

all-important kitchen, together with the dining room, a spacious living room, and a closet.

Blades House

Morphosis

Location: Santa Barbara, California, USA. **Date of construction**: 1996. **Architect**: Morphosis. **Scheme**: Single family house, garden, swimming pool, and garage. **Photography**: Morphosis.

In June 1990, a dreadful fire razed to the ground hundreds of single family homes built in the hills of the Santa Barbara coastline near Goleta, California (USA). All that remained, along with the ash, was a gently sloping landscape with scattered rocks and a group of native oaks. Morphosis' strategy was to build an elliptical wall and contain all parts of the house within it. This wall, which has an upper edge or lip suggesting that this exterior room is partly roofed, is made of exposed aggregate concrete. Opposite the ellipsis of the garden, the house roof draws another curve in the vertical plane.

The floor area of the house is about 350 m² (3800 ft²), arranged into three large areas adjacent to five small exterior rooms. Each area is designed as a sequence of superimposed zones in which the boundary between communal and private space has been deliberately blurred.

Check House

KNTA

Location: Singapore, Malaysia. **Date of construction**: 1995. **Architect**: KNTA. **Associates**: Joseph Huang, Ove Arup & Partners, Singapore (structural engineers); Hin Yin Choo, Michael Chorney, Finbarr Fin, Chee Meng Look, Bruce Ngiam, Ben Smart, Mong Lin Yap, Jacks Yeo, CCL Chartered Surveyors; Ee Chiang & Co. Pte Ltd. (main contractor), Ho Kong Aluminium Pte Ltd., Xin Hefen Engineering Pte. Ltd. (specialist contractors). **Photography**: Dennis Gilbert.

The plot on which the Check House stands is elongated, which is reflected in the design of both the house and the gardens. On the first floor, the shapes are curved and fluid, while on the second floor they are straight and angular. The house is designed as a series of stages and areas which follow each other naturally. A small paved road provides car access as far as the house, crossing the back garden. A curved ramp provides access to the entrance from the garage area, dominated by the sculptural image of a metal pergola suspended from a tensioning device on one side.

Concrete walls form the basic structure of the house. The various elements made of other materials are fixed to or hang from them.

All parts of the house converge on the double height living room, from which there are views over the front and rear gardens. The dining room, close to the front garden, is a circular room designed around a central, round table seating 12 people comfortably.

The rear garden houses the swimming pool, which is an open area surrounded by large windows. At the north end of the house, next to the swimming pool, there is a small pavilion made of glass blocks and a roof of two projecting wings supported on a single load-bearing beam.

Psyche House

Rene van Zuuk

Location: Almere, The Netherlands. **Date of construction**: 1991–1992. **Clients**: Rene van Zuuk and Marjo Körner **Architect**: Rene van Zuuk. **Photography**: Herman H. van Doorn.

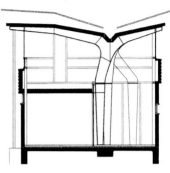

The project is a composition of interlinking areas, surfaces, and elements. It is designed on the basis of the materials, conscientiously rejecting the use of both passing fads and standard ideas. The house comprises two adjacent, longitudinal strips: one, double height, to the north; the other, with two levels, occupying the southern half. A curtain of translucent glass enters the house from the northwest corner, describing an arc which the sub-frame of the adjacent southern area joins at a tangent. Sheltered by the glass arc are four structures, four steel trees: their trunks split and the branches spread out, supporting the two wings of the roof. One of the trees is in the entrance area and the other three are interlinked by metal cross-tensioners inside the room, which dominate it. The structure is supplemented with another two Y-shaped supports, produced by I-shaped profiles, which support the more projecting wing of the roof running under the south façade.

House in Vaise

Jourda & Perraudin

Location: Vaise, France. **Date of completion**: 1990. **Architect**: Françoise-Hélène Jourda, Gilles Perraudin. **Scheme**: Single family home, garden, and garage. **Photography**: Stéphane Couturier.

This house is a direct representation of the architectural concepts of its designers, which have already been displayed in some of their previous works, such as the Paris City of Music and the Gandhi Cultural Center in New Delhi. The project clearly reflects its architects' concern to bring the inhabitants in contact with the external weather conditions and to integrate the building into its surroundings. The project is a direct testimony to a new philosophical focus on the relationship between living space and nature and connections between culture and countryside. The plot on which the house stands is a six-sided, irregular polygon. To retain as much greenery as possible, the architects decided on a layout of two, reduced height, rectangular floors. This arrangement suited perfectly the client family, with four children continually coming in and going out of the house. The layout consists of a living room/diner, kitchen, bedrooms, bathrooms, playroom, cellar, and terraces representing visual continuity between the inside and the outside. The architects achieved what they were initially seeking: to apply a biotechnological architecture where materials are used according to their specific function within the general structure.

Single family country homes

In modern society, where cities occupy the center ground and radiate their grid-like surroundings and their speed, the country means a move towards another type of activity. Anyone who decides to build a house in a meadow or near a wood takes a basic decision. They are expressing a desire for isolation, for the achievement of greater tranquillity, and for the start of a dual journey: proximity to more simple, fundamental things and gradual detachment from urban networks of relationships and obligations. We have included here houses which have a specific and recognizable shape. All the projects relate to nature in different ways: they adapt to the countryside, alter it, embellish it, and reveal the motives of those who live in them.

Villa M

Stéphane Beel

Location: Zedelgem, Belgium. **Date of construction**: 1994. **Architect**: Stéphane Beel. **Associates**: Dirk Hendriks, Paul van Eygen, Hans Verstuyft, Harm Wassink, Hans Lust, Philippe Viérin (design), SCES (structural engineering), R. Boydens (fittings). **Photography**: Lieve Blancquart.

The site for the Villa M is a clearing in a wood approximately 1 ha (2.5 acres) in area; it is completely flat.

The villa is an elongated structure (60 m, 197 ft in length by 7 m, 23 ft wide), built parallel to one of the existing walls. The different areas are set out along the length of the house in a sequence, separated by patches of architectural silence which may take the form of small patios or areas not dedicated to any particular purpose, which accommodate the services. These silent areas serve the purpose of keeping adjacent rooms at a distance from one another. Although there are no doors to interrupt the spatial continuity, the rooms are nevertheless separated, with the kitchen isolated from the dining room and the living room. From the garden, when the light starts to wane, the interior of the building takes on the appearance of a scenery backdrop: the enormous glass windows allow for movements to be seen, as the people inside pass from room to room.

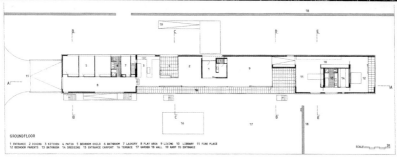

GROUNDFLOOR

1 ENTRANCE 2 DINING 3 KITCHEN 4 PATIO 5 BEDROOM CHILD 6 BATHROOM 7 LAUNDRY 8 PLAY AREA 9 LIVING 10 LIBRARY 11 FIRE PLACE
12 BEDROOM PARENTS 13 BATHROOM 14 DRESSING 15 ENTRANCE CARPORT 16 TERRACE 17 GARDEN 18 WALL 19 RAMP TO ENTRANCE

SCALE ___ 5M

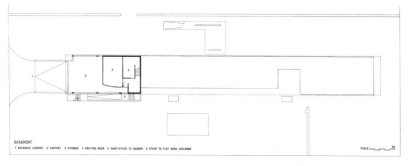

BASEMENT

1 ENTRANCE CARPORT 2 CARPORT 3 STORAGE 4 HEATING ROOM 5 RAMP/STAIR TO GARDEN 6 STAIR TO PLAY AREA CHILDREN

SCALE ___ 5M

Villa M 951

Villa in the woods

Kazuyo Sejima

Location: Chino, Nagano, Japan. **Date of construction**: 1994. **Architects**: Kazuyo Sejima. **Associates**: R. Nighizawa, S. Funaki, Matsuvi Gengo + O.R.S. **Scheme**: Single family home. **Photography**: Nacása and Partners.

The villa in the Tateshina woods occupies a position almost of defense in the face of the wilderness, creating a point with an ordered identity in the midst of natural chaos. Kazuyo Sejima chose a circular site to express the sense of homogeneity which the woodland created within him. This dense encirclement of vegetation does not allow for an axis to be identified; the sun's rays filter through the branches and make orientation difficult. The client, a gallery owner from Tokyo, wanted a house which he could use as a second home, in which he would be able to receive visitors, and was also provided with an exhibition area, the atelier. This scheme is arranged around a central circular space which meets these requirements, and which creates, by its perimeter, a ring in which the architect brings together the areas providing for the basic functions of a home.

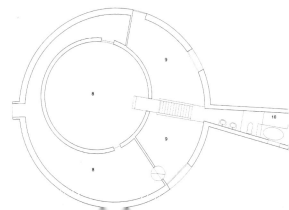

House at Tateshina

Iida Archischip Studio

Location: Tateshina, Nagano, Japan. **Date of construction**: 1994. **Architects**: Yoshihitko Iida. **Associates**: Niitsu (construction). **Scheme**: Single family home, landscaping, and external, double height covered walk. **Photography**: Koumei Tanaka.

The house is located in a holiday area, at the foot of Mount Tateshina, in Nagano. The site is on a gentle slope to the southwest, with the building surrounded by woodlands. Iida's project involved the construction of two parallel elements on a rectangular plot, somewhat displaced in relation to one another. Both are sited so as to follow the slope of the ground; access is through the more elevated end, and from the vestibule a ramp descends, following the natural inclination of the mountain side, and leads the visitor to the living room and the large wooden terrace. The ramp continues until finally losing itself again in the woods. A second ramp rises from the vestibule to a small bridge which connects to the adjacent building. The bathroom is on the second floor. This is an unusually open structure, with panoramic views over the woods, inviting one to spend hours relaxing in the bath and enjoying the scenery.

Barnes House

Patkau Architects

Location: Nanaimo, British Columbia, Canada. **Date of construction**: 1993. **Architects**: Tim Newton, John Patkau, Patricia Patkau, David Shone, Tom Robertson. **Associates**: Fast & Epp Partners (structural engineering), Robert Wall Ltd. (contractor). **Scheme**: Single family home and landscaping. **Photography**: Undine Pröhl.

According to the owners, John and Patricia Patkau, the Barnes House is part of an investigational process exploring architecture which started some years ago and is still going on. This journey is focused on the quest for the specific, the real, and the heterogeneous elements. In the case of the Barnes House, the specific is basically the location and the lively landscape which surrounds the building, rocky outcrops rich in vegetation, with views of the Strait of Georgia and Vancouver Island. The scheme by John and Patricia Patkau plays with both themes; on the one hand, the landscape, the topography, and the panoramic views; and, on the other, the abrupt, rocky site, resplendent with edges, changes of level, and sharp profiles. In a certain way, the forms of the house itself evoke both aspects of the landscape, and bring them to an intermediate scale.

Typical/Variant House

Vincent James, Paul Yaggie

Location: Wisconsin, USA. **Date of construction**: 1996. **Architects**: Vincent James, Paul Yaggie. **Associates**: N. Blantard, N. Knuston, A. Dull, S. Lazen, K. Scheib, Coen + Stumpt (landscaping), Yerigan Construction (building contractors). **Scheme**: Single family home, landscaping, and garage. **Photography**: Don F. Wong.

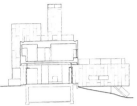

The owners embodied in the project a concept which fascinated them and for which they coined the term "typical/variant." The Typical/Variant House is a collection of spaces which accord with the rhythms and outlines of domestic life. Making use solely of elements which resemble wooden boxes, a variety of different contiguous architectural situations were created. Each one of them has its own specific proportions, orientation, and natural lighting. In parallel with this, the turns and angles of the different parts of the building define different semi-enclosed spaces on the outside. Both the rooms and the patio areas of the house are conceived as immediate, unadorned spaces, straightforward in form, which acquire life from the daily cycle of use. The structural solutions and the types of finish chosen are inspired by the typical rural architecture of the northern United States. The final result is at once abstract and yet familiar, satisfying the owners' desire for their home to be rustic and warm, allowing them to establish a feeling of intimacy and love. The external materials, mainly copper sheeting and bluish stone, are arranged in distinct sections which create a rich variety of rhythms and textures in the façades. As time passes, so the copper turns from a bright honey tone to a bluish-purple colour, then to a rich brown, and finally to a whitish-green shade.

Huf House

Ernst Beneder

Location: Blindenmarkt, Lower Austria. **Date of construction**: 1990–1993. **Client**: Dr. Josef Huf and Maria Huf. **Architect**: Ernst Beneder. **Associates**: Anja Fischer. **Photography**: Ernst Beneder, Marguerita Spiluttini.

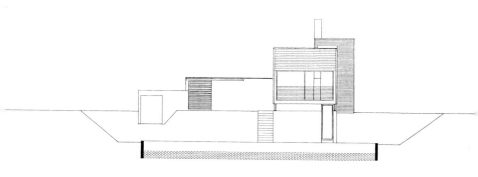

The Huf House was created as a second home, covering an area of 75 m² (807 ft²) and simple in scope. The site, surrounded by the wetland woods of the River Ybbs, is located adjacent to a large artificial pool. Bordered by the roadway on the north side, the house is shaped as a longitudinal prism, faced in timber, supported on the flat surface of the site and rising above the slope down to the edge of the water.

The interior is designed as a single space in which objects are then arranged; the staircase, which rises from the patio to the roof, stands next to the chimney and above the fittings of the kitchen in an entirely natural manner. The prism structure is supported on a concrete base, partially underground, and in turn supports a robust aluminum tower containing the bathroom on the lower floor and a gallery-cum-bedroom on the intermediate floor. The bathroom, which projects outside the perimeter of the prism structure, is separated by a semi-transparent door. One of the bedroom windows faces onto the patio, while the other opens onto the terrace and the dining room, across the stairway. Just at the point at which the site starts to fall away, the interior floor rises by five steps, merging into the parquet floor in the living room area.

Outside on the patio the batten framework adds warmth to the open space.

Häusler House

Karl Baumschlager and Dietmar Eberle

Location: Hard, Austria. **Date of construction**: 1993. **Architects**: Karl Baumschlager and Dietmar Eberle. **Area**: 230 m² (2500 ft²). **Scheme**: Single family house and landscaping. **Photography**: Eduard Hueder/Ardi-Photo Inc.

The Häusler House is a single family home in Hard, Austria, located on a flat and open site, and consisting essentially of a rectangular structure, characterized by a gray concrete texture, within which the project develops. The access façade and the side elements are practically closed off to the outside, and only the southern face is open. This façade consists of a regular concrete structure forming a uniform latticework, with timber facings, and recessed to a greater or lesser extent, from which a number of different floors branch off. The northern façade, the area of access, is a rectangle of gray concrete, which accommodates, as its only compositional elements, the aperture for the entrance and a horizontal window, extended and elongated, on the right, which runs as far as the corner. The house is reminiscent of the concrete creations by the North American artist Donald Judd: pure geometrical forms, of large dimensions, set in open landscapes, and creating a strange and disconcerting form of order.

Häusler House 963

Dub House

Bolles + Wilson

Location: Münster, Germany. **Date of construction**: 1994. **Architects**: Bolles + Wilson. **Scheme**: Single family home, interior courtyard, and landscaping. **Photography**: Christian Richters.

The scheme for the Dub House involved the reshaping (small-scale modification) of a house dating from the 1960s, in the modern style.

The first "extra," the word which the people involved use themselves, was an earthenware ceramic wall of vivid blue on the interior courtyard, a bold and optimistic explosion of color. The second element was a studio located next to the blue wall, somewhat lower, faced in zinc on the outside and wood on the inside. This second wall incorporates a set of windows of different sizes, as references to a neoplastic style. The third extra, by contrast with the first two, is a flat horizontal surface with a pergola of zinc bars which occupies the space created by the slight displacement of the two walls already described, between which the access to the building has been constructed.

On the inside there are two more new elements, a chimney formed of geometric shapes, with a circular aluminum fume extraction pipe, and a substantial wooden swing door, which almost amounts to a revolving wall in appearance.

Aktion Poliphile

Studio Granda

Location: Wiesbaden, Germany. **Date of construction**: 1989–1992. **Client**: Galerie z.B., Frankfurt. **Architects**: Studio Granda. **Photography**: Norbert Migueletz.

The scheme involves two houses, located above the fertile fields to the north of Wiesbaden, Germany: the Saturn House and the Delia House. Saturn symbolizes the concept of the paradox of time, which creates only subsequently to destroy its own creation. Its successor, the Delia, is a symbol of the fount of youth, energy, and health. Delia symbolizes modern times. Its hidden side, discreetly concealed, reflects the shadowy cold sadness and slowness, of its neighbour Saturn, both houses so forming a single private system. Saturn is solid and impenetrable, its roof formed of lead and the walls of a dark red plaster. Nothing passes across its face, its walls have no characteristic adornments or features, with the exception of a short arcade on the flank of the wall. From the shelter of the garden a deep groove, of double height, reveals the interior, showing through a series of smaller gaps in the side of the wall. Moving to the north wall of the building, we find a latticework of great beauty and originality, which likewise has a strong sense of symbolism. Saturn and Delia, wood and stone, fragility and strength. Symbolism, beauty, and practicality; three words which when taken together give meaning to the Aktion Poliphile, three words which, in harmony, join within this project, providing a masterly lesson for those who cling to the old adage that beauty always strives against the pragmatic. Symbolism, beauty, and practicality; neither the one nor the two prevail, only the three, and their perfect interdependence is mirrored in the Aktion Poliphile houses.

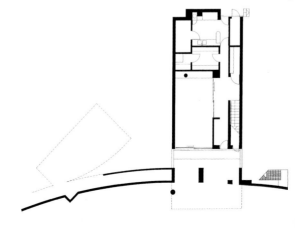

Bom Jesus House

Eduardo Souto de Moura

Location: Braga, Portugal. **Date of construction**: 1994. **Architect**: Eduardo Souto de Moura. **Scheme**: Single family home and landscaping. **Photography**: Luis Ferreira Alves.

The conceptual simplicity and the architectural language which characterize the Bom Jesus House are a clear example of how to provide a response to the physical circumstances which already prevail, a response which is appropriate yet understated and subtle. The composition of this single family house incorporates two elements which represent two different schemes and two different construction systems, uniting two houses in the same project. One structure in natural stone, which, springing from the irregular configuration of the ground, spans the building, and a cube of concrete and glass which rests on the platform delimiting the stone wall, symbolize the meeting between that which already exists and that which is

new. The Bom Jesus House stands on a site with a pronounced slope towards the southwest, facing towards the anarchic silhouette of the city of Braga. Access to the property from lower levels, coincides with the upper limit of the site, merging into a paved path which rises gently in a semiritualistic pattern.

Grotta House

Richard Meier

Location: New Jersey, USA. **Date of construction**: 1988. **Architect**: Richard Meier.

This house is sited on a slightly inclined surface, with woodland to the northwest and beautiful views to the south and the east. Two axes drawn from the center of the building form right angles with the main buildings, projecting the interior of the house into the natural landscape surrounding it, and providing a position of privilege in a location which is otherwise difficult to define. The circles and squares are stylistic elements of great importance and value to New York architect Richard Meier. The latest owners of the house, two art collectors, also acquired a love of architecture, inspired by the geometry of this design. The building is constructed around a cylindrical center space, two stories in height; this virtual structure is partially absorbed by the orthogonal body, in which it is integrated in turn within a square base. The house is a clear example of many of the themes which arise in Meier's work, such as the use of white; the building is almost completely white, the architect's preferred color, so sharpening the perception of the colors which exist in natural light and within nature itself. The interplay between light and dark, between mass and volume, can be better appreciated thanks to the contrast with the white surface of the building.

Bernasconi House

Luigi Snorzzi

Location: Carona, Switzerland. **Date of construction**: 1988–1989. **Client**: Raffosio Bernasconi. **Architect**: Luigi Snorzzi. **Associates**: Gustavo Grosman, Hans Peter Jenny. **Photography**: Filippo Simonetti.

The building is located in the Carona valley, in an area characterized by a pronounced upward slope in a southerly direction, and a broad vista to the northern flank. Access to the building is via an area on the highest side of the site, where the parking area is located and the view from the house is to the southwest. The functional arrangement of the interior is of a residential house located on three floors, added to which is a basement where the storage areas are located. The simplicity of the interior is reflected in the façades: visible concrete, simple structures, and strategically located apertures. The view of the building from the access area discloses the presence of two prismatic modules: the first, generally horizontal in arrangement, accommodates the residential areas proper, while the second, with a vertical superimposed perspective, provides the communicating link between the remote surfaces. The peaceful harmony between the visible concrete and the glass is supported by the use of the glass in the transitional area as both the floor paving and for the access stairways. The use of this material brings about a subtle change in the light effects on the changing levels of the stairway and at the ends of the floors.

Neuendorf Villa

Claudio Silvestrin

Location: Majorca, Spain. **Date of construction**: 1988–1991. **Client**: Hans and Carolie Neuendorf. **Architects**:
Claudio Silvestrin. **Associates**: Tietz & Partners (engineering), J. Salis Construcciones (construction).
Photography: Marco de Valdivia.

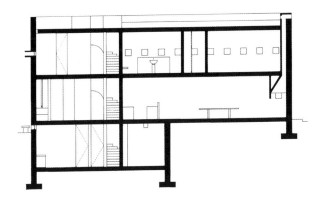

sense of emotion and dynamic energy to the whole complex. The structural forms and limits are a clear manifestation of the minimalist language of the project. Free of any element alien to the spiritual essence of the building, the ideas of space, light, and freedom have full rein.

The house is made of natural local materials. As a response to the arid and reddish surroundings, the walls are practically bare, with vertical clefts echoing the scoring of the ground and the interplay of light and shadow created by the slender trees which surround the building. The house was not designed to be directly accessible by car. The country lane which approaches the site leads to a shady parking area, from which a ramp 110 m (120 yds) in length rises to the villa. The swimming pool is designed to be an extension of the structure, with a length of nearly 40 m (44 yds) but a width of just 3.4 m (3.7 yds.) Despite the simplicity of the building's design, with

its tendency towards cubic shapes, each of the four façades offers a specific and individual aspect to the outside. After passing through the narrow hollow which gives access to the building, an interior patio measuring 12 x 12 m (39 x 39 ft) appears, around which the body of the villa extends in the shape of an L. Simple rectangular apertures, in generous dimensions, provide entry to the basic elements of the building, set out on two stories. The first floor contains the household areas, and the bedrooms and associated facilities are located on the upper floor. The movement of the light over the upper areas and rooms creates dramatic visual effects, and adds a

Single family homes by the sea

The environment has a profound influence on human development, to the degree that every site has its own territorial spirit. A good house needs to be in tune with, and provide a direct response to, not only the climate and other environmental conditions of the area in which it is located, but also the traditional way of life of the inhabitants. The coastline is characterized in minute detail by its highly significant geographical and social diversity; this means it is impossible to generalize about a shoreline, and it is far better to make a more specific and detailed study of small stretches. This section considers schemes which are located in an environment which is both beautiful and unique the seashore. These are buildings which engage in dialogs with the landscape that are especially interesting, a landscape which is constantly different, and constantly changing. And, in addition to their residential function and their vacation and leisure use, the frontage to the beach provides the ideal environment to escape the noise and stress of the big city.

Extension to the Neutra House

Steven Ehrlich Architects

Location: Santa Monica, California, USA. **Date of construction**: 1996–1998. **Architects**: Steven Ehrlich Architects. **Scheme**: Extension/annex to a single family home. **Photography**: Tom Bonner.

The Lewin residence in Santa Monica was designed by Richard Neutra in 1938. It is located at the foot of a rocky outcrop on the beach, and initially occupied an area of 550 m² (5900 ft²). The present owners wished to add a leisure area to this, with a swimming pool, an extension to the garage, and areas for services. To cut out the noise from the adjacent highway, Steven Ehrlich opted to locate the new garage and the service areas in such a way as to form an effective noise barrier. This arrangement creates a first patio common to both sections of the building, while the second patio encountered on the way from the road also has the original Neutra House as a backdrop, and establishes a visual link between the old living room and the new pavilion structure which accommodates the leisure facilities. A glazed bridge element crosses this outside space to connect the two areas. The meticulous care and attention, both in general planning as well as in detail, make this a residential project unique in terms of comfort as well as elegance of style.

House at Sag Pond

Mario Gandelsonas, Diana Agrest

Location: Sagaponack, Southampton, New York, USA. **Date of construction**: 1989-1992. **Client**: Richard Ekstract. **Architects**: Mario Gandelsonas, Diana Agrest. **Associates**: Wal-Siskind (interiors); Claire Weisz (architectural plan); Tom Bader, Peter Frank, Maurice Harwell, Thomas Kalin (consultants); Robert Silman Associates (structural engineering); David Dominsky (contractor). **Photography**: Paul Warchol.

The house, surrounded by fields, consists of six towers connected by bridges, spanning a void some 33 m (108 ft) in length facing north. The void accommodates the communal areas of the building, while the bridges and towers contain the private rooms, in two independent wings. One wing, facing south, houses the main bathroom and the master suite; the other, facing north, contains the bedrooms, which have independent stairways for guests. The formal structure of the building is developed over the width of these two geometric forms, the juncture of which creates the triangular shape of the hall, incurring a reverse perspective distortion of the stairways and imposing torsion on the parabola of the roof. This movement in turn affects the structure of the chimneys and the storeroom which separates the principal spaces and communal areas of the void. The cylindrical greenhouse structure is the only tower of which the structure is composed of vertical steel columns and timber rings.

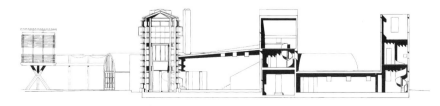

Cashman House

Ed Lippmann

Location: Sidney, Australia. **Date of construction:** 1996. **Architect:** Ed Lippmann. **Associates:** O. Arup (engineering). **Scheme:** Single family home. **Area:** 200 m². **Photography:** Peter Hyatt.

This house was built for a family who wanted to spend their weekends and summer vacations away from the big city. The site is located on a beach which is difficult to access, and is surrounded by thick vegetation that forms part of a nature reserve.
A geotechnical survey indicated that the structure ought to be very light: this is an area prone to torrential rainfall, its soil of very low consolidation and with serious erosion problems. The building was constructed with a light metallic structure and a cladding of undulating metal sheeting.
The house was designed as an open pavilion, with substantial glazing, almost as if it were a large covered terrace. The living area is divided into two parts, one of a single floor which accommodates the communal areas (living room, dining room, and kitchen), and one of two stories, containing the bedrooms and bathrooms.

House at Capistrano

Rob Wellington Quigley

Location: Capistrano Beach, California, USA. **Date of construction**: 1994. **Architect**: Rob Wellington Quigley. **Associates**: T. Cruz, C. Herbst, M. Falcone. **Scheme**: Single family home, kitchen garden, garage. **Photography**: Undine Pröhl.

Capistrano Beach is a locality on the coast of California where a series of single family houses have been constructed on the shoreline, above the sand of the beach itself. They form a gathering of individual fragments, a discontinuous formation spread over the uniformity of the beach. Their architecture is narrative and figurative, and, at the same time, abstract; this paradox and sense of dissonance are their essential aesthetic strategy. This complex of juxtapositions, tensions, and integrated fragmentation creates a difficult final unity, but nevertheless a unity which is capable of forming its spaces into a coherent whole. The faces, to the east and west, form parallel surfaces which contain the mass of the residential section. On the north and south faces, these rigid planes become blurred and at some points open to reveal the interior, such that the sea winds through the openings and domestic life overflows to the beach beneath. This house is a sensitive sequence of spaces with widely differing dimensions, different ways of obtaining light, and contrasting stylistic points of reference.

Schnabel House

Frank O. Gehry

Location: Los Angeles, California, USA. **Date of construction**: 1987–1989. **Architect**: Frank O. Gehry. **Photography**: Mark Darley

the west, a slender prism-shaped extension has been built outwards, which accommodates the garage. Above this is another smaller structure, arranged around the axis of the first, which houses the services; to connect this module to the kitchen,

Gehry has provided an arcaded gallery, supported by columns with cladding of natural copper and passing over part of the landscaped area.

The site provided for the building is a large plot of somewhat dull topographic features, a rectangular area which ended in an irregular trapezoidal area, approached by a descent in level to create an area of greater privacy in relation to the building's surroundings.

On the lower level, the main section of the rectangular site contains the kitchen, a split-level living room with central ceiling lighting, and a small studio. On the upper floor there are two bedrooms with en suite bathrooms, arranged around the structural void created at that level by the living room.

The appearance of the outside is characterized by a simple steel-gray stucco effect on the walls.

In the site access area, to

House in Venice

Antoine Predock

Location: Venice, California, USA. **Date of construction**: 1990. **Architect**: Antoine Predock. **Photography**: Timothey Hursley.

bathroom and dressing room, and a large terrace from which a stairway leads to a solarium. The most impressive aspect of this house is the use of materials and techniques, which reflect the actual use of the different areas, where ceramics in dark colours are combined with moquette floorings of natural materials, and the use of the water, in such a way that the image produced is always present but remains inverted.

A retaining wall with black granite facing, over which the water flows, is the only element which separates the building from the public highway. The sash window, with a red metal frame, located at the end of the axis of the building, pivots horizontally and forms an opening 33 cm (13 in) high with views of the ocean. Inside the building, areas illuminated by natural light combine with those of diffused lighting provided by a system of concealed glass panes.

This house, built right on the edge of the beach, is mounted on a rectangular base and extends over three separate floors. A basement, at ground level and partially concealed by concrete walls, serves as a garage and area for services. The first floor accommodates a spacious living room, the dining room, and the kitchen; the other wing contains a studio room and a bathroom. The top floor is the location for the bedrooms, the largest of them with an en suite

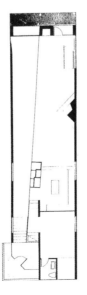

Villangómez House

Salvador Roig, F. J. Pallejà, J.A Martínez Lopeña, Elías Torres

Location: Ibiza, Spain. **Date of construction**: 1988–1990. **Clients**: Mariano and Alejandro Villangómez.
Architects: Salvador Roig, F.J. Pallejà, J.A. Martínez Lopeña, Elias Torres. **Photography**: Hisao Suzuki

The scheme for the building is conventional: a single family house with three bedrooms and an interior patio, the various sections of which are intended to merge as harmoniously as possible with the surrounding landscape, as well as providing interior light. The structure can be divided into two blocks of prismatic design, which are laid out essentially in an L shape. The intersection element between these blocks is oblique, triangular in shape, and intended to define an internal space facing the sea which acts as a patio and, at the same time, establishes and arranges the physical and visual communications of the entire structure. To provide the essential sense of intimacy, the architects have made use of two strategies: firstly, both the house and the patio are elevated some 60 cm (2 ft) above the natural ground level, so as to exploit to the full the views of the outside; and, secondly, the open section of the patio facing the sea is delimited by sketching out a series of open and unconnected facings between which the surrounding landscape can be glimpsed, as well as the permanent view of the sea, providing a vision from the terrace and the inside of the house of vertical fragments which then create one single horizontal reality. The house can be seen by passers-by between the trunks of the trees, as a fragmented vision, an impression which is heightened by the arrangement of different elevations, with specific solutions to suit the opposing landscape.

House on Lake Weyba

Gabriel Poole

Location: Noosa Heads, Australia. **Date of construction**: 1996. **Architect**: Gabriel Poole. **Associates**: Elisabeth Poole (design), Rod Bligh-Bligh Tanner (structural engineering), Barry Hamlet (aluminum). **Photography**: Peter Hyatt.

Poole arranged the space available into three separate and distinct pavilion structures, based on the life inside a residential house. Located at one end, the entrance element contains the kitchen, office, dining room, and living room-cum-studio. The area occupied can be doubled by extending the vinyl and steel panels and so creating a covered walkway area. The limits of the interior space can be constantly changed thanks to the use of movable interlocking elements and the enlargement of the floor surface beyond the line which delineates the structure. The second pavilion element houses the bathroom area, with shower and washroom sections. The colours of the individual facings contrast with the monochrome fiber-cement walls. The third pavilion is occupied by the main bedroom. The roof is the most immediately striking feature of the house; its polycarbonate cladding and its pitch, its edges, and its surrounds demonstrate clearly the way in which the residents face up to the elements.

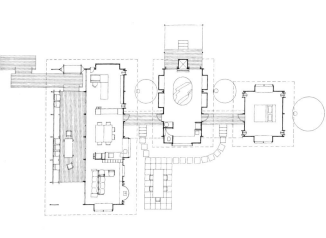

House in Sausalito

Mark Mack

Location: Sausalito, California, USA. **Date of construction**: 1987. **Architect**: Mark Mack.

This is a single family house which extends along the northwest axis of a site located on the crest of the Wolfback ridge in California, and is set in a landscape of exceptional beauty, offering simultaneously views of the Pacific Ocean and of San Francisco Bay.
The house is set on an irregular base, slightly curved, and extending over

two storys. The different parts of the building, separated according to their functions, are divided into the northern face, the public part of the building, closed and solid, and emphasized by the chamfered frames of the windows; and the south facing section, the private area, open and airy, with large windows and terraces giving dramatic views of the Bay and the Pacific.
In addition to this, the interior spaces are developed on both floors around the structure of the chimney, located at the epicentre of the structure, and which serves as both a functional element and a means of division.

Ackerberg House

Richard Meier

Location: Malibu, California, USA. **Date of construction**: 1986. **Architect**: Richard Meier.

Influenced by the traditional style of courtyards typical of Southern California, this house is located among the mountains extending alongside the coastal highway and the beach which borders the Pacific Ocean. The site chosen for the construction of the building consists of three flat areas and the adjacent plots, facing Malibu Beach. The building stands on an L-shaped base, and consists of two floors, the private family area and the living room area. Main access is from the north front, from where, passing through a covered walkway, a vestibule is reached with floors set at different levels, and surfaces set with glass.

This area leads on to the living room, the dining room, the kitchen and the bathrooms, the interior courtyard, and the guest rooms. Going up the stairs to the second floor, which is linked to the first floor by means of the open space of the living room, we come upon a suspended shelving area opening onto the lower level. A number of rooms and a suite with dressing room and washroom complete the basic ground plan. This free spatial sequence is supplemented by a tennis court already in place in the southern section, and a recently constructed swimming pool on the west side.

The World of Contemporary Architecture

Project Management: Arco Editorial, S.A., Barcelona, Spain
Author: Francisco Asensio Cerver
Editor: Paco Asensio
Design: Mireia Casanovas Soley
Layout: Ricardo Álvarez, Jaume Martínez Coscojuela, Emma Termes Parera
Language Editing: Paco Asensio, Ivan Bercedo, Aurora Cuito
Front Cover: © Mitsuo Matsuoka, Shigeo Ogawa
Back Cover: (from top to bottom) © Juri Havran, © Eugeni Pons, © Sasaki
and Associates, © Eugeni Pons

Original Title: *Atlas de arquitectura actual,* Francisco Asensio Cerver
ISBN 978-3-8331-1769-5

Copyright © 2005/2007 for this English edition:
Tandem Verlag GmbH
h.f.ullmann is an imprint of Tandem Verlag GmbH

Translation from Spanish: G. Bickford, M. McMeekin, M. Reece and
S. Wiles in association with First Edition Translations
English Language Editing: Kay Hyman in association with First Edition
Translations
Typesetting: The Write Idea in association with First Edition Translations
Project Management: Beatrice Hunt for First Edition Translations,
Cambridge, UK
Project Coordination: Nadja Bremse
Cover Design: Oliver Hessmann

Printed in China

ISBN 978-3-8331-4638-1

10 9 8 7 6 5 4 3 2 1
X IX VIII VII VI V IV III II I

The World of Contemporary Architecture

Francisco Asensio Cerver

*h.f.*ullmann

THE

ROBYN GRADY

RULES

ELLE KENNEDY

OF

JENNIFER LOHMANN

PLAY

MILLS & BOON

CONTENTS

The Fearless Maverick
Robyn Grady

One Christmas long ago, **ROBYN GRADY** received a book from her big sister and immediately fell in love with the story of Cinderella. Sprinklings of magic, deepest wishes come true—she was hooked! Picture books with glass slippers later gave way to romance novels and, more recently, the real-life dream of writing for Harlequin Books.

After a fifteen-year career in television, Robyn met her own modern-day hero. They live on Australia's Sunshine Coast, with their three little princesses, two poodles and a cat called Tinkie. She loves new shoes, worn jeans, lunches at Moffat Beach and hanging out with her friends at www.millsandboon.com.au. Learn about her latest releases at www.robyngrady.com and don't forget to say hi. She'd love to hear from you!

CHAPTER ONE

THE MOMENT ALEX WOLFE'S car went airborne, he knew the situation was bad. That's 'serious injury' or possibly even 'get ready to meet your maker' bad.

He'd been approaching the chicane at the end of a straight at Melbourne's premier motor racing circuit and, misjudging his breaking point, he'd gone into the first turn too deep. He'd tried to drive through the corner but when the wheels had aquaplaned on standing water, he'd slid out and slammed into a tyre stack wall, which provided protection not only for runaway cars and their drivers but also for crowds congregated behind the guard rail.

Like a stone spat from a slingshot, he'd ricocheted off the rubber and back into the path of the oncoming field. He didn't see what happened next but, from the almighty *whack* that had spun him out of control, Alex surmised another car had T-boned his.

Now, as he sliced through space a metre above the ground, time seemed to slow to a cool molasses crawl as snapshots from the past flickered and flashed through his mind. Anticipating the colossal *slam* of impact, Alex cursed himself for being a fool. World Number One three seasons running—some said the best there'd ever been—and he'd broken racing's cardinal rule. He'd let his concentration slip. Allowed personal angst to impair his judgement and screw with his performance. The news he'd received an hour before climbing into the cockpit had hit him that hard.

After nearly twenty years, Jacob was back?

Now Alex understood why his twin sister had persisted in trying to contact him these past weeks. He'd been thrown when he'd received her first email and had held off returning Annabelle's messages for precisely this reason. He couldn't afford to get wound up and distracted by—

Driving down a breath, Alex thrust those thoughts aside.

He simply couldn't get distracted, is all.

With blood thumping like a swelling ocean in his ears, Alex gritted his teeth and strangled the wheel as the 420-kilo missile pierced that tyre wall. An instant later, he thudded to a jarring halt and darkness, black as the apocalypse, enveloped him. Momentum demanded he catapult forward but body and helmet harnesses kept him strapped—or was that *trapped*?—inside. Wrenched forward, Alex felt his right shoulder click and bleed with pain that he knew would only get worse. He also knew he should get out fast. Their fuel tanks rarely ruptured and fire retardant suits were a wonderful thing; however, nothing stopped a man from roasting alive should his car happen to go up in flames.

Entombed beneath the weight of the tyres, Alex fought the overwhelming urge to try to punch through rubber and drag himself free, but disorientated men were known to stagger into the path of oncoming cars. Even if he *could* claw his way out, procedure stated rescue teams assist or, at the least, supervise occupants from any wreck.

Holding his injured arm, Alex cursed like he'd never

cursed before. Then he squinted through the darkness and, in a fit of frustration, roared out in self-disgust.

'Can we try that again? I know I can cock up more if I really set my mind to it!'

Claustrophobic seconds crept by. Gritting his teeth, Alex concentrated on the growl of V8s whizzing past, rather than the growing throb in his shoulder. Then a different group of engines sped up—medical response units. Surrounded by the smell of fumes and rubber and his own sweat, Alex exhaled a shuddery breath. Motor racing was a dangerous sport. One of the *most* dangerous. But the monumental risks associated with harrowing speeds were also the ultimate thrill and the only life to which Alex had ever wanted to ascribe. Racing not only gave him immense pleasure, it also provided the supreme means of escape. God knows there'd been plenty to run from growing up at Wolfe Manor.

The muffled cries of track marshals filtered through and Alex came back to the present as a crane went to work. Bound stacks of tyres were removed and soon shafts of light broke through.

A marshal, in his bright orange suit, poked his head in. 'You all right?'

'I'll live.'

The marshal had already removed the steering wheel and was assessing what he could of the car's warped safety cell. 'We'll have you out in a minute.'

To face a barrage of questions? The humiliation? And at some stage he'd have to tackle that other problem, which had set off this whole shambles.

'No chance of leaving me here, I suppose.'

The marshal took in Alex's sardonic smile and sent a consoling look. 'There'll be more races, son.'

Alex set his jaw. *Damn right there will be.*

The Jaws of Life arrived. Soon, sure hands were assisting him out and a world of fire-tipped arrows shot through that injured joint. Biting down, Alex edged out of the debris aware of fans' applause resonating around the park. He let go supporting his right arm long enough to salute to the cheering crowd before sliding into a response unit.

Minutes later, inside the medical tent and out of his helmet and suit, Alex rested back on a gurney. Morrissey, the team doctor, checked out his shoulder, applied a cold press, then searched for signs of concussion and other injuries. Morrissey was serving up something for the pain and inflammation when team owner, Jerry Squires, strode in.

The son of a British shipping tycoon, Jerry had lost an eye as a child and was well known for the black patch he wore. He was better known, however, for his staggering wealth and no-nonsense attitude. Today, with his usually neat steel-grey hair mussed, Jerry spoke in gravelled tones to the doctor.

'What's the worst?'

'He'll need a complete physical evaluation… X-rays and MRI,' Morrissey replied, his glasses slipping to the tip of his nose as he scribbled notes on a clipboard. 'He's sustained a subluxation to his right shoulder.'

Jerry sucked air in between his teeth. 'Second race of the season. At least we still have Anthony.'

At the mention of his team's second driver, Alex pushed to sit up. Everyone was jumping the gun! He wasn't out of the game yet.

But then the pain in that joint flared and burned like Hades. Breaking into a fresh sweat, he rested back on the elevated pillows and managed to put on his no-problem smile, the one that worked a charm on beautiful women and bristling billionaires.

'Hey, settle down, Jer. You heard the man. It's not serious. Nothing's broken.'

The doctor lowered his clipboard enough for Alex to catch the disapproving angle of his brows. 'That's still to be determined.'

A pulse beat in Jerry's clean-shaven jaw. 'I appreciate your glass-half-full attitude, champ, but this is no time for a stiff upper lip.' Jerry glanced out the window and scowled at the churning weather. 'We should've gone with wets.'

Alex flinched, and not from physical pain. In hindsight, granted, he should have opted for wet-weather tyres. He'd explained his rationale to the team earlier when other pit crews were changing over. Now he'd reiterate for the man who forked over multiple millions to have him race as lead driver.

'The rain had stopped ten minutes before the race began,' Alex said, feeling Morrissey's eagle eye pressing him to button up and rest. 'The track was drying off. If I could make it through the first few laps—get a dry line happening— I'd be eating up the k's while everyone else would be stuck in the pits changing back to slicks.'

Jerry grunted again, unconvinced. 'You needed extra traction going into that chicane. Simple fact is, you called it wrong.'

Alex ground his back teeth against a natural urge to argue. He hadn't called it wrong...but he had made a fatal error. His mind hadn't been one hundred percent on the job. If it *had* been, he'd have aced that chicane *and* the race. Hell, anyone could drive in the dry; handling wet conditions was where a driver's ability, experience and instinct shone through. And usually where Alex Wolfe excelled. He'd worked bloody hard to get where he was today—at the top—which was a far cry from the position he'd once filled: a delinquent who'd longed to flee that grotesquely elaborate, freakishly unhappy English manor that still sat on the outskirts of Oxfordshire.

But he'd left those memories behind.

Or he had until receiving those emails.

While Jerry, Morrissey and a handful of others conversed out of earshot, Alex mulled over his sister's message. Annabelle had said Wolfe Manor had been declared a dangerous structure by the council and Jacob had returned to reinstate the house and grounds to their former infamous glory. Images of those centuries-old corridors and chunky dusty furniture came to mind, and Alex swore he could smell the dank and sour bouquet of his father's favourite drop. The veil between then and now thinned more and he heard his father's drunken ravings. Felt the slap of that belt on his skin.

Clamping his eyes shut, Alex shook off the revulsion. As the eldest, Jacob had inherited that mausoleum but, if it'd been left to him, Alex would gladly have bulldozed the lot.

Still, there'd been some good times as kids growing up. Alex had surrendered to a smile when Annabelle's email also mentioned that Nathaniel, the youngest of the Wolfe clan—or of the legitimate children, at least—was tying the knot. A talent behind the lens for many years now, Annabelle was to be the official photographer. Alex had followed recent news of his actor brother in the papers…the night Nathaniel had walked out on his stage debut in the West End had caused a terrific stir. Then had come his Best Actor win last month in LA.

Alex absently rubbed his shoulder.

Little brother was all grown up, successful and apparently in love. Made him realise how much time had passed. How scattered they all were. He best remembered Nathaniel when he was little more than a skinny kid finding his own form of escape through entertaining his siblings, even at the expense of a backhand or two from the old man.

Voices filtered in and Alex's thoughts jumped back. Across the room it seemed Jerry and Morrissey had finished their powwow and were ready to join him again.

His eyebrows knitted, the doctor removed his glasses. 'I'll attempt to reduce that joint now. The sooner it's intact again, the better. We're organising transport to Windsor Private for those follow-up tests.'

'And when the tests come back?' Alex asked.

'There'll be discussions with specialists to ascertain whether surgery's needed—'

Alex's pulse rate spiked. '*Whoa*. Slow down. Surgery?'

'—*or* more likely some rest combined with a rehabilitation plan. It's not the first time this has happened. That shoulder's going to need some time,' Morrissey said, tapping his glasses at the air to help make his point. 'Don't fool yourself it won't.'

'So long as I'm back in the cockpit in time to qualify in Malaysia.'

'Next weekend?' Morrissey headed for his desk. 'Sorry, but you can forget about that.'

Ignoring the twist of fresh pain, Alex propped up on his left elbow and forced a wry laugh. 'I think I'm the best judge of whether I'm fit to drive or not.'

'Like you judged which tyres to kick off the race?'

Alex slid a look over to Jerry Squires at the same time

his neck went hot and a retort burned to break free. But no good would come from indulging his temper when the frustration roiling inside of him should be directed at no one other than himself. No matter which way you sliced it, he'd messed up. Now, like it or not, he needed to knuckle down and play ball...but only for a finite period and largely on his own terms. Because make no mistake—if he had to miss the next race, he'd be in Shanghai for Round Four if it killed him.

First up he'd need to shake any press off his tail. After such a spectacular crash, questions regarding injuries and how they might impact on his career would be rife. The photographer jackals would be on the prowl, desperate to snap the shot of the season—the Fangio of his time, the great Alex Wolfe, grimacing in pain, his arm useless in a sling. Damned if he'd let the paparazzi depict him as a pitiful invalid.

Privacy was therefore a priority. Any recuperating would happen at his reclusive Rose Bay residence in Sydney. He'd source a professional who understood and valued the unique code elite athletes lived by. Someone who was exceptional at their work but who might also appreciate a lopsided grin or possibly an invitation to dinner when he was next in town, in exchange for which she would provide the medical all clear needed to get him back behind the wheel in time for Round Four qualifying.

As the painkiller kicked in and the screaming in his shoulder became more a raw groan, Alex closed his eyes and eased back against the gurney.

When his shoulder was popped back in and those initial tests were out of the way, he'd set his assistant, Eli Steele, on the case. He needed to find the right physiotherapist for the job. And he needed to find her fast. He'd lost far too much in his life.

God help him, he wasn't losing this.

CHAPTER TWO

AS HER CAR cruised up a tree-lined drive belonging to one of the most impressive houses she'd ever seen, Libby Henderson blew the long bangs off her brow and again spooled through every one of her *'I can do this'* and *'There's nothing to be nervous about'* affirmations.

As her stomach churned, Libby recalled how not so long ago she'd been a supremely self-confident type. Nothing had frightened her. Nothing had held her back. That verve had propelled her to dizzy heights—a place where she'd felt secure and alive and even admired. Twice Female World Surfing Champion. There were times she still couldn't believe that fabulous ride had ended the way it had.

From an early age she'd taken to the surf. Libby's parents had always referred to her as their little mermaid. Growing up she'd trained every minute she could grab—kayaking, swimming, body surfing, as well as honing her skills on a board. Nothing had felt better than the endorphins and burn she'd got from pushing beyond her limits.

Being a world champion had been the ultimate buzz—fabulous sponsors, high-end magazine spreads, the chance to speak with and even coach youngsters eager to surf their way up through the ranks. Out ahead, for as far as she could see, the horizon shone with amazing possibilities. Her accident had changed that.

But, thankfully, there'd been a life after celebrity and elite athlete status, just a different life. When she'd overcome the worst of her accident, she'd thrown herself into the study she'd previously set aside and had attained a Bachelor of Health Sciences in Physiotherapy at Sydney's Bond University. She was beyond grateful her determination and hard work was paying off—today better than she'd ever dreamed.

As she swerved around the top end of the drive now, Libby recalled this morning's unexpected phone call. None other than Alex Wolfe, the British-born motor racing champ who'd come to grief at the weekend, had requested her services. Mr Wolfe's assistant, an efficient-sounding man by the name of Eli Steele, had relayed that he and Mr Wolfe had researched specialists in her profession extensively and had decided that her credentials best suited Mr Wolfe's current needs with regard to the shoulder injury he'd sustained. Libby had to wonder precisely what credentials Eli referred to.

She worked almost exclusively with injured athletes but she'd never treated anyone near as renowned as this man. Perhaps Alex Wolfe, or his assistant, was aware of her former life, Libby surmised, slotting the auto shift into park and shutting down the engine. But had they dug deep enough to unearth how the final chapter of that part of her life had ended?

After opening the car door, Libby swung her legs out. Pushing to her feet, she surveyed the magnificent ultramodern home as well as the surrounding pristine lawns and gardens. Rendered white with ultramarine and hardwood trims, the Rose Bay double-storey mansion spanned almost the entire width of the vast block. She imagined numerous bedrooms, each with their own en suite and spa bath. An indoor heated pool would provide luxurious laps during winter while an Olympic-size outdoor pool with trickling water features and, perhaps, a man-made beach would be the go during Sydney's often scorching summer months.

Straightening the jacket of her cream and black-trim pants-suit, Libby craned her neck. A grand forecourt, decorated with trellised yellow-bell jasmine and topiaries set in waist-high terracotta pots, soared around her. Her eyes drifting shut, she inhaled nature's sweet perfume and hummed out a sigh. In her sporting heyday, she'd earned good money but nothing compared with this unabashed show of wealth. Of course, the lucrative runoffs from the Alex Wolfe range of aftershave, clothing and computer games would contribute handsomely to his fortune. Charm, money, movie-star looks. Hell, Alex Wolfe had it all.

A thoroughly sexy voice, with a very posh English accent, broke into her thoughts.

'I agree. It's a cracking day. Perhaps we ought to chat out here.'

It started in her belly…a pleasant tingling heat that flooded her body in the same instant her eyes snapped wide open. On that extensive front patio, directly in front of her, stood a man. *The* man.

Alex Wolfe.

An embarrassing eternity passed before her stunned brain swam to the surface. Frankly, she'd never experienced a sight—a *vision*—quite like the one openly assessing her now. His lopsided grin was lazy, carving attractive grooves either side of a spellbinding mouth. His hair was a stylishly messy dark blond, the length of which curled off the collar of a teal-coloured polo shirt. And what about those shoulders! Mouthwateringly broad. Ubermasculine.

And let's not forget, Libby warned herself, sucking down a breath, the *only* reason she was here.

Stopping long enough to think about which foot to put forward first, Libby pinned on a warm but businesslike smile and moved to join her newest client, whom, she noticed now, also wore a navy blue immobiliser sling.

'I believe you were expecting me. I'm Libby Henderson. I was just admiring your home and gardens.'

He surveyed the vast front lawns and nodded as a gentle harbour breeze lifted dark blond hair off his brow. 'I always enjoy my stints in Australia,' he said. 'The weather's brilliant.' Gorgeous soft grey eyes hooked back onto hers as he cocked his head. 'I'd offer you my hand but...'

'Your right shoulder's giving you problems.'

'Nothing too serious,' he said, stepping aside to welcome her in.

Entering the foyer, which gave the modest size of her Manly apartment a decent run for its money, Libby considered his last comment. If Mr Wolfe's injury had been enough to land him in hospital and warrant subsequent intensive treatment ordered by his team doctor, clearly it was serious enough. Her job was to make certain that full range of motion and strength returned and, despite any downplaying on his part, that's precisely what she intended to do. Men like Alex Wolfe wanted to get back to it, and *now*. She understood that. Unfortunately, however, sometimes that wasn't possible.

Forcing herself not to gape at the storybook multi-tiered staircase or the mirror-polished marble floors, Libby instead turned to her host as he closed the twelve-foot-high door. She suppressed a wry grin. Must be the butler's day off.

'Can I offer you a refreshment, Ms Henderson?'

As he passed to lead her through the spacious white, almost austere vestibule, Libby's thoughts stuck on what should have been a simple question. But his tone implied that rather than coffee, any refreshment he offered might include something as social as champagne.

'I'm fine, thank you,' she replied, unable to keep her gaze from straying to the fluid style of his gait in those delectable custom-made black trousers as he moved off. Would he detect any peculiarities in her stride if their positions were reversed—she in front, he behind? But surely a man who'd dated supermodels and at least one European princess wouldn't be interested enough to notice.

'We'll talk in the sunroom.' Stopping before a set of double doors, he fanned open one side and she moved through.

After he'd closed this door too, he headed for a U-shaped group of three snowy-white leather couches. Beyond soaring arched windows sat that magnificent outdoor pool she'd imagined as well as a glamorous spa and stylish white wicker setting. A pool house, which mimicked the main building's design, looked large enough to accommodate a family of four as well as friends. Positioned beyond the pool area was a massive storage block—she suspected a huge garage. All the world knew Mr Wolfe liked his cars.

He gestured to the closest couch. 'Please make yourself comfortable.'

Libby lowered back against the cushions and set her feet neatly together. Rather than taking up position on the opposite couch, Alex Wolfe settled down alongside of her. A flush crept up her neck and lit her cheeks. This man's magnetism was a tangible, remarkable thing. His proximity to her on this couch couldn't be deemed as inappropriate—at least an arm's length separated them—and yet she couldn't ignore the *pull*. Not that Mr Wolfe would purposely be sending out those kinds of vibes. He was simply…well, he was only…

Oh, dammit, he was *sexy*—beyond anything she'd ever experienced before.

As a film of perspiration cooled her nape, Libby edged an inch away while, holding the sling's elbow, Alex stretched his legs out and crossed his ankles. His feet were large, the shoes Italian. She noticed those things nowadays.

'So, Ms Henderson, what do you have for me?'

'I've studied the MRI scans,' she began, her gaze tracing the line of that sling, 'as well as the orthopaedic surgeon's report outlining the details of the injury. Seems your shoulder didn't suffer a complete dislocation, but rather a subluxation. Do you know what that means?'

'My shoulder didn't pop completely.'

She nodded. 'In layman's terms, that's precisely it.'

When that amazing subtle smile lighting his eyes touched his mouth, Libby's tummy fluttered and she cleared her throat. *Yes, he's an incredibly attractive man but, for God's sake, concentrate!* Her goal here wasn't to get all starry-eyed but to have Alex Wolfe walk away from this episode fully recovered and bursting with glowing reports of her services. Hopefully, then, more of his ilk would follow and her reputation in her present career would be secured.

When she'd returned to her studies, she'd decided she wanted to work with elite athletes, that special breed that needed someone who not only understood how their bodies worked but also their minds, and who were prepared to do whatever it took to get back on top. Libby only wished she'd been given that option.

Centring her attention again, she threaded her fingers and set them on her lap. 'Your medical records outline ligament damage to that shoulder in your teens.'

His eyes clouded over for an instant, so stormy and distant she might have mentioned the devil. But then his smile returned, and more hypnotic than before.

'I came off a motorbike.'

She nodded. A natural thrillseeker, of course he'd have started out on two wheels. 'I see.'

'Do you like motor sports?'

'I was more a water girl.'

'Swimming? Skiing?'

That flush returned, a hot rash creeping over the entire length of her body. Feeling colour soak into her cheeks, she glanced down, unclasped her hands and smoothed the centre creases of her trousers. They weren't here to discuss her history.

'I have another appointment this afternoon, so perhaps we'd best stay on point.'

His gaze sharpened, assessing her, and he sat back. 'I imagine your practice keeps you busy, Ms Henderson.'

'Busy enough.'

'But not on weekends.'

'I work some Saturdays.'

'Not Sundays?'

She blinked. 'You think you'll need me Sundays too?'

'Let's make it every weekday for now.'

'Much of the work you can do without my help. Every second day would be sufficient.'

'Every week day,' he reiterated before smiling again.

'Don't worry, Ms Henderson. I promise my current predicament is extremely short-term.'

Libby's breath left her lungs in a quiet rush. This man was a living legend. Revered by millions all over the world. He was the sporting hero that boys chasing one another in parks pretended to be. Was he being intentionally snide? Or just plain 'I am invincible' arrogant? Libby knew better than most.

No one was invincible.

'We were discussing your previous injury,' she went on in an implacable tone, 'which could well have made you more susceptible to subsequent injuries. Let me explain.' She shifted back against the cushions. 'A joint dislocation, or *luxation* from the Latin, occurs when bones that join become displaced or misaligned usually through a sudden impact. The joint capsule, cartilage and ligaments become damaged. A subluxation, as occurred in your situation, Mr Wolfe, is a partial dislocation, which can occur as a result of previous damage to the surrounding structures of the shoulder. Either way there will be a weakening of the muscles and ligaments which need physiotherapy to help stabilise the joint.'

He was looking at her, his head slightly angled, a peculiar, flattering gleam in his eyes.

'I see.'

She held her breath against an unbidden flare of emotion, cleared her throat and focused again. 'With your hands on the wheel, the impact from the accident jarred your right humerus, which then sat anteriorly from the—'

His deep soft laugh interrupted her. 'Rewind a little, doc.'

'I'm not a doctor.' She wanted to be clear on her qualifications. 'I have a Bachelor of Health Sciences with honours and am a member of the Australian Physiotherapy Association.'

'And for now you are the lady who holds my future in the palm of her hand. I'll call you "doc." With your permission, of course.'

Libby stiffened. Talk about pressure. But then, he was paying the bill. She gave a hesitant half-shrug.

'I suppose…if it makes you feel more comfortable.'

His gaze dipped to her lips, then caught her eyes again. 'So—*doc*—you were saying.'

'Your humerus—' She stopped and bunched one hand to demonstrate. 'The *ball* slid partially out of its joint and needed to be manipulated back into the centre of your glenoid cavity, or socket.' She cupped her palm, pushed her fist in and locked the 'ball,' then disengaged it again.

'Right. The ball—' his own hand bunched '—goes into the socket.' He fit his big hard hot fist inside her still-elevated palm.

At the instant of contact, Libby's internal alarm blared and she jerked away.

Their eyes locked—his questioning, hers, she knew, wide and exposed. That tingling in her belly had intensified and the suddenly sensitive tips of her breasts tightened and ached.

But when one corner of his mouth hooked up the barest amount, Libby was brought back. As casually as possible, she scooped some hair behind an ear and willed her cantering heartbeat to slow. Crazy to even consider but…

Was he *flirting* with her? She couldn't be sure. He was a superstar and…

It'd been such a long time.

Her last intimate relationship had ended four months after

her accident. She'd thought fellow pro surfer Scott Wilkinson had been the sexist man alive, but Scott was an amateur compared to Alex Wolfe. This man's power to captivate with a simple look, the slightest touch, was palpable. She'd like to meet the woman who was immune to the magic of that smile. Charm was as instinctive to this man as his taking a corner at death-defying speeds. That wasn't to imply he would in any way be interested in checking her track out, so to speak.

More to the point, *she* wasn't interested in a quick spin with him either.

Schooling her features, Libby straightened her spine and focused on business. 'We'll need to concentrate on a series of strengthening rehabilitative exercises.'

'Sounds good.'

'When would you like to begin, Mr Wolfe?'

'Call me Alex.'

A perfectly reasonable request, she decided, noticing how his grey eyes seemed to sparkle at her nod of accent. 'What if I set up a timetable—?'

'I thought we could start tomorrow.'

'Tomorrow's fine.' Her voice lowered to a serious note. 'I'm sure I don't have to tell you that we'll need to work hard. Consistently.'

'I've no doubt you'll bring me through in time.'

Frowning, she cast her mind back. Had she overlooked something?

'In time for what?'

'I'll miss Round Three this weekend.' A muscle in his cheek flexed twice. 'Can't be helped, I'm afraid. Round Four's three weeks subsequent to that.'

Libby almost laughed. He was joking. But while his expression might be relaxed, the set of his square jaw was firm. He'd never been more serious in his life.

'I was told you'd been declared unfit by your team's doctor to drive professionally for at least six weeks.'

'We'll prove him wrong.'

She sat forward. He should be set straight.

'Your trackside physician wasn't able to perform the reduction. As you'd have been told many times now, delay can cause complications. An axial view showed stripping of the inferior glenoid and rotator cuff tearing...'

Her words dropped away as any patience she'd seen in his eyes on the subject cooled.

'My assistant informs me,' he said, 'that your clients think you perform miracles.'

'I'm not a saint, Mr Wolfe.'

'*Alex*. And, believe me, I'm not after a saint.'

His eyes smouldered and that hot pulse in her belly squeezed and sizzled. When the beating slid to a lower dangerous point, Libby pushed to her feet, too quickly as it turned out. She tipped to one side and threw out an arm to steady herself. But Alex Wolfe was already there, standing close, an arm circling her waist, his solid frame effortlessly providing the support she needed.

She was five-six, but she had to arc her neck way back to look into his face...which was a mistake. When those entrancing lidded eyes fused with hers, she imagined that his hold around her middle cinched, bringing her front to within a hair's-breadth of his...close to his chest...to those legs.

Giddy, she broke his hold and took two steps back.

As she willed the fire from her face and got herself together, he asked, 'Are you all right?'

'Perfectly. Thank you.' Shifting the bangs off her cheeks,

she gathered herself and resumed a businesslike air. 'I presume you know where my practice is.'

'All treatments will be conducted here.'

Her brows shot up. 'My equipment's at work.'

'I'll be honest.' His free hand slid into his trouser pocket and his legs braced wider apart. 'I'm concerned about the press. I have enough on my mind without watching out for headlines speculating on whether I'm a washed-up cripple.'

Her insides wrenching, Libby flinched.

In the second it took to compose her expression, Alex frowned as if he'd glimpsed and wondered at her lapse. With knees locked, she offered an indulgent smile.

'I understand you might want to shield yourself. But I'm afraid—'

'Everything you need will be brought in. I'll have my assistant organise it. And I'll double your fee to cover any inconvenience and time difficulties.'

She shut her dropped jaw.

Was she reading him right? *Double your fee...? We'll prove him wrong...? You'll bring me through...?* Did he think he could bribe her into cutting short his treatment so he could make his Round Four? Clearly Alex Wolfe wasn't familiar with the terms *caution* or *compromise*. He knew only one way to get things done. *His* way. If she didn't agree to his conditions—his offer—no doubt he'd find someone who would.

Which left her two choices.

She could bow to the inevitable, agree that all work be carried out on his private premises and take the fortune he offered as well as give the all clear when he deemed, whether he was fit to return to driving in her opinion or not. Or she could tell him she couldn't be manipulated by his charm or his pride. That her ethics were more important to her than money. More important than anything.

But there was a third option.

Decided, she looked him in the eye. 'I'll speak with your assistant. Get the ball rolling. We'll start tomorrow morning.'

A shadow swept over his expression, so fast she almost missed it. She recognised the emotion. Disappointment. He'd thought she'd put up more of a fight before capitulating to his terms, even for show's sake. Pity she couldn't set him straight, but that would come…when the time was right.

She headed for the door. 'I'll be back in the office in half an hour. Your assistant can call me any time after that.'

With long fluid strides he caught up, a satisfied smile tilting his lips. 'I do believe I'll enjoy working with you, doc.'

Doc. Walking side by side down the hall, Libby grinned.

'Perhaps I ought to wear a white coat and stethoscope when I call next,' she said, a slightly mocking edge to her voice.

'Feel free to wear whatever makes you comfortable. I will.'

'Oh, there won't be much need for clothes,' she said, stopping before the front doors. 'On your part, at least.'

His hold on the handle froze.

Swallowing the grin, she brushed his hand aside, opened the door and stepped out. 'See you tomorrow. Nine sharp.'

Walking away, she felt his surprise and curiosity drilling her back. But if her last comment was loosely inappropriate, she was okay with it. He'd needed to be pulled up and using his own level of language.

Alex Wolfe didn't know how well she understood his mind. She knew about burning passions. About setting a goal and never losing sight of it. She also knew how it felt to lose the capacity to chase and hold onto your dream. To have to reinvent yourself and leave that other more natural you behind.

Six weeks rehabilitation? Hell, Alex Wolfe didn't know how lucky he was.

But slow and steady won the race. *This* race anyway. She'd get him into a routine, he'd feel the positive results and when the time came she'd make him see how detrimental—possibly catastrophic—returning to the track too soon could be. Until then she'd be on her guard. She couldn't deny that those subtle looks, his unmistakable body language, his casual touch, affected her, and Alex knew it. He assumed he could manipulate her, charm her, perhaps even intimidate her into getting what he wanted.

Unfortunately for Alex Wolfe…not a chance.

Libby slid into the driver's seat. She was about to turn the ignition when her stomach twisted, like it had earlier when he'd tossed off that unconscious slap in the face. Her hand ran down her left thigh, over the patella. Then her fingertips traced the line where she and the lower limb prosthesis became one.

Washed-up cripple…

Long ago she had finished crying and asking herself, *What did I do to deserve this?* With the support of family, friends and professionals she'd moved from beneath those dark clouds of self-pity. Helping to rehabilitate others had brought new and worthwhile meaning to her life. But sitting here, remembering the gleam in Alex Wolfe's eyes when he'd looked at her that certain way, she couldn't mistake the pang in her chest or the choking thickness in her throat.

Her hand skimmed the shin she couldn't feel.

Would Alex Wolfe see her as less of a woman if he knew?

CHAPTER THREE

LEANING HIS GOOD shoulder against a patio column, Alex kept his eye on Libby Henderson's silver sedan as it looped the circular drive and headed out. An intrigued smile lifted one corner of his mouth.

Ms Henderson was an attractive prospect, particularly with those large amber-coloured eyes that seemed to both cloak her emotions as well as swirl with boundless possibilities. Her hair, which flowed past her shoulders in soft waves, was a captivating silvery blond, a consequence, no doubt, of a lifetime spent in Australia's surf-and-sun conditions. Of medium height, her lithe figure had curves in all the right places. If she'd tried to hide that fact beneath her designer business suit, she'd failed and she knew it.

Perhaps best of all, he thought as he watched her car disappear beyond the auto iron entry gates, Libby Henderson had spunk.

She'd as good as accepted his offer—to work here on him, *with* him. However, she'd let him know that he didn't intimidate her, even if they were aware of each other in a primal man-wants-woman way. When her palm had cupped his fist, she'd felt the zap as much as he had. But her comeback regarding the insignificance of what clothes he did or did not wear during their sessions had been priceless. Few people could pull him up like that. Coming from Ms Henderson, he couldn't say he minded.

Clearly, she was the right person for the job. With his past, he didn't wait around for miracles, nevertheless he had faith that Libby Henderson's clients believed she could work them. Regardless, he would have little trouble persuading her and, as a consequence, others that he was indeed fit to drive again when he deemed it should be so. And if she needed a hand in helping her decision along, he wasn't opposed to the idea. In fact, now that he'd met her, he was more than intrigued by the prospect.

Recalling the natural wiggle in her walk, he pushed off the column.

Until that time, he needed to focus elsewhere. Needed to keep busy. Tomorrow midday, a videoconference with the Australian CEO of his best-selling signature-brand aftershave was scheduled. Before then, he'd go through projection figures for an additional anticipated range. Along with earnings from his extensive investment portfolio, he certainly didn't need the money, but a man would be a fool not to strike when his iron was hot. Current and potential sponsors agreed: Alex Wolfe was *steaming*. He intended to keep it that way.

About to head in, he pulled up. Eli Steele's sleek black sports car was slinking up the drive. Grinning, Alex crossed back to the patio's edge. Not only was his assistant smart in a business sense, he had a good head for cars. Eli wouldn't be working for him if he didn't.

'I take it that was your physiotherapist driving off,' Eli said, easing out the driver's side door. 'How'd it go?'

'Well.' After Eli made his way up the steps, Alex clapped his friend on the back with his free hand. 'You did a fine job finding her.'

Eli drove a set of fingers over his scalp, ruffling his neat dark hair. 'So she's on board?'

'I've explained I need to be back in the seat no later than Round Four.' Two weeks shy of the six weeks the team doctor had insisted upon, which would leave him in a good position to retain his title.

Inside the vestibule, they hung a right and sauntered down the hall which led to Alex's home office.

'And she said she can accommodate?' Eli asked.

'Was there any doubt?'

'Only on my part, it seems.'

Frowning, Alex stopped. 'Run that by me again?'

Eli kept walking. 'Don't get me wrong. I'm convinced she does great work, but from what I've read she seems to have a granite mindset as well. I didn't think she'd roll over and agree to your time frame that easily.'

Outside the billiards room, Eli waited for his boss to catch up.

Digesting the information, Alex began to walk again. 'You sound unhappy about her being onside.'

'You want to race,' Eli explained, 'and you want to win. Clearly you can handle pain. But, Alex, you don't want to risk this injury getting worse. This is the second time that joint has given you trouble. Third time it'll be easier to damage still. If that happens you could be out for a lot longer than six weeks.'

They entered the office, its walls lined with framed shots capturing some heady moments on the track as well as the winner's podium—holding up a plate at Monaco, shooting champagne over an ecstatic crowd. Alex's favourite trophy by far was a homemade medal, which hung on a haberdashery store's dark blue ribbon. Made out of an inexpensive key ring and a portion of a wheel spike, the good-luck charm had been given to him many years ago by his mentor, a man to whom Alex owed everything—Carter White. Encouragement, belief. Carter had given the rebel teen Alex had once been the tools needed to succeed, which included the gift of a caring father figure Alex had sorely lacked at home. He really ought to pick up the phone and call Carter sometime.

Crossing to his desk, Alex collected the documents he'd received from that CEO and the bold *Alex Wolfe* logo caught his eye. Everyone was eager to see how far his brand-name net would fly and Eli was great to bounce new ideas and strategies off. He was more than an assistant; Eli was a first-class friend. They'd known each other only three years and yet Eli was closer to him than any of his brothers. Not that Alex blamed anyone for that…or, rather, he blamed no one other than the man who had single-handedly torn his own family apart: William Wolfe, may he rot in hell.

And he was seriously giving too much thought to all this lately but, for once, he couldn't seem to avoid it.

Staring blindly at those documents, Alex recalled how he'd waited until he'd left the hospital to reread Annabelle's email and compose an adequate reply.

Great to hear about Jacob's return and Nathaniel's upcoming nuptials, it had said. *Can't believe he's old enough to tie the knot! Will be in contact again soon. Hope you're well. Love to you, Alex.*

He'd thought about phoning; he had her number. But he knew Annabelle favoured email. Frankly, in this circumstance, so did he. Not that he and Annabelle didn't speak every couple of years or so…but never about that night. Not about what a different girl Annabelle was now from the lively chit she'd once been.

Alex lowered into his high-back leather chair, only half hearing Eli's last remark.

'… I'm sure Libby Henderson explained that to you.'

Alex's thoughts slid all the way back. Eli was talking about the increased chance of incurring a similar injury to his shoulder in the future.

'I'll keep up the exercises,' Alex said, 'and whatever else she prescribes.'

'As long as you don't screw it up permanently in the meantime by going back to the track too soon.'

Alex tossed a wry look around the walls, covered with victory memorabilia. 'I think I've done fairly well so far.'

But when Eli's dark blue gaze dropped and he rubbed the scar above his temple the way he did whenever he had something more to say, Alex blew out a breath and set the document down on the desk with a slap.

'Spit it out.'

Eli edged a hip over the corner of the polished rosewood desk and gave a shrug that said he was perplexed. 'I guess I'd expected Libby Henderson to put up at least a half-decent fight.'

In truth, Alex had expected that too. She'd almost agreed *too* easily to his generous offer. Nevertheless, 'Money's a strong motivator. With that kind of dosh on the table and the endorsements I'll flick her way, she'd be a fool not to jump at this chance.'

'I wouldn't have thought she'd be motivated by money any more than you are.'

'Why's that?'

'You seriously don't recognise the name?'

Alex rolled it over in his mind and came up a blank. 'Sorry.'

'Elizabeth Henderson was World Surfing Champion a few years back.'

Alex recalled her radiant can-do glow, the determined look in those swirling amber eyes, not to mention the alluring beach-babe hair and tan. Elizabeth Henderson, world champion surfer? He grinned. Sure. It fit.

'I had no idea,' he admitted. 'Water sports aren't my thing.' He and Libby had even had that discussion. 'I don't much follow female sport either. Do they televise women's surf championships?'

With a sardonic grin, Eli collected the document Alex had set aside. 'For a smart man, you're one hell of a chauvinist.'

Alex held his heart. 'You've wounded me.' Then he offered up a conciliatory smile. 'Don't worry. I'm on top of it. When Libby Henderson sets her mind to something, she does it her way and leaves the rest for dead. Which can only bode well for her performance as a physio.'

Dark brows knitted, Eli was flicking through the document, sifting through data. Eli was a hound for tracking down and assimilating facts. Which begged the question…

Eyes narrowed, Alex swung his chair one way, then the next. Finally he asked, 'Why didn't you tell me about Libby Henderson's past first-up?'

Eli continued analysing the pages. 'I wanted you to meet her without any preconceptions.'

'I don't see how knowing about her sporting acumen could hurt.'

When Eli kept his focus on the document, Alex's antennae began to prickle. Had being cooped up without driving privileges brought out a paranoid streak? Or was there something more to Libby Henderson? Something that Eli, for some curious reason, preferred his boss not discover?

He'd set out to hire someone who would be malleable to his needs. That objective hadn't changed. And yet after a single meeting he couldn't deny he was intrigued to learn more about this former surf queen turned sports star physio. Was his curiosity in part due to the fact that Libby reminded him of his sister? She and Annabelle conveyed a similar almost regal reserve, although Alex well remembered his sister in her younger years—open and vibrant. So eager to experience all life had to offer. He'd wager Libby harboured a more effervescent side as well. Either way…

Eli leaned over to point out some anomaly in the document but Alex found his thoughts still on Libby.

An attractive option. Boundless possibilities.

Yes. When Ms Henderson visited next, he'd be certain to dig deeper.

CHAPTER FOUR

HALF AN HOUR LATER, Libby walked through the entrance of her city office. Behind the front desk, her twenty-one-year-old receptionist, Payton Nagle, flicked back her waist-length chestnut hair and beamed out an enthusiastic smile.

'So*oooo*...how was the superstar?'

Containing a grin, Libby crossed over and scooped up the morning mail from the counter's top shelf. 'Still shining bright.'

'What's he like?' Eyes round, Payton tipped forward. 'Is he as sexy in real life as he is on the TV?'

'I'd have to say sexier,' Libby replied, matter-of-factly. The man was *so* sexy, it was criminal.

Falling back in her seat, Payton sighed long and hard at the ceiling. 'That strong square jaw, that deep to-die-for Brit accent... Honestly, Libby, I don't know how you stopped from swooning.'

'I'm a professional, Payton,' Libby said, shuffling through letters and invoices. 'Professionals aren't allowed to swoon.' Or rather they weren't allowed to let those kinds of unprofessional feelings show.

She set down the mail and drilled her receptionist with

her most serious gaze. 'Remember, not one word about my appointments with Alex Wolfe to anyone. He wants the press to think he's flown back to the UK or the paparazzi would be all over this. He doesn't want the situation with his shoulder made out to be any worse than it is.'

Didn't want to be projected as a cripple.

Shaking off that thought, Libby stretched toward the keyboard to check her email account while Payton crossed her heart to seal the promise. 'Did you tell him about your surfing?'

Libby recalled her thoughts from earlier, when she'd left Alex Wolfe and his premises. Other than the everyday reminder below her left knee, 'That part of my life's behind me.'

Payton's brows tugged together. 'But being a world champion…it's something you'd have in common.'

'I'm not there for chitchat.'

Or here, for that matter.

Setting her mind squarely back on business, Libby moved toward her office. A long low whistle, the sound of a missile falling, came from behind.

Hands on hips, Libby rotated back.

Payton was twirling a thick strand of hair around an index finger. 'You really like him, don't you?'

Libby's eyes bugged out. *Like* him?

'Payton, he's impossibly arrogant. Consumed by his own celebrity. And besides that…' Libby's fists loosened, her inflexible look melted and, beaten, she exhaled. 'Besides that, any woman with her full quota of hormones couldn't *help* but like him.' She shrugged. 'He's *drugging*. Same way honey is to a bee.'

'I wonder…' An eyebrow arched as Payton twirled more hair. 'Are you the honey or the bee?'

Libby coughed out a laugh. If Payton was suggesting that Alex Wolfe found *her* irresistible…!

'I'm neither,' Libby replied in an end-of-conversation tone. 'I'm a physiotherapist who has a full day ahead of her. As does her receptionist.'

Moving into her office, Libby shut the door and took two calming breaths to rein in the cantering pace of her heartbeat. She and Payton might be friends but foremost she was the younger woman's employer. Someone Payton should be able to hold up as an example. Revealing a vulnerable side—the purely female side that found Alex Wolfe absurdly attractive—had been foolish. And a one-time mistake.

Crossing to her desk, Libby told herself that Mr Wolfe had fleets of starry-eyed admirers the globe over, women who dreamed about being with him, talking to him, *doing* for him. They would also dream about how that kissable mouth might feel sensually closing over theirs, or the way he might move when he made hot, unhurried love deep into the night.

Resigned, Libby dropped into her chair.

Hell, she wasn't so different to those other mesmerised hoards. And that had to stop.

She knew Alex Wolfe's type. World Number Ones were all about staying on top. He would use anything and everything within his means to have her capitulate, wave her physio's green flag and get himself back on the track whether his injury was sufficiently healed or not. But no matter how distracting Mr Wolfe's looks and charm, she would *not* let herself be manipulated. There was only one thing for it.

Spine straight, knees together, she swept up her schedule.

From now on she would be nothing but objective in his company. Ruthlessly ethical. A consummate, non-sexual, iron-willed professional.

Ready to sort through the papers on her desk, Libby had collected a pen when a pang in her chest had her catching her breath. The thought had crept up on her like a frost on nightfall, and now that the reflection was formed she couldn't blot it out. Couldn't shake it off.

After her accident she'd thrown herself into study, then the practice. No energy was left over for window-shopping for knee-high dresses she would never wear or wondering if sometime, somewhere, she might meet someone new. She was too busy—too focused—and she preferred her life that way.

Now, for the first time in so long, she gave into the impulse, closed her eyes and remembered what it was like to be kissed by a man. How wonderful it could feel to be desired. She remembered the swell of want when tender words were whispered and steaming hungry flesh met flesh. Then she recalled the pure elation of spearing through a saltwater mountain and shooting free the other side. Her mind joined the two and drew a picture of a tall strong man, the lacy fringes of ocean waves swirling around his ankles, grey eyes smiling.

Squeezing the pen, Libby bowed her head. As well as she knew her own name, she was certain she would never return to the ocean. As much as she missed the water that was one challenge she didn't need to face. But would she ever know romantic love again?

She hadn't let herself dwell before now but, in truth, she missed the company, the sense of sharing, the special warmth of intimacy. And as silly as it sounded, she couldn't help but wonder...

What would it be like to have all that with Alex?

THE NEXT MORNING, her professional mask firmly in place, Libby arrived at Alex Wolfe's elite address smack on nine. As he had the day before, Alex greeted her at the door, escorted her inside, then led her into a spacious room—an elaborate home gym toward the rear of the enormous house.

Libby almost gasped. She'd seen licensed gyms less equipped than this. Every type of weight equipment, three state-of-the-art treadmills, six rowing machines, various balls, mats, presses and bars. A small double-glazed window set in an adjacent wood panelled wall indicated a sauna. Did the man host boot-camp parties? That indoor pool she'd imagined must be close by. Not that they'd be using it. She would always love the smell and look of water any way it came—sea, chlorinated or fresh from the sky. But her mermaid days were long over.

Arm in its sling, Alex sauntered over to join her. 'Should we start with a cup of strong tea before getting into the tough stuff?'

As usual that deep accented voice seeped through Libby's blood, making her syrupy warm all over. Ignoring the heat, aware of the dangers, she steeled herself, met his gaze and set her work bag on a nearby table. He might be king of his profession but during these sessions, like it or not, she was in charge.

'We'll begin with a full assessment.' She nodded at his immobilised arm. 'Now that we'll be concentrating on strengthening your shoulder, there won't be a need for that.'

With a speculative smile, Alex reached for a fastener. 'My shirt will need to come off too, I presume.'

'I'll help with the buttons.'

· When she didn't hesitate to step forward and assist, his brows hiked but she didn't react. He could turn on the wicked charm all he liked, but if he'd hoped to put her off balance again today, he could think again. She'd made a pledge and she intended to keep it.

Iron-willed.

Asexual.

Professional.

With the sling removed, she deftly unbuttoned his freshly laundered chambray shirt. The subtle smell of lemons drifted into her lungs, but the scent that truly caught her senses was musky. Pure male. A scent she wasn't unfamiliar with in her everyday work. But, of course, Alex Wolfe went a mile beyond 'everyday.'

Last button attended to, she eased the shirt off those dynamite shoulders, then manoeuvred around to release the fabric from his back. As the shirt fell away, her gaze gravitated to the muscular contours, the straight-as-a-die dent of his spine, the lean measure of his hips. Her heart began to pound. She thought she'd prepared herself but, frankly, the sight of this man half naked stole her breath away.

Thrusting back her shoulders, she once again set her mind on the specialist straight and narrow.

'Let's start with testing your range of movement.'

She asked that he first raise his arms in front, palm down, as high as possible, then at his sides. Next, internal and external rotation, with his hands behind his back.

While making notes—the ROM around the joint was

not full, which meant passive work to help it improve—she said, 'Now we'll test the strength.'

His good shoulder squared. 'Ready when you are, doc.'

Navigating around to face him, Libby found herself analysing that amazing chest and powerhouse arms from a female rather than professional point of view. Big mistake. Her brain began to tingle at the same time her bones seemed to liquefy. She'd laid awake half the night telling herself she could handle whatever today might bring and yet she'd missed the turn-off coming here because she'd been contemplating precisely this moment.

Resisting the urge to wet her lips, she eased her gaze higher and met his amused look. Then one corner of his mouth slowly curved and her face flooded with heat. Caught out, she stuttered an excuse. She hadn't been ogling. Merely...*assessing*.

'You, uh, obviously work out,' she said, and then inwardly cringed.

Stupid. He was a World Number One. Of course he worked out. No doubt there'd be gyms in his other houses around the world, and the best personal trainers, as well as a food plan to sustain the mind and might of a champion.

She cleared her throat. 'What I mean to say is...despite your injury, you look great.'

His lips tilted more at the same time he seemed to move slightly closer, lean faintly nearer, and the heat in her cheeks exploded, raging out of control as that natural male scent enveloped her completely.

His gaze skimming her cheek, he murmured, 'Thank you.'

Gulping back a breath, she averted her gaze and muttered, 'You're welcome.'

She imagined that he chuckled to himself before he asked, 'Where would you like me?'

With unsteady steps, she crossed to a mirror that covered an entire wall. 'We'll start here. You in front facing the mirror. I'll stand behind.'

He took up his position, steely legs in black athlete's shorts pinned apart. His slightly cleft chin angled up. 'How's this?'

Libby was torn between sighing and smirking at the magnificent reflection. As if he didn't know he looked better than fabulous.

'That's fine. Now hold your arms out at right angles to your body.' His arms rose easily. 'Any pain?'

'It feels…' The chiselled planes of his face pinched. 'A little weak.'

She grunted. She'd bet more than 'a little.'

'I'm going to test that strength. I'll put one hand here on the uninjured arm and the other here, on your recovering arm.'

As she laid a palm on each bicep, she felt the vibration… his chest rumbling, the sound of a big cat anticipating a full bucket of cream or, perhaps, defending it.

Locking off her imagination, she continued. 'Now I'll push lightly.'

'Would you like me to push too? You know—' his left bicep flexed twice beneath her hand '—push up?'

She met his poker-faced reflection and simmered inside. Damn the man! He'd done that little trick on purpose. This wasn't a contest or a show. Every session, every minute, counted. He needed to take this seriously.

Filling her lungs, she reassembled her patience. 'I'll push down and you try to resist.'

Gently she put weight on each arm. His left stayed parallel. His right came down.

His cool expression dissolved and a crease cut between his brows. 'That's no good.'

'With your injury, it's normal. We'll get there.'

'Yes, we will. In time for China.'

She held off gaping at his implacable tone. But she had no intention of arguing that particular point now. She had a job to do. His shoulder would be fit for a return to the track when she said it was and not a moment before.

'Would you go over there and lie down, please?'

Holding his injured arm, Alex looked her up and down, as if deciding whether it would weaken his position to comply. Then he reluctantly crossed the room, hitched up on the bed's white sheet and spread out.

Edging closer, she scanned the exquisite form lying before her and swallowed against the rapid pulse beating high in her throat. He looked even better on his back than he had standing. The rectus abdominis had been sculpted by a god. The tone of his trapesius and deltoids were exceptional. The pectoralis majors, dusted with crisp hair, were as first-rate an example as she'd ever seen—and she'd seen a few. Powerful, firm, prime flesh. Below that waist band, Libby imagined another well defined muscle and her mouth went dry.

He pushed up on his good arm and his broad shoulders slanted toward her. 'Maybe we should start with something more strenuous. You know, get the show on the road.'

'No, Alex. We shouldn't.'

His jaw shifted and eyes narrowed. 'I can't see what lying around will achieve.'

'Leave that to me.'

His gaze pierced hers, challenging, testing. Finally he

rolled back down, looking like a third grader forced to face some senseless spelling bee he hadn't studied for.

He stared blindly at the ceiling. 'What now?'

Alongside of him, Libby took both his hands, which felt as hot and strong as the rest of him looked. Her fingers curled around his and she brought them to lie near his navel. She refused to acknowledge the trail of dark hair descending in a particularly tantalising line to the loose band of his shorts, much less the subtle bulge further down.

'No pain?' she asked in a remarkably composed voice.

His gaze met hers and, confident, he grinned. 'Not a hint.'

'Good. Now slowly lift your arms.'

'How high?'

'See how you go. I'll go through the exercise with you first.' With his hands sandwiched between hers, a hot pulse beating through her blood, she began to move with him. 'Up, two, three…hold and…down, two, three.' Her words were even, regulated, the opposite of her clambering heartbeat. 'How's that feel?'

'Up. Down. Up. Down.' She felt his curious gaze on hers. 'How much longer?'

'A few more times.'

Any moment she expected him to protest again but as their breathing synchronised with the movements, he seemed to accept the inevitable. So while they finished the set, she focused on his shoulder, as well as his expression for signs of discomfort. Her gaze drifted to gauge the steady breathing of that glorious chest and before she could rein her straying thoughts in, she imagined her palms gliding over that granite surface and her lips brushing those small dark discs.

Hauling herself back with a start, Libby lowered their hands a final time and took a resolute step away.

'That's it?' he asked, sounding pleased.

She patted her hair, which she'd worn in a low bun with multiple pins today. 'Now I'll show you an easy exercise to continue with.' An active as opposed to passive version of the exercise they'd done together. 'And we'll work in some remedial massages along the way.'

But he growled. 'I don't need massages. I don't want easy.'

What he really meant was, *This soft stuff is a waste of time*.

Tucking in her chin, Libby took stock.

This time with Alex Wolfe would be more difficult than she'd thought. She knew Alex was beyond eager to get back onto the track and that he was beyond confident about his abilities. She respected where that energy came from…an unconquerable winner's spirit. That quality, however, did not excuse his veiled attempt to bribe her, suggesting she convince the team doctor that he was fit and well to drive whether he was or he wasn't. Nor did it excuse that forceful tone.

Regardless, the bottom line was that she'd taken on this case, which meant she would give it her all and then some, whether Alex Wolfe appreciated her own brand of zealousness or not. If he decided their relationship wasn't working, he could sack her, but she wasn't about to quit, or double guess herself at every turn. He'd thought enough of her credentials to hire her in the first place after all.

'Alex, I appreciate your…enthusiasm, but I'm going to ask you to leave the program to me.'

'Just as long as we're in tune with what I need.'

What I expect, he should have said.

Her smile was thin. 'I know precisely what you need.'

His gaze pierced hers and she thought he might push his point to make himself clear. The simmering in his eyes said he would miss not one more race than he thought he had to. Every round he didn't drive took him further away from the means to retain his title, and anyone who tried to stop him was public enemy number one.

But then the thrust of his shadowed jaw eased, his trademark grin returned and he added in a placated tone, 'Pleased to know we're on the same page.'

They continued to work out with similar isometrics. After thirty minutes, she caught him flinching so she called an end to their first session.

'That'll do for today,' she said, heading off to collect her bag.

He was standing, hands threaded behind to allow a gentle stretch between the blades. With his brow damp from rehabilitative work his body wasn't used to, he joined her. 'So you're leaving?'

'I have other appointments.'

She was sure he wouldn't be lonely. He must have acquaintances in Sydney he could catch up with. No doubt many wore skirts.

While she found her car keys, he eased into his shirt. Leaving it unbuttoned—an unabashed encore, she supposed—he escorted her out of the gym. Halfway down the long northern hall, that enormous storage block, visible beyond a set of soaring windows, caught her eye.

Curious, she slowed up. 'What do you keep out there?'

'Three guesses.'

She only needed one. 'Cars.'

He laughed and the deep, easy sound—as warm as a blanket on a cold night—made her forget what a privileged pain in the butt he could be at times.

'Come and have a look,' he said. When she opened her mouth to object, he broke in. 'Surely you can spare five minutes.'

Libby thought it over. Her next appointment wasn't for an hour, and she was intrigued as to how many and what types of cars a motor racing champion owned. She knew Payton would be interested to hear.

Relenting, and more than a little excited, she nodded. 'Five minutes.'

His grey eyes smiled, but in a different way—as if he truly appreciated her interest—and together they walked out the house, past the magazine lift-out pool and over the immaculate emerald-green lawn.

'Where did it all start,' she asked, 'this love affair with cars and speed?'

'My father owned prestige automobiles, everything from vintage classics to top-of-the-range sports cars. Every now and then I'd take one out.'

'He must have trusted you a great deal.'

'Oh, I didn't ask. I became quite well known throughout Oxfordshire for my jaunts.'

'Known to the authorities?' He only grinned, his gaze distant and mischievous as he remembered back. 'What did your father say when he got a hold of you?'

He opened the huge end door and flicked a switch. An enormous space, filled with rows of gleaming prestige cars, materialised before them.

'What's your poison?' he asked. 'The red Ferrari F430 is

extremely popular. Then there's the classic British sports car, which I can assure you is a very nice ride.'

The spectacle greeting her was so out of the world 'rich and famous,' Libby put her hand to her chest to try to catch a gasp. 'I hate to think of your insurance bill. Do you have as many cars in your other homes?'

They strolled further inside, under the overly bright lights, surrounded by automobile excellence and an atmosphere of wealth at its decadent best.

'This is my main stash. I have another healthy group hidden away in the French countryside. Some in England too.'

'Must leave your dad's collection for dead.'

Without commenting, he strolled on, and it clicked that he hadn't answered her previous question. What had his father done when he'd caught his son driving his prize cars? But then the obvious dawned and she guessed why he didn't want to speak about it.

She put a compassionate note into her voice. 'Is he still alive?'

Alex frowned over. 'Who?'

'Your father.'

He ran his left hand over the bonnet of a deep-blue muscle car. 'He's dead.'

Expecting that answer, she nodded. 'I'm sorry.'

'You must be the only person alive who is.'

Libby blinked several times and was about to ask him to explain. But his eyes were suddenly so shuttered, his face expressionless. Clearly this was a touchy subject. Seemed there was more to motoring superstar Alex Wolfe than met the eye, an obvious bitterness toward his deceased father for one. What else lay beneath his polished public persona?

But she was being no better than the press. Everyone was entitled to keep their past private, she and Alex included.

Still walking, she crossed her arms and looked down. 'I apologise. I shouldn't have dug.'

He tugged an ear and, thoughtful, focused on some far-off point. 'Quite a bit of digging's been going on recently,' he admitted.

About his past? Who was digging? 'Someone from your family?'

'Yes. From the family.'

'Who?'

'My twin.'

'You have a twin brother?'

'Sister.'

'What's her name?'

It took a few seconds for him to answer.

'Annabelle.'

'Alex and Annabelle.' She smiled. Cute.

'She was in contact before my accident.'

'Something to do with your father?'

'His estate,' he replied. Then he turned back to face her and his demeanour purposely lightened. 'Seems our oldest brother has made an appearance out of the distant blue to renovate old Wolfe Manor before the council tears it down. A sound idea, if you ask me.'

'This is back in England? Oxfordshire?'

'An estate overlooking a quaint little village by the name of Wolfestone.'

Libby shook her head, amazed. How many people had a village named after their family? But Alex didn't seem impressed by any of it. The timbre of his voice was casual again but the light in his usually entrancing grey gaze had dulled.

'How long since you've seen this mysterious brother?' she asked, knowing she was being nosy again.

But Libby knew ghosts from the past could creep up when a person had time on their hands, and Alex wouldn't be used to being confined, cut off, the way he had been these past days. If he wanted to share—about his family and old Wolfe Manor—anything he said wouldn't go beyond her.

'Jacob left Wolfe Manor almost two decades ago. Disappeared one night without a goodbye.' He looked down at the same time his brow furrowed. But then he seemed to shore himself up, particularly when his gaze hooked onto another sporty car. 'I'd offer you a ride in my Sargaris TVR but I really need two hands to control it.'

She'd lost interest in cars. 'Do you have other siblings other than those two?'

'Three shy of a football team.'

'Do you see them often?'

'Not regularly. Never all together. I haven't seen Jacob since he left.' Alex hunkered down to inspect something that seemed to trouble him about one of the car's tyres. 'What about you?'

'Me?'

'Do you have brothers and sisters?'

'I don't have any siblings.'

'Your parents alive?'

'And well.'

'What did you do before becoming a physio?'

As he pushed to his feet, she saw a certain glint in his eye and her insides wrenched. Seemed he had a few questions of his own…questions she wasn't entirely comfortable with answering Time to pull up the brake.

She curled some hair behind an ear. 'I didn't mean to pry so deeply. We got sidetracked and I was interested…'

Her words trailed off as he angled more toward her. The air between them seemed to crackle when he said in a deep sure tone, 'I'm interested too.'

She let out a pent-up breath. The emotion in his eyes looked sincere. But how much was she prepared to divulge? Although her accident and subsequent amputation weren't federal secrets, she'd made it her policy not to wallow in the past. She certainly didn't want pity, which was often people's first reaction.

Dismissive, she hitched up one shoulder. 'My family history isn't that exciting.'

'I'm sure being the female world surf champion would've been anything but boring.'

Her stomach pitched and a chill crept over her scalp. She felt unsteady. Worse, she felt like a downright fool. He *knew* about her past? And he'd said nothing! What other information had he gathered?

Although she was boiling inside, somehow she kept her tone civil. 'You should have mentioned that you knew.'

'Perhaps you should have mentioned it first.'

Her hands balled. He might be world famous but, honestly, who did he think he was?

'My past, Mr Wolfe, is hardly detrimental to my current career. If anything, it's advantageous.'

He quizzed her eyes and the unspoken question hung between them. *Then why not put it in your résumé?*

The uncomfortable silence stretched out. Feeling off

centre—trapped—she forged a look at her watch. Way past time she was gone.

'I should leave,' she said, rearranging her bag's shoulder strap. 'I'll be late for my next appointment.'

After hesitating only a heartbeat, he nodded and agreed. 'I'll see you out.'

He moved to take her elbow. Instinctively she jerked away. Too friendly.

'No need,' she said. 'You lock up here. I'll see myself out.'

As she turned away, at the far end of the garage parked near a battered dartboard, a car caught her eye. Rusted, uncared for, the bonnet was buckled, as if the driver had slammed into a tree. What was that wreck doing among these trophies? But she wasn't about to ask. This conversation had got way too personal already.

Leaving Alex behind, she made a beeline for the garage's exit.

From now on she would keep her thoughts and questions to herself. And, as much as she could, her hands as well.

CHAPTER FIVE

TWO WEEKS LATER, Alex was shunting a hand through his hair, pacing the floorboards of his home office. Libby Henderson had left thirty minutes earlier. As usual she'd been the consummate professional at their regular morning session. Had performed her duties with routine perfection.

Alex stopped and glared at his feet.

That woman was driving him mad.

Not because she was inadequate with regard to his treatments. From time to time he might hint that things weren't moving quickly enough, but in truth her slow and steady approach seemed to be paying off; his shoulder was twice as strong as it had been. His problem with Ms Henderson— what niggled him to the core—was far more complicated than that.

Other than the brief time he and Libby had spent in his garage when they'd exchanged titbits about each other's pasts, she was a clam. Tight-lipped, focused only on business and, more to the point, doing it all *her* way. Although he hadn't wanted to commit to paper his confidential proposition with regard to China—fine fodder for blackmail should it fall into the wrong hands—he believed he'd been clear when they'd struck their deal. In conjunction with therapy, he needed her help returning to the track in not six but *four* weeks. In exchange for this service, he would pay an exorbitant fee and sing her praises the world over. She'd agreed they were on the same page. However, despite her verbal acceptance of his terms, he was far from convinced that Libby Henderson was anyone's man, so to speak, but her own. That troubled him.

But there was more.

When they were together in the mornings, despite her pronounced reserve, he'd become more aware of a certain thrumming connection. The soothing sound of her voice. Her unconscious habit of curling hair behind an ear. The slant of her smile when he'd performed some exercise to her satisfaction. She'd grown on him, and the longer she maintained her emotional distance, the thicker the wall she put up, the more determined he was to knock it down. But neither charm nor mutual silence—not even obvious agitation—seemed to make a dent in her brickwork.

The homemade medal, hanging on its ribbon on the wall, seemed to call. As usual, memories of his gratitude to Carter and earliest commitment to his sport swam up. Alex couldn't change his mind about Round Four. He lived to race. To *win*. China meant valuable points that would tally toward this year's championship. So what to do about Libby? Would she or wouldn't she give him what he needed?

Other than Annabelle, he'd never met a woman like her. Polite but also unremittingly cool. This morning he'd asked how often she surfed nowadays. The look she gave could freeze the Gobi. Was conversing with him so distasteful?

Or was her reserve caused by something deeper...some past hurt perhaps? He'd never tried to penetrate Annabelle's veneer; neither brother nor sister wanted to dig around those old wounds. But Libby…

Filling his lungs, Alex hunted down his phone, punched in a speed dial and, mind set, waited to be connected. He'd been as good as locked away here, hell-bent on withholding any ammunition about his condition or imminent comeback to the press. But his arm was out of its sling. No one would guess anything was wrong with his shoulder. Frankly, he'd go stir-crazy if he didn't break out and soon.

He knew the perfect person with whom to share some R and R. The same person who needed to be asked a straight question and, in return, give a straight answer.

Phone ringing in his ear, Alex lowered into his chair, smiling.

He only needed to create the right atmosphere.

IN HER CITY PRACTICE, Libby sat at her desk, staring at a scramble of near-legible notes. Almost noon and she hadn't got close to nutting out the speech she needed to give this time next month. A formal national dinner with her peers, she wanted her words on the podium to shine and inspire. And yet here she was, scrubbing her brow, wishing she could focus on her words.

Instead she was thinking about the irascible Alex Wolfe and his penchant for being alternately charming or painfully difficult.

Each morning she'd show up at Alex's mansion, and just as routinely he would complain about whatever exercise she asked him to perform. Although his shoulder was free of its sling and they'd progressed to using resistance bands and light weights, clearly he considered the work needlessly repetitive and beneath him. But even demigods had to show humility and face their vulnerabilities sometime. Alex's time was now. Either that or he might find himself in hospital again—this time, perhaps, under the knife.

Lately, she felt at her wits' end. After that day in his garage when personal details had cropped up to momentarily misalign their relationship, she'd let him know that she was there for business and business only, and yet no matter what she suggested or how she suggested it, he seemed more committed to challenging her efforts or creating a more casual atmosphere than anything else. Clearly he didn't comprehend the possible consequences. But she wasn't about to roll over and let him run her show, even if a part of her understood his reluctance.

Doodling a shell alongside her speech salutation, Libby recalled a time when she hadn't let anyone get through to her either. Where Alex was too 'above it all,' during the first weeks of her rehabilitation she'd been filled with anger and frustration. She'd lost the surf, her fiancé...heck, she'd lost a *limb*. To her mind she didn't need to work at getting well. What was the point?

Thank heaven that phase had soon passed and she'd come out the other end valuing, beyond anything, the perseverance of people who had not only stood by her, but had also said, with both patience and courage, how things needed to be if she wanted to get the most out of life. Like those people who had helped her, she wouldn't give up on Alex, no matter what trivialising tactic he used to try to manipulate the situation. His recovery meant a lot to him. It meant a lot to her too.

A harried padding of footfalls sounded on the corridor carpet. Short on breath, face flushed, Payton rushed into the room.

'You'll never guess who's here!'

Putting a lid on her surprise, Libby calmly set down her pen and sat straighter. 'Given that blush, I'm guessing Alex Wolfe.'

A tall broad-shouldered figure was already stalking up behind Payton. Then Alex was standing in her doorway, smiling that irrepressible smile. Her autonomic reaction to his presence never failed to astound Libby. Her stomach muscles contracted, her insides warmed and glowed and, immediately light-headed, her gaze soaked up the hypnotic message in his eyes, then dipped to appreciate the intoxicating masculine tilt of his lips.

No wonder poor Payton was beside herself.

Looking as if she were about to melt, Payton kept her gaze on their visitor. 'I said you wouldn't mind if he came straight through.'

'That's fine, Payton.' Libby pushed up on slightly unsteady feet. 'The front bell just rang, if you'd like to see who it is.'

Edging around their visitor, Payton reluctantly headed off.

When they were alone, Libby skirted her desk and, leaning against the edge, crossed her arms. 'This is a surprise.'

His brows shot up. 'You don't remember?'

Libby stopped breathing. Did they have an appointment she'd forgotten? Not possible.

'Remember what?'

With that lazy delectable stride that sent her heartbeat racing all the more, he sauntered forward. 'It's our two-week anniversary.'

Libby couldn't help it. She laughed. In between being chronically difficult, Alex could also be infinitely charming.

'So it is. Happy anniversary.' Her eyebrows snapped together. 'You didn't drive here, did you?' She'd told him this morning that another couple of days off from civilian driving was safest.

'Although I'm sure I could,' he told her, 'I got a ride.'

'A taxi?'

'Limo.'

Libby's head kicked back. Hardly the transport of a man who wanted to remain inconspicuous.

'I thought you wanted to lay low?'

He shrugged. 'My accident is old news now.'

She understood his point; today's headline was tomorrow's back page small print. Although she couldn't imagine any member of the paparazzi passing on the chance to catch a celebrity of Alex's stature off the clock.

Then again Alex might have decided that now his arm was sling-free and stronger, he wouldn't mind a spot of *positive* publicity. Either way his rationale on that subject had less than nothing to do with her.

Casually inspecting her office walls—her degrees, photos and that black-and-white aerial of Sydney circa 1960, predating the Opera House—he strolled further into the room.

'Are you busy?' he asked.

'I'm always busy.'

'But you'll need to stop to eat.'

'I usually get in a sandwich,' she said, vaguely suspicious now.

He rotated to face her. 'No sandwich today. Grab your coat.'

'I beg your pardon?'

'I'm taking you to lunch.'

Libby's hands fell to clasp the edges of the desk either

side of her hips. Not for one moment had she imagined this visit was linked to anything other than his therapy. Since that day in the garage, she'd avoided any talk of a private nature. Having him acknowledge a two-week anniversary was curious enough. Now he was inviting her to lunch? She was near speechless.

She shook her head. 'I don't think it's appropriate that our relationship should include...'

But her words trailed off. Was that a puppy-dog face he was pulling?

'You don't want to hurt my feelings, do you, doc?'

'Feelings,' she announced, 'have nothing to do with it.' She rounded the desk and lowered purposefully back down into her seat. When their eyes met again, that knee-knocking smile had only spread wider.

'Would it help if I said please?'

'I'm sorry.' Collecting her pen, she pretended to focus on her notes. 'But I have work to do.'

'Client appointments?'

'Guest speech.'

'I'm good with speeches. We can discuss it over lunch.' From beneath her lashes, she saw him saunter across and her heartbeat began to flutter. 'Or I can organise take-out. We can have a picnic in here.' His attention zeroed in on a photo framed behind her. He squinted, then chuckled. 'Hey, that's *you*.'

Libby groaned. *This* is why she'd never wanted him in here. Questions. The answers of which were her business and nobody else's.

Nevertheless, she acknowledged what was obvious. 'Yes, that's me, but a long time ago.'

She braced herself, waiting for him to ask about her current surfing habits again like he had this morning; she'd rather not discuss it. Instead his gaze swept over and he smiled.

'C'mon, doc. The limo's waiting.'

She reclined back and studied him for a drawn-out moment. Finally she huffed. 'You're not giving up, are you?'

'I've done everything you've asked these past two weeks. We deserve some time-out.'

'You've done *everything* I've asked?'

At her unconvinced look, he let slip a grin. 'Well, sometimes you might've needed to ask twice…'

A runaway smile stole across her face. Then her gaze fell to her disarray of notes. She'd vowed to have this first draft down by the end of the week. But her stomach did feel empty. Maybe her brain would work better after a good meal. And that was the *only* reason she was going. Although to believe conversation wouldn't vie toward the personal was naive. She couldn't help but wonder if he'd heard from his sister about his mysterious brother again.

Giving in, she unfolded from the chair, raised her chin and stipulated, 'One hour.'

'One hour?' Alex broke into a broad smile. 'We'll discuss it over lunch.'

TWENTY MINUTES LATER, Alex's chauffeur-driven limousine parked outside a quaint-looking restaurant. The high-pitched ornate roof and rattan features suggested an oriental bent. Then Libby caught a whiff of spicy aromas and saw the establishment's name.

Malaysian Pearl.

As the uniformed driver assisted her out, Libby sent Alex a look. 'Is this place supposed to be a hint of some kind?'

'I figure since I missed the race in Sepang I ought to enjoy some of the flavours of the country I won't get to visit this year.'

'You're a fan of Malaysian food?'

Joining her, he set his palm lightly on the small of her back and winked. 'The hotter, the better.'

Libby moved away from his touch. She wasn't certain he was speaking about curries.

They moved up the timber plank path, past the peaceful trickling of a rock pebble water feature. Inside they were seated in a private corner, which was cloaked by palm fronds, bamboo dividers and bordered by generous windows overlooking the blue silk-stretched waters of the bay. The interior reflected Eastern symmetry, simplicity and serenity—a smiling Buddha sat on a podium facing the entrance, authentic wooden lamps featured on each table and background music offered the tranquil strains of flutes and tinkling bells.

Settling in, Libby set her bag aside. 'You enjoy your stays in Malaysia?'

'I don't usually see much outside of Sepang. That's the town and district where the race is held each year. It's a hop from the international airport to the circuit.'

Alex sat back while a waiter, who had already seen to the placement of Libby's linen napkin, now laid a starched white square on the gentleman's lap. As Libby took in the surrounds and her compelling company, a thought struck her. This was the first time she'd been with Alex in public and she sensed others in the room absorbing and reacting to his appealing air of authority too.

Was it that some people in the restaurant, including the waiter, recognised Alex out of his racing gear? Or was it as she suspected? That no matter where he might be, Alex Wolfe radiated a presence that commanded attention. Even deference.

As the waiter moved off, Alex continued. 'I plan to visit Malaysia purely for a vacation one day.'

'Ever get tired of living out of a suitcase?' she asked, feeling the beat of her pulse increase at the way his big tanned hand brushed the white tablecloth. His eyes searched hers and he considered her words.

'That's an interesting question coming from one who would know about such things.'

A wistful feeling drifted through her. She didn't think often of those days, travelling the world over for her sport. Better to concentrate on the blessings she'd kept and new opportunities she'd created. But she could easily admit, 'I loved the travel. Around Australia as much as around the world.'

His grey eyes glittered. 'Your favourite port?'

'Brazil is awesome. Malibu for the nostalgia. But... Maui.' Remembering the thrill of riding those two and a half metre barrels, she smiled. 'Yeah. Definitely Maui.'

'Sounds as if you were Australia's answer to *Gidget*.'

She smiled at the connection. 'A lot of people don't realise the girl from that old movie and series was based on a real person.'

'The first female world champion?'

'*Gidget* was written in the fifties.' Libby still owned the copy she'd picked up at a second-hand store the summer she'd turned thirteen. 'The first female championship wasn't until 1964. Won by a Sydneyite,' she noted with pride. 'She was awarded two hundred and fifty dollars, a new surfboard and several packets of cigarettes.'

He laughed, an easy sound that made Libby feel as if they'd known each other for years. 'The things you learn on a date with your physio.'

Libby's smile fell at the same time her heart rolled over. This wasn't a *date*. This was lunch with a client. A handsome client with incredibly strong features and soft grey eyes that seemed to be inviting her in.

Shifting in her chair, Libby collected her food menu, although she suddenly felt so flustered she couldn't concentrate on the words.

Alex collected his menu too, and after a time commented, 'I rang my brother.'

Her gaze shot up and menu went down. 'Jacob?'

'Think I told you we haven't seen each other since he left all those years ago.'

'That must have been hard. Your oldest brother leaving without a word.'

'I don't think he had any option.'

When he beckoned the waiter over, Libby leaned forward. Elbows on the table, she laced her fingers and rested her chin on the bridge. After that day in his amazing garage when she'd learned Alex knew of her surfing history, she'd been taken so off guard, had felt so undercut, she vowed never to talk personal again. And she'd stuck to that.

But so what if the fact she'd had an accident happened to come up? It would make no difference to her attitude or commitment to their sessions, and shouldn't she give Alex the benefit of the doubt that he would still value her abilities as a physio? As a human being?

And what harm could come from hearing more about the mysterious Wolfe clan? In truth, she was beyond intrigued. A father nobody missed. A brother who'd escaped in the dead of night. Eight siblings in all, one of whom was Alex's twin, the sister who'd contacted him before his terrible crash.

After Alex ordered a bottle of cabernet sauvignon, Libby said, 'You and your brother must have had a lot to talk about.'

'It was a little awkward speaking again after so many years. I was only fourteen when Jacob left. But we'd always got along.'

He wove a fingertip aimlessly over the pearl etched on the menu, perhaps wondering if he ought to divulge anything more. For a moment she thought she glimpsed pain lurking in the shadows of his gaze and words of support rose up. Yes, she was curious but they could talk about something else if the past hurt too much to discuss. She understood, more than he might ever know.

But then he swept up his water glass, took a sip and met her gaze again.

'Wolfe Manor has been declared structurally unsafe and a danger to the community,' he said. 'Jacob wants to repair the damage. No easy feat.'

Repair the damage… Libby had the feeling Alex was speaking about more than fixing some dilapidated ancient house.

'Does Jacob think it's salvageable?'

'Rising damp, holes in the roof, crumbling brick, grounds grown wild. Vandals did a number on it too. But apparently Jacob's an architect now. He plans to refurbish the manor completely, then sell it on.' His jaw tightening, Alex seemed to look inward. 'Frankly, I can't see how he can set foot in that place again.' His gaze cleared as it darted over her shoulder and his chin kicked up. 'Here comes the wine.'

As the waiter presented the label for Alex to acknowledge, Libby pressed her lips together. These weeks she'd tried to keep a professional distance between herself and Alex. He was the kind of man any woman could get distracted by. And in only a few moments of conversation, she was looking at him not as a client or even a world-renowned top athlete but a real person, with regrets and fears as well as the courage to overcome them.

She wanted to hear more about the ghosts that seemed to inhabit Wolfe Manor. She imagined streams of cobwebs, fallen-down stairs, skeletons in every closet. But how much more was Alex prepared to divulge?

Wine poured, Alex raised his glass. 'Here's to my speedy recovery.'

'Here's to a healthy future.'

He grinned over the rim of his glass and sipped.

'What other news did your bother have?' she asked, savouring the wine's oaky flavour while lowering her glass.

'Now this is interesting.' When he tipped forward, his shoulders seemed to grow as the space between them closed. Libby's nerve endings began to hum. Thank heaven they would never kiss. She might go up in flames!

'Another brother, Lucas, is involved with Hartington's.'

'The big UK store?'

Alex nodded. 'The venue which was supposed to host the company's centennial party pulled out at the last minute and Lucas ended up hosting the bash on the Wolfe Manor grounds. The place was apparently surrounded by scaffolds, but they'd restored a good portion of the lawns to their former aristocratic glory. Another brother, Nathaniel, was there on the night.'

Libby's mind wound back. That Christian name gelled with Alex's surname and then exploded in her head.

'Not Nathaniel Wolfe the actor? The movie star who won that big award a couple of months ago?'

'One and the same. There was a scandal surrounding his West End debut.'

'I read about it.'

'He hid away on a privately owned island off the coast of South America.'

'Nathaniel owns an island?'

'No. Another brother, Sebastian.'

Near overwhelmed, Libby blew out a breath. 'The Wolfe kids did well for themselves.'

'Despite all odds.'

Again Libby saw that shadow darken his gaze, drag on his mouth, and she shivered. Just how bad had his childhood been?

'Anyway,' he went on easily, pretending to himself that his past didn't worry him when it was obvious that it did, 'seems Nathaniel fell in love with the woman he kidnapped—'

She frowned. 'Oh, now you're making it up.'

He raised a hand—Scout's honour. 'And at this centennial night they announced their plans to marry.'

Emotion flooded her throat and a mist came over her eyes. Silly to have such a strong emotion, but that evening sounded like a fabulous fairytale ending. One any girl might dream of. *If* she were ready for that kind of thing. If she'd found the right one.

'I hope they'll be very happy,' Libby said with the utmost sincerity. 'Are you invited to the wedding?'

'I have a previous engagement.'

Questioning, she angled her head and realised he was talking about a race. But she didn't want to put a damper on their conversation, ask about dates and then get into the old 'you might not be fit to drive' argument. Today she didn't want to discuss that at all.

The waiter appeared, refilled their near-empty glasses and enquired, 'Are you ready to order, sir?'

'Five minutes,' Alex replied, and pulled a mock guilty face as the waiter walked away. 'Guess we ought to make some decisions.'

Libby glanced at her watch and gasped. 'Where's the time gone?'

'Seems you won't make it back to the office in an hour.'

'That speech won't go away.'

'Precisely. It'll be there tomorrow. So let's enjoy what's left of today.'

When he raised his glass, she hesitated but then lifted hers too. Just this once, who said life had to be all work and no play?

CHAPTER SIX

HE AND LIBBY took their time with their meals, savouring the exotic flavours and brilliant bay views. A dessert wine was ordered to go with pineapple tarts to end off. Now as the waiter took the empty dessert dishes, Alex moved to fill his companion's glass again, but Libby held up both hands.

'Thank you, but I've had more than enough.'

'You're not still pretending that you're going back to work,' he chided.

'But it's only—' She checked her watch, then, amazed, glanced around the near-deserted restaurant. 'Four o'clock?'

Alex smiled. He hadn't known hours could melt away so quickly either.

Libby was a different person away from her work—not cool or reserved at all. They'd talked about the places they'd travelled. The different aspects of their chosen sports. He'd learned more about her background, growing up on Sydney beaches with parents who cared about her and her dreams. Even now he couldn't imagine what it must be like to be the product of a happy home. Made him wonder for the first time about being a parent himself.

What kind of father would he make? Would he be overly

protective because of his unhappy history or would the shadow of William Wolfe try to descend upon and direct him as it once had his older brother?

During their recent phone conversation, Jacob had opened up. He'd explained how he'd become increasingly agitated after the court case involving the death of their father and had jumped down poor Annabelle's throat that last day he'd spent at Wolfe Manor twenty years ago. Jacob had been afraid that if he stayed, he'd become the monster their father had been.

If Alex had been Jacob, he'd have run too. Better than filling his siblings, who had looked up to their oldest brother, with loathing and fear. He supposed they all had their crosses to bear, scars from their childhood at Wolfe Manor, but perhaps none more than Annabelle. While Jacob had been there to save her that dark night, Alex had been the brother who had unintentionally sent his beautiful twin to face a horrible fate. It was all so many years ago and yet lately the memories had become more vivid. Harder to escape or play down.

Clearly because he had too much time on his hands.

With renewed energy, he set the bottle back in its ice bucket. 'What say you give me a lesson?'

Libby was folding her napkin. 'Lesson?'

'Surfing.' He cupped his right shoulder. 'Might be just what the ol' boy needs.'

She held his gaze before pushing her folded napkin away. 'There's lots of professionals who teach for a living.'

'I was thinking more for fun.'

A diversion. Like today.

She sent a mild censuring look. 'We'll stick to our regular exercises.'

He persisted. 'After listening to your surf tales, I'm obviously missing something pretty special.'

And he couldn't think of anyone he'd rather have teach him. He couldn't think of anyone he'd rather see in a bikini. Or out of one, for that matter.

Although he understood Libby's attire during their sessions was meant to match her professional demeanour, those long white drawstring pants she wore weren't terribly flattering. Once in a while a sensible pair of shorts wouldn't hurt; a not so sensible pair wouldn't either. Unfortunately he couldn't see a change of wardrobe during work hours. Which meant he'd need to suggest some outing that would invite a less...*restricted* look.

Yes. He wanted to see more of Libby and, after today, he believed she'd like to see more of him. Most importantly, this spending time outside of work-related matters had eased his mind about China. The open, supportive Libby he'd come to know today wouldn't hold him back. And rather than pushing his point and possibly getting her back up, now he thought it wiser to simply keep her onside. When the time came, just as she'd accepted today's invitation to lunch, she would also give his shoulder an early checkmark.

After signing the bill, Alex escorted his lunch date outside. They passed a wall displaying the restaurant's logo—a shimmering pearl bedded in a clamshell.

'If you were known as a mermaid,' he said, his palm coming to rest against her lower back, 'I'm betting pearls are your bling of choice.'

As she'd done earlier, she wound away from his touch. 'I'm not so much into jewellery.'

He cast a doubtful look. 'I thought every woman was into diamonds, at least.'

'Not this woman.'

Her smile was almost tight, which, after such a relaxing lunch, made him wonder.

Obviously she thought she needed to explain. 'It's not that I don't think gems are pretty. As a matter of fact, I think pearls are beautiful. I just don't own any. I'm more of a practical type.' She held up her wrist. 'I own a watch.'

Examining the piece, he frowned to himself. A sports dial, not at all feminine. He supposed some females weren't into rings and things. Or would Libby be flattered, like most women, to be given a stunning necklace, bracelet or something even more special?

As they slid into the limo, Alex stole a glance at his companion's hands while she excused herself to check her mobile for messages. Those fingers had been on display practically every day for two weeks. He'd known she wasn't engaged. That had come out in Eli's initial research. But was she seeing anyone on a more casual basis?

When his gut kicked, he scrubbed his jaw.

Well, why wouldn't she be? She was an extremely attractive, highly intelligent woman with a great deal to offer a man. And if she were indeed seeing someone, her usual 'I'm only about work' demeanour—the way she avoided his casual touch—made more sense. As for accepting his invitation to lunch today... An important client showing up out the blue? He hadn't given her much choice.

He swallowed a curse.

Just when he'd felt better about this whole situation. But the day wasn't over yet. Still time to find out more.

'It's going on four-thirty,' he said, when she slid her phone away. 'Too late to go back to the office. And you can't drive after the wine. I'll drop you home.'

Libby gazed off, no doubt considering her options. Clearly seeing the merit in his suggestion, she nodded and gave the driver her address, which was less than five minutes away. When the limo pulled up, Alex swung out, then helped her onto the footpath. With an almost shy smile, she looped her bag more securely over a shoulder.

'Lunch was a lovely surprise. Thank you.'

'I'll see you to the entrance.'

Other than her pupils dilating, her expression remained unaffected. 'There's really no need.'

'You'll offend my sense of chivalry.'

She blinked as though she wasn't sure if he were joking. While he kept a straight face—he *always* walked his dates to their doors—she thought it through, finally gave in to a shadow of a smile and walked alongside him toward her building. Once they reached the glass security door, however, she pulled up to her full height and faced him.

End of the line.

'Well, here we are and, uh—' she peered around him '—your driver's waiting.'

'That's what I pay him for,' he said. 'Driving and waiting.'

Done with pretext, she eased out a breath. 'I know what you're thinking. We've had a nice few hours and you'd like me to invite you up.' She shook her head. 'Not a good idea.'

'I disagree.'

Her amber eyes flared. 'Neither of us want this to get complicated.'

'Who said it has to be complicated?'

Growing more nervous, she wet her lips. 'We have a working relationship we need to maintain.'

'This is working for me.' He stepped closer and his head lowered, close to hers. 'How about you?'

He hadn't set out to kiss her, but his mouth found hers, nevertheless. Then he told himself to keep it light, no more than a lingering brush of his lips over hers. But as they touched, an overwhelming need to explore broke through and instinctively his hands found her shoulders and winged them gently in.

White heat unfurled high on each thigh as the heavy beat of his heart echoed through his veins. He urged her nearer, until her breasts pressed low against his chest and, as he kneaded her flesh, the tight beads pushing against her blouse rubbed and hardened more. His tongue ran over her teeth and when her mouth opened wider, inviting him in as she dissolved, Alex forgot they were in public, in broad daylight, doing what should be enjoyed behind the privacy of closed doors. He forgot everything except the wonderful way Libby felt in his arms and his desire to know more.

He was taken off guard when her palms spliced up between them and, groaning, she pushed away. Short on breath, Libby avoided his gaze as she flattened a hand against the entry door to steady herself. 'Why did you do that?'

'You have to ask?'

Other than the deep rise and fall of her chest, she didn't move. Her cheeks scorched red, she merely lifted her gaze and glared at him. 'Alex, don't *ever* do that again.'

'Because you're my physio?'

Pressing her glistening lips together, she nodded deeply. 'Exactly. And…' She rose up a little. 'I'm not after a relationship right now.'

He smiled softly. 'That's a shame.'

A flame leapt in her eyes and for a moment he thought she might reconsider and ask him up but then she punched a number into the security pad and, in a blink, disappeared inside.

On his way back to the limo, Alex went over every second of that delectable kiss as well as the steps which had led him to this unique point in time. He'd gone from admitting that Libby Henderson had grown on him to openly confessing he wanted to broaden the scope on their relationship. This morning he'd merely wanted to get to the bottom of what lay behind her ice queen act, as well as confirm that she was still onside with regard to his plans for China. And yet now he found himself enjoying a woman's company like he never had before. Hell, he'd even winced at a spike of jealousy when he'd thought of Libby with another man.

Not good.

Standing guard by the limo, the driver opened the back passenger's door. Rubbing the back of his neck, Alex climbed inside.

He couldn't remember being rejected by a lady since tenth grade. Hands down it wouldn't matter so much if it weren't this particular one, because the bald-faced truth was that Libby had done *more* than grow on him. She'd burrowed under his skin. Was playing more and more on his mind. And that was a condition he was less than happy to entertain; he had enough on his mind as it was.

He needed to avoid unnecessary complications. Ipso facto, this state of affairs had to cease and desist. If Libby wasn't interested in having him hold her, getting involved, as of this moment that went double for him.

CHAPTER SEVEN

THE NEXT MORNING, Libby strode into that lavish Rose Bay home with her head down and nothing but work on her mind. Or that's what she needed Alex Wolfe to believe.

He'd caught her unawares yesterday afternoon. After their lunch, she'd known he was hinting at an invitation upstairs into her apartment, but when she'd knocked him back she'd never expected him to *kiss* her. And what a kiss! For one dizzy moment, she'd almost reconsidered and dragged him inside. But then all those old fears had come creeping back in.

Although they'd had a better than good physical relationship, after her accident Scott hadn't wanted to be around, let alone *touch*, her. She'd thought Scott was the one, but when she'd needed him most—needed to know she could still be desirable—he'd not only let her down, he'd left her with a huge question mark hanging over her head. She hated to be a glass-half-full type and yet there were times when she couldn't help but wonder…

What man wouldn't view her the same way Scott had?

Although she felt Alex's eyes simmering over her now as she moved off in front and down that long hall, she kept her demeanour neutral and, as she'd done every day for the preceding two weeks, set her bag down in its usual place in the gym. Despite her bravado, she felt the telltale signs of his close proximity already at work on her. Fluttering heart-beat. Elevated breathing pattern. The effervescent buzz her blood acquired simply knowing he was near. Those reactions had been bad enough in the past, particularly whenever her skin touched his. But after that heart-stopping kiss…

Libby's mind froze.

Would he try to kiss her again?

'How are you feeling this morning?'

On her way past a treadmill, Libby's step faltered. That was *her* usual pre-session question to Alex, not the other way round.

'Fine,' she replied, without meeting his gaze.

'I've already done some work on my shoulder this morning,' he told her in a level tone that suggested he wasn't comfortable with her being here today. Which answered her question about whether he might try to kiss her again.

Well, if he felt uncomfortable, she thought, taking up her position before the mirror, he had only himself to blame. If her rejection had stung, maybe he ought to join the rest of humanity and toughen up.

'Let's see where we are with your range of motion.' She felt his eyes on her reflection but she kept her focus on his shoulder and her mind on work. Finally, brooding, he wound out of his shirt and she instructed, 'Arms out front, please.'

As if his soles were lined with lead, he angled toward the mirror, braced his legs and both arms gradually went out.

'Raise them slowly,' she said.

She stole a glance at his expression. His unshaven jaw was drawn tight and his gaze was distant and stormy. If he wanted to make this morning more difficult than it needed to be, he could do his worst. As far as she was concerned—and, it seemed, he too—yesterday's indiscretions were behind them. Doubly good because now she didn't need to ponder over how Alex might behave if he discovered she wasn't all he presumed.

Alex was already lowering his arms but she noted he hadn't lifted them as high as he had been. Not anywhere near.

She moved to stand in front. 'Again, please.'

A muscle beat in the tight angle of that jaw, then he raised both arms again to that same point he had the first time. When he let them drop as if he couldn't be bothered, he moved to sweep up the shirt he'd cast off.

'That's it for today,' he told her. 'I'm done.'

Her physio antennae tingling, Libby followed as he marched off. He wasn't hiding anything. She'd caught his wince before he'd lowered his arms.

'Your shoulder hurts?' Knowing the answer, she went on. 'Describe the pain.'

He eased his right arm through its sleeve. 'It's nothing.'

'You said you'd already worked out this morning.' She crossed to her bag, retrieved her apricot kernel oil and moved to the massage table. 'Can you come over here and lie down?' She added over her shoulder, 'Shirt off again, please.'

'Libby, I don't want a massage.'

She tried to ignore the ripple of frustration in his tone. Whether this morning was awkward was inconsequential. He'd overdone his exercises and a remedial massage was the right call. If he wanted to get back on track, he'd best suck it up and do as he was told.

'Sounds as if you've overexerted the muscles,' she said. 'I'm going to work over the accumulation of trigger points— those painful knots—that are restricting your range of movement.' His chin down, he exhaled and continued to glare the other way. She fisted her hands on her hips. 'Do you want to get back as soon as possible or don't you?'

His penetrating gaze hooked back onto hers at the same time his palm slid up his right arm. She wondered if his ego was dented enough that he might be done with it and order her out. But then he shrugged back out of his shirt and joined her.

Her stomach muscles squeezed like they did whenever he was near—particularly when he was half naked—but she clicked her mind onto professional mode, uncapped the oil and arranged some towels, which were laid on a tray near the table.

'Spread out,' she said. He hoisted himself up and lay down. 'Now just relax and we'll have those muscles loosened up in no time.'

Starting lightly, she kneaded the area to warm up the tissue. After finding several trigger points, she used her thumbs and fingers to press and manipulate, gradually applying more and more pressure. Five minutes in, when she began to drill a particularly stubborn knot, he jumped.

'*Aahh!* You're a bit vigorous there, doc.'

'Stay with me,' she said. 'We'll work out these problems, then you'll need to drop down your exercises for a few days and start back with lower repetitions.'

'I don't have that time.'

Setting her jaw, she stopped rubbing. *Enough.*

'If you'd prefer, I can help you find someone else.'

Dammit, she knew what she was doing and he could either work with her or find another physio. She was over the tiptoe show, on every level. It was difficult but if she could control her inappropriate feelings toward him, surely Alex could shelf his as well.

The tension locking his scapulas loosened. He faced the sheet once again and muttered, 'Do what you have to.'

Half satisfied, Libby applied more oil and soon she was in the zone again, doing what she did best—letting her fingers work their magic, giving a client's impaired muscles new life.

ALEX LAY ON that table like a good patient, gritting his teeth as Libby kneaded and rubbed and slid her hands over his apricot-scented knot-infested back. When she hit a spot that shot a hot bolt screaming through to his chest, this time he curled his toes and bit off the groan. He and remedial massages weren't strangers but he could tell *this* technique was truly hitting the mark. Not only that. The touching and rocking was also expelling barrel loads of all kinds of endorphins. Given he'd decided it wiser not to pursue those feelings where Libby was concerned, this was not a good thing.

For Libby's part, he knew this time was strictly about his shoulder. Nothing lay behind her tactile attentions other than her need to do the best she could for his recovering injury and rectify the setback he had brought about; trying to work Libby and memories of that kiss out of his system, he'd pushed himself too hard with the bands this morning. From *his* current position, however—a purely male point of view—her organic manipulations were working more than one kind of wonder.

He and Libby had touched before. Yesterday when they'd

embraced, he'd dwelled on how good it would feel to experience more. Now, through this ultra hands-on method, he'd got a big insight into that and the buzz was having its effects in places he couldn't control.

'How does that feel?' she asked.

Eyes closed, he sighed. To be honest? 'Fabulous.'

Her palm gave one last glorious sweep of his warmed skin. 'Make sure you rest over the weekend.'

Frowning, he cracked open one eye. It was over?

'You can't leave yet.' He groaned, groggy—aroused—then, knowing insistence wouldn't work, he appealed to her professional sense of compassion. 'There's still a twinge in my traps.'

Her brows jumped. 'Oh?'

She inspected the area, shook out more oil and then her hands were working over his back again and that delicious buzz circulating through his system grew stronger. Burned brighter.

After a few moments, she asked, 'Does that feel better?'

With his cheek rubbing against the sheet, he hummed out a smile. 'Definitely.'

When her fingers lingered, then trailed slowly away, he wondered if a smidgeon of private pleasure had leaked into her professional sphere as well. After that kiss he didn't buy that she wasn't interested in him in a XY kind of way. He was close to certain she wouldn't stymie his return to the track earlier than Morrissey had subscribed. Therefore he didn't need to worry about building up more of a rapport... doing what he could to make certain she was on his side. In fact, he'd decided trying to push the intimacy point now might prove detrimental to his primary goal.

Better for everyone concerned if he simply backed off, no matter how his current testosterone levels might object.

She left off to wipe her hands. 'All the bumps are gone now,' she said.

That wasn't entirely true, he thought as he pushed up and gingerly swung his legs over the table's side. Beneath his shorts, his erection was of the opinion that all this rubbing was deeply personal. Grabbing a towel off the tray, he let its tail hang and cover the front of his shorts as he fake-rubbed his chest.

'Drink plenty of water.' Recapping her oil, she gave a practiced smile. 'I'll see you Monday.'

As she crossed to her bag, still holding his towel, he edged off the table. No question, he should let her be on her way. Then maybe he could call up a few friends, organise a weekend in Paris or Milan. Anywhere away from here. All this tension… He merely needed to shake loose and get out.

So what was stopping him?

He took two steps toward her, stopped, then, driven, took another.

'About yesterday…' he began.

'It's in the past. There's nothing to say.' She stuffed the plastic bottle away and lobbed the bag over her shoulder.

He exhaled. Absently rubbed his chest again. She was right. He even said it aloud.

'You're right.'

'Remember, take a rest until I see you next.'

Clutching that towel, he walked forward to see her out. 'I won't lift a single weight,' he confirmed. 'I won't even think of this room.'

I definitely won't think of you.

Her brow slowly creased; she'd noticed him advancing and took a step back. 'I can see myself out.'

'If you prefer. There's just one thing.'

'What's that?'

'What happened...' His hand fisted in the towel before he tossed it aside. 'It's not in the past.'

Her eyes rounded with alarm. 'Alex, you agreed. There's nothing more to say.'

'Correct. I'm all done talking.'

With his good arm, he reached and drew her near. He saw her eyes flare and knew a moment when she might have told him to back off and let her be. But then the breath seemed to leave her body, her lids grew heavy and he saw her heart glistening there in her eyes. He was right. This situation—this maddening push and pull—couldn't go on. Now was the time to end it. And end it his way.

EVEN AS ALEX'S head slanted over hers and Libby drifted off into the caress, some weak, desperate part of her cried out that this should not, *could* not, happen. But as the kiss deepened and her head grew light, eventually she forgot the reasons why. The slow velvet slide of his tongue over hers, the way his hands pressed her gloriously near...she could only wonder at the amount of strength it had taken yesterday to tear herself away.

This may be dangerous, but it felt so infinitely right. This minute she only knew she was absorbed by sensation. Absorbed, and lifted up, by him.

Her palms ironed up over his bare hot chest at the same time his hands pressed down over her back. His head angled as he curled over her, his touch sculpting her behind, hooking around her thigh and urging it to curl around his hip as his pelvis locked with hers. She felt the perspiration building on his skin, the glide of his hand scrooping around her thigh, sliding lower toward her knee—

Breathless—terrified—she yanked away.

Oh, God, she'd vowed this wouldn't happen again.

She didn't want him to know.

'This is a working relationship,' she grated out, trembling.

'Who says it can't be more?'

Alex gathered her in and the next she knew they were kissing again, and this time he wasn't playing. Now he delivered his full punch, and the effects left her reeling, helpless. Giddy. He whipped up a hurricane inside of her, a dark powerful storm that tossed her off course and hurled her places that promised such blissful satisfaction. But the edges of her mind were still calling. As much as she might want to—and she wanted to so badly—she couldn't go through with any of this.

This time when she broke the kiss, their lips remained close. She couldn't get enough air. Couldn't stop the hot flood of emotion.

'You don't…don't understand.'

His brow furrowed and eyes turned dark. He shook his head. 'No, Libby, I'm afraid I don't.' He searched her eyes. 'Has someone hurt you?'

She wanted to tell him everything. Say, yes, as a matter of fact she *had* been hurt and deeply. She'd had a wonderful life, what she thought had been a wonderful fiancé, then the world had crashed in and she hadn't been with a man since. When Scott had rejected her—when his tight expression had told her the thought of touching her repelled him—it had left scars that made her leg injury seem like a scratch.

Alex's gaze pierced hers as a different light flashed in his eyes. 'Are you seeing someone else?'

As if.

'The point is, Alex, I didn't sign up for this.'

'Sometimes life throws us a curve ball.'

She coughed out a humourless laugh. 'Thanks for the tip.'

He studied her and finally blew out a long defeated breath. He even slid a foot back. 'Look, what if we calm down and give each other a break?'

'I like that idea. On one condition.' She implored him with her eyes. 'You don't ever try to touch me again.'

As LIBBY WALKED OUT, Alex's every muscle clenched, ready to leap and drag her back. Because he didn't believe her. She *wanted* him to hold her again. Kiss her again. What the hell was stopping her?

He tried to put himself in her shoes. Seemed her job meant everything to her, as much as his career meant to him. She didn't want to jeopardise her reputation or professional integrity by becoming intimately involved with a client who had made no secret of his need to attain an early checkmark for his shoulder.

But her need to avoid him went deeper than that.

Imagining her marching out his front door, Alex strode in the opposite direction, down toward the rowers, then he strode back and, fuelled by frustration, kicked a treadmill, and kicked it again. He hadn't felt this keyed up since he was a kid with no good way to expend his energy. But huffing around and fracturing his foot wouldn't help. Learning more about Libby might.

His mobile sat on the ledge outside the sauna. He snapped

it up. When Eli answered, he got to the point. 'What else do you know about Libby Henderson?'

Silence echoed down the line before Eli replied, 'What's wrong? She's not doing her job?'

'Eli, I'll give you three seconds. What else do you know?'

Eli blew out a long breath before he began to talk, and as he explained and the pieces fell into place, Alex sank lower and lower until he was sitting, gobsmacked, on the floor. He cursed under his breath. Tried to shake off the tingles racing over his skin. He'd had no idea. Not a bloody clue. But now when he thought about Libby's cool facade, about the way she'd literally jumped out of her skin today when he'd reached for her leg...

His gut twisted and his head dropped to his knees.

How did you tell someone something like that? He'd never told anyone about *his* deepest wounds...the hurts, and shame, he pushed aside every day.

'Alex? You there?'

His stomach churning, Alex lifted his head. He felt wrung out, as if he'd spent a day behind the wheel navigating the toughest track on the circuit.

'Yeah,' he groaned, holding his brow. 'I'm here.'

'I'll come over.'

'*No.* I'm fine.'

'It shouldn't make a difference—'

'You're wrong, Eli,' he cut in. 'It makes a difference.' Then he asked the obvious. 'Why didn't you tell me?'

'Because you didn't need to know.'

Alex let go the breath he'd been holding. His friend was right. He hadn't needed to know about Libby's accident.

When he'd hired her, those kinds of personal details were none of his business. Now…

He pushed to his feet.

That detail changed everything.

CHAPTER EIGHT

AFTER A VERY unsettling day that had started in the most unsettling way, Libby let herself into her apartment. Dropping everything, she filled the tub, peeled off her clothes, then sank into the wonderful warm suds. Her head resting against a vinyl pillow, she closed her eyes and sighed. She felt drained. Confused.

What was she supposed to do now?

This morning, despite her best efforts to avoid another incident, Alex had kissed her soundly again, and for a second time she'd kissed him back. Even now her cheeks burned remembering how easily she'd succumbed. Worse, despite ultimately turning her back and walking away, a silly self-destructive part of her couldn't help but wish he would take her in his arms again. One dose of Alex Wolfe had been bad enough. Now that she'd tasted him twice, she was in grave danger of becoming addicted.

After Scott, she'd let herself get close to only one man. Leo Tamms had gone to her university, majored in civil engineering and had asked her out three times. She thought they'd got on well. On their last date, they'd even kissed goodnight. One day in the cafeteria he'd asked why she walked with a limp—she hadn't perfected her gait back then. In his eyes she could see Leo suspected anyway, so she'd garnered her strength and told him her story. Leo had seemed interested, sympathetic, but he hadn't asked her out again. In fact, whenever he saw her coming, he slipped a one-eighty and streaked the other way.

That episode had hurt almost as much as Scott's rejection. It confirmed the doubt that had lurked at the back of her mind since the accident—that many people were shallow enough to judge others by their wrapping rather than what they really offered, which was underneath. Was Alex Wolfe one of those people?

Twenty minutes later, feeling more relaxed, Libby dried off. Tying the ribbon sash of her floor-length negligee, she moved into the kitchen, opened the fridge and eyed some leftover chicken stir-fry. But her appetite had been MIA all day. Her stomach was too full of butterflies with her wondering what would come next in this ill-fated game Alex seemed intent on playing. So she poured a glass of milk to line her stomach and, sipping, crossed into the living room.

She could work on that speech, she supposed, or put on a movie, read a book. Or sit here all night wishing life weren't so complicated. She'd been content before Alex Wolfe had inserted himself into her life. She'd been at peace with herself and what she'd accomplished. Now it seemed she was weighed down with questions. Sometimes, like at lunch yesterday, she could almost convince herself that Alex was sincerely interested in her. But common sense said he was far more interested in how he could use her…what she could give: a free pass to China.

When the building entrance buzzer sounded, Libby stiffened. But then she siphoned down some air and got a grip.

Her imagination would be the death of her. Of course it wasn't Alex Wolfe buzzing. It was a friend dropped by. Or a delivery of some kind.

Chiding herself, she headed for the intercom, thumbed a button and said hello. The voice that resonated back was deep and hauntingly familiar.

'I hoped I'd find you home.'

Libby held her stomach as her midsection double clutched and a lump of anxiety lodged in her throat. She took one shaky step back and clapped shut her hanging jaw. Then she got her thoughts and courage together and, resolute, leaned toward the speaker.

'What are you doing here?'

'I brought you something.'

She frowned. Brought her what exactly? But she didn't want to know. He needed to leave.

He needed to leave *now*.

'You can give me whatever it is on Monday.'

'It might be dead by then.'

She stopped to think. Did he say *dead*?

His voice lowered. 'Please, Libby, let me up.'

She hugged herself as her stomach looped again and her thoughts scurried on. She ought to tell him to get in his limo, if that's how he'd got here, and cruise straight back to his palatial home. God knows she didn't need this aggravation.

The intercom crackled. 'Libby, I need to apologise for today.'

Her chest twisted and she screwed her eyes shut. She raised her voice. 'Go away.'

'Five minutes, then I promise to leave.'

Feeling ill, she bowed over. She didn't want to let him in. But then she wanted to so much. More to the point, Alex's mind seemed set. He wanted to apologise in person for his behaviour this morning and instinct warned her that he wouldn't leave until he did. That kind of one-eyed determination was a big part of the reason he was a World Number One.

Groaning, she hit the entry button, then retrieved a wrap from her wardrobe to cover her negligee. By the time she made it back, a knock was sounding on her door. After driving her damp palms down her sides, for better or worse, she reached for the handle and prepared to open up.

ALEX WAITED OUTSIDE the apartment door, clearing his throat, rocking on his heels, more nervous than he'd been in a long time. Since Eli had revealed Libby's secret earlier today, he'd thought of nothing but. The fact he'd seen her only in those long white pants, the way she wove away if ever he got too close...now it all made sense.

His interest in her had started out as purely mercenary. He'd been determined to do what was necessary to keep his pretty physio onside and willing to sign off early on his injury. But even before this week's lunch date, he'd begun to see Libby Henderson differently. After that first kiss—the way she'd cut him off and strode away—he'd told himself no matter how much she intrigued him, it would be wiser to play the attraction down and forget that caress had ever happened.

Not possible.

This morning he'd kissed her again. After the initial merging of mouths and climbing of heat, she had broken away and served up an even frostier dismissal. *Don't ever try to touch me again.*

He couldn't do that.

Shifting his weight, he told his jangling nerves to quieten at the same time he looked down to inspect what he'd brought. A way to break the ice, get them talking. Hopefully get beyond this impasse.

God, he hoped she liked it.

LIBBY FANNED OPEN the door to find Alex standing on her threshold, looking as amazing as he had the other day when he'd appeared at her office out of nowhere. But tonight the sight of his tall broad-shouldered frame was beyond overwhelming. That slanted smile became more alluring—more tempting—every time they met.

Stepping closer, he held out his gift. 'This is for you.'

Her gaze dropped and, perplexed, she lifted one shoulder and let it drop. 'You're giving me a stick of bamboo?'

'It's a peace offering.'

'An unusual one,' she decided, accepting the stick. Then she noticed a fan of delicate flowers hanging from a shoot.

'Most bamboo only flower once every few decades.'

Really? 'I didn't know that.'

'It has deep symbolic meaning in Asian countries.'

Understanding the connection, she half grinned. 'You mean like Malaysia.'

'There they speak of a legend where a man dreams of a beautiful woman while he sleeps under a bamboo plant. When he wakes, he breaks the bamboo stem and discovers that the woman is inside.'

Libby's heart beat high in her throat. Was he in some way comparing the couple in the legend to them? Gathering herself, she cleared her throat.

'That's a lovely story.'

'An old man in Sepang once told me that bamboo bends

in a storm—' he took the top of the stem she now held and slanted it to the left '—and when the storm is over it stands straight again.' He set it right. 'It never loses its original ground…its integrity.'

She held her breath against a push of emotion. Now he was definitely talking about her…telling her that bending here, now, with him, wouldn't affect the respect she'd earned in her profession. He'd gone to a lot of trouble—finding this flowering piece of bamboo, looking into legends and symbols of the East. She was touched, and yet the voice of caution implored her to beware.

'Alex, why are you here?'

His gaze lingered over her lips and his voice dropped to that deep drawl that sent her heart pounding and common sense melting into a puddle.

'You know why I'm here.'

When his hand slid down the stem and covered hers, his skin on hers felt so good. In a strange way, familiar. Two minutes together, one small touch, and already she felt about to crumple.

But then she bit her lip and shook her head. She wanted to believe what she felt when they'd kissed was real. She wanted to be like so many other women who took a chance and were willing to see where things led. But she couldn't take the next step.

She was frightened to.

She lifted her chin. 'This shouldn't happen. We shouldn't get involved.'

The back of his free hand brushed her cheek. 'Too late.'

She was shaking inside and when his head lowered and his mouth skimmed her brow, overcome with deepest longing, she quivered to her toes.

Against her hair, he murmured, 'Say you're not angry with me.'

When his lips grazed her temple and his warm breath brushed her ear, torn in two, she groaned. 'I'm angrier with myself.'

'Let it go,' he told her.

And then she was lost in his kiss, a caress more beautiful, more erotic, than any she'd known. Perhaps because this time she'd almost surrendered. Almost submitted to what seemed inevitable. But was this what she wanted? Did she need to open up this much to a man she'd known only two weeks? Even if he seemed so sincere?

Needing air—needing *space*—she broke away and held her forehead.

'Alex, you're confusing me.'

'I'm trying to be clear.'

His hands wound around her waist and his mouth claimed hers again. But she wanted to explain…needed to let him know…

The rest of that thought evaporated when reality ceased to exist and both her arms floated up to coil around his neck. His chest rumbled with satisfaction and she felt his smile as she liquefied like a dollop of creamy butter in the sun. But as his palm slid down over her hip, then her thigh, a sliver of reason shone through the drugging fog. If she truly intended to go through with this—make love—there was something he needed to know.

Reluctantly this time she drew away. His breathing heavy, he rested his brow against hers and smiled into her eyes. 'You're not going to say you're still confused.'

'There's something I need to tell you.'

His lips nipped hers as he brought her gently flush against his body. 'You don't need to tell me anything.'

Her stomach pitched. 'I really do.'

Stepping back, she caught her skirts and began to ease the satin up. But Alex kept his eyes on hers.

'Libby… I know.'

Her hands curled more tightly into the satin and, as her throat thickened, she frowned.

'You…know?' *About my accident? About my leg?* When he nodded, her throat swelled more, cutting off her air. Growing light-headed, she shook her head. 'You knew all the time?'

'Only after you left this morning. I guessed there had to be more to the way you'd acted. I ended up discovering that you and I are more alike than you know.'

Her mind was caught in a whirlpool. She didn't know which way to turn or how to respond, especially to that last remark.

'Don't tell me you wear a prosthesis because that's something I wouldn't have missed.'

His smile was brief and…understanding. 'I know what it's like to live with the consequences of the past. To want to whitewash or, better yet, forget they ever happened.'

Her defences sprang up. 'I don't have anything to prove,' she lied.

'Then let me prove something to you.'

He kissed her again, this time with a deliberate care that asked for her consideration and her trust. When he angled down and swept her off her feet, this time she surrendered and didn't shy away. She did, however, think to murmur, 'Carrying me…you might hurt your shoulder.'

He began to walk. 'It'd be worth it.'

WITH HER CRADLED in his arms, Alex crossed to the centre of the living room, then spotted a quilted bed beyond an opened door. Moving through, he manoeuvred to flick the light switch with his shoulder, but Libby stiffened.

'Could we leave the light off?'

Alex studied the concern in her gaze. Perhaps it was the bond they shared through love of their individual sports. Maybe it was as simple as sexual chemistry combining and setting off sparks that wouldn't die. Whatever the reason, in a short time Libby had come to mean far more than an early ticket back on the track or just another available female. What he'd learned about her accident made no difference to those feelings. But he needed to let her discover that in her own time. In her own way.

In the shadows he smiled into her eyes. 'Whatever you want.'

He crossed the room and, beside the bed, he set her on her feet, eased back the covers, then returned to trail a series of soft kisses around her jaw while he untied the gown's sash and carefully peeled the sleeves from her arms. The tip of his tongue drew a deliberate line from the tilt of her chin down the curve of her throat while his touch drifted and cupped to measure the sensual swell of her breasts. Groaning at the jolt of pleasure, he grazed the pads of his thumbs over her nipples, making the already tight beads harder still.

While her fingers combed his hair and she told him with a breathy sigh how wonderful he felt, he bit down against the urge to go about this consummation with a little more haste. If she thought he felt good, she felt better than heaven. Better than anyone, or anything, he'd known before.

He tugged the silk bow beneath her bust as his mouth

worked soft scorching kisses along the sweep of her collar-bone. When he slid the thin straps from her shoulders and her satin sheath fell to the floor, he lifted his head to hold her with his eyes while his erection throbbed and hardened more. In the dim light, he saw the wince, her gaze drop away, and all the breath left his lungs.

She'd never wanted him to know about her leg. Now she was worried over what he might say or think when she had nothing to hide behind. And for a terrifying heartbeat, he wasn't certain *what* to do. Libby was beautiful. More than anything, he wanted to make her feel that way. What if he somehow botched this by saying or doing something unintentionally thoughtless? Where his apprehensions over Annabelle were concerned, that had translated into saying and doing very little indeed. Damned if he'd turn away from this, but how should he reassure Libby?

But then a feeling—a unique sense of awareness—settled over him and, like a light turning green, he knew and could go forward. He only needed to be honest. In coming here tonight, he'd put himself out on a limb. Now he would do everything in his power to let her know it was safe to do the same. With every stroke, every kiss, he'd let her know he was glad their meeting had come to this. Most important, he hoped she felt the same way.

He cupped her shoulders and murmured close to her ear, 'I'm one very lucky man.'

He heard her intake of air at the same time she tipped slightly back. In the shadows, her wide luminous gaze met his, then, gradually, a guarded smile touched the corners of her mouth.

'I should warn you…it's been a while.'

He grazed his cheek tenderly against hers. 'Then we'd best make up for lost time.'

He swept her up and laid her on the sheet.

LIBBY WAS A quaking bundle of nerves. She wanted to do this, be with Alex this way, but she was also terrified to the marrow of her bones. One part of her cried out to trust him. He was a mature man who, better than many, understood about life; that she wore a prosthesis didn't factor into his feelings here. Another part, however, had reverted back to the uncertain, confused girl she'd been the first year after her accident. She felt lacking. Odd and incomplete.

But then he undressed, lay down, gathered her close and when his mouth covered hers again, those torturous dark feelings little by little fell away. Soon her arms went out, wrapping around his neck, then her fingers were splaying up through the back of his hair as they kissed hungrily, with all the passion they'd both tried at one time or another to deny.

Sighing into his mouth, she gave herself over to the magic. Let all her inhibitions wash away. The way he stroked her, adored her, was the highest form of bliss. Making love—*being* loved—had never felt like this.

When his lips left hers and his teeth grazed down one side of her throat, every nerve ending sizzled and her mind went to mush. Then he was dabbing warm firm kisses over her breasts, drawing one nipple into his mouth while he teased the other between a forefinger and thumb. All her other sensibilities fell away. She only knew his flesh on her flesh. Only felt his mounting desire stirring with hers. But when the caress of his mouth slid lower, and the glide of his hand did the same, all Libby's fears plumed up again, so thick and fast that they cut off her air.

On reflex, she gripped his hand.

In the misty light, his gaze snapped up and she saw his eyes round in surprise. He'd forgotten. Heck, she'd almost forgotten too.

Now, however, every muscle and tendon was gridlocked. Her heart was galloping but with an anticipation that had nothing to do with desire. In good faith, Alex might want to believe the state of her leg didn't matter, but, truth was, experience said that it did. And yet she hated herself for doubting his sincerity, for feeling this…diminished.

With a raw ache pressing on her chest and her stomach sinking fast, she closed her eyes, turned her head and gently but firmly urged his hand away.

ALEX FROZE, as rigid and tense as Libby clearly was. He hadn't planned any moves. He was doing what felt good. What felt right. But as Libby had said, for her it had been a while. Had she not made love since her accident?

He wanted her to be comfortable with this. With him. At the same time, he wanted this joining to be everything it could be. Everything she deserved. For that to happen— to reassure her—he needed to persist. He wasn't giving up.

Tenderly, he brushed her cheek with the back of his hand. 'Did I hurt you?'

Keeping her eyes closed, facing away, she inhaled and shook her head. 'No.'

He tipped her chin toward him and waited until her glistening eyes dragged open. Then he willed her to feel, to understand. To find the kind of confidence in deep affection that could be borrowed from and fostered by another. That was here. She only needed to accept it.

In the soft shadows, he searched her eyes. 'Trust me, Libby. Trust yourself.'

Prepared to wait all night if need be, he smiled into her eyes and bit by bit the worry faded and her physical tension unlocked and eased. As he continued to stroke her cheek, gradually she began to smile too. When he was certain she was ready, when there was little chance she'd flinch again, he nuzzled against her neck and as his touch trailed lower—down her thigh, past that knee—he murmured near the shell of her ear.

'It makes no difference…it doesn't matter….'

He gave her more time, letting his fingers glide, pressing meaningful kisses over her brow, at her temple. When her breathing had changed and he felt her stirring in that way that said she was drifting again, he let his mouth trail from her throat to the dip between her breasts. Finally his mouth closed over that pert tip again. As he drew her deeply in, her hips gradually arced up and his touch slid across.

He groaned with unreserved want.

She was so ready for him, wet and swollen.

He drew a flowing line up and down her cleft, then slowly circled and pressed that sensitive bud. When her hand wrapped around his and she trembled, he imagined her fire building, leaping higher, almost ready to consume. He could barely wait for the flames to take them both.

As her free palm fanned over and kneaded one shoulder, he moved up and stole another penetrating kiss while he brought her to the teetering brink. When she was trembling beneath him, he wove down the length of her body until he was kissing her again and hoping she could hold out longer even while feeling compelled to do everything within his power to make sure she couldn't.

Pleasure-filled noises hummed in her throat as he scooped under her behind and the tip of his tongue swirled and flicked. All too soon she was pressing down into the mattress, clutching the sheet, convulsing and flowing while her thighs clamped around his jaw.

He let her float all the way down before he slid back up and, in the shifting shadows, searched her eyes. They were happy, dreamy, more content than he had hoped. As her arms curved around the pillow beneath her head, with her hair splayed out, a silvery aura framing her glowing face, he knew he'd never know another moment like this, where he felt as if he'd seen and felt everything and yet still had so much to learn.

LIBBY SLOWLY OPENED her eyes and put out her arms as the length of Alex's hard body joined with hers. Her mind was still spinning with tingling stars when he nudged inside. The pressure felt entirely natural and yet magical, like a king tide growing beneath a full moon, swelling so quickly, those stars were already building again. She arched up to meet him and, groaning against her lips, he thrust in deeply and all at once.

He hit a spot so high, so hot, she gripped his shoulders and gasped.

Pulling away, he combed the hair from her cheek and, concerned, searched her eyes. 'Libby, are you all right?'

Recovering, ready for more, she eased out a breath and nodded as her palms ran down his slick sides. 'Way better than all right.'

His smile came slowly. Then he filled her again. She felt his lidded eyes on her as the heat increased and the burn at her core condensed. When she didn't think the friction he'd built could spark any brighter, his movements came faster, he drove in harder and a moan escaped her throat. She'd given herself over totally to this delicious sizzling sensation…the intense force boiling through her blood. When the pressure seemed too much, when she was on the scorching cusp again—

HE DROPPED HIS head into her hair and, inhaling the floral scent, let the tide rise to an unprecedented high. He murmured her name, drove in to the hilt and held himself there, deep inside, while she moved and clutched around him. He didn't want the feeling to end, never wanted to let her go. The force was so great. The pleasure too extreme.

At the instant his orgasm imploded, Alex arced his neck back and gave into the shuddering release that rocked every cell in his body. The climax throbbed again and again, and all the while a chorus hummed through his head and his heart.

I'm one very lucky man…

GAZING THROUGH HER bedroom window, Libby watched the glittering stars, listened to the rolling surf and cuddled up against her scrumptious man. After making love again she felt both exhausted and raised up. Her every surface buzzed from his attentions. Her mouth and breasts burned from the graze of his stubble. She'd never been more sated. Never wanted to know anything again so much.

Alex Wolfe was more than she could ever have imagined.

His deep voice rumbled out from the shadows.

'You sleepy?'

'No.' She snuggled in closer. 'You?'

Rolling to face her, he drew a tender line around her cheek. 'Wide awake.'

Libby blew out a quiet contented breath. Was it imagination or did he feel as blissful lying here as she did? Amazing, given she'd had little to no confidence these past few years as far as intimacy with a man was concerned. This was the first time she'd made love since before her accident but, with his help, she'd overcome her nerves. In fact, she felt more whole and desirable than she ever had.

For long peaceful moments, she lay there, absorbing the way he watched his fingers toy with her hair, sweeping back strands, curling a section behind her ear.

'I bet you looked unbelievable on a board,' he said.

She held her breath but the regret she sometimes felt when she recalled that lost part of her life didn't surface. Rather, this time when she thought back, she was filled with nothing but a sense of happy nostalgia.

'It came naturally,' she said. 'My gran said I could swim before I could walk.'

'Guess our talents come out early. I rode a pushbike at a little over two. Was doing stunts and mad stuff when I was six.' He touched his nose. 'Almost lost this when I came off shooting down a hill at warp speed.'

Imagining the blood, she flinched. 'Your mother must've been beside herself.'

A muscle in his jaw flexed. 'My mother died before my second birthday. Drug overdose.'

Libby's heart sunk. She couldn't imagine it. She'd known his childhood had been tough but to have lost a mother as well, and in such circumstances...'You wouldn't remember anything about her, then.'

From the wooden look on his face, she thought he might

simply close the subject. He often looked so troubled when talk turned to his past. But then he tugged his ear and even found a lopsided smile.

'Apparently Amber, my mother, was a bit of a party girl but not much good at bath times or changing nappies. Still, from what I was told she loved her children. There are snaps of her dressing us up for games, taking us to the beach to build massive sandcastles. William even came along a couple of times. In their own unhealthy way, I think my parents might have been happy. Amber seemed to bring out the best, as well as the worst, in him. A lot of people did.'

He dropped his gaze but not before she glimpsed the pain and regret lurking in the shadows of his eyes. Clearly he hadn't meant to go that deeply into it. Given just how dark his past was, she more than respected that. She wished she could go back in time and protect the innocent little boy Alex once had been. Since she couldn't, perhaps shedding a bit more light on her own yesterdays might help.

'I was surfing up in North Queensland on holiday with a friend when my accident happened,' she began. 'It was my fault. I should have been more careful.'

Focused again, he pushed up on one elbow. 'In what way?'

'Firstly, I should've waited for my friend before I plunged in. There was nobody else around. Number one rule broken.'

'If you get in trouble there's no one to help.'

She nodded. 'An onshore breeze was forecast. They turn a good swell to mush. But that morning when I first ran in, the waves were pumping.'

A shiver chased over her skin and she shrugged. 'I didn't realise there was coral nearby. After twenty minutes or so,

I did see the fin, however. That's when I decided to double time it back in.'

He held her hand and squeezed. 'A shark.'

'I found out later it'd been cruising the bay for weeks. Should have done my homework. I caught a last wave in but it closed down.' She explained, 'The wave broke along its entire length all at once. When I wiped out, I felt a stab on my calf—the coral—and came up disorientated. I'm grateful I didn't see the fin a second time. Just felt the tug.'

His face pinched, Alex swore under his breath and squeezed her hand again.

'My buddy had arrived in time to see my spill.' She smiled, remembering how brave Barb had been. 'I've never been able to thank her enough for swimming out and saving me. She did what she could using regular first aid know-how, but we were miles from civilisation, surrounded by sand and palm trees. She sent out an SOS on her phone. A rescue boat patrolling close by picked us up. At first the doctors thought they could save my lower limb but an infection set in and, well...that was that.'

He blew out a long breath. 'My shoulder injury seems pathetic compared to what you've gone through.'

'It was hard at first.' She thought more. 'Confusing, really. But I was walking six months later. These days, people who don't know about the accident can't tell.'

'How do you feel when you go into the water now?'

She tugged the blanket up around her neck. 'I haven't been in since.'

'There must be a part of you that wants to?'

Her stomach muscles knotted. Odd. She could recall that day, her injury and recuperation, and be as close to okay with it as a person could be. But the thought of going back in the water...

Shuddering, she drew the blanket higher still.

She didn't want to push herself that far. She simply wouldn't feel safe. But fearless Alex Wolfe didn't need to know that. Tonight she didn't want a pity party, then a pep talk.

'One day I might,' she said lightly, then added more truthfully, 'I bought an apartment on the esplanade so I'd be close to the sound and smell of the ocean. Hasn't enticed me yet.'

He lifted her hand and pressed his lips to her inside wrist. 'You must have had good people there for you afterward.'

'Unfortunately one of them wasn't my boyfriend.' When Alex's brows jumped, she qualified, 'Fiancé actually. We'd planned to be married.'

A growl rumbled in his throat. 'Please don't tell me he dumped you because of the accident.'

'Scott was a surfing pro with titles like me. We both lived for the water. At the time it seemed we lived for each other. We surfed the world's hot spots together. We were both totally dedicated to our sport. But after my accident, things changed. *I* changed. Scott didn't have too deep of an insight into how my injury had affected me...affected every aspect of my life. Truth was he wasn't much interested in spending the time or the effort to try to understand. Seemed if we couldn't surf together,' she explained, 'we had absolutely nothing in common.'

She cast her mind back and felt that same twinge of regret and awareness she'd acknowledged back then.

'Scott came to see me less and less often,' she went on. 'When he did visit, we had little to say. Our relationship had been that superficial—more about how I looked hanging off his arm at events than anything.'

She didn't add that he'd never touched her again after her injury, although from Alex's keen expression she wondered if he'd guessed.

Alex's voice resonated in the semi-darkness. 'So he broke it off.'

'I did. When I realised how separate we felt without the ocean bringing us together, seemed there was only one choice.'

Alex grunted. 'I hope he and his surfboard are happy together.'

She gave a wry grin. 'I'm sure they are. And I'm not bitter about that. I had friends who were fabulous through the whole thing. My parents, and Gran, of course…even when I was being a pain and down on myself,' she admitted.

When he brought her close and grazed his lips over her crown, she closed her eyes and absorbed his masculine smell as well as his strength.

'You're being too hard on yourself,' he murmured.

She didn't bother saying she knew that she wasn't. But she'd survived—and flourished, in some ways, at least. Tonight with Alex had helped even more.

'I needed something else I could put my heart and soul into,' she said. 'Turned out to be something that I ended up believing in a thousand times more than collecting sports awards.'

'Helping others recover from their injuries. And you're wonderful at it.'

Her heart swelled. 'You really think so?'

'I know I've given you a rough time but I appreciate everything you've done. In fact, I think I'm in need of a little therapy right now.'

Alarmed, she studied his eyes for signs of physical pain. They had been pretty energetic beneath the sheets. 'Is your shoulder hurting?'

'Higher. A little ache—' he tapped his lips '—right here.'

Relaxing, she laughed. 'I can fix that.' She came forward and her kiss skimmed his bristled jaw. 'How does that feel? Or maybe I should try this technique.' Her tongue slid down to the beating hollow at the base of his throat.

He rolled her over and murmured against her parted lips, 'Libby, I'm aching all over.'

CHAPTER NINE

THAT MORNING HE and Libby ate breakfast at a local Manly café.

With the waves washing on the beach and traffic, both pedestrian and motor, passing at a leisurely weekend clip, they took an outside table and enjoyed the perfect autumn sunshine while ordering—fruit and toast for the lady, a full breakfast with bacon, eggs, fried mushrooms and tomatoes for him. He'd worked up quite an appetite, Alex realised, setting his napkin on his lap and considering something sweet to finish with...not that he hadn't enjoyed 'sweet' all night long.

There had been a sour note, however, when Libby had told him about her so-called fiancé. She had to know she was better off without that dolt. What kind of a man would commit himself by giving a beautiful girl a ring and then—

The fork stopped midway to Alex's mouth.

What had happened to Libby's engagement ring? Was that why she wasn't into jewellery now? Bad memories of a lying solitaire?

Alex stabbed more egg on his fork.

He hoped she'd dropped it in an express post bag and sent it back to that son of a—

'Do you eat like that every morning?'

Snapping back, Alex assembled a smile. 'Today I was famished.' Before he brought the fork to his mouth again, he added, 'That's your fault.'

'We didn't get much sleep,' she admitted beneath lowered lashes as he chewed and set his cutlery aside.

'Sleep's overrated.'

'Why sleep when you can race, right?' She slanted her head and a waterfall of silvery blond cascaded over her shoulder as she leaned back. 'How did it all start? You mentioned taking your father's cars out and earning yourself a reputation.'

Needing time, Alex patted his mouth with the napkin. The subject of his father could get tricky. Plainly put, he didn't like to discuss it. The topic caused his insides to crawl and made him ashamed that his last name was Wolfe. Still, if Libby had the courage to open up and come clean about her slug of an ex…

Alex cleared his throat and sat back.

Guess he could share a little more.

'The first time I took off,' he began, 'I wasn't quite fourteen. My father…' Alex's throat tightened and he grunted, remembering too well. 'William was being his usual obnoxious self. I needed to escape so I lifted his favourite sports car and tore off. That's the moment I knew what I wanted to do. How I wanted to live. I felt at home with the top down, the wind on my face, racing away as fast as four wheels could take me.'

Like it was yesterday, he recalled the thrill of that first time pitting himself against the curves and dips in the road, against the bona fide danger of excess speed. It never got old.

'And your father never caught you?'

Before he could contain it, Alex flinched. In time he hid the subsequent shudder. No wonder he'd rather not speak of those days. Preferred never to think of them, full stop.

Reaching for his juice, he resumed his more casual mask. 'Eventually he caught me. By that time, sneaking out with one of his cars had got to be addictive…a regular event. He used to spot a scratch or dent now and then.'

The beatings that followed had been worth every minute he'd got to spend behind the wheel.

Libby's glistening eyes said she didn't know whether to be amused or shocked. 'You're lucky you didn't kill yourself. Or someone else.'

Of course she was right. Thank God he'd hooked up with someone who had taught him early about respect—for himself, for cars, as well for others on the road.

'If it's any compensation, my joyrides got me expelled at the end of summer term '91.'

Her face fell. 'Oh, Alex…'

'They also got me noticed by a gang who loved fast cars as much as I did.' He smiled. Good times. 'I bought myself a souped-up dirt bike and competed with the other guys in weekend meets. That's where I got a taste for winning. We had our own races organised in the back streets on quiet weekends.'

Her smile was wry. 'Sounds like a wild crowd.'

'There were some parties,' he admitted, taking a sip of his drink. Given that last one… He set down his glass and pinned back his shoulders. 'Probably too many parties.'

But that was a whole other story and one he refused to broach with Libby now. With anyone *any time*.

A touch on his arm had him glancing up to find her worried gaze.

'Alex…you okay?'

He shook off the image of Annabelle after that night and pasted on a smile. 'Fine. I'm fine.'

'Did you ever get in trouble with the law?' she asked.

'There was one night,' he said carefully. 'A policeman took pity on me. Said he'd look the other way if I put my so-called talent to good use rather than playing the lunatic. He gave me the name of a racing buddy of his. A mechanic in Oxfordshire.'

Elbow on the table, she set her cheek in the bed of her hand. 'And he took you under his wing?'

That's when life took its first good turn.

'Carter White became my coach in life as well as on the track.' Alex's chest grew warm the way it did whenever he thought of the difference that one man had made. 'When I first went to his shop, I wanted to jump in the first car I could and tear up the road. But Carter taught me to value my skill and the vehicles I drove. He also made me promise to catch up on classes I'd missed after I was expelled for truancy.'

'I thought you said you were expelled because of joy-riding.'

His grin was lopsided. 'That too.'

She coughed out a laugh. 'Did this Carter White own a bag of fairy dust? How did he manage to turn such a wayward kid around?'

'With a chronically slow and steady approach.' Much like the technique Libby used on his shoulder, come to think of

it. 'He had me work on cars and motorbikes for months before he let me drive or ride. At first I thought he was doing it
simply to annoy me, but it didn't take long before I learned
a deep appreciation for the way engines worked, the way
bodies were put together. I learned to admire their beauty
and power. After five years as a team, I thanked him and
took off to pursue the bright lights.'

'Just like that?'

Her brows knitted…as if she thought he ought to have
stayed?

'It was with his blessing,' Alex pointed out. Carter had
wanted his protégé to advance as much as Alex had needed
to move on. 'He gave me a memento of our time together
and to remember the faith he'd put in me. He made the
medal himself. It has a big number one plunging through
its centre.' Anyone who cared to read up on Alex Wolfe
knew about the significance of that piece. 'Whenever and
wherever I race, I carry that medal for good luck'. Ironic
that after Annabelle's last message he'd forgotten to slip
it into his suit before his crash. He'd never forget it again.

'It means a great deal to you.'

Understatement. 'That chunk of metal means more than
all the cups and trophies I could acquire in a lifetime of
championships.'

It represented not only everything he'd gained but everything he'd left behind and never wanted to visit again.
Carter had told him to pass it on when he didn't need it
anymore. To give it to someone who did. Hell, he'd rather
cut out his own heart. He could never give it up, just as he
could never give up racing.

'When did you see him last?' she asked.

And Alex's breath caught in his chest. He couldn't remember the last time. He glossed over it.

'We keep in touch.'

'By email?'

He thought about it and nodded. 'Usually.'

Her gaze probed his as if she wanted to dig more but then she carried on with her earlier thread.

'They say you're fearless on the track. That there's never been a more focused champion.'

With a jaded grin, he gestured for the bill. 'Guess the press are good for something.'

'Did the other Wolfe children go off the rails before making good?'

God knows they'd all had their moments. 'The second eldest, Lucas, was always a handful. He never knew his mother. Never even knew her name. He was dropped on the Wolfe Manor doorstep when he was a newborn.' He squashed a spike of unease. Poor bastard. 'Our father took a particular dislike to him. Can't blame Luc for growing up to like women and booze a bit too much. But in her most recent email Annabelle said our shameless playboy sibling has found true love.' His grin was warm. 'Difficult to believe. She must be an exceptional girl.'

Alex's thoughts again turned to the woman sitting across from him. Seemed he'd met an exceptional woman too. Not that he was after marriage. Time, lifestyle, an unhappy childhood without parents…there were a hundred reasons to remain single. Where women were concerned, he was careful not to insinuate anything else. He had never and *would* never promise what he couldn't deliver. Not like the jerk who'd let Libby down.

'What about Jacob?' she asked. 'Didn't you wonder about him after he walked out and never came back?'

'He…had a lot weighing on his mind.'

She cocked her head as if trying to read his expression. 'Sounds as if you all had terrible things to reconcile.'

'Jacob perhaps more than any of us.'

Alex's back teeth ground together. He'd like to be completely honest but he didn't discuss that particular episode of his life. Still, sitting here with Libby now…

For the first time in his life Alex felt an urge to open up.

'A year before Jacob left there was…an incident,' he said. 'Charges were laid.'

Her face paled. 'Serious charges?'

The waiter left the bill. Alex scrawled his signature and set the pen down. 'Want to walk for a while?'

She scraped back her chair. 'Love to.'

Five minutes later, they were strolling along the esplanade, the road on one side and the tumbling surf on the other. He wound his arm around her waist, then, looking out over the glittering blue-green waves, asked, 'You okay with this?' *Being so close to the water?*

With the breeze combing through her flaxen hair, she nodded. 'I often walk along here. Just haven't managed to get any sand between my toes lately.' She snuggled up against his arm. 'But we were talking about Jacob.'

Alex focused and suddenly all those old fettered memories strained to break free, pinpricks of murky light struggling through tears in a dark smelly rag. Looking back he didn't know how he'd ever lived through those tragic years. How any of the Wolfe children had. But that was the secret, he supposed. Even with storms of brutality and madness and

death swirling all around, the Wolfe kids had remained individual and strong—he grinned to himself—like bamboo.

'My father had a foul temper,' he began, looking out over
today's thunderous waves crashing on the shore, 'which was
a hundred times worse when he drank. And he drank often.
We all suffered at his hand. All but one. Then one night—'

He bit off the rest. He didn't need to go there.

Libby jumped to her own conclusion. 'Alex, your father
didn't *kill* anyone?'

'He might as well have.'

'Who?'

Alex's gut wrenched. Even now those memories left him
stone-cold. He blew out a long steadying breath and grated
out the words he'd never wanted to utter.

'He assaulted my sister.'

Libby's heels dug into the pavement as her face filled
first with anger, then with pain.

'Annabelle?'

'He'd been out riding all day. Drinking most of it too.
When Annabelle came home he said she wasn't dressed
appropriately.'

Alex remembered the micro mini, skyscraper heels and
carefully applied makeup Annabelle had worn that night.
She hadn't looked like a fourteen-year-old. She'd looked
more like a woman who knew precisely what was what.
Truth was that Annabelle *was* an innocent. Or had been
until that evening when innocence had been destroyed forever.

'Our father railed at her, then pulled out his riding
crop....'

Closing his eyes, Alex tried to shut out the scene he'd

heard about second-hand. He couldn't bring himself to say the words. To face the shame. His father's or his own.

Libby had covered her mouth but her gasp escaped. 'That poor girl.'

Alex studied her face. Libby had no idea that the revulsion she felt was as much his to bear as his father's. Of all his siblings, he loved Annabelle best and yet he'd let her down, fobbed her off, when he should have been there to look out for her. Thank God Jacob came home when he did.

'Jacob tried to protect her and pushed William away,' he went on, his pace down to a crawl now. 'My father staggered back and struck his head on the corner of the staircase. He died instantly.'

'But surely it was self-defence.'

'The jury acquitted my brother of all charges. But the weight of what he'd done ate away at Jacob.'

It sure as hell had eaten away at *him*.

Her gaze filled with sympathy and support, Libby stopped and held his gaze. 'Do you and Annabelle ever talk about it?'

His stomach lurched and he frowned. The very idea knocked him completely off balance.

'Why *would* we?'

He'd all but snapped it out, and Libby blinked several times before her gaze sharpened, trying to see through to places he didn't care for her to go.

'Is there something more, Alex?' she asked quietly. 'Something you're not telling me?'

His heartbeat thumping, he started off again. He'd said enough. The incident had forever changed his sister and it was largely his fault. How could he and Annabelle ever talk about such cruelty, about her maiming—

'Alex…?'

He brought himself back and was about to change the subject when a group, congregated around a picnic table, caught his attention. One woman held a folded magazine and was pointing their way. Looked like he was back in the news.

Defiant, he lifted his chin.

And so what if he was? His arm was out of its sling. Thanks to Libby, he was on his way to full recovery and after two and some weeks cooped up, worried about his future, he felt the greatest urge to venture out.

His gaze slid to his companion. Maybe she'd enjoy a break as well, to continue what they'd started here. Something fun and light, of course. Like the past few hours had been.

As the thought took form, his mouth went dry and Alex wanted to laugh. He was *nervous* about inviting Libby? Amazing what a couple of weeks away from regular social contact could do. She wouldn't say no.

Would she?

He cleared his throat, tugged his ear. 'What would you say to getting out of here for a while?'

She tossed a wary look around. 'You mean, off the street?'

'I mean out of Sydney.'

LIBBY FROZE. She'd heard Alex's suggestion. That he—that *they*—should escape the city. And when the shock wore off, her first reaction was to clasp her hands and exclaim, 'When do we head out?' What girl, who'd spent the night with such an amazing man, would think to refuse?

But at the same time a cloud blocked out the sun, darker reality sank in.

She glanced around. Alex's presence radiated out even in this casual crowd, same way his charisma had turned heads in that Malaysian restaurant. An animated group by that picnic table had certainly picked up on who he was. It seemed, now that his shoulder was on its way to full recovery, he was no longer reticent about getting out and being seen. He didn't seem perturbed by that crowd's attention. Wherever he went, he'd be noticed. Which meant, if she were with him, she'd be noticed too.

Two things wrong with that.

Firstly, she didn't think it wise to make a habit of parading around with Alex as if they were romantically involved, which, she guessed, they were. Even here, in relatively relaxed Manly, people had phones with cameras and video capabilities and weren't afraid to use them. Maybe Alex accepted those kinds of intrusions into his private world but she was no longer a celebrity and didn't miss the spotlight. She didn't need her life, present or past, speculated upon in magazines or the internet.

He wanted to whisk her away?

While her teeth rolled over her bottom lip, he raised a brow.

'I see you're not racing home to pack a bag.'

'Alex, what if you're recognised?' She rephrased. 'Make that, what happens *when* you're recognised?'

'And someone snaps our picture for some celebrity magazine?' He leaned forward and stage whispered. 'We'll survive.'

He'd survive. But, 'You can understand that the perception that I'm involved with a high-profile client could damage my career.'

'We could wear dark glasses and Hungarian moustaches?'

He chuckled and, despite it all, she smiled too. Was she overreacting? Like she had when she'd thought he wouldn't be interested if he found out about her leg?

'Look,' he said more levelly, 'if you rather not, we'll stay in. I understand you want to shield yourself.'

She sighed. Now she felt bad.

What was so wrong with being the girl who'd experienced an incredible night and couldn't deny herself more? Life could be uncertain, but there didn't have to be a shark lurking behind every shadow. She'd felt so safe with Alex these past few hours. Where was the crime in wanting to prolong that?

She made a decision. Stood up tall.

'No. I want to go.'

He gauged her expression. 'You're certain?'

Libby held her breath. Her head told her not to go but her heart was saying loud and clear, *What's the worst that can happen?*

The sun came out at the same time she smiled broadly and announced, 'Commander, lead the way.'

ELI WAS SITTING on the forecourt steps when Alex arrived home an hour later. Alex bet the magazine his assistant held was the same edition the picnic table crowd had been ogling earlier. Obviously it contained a shot of him. A file shot speculating on his comeback? Or had he somehow been snapped in Sydney these past weeks?

As Alex swung out of the limo and the driver headed off,

Eli pushed to his feet. Alex's step slowed on his way up the steps. His friend's expression was closed. Not a good sign.

Eli offered the magazine, folded to a celebrity page. 'No prizes for guessing where you spent the night.'

Alex zoomed in on a picture; a chill sped up his spine and he swore.

Eli scratched his temple. 'I, er, take it you weren't aware this was out?'

'I…had some idea.'

Alex let them inside and headed toward the office, that photograph imprinted at the forefront of his mind—he and Libby standing outside her apartment building, embracing. Kissing.

'Her face is hidden,' Eli said, following Alex down the hall. 'And her name isn't listed, but people will want to know who your new love interest is. What'll I say when the phone starts ringing?'

'No comment.'

'They'll find out one way or another. Could be better coming from us.'

Alex swept into his office, fell into the chair behind his desk and came clean.

'I asked Libby to come away with me this weekend.'

Eli's brows jumped, then he slid his hands into his trouser pockets. 'Somewhere secluded?'

'I was thinking the Gold Coast.'

When Libby had brought up her concerns over how she might be perceived should the press spot them together, he'd acquiesced. Speculations about sleeping with a high-profile client… He understood Libby wanted to look out for her reputation. But he was pleased she'd decided to go with her heart and had agreed to a quick trip away. After this, however…

Eli sauntered forward. 'I might be wrong but when I spoke with Libby Henderson she didn't seem the type to want back in the limelight. In fact, she seemed reserved. Private.'

'Anyone knows if you work with celebrities some of the shine is bound to rub off.'

'She's doing more than *working* with you.'

Alex's gaze snapped up from his hands, clasped on the desk. 'She's over twenty-one.'

Eli's nostrils flared, then he held up his hands. 'You're right. It's none of my business.'

Alex scooted the chair over to his laptop.

Eli was dead on. It wasn't his business.

After tapping a few keys, images of a cosmopolitan sky-line, bordered by miles of golden beach, flashed onto the screen. An hour's flight, relaxed and at the same time full of life. Just the place for an overnight escape.

'Can you organise the jet to fly out for the Gold Coast this afternoon at three?' Alex asked his assistant. 'I'll need a car and driver at the airport and reservations for a pent-house suite at the casino.'

'Nothing like keeping a low profile,' Eli muttered.

Alex ignored it. 'Book tickets for the show too.'

'And if it's booked out?'

Alex pasted on a smile. 'As always, I know you'll come through.'

When Eli saluted his chief and strode out to get plans underway, Alex sat back and took stock.

He shouldn't be cut at Eli for having his say. That's what he paid him for and he only had his and Libby's best interests at heart. Certainly Libby was a nice lady who ought to be treated well—protected—particularly after that failed episode with her ex. But, as he'd told Eli, he wasn't taking advantage of Libby. She was an adult who wanted to make the most of what they'd shared while they could. She wouldn't be thinking long-term, not when she knew better than most how his work ate up practically all his time and energy.

Simply put, he wasn't the marrying kind. Eli knew it. All the *world* knew it. After hearing more of his lacklustre childhood today, surely Libby was smart enough to know it too.

CHAPTER TEN

As COMMERCIAL AS the Gold Coast had become, Libby had always adored this laidback yet glitzy part of the world. Many considered the beaches to be the whitest and finest of any. The restaurants and nightlife were first-rate. Still, when Alex had invited her to join him on a one-night whirlwind stay at Jupiters Casino at Broadbeach, initially she'd been reluctant. Even landing at Coolangatta Airport fifteen minutes earlier, despite her enthusiasm in accepting, she'd still had her doubts.

Catching a sidelong glance at Alex's classic profile now, sitting alongside him in another chauffeur-driven limo, Libby's cheeks toasted remembering the glorious hours they'd spent together last night. This morning when they'd woken and had gone to breakfast, she'd felt so comfortable in his company, almost as if they'd been 'a couple' for years. Alex had delved more into his childhood and the shocking Wolfe family secrets. She'd ended up all the more in awe of what this man had achieved under such oppressive conditions growing up. She also felt lucky to know that he trusted her enough to share the information. She trusted him more now too. Coming away with Alex this weekend felt right. If a photographer happened to catch them together...

Her hands locking in her lap, she focused out the limo window at the beach shacks intermingled with high-rise resorts flying by.

She needed to take one step at a time...even if secretly she'd caught herself daydreaming about joining Alex on other flights, to Spain, Turkey, Monte Carlo... She shouldn't let her imagination roam like that, but they seemed well suited on so many levels, not least of all in the bedroom. When they were together, she didn't think about her deficiencies. She only felt desired and beautiful.

Of course she wasn't anywhere near as refined as the women he usually dated. Not anywhere near as glamorous. But the way Alex had treated and confided in her, she was convinced he wasn't as shallow and mercenary as she'd first thought. In fact, he was anything but.

Alex's voice broke into her thoughts.

'I did mention the show tonight.'

Knowing the production, Libby crooned out a line about still calling Australia home and, while Alex chuckled, she added, 'I've heard it's fabulous.'

'You like music?'

'Sure.'

'Dancing?'

'Oh, I haven't danced in years.'

'We'll have to change that.'

In all honestly she wouldn't say that she *couldn't* dance. Despite her prosthesis she was certain she had the stability and balance needed. Handling the surf was a different matter. In the ocean your balance was constantly challenged. When she'd been younger, leaping over the waves had seemed as natural and fun as eating ice cream. Now she could barely bring herself to think about finding the courage to venture out again.

The limo eased up the casino's resort-style drive. The massive tiered building had been visible from the road for some time. With the huge orange sun sinking rapidly behind the hinterland horizon, banks of lights began to flicker on—iridescent gold and blue—creating the image of a colossal elaborate staircase, which led to the complex's middle floors. The grounds were pristine and subtropical with masses of palm trees and colourful seasonal flowers in bloom. Libby felt as if she'd truly arrived in paradise.

As the limo rolled into the forecourt, a uniformed doorman strode up and opened the passenger's door. Alex assisted her out and together they entered an establishment where multiple millions were gambled, won and lost, each day. Moving into the lobby, Alex kept his sunglasses on, surely not because he thought they might disguise who he was. He couldn't walk into a room and go unnoticed anymore than Russell Crowe. From the way her green eyes widened, the brunette behind the reception desk knew precisely who this handsome guest was.

After checking in, they rode a lift to the top, while peering down over the lower floors through the clear windows of the cabin. When he opened the door of their penthouse and ushered her inside, overwhelmed, Libby sighed long and loud. She felt thoroughly spoilt by the plush crimson carpet, extravagant matching window dressings and sumptuous leather furnishings. But she also felt strangely at home, or at least more at home than in Alex's grand Rose Bay residence. His house was beyond beautiful, but so large and a little sterile for her tastes. This suite, on the other hand, was big but also had colour and something of a cosy feel even amid all the crystal and gold fittings. She just knew they'd have a wonderful time here.

Alex wandered up behind her. His arms slid around her waist as his warm lips nuzzled her ear.

'You like?'

Smiling, she nodded. 'It's gorgeous.'

'I could extend our reservation.'

Her heart leapt, but there was no way. 'I have to be back in the office Monday.'

His hands skimmed down the front of her trousers. 'No chance of putting back your appointments?'

She didn't bother to reply. He knew her well enough to understand she would never put her personal agenda ahead of clients' prearranged appointments.

He chuckled against the sensitive sweep of her neck. 'I'll take that as a no. So until Sunday night, then—' he eased her around '—let's focus on us.'

He tilted her chin up, his mouth covered hers and the effects of his kiss spiralled through her centre, leaving her weak and instantly wanting. She'd been right agreeing to come here with Alex today. Everything felt so perfect. His body pressed against hers. His words. Most of all, his kiss.

His lips left hers slowly but his mouth stayed close. 'You sure you want to go see this show? We could always stay in.'

Libby's pulse rate leapt. She was tempted but, 'I'm sure the tickets weren't easy to get a hold of.'

'Neither were you.' He took her handbag and blindly set it on the lounge while his eyes smouldered into hers. 'I'll order up champagne and we can sip it in bed.'

In the middle of another penetrating kiss, Alex's phone buzzed and he mumbled, 'Ignore it.'

Dreamy, she murmured back, 'Could be important.'

'Don't care.'

When the buzz sounded again, however, he groaned and reached for his phone. About to turn it off, he looked at the message ID and drew in a quick breath.

'It's Annabelle.'

He retrieved the message. When his brows crept in, Libby asked, 'Is something wrong?'

'She's texting to see if I'll be attending Nathaniel's wedding next weekend. I've already said I'll be racing.'

Libby's insides pitched. He meant racing at his all-important Round Four in China. Holding her stomach, she moved off toward the palm-and-surf-fringed view. She couldn't avoid it any longer.

'We're actually not certain about that yet.'

Feeling his eyes boring a hole in her back, Libby waited on tenterhooks. Although from the get-go she'd known that he'd planned to have her sign off on his injury before the stipulated six weeks, she'd never agreed to anything. Neither had she dismissed his goal outright. Nothing was impossible. Similarly nothing was set in cement.

In the preceding weeks, she'd wrangled her way around the issue. Now, for more reasons than one, she needed to be clear.

Assuming her professional mask, she rotated around. 'Your shoulder is doing extremely well. But given that your doctor was firm about the time frame for recovery, I can't make any decisions for or against just yet.'

His eyes narrowed. She could sense his mind ticking over as his chin came slowly up and he sauntered toward her. 'You could give me a full evaluation early.'

'Your cuff and lesser muscles have been under a great deal of strain, and after the setback yesterday—'

'There's no reason we can't go through the exercise, is there?'

Well…

Cornered, she exhaled. 'No. There's no reason.'

'Then I'd like the evaluation.' The tension in his jaw eased but his gaze still held that glint.

'I need you to know that I won't falsify my records.' She wouldn't do that for anyone for any reason. He must know that.

His gaze probed hers and a slight grin hooked one corner of his mouth. 'Of course you wouldn't.'

As her heartbeat thudded, she tried to read his eyes.

When they'd first met she'd believed she'd had his number. Nothing was taboo when it came to Alex Wolfe securing what he needed to benefit his racing career, including seducing his physiotherapist. Remarkably, in the past twenty-four hours, she'd come to respect Alex. Last night, this morning, flying here this afternoon, she'd even come to trust him…trust that he wouldn't intentionally use or hurt her. Whatever his plans before they'd met, he would never try to manipulate her now.

'When do you need to let your doctor know?' she asked.

'I can call him Monday with a standby and give the heads-up as late as Wednesday.'

She kept her gaze on his, then eyed his injured shoulder, which looked as magnificent as the other beneath his casual cream button-down *sans* tie. He'd been superbly fit to begin with. His muscles and tendons had responded well to her program. In her opinion he wasn't there yet…

But if they had until Wednesday and she tested his shoulder then, holding absolutely nothing back…

She tilted her head. She had to ask.

'And if I decide your shoulder's not fit to race?'

He shrugged. 'Then we'll go to my brother's wedding in London.'

She coughed out a laugh, then realised he was serious. 'You said your other brother's hotel is off the coast of *South America*.'

'Yes, but Sebastian owns hotels worldwide. He has another hotel in London, that's where the wedding is being held. You have a passport?'

The room began to spin. Alex was asking her to a wedding? And not just *any* wedding. A Wolfe family occasion, with his brothers and the twin sister he so clearly adored. And missed, though he didn't want to admit it.

'I'd much rather take you to China with me,' he added, closing the distance left separating them. 'But let's make the Grande Wolfe Hotel our backup plan. For now…' He took her hand and led her to the bedroom. 'Let's not wait for champagne.'

THEY DINED IN an award-winning restaurant overlooking the casino's dazzling atrium. The redwood and granite decor was exquisite, a perfect setting for the haute cuisine. They enjoyed basil salmon terrine and roast duckling before moving into the theatre to view a show that equalled in talent and score any lavish Vegas production.

Afterward, when they crossed out into the main area, close to where the gaming took place, Libby had thought she, at least, should be tired; the previous night had been a long one and she was an early-to-bed type of girl. And yet this evening had been so enlivening, the atmosphere so electric, she couldn't think about retiring to the quiet of their suite just yet. It was as if her every cell was on celebratory mode. Particularly when she thought about his suggestion that she accompany him to the Wolfe wedding. She would get to meet all the larger-than-life characters she'd heard so much about.

It all seemed surreal.

Of course, she couldn't pretend that she was the kind of woman others might expect to see accompanying Alex to such an event. She didn't have a manicure every week, or worry too much about fashion and A-lists. Eventually, she supposed, word would leak that she and Alex were involved. And when it did, what anyone else thought wouldn't matter.

But she was thinking too far ahead.

Slipping through the crowd, looking like the silver screen's latest version of James Bond in his dinner suit, Alex wrapped her arm around his and slid over a wicked grin.

'I think you ought to wear that gown to therapy Monday morning, doc.'

Libby swallowed a laugh. She did feel a little like a princess in this evening dress, which she'd bought for the physio guest speaker dinner next month. Beneath the sweetheart neckline, the strapless bodice, which was decorated with beads, fit snug to the hips. The gold leaf coloured satin skirt fell straight to the floor and featured an elegant chapel train. Beyond beautiful to wear on a special evening, however…

She arched a brow. 'It wouldn't be so practical in your gym.'

'Who cares about practical?' He came close, nipped her ear and a bevy of tingles flew through her. 'Will we put a few in the slot machines?' he asked, changing the subject as he tipped away. 'Or are you more a blackjack fan?'

'I know we're in a casino, but I don't gamble. I don't mind watching the excitement though.'

He studied a croupier sweeping a tower of chips to the house and admitted, 'Not my vice either.' His eyes flashed. 'I know what I promised we'd do. *Dance.*'

Libby stilled. She was so not comfortable with that idea, but she didn't want to seem like a coward. Or…inadequate.

Casting a quick glance around at patrons enjoying the beating lights and ringing bells, she hitched up her shoulders and let them drop. 'I don't think they have a dance floor.'

'Of course they do.' His eyes lighting up, he snapped his fingers. 'I have an idea.'

Before she could object, they were headed toward the reception desk. After leaving her by an elaborate water feature, he stopped by the concierge and spoke briefly to a middle-aged man who nodded enthusiastically and handed something over. Joining her again, Alex snatched a kiss from her cheek.

'All set.'

He wouldn't explain further, only led her to the casino foyer and out into the forecourt, where a sleek black sports car awaited. When a uniformed porter opened the passenger's side door, Libby hesitated only a moment before giving into the spirit of adventure and sliding into the sumptuous dark leather cabin. After buckling up, Alex ignited the engine and, incredibly low to the ground, the car zipped out the hotel grounds.

Anticipation balling in her stomach, Libby looked across and took in Alex's classic profile, dramatically silhouetted against the moon and streetlights. 'So, where are you whisking me away to now?'

His mouth hooked into a grin. 'That's top secret, I'm afraid.'

They headed away from the bright lights until, looking around, Libby realised there were few lights at all. Minutes later, he drove into a darkened and otherwise empty car park positioned one side of a quiet stretch of sand dunes. While Libby racked her brains, trying to work out what came next, her door opened and Alex offered a hand.

A cool salty breeze filed through her hair as she pushed to her feet and scanned the peaceful scene. The hum of traffic and lights from the city seemed an eternity away while the stars were a hundred times brighter and nearer than she'd ever seen. Beyond the dunes, the rhythmic wash of waves called. Seemed that Alex heard their call too. His hand folded around hers and he gave an encouraging tug.

'Let's walk.'

Her heart flew to her throat. 'On the *beach*?'

'Sure.' He squeezed her hand. 'Slip off your shoes.'

'Alex, you know I haven't—' Her throat convulsed and she swallowed. 'I haven't…'

Cupping her face, he smiled into her eyes. 'You haven't been on a beach since your accident. Tonight, I think that should change.'

Tonight? Right *now*? 'You're serious?'

'More than you know.'

When he slipped off his shoes, Libby's breath hitched in her chest. Barefoot, he headed toward the dunes, then threw a glance back. 'You coming?'

Libby took a few deep breaths but her head still tingled

with the heavy scratchings of panic. He didn't know what he was asking.

'The sand's cool and soft,' he said before lifting his nose to the air. 'I can feel the salt spray on my face.'

Closing her eyes, Libby lifted her face too. As moist briny air filled her lungs, pictures of her playing in the sand as a girl rushed up—carefree, innocent—and an unexpected urge gripped. When she opened her eyes, her pulse was thumping with the beginnings of excitement.

Do it. Just do it!

Before she could change her mind, she swept off her shoes and hurried to meet him on top of the grassy dune. Laughing, he snatched a kiss, grabbed her hand and together they navigated the downward sandy slope.

Libby found herself laughing too. Yes, the sand was cool and powder soft. It felt so good, she had to fight the impulse to fall to her knees and scoop the grains up in her arms like she used to. Should she have tried to do this sooner, or was now simply the right time? With the right person. She couldn't say that she was completely anxiety free. But with Alex walking alongside of her, his hand fitted so firmly around hers, she could handle the unease and focus on the great memories rather than the sad.

Libby's gaze slipped to Alex's thoughtful profile as he watched the waves folding in several metres away. Was he thinking of how his mother had once taken him to the beach? Was he wishing he'd been old enough to remember? Good memories mixed with sad…

Alex seemed to come back from wherever his mind had been and glanced down at her feet. 'How's it feel?'

'Weird,' she replied, then admitted with a happy grin. 'Nice. Very nice.'

The sparkle in his eyes said he was pleased. 'Someone once told me our only restrictions are the ones we place on ourselves.'

'Carter White?' He nodded and it made sense. But, to be fair, as Alex well knew: 'Sometimes it can be a challenge to conquer them.'

Beneath a glittering stream of stars, his gaze intensified. Was he thinking of the limitations he put on himself in later life? Personal boundaries, cut-off lines he didn't want to revisit even with all his success and world acclaim?

His pace slowed and he gestured to something up ahead. 'Looks as if we're expected.'

Libby's spirits dropped. She'd thought they were alone, just them and the stars and the sea. But, yes, ahead up the beach sat a small enclosed marquee, barely illuminated by a handful of misty lights. Then the gentle strains of a symphony seemed to fade up out of nowhere. Violins, saxophones...an invisible orchestra was playing.

But as they ventured closer, it became apparent that the marquee, and immediate area, was vacant. Libby darted a look around and pricked her ears to catch any sounds of company. But Alex didn't look the least surprised or curious.

Finally coming up to speed, she set her hands on her hips. 'You organised this, didn't you?'

He only laughed. 'Guilty, Your Honour.' He moved to an ice bucket, proceeded to inspect the champagne bottle's label, then exclaimed, 'Exceptional year. But we'll open it later. For now...' After replacing the bottle, he returned to stand before her. His warm hand twined around hers, he pressed a light kiss to her knuckles, then brought their clasped hands to his lapel. 'We're going to dance.'

'Here?'

'Yes, Libby. Here. Now.' His gaze roamed her face. 'You're going to dance with me.'

Panic fisted in her windpipe. 'But the sand…it's so uneven.'

His other hand scoped around to support her back. 'I've got you.'

Libby was ready to insist. She didn't feel like dancing. Wasn't getting her on the beach after so long breaking down a big enough fence for one night? But as his gaze continued to hold hers and his confidence in her radiated out, she pressed her lips together, inhaled one big steadying breath and, sucking it up, let the music filter over her.

As the chorus of a well-known love song grew slightly louder, Alex took one step, then another, and gradually something strong and instinctive took over and Libby began to move too, stilted at first, feeling uncertain…awkward. But he continued to move along with her, then move a little faster. Next he was winding her under his arm. When he brought her back, he swayed with her again before the music segued into something more dramatic.

He rested his forehead against her. 'What do you think? Ready to go to town?'

Before she could say, 'No! Definitely not!' he did some incredible move and wound her under his arm again before dipping her Valentino style and leading her in a dramatic tango charge. Stunned—*amazed*—at any moment Libby fully expected to fall flat on her face. But although her moves were hardly smooth, she kept up. Kept up and more! When he changed direction and slid back the other way, she gave herself over to the impulsiveness of it, to the freedom. To the trust. And for the first time in years, it was true.

She lifted her face to the moon and laughed out loud.
She was *dancing*!

THEY DANCED UNTIL the night air grew too cold on her arms.
Alex removed his jacket and, moving behind her, drew the
warm black fabric over her shoulders. As he stood once
more in front of her, she peered up into his gaze, dark grey
and intense in the shadows, and suddenly the awareness of
what throbbed between them, of what they'd shared in just
over a day, became too much.

She thought she'd loved Scott but the feelings she had for
her ex seemed childish beside the intensity of the sensations
Alex brought out in her. From the first moment they'd met,
he'd touched a place within her she hadn't known about.
What she felt now was beyond anything she could ever have
believed could exist between a man and woman. It was exhilarating. Thrilling. And way more than a little scary.

She was feeling so much so soon. For so many reasons it
wouldn't be wise to let herself feel too much more.

Libby blew out a shaky breath and stepped back. She
needed some space to get her whirling thoughts together,
so she headed toward the water and gazed out over the dark
undulating blanket of the sea. She filled her lungs with fresh
briny air, not surprised that the constant crash of waves, the
ocean's thunderous heartbeat, matched her own.

At her back, Alex's natural heat enveloped her and his
rich voice touched her ear, spreading ripples of intense pleasure over every inch of her skin.

'You're still cold?'

Smiling, she snuggled down into his jacket and huddled
back against him. 'I'm just right.'

'Are you sure? That breeze is fresh. I flicked on the heater in case.'

She angled around. Sure enough, a tall outdoor heater was set up to one side of the marquee. Its large grate was glowing red. Deep inside the softly lit tent sat a plush divan with piles of comfy-looking cushions. A fluffy white blanket lay folded at one end.

She arched a brow. 'This is all very convenient.'

Not bothering to hide a grin, he ushered her toward the divan. 'Isn't it?'

After settling back against a pile of pillows set in one corner, she waved away his offer of champagne. She only wanted to snuggle beneath that blanket and drink in the enchanting view with Alex's strength and heat supporting her.

When Alex joined her, he shook out the blanket and tucked the soft folds in. 'Warm enough?'

Burrowing into him, she sighed against his chest. 'Now I am.'

They sat together, her legs curled up to one side, the heater emitting a warm ghostly glow while the moonlit sea stretched out before them to infinity.

With her cheek resting against his chest, he was stroking her shoulder when he noted, 'The moon on the water looks like a net cast with pearls.'

She examined the sea, then sat up and gave him a curious look. 'You really have a thing for pearls, don't you?'

He chuckled. 'Not before meeting you, I swear. Maybe it was our conversation the other day over lunch—' his palm traced over her crown '—or perhaps it's the lustre of your hair that reminds me whenever we're together.'

Libby considered his words. She supposed pearls could be the jewel for her. Diamonds sure as heck hadn't worked. The cluster she'd worn as an engagement ring had been gorgeous but had never been truly special to her, no doubt because Scott hadn't presented her with a ring when he'd proposed. After many embarrassing questions from friends and family, she'd gone and bought her own. After everything had fallen apart, she'd been so disillusioned she'd sworn never to wear another diamond on her finger. But pearls...

Yes. Maybe pearls.

But then, 'My gran used to say pearls mean tears.' Guess that suited too; she'd shed a few in her life.

'In some religions pearls represent completeness.'

She laughed. 'Is there anything you're not an expert on?'

He leaned forward and his lips skimmed hers. 'I plan to learn a lot more about you.'

His mouth slanted over hers and any chill in the air seemed to evaporate into steam. As the temperature beneath the blanket climbed, Libby's thoughts drifted back to pearls, the mysteries they seemed to conceal, and how Alex continued to uncover so many previously depressed levels inside of her.

She trembled at the welcome pressure of his hand ironing over her bodice. Then he was delving beneath the cup, the pad of his thumb rubbing the tight aching peak and reducing her insides to liquid fire. Leaning in, she measured the broad expanse of his chest beneath his shirt, marvelling at how something as simple as feeling the crisp crinkle beneath her palm could bring out such intensely charged emotions. The invisible zip at the side of her gown came down and her breasts, and any remaining inhibitions, were freed.

As his touch brushed bare skin, remembered sensations from the night before and this afternoon transformed and condensed into a physical need, pulsing and burning until she thought she might faint from the hunger.

When he broke the kiss and urged her gently away, her nerve-endings were sizzling. She didn't want him to stop. She only wanted to feel him naked and bearing down. But when he lifted her chin, her heavy eyelids dragged open and she realised with a start where they were. Away from prying eyes but still in a public place.

And she couldn't care less.

His voice was a drugging whisper at the shell of her ear. 'Your gown will be crushed.'

'Do you think I care?'

He smiled and she tilted her weight against him until he lay back on the pillows, then she made short work of his trouser fastenings. Over the distant thunder of waves, she heard the metallic burr of his zipper easing down. Alex's chest expanded on a giant breath and, his gaze burning, he tugged off his trousers at the same time she leaned forward and dropped a lingering kiss an inch above his navel.

Her tongue wove a trail down the arrow of dark hair that led to his thighs and soon her mouth connected with that part of him that didn't know the meaning of the word *reserved*. Circling the top of his shaft with her hand, she dragged her fingers down, then looped her tongue around the hot tip twice.

His hips arched up and he clutched a sequined pillow near her head. With him braced, she slid her lips down over the head of his erection at the same time her fisted hand came back up.

'Libby...' She heard him swallow. 'This could get dangerous.'

She hummed out her approval and went down again.

AFTER ORGANISING A late checkout from the penthouse, she and Alex spent the remainder of the day in Surfers.

Midmorning they enjoyed an ice cream in famous Cavill Avenue, where great restaurants, beach umbrellas and micro bikinis ruled. For a bit of fun, they checked out the Wax Museum, the largest in the southern hemisphere, and marvelled at the lifelike replicas of so many singers, royal members and notorious villains. Libby commented in all sincerity it shouldn't be long before they commissioned a likeness of him.

For lunch, they stopped in for some live music, a couple of thick-cut steaks and Queensland ales at the Surfers Paradise Tavern, a local icon established back in 1925 when Surfers was a small isolated town that went by the name of Elston. When someone started belting out the chorus of a famous Slim Dusty tune, everyone joined in, including Alex.

Alex was certainly a complex character—he could be alpha-annoying, inherently charming, and there were also times when he seemed so distracted and remote. But as Alex laughed and clapped and sang along with the crowd now, Libby knew this was who he wanted to be. Who he *could* be. Relaxed. Real.

Midafternoon, the limo collected them and started inland. No matter how much she begged, Alex wouldn't let on where they were going. Thirty minutes later they pulled into a magnificent rural property, with an extravagant ranch-style mansion.

Slipping out of the limo, Libby took in the spectacular far-reaching grounds. 'This is yours?'

'A friend's.'

'You want to catch up while we're here?'

'He's in Italy.'

She frowned. 'I don't understand.'

'Darren's an old driving buddy. When he retired, he missed the thrill so much, he built his own track.'

Understanding, she smiled. 'You're going to take a car for a spin.' With her watching. Frankly, she couldn't wait to see Alex in action—as long as he, and his shoulder, didn't overdo it.

'I am indeed going for a spin.' He took her hand. 'And you're coming with me.'

Libby's heart tripped over several beats. In her own car, she hated to go past 100 k's. Surfing had its dangers, certainly, but simply thinking of the kind of speeds Alex merely cruised at on a track left her mind reeling and stomach somersaulting.

She stammered and stuttered and said she couldn't possibly but, as usual, Alex wouldn't take no for an answer. And when Libby remembered the night before—walking along the beach, dancing beneath the stars—amazingly she found she could find the courage for this as well.

Ten minutes later they had donned helmets and were buckling up. The track unwinding before them looked very much like the professional circuits Libby had seen on cable. As Alex kicked in the engine, she told herself to relax and enjoy the experience. Didn't help that her knuckles had turned white, gripping her thighs.

'This here is one fast car.'

'Convertible,' she added, feeling even more vulnerable with the top down. She moistened dry lips. 'Just how fast are we going to go?'

He reached for her knee and squeezed. 'You don't want to know.'

Alex stepped on the pedal—floored it, in fact. The car flew off and Libby left a screaming laugh behind.

They went from naught to three thousand kilometres per hour in three point five seconds. Or that's how it felt. With wind blasting through her hair, scared out of her wits, Libby hung on and told herself she was not only in the hands of a professional, she was in the care of the best. Everything might be belting by in a blur. Common sense said if they crashed they would die. Just when she thought her pulse couldn't race any faster she saw the sweeping bend up ahead.

Her jaw dropping, she swung a horrified look at Alex's concentrated profile. His eyes were narrowed, his hands firm on the vibrating wheel, a smile of pure exhilaration tugged on his lips. He changed down, she held her breath and they took the turn with his foot still down. All four tyres skidded sideways, drifting around the arching corner as if they'd hit black ice.

Libby let go a wailing scream.

OVER THE ROAR of the engine and whistle of the wind, Alex heard Libby's shriek of horrified delight and, righting the car, laughed out loud.

Priceless.

It hadn't hit until this minute but he'd never been in this situation before—in a car on a track with a woman. Until today, he'd never considered the possibility. But as he gunned the 650 horsepower engine down the far straight, he realised this was a first in more than one way.

Whenever he hit a track, he was unfailingly focused on bettering himself, achieving his best, but today wasn't about career or proving anything. Not in the typical sense, in any case. He only wanted to have fun or, more correctly, he wanted *Libby* to have fun. From what he could see of the stretched smile on her face through the hair whipping around her head, it seemed he'd achieved precisely that.

BY EIGHT, they were back at Sydney Airport, where the limousine was parked ready to take them home. But Libby's mind was still spinning. The night away had been amazing enough without that unbelievable experience on the track this afternoon. She thought she had a good grip on who Alex Wolfe was, but she'd only known half of it. After that wild, hair-raising ride, she'd come to appreciate in a way she couldn't have before what got him so jazzed about racing and why he was fighting tooth and nail to keep on top: to hold onto that fabulous sense of freedom combined with the ultimate sense of control.

Alex waited until they'd pulled up outside her apartment block before he took her hand and said, 'Come back to Rose Bay with me.'

Wanting to so badly, she closed her eyes and shook her head. 'That's not a good idea.'

'I think it's a great idea.'

He leaned closer—his shoulders, his mouth—but she put both hands against his chest and explained, 'I need to be up early, and if I go back to your house I won't get any sleep.' They were both running on adrenaline as it was.

He seemed to think her excuse through, then reluctantly agreed.

'In that case...' He reached into the limo's side door pocket and retrieved a small pink plastic bag. He looked at it awkwardly as if debating what to do with it. Then he offered it over.

'I bought you a gift.'

She blinked first at him, then at the bag. 'What is it?'

'Open it and see.'

With an uncertain smile, she accepted the bag and slid the contents into her palm. She sighed at what she saw. A gold clamshell, the size of a dessertspoon, held a bed full of glittering light blue stones. Dotted amongst those stones sat three separate creamy beads the size of freshwater pearls. A clasp was linked to the top of the shell.

Beside her, Alex leaned close. 'I picked it up at one of those tourist stores. The blue stones symbolise the sea. The pearls represent the past, present and the future. I thought it suited you.'

Libby's heart beat high in her throat. It was a trinket, an inexpensive charm that he'd put real thought into, and she *loved* it!

Over the thickness in her throat, she murmured, 'It's perfect.' She'd never known anything *more* perfect.

He curled some hair away from her flushed cheek. 'I'll walk you up.'

She lowered the charm. It had been an incredible couple of days but she couldn't think about saying goodnight to Alex at the building entrance or her apartment door. He might suggest coming in and, the way she felt now—the way she'd felt all weekend—she wouldn't be able to turn him away. Tonight she needed to.

'If you walk me to the door,' she said, 'you'll kiss me and, before I know it, I'll be tugging you inside. We both need some sleep.'

His brow furrowed and a muscle in his jaw flexed twice but finally he nodded and knocked on the glass partition, signalling the driver to collect her luggage and open her door.

'Thank you for a wonderful weekend,' she said, her heart so full she thought it might burst.

'We'll do it again soon.'

But he didn't mention specifics…didn't mention the wedding…and after an all-too-brief kiss goodnight, the driver opened her door and carried her luggage to the building entrance. She let herself in, heard the purr of the limo's engine as it pulled out from the curb, then she gazed down again at the pearl charm in her hand. If not for this, she might think it was all some fantastic dream.

Feeling so churned up inside, she held her stomach. Before this weekend she'd known Alex was scorching. Now she found his company positively irresistible and for way more reasons than his looks and his charm. Everything she'd learned about him…everything she'd confessed about herself…

Alex Wolfe was a complex person. A world-renowned celebrity. A man who had helped her face some fierce, long-held fears. He was more than any woman could hope for and Libby simply couldn't deny it any longer.

She was falling in love.

CHAPTER ELEVEN

THE NEXT MORNING, Libby dragged herself into her office. She felt groggy. Not surprising given her lack of sleep the night before. After tossing and turning till dawn, in hindsight, it might have been easier if Alex *had* walked her to the door. At least she wouldn't have woken up lonely.

Instead she'd placed the pearl charm on her bedside table and had lain awake watching the imitation jewels sparkle in the moonlight while going over every moment of her amazing weekend with Alex Wolfe...her client. Her lover.

The superstar sportsman with the shoulder she'd agreed to put through a thorough examination two days from now.

If she found him unfit to drive, Alex had said he'd take her to that family wedding. But he hadn't mentioned it last night when he'd dropped her home. He was banking on his injury passing her assessment. And if she found his joint needed more time to heal... The former athlete in her said he wouldn't take the news well.

But she couldn't give him a green light simply to make him happy, she told herself, crossing her office's reception area. And if he was half the man she'd come to believe him to be, even if he were unhappy, Alex would understand her position. He might be upset with the situation but he wouldn't be angry. At least, not with her.

Behind her desk, Payton glanced up. Her mouth rounded before she dropped her head and disappeared behind the counter's top lip.

Libby looked around. Had she missed something?

'Payton…everything all right?'

Peering back over the counter, Payton gave a coy look. 'How was your, uh, weekend?'

'My *weekend*?' Libby's stomach flip-flopped twice. 'How did you know—?'

Then she saw a celebrity magazine open on the desk and the half-page shot of her and Alex checking in at the casino Saturday afternoon. All her strength funnelled through her middle and out her toes. Baby-fawn weak, she let the counter help hold her up while she croaked out, 'Is that the only picture?'

'In *this* magazine. There was another one out on Friday.'

From her desk's top drawer, Payton slid out another magazine, folded to a page, to a snap, of Alex and some unidentifiable female he was kissing in the entrance of an apartment block.

Looking uncomfortable, Payton wriggled back in her seat. 'I'm guessing the woman Alex Wolfe's kissing is you.'

Libby remembered Alex's hesitation on the Manly esplanade on Saturday morning when he'd noticed a small group studying him. She remembered that one of the group had held a magazine. Now she knew what had amused them so much: they'd seen her and Alex walking together and were speculating on whether he was really *the* Alex Wolfe and if she was the woman in the photo.

Slipping against the counter edge, Libby held her woozy

head. This was worse than she'd ever imagined. As Payton suggested, it wasn't certain who the woman in that kissing photo was but it wouldn't be hard to put two and two together after this additional *clearer* shot taken on the Gold Coast.

She'd known this kind of a leak was a possibility and yet she'd gone ahead and continued to see him intimately anyway. Now the stark reality glared out at her. If she gave Alex what he wanted on Wednesday after her evaluation, who would believe she hadn't been charmed or, worse, bribed?

She slipped her bag, holding the pearl charm, behind her back and muttered as she headed off, 'I'm unavailable for calls.'

But Payton wasn't letting her friend off that easily.

'Libby, please. Talk to me. This is so *huge*. I mean... ohmigod... Alex *Wolfe*!' She held her heart as if it were pounding and said solemnly, 'I bet he's an unbelievable kisser. Did you ever think for one moment that he'd fall for you like this?'

Libby stopped, shuddered and walked haltingly back. Maybe there were some photos she hadn't seen yet. Good Lord, she hoped there hadn't been any telescopic lenses pointed at the beach that night!

'I was telling my friend, Tawny,' Payton went on, 'that when he was here the other day I thought he was looking at you with a real sultry gleam in his eye. And then when you didn't come back from lunch at all that day, I didn't want to say anything but my imagination went through the roof—'

'*Payton.*' Feeling her entire body erupt in a blush, Libby threw a worried glance toward the front entrance. 'I don't want you spreading gossip like that.'

Payton's eyebrows slanted in. She looked confused. Hurt.

'But, Libby, *everyone* knows. It's all over the papers and the internet. What's wrong? If I were you, I wouldn't give a tinker's tap what the press is saying.'

Her knees gone to jelly, Libby had slumped against the counter. The internet? She felt gutted. No. She was *numb*.

Libby stumbled into her office, fell into her chair and, holding her flushed cheeks, groaned. Once upon a time she'd thrived on publicity. In her day, she'd adored being Australia's poster girl. She'd been on fire, but she wasn't so hot anymore, and a huge diversion from Alex Wolfe's usual female fare. He had a reputation for seeing starlets and supermodels and positively no one who came close to resembling her. The press would try to crucify her.

But strangely she didn't care about that aspect. She knew how Alex felt about her. How he saw her and had helped her see herself that way again too. She might have given back mobility and strength to his arm but he'd given back infinitely more.

A scratching on the window had Libby swinging around. Through the glass she caught the fervent expression of a man with shaggy coffee-coloured hair before the flash of a professional camera went off and blinded her. Shielding her eyes, she lunged over and snapped shut the blinds at the same time Payton flew through the doorway.

'Libby, a reporter's in the foyer.'

A person was on Payton's heels. Peering over her shoulder, the young man with silver framed eyeglasses held up a mini recorder. 'I'm after a quote, Ms Henderson. People want to know about Alex Wolfe's latest love interest.'

For an instant, rather than the reporter, Libby saw Alex standing there as he had almost a week ago when he'd asked her to lunch and she'd taken that first step toward her ordinary life being turned on its head. She loved being with Alex, but she wanted no part of this.

While Payton tried to crowd the reporter back, Libby struggled to assemble her thoughts, but the intruder was beyond eager to snare this ripe opportunity.

'You were Female World Surfing Champ years ago, Libby. Do you have any comment on your accident? Does Alex know that you wear a prosthesis? Do you compare yourself to the women Alex Wolfe usually dates?'

Growling, Payton grabbed the reporter's arm and tried her best to wrestle him out. But when Libby came steadily forward, the two stopped their battle, the reporter clearly anticipating a gossip worthy response.

'You'd like a reply,' Libby asked, and the reporter nodded. So she first held the doorjamb for ballast, swung back a leg and kicked him as hard as she could in the shin. When he jumped and howled, she announced, 'That's my answer.'

Payton gave an astonished way-to-go look before Libby closed and locked the door.

Libby listened to her friend herding the reporter away while delayed tears threatened to rise. The reporter hadn't said anything new…about her accident…her leg…most particularly the fact that it seemed an anomaly that a man like Alex Wolfe should find her appealing. *Sexy.* Scott certainly hadn't after that day.

But they were different men. Different on so many levels.

Her cell phone rang. She reached her bag and retrieved the call at the same time she saw the screen blink out the caller's name. Alex Wolfe.

'Are you available for lunch?' he said down the line. 'There's a restaurant I want to take you to but it's difficult to get a reservation. I wanted to call early.'

'You know about those magazines, don't you?' she asked straight out.

The silence on the line finally ended in an expulsion of air. 'Yes.'

'That's why you phoned. To see if I knew too.'

He exhaled again. 'I'm sorry, Libby.'

'It's not your fault,' she said. 'It was bound to happen. I knew that as well as you did.'

'You're okay with it?'

Libby thought about the photographer scratching at her window, the reporter barging into her office and asking the rudest questions. But she wouldn't tell Alex what that obnoxious man had said. No doubt the press would do all they could to ask Alex the same.

What did he find appealing about a cripple like Libby Henderson?

'Libby?'

'I'm fine,' she said, then took a breath and told herself that she was. She'd weathered worse. She'd survive. 'I'll be over by nine for our session but I can't go to lunch.'

'Can't or won't?'

'Alex, we have some intense days ahead of us. Let's concentrate on that.'

His voice deepened. 'You're sure you're okay?'

She said yes but wanted to add, *Or I will be.*

She couldn't wait for Wednesday to come and go. She knew Alex couldn't either.

SHE AND ALEX worked diligently together on Monday and Tuesday. She told him she'd feel happier not to see each other on an intimate basis until these hard yards were out the way. They didn't discuss those photographs again. He didn't mention whether any reporters had tried to get a quote. She couldn't bear to go near her computer or the internet and told Payton to do her a favour and not fill her in on any goss.

When Wednesday dawned, Libby rocked up at the Rose Bay mansion and tested Alex's shoulder. She held nothing back and was vigilant for any sign of weakness or pain, but he showed no trace of fatigue. Never came near wincing. After their setback on Friday, she found it difficult to believe. She didn't want to make a mistake or have anyone assume she'd forfeited her ethics for her 'boyfriend.' Her client's best interests always came first. And in this case, it seemed, Alex's interests would be best served by returning early to the track.

Of course the team doctor would want to perform his own evaluation. But she couldn't see that he wouldn't concur. Seemed Alex Wolfe would be racing in China after all. Hopefully he would surge back to the top, and her reputation would be left intact. Of course they wouldn't be attending his brother's wedding, but she had a feeling that with the eldest brother's unexpected appearance after twenty years, there would be many more Wolfe reunions in the future. Hopefully she and Alex would continue to see each other…which meant her privacy would be affected. She could barely tolerate the thought of being corralled by heartless members of the paparazzi as she had been on Monday. But it was a price she was prepared to pay.

With the evaluation complete, Alex shrugged back into his shirt. 'Well, doc, what's the verdict?'

Standing alongside him before the mirror, she crossed her arms and raised her chin. 'I have to say that based on what I've seen today and the progress that you've made…'

He stopped buttoning and almost frowned. 'Is it a green light or a red?'

She smiled. 'Green. In my opinion your shoulder is strong enough to cope well under professional car racing conditions.'

Ecstatic, Alex punched the air, but he was wise enough to do it with his left arm. Then he brought her close and kissed her with a tender passion that left her heart banging against her ribs. When his mouth released hers, he smiled into her eyes and then, relieved and so pleased, he laughed and Libby discovered she was laughing too. She'd made the right decision, and now she only had to wait for Alex to win that race in Beijing and then contact her to discuss how, where and when they would celebrate. The world might see her as 'not up to par' but Alex wouldn't use her emotions, use her growing affection and trust, to get what he needed. Not after everything they'd shared.

Alex strode over to collect his phone off a ledge near the treadmills. 'I need to call the team manager. The test driver needs to be told and forms have to be signed.'

Understanding completely, Libby headed off to collect her bag. 'Absolutely. I'll be on my way.'

Phone in hand, Alex quizzed her eyes. 'Do you need to write up a letter? Sign something?'

'I'll fix it with your assistant when I get back to the office.'

He held her gaze, his expression lighter than she'd ever seen, but somehow she knew he wasn't really seeing *her*. Rather he was imagining the crowd cheering him on this weekend. He was anticipating the challenge and thrill of being back in the driver's seat, of doing what he was born to do. Race and win. He was excited. He had every right to be.

Of course he'd need to keep up with the specific stretches and strengthening exercises, not only for the short-term but for the rest of his life. He'd need regular physio checkups to be on the safe side. Given he wasn't permanently stationed here in Sydney, it didn't necessarily have to be her.

Libby chewed her lip.

How much time did Alex actually spend in Australia?

As if he'd read her thoughts, Alex set the phone aside and strode over. Looking proud and happy, but also distracted, he held her upper arms and spoke in an earnest voice she hadn't heard before.

'We can celebrate next week. In the meantime…can you fly out later today?'

She could only gape. *Fly out?*

'You mean to *China*?'

'Practice laps start tomorrow.'

Libby held her swooping stomach. She couldn't get her mind around what he'd asked. She'd assumed that he'd board his private jet and, focused only on the finish line, leave her behind. He wanted her to fly with him to Asia?

But, 'I—I can't. I have appointments.'

Responsibilities. He knew that.

His mouth pressed into a thin line. 'There's no use trying to convince you, I suppose. But I can be back by Tuesday. We'll go out on the town then.'

Holding that thought, she nodded, snatched a kiss and, grinning, headed for the door. 'Great. Then I'll leave you with it.'

'I'll see you out.'

'No. Really, I'm fine.'

But he was already a step ahead of her.

As they walked down the hall, she tried not to dwell on

the fact that he didn't take her hand or rest his palm against her back as he had these past days. His mind was thousands of miles away. Understandable. She remembered well how intense psyching up before a competition could be.

After opening the front door, he accompanied her out on to the patio. Suddenly uncertain of whether to kiss him again, shake his hand or perhaps simply send a salute, she muttered a quick, 'Good luck,' then headed for the steps. About to take the first, a hand on her elbow pulled her up.

She turned and peered up into his smiling eyes. 'One more kiss and I'll let you go.'

He was bringing her near when Libby's thoughts leapt upon those intimate shots taken of them last week. Then she thought of those horrible questions that reporter had shot at her, and she flinched and pulled away.

'Let's not.' She skipped a glance around. 'There could be some lenses pointed this way.'

But, smiling still, he only slid a step closer so Libby took a step back. Then the ground seemed to vanish from beneath her and she was falling backward with nothing to grip. Her arms had flailed in an arc over her head and her body was going horizontal when her waist was lassoed and she was tugged back up and onto her feet.

Out of breath, she got her balance, then her bearings. She looked over in time to see Alex's right arm fall away from its hook around the nearby patio column…in time to see him grimace and hold his shoulder while his jaw clenched tight. When he saw her studying him, his hand dropped away, the contorted expression vanished and he rolled back his shoulders.

Holding her roiling stomach, she came closer and reached to touch the joint. 'Oh, God, Alex, you're hurt.'

Winding away, he seemed stuck between a scowl and a smile.

'I'm *fine*.'

'Please, Alex, let me see.'

He caught her hand. 'You were on your way to write a letter.'

'Are you in much pain?'

'Not even a twinge.'

She studied his darkening gaze and swallowed back worry and regret. Her voice was choked. 'I'm sorry—' sorrier than he could ever imagine '—but I don't believe you.'

His eyes narrowed at the same time his nostrils flared and a vein pulsed down the side of his throat. 'You want proof?' He fisted his right hand and brought it almost level to his waist before bringing it down again. Dying inside, Libby bit her lower lip. He hadn't been able to lift his arm any higher.

She put a professional note in her voice. 'We'll get another MRI.'

'No more tests, dammit! I'm ready to drive.'

'I'm sorry, Alex, I'm so sorry.' She knew what it meant to him. What he thought he was losing. *Everything*. 'But I don't think you are ready.' She raised her hands in a calming gesture. 'We'll work on it, okay? Your next race after China is when? Two weeks? If we put all our effort into—'

'Right now I need to make a phone call,' he cut in, something like rage and betrayal darkening his face. 'If you'll excuse me.'

He turned on his heel and left Libby gaping as the door shut in her face.

AT ONE IN the afternoon, Eli Steele arrived at Libby's practice. Payton led him straight through to her office.

Eli was a tall, attractive man. Well-mannered, Libby remembered as she rose from behind her desk. And one hundred and ten percent dedicated to Alex Wolfe. She wondered if Alex had ever abused his assistant's trust like he'd so recently abused hers. Having that twelve-foot-high door shut in her face wasn't an event she'd soon forget.

'I have communication here from Alex,' Eli said, after taking her hand in a professional greeting. 'I wanted to deliver it in person.'

Her stomach churning, Libby murmured that she appreciated that and with shaking hands opened the sealed envelope. Holding her breath, she scanned the lines.

> *Libby,*
> *Thank you for all your efforts. After discussions with my team manager and doctor it's been decided my situation may well benefit from a different approach. I thank you for your time and dedication to date. I will be in contact after I'm back behind the wheel.*
> *Sincerely, Alex Wolfe*

Feeling as if a bomb had exploded in her face, Libby set down the letter.

'He's...disappointed,' Eli explained, as if that could be an excuse.

Alex was disappointed?

She sank into her chair. 'So am I.'

Particularly that he'd had Eli do his dirty work. Bet it wasn't the first time.

Like a good assistant, Eli made an excuse. 'You have to understand...racing is Alex's life. He couldn't be a champion if he didn't concentrate everything he had on showing up and winning.'

But she was still digesting the brevity and formal tone of that note. *I thank you for your time and dedication to date.*

Her fingers balled up the paper.

Where did he come off thinking he could treat her, treat *any* woman, this way? Three days ago they were together, laughing, racing around that track at incredible speeds. Making love. *Sharing!*

Swallowing the hurt and disbelief, she set the note aside. 'You can tell Mr. Wolfe that I expected more from him… but I shouldn't have. I hope you don't mind me saying, Eli, neither should you.'

Alex cared only about himself—his career—and he would use anyone for any purpose to get what he needed to get to and stay on top.

Eli rearranged his feet. Nodded at the ground. Then he blew out a breath and headed out. 'Good luck, Libby.'

Libby was still sitting, getting more incensed by the second, when Payton edged in and closed the door.

'Want to talk about it?'

'I was an idiot,' Libby admitted, her face unbearably hot. 'I did precisely what I swore I wouldn't. I got involved with a client—and not just *any* client.'

She remembered Alex reaching to kiss her and how, worried about photographers, she'd pulled away. He must know, above all else, she only wanted his shoulder to mend. This morning had been a terrible accident. Like his spin-out on the track. Like her incident in the surf. But that didn't help, did it?

She should have stuck to the original plan, the one that would've worked for everyone. She should have kept their relationship professional, no matter the temptation. Instead she'd let herself be charmed, then dumped like an old pair of jeans.

She glared at the bunched note.

She'd never told Scott how little she'd thought of his behaviour toward her after her accident. Years on she wasn't so magnanimous. How dearly she wanted to teach this particular pompous ass a lesson in decency.

On returning from Rose Bay this morning, she'd told Payton everything. Payton had hugged her for a long time. Now her friend hugged her again.

'Libby, this wasn't your fault. You're only human.'

Libby groaned. 'Seems Alex doesn't have that problem.'

How would he have acted if she hadn't signed off on his injury after the evaluation this morning? Would he have closed the door in her face anyway, as he'd done after he'd caught her on the porch?

Feeling ill, she leant back in her chair and stared blindly at the ceiling.

She had to face facts. He'd used her. She wasn't inadequate as the press had depicted. It was worse.

She was an outright fool.

CHAPTER TWELVE

TWO WEEKS LATER, standing in the pits in Catalunya, Spain, Alex watched over his team as they ran their battery of checks on his car's precision instruments.

He usually got off on the noise of the pits...tools clanging, crews conversing, motors revving. The smell of oil and rubber and elbow grease was normally a great stimulus. The anticipation of feeling tyres gripping asphalt as he zipped around another competition track was a huge buzz. Alex thought he'd never grow tired of it.

And yet today those much loved highs were noticeably absent. In fact, his gut was mincing, and not with its usual healthy mix of pre-performance nerves and adrenaline. His malady wasn't because he didn't believe in his ability, he decided, heading toward the team manager, who was watching a sequence on a monitor at the rear of the pit. He would not only race this weekend, he would *win*. He'd made sure he'd set Libby Henderson well outside his radar so he wouldn't have that distraction playing on his mind. No way did he need to combat the same kind of turmoil he'd endured before charging out at the track before his accident.

Six weeks on, he'd digested all the family news. Jacob

had returned to the scene and was working to restore old Wolfe Manor. According to Annabelle's latest communication, Nathaniel was happy and married to his new bride. She'd even sent photos of the day. Sebastian's five-star hotel—the London Grand Wolfe—was certainly something.

And Annabelle…

Frowning, Alex remembered Libby's question about whether brother and sister had ever discussed that tragic night. For twenty years he'd managed to keep those thoughts—his sense of guilt—from intruding on his life too much. And yet lately, the more he thought about that time, the more the fact that he'd never had the courage to look Annabelle in the eye afterward niggled the hell out of him. The real kicker was that in his heart he'd always known that by avoiding her gaze, brushing the subject under that mat, he'd only hurt her more.

His focus wandered over to the recording that the team manager was watching on the pit monitor. He recognised the track, the car. He sure as hell remembered the crash. Alex shuddered. He understood everyone was eager for that kind of incident never to occur again. Every factor leading up to, as well as the accident itself, would be mulled over and dissected again and again in a bid to avoid a repeat performance. But, dammit, he couldn't bear to watch it even one more time.

As he pivoted away, that tendon in his shoulder twinged again. He hid his flinch, then slid a casual glance around. No one had noticed. Cupping the joint, he rotated his arm and felt the faint ache again, just for a second. His strength in his injured shoulder was so much better than it had been two weeks ago. Still, every now and then…

Deep in thought, Alex moved out toward Pit Row.

Morrissey has been in communication with the replacement physio Alex had hired, and was happy with the subsequent report. After his own examination, Morrissey had cleared Alex for this round. Jerry Squires, however, had offered a stinging remark. 'If your shoulder doesn't hold up because of the incident with that woman, I'll sue for malpractice.'

Alex hadn't been certain which incident the team owner meant. Libby's fall, which Alex had caught and the new physio had reported on, or the affair?

Either way, no matter how their relationship had ended—and it hadn't ended well—Alex would never allow Libby to be hurt because of him. He'd hurt her enough already by refusing to see her. By saying goodbye with nothing more than a note. After what they'd had together, she must despise the sound of his name.

Alex pushed those thoughts aside as his ears pricked to a different kind of hype. Before a major competition, certain members of the public were permitted down Pit Row to see, firsthand, their favourite teams and drivers prepare for the big day. Rotating the arm again, Alex moved outside and scanned the clutches of people. His attention hooked on a particular boy, perhaps twelve or thirteen, wearing a shirt sporting Alex's team logo. When the boy recognised the World Number One, he bounced on the spot and his face split with a smile that warmed Alex's heart to its core.

Remembering a time he'd been that young and enthusiastic, Alex came forward.

'You like racing?' he asked the boy.

'*Muchas. Sí.*' He translated into English. 'Very much.'

Smiling, Alex nodded. 'What's your name?'

'Carlos Diaz.'

'When you grow up, you'd like to race?'

Carlos's dark eyes flashed and his little chest puffed out. 'I want to be like you. Brave. Smart. The best there is, *señor*!'

His mother patted the boy's dark head and apologised. '*El chico*, he has no father, but he has his dreams.'

Lowering his gaze, Alex remembered back and murmured, 'Reaching for dreams is what keeps us alive.'

The boy beamed at him—all faith and pride and resolve—and a shiver chased over Alex's skin as he was taken back to a time when he'd raced through the Oxfordshire countryside, chasing wild dreams with no one of patience or knowledge to guide him. Then Alex felt that homemade medal resting in his pocket, heavy as it never had been before.

Thoughtful, he fished the medal out and examined the tarnished surface of his most prized possession. The rough-hewn circle had become so much a part of him; Alex had believed he would carry it to his grave. This medal represented the opening of his gate. His escape. A new beginning. But maybe after all this time…

As he weighed the medal in his palm, his gut knotted and his fingers reflexively curled over to make a fist. But then an odd sense of calm settled over him, like a friendly hand squeezing his shoulder or patting his back, and exhaling, smiling, he reached out his hand to the boy.

'This might not look like much,' Alex said, revealing the medal again, 'but for me, it's worked miracles. It represents hope and determination and most of all it's about belief. Belief in yourself.' His opened hand nudged nearer. 'I want you to have it, Carlos.'

The boy's eyes bugged out. A heartbeat later he exploded

into a barrage of animated Spanish. His mother was beside herself, holding her brow and thanking Alex repeatedly too. A sense of relief—and right—washed over him.

Alex clapped the boy's shoulder, then ruffled his hair.

'I'll have my assistant come over and get your contact details. Let's see if we can get you started.' He held up a warning finger. 'But first you'll need to learn everything there is about cars. You need to learn to appreciate their power.'

Then you can learn to harness and direct your own.

Carlos grabbed Alex's hand and pressed his mouth to the knuckles. '*Gracias, gracias*, Señor Wolfe.'

As he walked away, first to find Eli to have him speak with the boy, then to the team manager to relay his decision about stepping aside, Alex faced the cold hard truth of what he had done and immediately found peace with it.

He might want to tell himself different, but he was less than a hundred per cent fit to drive. He might be fit enough in the future. He couldn't know that for certain. What Alex *did* know was that he was able and willing to face that reality, look it in the eye, no matter how uncomfortable. And Libby Henderson had helped him do that.

After such a horrendous start, he was grateful for the significant life racing had provided. Grateful for his fans and his sponsors. But today he understood there was more. So much more. Question was...

After what he'd put her through, would Libby ever let him reach out and claim it?

CHAPTER THIRTEEN

WHEN LIBBY'S CELL phone rang, she reached to pick up. Then she saw the ID and her hand snatched back.

She had no appointments this morning. She'd told Payton she'd be in late—her bookkeeping needed attention and she could do that away from the office. After dressing, she'd packed up her laptop, took a walk and had ended up here, at the café where she and Alex had breakfast together those weeks before. She'd ordered pancakes and had forced her mind upon work. Too much time had been wasted on the frustrating question of Alex Wolfe.

Whenever thoughts of the weekend they'd spent together seeped in, she thrust them away. Two weeks on, those couple of days simply didn't seem real. If she hadn't kept the magazine shots and pearl charm, she might think that time with Alex was nothing but some fantastic dream.

The public must have thought so too. After the day that obnoxious reporter had hounded her, the paparazzi's interest had died. Instinct must have told them there wasn't an ongoing story and instinct was right.

So why was Alex calling now? What did she have that

he could possibly want? After the way he'd treated her, she sure as hell wanted nothing from him.

By the time her mind stopped spinning, the phone had quit ringing, and the smell of coffee and natter of early-morning café patrons filtered back. With a pulse drumming in her ears, Libby retrieved the message. As she listened to the rich timbre of his voice, her head began to tingle and, after a time, she remembered to breathe.

Alex wanted her to come to his Rose Bay home. He was there, waiting for her now. He could send a car if she preferred. Then his voice deepened and he said that he was sorry for the way he'd behaved, the way he'd dismissed her when she'd obviously felt so bad about what had happened.

Libby's back went up.

He was sorry?

So he *should* be.

But then she wondered. Today, Friday, was the first qualifying round in Spain. In the paper, on the sports news, everyone had been saying that Alex Wolfe was back and ready to take pole position this Saturday in Catalunya. And yet he was here in Sydney?

Libby quarrelled with herself for another ten minutes before she packed up, slid into her car and drove to Rose Bay with her fingers clenching the wheel and her heart in her throat the whole way. If he wanted to see her, hey, she wanted to see him too, but not for let's-kiss-and-make-up time, if that's what he expected. She could think of only one reason for Alex being here rather than in Spain. He'd re-injured that shoulder during practice and had decided to reinvest in his original blindly trusty physio. To even *think* he believed she would roll over and do his bidding after the way he'd cast her off made her blood boil.

When she pulled up at his lavish home, memories of that fateful first day resurfaced. Unbelievably, the nerves mixing in her stomach were even worse today. But that wouldn't stop her from finally giving Alex a piece of her mind. He'd better have hold of his seatbelt.

Stealing herself, Libby moved up those front steps, pressed the doorbell and, counting her heartbeats, impatiently looked around. About to press again, the door fanned open. She thought she was prepared for this meeting, but standing framed by that soaring doorway, Alex looked so regal and fresh and handsome and...

Near.

Coming back, Libby straightened and balled up her hands. She would *not* let herself be distracted. She had a score to settle—an ego to cut down to size—and this was the time to do it.

Libby nodded a cool greeting. 'How are you, Alex?'

'I'm good. Great actually.' With his usual casual grace, he stepped aside. 'Please, come in.'

'I thought you'd be busy on the track,' she said with remarkable poise as she skirted around and moved inside.

As he shut the door, she turned, ready to tell him that if his shoulder was still troubling him, he had better find someone else because she was no longer available. And if purple pigs had begun to fly and he was after some female companionship, he could wind out his string and go fly a kite. But before she could start, Alex was explaining about Spain.

As they stood in the massive foyer's soft fans of light, he recalled the excitement in the Spanish pits and how his team manager had watched and re-watched his spectacular crash. He admitted that, although his shoulder had been cleared in time for Spain, at the last moment he accepted that his current weakened condition wouldn't do his team any favours. And so, unbelievably, he'd stepped aside from racing until further notice. Then he described a young boy he'd met in Pit Row. A boy who dreamed of racing and being just like his hero, Alex Wolfe.

Despite her agenda, as Alex's story unfolded, Libby found herself absorbed.

'I gave Carlos, that boy,' he explained, 'my medal from Carter White.'

Libby's head kicked back. The medal his mentor had made and given him all those years ago? It meant so much to Alex. She couldn't accept that he'd handed it over to a stranger.

'But why?' she asked.

'It was time.'

'Time for what?'

'To accept the past and move ahead with my future.'

He said this boy, Carlos, had no father. Alex had set up a personal sponsorship to help with the boy's education and passion for cars. While he was on sabbatical he intended to scout for more talented teens who could use a little help.

When he took her hand, Libby was so taken aback by all she'd heard, she lacked the presence of mind to pull away.

'I came back, Libby. I've missed you.' He searched her eyes. 'I was hoping that you'd missed me too.'

He looked at her with such intense emotion. With obvious desire. But instead of being moved the way he so obviously hoped she would be, all the feelings she'd unintentionally put on the backburner since stepping into this house came bubbling up in a thick hot rush. Tears prickled behind her eyes. How dare he lay all that on her, then tell her that he missed her, as if he hadn't discarded her so callously before he'd left. As if he truly cared.

'You haven't mentioned the note you had Eli deliver to me,' she said, struggling to keep her voice level. She was angry. Hurt. And, dammit, justified in feeling that way.

He looked sheepish. 'I needed to get back on track.'

'Pity you didn't quite manage it.'

His eyes flashed before he stepped closer and she had to arch her neck to look into his stormy gaze. 'Don't you understand what I'm telling you? Don't you know why I'm here?'

'Not to have me work on your shoulder?' she mocked.

His brows drew in. 'Of course not.'

'Then I'm guessing you'd like to sleep with me again.'

'Don't reduce it to that,' he growled.

Emotion swelled and clogged her throat. 'You shut the door in my face,' she ground out, 'flicked me away like a fly, and you honestly think I'll throw my arms around you now?'

'I said I was wrong,' he stated. 'I apologised.'

She glared at him, then turned to leave.

Apology not accepted.

But he caught her wrist. When her fiery gaze met his, his expression was set, assured...and at the same time wary.

He almost smiled. 'You don't want to go.'

'You don't know what I want.'

'Then I'll tell you what *I* want.'

He scooped her close, and before she could think to wind away, his mouth was covering hers and all the nights she'd spent dreaming of him, all the times she'd wanted to cry, came leaping up. He'd left her. She'd thought he was never coming back, and yet here he was, holding her, kissing her, telling her that...

That he still wanted her.

She didn't want to kiss him back. She wanted to break away. *Run* away. She had more self-respect, more moral strength, than this.

But as the kiss deepened, and the flames licking at her veins multiplied and spread, gradually, somehow effortlessly, she felt her arms lift, circling and helping to press her body against his. If this was a dream, God help her, she never wanted to wake up.

An eternity later, the kiss ended softly but the heat of his lips remained close. He murmured one simple word.

'Stay.'

Her heart squeezed. Despite everything she knew and feared, she wanted to. But she couldn't. She couldn't let her heart railroad her head when she knew later she'd regret it. She shouldn't have kissed him back. She should never have come. She dropped and shook her head.

'No.'

He folded hair back from her face. 'What's stopping you?'

'Sanity,' she said. 'Pride.'

'They're both overrated.'

She gave into a grin but then swallowed it back down. 'Dammit, Alex, I'm not supposed be amused. I'm supposed to be—'

But when his lips grazed hers, the tail of that thought evaporated as a tingling wondrous thrill ripped through her. The final bricks of that wall crumbled and fell, and any remaining doubt or annoyance were replaced by an energy of a different kind—an awareness so consuming and overpowering that the battle was all over.

She was lost.

Taking soft slow kisses, he kneaded her upper arms, making her blood heat and hum. He'd missed her.

She sighed against his lips.

She'd missed him more than air.

Seconds melted into scorching minutes. As he gathered her closer, she ironed her palms over his shoulders, his chest. Her fingers twined around his shirt buttons while their kisses grew steamier still. With him leading her, they blindly headed for the stairs. His shirt fell halfway up, her shirt followed close behind. At the top of the stairs, breathing laboured, his mouth broke from hers long enough to smooth the pad of his thumb sensually over her lower lip, then guide her into the master suite.

The room was cool and dark and predictably large. The carpet and satin spread on the king-size bed were steely grey. The sheets were already folded down and the heavy curtains pulled against the morning sun.

He took her hand and, his eyes on hers, led her to one side of the bed before deliberately lowering his mouth to the curve of her throat. When his teeth grazed the skin, she shivered and sighed until all her breath was gone, then she arched her neck and offered more.

Their clothes came off quickly while they were standing, sitting, finally while they were caressing and writhing amongst the sheets. As he explored her every curve and valley, she gave herself over to the fantasy, only wishing it would never end. She thought she'd lost the chance to ever feel this beautiful again, and as he gently rolled her onto her stomach and traced slow hot kisses down her back, she had to be glad she'd succumbed one more time. She'd need these memories when it was time to let that harsh light back in.

By the time his mouth joined hers again, sparks were firing through her veins and that smouldering kernel of need at her core had begun to throb and burn. His body angled and covered hers, then he was filling her, moving with long measured strokes that pushed her, inch by inch, higher up that growing wave. His head dropped into her hair at the same time his hand fanned and gripped her thigh. He murmured her name and moved against her faster, until the powder ignited, the kindling went up and she was thrown a thousand leagues into the air.

Still throbbing above her, he dotted kisses over her brow, her cheek. When he shuddered one last time and exhaled on deep satisfaction, she drew her fingers around his bristled jaw and, short of breath, tipped up to feel his lips on hers one last time.

His mouth trailed her cheek, around her jaw. He murmured things close to her ear that almost had her believing that she was and would remain the most important thing in his life. When he reluctantly shifted to lie beside her, her mind set, she rolled to her side off the bed. As she reached to collect her bra and panties off the floor, uncertain of what she was up to, Alex sat slowly up.

'Don't get dressed,' he said lightly. 'If you have appointments this afternoon, just this once, cancel.'

'I don't have any appointments,' she said, fitting the bra's clasp.

He leaned over and warm fingers traced her back. 'Then lie down. I want to hold you.'

Lord, she was tempted. But it was out of the question. Alex had to know that. After what they'd shared, she didn't want to argue. Still she had to say this and say it now. Sitting on the edge of the bed, she turned and looked him in the eye.

'Alex, this won't happen again.'

His brows knitted, then he sat up straighter and ran a hand through his thick crop of hair. Finally he shook his head.

'What are you talking about?'

'Right or wrong, I love being with you. You can make me forget...*everything*. It's almost enough...' Emotion stuck in her throat and, wishing this was over, she lowered her gaze.

'Enough for what?'

'To make me forget what you did. How you treated me.' *How you used me.*

'Libby, for God's sake. I did what you wanted. I wasn't sure about my shoulder so I threw it all in and came back.' He reached and gripped her hand. 'I came back to *you*.'

Who was he trying to fool? 'You shouldn't have left like that in the first place!'

'You honestly can't understand what I was going through?'

'I know what it's like to be on top,' she said, 'and then have the rug pulled out from beneath you. It's a huge shock. It hurts like hell. I *get* it.' Of course she did.

His gaze pierced hers for a heart-stopping beat, then he flung back the sheet and, in a temper, leapt out of bed.

'Don't make it sound like I'm washed up. Like I'm a has-been with nothing to look forward to.'

A surge of indignation ignited her cheeks. Of course he would see her as 'nothing.'

Clenching her jaw so hard her teeth ached, she thrust her feet through her trouser legs. She didn't need to stay here to listen to this. To Alex defending his precious title, even in the bedroom.

By the time her shoes were on, he seemed to have contained himself, although his voice was tellingly tight. 'I don't know why you can't put it behind you.'

'Same way you hope Annabelle's put it all behind *her*?'

She rotated to see his powerful silhouette seeming to grow larger against the shuttered light. A measure of her bravado slipped when he strode around the bed and, rigid with anger, loomed over her.

'I apologised, damn it. I've *explained*.' His eyes blazed with outright frustration. 'What the hell do you *want* from me?'

She sized him up. He wasn't blind. Neither was he stupid. If he couldn't see what she wanted—what any woman in her position would want—she sure as hell wouldn't tell him.

Defiant—poised—she crossed her arms. 'I don't want anything from you.'

A pulse in his cheek beat erratically at the same time his grey eyes darkened, like twin thunderstorms about to unleash. But then the breath seemed to leave his body and, after two long torturous beats, his chin tipped up.

'You want to punish me for what I did. But, Libby, you're punishing us both.'

'Punishing? Or protecting?'

A patronising look on his face, he reached for her but she wound away. His mouth pressed into a hard line at the same time his jaw shifted. When he reached for her again, this time he didn't try for her wrist. Now he demanded her full attention. As his hands seized her upper arms, his mouth tilted on a sardonic smile.

'Don't tell me you're sorry that today happened. Don't try to tell me you really want to go.'

'You're right.' *Dear God.* 'I want to stay.'

But she couldn't forget Scott, or Leo. More so, she couldn't forget how Alex had dismissed her so heartlessly two weeks ago. Tears building in her eyes, she tried but couldn't swallow past the claw opening in her throat.

'But no matter how much I'd like for you to hold me—' *kiss me* '—I won't lay myself open to that kind of hurt again.'

The world seemed to shrink and press in on her lungs, on her heart, as the hold on her arms tightened. She wondered what he'd do next. Throw her out? Turn his back. Before her mind could grasp a third possibility, his mouth came crashing down, capturing and claiming hers without apology. Without reserve.

His caress was like a giant vacuum, devouring all memory other than the sublime sensory. As she lost herself to sensation, Alex curled over her more, driving her to surrender. Convincing her that she couldn't break free. He wouldn't allow it.

When his lips finally, grudgingly, left hers, their breathing was ragged and the room was spinning. His palms slid up over her shoulders to rest either side of her neck, and as his heavy gaze penetrated hers, she recognised the appeased certainty glowing in his eyes. His chest expanded as his focus dropped to her parted lips and his thumbs drew coaxing circles beneath her lobes.

'Now did *that* feel as if I want to hurt you?'

'I never said you wanted to,' she got out, feeling giddy. Weak. 'That doesn't mean you won't.' That you won't *again*.

His gaze hardened. 'I won't let you do this. I won't let you push me away.'

'No. You'd rather keep me hanging around until you're ready to get back to what's really important.' His only true passion. Racing.

Growling, he threw his hands away from her and made to hold his head as if legions of demons were scratching at his brain.

'Damn it, Elizabeth! Why do you have to be so *difficult*.'

'Would you rather I was more like Annabelle?' she shot out. He'd never been honest and open with her and, for whatever reason, his sister had let it slide.

His voice lowered to a dangerous pitch. 'Keep her out of it. You know nothing about Annabelle.'

'What's worse is neither do you.'

'Do not change the subject.'

As he enunciated each word, emotion filled her throat, stung her eyes, but she wouldn't keep quiet. She wasn't poor Annabelle.

'You *use* people, Alex. You'd do anything—use anyone— to keep in front of the pack. You used Carter White. You use Eli Steele. You use your fans and your team and your money to put a divider between you and your past. You set out to use *me*—'

'That's not *true*!' His roar echoed through the room before his resolute gaze wavered and finally dropped away. 'Not after I got to know you.'

Libby slumped. But why should she feel so disappointed? Hadn't she known it all along? Then. Now. She was no more than a tool for Alex to manipulate to get what he needed.

When he sank down to sit on the edge of the bed, suddenly all the fight went out of her too. What was left was dull, deep acceptance. The realisation this was over and it needed to be. She stood and, leaving him behind, made her way down the stairs and out that door one last time.

She understood why Alex was happier living behind his safety nets. She was guilty of it too. It hurt less. But no matter how hard Alex pretended to be together—whole— the sad lonely truth was he was more damaged than she'd ever been.

CHAPTER FOURTEEN

'THOUGHT I'D FIND you here. Which one are you thinking of taking out?'

At the sound of Eli's voice, Alex held off throwing his third dart and turned to see his friend entering the Rose Bay backyard garage. After this morning's emotional roller-coaster ride with Libby Henderson, he could use a little uncomplicated male company.

When Libby had left earlier, Alex had been at a loss. Since he'd received that email from Annabelle weeks ago his life had been like a dodgem car race, complete with bang-ups and standstills and mind-spinning turnarounds. He'd done the right thing in Spain. He felt good about mentoring that boy. As far as pulling out of the race, given the intermittent pain in his shoulder, he'd had no choice but to step aside. He hadn't been so sure in predicting Libby's reaction to his invitation to his home. Their meeting had started off fiery. When they'd moved to the bedroom things had only got hotter. After making love he'd assumed their differences were all squared away.

Not even close.

Alex hurled the last dart and hit an inch off bullseye—

not bad for left-handed. Then he ambled forward, past the old beat-up wreck in the corner, and wriggled the darts from the cork.

'I don't feel like driving.' Alex offered up the darts to his friend. 'Want a throw?'

Eli tugged his ear. 'I need to rush out and buy a hearing aid. Did you say you don't feel like *driving*? Has your arm got worse? I thought you were fine for everyday conditions.'

He gave a shrug that let Eli know that wasn't it.

Alex sat on a stool and twirled the darts between his fingers, watching the red and black feathers swirl one way, then the other, while he thought over what Libby had said... about Annabelle and Carter and Eli. He couldn't get her words out of his mind.

'Have you ever let a woman get to you?' Alex finally asked.

'Get to me?'

'You know. Get into your blood. Screw with your brain. She haunts me, Eli, and, I tell you, I'm done with it. I want her gone—' determined, he flung all three darts at the board at once '—out of my head.'

Eli pulled up a stool. 'You mean out of your heart.'

Alex stood to retrieve the darts. 'Don't talk to me about what I think you're going to talk to me about.'

'In three years, that's the first time I've heard you ramble.'

Alex grunted and, darts in hand, took up his position behind the line. 'That's her fault.'

'You're one stubborn SOB, you know that?'

'Nothing but compliments today.' He threw the darts, one, two... When the last one hit the wall, he took stock and caught Eli's eye and apologised, which he didn't do often.

'Sorry. I'm out of sorts today.'

'You've been on your own a long time, Alex.'

Halfway to the dartboard, Alex stopped and looked at his friend hard. 'You're not going all Dr Phil on me, I hope.'

'What is it about Libby that frightens you?'

'Why would I be frightened?'

'Make that terrified.'

Alex wriggled the darts out again. 'I simply know what I'm capable of.'

Or he thought he'd known.

She'd asked him if she was protecting them both and she'd had a bloody good point. He loved being with her. He couldn't imagine finding that kind of connection again. But he wouldn't pretend that he could promise anything and Libby had known it. He didn't do commitment unless it was to the track.

'If you ask me,' Eli said, 'and you did, you need to look at this from a wider perspective.'

'It's cut and dried. She wants something from me that I simply can't give.'

'Commitment. Maybe marriage.'

That's what she wanted, all right. Then, like magic, the goodbye note and door shut in her face would be forgotten. *Poof!*

Alex pointed out, 'I've known her a matter of weeks.'

'And despite that she put her reputation on the line when she agreed to that early evaluation.'

'That point is moot.'

After he'd hurt his shoulder again—catching Libby when she'd spilled off the patio—her evaluation had meant nothing. He'd had to start physio again. But he'd needed to work with someone else. He couldn't abide any more distractions. His life had become too complicated as it was.

Eli pushed up to his feet, walked around the stool and crossed his arms. 'Right. You don't want to drive. Seems like you don't want to talk. I'm sure you don't want to sit around all week wishing you could swap these toys for a chance to be with her again.' He paused to consider. 'Did you tell her you understood how she felt?'

'I'm pretty sure I showed her, Eli.'

'Did you say you were sorry? It's not so easy for us guys, I know.'

Alex was about to say yes, he'd apologised, and more than once. But then the words slipped away and he was left with the image of Libby, sitting beside him while he screeched around that private Gold Coast track. He was struck by the memories of how exhilarated and, to some extent, shaken he'd been afterward, knowing he'd never shared anything like that kind of experience before.

Wondering more, he angled his head.

Was he….could he be…in *love*? Did he *love* Libby Henderson in the forever-after way? Marriage, family, 'can I truly move on from my gritty childhood' way? She brought out emotions and admissions no one else could.

But then another image faded up… Annabelle. And the old scarred memories that he wished to Hades he could forget came crashing down again. All those years ago Annabelle had so desperately wanted to be part of his 'cool' crowd. Instead of listening to her, protecting her that night, he'd shoved her off home—shut the door in her face—and continued on with his own thing. As if it were yesterday he remembered the next morning, running from the police in that beat-up blue sedan over there, then facing the truth about the obscenities that had occurred the night before.

He'd felt responsible for so much of Annabelle's hurt and shame. If he hadn't turned her away, she wouldn't have been beaten by that worthless sod who'd dared call himself their father. Jacob wouldn't have had to bear the guilt of committing patricide, even if he was subsequently acquitted of all charges. Self-defence. He'd defended Annabelle. Defended them all. And Alex had lacked the courage to apologise to his twin for casting her off that night, for handing her over to that animal on a platter.

They all had their wounds. But was it too late to talk about it now? To give a part of himself he hadn't ever thought worth giving.

Alex dropped his head into his hands and, his chest aching, groaned aloud, 'Is it too late?'

'I don't think so,' Eli replied. 'But do it soon, mate. For both your sakes.'

After Eli left, Alex went into his office and clicked into his email account. He brought up Annabelle's address but then his gaze flicked to the phone. His sister, once so lively, was so reserved these days. She preferred a less personal form of communication but this time he needed to hear her voice, and she needed to hear his.

He punched in her quick dial, but when his stomach flipped he disconnected and dropped the phone on the desk. After such a long silence, did he want to do this? *Could* he bring up the most traumatic night of both their lives and be certain it wouldn't do more harm than good? What if she confirmed what he'd always feared most? That she hadn't forgiven him for thrusting her aside. Letting her down.

Just like he'd let Libby down.

His gut churning, Alex fell into the chair and held his brow.

These past weeks, this unease about the past had built until now he felt as if he were drowning. At this moment, it pressed down so heavily he could barely breathe. Even if Annabelle's reaction was less than accepting, he *had* to get this off his chest. He had never meant to hurt his sister.

And Libby…?

Setting his jaw, he collected the phone, punched in the quick dial again and, on tenterhooks, waited to hear if Annabelle picked up when she saw his ID.

Six rings. Seven.

A click and then…

'Alex? Is that you?'

'Annabelle.' His pent-up breath came out in a rush. 'It's good to hear your voice.'

'Do you know what time it is? What's wrong?'

He glanced at the wall clock and cursed under his breath. He hadn't considered the time difference. She'd be half asleep. His throat tightened. Maybe he ought to phone back.

'Alex? Are you all right?'

Concern had deepened her tone. If he hung up now, she might be up half the night worrying. This might feel a thousand times more difficult than it should be but, for better or worse, he was committed.

He cleared his throat, pushed to his feet and rushed a hand through his hair.

'There's something I need to say. I'd rather say it in person, but I'm afraid it can't wait.' This had waited long enough. He swallowed his fear and confessed after twenty long years.

'Annabelle, I'm sorry I wasn't there for you. I'm sorry I turned you away.'

A long silence echoed down the line before, sounding unsure, uneasy, his sister replied, 'What are you talking about?'

'That night.' The night no one ever mentioned. 'I'm sorry I was a jerk and booted you out of that party when I should have taken care of you. I'm sorry—' His voice caught and he found himself swallowing hard against the pit in his throat. 'I'm sorry I wasn't there for you afterward. I didn't know...' He exhaled and, broken, admitted, 'I felt guilty... I didn't know what to say. How to say it.'

When more silence wound down the line, a withering feeling sailed through him. He shouldn't have rung. Annabelle had built up a wall just as he had done. He had no right trying to break it down after so long. He should have left this buried—

But then he heard a snuffle, then a sigh, and a spark of hope lit in his chest.

'All these years,' Annabelle murmured, her voice soft and thick, 'I thought you were angry with me for causing so much trouble that night.'

Astounded, Alex coughed. 'What? *No.* I was never angry with you. I was angry with me.'

'We were children.' He heard the strain in her voice and imagined the glistening tears edging her eyes. 'It was nobody's fault.'

Wondering, Alex's hand tightened around the phone. Nobody's fault? Surely she hadn't forgiven their father. But something kept him from asking. William Wolfe was the monster behind all this pain, but Alex didn't want that name mentioned in this conversation. This was about him and Annabelle. About finally making it right between brother and his wounded and much loved sister.

'Can you forgive me?' he asked, trying not to flinch as his mind's eye called up that single red welt marring her still-beautiful face.

'Oh, Alex. No matter how far apart we've seemed, you're my other half. You always will be.'

His eyes misting over, Alex lowered into the chair and as he and Annabelle spoke more, for the first time in his life he knew a sense of true belonging. When he'd finished that phone call, despite knowing the time difference now, he called and spoke to his old friend, Carter White, and vowed to keep in touch.

He was finally making peace with himself and people from his past but he wouldn't rest until he had at least one other's. The person who had set this all in motion.

He'd given Libby parts of himself he'd never allowed anyone else to glimpse. But he'd given her much more than that. He'd given her his heart.

God knows he hadn't meant to. The very idea was as foreign as it was...*healing*. Although, after their argument today, he suspected Libby would rather consume hot coals than admit it, Alex more than sensed she felt the same way. He'd hurt her—deeply—just as he had Annabelle, and Libby wasn't prepared to be hurt again. He couldn't blame her. But now he knew to the depths of his soul what they could have together. What they *both* wanted and needed.

If it took the rest of his life, he wouldn't take her no for an answer.

CHAPTER FIFTEEN

'YOU AMAZE ME, LIBBY. So many talents and you know your way around a hotplate as well.'

Collecting the plates from her dining table, Libby sent Payton an amused look. 'Chicken and roast vegetables aren't exactly haute cuisine.'

'It is the way you do them,' Payton said, following her friend into the kitchen.

Libby had invited Payton over for a meal, or rather Payton had suggested they go out, grab a bite, maybe catch a movie. But Libby had baulked at venturing out in public. Since breaking off with Alex last week, she'd tried her best to stay upbeat but, in truth, she hadn't felt much like company.

Friday afternoon last, she'd confided in Payton about the goings-on of that morning. How she'd confronted Alex and things had taken a left turn. Although walking away that day was the right thing to do, her sense of loss cut so deep that sometimes it hurt to breathe. Reason told her that she had everything to live for and yet she had the hardest time convincing her heart to listen. When she forced her mind on work, she felt in some ways happier, but when she was alone she couldn't help but remember and wish things had turned out differently. Payton had noticed her mood, which was why she'd prescribed some R and R tonight.

While Libby rinsed the plates, Payton put away the condiments. 'If you're not tired, I could go pick up a DVD. Or we could just talk.'

Libby appreciated the gesture, but it was getting late and they both had work tomorrow. She looked up from the running tap.

'I'm fine, Payton, honest.' She stacked the rinsed plates on the drainer. 'You go home and get some shut-eye.'

'Are *you* ready for bed?'

'I might go for a walk.'

'At this time of night?' Payton disappeared into the living room. Libby found her shrugging into her bright pink coat. 'I'll come with you.'

Libby smiled. Payton could be a little on the flighty side but her heart was big and her concern was always sincere.

'The path along the esplanade's well lit.' Joining Payton, Libby touched her friend's arm. 'I'll be fine.'

Payton's mouth pulled to one side before she let out a lungful of air. 'Well, if you're sure you don't want the company.' She lowered her gaze, then caught Libby's again. 'You know there's no one I admire more than you. You're the strongest person I know.'

Libby's throat constricted. She'd always tried to tell herself strength was what mattered. If you kept that, you could do anything. She was alive and had wonderful family and a great practice and excellent friends. One day she'd find romantic love again.

One day...

After she and Payton said goodbye, Libby packed the

dishwasher, then wandered over to the opened curtains. Feeling hollow, she let her gaze trail over the moonlit waters of tonight's calm ocean. Once she'd been a mistress of those waves, and when that world had collapsed she'd knuckled down and had built another. In time this dull dead ache in her stomach would fade. Sometime in the future she would get over Alex Wolfe and his dazzling smile, his dynamite personality...the unbelievably beautiful way he made love....

Growling at herself, Libby grabbed a light jacket and headed out to find that fresh air. She needed to get over this bout of self-pity, she decided, taking the lift to the ground floor. Maybe she ought to learn how to jog again. Nothing cleared the cobwebs and left you exhausted like a solid four-k run. And she really needed a holiday. Perhaps Thredbo. If she could dip and do the tango, there was no reason she couldn't relearn how to snow ski.

Five minutes later, she was moving down the same esplanade pathway Alex and she had enjoyed strolling along weeks earlier. The three-quarter moon smiled down, the powerful ocean breathed in and out, and yet, with all her tentative go-slay-'em plans, Libby's heart still felt horribly empty.

Stopping at a stairway leading to the beach, her heartbeat began to skip. The only time she'd felt sand between her toes since her accident had been that incredible night she'd spent with Alex. He'd forced her to face that fear and she'd conquered it. It had been a gigantic step. Would she ever have found the courage if not for him?

Libby took in a lungful of air, and another, then headed down the stairs. When she hit the uneven soft sand, she tipped sideways but not nearly enough to fall. Regaining her balance, she focused on her feet, half buried. She lowered onto the bottom step and removed her shoes.

A moment later, her toes dug into the cool powdery grains and Libby's heart flew to her throat as a thousand wonderful memories flooded her mind...of when she was a child with her family, then as a teen with the world at her feet, and finally as a woman, finding true courage again while falling in love.

Gradually she pushed to her feet, then drew the clamshell pearl charm from a pocket. As she rotated the piece in her palm, the moonlight caught the stones and threw back dazzling prisms of blue light. In some ways, at least, she must have meant something special to Alex.

Hadn't she?

A bus roared past and Libby glanced off to the road. Tonight there seemed to be more traffic than usual—family cars, lorries, motorbikes. But their noise was gradually swallowed up by the throatiest, roughest engine ever slapped together. Libby pivoted further around and peered up the street. Was someone taking their steam train for a run?

The streetlights reflected in her eyes but when she squinted and refocused, she recognised the car. Her stomach pitched. It was one of a kind and she could imagine only one person ever driving it.

Same dull powder-blue paint job. Same massive dents and scratches. She took a few disbelieving steps nearer.

Why was Alex driving that wreck?

What was Alex doing *here*, full stop!

The car swerved into a park and the volcanic rumble from its engine shut down. Libby gathered herself as a rusty door squeaked and slammed shut. Alex glanced first at the building, then, as if guided by radar, swung his gaze around.

With half a football field between them, their eyes connected. The next instant he was leaping the beach wall and landing with an athletic grace and determination that left her weak. Without missing a beat, he continued his beeline to the spot where she stood.

When he stopped before her, looking larger than life and more handsome than she'd ever seen him, Libby wished she had a prop to lean against. He left her off balance. Dizzy with a flurry of emotions.

As a sea breeze tugged at his hair and his billowing shirt, she swallowed against the great lump in her throat. The question *Why did you come?* burned the tip of her tongue but she didn't feel ready to hear his response.

Instead she asked, 'Why are you driving that wreck?'

He owned so many amazing cars. That one sounded as if it were ready to cough out its last breath.

'I decided it was time to settle up with slices of my past and either unload or re-embrace them.' He jerked a thumb back at the bomb. 'I'm going to do her up again. She's still beautiful despite the beating she took. I owe it to her—me too—to make it right.'

Libby quizzed his committed gaze. There was more to what he'd said—to the expression on his face—but before she could ask, he went on. 'I didn't expect to find you down here, walking on the sand.'

She stole a glance over her shoulder, saw the tide was on its way in, and instinctively took two steps toward the road...toward Alex. And that was dangerous. Whatever he was doing here—to apologise again, to seduce her because he knew he could—no matter what her heart said, she didn't want to hear it.

'I thought you'd be in another country by now,' she stated stiffly.

Beneath the moon- and streetlight, a ghost of a smile touched his lips. 'I have business to attend to.'

'Business?'

Holding her with his eyes, he stepped closer. 'Of the utmost importance.'

With her heartbeat pounding in her ears, she managed an offhanded shrug. 'Something to do with your aftershave?'

'Something to do with you, Libby. To do with us.'

When that smile reached his eyes, her skin flashed hot. She dropped her gaze to the wet sand at her feet and held herself tight. His coming here, playing with her like this…it wasn't flattering or charming. After the way they'd parted, knowing the way she felt, this was plain cruel.

'I need to go.'

She moved to angle around him but he blocked her path.

'Libby, listen to me. *Please.*'

Trembling inside, she kept her gaze lowered on the damp ripples left on the sand by the tide. If she peered into those soft grey depths now, he might talk her into anything.

With a knuckle he lifted her chin and, when their eyes met, his searching hers so deeply, she felt her will being sucked away.

'You said yourself. We understand each other. We appreciate each other too—' his brows nudged together '—even if there were times I didn't let you know like I should have. Maybe we wouldn't share that understanding if our lives had been spared the tragedy. I wish my childhood had been different, that my father had been a loving, caring man who had cheered me on instead of either ignoring me or trying to crush me beneath his heel. I wish

I'd known my mother.' He took both her hands in his, so warm and firm. 'And you must wish that you hadn't gone into the surf that day. We've been dealt some bad cards but it's the only hand we had to play.' His arm slipped around her waist and he smiled softly. 'We're survivors. We brush ourselves off and we find a way to go on.'

A ragged breath caught in her chest. Her heart was squeezing so much her lungs hurt. And plump tears were rising, welling in her eyes. Dammit, he wasn't playing fair.

'You know how I feel about your childhood.' She wished she'd been there as an adult to have rescued them all. 'But what happened back then...' She swallowed against raw emotion. 'Alex, it doesn't have anything to do with now.'

'I think it does.' His voice lowered. 'Everyone's destined to take some wrong turns, like me suggesting at the start that you go against your conscience. Like shutting you out that day.' A pulse beat in his throat as he drew her gently near. 'That was wrong. I knew it, but I was trying to convince myself that retaining the championship was more important. I wanted to keep what I had. What I knew. But being with you...' His gaze intensified as it roamed her face. 'You've taught me there's more than wanting to drive fast cars. I've learned that I *want* more. Can *give* more. That I'm ready.'

Just as he'd asked, Libby had listened, with the wash of the waves coming closer and the hope of his words reaching mercilessly deep.

Her question was a hoarse anxious whisper. 'How much more?'

'I want it all,' he said simply. 'Marriage, kids. But only with you. I want us to have a life. Together I know we'll do it right.' His gaze dropped to her lips before finding her eyes again. 'I love you, Libby. I love you so much.'

She sucked down a breath at the same time a hot tear sped down her cheek. Was this a dream? Had she heard right?

'Are you saying…?'

'I'm asking you to marry me.' His warm lips brushed her temple. 'God knows I can live without chequered flags. I can't live without you.'

Another tear fell, and another. He wanted her to believe in him. He *loved* her. Couldn't live without her. She wasn't sure which way to turn. What to say.

She swallowed back disbelieving, happy tears again. 'You're sure?'

'As sure as I know that together we can do anything. Go anywhere. Have everything.'

She gave in to the feelings that had haunted her these past days and, wanting so much to trust—to believe—she finally surrendered and let the words come.

'I love you too.' Her throat ached with the depth of her love. 'You can't imagine how much.'

Her words were barely out before his mouth claimed hers and every fibre in her body sparked like tinder and caught light. As his arms drew her closer still, she submitted, to his kiss, to his belief in them both. Most of all she submitted to their love.

A series of car horns, blaring from the street, brought her back. She and Alex glanced toward the road. Some young men in souped-up cars were beeping and hooting at the couple shamelessly embracing on the beach.

Laughing softly, Alex brought his gaze back to hers, then cocked a brow. 'You know what this means, don't you?'

'We'll probably wind up in tomorrow's newspaper?'

'In that case, let's give them something to talk about.'

His left arm hooked under her legs and then her feet were swinging in the air and she was cradled firmly against his chest.

She gasped. 'Be careful! Your shoulder.'

'I'm strong enough for this.'

When he moved toward the water, Libby's blood pressure dropped and she stiffened to a board. *'What you are doing?'*

'Don't worry. We'll do it together.'

'You mean go into the water? *Now?*'

'Do it this once,' he said, 'then, if you want, you can put it behind you.'

Her head began to prickle. She broke out in an all-over sweat. 'I... I *can't.*'

But he began moving again, then she heard his feet swishing through the water and felt the cool spray of the sea on her skin.

'I'll keep you safe,' he said. 'From this moment on I'll always be here for you. I'll never turn away.'

Carefully she laced her arms around his neck but gasped when her foot swept through the cool wet.

Concerned, he pulled up. 'You okay?'

She nodded, at first in reflex, then a second time knowing, remarkably, that she was, indeed, better than fine. Alex was right. She'd always needed to do this at least once, and now, safe in his arms, she knew that she could.

As the water reached higher, she told herself to relax and soon the familiar roll of the waves was lapping her body, as it had so many times before, and Alex was smiling down at her, love and pride shining in his eyes.

'How's that?'

'A little weird,' she admitted, 'but mostly…like I'm saying hello to an old friend.'

His smile said he'd known it all along.

'So how about it, Libby? Will you be my bride?'

Tears slid from the corners of her eyes. Happy tears. Tears that made her feel as if she were the luckiest, most beautiful woman alive.

Alex Wolfe, the man she loved with all her heart, wanted to marry her.

'There's nothing I want more.' She held his bristled jaw in her palm as the gratitude inside her swelled. 'I love you.'

Those gorgeous grey eyes glistened and smiled into hers. 'Say it again.'

As the waves gently lapped, she grazed her thumb over his bottom lip and confessed, 'I love you…like I didn't know existed.'

As he kissed her again, he waded in deeper and those old affirmations swirled back into her mind.

I can do this…. There's nothing to be nervous about…. No need, Libby, to be *scared.* And then that pleasant tingling heat flooded her body in the same instant a perfect sense of serenity descended and her eyes drifted shut.

The past would always be there but as long as she and Alex were together—for the lifetime that they'd share and be in love—their lives, their future, would be an open road. An accepting sea.

Nothing and no one would ever stand in their way.

* * * * *

Body Check
Elle Kennedy

I could not have written this book without my fantastic critique partners, Lori Borrill and Jennifer Lewis, two incredible authors in their own right and the best support system a girl could have.

I'd also like to dedicate this book to… My family and friends, for not letting me give up. Tyler, Amanda and Brad, for all their help with this story.

My fabulous editor, Laura Barth. And senior editor Brenda Chin for taking a chance on me and my hockey-playing hero!

CHAPTER ONE

"I REALLY NEED to get laid," Hayden Houston said with a sigh. She reached for the glass on the smooth mahogany tabletop and took a sip of red wine. The slightly bitter liquid eased her thirst but did nothing to soothe her frustration.

The pictures staring at her from the walls of the Ice House Bar didn't help, either. Action shots of hockey players mid slap shot, framed rookie cards, team photos of the Chicago Warriors—it seemed as if the sport haunted her everywhere she went. Sure, she was a team owner's daughter, but occasionally it would be nice to focus on something other than hockey. Like sex, perhaps.

Across from her, Darcy White grinned. "We haven't seen each other in two years and that's all you've got to say? Come on, Professor, no anecdotes about life in Berkeley? No insightful lectures about Impressionist art?"

"I save the insightful lectures for my students. And as for anecdotes, none of them involve sex so let's not waste time with those."

She ran her hand through her hair and discovered that all the bounce she'd tried to inject into it before heading to the Ice House Bar had deflated. Volume-enhancing mousse?

Yeah, right. Apparently nothing could make her stick-straight brown hair look anything other than stick-straight.

"Okay, I'll bite," Darcy said. "Why do you have sex on the brain?"

"Because I'm not getting any."

Darcy sipped her strawberry daiquiri, a drink she'd confessed she hated but drank anyway, claiming men found it sexy. "Aren't you seeing someone back in California? Dan? Drake?"

"Doug," Hayden corrected.

"How long have you been together?"

"Two months."

"And you still haven't done the mattress mambo?"

"Nope."

"You're kidding, right? He's not down with getting it on?" Darcy paused, looking thoughtful. "Or should I say, he's not *up* with it?"

"Oh, he's up. He just wants, and I quote, 'to get to know each other fully before we cross the intimacy bridge.'"

Her friend hooted. "The intimacy bridge? Girl, he sounds like a total loser. Dump him. Now. Before he brings up the intimacy bridge again."

"We're actually on a break right now," Hayden admitted. "Before I left I told him I needed some space."

"Space? Uh-uh. I think what you need is a new boyfriend."

God, that was the last thing she wanted. Toss her line in the dating pool and start fishing again? No, thank you. After three failed relationships in five years, Hayden had decided to quit falling for bad boys and focus on the good ones. And Doug Lloyd was definitely a good one. He taught a Renaissance course at Berkeley, he was intelligent and witty, and he valued love and commitment as much as she did. Having grown up with a single father, Hayden longed for a partner she could build a home and grow old with.

Her mom had died in a car accident when Hayden was a baby, and her dad had given up on finding love again, opting instead to spend more than twenty years focusing on his hockey-coaching career. He'd finally remarried three years ago, but she suspected loneliness, rather than love, had driven him to do so. Why else would he have proposed to a woman after four months of dating? A woman who was twenty-nine years his junior. A woman he was in the process of divorcing, no less.

Well, she had no intention of following her dad's example. She wasn't going to spend decades alone and then jump into marriage with someone totally unsuitable.

Doug held the same mind-set. He was a traditionalist through and through, a believer that marriage should be valued and not rushed into. Besides, he had a rock-hard body that made her mouth water. He'd even let her touch it…once. They'd been kissing on the couch in the living room of her San Francisco town house and she'd slid her hands underneath his button-down shirt. Running her fingers over his rippled chest, she'd murmured, "Let's move this into the bedroom."

That's when he'd dropped the no-intimacy bomb on her. He'd assured her he was unbelievably attracted to her, but that, like marriage, he didn't believe sex should be rushed. He wanted the first time to be special.

And no amount of chest rubbing could persuade him to let go of his chivalrous intentions.

And therein lay the problem. Doug was simply too *nice*. At first she'd thought his views on making love were really very sweet. But two months, coupled with *eight* months of celibacy prior to meeting Doug, added up to extreme sexual frustration on her part.

She loved that Doug was a gentleman but, darn it, sometimes a girl just needed a *man*.

"Seriously, this Damian guy seems like a wimp," Darcy said, jerking her from her thoughts.

"Doug."

"Whatever." Darcy waved a dismissive hand and tossed her long red hair over her shoulder. "Screw intimacy. If Dustin won't have sex with you, find someone who will."

"Believe me, I'm tempted."

More than tempted, actually. The next couple months were bound to be pure hell. She'd come home after final exams to support her father through his messy divorce, to be the good daughter, but that didn't mean she had to like the situation.

Her stepmother was determined to squeeze Hayden's dad for every dime he had. And, boy, did he have a lot of dimes. Though he'd spent most of his life coaching, Presley had always dreamed of owning a team, a goal he'd finally reached seven years ago. Thanks to the substantial insurance settlement he'd received after her mom's accident, and his wise investment in a pharmaceutical company that had made him millions, he'd been able to purchase the Chicago Warriors franchise. Over the years he'd continued investing and building his fortune, but his main priority was the team. It was all he ever thought about, and that's what made coming home so difficult.

Her childhood had been chaotic, to say the least. Traveling with her dad across the country for away games, living in Florida for two years when he'd coached the Aces to a championship victory, five years in Texas, three in Oregon. It had been tough, but Hayden's close relationship with her dad had made the constant upheaval bearable. Her father had always shown an interest in her life. He'd listened while she babbled about her favorite artists, and taken her to countless museums over the years.

Now that she was an adult and he was busy with the team, he no longer seemed to care about making time to connect with her outside of the hockey arena. She knew other team owners didn't get as involved as her father did, but his background as a coach seemed to influence his new position; he had his hand in every aspect of the Warriors, from drafting players to marketing, and he thrived on it, no matter how time-consuming the work was.

That's why three years ago she'd decided to accept the full-time position Berkeley had offered her, even though it meant relocating to the West Coast. She'd figured the old absence-makes-the-heart-grow-fonder cliché might kick in and make her father realize there was more to life than hockey. It hadn't.

So she'd come back to see him through the divorce in hopes that they could reconnect.

"Have you become a nymphomaniac since you left town?" Darcy was asking. "You never mentioned it in your e-mails."

Hayden forced herself to focus on her best friend and not dwell on her issues with her dad. "I haven't become a nymphomaniac. I'm just stressed-out and I need to unwind. Do you blame me?"

"Not really. The evil stepmother is throwing poison apples all over the place, huh?"

"You saw the morning paper, too?"

"Oh, yeah. Pretty crappy."

Hayden raked her fingers through her hair. "Crappy? It's a disaster."

"Any truth to it?" Darcy asked carefully.

"Of course not! Dad would never do the things she's accusing him of." She tried to control the frustration in her tone. "Let's not talk about this. Tonight I just want to forget about my dad and Sheila and the whole messy business."

"All right. Wanna talk about sex again?"

Hayden grinned. "No. I'd rather *have* sex instead."

"Then do it. There are tons of men in this place. Pick one and go home with him."

"You mean a one-night stand?" she asked warily.

"Hell, yeah."

"I don't know. It seems kind of sleazy, hopping into bed with someone and never seeing them again."

"How is that sleazy? I do it all the time."

Hayden burst out laughing. "Of course you do. You're commitment-phobic."

Darcy went through men like socks, and some of the details she shared in her e-mails made Hayden gape. *She* certainly couldn't remember ever experiencing seven orgasms in one night, or indulging in a ménage à trois with two firefighters she'd met—figure this one out—at an illegal bonfire in Chicago's Lincoln Park.

Darcy raised her eyebrows, blue eyes flashing with challenge. "Well, let me ask you this—what sounds more fun, having a few screaming orgasms with a man you may or may not see again, or hiking across the intimacy bridge with Don?"

"Doug."

Darcy shrugged. "I think we both know my way is better than the highway. Or should I say the bridge?" She fluttered her hand as if waving a white flag. "Sorry, I promise to refrain from any further bridge comments for the rest of the evening."

Hayden didn't answer. Instead, she mulled over Darcy's suggestion. She'd never had a one-night stand in her life. For her, sex came with other things, relationship things, like going to dinner, spending a cozy night in, saying *I love you* for the first time.

But why did sex always have to be about love? Couldn't it just be purely for pleasure? No dinner, no I-love-you's, no expectations?

"I don't know," she said slowly. "Falling into bed with a man when last week I was still with Doug?"

"You asked for space for a reason," Darcy said. "Might as well take advantage of it."

"By going to bed with someone else." She sipped her wine, thoughtful and hesitant at the same time.

"Why not?" Darcy said. "Look, you've spent years searching for a guy to build a life with—maybe you should try looking for one who jump-starts your libido instead. The way I see it, it's time for you to have some fun, Hayden. I think you need fun."

She sighed. "I think so, too."

Darcy's grin widened. "You're seriously considering it, aren't you?"

"If I see a guy I like, I just might."

Her own words surprised her, but they made sense. What was so wrong with hooking up with a stranger in a bar? People did wild things like that all the time, and maybe right now she needed to be a little wild.

Darcy twirled the straw around in her daiquiri glass, looking pensive. "What's your pseudonym going to be?"

"My pseudonym?" she echoed.

"Yeah. If you're going to do this right, you need total anonymity. Be someone else for the night. Like Yolanda."

"No way," she objected with a laugh. "I'd rather just be myself."

"Fine." Darcy's shoulders drooped.

"We're getting ahead of ourselves, Darce. Shouldn't I pick the guy first?"

Darcy's enthusiasm returned. "Good point. Let's spin the man wheel and see who it lands on."

Stifling a laugh, Hayden followed her friend's lead and swept her eyes around the crowded bar. Everywhere she looked, she saw men. Tall ones, short ones, cute ones, bald ones. None of them sparked her interest.

And then she saw him.

Standing at the counter with his back turned to them was the lucky winner of the man wheel. All she could see was a head of dark brown hair, a broad back clad in a navy-blue sweater and long legs encased in denim. Oh, and the butt. Hard not to notice that tight little butt.

"Excellent selection," Darcy teased, following her gaze.

"I can't see his face," she complained, trying not to crane her neck.

"Patience, grasshopper."

Holding her breath, Hayden watched the man drop a few bills on the sleek mahogany counter and accept a tall glass of beer from the bartender. When he turned around, she sucked in an impressed gasp. The guy had the face of a Greek god, chiseled, rugged, with intense blue eyes that caused her heart to pound and sensual lips that made her mouth tingle. And he was huge. With his back turned he hadn't seemed this big, but now, face-to-face, she realized he stood well over six feet and had the kind of chest a woman wanted to rest her head on. She could see the muscular planes of his chest even through his sweater.

"Wow," she muttered, more to herself than Darcy.

A shiver of anticipation danced through her as she imagined spending the night with him.

Beer in hand, the man strode toward one of the pool tables at the far end of the bar, and headed for the cue rack. Setting his glass on the small ledge along the wall, he grabbed a cue and proceeded to rack the balls on the green felt table. A second later, a tall, lanky college-age kid approached and they exchanged a few words. The kid snatched up a cue and joined Mr. Delicious at the table.

Hayden turned back to Darcy and saw her friend rolling her eyes. "What?" she said, feeling a bit defensive.

"What are you waiting for?" Darcy prompted.

She glanced at the dark-haired sex god again. "I should go over there?"

"If you're serious about doing the nasty tonight, then, yeah, go over there."

"And do what?"

"Shoot some pool. Talk. Flirt. You know, look under the hood before you commit to buying the car."

"He's not a car, Darce."

"Yeah, but if he was, he'd be something dangerously hot, like a Hummer."

Hayden burst out laughing. If there was one thing to be said about Darcy, it was that she truly was one of a kind.

"Come on, go over there," Darcy repeated.

She swallowed. "Now?"

"No, next week."

Her mouth grew even drier, prompting her to down the rest of her wine.

"You're seriously nervous about this, aren't you?" Darcy said, blue eyes widening in wonder. "When did you become so shy? You give lectures to classes of hundreds. He's just one man, Hayden."

Her eyes drifted back in the guy's direction. She noticed how his back muscles bunched together as he rested his elbows on the pool table, how his taut backside looked practically edible in those faded jeans.

He's just one man, she said to herself, shaking off her nerves. Right. Just one tall, sexy, oozing-with-raw-masculinity man.

This would be a piece of cake.

BRODY CROFT CIRCLED the pool table, his eyes sharp as a hawk's as he examined his options. With a quick nod, he pointed and said, "Thirteen, side pocket."

His young companion, wearing a bright red Hawaiian T-shirt that made Brody's eyes hurt, raised his eyebrows. "Really? Tough shot, man."

"I can handle it."

And handle it he did. The ball slid cleanly into the pocket, making the kid beside him groan.

"Nice, man. Nice."

"Thanks." He moved to line up his next shot when he noticed his opponent staring at him. "Something wrong?"

"No, uh, nothing's wrong. Are—are you Brody Croft?" the guy blurted out, looking embarrassed.

Brody smothered a laugh. He'd wondered how long it would take the kid to ask. Not that he was conceited enough to think everyone on the planet knew who he was, but seeing as this bar was owned by Alexi Nicklaus and Jeff Wolinski, two fellow Warriors, most of the patrons were bound to be hockey fans.

"At your service," he said easily, extending his hand.

The kid gripped it tightly, as if he were sinking in a pit of quicksand and Brody's hand was the lifeline keeping him alive. "This is so awesome! I'm Mike, by the way."

The look of pure adoration on Mike's face brought a knot of discomfort to Brody's gut. He always enjoyed meeting fans, but sometimes the hero worship went a little too far.

"What do you say we keep playing?" he suggested, gesturing to the pool table.

"Yeah. I mean, sure! Let's play!" Mike's eyes practically popped out of his angular face. "I can't wait to tell the guys I played a round of pool with Brody Croft."

Since he couldn't come up with a response that didn't include something asinine, like "thank you," Brody chalked up the end of his cue. The next shot would be more difficult than the first, but again, nothing he couldn't manage. He'd worked in a bar like this one back when he'd played for the farm team and was barely bringing in enough cash to feed his goldfish, let alone himself. He used to hang out after work shooting pool with the other waiters, eventually developing a fondness for the game. With the way his schedule was now, he rarely had time to play anymore.

But with rumors about a possible league investigation swirling, thanks to allegations made in a recent interview with the team owner's soon-to-be ex-wife, Brody might end up with more free time than he wanted. Mrs. Houston apparently had proof that her husband had bribed at least two players to bring forth a loss and that he'd placed substantial—*illegal*—bets on those fixed games.

While there was probably no truth to any of it, Brody was growing concerned with the rumors.

A few years ago a similar scandal had plagued the Colorado Kodiaks. Only three players had been involved, but many innocent players suffered—other teams were reluctant to pick them up due to their association with the tarnished franchise.

Hell would freeze over before he'd accept a payout, and he

had no intention of being lumped in with any of the players who might have. His contract was due to expire at the end of the season. He'd be a free agent then, which meant he needed to remain squeaky clean if he wanted to sign with a new team or remain with the Warriors.

He tried to remind himself that this morning's paper was filled with nothing but rumors. If something materialized from Sheila Houston's claims, he'd worry about it then. Right now, he needed to focus on playing his best so the Warriors could win the first play-offs round and move on to the next.

Resting the cue between his thumb and forefinger, Brody positioned the shot, took one last look and pulled the cue back.

From the corner of his eye, a woman's curvy figure drew his attention, distracting him just as he pushed the cue forward. The brief diversion caused his fingers to slip, and the white ball sailed across the felt, avoided every other ball on the table and slid directly into the far pocket. Scratch.

Damn.

Scowling, he lifted his head just as the source of his distraction drew near.

"You could do it over," Mike said quickly, fumbling for the white ball and placing it back on the table. "It's called a mulligan or something."

"That's golf," Brody muttered, his gaze glued to the approaching brunette.

A few years ago an interviewer for *Sports Illustrated* had asked him to describe the type of women he was attracted to. "Leggy blondes" had been his swift response, which was pretty much the exact opposite of the woman who'd now stopped two feet in front of him. And yet his mouth went dry at the sight of her, his body quickly responding to every little detail. The silky chocolate-brown hair falling over her shoulders, the vibrant green eyes the same shade as a lush rain forest, the petite body with more curves than his brain could register.

His breath hitched as their eyes met. The whisper of an uncertain smile that tugged at her full lips sent a jolt to his groin. Jeez. He couldn't remember the last time a single smile from a woman had evoked such an intense response.

"I thought I'd play the winner." Her soft, husky voice promptly delivered another shock wave to Brody's crotch.

Stunned to find he was two seconds away from a full-blown erection, he tried to remind his body that he wasn't a teenager any longer, but a twenty-nine-year-old man who knew how to control himself. Hell, he could control the puck while fending off elbows and cross-checks from opposing attackers; getting a hold of his hormones should be a piece of cake.

"Here, just take my place now," Mike burst out, quickly pushing his cue into her hands. His gaze dropped to the cleavage spilling over the scooped neckline of the brunette's yellow tank top, and then the kid turned to Brody and winked. "Have fun, man."

Brody wrinkled his brow, wondering if Mike thought he was graciously passing this curvy bombshell over to him or something, but before he could say anything, Mike disappeared in the crowd.

Brody swallowed, then focused his eyes on the sexy little woman who'd managed to get him hard with one smile.

She didn't look like the type you'd find in a sports bar, even one as upscale as this. Sure, her body was out of this world, but something about her screamed innocence. The freckles splattering the bridge of her nose maybe, or perhaps the way she kept biting on the corner of her bottom lip like a bunny nibbling on a piece of lettuce.

Before he could stop it, the image of those plump red lips nibbling on one particular part of his anatomy slid to the forefront of his brain like a well-placed slap shot to the net. His cock pushed against the fly of his jeans.

So much for controlling his hormones.

"I'm guessing it's my turn," she said. Tilting her head, she offered another endearing smile. "Seeing as you just blew your shot."

He cleared his throat. "Uh, yeah."

Snap out of it, man.

Right, he needed to regroup here. He played hockey, yeah, but he wasn't a player anymore. His love-'em-and-leave-'em ways were in the past. He was sick to death of women fawning all over him because of his career. Nowadays all he had to do was walk into a place—club, bar, the public library—and a warm, willing female was by his side, ready to jump his bones. And he couldn't even count the number of times he'd heard, "Do you like it rough off the ice, baby?"

Well, screw it. He'd been down the casual road, had his fun, scored off the ice as often as he scored on it, but now it was time to take a new path. One where the woman in his bed actually gave a damn about *him,* and not the hockey star she couldn't wait to gush to her friends about.

The sexual fog in his brain cleared, leaving him alert and composed, and completely aware of the flush on the brunette's cheeks and the hint of attraction in her eyes. If this woman was looking to score with Mr. Hockey, she had another think coming.

"I'm Hayden," his new opponent said, uncertainty floating through her forest-green eyes.

"Brody Croft," he returned coolly, waiting for the flicker of recognition to cross her features.

It didn't happen. No flash of familiarity, no widening of the eyes. Her expression didn't change in the slightest.

"It's nice to meet you. Brody." Her voice lingered on his name, as if she were testing it out for size. She must have decided she liked the fit, because she gave a small nod and turned her attention to the table. After a quick examination, she pointed to the ball he'd failed to sink and called the shot.

Okay, was he supposed to believe she genuinely didn't know who he was? That she'd walked into a sports bar and randomly chosen to hit on the only hockey player in attendance?

"So…did you catch the game last night?" he said with a casual slant of the head.

She gave him a blank stare. "What game?"

"Game one of the play-offs, Warriors and Vipers. Seriously good hockey, in my opinion."

Her brows drew together in a frown. "Oh. I'm not really a fan, to be honest."

"You don't like the Warriors?"

"I don't like hockey." She made a self-deprecating face. "Actually, I can't say I enjoy any sport, really. Maybe the gymnastics in the summer Olympics?"

He couldn't help but grin. "Are you asking or telling?"

She smiled back. "Telling. And I guess it's very telling that I only watch a sports event once every four years, huh?"

He found himself liking the dry note to her throaty voice when she admitted her disinterest in sports. Her honesty was rare. Most—fine, *all*—of the women he encountered claimed to love his sport of choice, and if they didn't truly love it, they pretended to, as if sharing that common interest made them soul mates.

"But I love this game," Hayden added, raising her cue. "It counts as a sport, right?"

"It does in my book."

She nodded, then focused on the balls littering the table. She leaned forward to take her shot.

He got a nice eyeful of her cleavage, a tantalizing swell of creamy-white skin spilling over the neckline of her snug yellow top. When he lowered his eyes, he couldn't help but admire her full breasts, hugged firmly by a thin bra he could only see the outline of.

She took the shot, and he raised his brows, impressed, as the ball cleanly disappeared into the pocket. She was good.

All right, more than good, he had to relent as she proceeded to circle the table and sink ball after ball.

"Where'd you learn to play like that?" he asked, finally finding his voice.

She met his eyes briefly before sinking the last solid on the table. "My dad." She smiled again. Those pouty lips just screamed for his mouth to do wicked things to them. "He bought me my own table when I was nine, set it up right next to his. We used to play side by side in the basement every night before I went to bed."

"Does he still play?"

Her eyes clouded. "No. He's too busy with work to relax around a pool table anymore." She straightened her back and glanced at the table. "Eight ball, corner pocket."

At this point, Brody didn't even care about the game Hayden was certain to win. The sweet scent of her perfume, a fruity sensual aroma, floated in the air and made him mindless with need. Man, he couldn't remember the last time he'd been so drawn to a woman.

After sinking the eight ball, she moved toward him, each step she took heightening his desire. She ran her fingers through her dark hair, and a new aroma filled his nostrils. Strawberries. Coconut.

He was suddenly very, very hungry.

"Good game," she said, shooting him another smile. Impish, this time.

His mouth twisted wryly. "I didn't even get to play."

"I'm sorry." She paused. "Do you like to play?"

Was she referring to pool? Or a different game? Maybe the kind you played in bed. Naked.

"Pool, I mean," she added quickly.

"Sure, I like pool. Among other things." *Let's see how she handles that.*

A cute rosy flush spread over her cheeks. "Me, too. I mean, I like other things."

His curiosity sparked as he stared at the enigma in front of him. He got the distinct impression that she was flirting with him. Or trying to, at least. Yet her unmistakable blush and the slight trembling of her hands betrayed the confident air she tried to convey.

Did she do this often? Flirt with strange men in bars? Looking at her again, now that he was able to see through the fog of initial attraction, it didn't seem like the case. She was dressed rather conservatively. Sure, the top was low-cut, but it covered her midriff, and her jeans didn't ride low on her hips like those of most of the other women in this place. And sexy as she was, she didn't seem to be aware of her own appeal.

"That's good. Other things can be a lot of fun," he answered, unable to stop the husky pitch of his voice.

Their gazes connected. Brody could swear the air crackled and hissed with sexual tension. Or maybe he just imagined it. He couldn't deny the hum of awareness thudding in his groin like the bass line of a sultry jazz tune, but maybe he was alone in the feeling. It was difficult to get a read on Hayden.

"So... Brody." His name rolled off her lips in a way that had his body growing stiff. That didn't say much, considering that every part of him was already hard and prickling with anticipation.

He wanted her in his bed.

Whoa—where had that come from?

Five minutes ago he was telling himself it was time to quit falling into bed with women who didn't give a damn about him and look for something more meaningful. So why the hell was he anticipating a roll in the hay with a woman he'd just met?

Because she's different.

The observation came out of nowhere, bringing with it a baffling swirl of emotion. Yes, this woman had somehow managed to elicit primal, greedy lust in him. Yes, her body was designed to drive a man wild. But something about her seriously intrigued him. Those damn cute freckles, the shy smiles, the look in her eyes that clearly said, "I want to go to bed with you but I'm apprehensive about it." It was the combination of sensuality and bashfulness, excitement and wariness, that attracted him to her.

He opened his mouth to say something, anything, but promptly closed it when Hayden reached out to touch his arm.

Looking up at him with those bottomless green eyes, she said, "Look, I know this is going to sound...forward. And don't think I do this often—I've never done this actually, but..." She took a breath. "Would you like to come back to my hotel?"

Ah, her hotel. An out-of-towner. That explained why she

hadn't recognized him. And yet he got the feeling that even if she did know what he did for a living, she wouldn't care.

He liked that.

"Well?" she said, fixing him with an expectant stare.

He couldn't stop the teasing twinge in his voice. "And what will we do in your hotel room?"

A hint of a smile. "We could have a nightcap."

"A nightcap," he repeated.

"Or we could talk. Watch television. Order room service."

The little vixen was teasing him, he realized. And, damn, but he liked this side of her, too.

"Maybe raid the minifridge?"

"Definitely."

Their eyes met and locked, the heat of desire and promise of sex filling the space between them. Finally he shoved his pool cue in the rack and strode back to her. Screw it. He'd told himself no more sleazy bar pickups, but damn it, this didn't feel sleazy. It felt *right*.

Barely able to disguise the urgency in his tone, he curled his fingers over her hot, silky skin and said, "Let's go."

CHAPTER TWO

DEAR GOD, HE'D said yes.

She'd invited a gorgeous stranger back to her hotel room for a *nightcap* (translation: sex) and he'd actually said *yes*.

Hayden resisted the urge to fan her hot face with her hands. Instead, trying to remain cool and collected, she said, "I'll meet you outside, okay? I just need to tell my friend I'm leaving."

His smoldering blue eyes studied her for a moment, making her grow hotter. With a quick nod, he exited the bar. Tearing her attention away from his criminally sexy backside, she spun on her heel and hurried back to Darcy, dodging people along the way. When she reached the table, Darcy greeted her with a delighted grin. "You bad girl, you," she teased, wagging her finger.

Sliding into the chair, Hayden swallowed hard and willed her heartbeat to slow. "Jesus. I can't believe I'm doing this."

"I take it he said yes?"

Hayden ignored the question. "I just propositioned a complete stranger. Granted, he's a very sexy stranger, but hell! I'm not sure I can do this."

"Of course you can."

"But I don't even know him. What if he hacks me to pieces and hides my dismembered body parts in the air-conditioning system of the hotel or something?"

"You have your cell phone?"

She nodded.

"If you see any sign of trouble, call the cops. Or call me and I'll call the cops." Darcy shrugged. "But I wouldn't worry. He doesn't seem like the serial-killer type."

Hayden blew out a breath. "That's what they said about Ted Bundy."

"You can back out, you know. You don't have to sleep with this guy. But you want to, don't you?"

Did she want to? Oh, yeah. As the image of Brody's chiseled face and scrumptious body flashed through her brain, some of her nervousness dissolved. He was hands down the most gorgeous man she'd ever met. And she got the feeling he knew his way around a bedroom. The raw sex appeal pouring out of him told her she might be in for a very stimulating night.

"I want to." Newfound confidence washed over her. "And I probably shouldn't keep him waiting."

Darcy winked. "Have fun."

"Are you going to be okay here alone?"

"Of course." Darcy gestured to her fruity pink drink. "This daiquiri will attract the fellows like flies to honey. For the purpose of this analogy, I'll be the honey."

Hayden laughed. "Whatever you say."

With a quick wave, she threaded through the crowd toward the door. When she stepped into the cool night air, she spotted Brody standing near one of the potted plants in the entrance, his hands slung in the pockets of his jeans. A shiver tickled her belly as she took in his profile. He really was spectacular. Her gaze lowered to his lips. She wondered what they would feel like pressed against her own. Would they be soft? Hard? Both?

"Hey," she said, her voice wavering.

She took a step forward just as he turned to face her. His expression, appreciative, anticipatory, sizzled her nerves. "Your car or mine?" he asked in a rough voice that made her toes curl.

"I don't have a car. My friend drove here." A squeak, her voice had come out in a damn squeak.

"My car's over there." He nodded, then began walking toward the parking lot. He didn't check to see if she was following. As if he just assumed she was.

This was her chance to walk away. She could hurry into the bar and pretend she'd never asked this man to come back to her hotel. She could phone up Doug, have a heart-to-heart, maybe entice him into engaging in some phone sex.... Ha! Fat chance.

She hurried to keep up with Brody's purposeful strides.

"Nice car," she remarked when they reached the shiny black BMW SUV.

"Thanks." He pulled a set of keys from his front pocket and pressed a button. The car's security system beeped as the doors unlocked, and he reached for the passenger door and opened it for her. Hayden settled against the leather seat and waited for Brody to get in.

After he'd buckled his seat belt and started the engine, he turned to her and asked, "Where to?"

"The Ritz-Carlton."

He raised his eyebrows but didn't say anything, just pulled out of the parking lot and made a left turn. "So where are you from, Hayden?"

"I was born in Chicago, but I've been living in San Francisco for the past three years."

"And what do you do out there?"

"I'm a junior professor at Berkeley. I teach art history, and I'm also working toward a Ph.D."

Before she could ask him what he did for a living, he said, "Sounds exciting."

She got the feeling he wasn't talking about her career anymore. Her suspicions were confirmed when his gaze swept over face and dropped to her cleavage. Under his brief—but appreciative—scrutiny, her nipples tightened against her lace bra.

She played with the sleeve of the green wool sweater she'd brought instead of a coat, focusing on the scenery along South Michigan Avenue, afraid to look at him again. If he got her this aroused from one hooded glance, what on earth would he do to her in bed?

Gosh, she couldn't wait to find out.

The rest of the car ride was silent. They reached the hotel, and Brody pulled into the lot and killed the engine. Still, neither of them spoke. As she unbuckled her seat belt, her pulse began to race. This was it. An hour ago she'd been complaining to Darcy about the lack of sex in her life, and now here she was, walking into the lobby of the Ritz with the sexiest man she'd ever encountered.

Her heart thumped against her rib cage as they rode the elevator up to the penthouse. Shooting her a quizzical look, he said, "You must make good money at Berkeley."

She simply nodded, her expression vague. She didn't want to tell him that the lavish penthouse actually belonged to her father. Her dad had lived here up until three years ago, before he'd married Sheila. He kept the place so Hayden would have somewhere to stay when she came to visit. But she didn't want to tell Brody, mostly because that would lead to questions like *what does your father do*? Which would then lead to questions about her dad's hockey team and that was one topic of conversation she tried to avoid.

With the exception of Doug, most of the men she'd dated over the years had gone a little crazy when they found out her father owned the Warriors. Once, she'd dated a man who'd badgered her constantly to get him season tickets—which had driven her to promptly break up with him.

She understood the sports obsession that came with most males, but just once it would be nice if *she* were the source of a man's infatuation.

The elevator doors opened right into the living room. Decorated in shades of black and gold, the room boasted four enormous leather couches in the center, all positioned in the direction of a fifty-six-inch plasma television mounted on the far wall. The suite had three large bedrooms, as well as a private covered balcony with a ten-person hot tub. In the corner of the main suite was a wet bar, which Hayden made a beeline for the second they stepped inside.

She wasn't a big drinker, but her nerves were shaky, making her hands tremble and her heartbeat erratic, and she hoped the alcohol might calm her down.

"What can I get you?" she called over her shoulder. "There's beer, scotch, whiskey, bourbon—"

"You." With a soft laugh, Brody eliminated the distance between them.

Oh, God, he was huge. She had to fully tilt her head up to look at him. At five feet three inches, she felt like a dwarf next to him. Her heart jammed in her throat as he stepped even closer. She could feel his body heat, his warm breath tickling her ear as he leaned down and whispered, "That was the nightcap you were referring to, wasn't it?"

His low, husky voice heated her veins. When she met

his eyes, she saw the unmistakable desire glittering in their cobalt-blue depths. "Well?" he prompted.

"Yes." The word squeaked out of her mouth.

He settled his big hands on her waist, yet didn't press his body against hers. Despite the pounding of her heart, anticipation began to build in her belly, slowly crept up to her breasts like a vine and made them grow heavy, achy. She wanted him closer, wanted to feel his firm chest on her breasts, his hardness between her thighs.

Brody lifted one hand and brushed his thumb against her lower lip. "If you want to change your mind, now's the time."

He waited for her answer, watching her closely. Her throat grew dry, while another part of her grew wet.

Did she want to change her mind? Maybe she should call her own bluff now, before things got out of hand. But as she studied his handsome face, she realized she didn't want him to leave. So what if this wouldn't result in I-love-you's and cosigning a mortgage for a house? Tonight wasn't about that. Tonight she was stressed and tired and sexually frustrated. And just once she wanted to be with a man without thinking about the future.

"I haven't changed my mind," she murmured.

"Good."

He skimmed his hand over her hip, moving it to her back, grazing her tailbone. Then he stared at her lips, as if pondering, debating.

His slow perusal lasted too long for her throbbing body. She wanted him to kiss her. Now. She let out a tiny groan to voice her anguish.

Amusement danced across his features. "What? What do you want, Hayden?"

"Your mouth." The words flew out before she could stop them, shocking her. Since when was she this forward?

"All right." He dipped his head and planted a soft kiss on her neck, lightly biting the tender flesh with his teeth.

She whimpered and he responded with a chuckle, his warm breath moistening her skin. He trailed his tongue up to her earlobe, flicked over it, licked it, then blew a stream of air over it, making her shiver.

Fire began simmering in her blood, heating all the parts that already ached for him. She reached up and touched his dark hair, relishing the silky texture. She'd never known a simple kiss could have such a slow buildup. Most of the men in her past had thrust their tongues into her mouth and quickly followed suit by thrusting themselves into her.

But Brody, he took his time.

He tortured her.

"Your skin tastes like…" He kissed her jaw, then nipped at it. "Strawberries. And honey."

All she could do was shiver in response.

"Take off your clothes," he said roughly.

She swallowed. "Now?"

"Now would be a good time, yes."

She reached for the hem of her sweater, trying to fight the insecurity spiraling through her. She'd never stripped for a man before. Was she supposed to put on a show? Dance? Well, forget that. No matter how much she wanted him right now, she wasn't going to pretend to be the sexy seductress she wasn't.

She pulled her sweater and tank top over her head, pleased to hear Brody's breath hitch at the sight of her lacy wisp of a bra. When she reached for the front clasp, he shook his head. "No. Not yet. First the jeans."

Well. Commanding, wasn't he?

Obligingly, she wiggled out of her jeans and let them drop to the floor. Her black panties matched her bra, and they, too, left little to the imagination.

Brody's eyes widened with approval. She was starting to get the hang of this stripping thing. Hooking her thumbs under the spaghetti-thin straps that constituted a waistband, she pulled her panties down her thighs, slowly, bending over a little so he could get a peek at her cleavage.

Naked from the waist down, she held his gaze. "Like what you see?"

His serious expression never faltered. "Very much. Now the bra."

In one slow, fluid movement, she unclasped her bra and tossed it aside. Strangely enough, she no longer felt insecure.

"I like—" he stepped closer and brushed his thumb over the swell of one breast "—these. A lot."

She wondered if he realized he still hadn't kissed her lips. Though the way his eyes burned every inch of skin she'd just exposed to him, she felt thoroughly kissed.

"Your turn. Get rid of your clothes."

He grinned. "Why don't you do it for me?"

The thought of undressing him was so appealing that her nipples hardened. He didn't miss the reaction, and his grin widened.

"Gets you going, doesn't it, the thought of peeling these clothes off my body?" he taunted.

"Yes," she blew out.

"Then do it."

With a shaky breath, she grasped his sweater, bunching the material between her fingers before lifting it up his chest and over his head. That first sight of his bare chest stole the breath from her lungs. Every inch of him was hard. His defined pectorals, the rippling abs and trim hips. He had a two-inch scar under his collarbone, and another under his chin that she hadn't noticed before, but the scars only added to his appeal, making him appear dangerous.

A badass tribal tattoo covered one firm bicep, while the other boasted a lethal-looking dragon in mid-flight. It reminded her of her own tattoo, the one she'd gotten for the sole purpose of pissing off her father after he'd grounded her for missing curfew when she was seventeen. Even now the spontaneity of her actions—getting a *tattoo!*—surprised her. Darcy always teased that she had a secret wild side, and maybe she did, but it rarely made any appearances.

Tonight, though, her wild side had definitely come out to play.

"Like what you see?" Brody mimicked, the heat in his eyes telling her he was enjoying the attention.

She licked her lips. "Yes." Then she reached for his fly, unbuttoned it and pulled the zipper down. She bent over to slide his jeans off, admiring his long legs and muscular thighs and the erection that pushed against the black boxer briefs he wore, a thick ridge that made her mouth water.

Dear God, this was insanity.

Stumbling to her feet, she tugged at his waistband and helped him out of the briefs. Leaving him as naked as she was.

She shyly appraised his body, which was toned, muscled and unbelievably *male.* She eyed his impressive erection, then trembled at the thought of that hard, pulsing cock buried deep inside her.

Suddenly she could no longer bear it.

"For God's sake, kiss me," she blurted out.

"Yes, ma'am." His eyes gleaming, Brody pressed his body against hers and finally bent down to capture her mouth.

Oh, sweet Jesus.

He felt and tasted like heaven. With skilled ease, he explored her mouth, swirling and thrusting his tongue into every crevice, hot and greedy. When he sucked on her bottom lip, she let out a deep moan then pulled back and stared at him in awe.

Brody seemed to know exactly what to do, turning her on in a way she'd never anticipated. He fondled her breasts for an excruciatingly long time before finally dipping his head and sampling one mound with his tongue.

He sucked the nipple hard, flicked his tongue over it, nibbled on it until she cried out with pleasure that bordered on pain, and just when she thought it couldn't possibly feel better than that, he turned his attention to her other breast.

Arousal drummed through her body, until her thighs grew slick from her own wetness, and she found herself choking out, "We need a bed. Now."

DAMN, HE HADN'T expected her to be like this. Deliciously demanding and so gorgeous. Something about Hayden sent lust and curiosity spinning through him, the need to both claim her and unravel the mystery of her.

And there was definitely plenty to learn about this freckle-faced professor who had initiated a one-night stand when it was obviously not in her nature.

He sucked on her nipple once more before pulling his head away and straightening his back. His mouth went dry as sawdust as he stared at the evidence of his handiwork on those high, full breasts. His stubble had chafed the hell out of her creamy white skin, leaving splotches of red, and the tips of her dusky pink nipples glistened with the moisture, making him want to feast on her again.

His eyes dropped to the wispy line of dark hair between her thighs. He knew it was called a landing strip and goddamn but he couldn't wait to land his tongue down there. The sparse amount of hair offered a mouthwatering view of her swollen clit.

His already hot and hard body grew hotter and harder.

"Where's the bedroom?" he groaned.

Hayden's mouth quirked. Without answering, she turned on her heel toward the unlit hallway.

Brody took two steps, then stopped when he noticed the tattoo on her lower back. Oh, man. In the shadowy corridor he could just make out the shape of a bird. A hawk, or an eagle. Dark, dangerous, incredibly sexy and completely surprising. He'd known this woman was different. Her tattoo was so tantalizing he marched up to her and gripped her slender waist with both hands.

The top of her head barely reached his chin. How had this saucy little woman reduced him to a state of foolish hunger?

As his hands trailed down her hips, she twisted her head slightly to send him a look that said she was curious about his next move.

His next move consisted of dropping to his knees and outlining the tattoo with his tongue.

Hayden shuddered, but he kept one hand on her waist, keeping her steady. "Why an eagle?" he murmured, kissing her lower back.

"I like eagles."

A very simple answer from a very complicated woman. He stroked her ass with his hand, then lowered his head and bit into the soft flesh.

"Bedroom," she gasped.

"Screw it," he muttered.

Still holding her secure with one hand, he slid the other around to her front and ran one finger over her clit. She hissed out a breath, then jerked forward, pressing her palms to the wall and raising that firm ass so that he got a very naughty view of her glistening sex.

He moved closer as if being pulled by a magnet. As his pulse drummed in his ears, he licked her damp folds from behind and used his finger to stroke her clit.

Hayden shuddered again. "That feels…" she moaned "…amazing."

"What about this? How does this feel?"

He shoved his tongue directly into her opening.

Her breath hitched.

He chuckled at her reaction, then thrust his tongue right back inside her enticing sex before she could catch her breath.

Hayden's soft moans filled the wide hallway. Her breathing grew ragged, her clit swollen beneath his thumb, her sex wet with arousal. He kissed her once more, then moved his mouth away and replaced it with two fingers.

"Are you trying to make me come?" she choked out.

"That was the plan, yeah."

He explored her silky heat, fingering her deftly, enjoying her soft whimpers of pleasure while at the same time trying to ignore his erection, which was threatening to explode.

Any second now his control would shatter, he knew it would, but he held on to that one tiny thread of restraint, feeling it slowly unravel and fray inside him. Hayden's cry of abandon made him move faster, increase his pressure over her clit and add another finger into the mix. And then she came. Loudly. Without inhibition. She pushed her ass into his hand as her inner muscles tightened and contracted over his fingers.

"Oh, God… Brody…" Her voice dissolved into a contented sigh.

A moment later she slid down to the carpeted floor, her

bare back pressing into his chest as he continued to trace lazy figure-eights over her clit.

She shifted so they were face-to-face, her green eyes burning with need, her face flushed from her climax. She looked so good that he leaned forward to push his tongue through her pliant lips, intent on exploring every recess of her hot, wet mouth, desperate to taste every part of this woman.

Without breaking the kiss, he rolled her gently onto her back and covered her body with his.

"I need to be inside you," he choked out.

It was a primal urge, an overwhelming desire to possess and one he never knew he had, but sure enough it was there, making his entire body tense with need, waiting to be released.

Tearing his mouth from hers, he stood up and left her in the hall. He returned a moment later with the condoms that had been tucked in his wallet. Only three condoms, he realized as he glanced down at his hand. Maybe he was being overly optimistic, but as he looked at Hayden, he suspected he might need to make a trip to the drugstore. She hadn't bothered getting up and she looked ridiculously sexy lying there on the floor beneath him. Sexy and trashy and so damn appealing his cock twitched with impatience.

The air was thick with tension, the hallway quiet save for their heavy breathing. Before he could tear open the condom packet, she sat up and murmured, "Not yet."

Then she wrapped her lips around him.

"Jesus," he mumbled, nearly keeling over backward.

The feel of her eager mouth surrounding him brought on an unexpected shudder. She took him deeper into her mouth, cupping his balls, stroking his ass and licking every hard inch of him.

A few moments of exquisite torture were all he could bear. Hard as it was to pull back from the best blow job of his life, he gently moved her head, so close to exploding he wasn't sure how he managed to hold back.

He lowered himself onto her again and Hayden sighed as one palm closed over her breast. "It's been so long..."

"How long?" he asked.

"Too long."

He lightly pinched her nipple before bending down to kiss it. "I'll take it slow then." He sucked the nipple deep in his mouth, rolled the other one between his thumb and forefinger.

She forced his head up and kissed him. "No." She took his hand and dragged it between her legs. "I want fast."

He swallowed when he touched her sex, still moist from her climax.

He grew even harder, wanting so badly to put the damn condom on and slide into her slick heat. But the gentleman in him argued to go slow, to taste every inch of her body and bring her over the edge again before he took his own release. Once more he tried to slow the pace, stroking her with his thumb.

His gentlemanly intentions got him nowhere.

"I'm ready," she said between gritted teeth. "I don't need slow. I need you to fuck me, Brody."

His cock jerked at the wicked request.

Oh, man. He'd never have pegged this woman as a dirty talker. But, damn, how he liked it.

Without another word, he rolled the condom onto his shaft, positioned himself between her thighs and drove deep inside her. They released simultaneous groans.

Burying his face in the curve of her neck, Brody inhaled the sweet feminine scent of her and withdrew, slowly, torturously, only to thrust into her to the hilt before she could blink.

"You're so tight," he muttered in her ear. "So wet."

"Told you I was ready," she said between gasps of pleasure.

He slammed into her, over and over again, groaning each time she lifted her hips to take him deeper. It was too fast for him, and yet it felt like everything was moving in slow motion. The way she dug her fingers into his buttocks and pulled him toward her, squeezing his cock with her tight wetness. The rising pleasure in his body, the impatient throb in his groin that forced him to move even faster.

She exploded again, quivering, shuddering, making little mewling sounds that had his entire body burning with excitement.

He continued plunging into her until finally he couldn't take it anymore. He came a second later, kissing her harshly as his climax rocked into him with the force of a hurricane. Shards of pleasure ripped through him, hot, intense, insistent. Uncontrollable. He fought for air, wondering how it was possible that the little woman beneath him had managed to bring him to the most incredible release of his life.

They lay there for a moment, breathing ragged, bodies slick, his cock still buried inside her.

Hayden ran her hands along his sweat-soaked back, then murmured, "Not bad."

Even in his state of orgasmic numbness Brody managed a mock frown. "Not bad? That's all you can say?"

"Fine, it was tremendously good."

"That's better."

With a small grin, she disentangled herself from his embrace and got to her feet. Her gaze ruefully drifted in the direction of the bedroom they'd never managed to reach.

"Five more steps and we could've been on my big, comfortable bed."

He propped himself up on his elbows, the soft carpet itching the hell out of his back. "Don't you worry, Hayden," he said with a rakish glint in his eye. "The night is still young."

CHAPTER THREE

"HOW MANY?" DARCY demanded the next day.

Hayden moved her cell phone to her other ear and maneuvered her rental car through afternoon traffic. Chicago's downtown core was surprisingly busy; tonight's Warriors game had probably compelled more than a few people to leave work early. Hayden, on the other hand, didn't have a choice in the matter. Whether she wanted to or not, she was about to spend the evening sitting next to her dad in the owner's box, watching a sport she not only found dismally boring, but one she'd resented for years.

God, she couldn't even count how many games she'd been dragged to over the years. Hundreds? Thousands? Regardless of the final tally, she was no closer to liking hockey now, at twenty-six, than she had been at age six, when her father took her to her first game. To her, hockey meant constant uprooting. Traveling, moving, sitting behind the bench with a coloring book because her dad hadn't felt right hiring a nanny.

A shrink would probably tell her that she was projecting, taking out her frustration with her father on an innocent little sport, but she couldn't help it. No matter how hard she'd tried over the years, she couldn't bring herself to appreciate or enjoy the damn game.

"I don't kiss and tell," she said into her cell, stopping at a red light. An El train whizzed overhead, momentarily making her deaf to anything but the thundering of the train as it tore down the tracks.

"Like hell you don't," Darcy was saying when the noise died down. "How many, Hayden?"

Suppressing a tiny smile, she finally caved in. "Five."

"Five!" Darcy went silent for a moment. Then she offered an awe-laced obscenity. "You're telling me the hunk gave you *five orgasms* last night?"

"He sure did." The memory alone brought a spark of heat to her still-exhausted body. Muscles she hadn't even known she had were still aching, thanks to the man who could definitely give the Energizer Bunny a run for its money.

"I'm stunned. You realize that? I'm utterly stunned."

The light ahead turned green and Hayden drove through the intersection. A group of teenagers wearing blue and silver Warriors jerseys caught her attention, and she groaned at the sight of them. She was so not in the mood to watch a night of rowdy hockey with her father.

"So how was the big goodbye and 'thanks for the five O's'?" Darcy asked.

"Strange." She made a left turn and drove down Lakeshore Drive toward the Lincoln Center, the brand-new arena recently built for the Warriors. "Before he left, he asked for my number."

"Did you give it to him?"

"No." She sighed. "But then he offered me *his* number, so I took it."

"It was supposed to be a one-night stand!"

"Yeah...but...he looked so dismayed. I made it pretty

clear that it was a one-night thing. You'd think he'd be thrilled about that. No strings, no expectations. But he was disappointed."

"You can't see him again. What if things get serious? You'll be going back to the West Coast in a couple months."

Darcy sounded surprisingly upset. Well, maybe it wasn't that surprising, seeing as Darcy found the idea of falling in love more petrifying than the Ebola virus. The phobia had taken form a few years ago, after Darcy's father broke up his marriage of twenty years by falling in love with another woman. Since then Darcy had convinced herself the same would happen to her. Hayden had tried to assure her friend that not all men left their wives, but her words always fell on deaf ears.

"Nothing will get serious," Hayden said with a laugh. "First of all, I probably won't see Brody again. And second, I won't allow myself to develop a relationship with any man until I figure out where things stand with Doug."

Darcy groaned. "Him? Why do you continue to keep him in the picture? Turn your break into a breakup, before he mentions the intimacy bridge and—"

"Goodbye, Darce."

She hung up, not in the mood to hear Darcy make fun of Doug again. Fine, so he was conservative, and maybe his comparison of sex to a bridge was bizarre, but Doug was a decent man. And she wasn't ready to write him off completely.

Uh, you slept with another man, her conscience reminded.

Her cheeks grew hot at the memory of sleeping with Brody. And somehow the words *sleeping with Brody* seemed unsuitable, as if they described a bland, mundane event like tea with a grandparent. What she and Brody had done last night was neither bland nor mundane. It had been crazy. Intense. Mind-numbingly wild and deliciously dirty. Hands down, the best sex of her life.

Was she a complete fool for sending him away this morning?

Probably.

Fine, more like absolutely.

But what else should she have done? She'd woken up to find Brody's smoky-blue eyes admiring her and before she could even utter a good-morning he'd slipped his hand between her legs. Stroked, rubbed, and brought her to orgasm in less than a minute. As a result, she'd forgotten her name, her surroundings and the reason she'd brought him home in the first place.

Fortunately, the amnesia had been temporary. Her memory had swiftly returned when she'd checked her cell phone messages and saw that both her father and Doug had called.

Brody had made it clear he wanted to see her again, and sure, that would be nice…okay, it would be freaking incredible. But sex wasn't going to solve her problems. Her issues with Doug would still be there, lurking in the wings like a jealous understudy, as would the stress of her father's recent struggles. And if Brody wanted more than sex, if he wanted a relationship (as unlikely as that was) what would she do then? Throw a third complication into her already complicated personal life?

No, ending it before it began was the logical solution. Best to leave it as a one-night stand.

She reached the arena ten minutes later and parked in the area reserved for VIPs, right next to her father's shiny red Mercedes convertible. She knew it was her dad's, because of the license plate reading "TM-OWNR." *Real subtle, Dad.*

Why had she even bothered coming home? When her

father had asked if she could take some time off to be with him during this whole divorce mess, she'd seen it as a sign that he valued her support, wanted her around. But in the week she'd been home she'd only seen her dad once, for a quick lunch in his office. The phone had kept ringing, so they'd barely spoken, and it was unlikely they'd get any time to talk tonight. She knew how focused her dad was when he watched hockey.

With a sigh, she got out of the car and braced herself for a night of watching sweaty men skating after a black disk, and listening to her father rave about how "it doesn't get better than this."

Gee, she couldn't wait.

"WATCH OUT FOR Valdek tonight," Sam Becker warned when Brody approached the long wooden bench on one side of the Warriors locker room. He paused in front of his locker.

"Valdek's back?" Brody groaned. "What happened to his three-game suspension?"

Becker adjusted his shin pads then pulled on his navy-blue pants and started lacing up. For thirty-six, he was still in prime condition. When Brody first met the legendary forward he'd been in awe, even more impressed when he'd seen Becker deke out three guys to score a shorthanded goal, proving to everyone in the league why he still belonged there.

And what had impressed him the most was Becker's complete lack of arrogance. Despite winning two championship cups and having a career that rivaled Gretzky's, Sam Becker was as down-to-earth as they came. He was the man everyone went to when they had a problem, whether personal or professional, and over the years, he'd become Brody's closest friend.

"Suspension's over," Becker answered. "And he's out for blood. He hasn't forgotten who got him suspended, kiddo."

Brody ignored the nickname, which Becker refused to ease up on, and snorted. "Right, because it's my fault he sliced my chin open with his skate."

A few more players drifted into the room. The Warriors goalie, Alexi Nicklaus, gave a salute in lieu of greeting. Next to him, Derek Jones, this season's rookie yet already one of the best defensemen in the league, wandered over and said, "Valdek's back."

"So I've heard." Brody peeled his black T-shirt over his head and tossed it on the bench.

Jones suddenly hooted, causing him to glance down at his chest. What he found was a reminder of the most exciting sexual experience of his life. Over his left nipple was the purple hickey Hayden's full lips had branded into his skin, after he'd swooped her off the hallway floor and carried her into the bedroom—where he'd proceeded to make love to her all night long.

This morning he'd woken up to the sight of Hayden's dark hair fanned across the stark white pillow, one bare breast pressing into his chest and a slender leg hooked over his lower body. He'd cuddled after sex plenty of times in the past, but he couldn't remember ever awakening to find himself in the exact post-sex position. Normally he gently rolled his companion over, needing space and distance in order to fall asleep. Last night he hadn't needed it. In fact, he even remembered waking up in the middle of the night and pulling Hayden's warm, naked body closer.

Figure that one out.

"Remind me to keep you away from my daughter," Becker said with a sigh.

Next to him, Jones guffawed. "So who's the lucky lady? Or did you even get her name?"

Brody's back stiffened defensively, but then he wondered why it bothered him that his teammates still viewed him as a playboy. Sure, he *had* been a playboy, once upon a time. When he'd first gone pro, he couldn't help letting it all go to his head. For a kid who'd grown up dirt-poor in Michigan, the sudden onslaught of wealth and attention was like a drug. Exciting. Addictive. Suddenly everyone wanted to be his friend, his confidante, his lover. At twenty-one, he'd welcomed every perk that came with the job—particularly the endless stream of women lining up to warm his bed.

But it'd gotten old once he'd realized that ninety percent of those eager females cared most about his uniform. He didn't mind being in the limelight, but he was no longer interested in going to bed with women who thought of him only as the star forward of the Warriors.

Unfortunately, his teammates couldn't seem to accept that he'd left his playboy days in the dust. It was probably a label thing; the guys on the team liked labels. They all had 'em—Derek Jones was the Prankster, Becker was the Elder, Craig Wyatt was Mr. Serious. And Brody was the Playboy. Apparently admitting otherwise screwed up the team dynamic or something.

Ah, well. Let them believe what they wanted. He might not be a Casanova anymore but he could still kick their butts any day of the week.

"Yes, I got her name," he said, rolling his eyes.

Just not her number.

He kept that irksome detail to himself. He still wasn't sure why it bugged him, Hayden's refusal to give him her phone number. And for the life of him, he also couldn't make sense of that bomb of a speech she'd dropped on him earlier.

I'd rather we didn't see each other again. I had a great time, but I never had any intention of this going beyond one night. I hope you understand.

Every man's dream words. He couldn't remember how many times he'd tried to find a way to let a woman down gently when she asked for something more the morning after. Hayden had pretty much summed up the attitude he'd had about sex his entire life. One night, no expectations, nothing more. In the old days he would've sent her a fruit basket with a thank-you card for her casual dismissal.

But these days he wanted more than that. That's why he'd gone back to Hayden's hotel room, because something about the woman made him think she was the one who could give him the *more* he desired. A sexy professor who hated sports and set his body on fire. Almost made him want to call up that *Sports Illustrated* interviewer and get a retraction printed: *Brody Croft is no longer attracted to leggy blondes.*

"Hope you didn't tire yourself out," Becker said. "We can't afford to screw up tonight, not in the play-offs."

"Hey, d'you guys get a look at the paper this morning?" Jones asked suddenly. "There was another article about the bribery accusations Houston's wife made." He frowned, an expression that didn't suit his chubby, *Leave It to Beaver* face. At twenty-one, the kid hadn't mastered his super-tough hockey glare yet. "Like any of us would take money to purposely put a loss on our record. Damn, I want to toilet paper that chick's house for all the trouble she's causing."

Brody laughed. "When are you going to grow out of these pranks? Grown men don't toilet paper people's homes."

"C'mon, you like my pranks," Derek protested. "You were laughing your ass off when I replaced Alexi's pads with those pink Hello Kitty ones."

From across the room, their goalie Alexi Nicklaus gave Jones the finger.

"Simmer down, children," Becker said with a grin. He turned to Brody, his eyes suddenly growing serious. "What do you think about the articles?"

Brody just shrugged. "Until I see the proof Mrs. Houston allegedly has, I refuse to believe anybody on this team threw a game."

Jones nodded his agreement. "Pres is a good dude. He'd never fix games." He paused, then chuckled. "Actually, I'm more intrigued by the other allegation. You know, the one from an unnamed source claiming that Mrs. H is hitting the sheets with a Warriors player?"

Huh? Brody hadn't read the paper yet, and the idea that the owner's wife was sleeping with one of his teammates was both startling and absurd. And worrisome. Definitely worrisome. He didn't like how this scandal seemed to be snowballing. Bribery, adultery, illegal gambling. Shit.

Jones turned to Brody. "Come on, admit it. It was you."

Uh, right. The thought of hopping into the sack with Sheila Houston was about as appealing as trading in his hockey skates for figure skates and joining the Stars on Ice. He'd only needed a handful of encounters with the woman to figure out she had nothing but air between her pretty little ears.

"Nah. My bet's on Topas." Brody grinned at the dark-haired right wing across the room. Zelig Topas, who'd won Olympic silver playing on the Russian team at the last Games, was also one of the few openly gay players in the league.

"Funny," Topas returned, rolling his eyes.

The chatter died down as Craig Wyatt, the captain of the Warriors, strode into the room, his Nordic features solemn as always. Wyatt stood at a massive height of six-seven, and that was in his street shoes. With his bulky torso and blond buzz cut it was no wonder Wyatt was one of the most feared players in the league and a force to contend with.

Without asking what all the laughter was about, Wyatt dove right into his usual pregame pep talk, which was about as peppy as a eulogy. There was a reason Wyatt was nicknamed Mr. Serious. Brody had only seen the guy smile once, and even then it was one of those awkward half smiles you pasted on when someone was telling you a really unfunny joke.

Needless to say, Brody had never clicked with his somber captain. He tended to gravitate toward laid-back guys like Becker and Jones.

Promptly tuning out the captain's voice, he proceeded to rehash this morning's conversation with Hayden, musing over her insistence that they leave things at one night. He understood wanting to end with a bang but...

Nope, wasn't going to happen.

Hayden might've neglected to hand out her number, but she'd left her calling card by inviting him to her hotel suite. After tonight's game Brody planned on strolling right back to the Ritz and continuing what he and Hayden had started last night. Just one night?

Not if he could help it.

"THERE'S NOTHING BETTER than this," Presley Houston boomed as he handed his daughter a bottle of Evian and joined her by the glass window overlooking the rink below.

They had the owner's box to themselves tonight, which came as a great relief. When she was surrounded by her father's colleagues, Hayden always felt as if she were one of those whales or dolphins at Sea World. Frolicking, swimming, doing tricks—all the while trying to figure out a way to break through the glass, escape the stifling tank and return to the wild where she belonged.

"Do you get to any games out in California?" Presley asked, picking an imaginary fleck of lint from the front of his gray Armani jacket.

"No, Dad."

"Why the hell not?"

Uh, because I hate hockey and always have?

"I don't have the time. I was teaching four classes last semester."

Her father reached out and ruffled her hair, something he'd done ever since she was a little girl. She found the gesture comforting. It reminded her of the years they'd been close. Before the Warriors. Before Sheila. Back when it was just the two of them.

Her heart ached as her dad tucked a strand of hair behind her ear and shot her one of his charming smiles. And her father undeniably had charm. Despite the loud booming voice, the restless energy he seemed to radiate, the focused and often shrewd glint in his eyes, he had a way of making everyone around him feel like he was their best friend. It was probably why his players seemed to idolize him, and definitely why *she* had idolized him growing up. She'd never thought her dad was perfect. He'd dragged her around the country for his career. But he'd also been there when it counted, helping with her homework, letting her take art classes during the off-season, giving her that painful birds-and-bees talk kids always got from their parents.

It brought a knot of pain to her gut that her father didn't seem to notice the distance between them. Not that she expected them to be bosom buddies—she was an adult now, and leading her own life. Nevertheless, it would be nice to at least maintain some kind of friendship with her dad. But he lived and breathed the Warriors now, completely oblivious to the fact that he'd pushed his only daughter onto the back burner of his life these past seven years.

She noticed that gray threads of hair were beginning to appear at his temples. She'd seen him six months ago over Christmas, but somehow he seemed older. There were even wrinkles around his mouth that hadn't been there before. The divorce proceedings were evidently taking a toll on him.

"Sweetheart, I know this might not be the best time to bring this up," her father began suddenly, averting his eyes. He focused on the spectacle of the game occurring below, as if he could channel the energy of the players and find the nerve to continue. Finally he did. "One of the reasons I asked you to come home...well, see... Diane wants you to give a deposition."

Her head jerked up. "What? Why?"

"You were one of the witnesses the day Sheila signed the prenuptial agreement." Her dad's voice was gentler than she'd heard in years. "Do you remember?"

Uh, did he actually think she'd forget? The day they'd signed the prenup happened to be the first meeting between Hayden and her only-two-years-older stepmother. The shock that her fifty-seven-year-old father was getting remarried after years of being alone hadn't been as great as learning that he was marrying a woman so many years his junior. Hayden had prided herself on being open-minded, but her mind always seemed to slam shut the second her father was involved. Although Sheila claimed otherwise, Hayden wasn't convinced that her stepmother hadn't married Presley for his money, prenup or not.

Her suspicions had been confirmed when three months

into the marriage, Sheila convinced her father to buy a multimillion-dollar mansion (because living in a penthouse was *so* passé), a small yacht (because the sea air would do them good) and a brand-new wardrobe (because the wife of a sports team owner needed to look sharp). Hayden didn't even want to know how much money her dad had spent on Sheila that first year. Even if she worked until she was ninety, she'd probably never earn that much. Sheila, of course, had quit her waitressing job the day after the wedding, and as far as Hayden knew, her stepmother now spent her days shopping away Presley's money.

"Do I really have to get involved in this, Dad?" she asked, sighing.

"It's just one deposition, sweetheart. All you have to do is go on record and state that Sheila was in her right mind when she signed those papers." Presley made a rude sound. "She's claiming coercion was involved."

"Oh, Dad. Why did you marry that woman?"

Her father didn't answer, and she didn't blame him. He'd always been a proud man, and admitting his failures came as naturally to him as the ability to give birth.

"This won't go to court, will it?" Her stomach turned at the thought.

"I doubt it." He ruffled her hair again. "Diane is confident we'll be able to reach a settlement. Sheila can't go on like this forever. Sooner or later she'll give up."

Not likely.

She kept her suspicions to herself, not wanting to upset her father any further. She could tell by the frustration in his eyes that the situation was making him feel powerless. And she knew how much he hated feeling powerless.

Hayden gave his arm a reassuring squeeze. "Of course

she will." She gestured to the window. "By the way, the team's looking really great, Dad."

She had no clue about whether the team looked good or not, but her words brought a smile to her father's lips and that was all that mattered.

"They are, aren't they? Wyatt and Becker are really coming together this season. Coach Gray said it was tough going, trying to make them get along."

"They don't like each other?" she said, not bothering to ask who Wyatt and Becker were.

Her dad shrugged, then took a swig from the glass of bourbon in his hand. "You know how it is, sweetheart. Alpha males, I'm-the-best, no-I'm-the-best. The league is nothing more than an association of egos."

"Dad..." She searched for the right words. "That stuff in the paper yesterday, about the illegal betting...it's not true, is it?"

"Of course not." He scowled. "It's lies, Hayden. All a bunch of lies."

"You sure I shouldn't be worried?"

He pulled her close, squeezing her shoulder. "There is absolutely nothing for you to worry about. I promise."

"Good."

A deafening buzz followed by a cheesy dance beat interrupted their conversation. In a second Presley was on his feet, clapping and giving a thumbs-up to the camera that seemed to float past the window.

"Did we win?" she asked, feeling stupid for asking and even stupider for not knowing.

Her father chuckled. "Not yet. There's five minutes left to the third." He returned to his seat. "When the game's done how about I take you for a quick tour of the arena?

We've done a lot of renovations since you were last here. Sound good?"

"Sounds great," she lied.

BRODY STEPPED OUT of the shower and drifted back to the main locker area. He pressed his hand to his side and winced at the jolt of pain that followed. A glance down confirmed what he already knew—that massive check from Valdek at the beginning of the second period had resulted in a large bruise that was slowly turning purple. Asshole.

"You took a shitty penalty," Wyatt was grumbling to Jones when Brody reached the bench.

The captain's normally calm voice contained a hint of antagonism and his dark eyes flashed with disapproval, also uncharacteristic. Brody wondered what was up Wyatt's ass, but he preferred to stay out of quarrels between his teammates. Hockey players were wired to begin with, so minor disagreements often ended badly.

Derek rolled his eyes. "What are you complaining about? We won the freaking game."

"It could've been a shutout," Wyatt snapped. "You gave up a goal to Franks with that penalty. We might be up by two games, but we need to win two more to make it to the second round. There's no room for mistakes." Still glowering, Mr. Serious strode out of the locker room, slamming the door behind him.

Jones tossed a what-the-hell's-up-with-him? look in Brody's direction, but he just shrugged, still determined to stay out of it.

Dressing quickly, he shoved his sweaty uniform into the locker, suddenly eager to get out of there.

On his way to the door he checked his watch, which read nine forty-five. Too late to pay a visit to Hayden's penthouse suite? Probably. Maybe inappropriate, too, but, hell, he'd never been one for propriety. Hayden had been on his mind all day and he was determined to see her again.

"Later, boys," he called over his shoulder.

The door closed behind him and he stepped into the brightly lit hallway, promptly colliding with a warm wall of curves.

"I'm sor—" The apology died in his throat as he laid eyes on the woman he'd bodychecked.

Not just any woman, either, but the one he'd been thinking about—and getting hard over—all day.

A startled squeak flew out of her mouth. "You."

His surprise quickly transformed into a rush of satisfaction and pleasure. "Me," he confirmed.

Looking her up and down, Brody was taken aback by the prim white blouse she wore and the knee-length paisley skirt that swirled over her legs. A huge change from the bright yellow top and faded jeans she'd worn last night. In this getup she looked more like the conservative professor and less like the passionate vixen who'd cried out his name so many times last night. The shift was disconcerting.

"What are...you're..." Hayden's eyes darted to the sign on the door beside them. "You play for the Warriors?"

"Sure do." He lifted one brow. "And I thought you said you weren't a hockey fan."

"I'm not. I..." Her voice trailed off.

What was she doing in this section of the arena? he suddenly wondered. Only folks associated with the franchise were allowed back here.

"Sorry to keep you waiting, sweetheart," boomed a male voice. "Shall we continue the tour—" Presley Houston broke out in a wide smile when he noticed Brody. "You played well out there tonight, Croft."

"Thanks, Pres." He looked from Hayden to Presley, wondering if he was missing something. Then a hot spurt of jealousy erupted in his gut as he realized that Presley had called Hayden *sweetheart.* Oh, man. Had he screwed around with Houston's mistress?

A dose of anger joined the jealousy swirling through him. He eyed the woman he'd spent the night with, wanting to strangle her for hopping into bed with him when she was obviously very much *taken,* but Presley's next words quickly killed the urge and brought with them another shock.

"I see you've met my daughter, Hayden."

CHAPTER FOUR

WHAT WAS HE *doing* here? And why hadn't he told her he played for the Warriors?

Hayden blinked a few times. Maybe she was imagining his sleek, long body and devastatingly handsome face and the hair that curled under his ears as if he'd just stepped out of a steamy shower—

He's not a hallucination. Deal with it.

All right, so her one-night stand was undeniably here, flesh and blood, and sexier than ever.

He also happened to be one of her dad's players. Was there a section in the league rule book about a player sleeping with the team owner's daughter? She didn't think so, but with all the rumors currently circulating about her father and the franchise, Hayden didn't feel inclined to cause any more trouble for her dad.

Apparently Brody felt the same way.

"It's nice to meet you, Hayden." His voice revealed nothing, especially not the fact that they were already very much...acquainted, for lack of a better word.

She shook his hand, almost shivering at the feel of his warm, calloused fingers. "Charmed," she said lightly.

Charmed? Had she actually just said that?

Brody's eyes twinkled, confirming that the idiotic reply had indeed come out of her mouth.

"Hayden is visiting us from San Francisco," Presley explained. "She teaches art at Berkeley."

"Art history, Dad," she corrected.

Presley waved a dismissive hand. "Same difference."

"So what position do you play?" Hayden asked, her voice casual, neutral, as if she were addressing a complete stranger.

"Brody's a left winger," Presley answered for him. "And a rising star."

"Oh. Sounds exciting," she said mildly.

Presley cut in once more. "It is. Right, Brody?"

Before Brody could answer, someone else snagged her dad's attention. "There's Stan. Excuse me for a moment." He quickly marched away.

Hayden's mouth curved mischievously. "Don't mind him. He often takes over conversations only to leave you standing in his dust." Her smile faded. "But you probably already knew that, seeing as you play for his team."

"Does that bother you?" Brody said carefully.

"Of course not," she lied. "Why would it?"

"You tell me."

She stared at him for a moment, then sighed. "Look, I'd appreciate it if you didn't tell my father about what…happened between us last night."

"Ah, so you remember." Amusement danced in his eyes. "I was starting to think you'd put it out of your mind completely."

Sure. Like that was even possible. She'd thought about nothing but this man and his talented tongue all day.

"I haven't forgotten." Her voice lowered. "But that doesn't mean I want to do it again."

"I think you do."

The arrogance in his tone both annoyed her and thrilled her. Jeez, how *hadn't* she figured out he was a hockey player last night? The man practically had *pro athlete* branded into his forehead. He was cocky, confident, larger than life. Something told her he was the kind of man who knew exactly what he wanted and did everything in his power to get it.

And what he wanted at the moment, disconcerting as it was, seemed to be *her*.

"Brody—"

"Don't bother denying it, I rocked your world last night and you can't wait for me to do it again."

She snorted. "There's nothing like a man with a healthy ego."

"I like it when you snort. It's cute."

"Don't call me cute."

"Why not?"

"Because I hate it. Babies and bunny rabbits are cute. I'm a grown woman. And stop looking at me like that."

"Like what?" he said, blinking innocently.

"Like you're imagining me naked."

"I can't help it. I *am* imagining you naked."

His eyes darkened to a sensual glitter, and liquid heat promptly pooled between her thighs. She tried not to squeeze her legs together. She didn't want him seeing the effect he had on her.

"Have a drink with me tonight," he said suddenly.

The word *no* slipped out more quickly than she'd intended.

Brody's features creased with what looked like frustration. He stepped closer, causing her to dart a glance in her father's direction. Presley was standing at the end of the hall, engaged in deep conversation with Stan Gray, the Warriors' head coach. While her dad seemed oblivious to the sparks shooting between her and Brody, Hayden still felt uncomfortable having this discussion in view of her father.

It didn't help that Brody looked so darn edible in gray wool pants that hugged his muscular legs and a ribbed black sweater that stretched across his chest. And his wet hair... She forced herself to stop staring at those damp strands, knowing that if she allowed herself to imagine him in the shower, naked, she might just come on the spot.

"One drink," he insisted, with a charming grin. "You know, for old time's sake."

She couldn't help but laugh. "We've known each other for all of twenty-four hours."

"Yes, but it was a very wild twenty-four hours, wouldn't you say?" He moved closer and lowered his head, his lips inches from her ear, his warm breath fanning across her neck. "How many times did you come again, Hayden? Three? Four?"

"Five," she squeezed out, and then quickly looked around to make sure nobody had heard her.

Her entire body started to throb from the memory. Nipples hardened. Sex grew moist. That she could experience such arousal in a hallway full of people—one of them her father—made her blush with embarrassment.

"Five." He nodded briskly. "I haven't lost my touch."

She resisted the urge to groan. He was too damn sexual, too sure of himself, which gave him a definite advantage, because at the moment she wasn't sure of anything.

Except the fact that she wanted to tear off her clothes and hop right back into bed with Brody Croft.

But, nope, she wouldn't do it. Sleeping with Brody again had Bad Idea written all over it. It had all been much simpler last night, when he'd just been an exciting, sensual stranger. But now...now he was real. Even worse, he was a hockey player. She'd grown up around enough hockey players to know how they lived—the constant traveling, the media, the eager females lining up to jump into bed with them.

And along with being involved in a sport she hated, Brody was so...arrogant, flirtatious, bold. Yesterday it had added to the allure of sex with a stranger. Today it was a reminder of why she'd decided bad boys no longer played a part in her life.

Been there, done that. Her last boyfriend had been as arrogant, flirty and bold as Brody Croft, and that relationship had ended a fiery death when Adam dumped her on her birthday because the whole "fidelity thing" cramped his style. His words, not hers.

She wasn't quite sure why she had such terrible judgment when it came to men. It shouldn't be so hard finding someone to build a life with, should it? A home, a solid marriage, great sex, excitement *and* stability, a man who'd make their relationship a priority—was that too much to ask for?

"Why are you so determined to see me again?" she found herself blurting, then lowered her voice when her father glanced in their direction. "I told you this morning I wanted to leave things at one night."

"What about what I want?"

She bit back an annoyed curse, deciding to go for the honest approach. "My life is complicated right now," she admitted. "I came home to support my father, not get involved with someone."

"You were pretty involved with me last night," he said,

winking. He uncrossed his arms and let them drop to his sides. "And you can't deny you liked it, Hayden."

"Of course I liked it," she hissed.

"Then what's the problem?"

"The problem is, I wanted one night. Seeing you again wasn't part of the plan."

"Plan, or fantasy?" he drawled, a knowing glimmer in his eyes. "That's it, isn't it? You fantasized about indulging in one night of wicked sex with a stranger and now that you have it's time to move on. I'm not judging you, just pointing out that the fantasy doesn't have to end yet."

The word *fantasy* sounded intoxicating the way he said it. Before she could stop herself, she wondered what other fantasies they could play out together. Role play? Bondage? Her cheeks grew warm at the latter notion. It turned her on, the idea of tying Brody up...straddling him while he lay immobile on the bed...

No. No, she was *so* not going there. She seriously needed to quit letting this guy jump-start her sex drive.

"The way I see it, you've got two options," he said. "The easy way or the hard way."

"I can't wait to hear all about it."

"Sarcasm doesn't become you." His cheek dimpled despite his words. "Now, the easy way involves the two of us heading over to the Lakeshore Lounge for a drink."

"No."

He held up his hand. "You haven't heard the rest." A devilish look flickered across his face. "If you choose to pass on the easy option, that's when things get a little...*hard*."

Heat spilled over her cheeks. Her eyes dropped to his groin, almost expecting to see the long ridge of arousal pressing against the denim of his jeans. Fine, no almost about it. He had an erection, all right, and the second she noticed it her nipples grew even harder.

"See, if you deny me this one harmless drink," he continued, "I'll be hurt. Maybe even a tad offended. Also, your father seems to be nearing the end of his conversation—yup, he's shaking Stan's hand. Which means he'll head back over here just in time to hear you say no, and then he'll ask you what you're saying no to, and I'm sure neither one of us wants to open *that* can of worms."

She turned her head and, sure enough, her father was walking toward them. Great. Although she knew her dad could handle the knowledge that his twenty-six-year-old daughter wasn't a virgin, she didn't want him privy to her sex life. Especially a sex life that involved one of his players.

Her dad might be totally gaga over his team, but he'd often warned her about the turbulent nature of hockey players. The latest warning had come during her last visit to Chicago, when she'd been hit on by an opposing player after a Warriors game. She'd declined the dinner invitation, but it hadn't stopped Presley from launching into a speech about how he didn't want his daughter dating brutes.

If he knew she'd gotten involved with Brody, it would just add to his stress.

"So how about that drink, Hayden?"

Her pulse quickened when she realized if she agreed to Brody's request, chances were they wouldn't get around to the drink anyway. The second he had her alone he'd be slipping his hands underneath her shirt, palming her breasts, sucking on her neck the way he'd done last night, as he'd slid inside her and—

"One drink," she blurted, then chastised herself for yet again letting her hormones override her common sense. What was *wrong* with her?

With a soft chuckle, Brody rested his hands on his trim hips, the poster boy for cool. "I knew you'd see it my way." He grinned.

THE LAKESHORE LOUNGE was one of those rare bars in the city that offered an intimate atmosphere rather than an intrusive one. Plush, comfortable chairs looked more suited to an IKEA showroom; tables were situated far enough apart that patrons could enjoy their drinks in privacy, and a pale yellow glow took the place of bright lighting, providing an almost sensual ambience. It was also one of the only establishments that still adhered to a strict dress code—blazers required.

It was a damn good thing he was Brody Croft. Even better that Ward Dalton, the owner of the lounge, claimed to be his number-one fan and turned a blind eye to Brody's casual attire.

Dalton led them across the black marble floor to a secluded table in the corner of the room, practically hidden from view by two enormous stone pots containing leafy indoor palms. A waiter clad in black pants and a white button-down appeared soon after, taking their drink orders before unobtrusively moving away.

Brody didn't miss the baffled look on Hayden's gorgeous face. "Something wrong?" he asked.

"No. I'm just…surprised," she said. "When you said we were going for a drink, I thought…" Her cheeks turned an appealing shade of pink. "Forget it."

"You thought I'd drive you right back to your hotel suite and pick up where we left off?"

"Pretty much."

"Sorry to disappoint you."

She bristled at the teasing lilt of his voice. "I'm not disappointed. In fact, I'm glad. Like I said before, I'm not interested in getting involved."

He didn't like the finality of her tone. For the life of him, he couldn't figure out why Hayden didn't want a repeat performance of last night. They'd been so good together.

He also couldn't decide whether or not she'd known who he was all along. Her father was Presley Houston, for chrissake. She didn't need to *like* hockey to know who the players were, especially the players on her own father's team. And yet the shock on her face when she'd bumped into him outside the locker room hadn't seemed contrived. He'd seen authentic surprise on her beautiful face. Not to mention a flicker of dismay.

No, she couldn't have known. It wouldn't bother her this much if she had.

He appreciated that she liked the man and not the hockey player, but that only raised another question—what held her back from getting involved with him? Was it the fact that he played pro hockey, or was it something else? *Someone* else, perhaps?

His jaw tightened at the thought. "What exactly is stopping you from pursuing this?" he asked in a low voice. "It's more than Presley's current problems, isn't it?"

The way she stared down at the silk cocktail napkin on the table as if it were the most fascinating item on the planet deepened Brody's suspicions.

He narrowed his eyes, unable to keep the accusation out of his tone. "Is there a husband waiting for you in California?"

Her gaze flew up to meet his. "Of course not."

Some of the suspicion thawed, but not entirely. "A fiancé?"

She shook her head.

"A boyfriend?"

The blush on her cheeks deepened. "No. I mean, yes. Well, kind of. I *was* seeing someone in San Francisco but we're currently on a break."

"The kind of break where you can sleep with other people?"

Whoa, he had no idea why he'd become antagonistic, or why his shoulders were suddenly stiffer than Robocop's.

What was up with this sudden possessiveness? They'd only had one night together, after all. Staking claims at this point was ridiculous.

"As I keep telling you, my life is complicated," she said pointedly. "I'm in the process of making some serious decisions, figuring out what my future looks like."

He opened his mouth to reply only to be interrupted by the waiter, who returned with their drinks. The waiter set down Brody's gin and tonic and Hayden's glass of white wine, then left the table without delay, as if sensing something important was brewing between them.

"And this boyfriend," Brody said thoughtfully. "Do you see him in your future?"

"I don't know."

Her tentative answer and confused frown were all he needed. He wasn't an ass; if Hayden had expressed deep love for the other man in her life, Brody would've backed off. He had no interest in fighting for a woman who belonged to someone else. But the fact that she hadn't answered a definite yes to his question told Brody this was fair game.

And nothing got him going more than a healthy bout of competition.

He lifted his gin and tonic to his lips and took a sip, eyeing her from the rim of his glass. Despite her prim shirt that buttoned up to the neck, she looked unbelievably hot. He could see the outline of her bra, and the memory of what lay beneath it sent a jolt of electricity to his groin.

"We're not doing it again," she said between gritted teeth, obviously sensing the train of thought his mind had taken.

He laughed. "Sounds like you're trying to convince yourself of that."

Frustration creased her dainty features. "We had sex, Brody. That's all." She took a drink of wine. "It was amazing, sure, but it was only sex. It's not like the damn earth moved."

"Are you sure about that?"

He pushed his chair closer, so that they were no longer across from each other, but side by side. He saw her hands shake at his nearness, her cheeks flush again, her lips part. It didn't take a rocket scientist to see she was aroused, and, damn, but he liked knowing his mere proximity could get this woman going.

"It was more than sex, Hayden." He dipped his head and brushed his lips over her ear. She shivered. "It was a sexual hurricane. Intense. Consuming." He flicked his tongue against her earlobe. "I've never been that hard in my life. And you've never been wetter."

"Brody…" She swallowed.

He traced the shell of her ear with his tongue, then moved his head back and lowered his hand to her thigh. He felt her leg shaking under his touch. "I'm right, aren't I?"

"Fine," she blurted out. "You're right! Happy?"

"Not quite." With a faint smile, he slid his hand under the soft material of her skirt and cupped her mound. Running his knuckles against the damp spot on her panties, he gave a brisk nod and murmured, "Now I'm happy."

Hayden's focus darted around like a Ping-Pong ball, as

if she expected their waiter to pop up in front of them any second. But the table was well secluded, and nobody could approach it without entering Brody's line of sight. He took advantage of the privacy, cupping Hayden's ass and gently shifting her so that her body was more accessible. He dragged his hand between her legs again, pushing aside the crotch of her panties and stroking her damp flesh.

The soft sounds of people chatting at neighboring tables excited the hell out of him. He was no stranger to sex in public, but he couldn't say he'd ever pleasured a woman in an upscale bar where any minute he could get caught.

A sharp breath hissed out of her mouth as he rubbed her clit in a circular motion. "What are you doing?" she whispered.

"I think you know exactly what I'm doing."

He continued to boldly rub her clit, then danced his fingertips down her slick folds and prodded her opening with the tip of his index finger. The wetness already pooling there made his cock twitch. He wanted nothing more than to shuck his jeans and thrust into that wet paradise. Right here. Right now. But he wasn't *that* bold.

"Brody...you've got...to stop," she murmured, but her body said otherwise.

Her thighs clenched together, her inner muscles squeezed his finger and a soft moan slipped out of her throat.

"You'll come if I keep doing this, won't you, Hayden?"

He looked from her flushed face to the neighboring table, several feet away and barely visible through the palm fronds separating the two tables. He hoped to hell the couple seated at that table hadn't heard Hayden's moan. He didn't want this to end just yet.

"Brody, anyone can walk by."

"Then you'd better be quick."

He pushed his finger into her core, smiling when she bit her lip. The look on her face drove him wild. Flushed, tortured, excited. He was feeling pretty excited himself, but he managed to get a handle on his own rising desire. He'd pressured her to spend the evening with him because he had something to prove, and what he wanted to prove wasn't that he was dying for a second go, but that *she* was dying for it.

Applying pressure to her clit with his thumb, he worked another finger inside her, pushing in and out of her in a deliberate lazy rhythm. His mouth ached with the need to suck on one of her small pink nipples, but he tightened his lips before he gave in to the urge and tore her shirt open. Instead, he focused on the heat between her thighs, the nub that swelled each time he brushed his thumb over it and the inner walls that clamped over his fingers with each gentle thrust.

Keeping one eye on Hayden's blissful face and the other on his surroundings, he continued to slide his fingers in and out, until finally she let out a barely audible groan and squeezed her legs together. He felt her pulsing against his fingers and resisted a groan of his own as a soundless orgasm consumed her eyes as well as her body.

She came silently, trembling, biting her lip. And then she released a sigh. Her hands, which at some point she'd curled into fists, shook on the tabletop, making her wine-glass topple and spill over the side of the table.

He quickly withdrew his hand as Hayden jumped at the startling sound of the glass rolling and shattering on the marble floor. Her sudden movement caused her knee to hit one of the table legs, making the table shake and the ice cubes in his drink collide into the side of the glass with a jingling sound.

From the corner of his eye Brody saw the waiter hurrying over, and yet he couldn't fight a tiny chuckle. Turning to meet Hayden's dazed eyes, he laughed again, swiftly fixed her skirt and said, "Still want to tell me the earth didn't move?"

CHAPTER FIVE

ABOUT TWELVE HOURS after experiencing her very first public orgasm, Hayden strode into Lingerie Dreams, the classy downtown boutique owned by her best friend.

She was in desperate need of Darcy right now. Darcy and her one-night-stand mentality would definitely help her get her thoughts back on the right track and *off* the track that sent her hurtling straight into Brody Croft's bed.

Funny thing was, he hadn't pushed her after their interlude at the lounge last night. He'd paid for their drinks, walked her out to her rental car and left her with a parting speech she couldn't stop thinking about.

The next move's yours, Hayden. You want me, come and get me.

And then he'd left. He'd hopped into his shiny SUV, driven off and left her sitting in her car, more turned-on than she'd ever been in her entire life. Though she'd been ready to go home with him, he'd made it clear it wouldn't happen that night, not when he'd had to twist her arm to get her there.

Oh, no, he wanted *her* to initiate their next encounter.

Something she was seriously tempted to do. Which was why she needed Darcy to talk her out of it.

The bell over the door chimed as she walked into the boutique. She sidestepped a mannequin wearing a black lace teddy and a table piled high with thongs, and approached the cash counter.

"Something terrible has happened," Darcy groaned the second she saw her.

"Tell me about it," Hayden mumbled.

But the look of dismay on Darcy's face made Hayden push the memory of last night aside for the moment. She caught a whiff of sweet floral scent, looked around and finally spotted a bouquet of red and yellow roses peeking out of the metal wastebasket next to the counter.

"Courtesy of Jason," Darcy sighed, following her gaze.

"Who's Jason?"

"Didn't I mention him?" She shrugged. "I hooked up with him last week after yoga class. He's a personal trainer."

Like she could actually keep track of all the men Darcy hooked up with. Hayden didn't know how her friend did it, wandering aimlessly from guy to guy.

"And he sent you flowers? That's sweet."

Darcy looked at her as if she'd grown horns. "Are you insane?" she said. "Don't you remember how I feel about flowers?"

Without waiting for an answer, Darcy leapt to her feet and checked to make sure the store was void of customers. Then she marched over to the front door, locked it and flipped the Open sign over so that it read Closed.

With her kitten heels clicking against the tiled floor, Darcy gestured for Hayden to follow her, drifting over to the fitting-room area. Along with four dressing rooms, the large space offered two plush red velvet chairs.

Hayden sank into one of the chairs and reached for the bowl of heart-shaped mints Darcy left out for her customers. Popping a mint into her mouth, she studied her friend, who still looked upset.

"Wow, this flower thing is really bugging you."

Darcy flopped down and crossed her arms over her chest, her face turning as red as the hair on her head. "Of course it bugs me. It's not normal."

"No, *you're* not normal. Men give women flowers all the time. It's not poor Jason's fault he picked you as the recipient."

"We went out for smoothies after yoga and fooled around in his car when he dropped me off at home." Darcy made a frustrated sound. "How in bloody hell does that warrant flowers?"

"What did the card say?" Hayden asked curiously.

"'I hope to see you again soon.'"

She was about to comment on Jason's thoughtfulness again but stopped herself. She knew how Darcy felt about relationships. The first sign of commitment had her fleeing for the exit and looking for the next one-night stand. But it really was too bad. This Jason fellow sounded as nice as Doug.

Shoot, she'd promised herself she wouldn't think about Doug today.

She still hadn't returned his phone call, and when she'd woken up this morning there had been another message from him on her cell. How could she call him back, though? She'd only been gone a week and already she'd jumped into bed with another man. She wondered how nice Doug would be when she told him about *that*.

"I'm going to have to find a new gym," Darcy grumbled, her blue eyes darkening with irritation. She started fidgeting. Crossed her legs, then uncrossed them, clasped her hands together, then drummed them against the arms of the chair.

Hayden could tell her friend was about to explode. Any minute now…no, any second now…

"What is the *matter* with the penis species?" Darcy burst out. "They claim that *we're* the needy ones, calling us clingy and high-maintenance, accusing us of being obsessed with love and marriage. When really, really, it's what *they* want. They're the mushy ones, sending flowers as if a smoothie and a backseat blow job qualify as a monumental event that needs to be celebrated…" Darcy's voice trailed and she heaved a sigh.

"I'm obviously going to have to set him straight," Darcy declared, reaching for a mint and shoving it into her mouth. She still looked aggravated, but her anger seemed to have dissolved.

"At least thank him for the flowers," Hayden said gently.

"I already called and did that. But I think I need to make another call and make sure Jason knows what happened between us won't go any further. Like the way you set your hunk straight."

"Right. About that…you're not going to believe this." She quickly filled her friend in on her visit to the arena and how she'd run into Brody outside the locker room.

"He's a hockey player? I bet you were just thrilled to find that out." Darcy grinned. "So, you told him to get lost, right?"

"Um…"

Darcy's jaw dropped. "Hayden Lorraine Houston! You slept with him again, didn't you?"

"Not exactly. I did go out for a drink with him, though."

"And?"

Hayden told her about the under-the-table orgasm. When her friend shook her head, she added, "I couldn't help it! He just started…you know…and it was really good…" Her voice drifted.

"You have no self-control." Darcy shot her a weary look and asked, "Are you going to call him?"

"I don't know. God knows I want to. But calling him defeats the purpose of a one-night stand." She groaned. "I just wanted some stress-busting sex. And now I'm even more stressed-out."

"So tell him to take a hike. You've got enough on your plate without an arrogant hockey player demanding overtime sex."

Hayden laughed. "He is pretty determined." She remembered the passion flaring in his eyes when he'd brought her to climax yesterday. "He's driving me crazy, Darce."

"Good crazy or bad crazy?"

"Both." A shaky breath exited her throat. "When I'm with him all I can think about is ripping off his clothes, and when I'm not with him all I can think about is ripping off his clothes."

"I don't see the bad part here."

She bit her bottom lip. "He's a hockey player. You know how I feel about that." She blew out a frustrated breath. "I don't want to be with anyone involved in sports. God, I hated it when Dad used to coach. No real place to call home, no friends. Hell, my friendship with you is the only one that lasted, and half of it took place via e-mail."

Reaching for another mint, she popped it into her mouth and bit it in half, taking out her frustration on the candy. "I don't want to date a guy who spends half the year flying to other states so he can skate around an ice rink. And besides, I'm dealing with too much other stuff at the moment.

The franchise is taking some heat, Dad's dumping all his Sheila problems on me, and Doug has already called twice wanting to talk about *us*. I can't launch myself into another relationship right now." She set her jaw, practically daring Darcy to challenge her.

Which, of course, she did. "You know what I think?" Darcy said. "You're making too big a deal out of this."

"Oh, really?"

Darcy leaned back in her chair and pushed a strand of bright red hair behind her ear. "You're only in town for a couple of months, Hayden. What's the problem with having some fun in the sack while you're here?"

"What happened to your one-night-stand speech?"

"Apparently it isn't working out for you." Darcy shrugged. "But you seem to believe it's black and white, one-night stand or relationship. You're forgetting about the gray area between the two extremes."

"Gray area?"

"It's called a fling."

"A fling." She said the word slowly, trying it on for size. She'd never been a casual-fling girl, but then again, she hadn't thought she was a one-night girl, either. Maybe a fling with Brody wouldn't be so disastrous. It wasn't like he wanted to marry her or anything; he just wanted to burn up the sheets for a while longer, continue the fantasy...

But if she agreed to let their one night lead into a fling, who's to say the fling wouldn't then lead to something more?

"I don't know," she said. "Brody is a distraction I can't deal with at the moment." She paused, her mouth twisting ruefully. "But my body seems to have a mind of its own whenever he's around."

"So take control of your body," Darcy suggested.

"And how do I do that?"

"I don't know, next time you get the urge to jump Brody Croft's bones, try an alternative. Watch some porn or something."

A laugh tickled Hayden's throat. "That's your answer? Watch porn?"

Darcy grinned. "Sure. At least you won't be thinking about Mr. Hockey when you're busy getting turned-on by other men."

"Right, because the men in porn are so wildly attractive," Hayden said with a snort. "What's the name of that guy who used to be really popular, the chubby one with the facial hair? Ron Jeremy?"

"It's not the seventies, hon. Male porn stars have come a long way. Trust me, just take a long bubble bath, put in a DVD and go nuts. You won't think about Brody even once."

"This is possibly the most ridiculous conversation we've ever had." Hayden rolled her eyes. "If I watch anything tonight, it'll be the van Gogh special on the Biography Channel."

Darcy released an exaggerated sigh. "A man who cut off his own ear is not sexy, Hayden."

"Neither is porn." She glanced at her watch, eyes widening. "Shoot. I've gotta go. I'm supposed to give a deposition today about Sheila's state of mind when she signed the prenup."

"Sounds like a blast. Unfortunately I left my party shoes at home so I can't come with you."

They got up and wandered over to the door. Darcy unlocked it and held it open, her attention straying back to the flowers poking out of the wastebasket. "At least your guy only wants sex," Darcy said, looking envious.

"Brody is not my guy," Hayden responded, hoping if she said the words out loud she might convince her traitorous body of it. "Are we still on for dinner tonight? I'm down as long as I get home in time to watch that biography."

"And I'm down as long as it's Mexican. I'm feeling spicy." Darcy waved as Hayden left. "Enjoy the deposition," she called out after her.

"Enjoy the flowers," Hayden called back.

She turned just in time to see her best friend flipping her the bird.

"THANK YOU, HAYDEN," announced Diane Krueger, Presley's divorce attorney. "We're finished here."

Hayden smoothed out the front of her knee-length black skirt and pushed back the plush chair, getting to her feet. Next to her, her father stood as well. On the other side of the large oval conference table of the Krueger and Bates deposition room, Sheila Houston and her lawyer were huddled together, whispering to each other.

Hayden couldn't help but stare at her stepmother, still as startled by Sheila's appearance as she'd been when the woman had first strode into the law office. The last time Hayden had come to town, Sheila had looked as if she'd stepped from the pages of a fashion magazine. Long blond hair brushed to a shine, creamy features flawless and perfectly made up, expensive clothes hugging her tall, slender body.

This time Sheila looked…haggard. Much older than her twenty-eight years and far more miserable than Hayden had expected her to be. Her hair hung limply over her shoulders, her normally dazzling blue eyes were distressed, and she'd lost at least fifteen pounds, which made her willowy shape look far too fragile.

Though she hated feeling even an ounce of sympathy for the woman who was making her father's life hell, Hayden had to wonder if Sheila was taking this divorce process a lot harder than Presley had let on. Either that, or she was devastated by the thought of losing that yacht she'd forced Presley to buy.

"Thanks for doing this, sweetheart," her father said quietly as they exited the conference room. "It means so much that you're going to bat for your old man."

For the third time in the past hour, Hayden noticed her dad's slightly glazed, bloodshot eyes and wondered if he'd had something to drink before coming here. His breath smelled like toothpaste and cigars, but she got a wary feeling when she looked at him.

No, she was being silly. He was probably just tired.

"I'm happy to help," she answered with a reassuring smile.

He touched her arm. "Do you need a ride back to the suite?"

"No, I've got my rental."

"All right." He nodded. "And don't forget about the party on Sunday night. Gallagher Club, eight o'clock."

Shoot, she'd already forgotten. There was a huge shindig at the prestigious gentlemen's club of which her dad was a member. And apparently her appearance was necessary, though she had no clue why.

Her father must have noticed her reluctance because he frowned slightly. "I'd like you to be there, Hayden. A lot of my friends want to see you. When you were here over the holidays you declined all of their invitations."

Because I wanted to see you, she almost blurted. But she held her tongue. She knew her father liked showing her off to his wealthy friends and boasting about her academic credentials—something he didn't seem to care about when they were alone.

She swallowed back the slight sting of bitterness. Considering they'd just spent an hour with the woman determined to bleed him dry, Hayden figured she ought to cut her dad some slack.

"I'll be there," she promised.

"Good."

They said their goodbyes, and she watched her father hurry out of the elegant lobby onto the street as if he were being chased by a serial killer. Not a stretch, seeing as the law firm was called Krueger and Bates. Hayden wondered if she was the only one who'd made the connection.

"Hayden, wait."

She stopped at the massive glass entrance doors, suppressing an inward groan at the sound of her stepmother's throaty voice.

Hayden turned slowly.

"I just..." Sheila looked surprisingly nervous as she plowed ahead. "I wanted to tell you there are no hard feelings. I know you're trying to protect your father."

Hayden's eyebrows said hello to her hairline. No hard feelings? Sheila was in the process of sucking the money out of Presley's bank accounts like a greedy leech and she wanted to make sure there were no hard feelings?

Hayden could only stare.

Sheila hurried on. "I know you've never liked me, and I don't blame you. It's always hard to watch a parent remarry, and I'm sure it doesn't help that I'm only two years older than you." She offered a timid smile.

"We really shouldn't be talking," Hayden said finally, her voice cool. "It's probably a conflict of interest."

"I know." Sheila ran one hand through her hair, her features sad. "But I just wanted you to know that I still care about your father. I care about him a lot."

To Hayden's absolute shock, a couple of tears trickled out of the corners of Sheila's eyes. Even more shocking, the tears didn't look like the crocodile variety.

"If you care, then why are you trying to take everything he owns?" she couldn't help but ask.

A flash of petulant anger crossed Sheila's face. Ah, *here* was the Sheila she knew. Hayden had seen that look plenty of times before, usually when Sheila was trying to convince Presley to buy something outrageous and not getting her way.

"I'm entitled to something," Sheila said defensively, "after everything that man put me through."

Right, because Sheila's life was *so* unpleasant. Living in a mansion, wearing haute couture, not paying a dime for anything...

"I know you think I'm the bad guy here, but you need to know that everything I've done is a result of... No, I'm not going to blame Pres." The tears returned, and Sheila wiped her wet eyes with a shaky hand. "I saw that he was spiraling and I didn't try to help him. I was the one who sent him into another woman's arms."

"Pardon me?" A knot of anger and disbelief twined Hayden's insides together like a pretzel. Sheila was actually insinuating that her father had been the one to stray? Her dislike for the woman quickly doubled. That she could even accuse a man as honorable as Presley Houston of adultery was preposterous.

Sheila eyed her knowingly. "I guess he left out that part."

"I have to get going," Hayden said stiffly, her jaw so tense that her teeth were beginning to ache.

"I don't care what you think of me," Sheila said. "I only want you to take care of your father, Hayden. I think he's started drinking again and I just want to make sure that someone is looking out for him."

Without issuing a goodbye, Sheila pulled an Elvis and left the building.

Hayden watched as her stepmother disappeared down the busy sidewalk, swallowed up by Chicago's afternoon lunch crowd.

She couldn't will herself to move. Lies. It had to be lies. Her father would never break his marriage vows by hopping into bed with another woman. Sheila was in the wrong here. She had to be.

I think he's started drinking again.

The comment replayed in Hayden's brain, making her toy nervously with the hem of her thin blue sweater. She'd thought her father's eyes had looked bleary. Fine, maybe he *did* have a drink or two before coming here, but Sheila's remark implied that Presley's drinking went beyond today. That at some point in time he'd suffered from an alcohol problem.

Was it true? And if so, how hadn't she known about it? She might not visit often, what with her hectic schedule at the university, but she spoke to her father at least once a week and he always sounded normal. *Sober.* Wouldn't she have suspected something if he had a drinking problem?

Lies.

She clung to that one word as she pushed the strap of her purse higher on her shoulder and stepped through the doors. Sucking in a gust of fresh air, she headed for her rental, forcefully pushing every sentence Sheila had spoken out of her mind.

BRODY LEFT THE locker room after a particularly grueling practice, wondering if he'd made a big fat mistake by pretty much telling Hayden the puck was in her end, the next move hers.

It had seemed like the right play at the time, but today, after two hours of tedious drills topped off by a lecture from the coach, he was rethinking the action he'd taken. Or more specifically, regretting the action he wouldn't be getting. His body was sore, his nerves shot, and he knew a few hours in Hayden's bed were all the medicine he needed.

He also knew she wouldn't call.

You got cocky, man.

Was that it? Had he been so confident in his ability to turn Hayden on that he just assumed she'd want him to do it again?

Damn it, why hadn't he taken her home with him? He'd seen the lust in her gorgeous eyes, known that all he had to do was say the word and she'd be in his arms again, but he'd held back. No, pride had held him back. He hadn't wanted to go to bed with her knowing he'd coerced her into joining him for that drink. He'd wanted it to be her choice, her terms, her desire.

It was almost comical, how this conservative art history professor had gotten under his skin. She was so different from the women he'd dated in the past. Smarter, prettier, more serious, definitely more pigheaded. She annoyed him; she excited him; she made him laugh. He knew he should just let her go since she obviously didn't want to pursue a relationship, but his instincts kept screaming for him not to let her out of his sight, that if he blinked, she'd be gone, and someone very important would be slipping through his grasp. It made no sense to him, and yet he'd always trusted his instincts. They'd never failed him before.

He kicked a pebble on his way to the car, feeling like

kicking something harder than a rock. His own thick skull, perhaps.

He pressed a button on the remote to unlock the doors, then swore when he realized his wrist was bare. Shoot. He must have left his watch back at the practice arena. He always seemed to misplace the damn thing. He hated wearing a watch to begin with, but it had been a gift from his parents in honor of his first professional game eight years ago. Chris and Jane Croft were ferociously proud of their son, and he witnessed that pride every time he went back to Michigan for a visit and saw them staring at that watch.

Sighing, he turned around and headed back to the entrance of the sprawling gray building. The Warriors practiced in a private arena a few miles from the Lincoln Center, a little unorthodox but Brody found it somewhat of a relief. It meant the media never filmed their practices, which took the pressure off the players to always be on top of their game.

The double doors at the entrance led to a large sterile lobby. A blue door to the right opened onto the rink. To the left were the hallways leading to the locker rooms, and when Brody strode into the arena he immediately noticed the two people huddled by the locker-room corridor. Their backs were turned, and Brody quickly sidestepped to the right, ducking into another hall that featured a row of vending machines.

"You shouldn't have come here," came Craig Wyatt's somber voice.

Brody sucked in a breath, hoping the Warriors captain and his companion hadn't spotted him.

He'd sure as hell spotted them, though.

Which posed the question: what was Craig Wyatt doing whispering with Sheila Houston?

"I know. I just had to see you," Sheila said, her voice so soft Brody had to strain his ears to hear her. "That meeting with the lawyers today was terrible..." There was a faint sob.

"Shh, it's okay, baby."

Baby?

Deciding he'd officially heard enough—and that he'd return for his watch another time—Brody edged toward the emergency exit at the end of the hallway. He turned the door handle, praying an alarm wouldn't go off. It didn't. Relieved, he exited the side door of the building and practically sprinted back to his car.

The drive to his Hyde Park home brought with it a tornado of confusion that made his head spin. Craig Wyatt and Sheila Houston? The player rumored to be having an affair with the owner's wife was *Wyatt*? Brody would've never expected it from the straight-laced Mr. Serious.

If it was true, then that meant the idea of bribes exchanging hands in the franchise might not be a lie after all. Craig Wyatt might have the personality of a brick wall, but he was the captain of the team, as well as the eyes and ears. He frequently kept track of everyone's progress, making sure they were all in tip-top shape and focused on the game. If he suspected anyone had taken a bribe, he would've investigated it, no doubt about it.

Jeez, was Wyatt the source Sheila had referred to in that interview? Had he been the one to tell her about the bribes?

Or...

Shit, had Wyatt taken a bribe himself? No, that didn't make sense. Sheila wouldn't draw attention to the bribery and illegal betting if her lover was one of the guilty parties.

Brody steered into his driveway and killed the engine.

He reached up and pinched the bridge of his nose, hoping to ward off an oncoming headache.

Damn. This was not good at all.

He didn't particularly care what or who Craig Wyatt did in his spare time, but if Wyatt knew something about these rumors...

Maybe he should just confront the man, flat out ask what he knew. Or maybe he'd ask Becker to do it for him. Becker was good at stuff like that, knew how to handle tough situations and still keep a clear head.

He rubbed his temples, then leaned his forehead against the steering wheel for a moment. Lord, he didn't want to deal with any of this. If he had his way, this entire scandal would just disappear; he'd play out the rest of the season then re-sign with the Warriors or sign with a new team. His career would be secure and his life would be peachy.

And Hayden Houston would be right back in his bed. A guy could dream, after all.

"I WILL NOT watch porn," Hayden muttered to herself later that night, stepping out of the enormous marble bathtub in the master suite of the penthouse. She reached for the terry-cloth robe hanging behind the door, slipped it on and tightened the sash around her waist.

Not that there was anything wrong with porn. She wasn't a nun, after all—she'd watched a few X-rated videos in her twenty-six years. But she'd never used porn to get over a man before, and besides, she'd had six orgasms in two days. She should be thoroughly exhausted by now and not thinking about having sex at all.

Unfortunately, she *was* thinking about sex, and it was all Brody Croft's fault.

At dinner, Darcy had again pointed out that a fling

wouldn't be the end of the world, but Hayden still wasn't sold on the idea. She got the feeling that if she gave Brody an inch, he'd take a mile. That if she suggested a fling, he'd show up with an engagement ring.

Barefoot, she stepped out of the bathroom into the master bedroom, pushing wet hair out of her eyes. She'd finally gotten around to unpacking her suitcase this morning, but the suite's huge walk-in closet still looked empty. She changed into a pair of thin gray sweatpants and a cotton tank top, brushed her hair and tied it into a ponytail, then headed for the kitchen.

Normally she hated hotels, but her father's penthouse at the Ritz-Carlton surpassed any ordinary hotel suite. He'd lived here before marrying Sheila, and the apartment had everything Hayden could possibly need, including a large kitchen that was fully stocked and surprisingly cozy. It reminded her of her kitchen back home, making her homesick for the West Coast. In San Francisco, she hadn't needed to worry about anything except how she was going to get her boyfriend into bed.

Here, she had her father's problems, her stepmother's lies and Brody Croft's incessant attempts to get *her* into bed.

Quit thinking about Brody.

Right. He was definitely on tonight's don't-think-about list.

After she'd made a bowl of popcorn and brewed herself a cup of green tea, she got comfortable on one of the leather couches in the living area and switched on the TV. She was totally ready to lose herself in that van Gogh biography. Since she was teaching an entire course on him next semester, she figured she ought to get reacquainted with the guy.

She scrolled through the channels, searching for the program, but couldn't seem to find it. The Biography Channel was telling the life story of a Hollywood actress who'd just been busted on cocaine charges. The History Channel featured a show on the Civil War. She kept scrolling. No van Gogh to be seen.

Great. Just freaking great. Could nothing go right in her life? All she'd wanted to do tonight was watch a show about her favorite artist and not think about Brody Croft. Was that really too much to ask?

Apparently so.

She skipped past a shocking number of reality shows, finally stopping on the Discovery Channel, which was playing a special on sharks. She sighed in resignation and settled the bowl of popcorn in her lap.

"The great white shark can smell one drop of blood in twenty-five gallons of water," came a monotone voice.

Hayden popped a few kernels in her mouth and chewed thoughtfully, watching as a lethal-looking shark swam across the screen.

"The great white does not chew his food. Rather, he takes massive bites and swallows the pieces whole."

Yeah, like Brody... *No Brody thoughts allowed, missy.*

"There have been reports of great whites exceeding twenty feet in length. They can weigh in at over seven thousand pounds."

Ten minutes and fifteen shark facts later, Hayden was stretching out her legs and wiggling her toes, wondering if she should apply some red nail polish. This shark documentary was getting old.

She pressed the guide button on the remote control, scrolled down, skipped the barrage of sports channels, stopped briefly on CNN, then scrolled again. She saw a listing for something called *The Secretary* and decided to click on it, but what came on the screen wasn't the sitcom her students at Berkeley were always raving about.

It was, of course, porn.

"You're a very fast typist, Betty."

"Thank you, Mr. Larson. My fingers have always been my biggest asset."

"I bet they have. Bring your hand a little closer."

"Ooh, Mr. Larson, that tickles."

"Do you like it?"

"Mmm, yes."

"What about this?"

"Mmm, even better."

Hayden had to bite her lip to refrain from bursting into laughter. On the screen, Betty and her boss began making out. Mr. Larsen's big hairy hand disappeared under Betty's conservative skirt. Loud moaning ensued.

She shook her head and pressed a button on the remote. Betty and Mr. Larson disappeared, replaced by a great white shark.

You want me, come and get me.

The sound of Brody's sandpaper-rough voice filled her head. She let out a long breath, exasperated. Why couldn't she stop thinking about the guy? And why couldn't she stop wanting him? She wanted him so badly she could practically feel those big muscular arms around her waist.

But sometimes the things you wanted weren't necessarily the ones you needed.

At the moment, she needed to concentrate on supporting her dad through his divorce and maybe finally call Doug back to tell him she'd slept with someone else and that it was time to turn their break into a breakup.

But what she *wanted* was one more night with Brody Croft.

It doesn't have to be black and white.

She sat there for a moment, chewing on her lower lip as Darcy's words buzzed around in her brain.

Was her friend right? Was she overanalyzing all of this? She'd always had the tendency to pick and prod at each situation until she'd sucked every last drop of fun or enjoyment from it. This wasn't an art history lecture she needed to plan for—it was just sex. Was there really anything wrong with delving into that gray area and enjoying a carnal ride with a man she found wildly attractive?

She turned off the television and reached for the phone.

CHAPTER SIX

THE CALL FROM Hayden came as a total shock. Brody had just stepped out of the shower, where he'd stood under the hot spray for a good half hour to get the kinks out of his muscles. He'd intended to grab a beer from the fridge and watch the highlight reel on ESPN, maybe give Becker a call to talk about Craig Wyatt, and then his cell phone began chirping out a tinny rendition of Beethoven's Symphony No. 9 and Hayden's throaty voice was on the other end.

Come over.

She'd only spoken those two words, then disconnected, leaving him both pleased and befuddled.

Obviously she'd finally changed her mind and taken him up on his offer to continue the fantasy she'd started two nights ago, but was it still just sex she craved? Or was she looking for something extra this time around?

Shit, he was getting ahead of himself here. Hayden was simply inviting him back into her bed for another wild romp, not offering to make a commitment.

He quickly put on a pair of jeans and pulled an old Warriors jersey over his head. Then he grabbed his car keys from the credenza in the hallway, shoved his wallet into his back pocket and left the house, breathing in the damp night air.

It was mid-May, which meant the nights were still cool and the chance of a thunderstorm or even a freak blizzard wasn't all that far-fetched, but Brody loved this time of year, when spring and summer battled for domination over Chicago's climate. He'd lived in this city almost eight years now, and he'd grown to appreciate and enjoy everything about it, even the indecisive seasons.

When he pulled up in front of Hayden's hotel, a light drizzle of rain was sliding across the windshield. He hopped out of the SUV and entered the lobby just as a bolt of lightning filled the sky. Thunder roared ominously in the distance, growing louder and louder until the rain became a steady downpour.

Shaking droplets of water from his hair, he approached the check-in desk and asked the clerk behind it to ring Hayden's suite. A moment later, the clerk walked him over to the elevator and inserted a key into the panel that would allow Brody access to the penthouse, then left him alone in the car.

The elevator soared upward, its doors opening into the suite, where Hayden was waiting for him.

"I have some ground rules," she said in lieu of a greeting.

He grinned. "Hello to you, too."

"Hello. I have some ground rules."

He tossed his car keys on a glass table beside one of the couches and moved toward her.

Even in sweats, she looked amazing. He liked how she'd pulled her hair back in a messy ponytail, how a few haphazard strands framed her face, which was devoid of makeup. He especially liked how her thin tank top didn't hide the fact that she wore no bra.

His mouth ran dry as he dragged his gaze across those gorgeous breasts, the outline of her dusky nipples visible through the white shirt.

Her fair cheeks grew flushed at his perusal. "Don't ogle. It's unbecoming."

He grinned. "Ah, I was wondering where Miss Prim and Proper had gone. Hello, Professor, nice to see you again."

"I am *not* prim and proper," she protested.

"Not in bed anyway…"

"Ground rules," she repeated firmly.

He released a sigh. "All right. Get it out of your system."

She leaned against the arm of the couch, resting her hands on her thighs. "This is only going to be sex," she began, her throaty voice wavering in a way that brought a smile to his lips. "Continuing the fantasy, or whatever it was you said. Agreed?"

"I'm not agreeing to anything yet. Is there more?"

"My father can't know anything about it." She paused, looking uncomfortable. "And I'd prefer if we weren't seen in public together."

His nostrils flared. "Ashamed of being linked to a hockey player?"

"Look, you already know the franchise is taking some heat, Brody. I don't want to make things worse for my dad by giving the media more fuel for the fire they're determined to start."

He had to admit her words made sense. After seeing Craig Wyatt whispering with Sheila Houston at the arena today, Brody had no interest in stoking the fire. Best-case scenario, if he was spotted with Hayden, the press would sensationalize the relationship the way they were currently sensationalizing everything else associated with the Warriors. Worst-case scenario, a jerk reporter would insinuate that the team owner's daughter knew of her father's guilt and was either trying to shut Brody up because he was involved, or sleeping with him to find out what he knew.

He didn't particularly like either of those scenarios.

Still, he wasn't about to let Hayden get her way entirely. He had a few demands himself.

"If I agree to your rules, you have to agree to mine," he said roughly, crossing his arms over his chest.

She swallowed. "Like what?"

"If you're in my bed, that's the only bed you'll be in." He set his jaw. "I won't share you, especially not with the guy waiting for you in California."

"Of course."

"And you have to promise to keep an open mind."

Interest flickered in her gaze. "Sexually?"

"Sure. But emotionally, too. All I'm saying is that if things between us get...deeper, you can't run away from it."

After a beat of silence, she nodded. "I can do that. And do you agree to keep whatever we do here to yourself?"

"I can do that," he mimicked with a grin.

"Then what are you waiting for?" she asked. "Take off your clothes already."

HAYDEN COULD BARELY contain her amusement as Brody pulled his jersey over his head and tossed it aside. He reminded her of a kid on Christmas morning. The eagerness practically radiated from his tall, powerful body, but when he pushed his jeans down his legs there was nothing comical about the situation anymore.

His cock sprang up against the material of his boxers, demanding attention and making Hayden's mouth grow dry.

No matter how unsettling she found Brody's terms, it was too late to reverse her decision. He wanted her to keep an open mind, fine. But she highly doubted things between them would get *deeper,* as he'd suggested. Their one-night stand may have turned into a fling, but she was confident it wouldn't go further than that.

Besides, right now she didn't want or need to think about the future, not when there were more important things to focus on. Such as Brody's spectacular body and all the things she wanted to do to it.

An impish grin lifted the corner of her mouth as she remembered what he'd done to *her* body the night before at the bar. Her next move suddenly became very clear.

"The keeping-an-open-mind part," she said mischievously. "It goes for you, too, right?"

Brody kicked aside his boxers and fixed her with an intrigued stare. "What do you have in mind?"

She didn't answer. Crooking her finger at him, she gestured for him to follow her down the hallway. They entered the bedroom, where she turned her finger to the bed and said, "Get comfortable."

Brody raised his brows. "Are you planning to join me?"

"Eventually."

He lowered himself onto the bed and leaned against the mountain of pillows at the headboard.

Fighting a smile, Hayden swept her gaze over Brody's long naked body sprawled before her.

"I'm feeling lonely," he murmured. "Are you going to stand there all night and watch me?"

"Maybe."

"What'll it take to get you to come here?"

She chewed on the inside of her cheek, thoughtful. "I don't know. You'd have to make it worth my while, give me a good reason to get into that bed with you."

He chuckled and grasped his shaft with his hand. "This isn't reason enough?"

She laughed. "God, you're arrogant." She stared at his erection, the way his fingers had curled around the base, and moisture gathered in her panties. There was something seriously enticing about watching this man touch himself.

"C'mere," he cajoled. "You don't really want to make me do this alone, do you?"

His gruff voice sent shivers through her, making her nipples poke against her tank top. "I don't know," she said again. "I'm getting pretty turned-on watching you right now…"

Still watching his hand, she strode toward the desk under the curtained window, pulled the chair out and lowered herself on it. "Tell me what you'd want me to do, if I was lying there with you."

Something raw and powerful flashed in his smoky blue eyes. "I think you already know."

"Humor me."

A hint of a smile lifted one corner of his mouth. Without breaking eye contact, he moved his hand up his shaft. From where she sat she could see a bead of moisture at the tip. Her sex throbbed.

"Well, I'd definitely encourage you to bring your tongue into play," he said, his voice lowering to a husky pitch.

He squeezed his erection.

Uncontrollable need raced through her body and settled between her legs.

"Some licking would have to be involved," he continued, propping one hand behind his head while his other hand continued stroking. "Sucking, of course."

"Of course," she agreed, shocked by the pure lust resonating through her.

Brody shot her a wolfish look.

She gasped when he quickened his pace. No man had ever done that in front of her before, and the sexual heat pulsating through her body was so strong she could barely breathe. There was something so kinky, so *dirty* about the way he was lying there, stroking himself while she watched. And that she was still fully clothed only made the situation hotter. It gave her the upper hand, reminding her of a fantasy she hadn't dared to think about in years. Scratch that—she'd thought about it only yesterday, when she'd seen Brody at the arena.

She licked her lips, debating whether or not to bring it up.

"What are you thinking about?"

She was certain her embarrassment was written all over her face. And yet the pang of embarrassment was accompanied by a jolt of excitement, because for the first time in her life she was thinking about making that particular fantasy come true.

"Hayden?"

He stopped stroking and she almost cried out in disappointment. "No, keep doing that," she murmured, meeting his eyes again.

"Not until you tell me what's on your mind."

"I...you'll probably think it's silly."

"Try me."

She couldn't believe she was considering confessing her deepest, darkest fantasy to a man she'd known less than a week when she'd never raised the subject around guys she'd dated for months. That in itself said a lot.

Try him.

She swallowed and got to her feet. Eyeing her expectantly, Brody let go of his shaft and leaned his head against both hands, waiting. "Well?" he prompted.

"Promise not to laugh?"

"I won't laugh. Scout's honor." He held up his fingers in a sign that she was fairly certain did *not* belong to the Boy Scouts, but, hell, at least he'd promised.

She took a breath, held it, then released it at the same time she blurted out the words. "I've always wanted to tie a man to my bed."

He laughed softly.

"Hey!" Heat seared her cheeks. "You promised."

"I'm not laughing at the request," he said quickly. "You just took me by surprise."

Relief washed over her, dimming her humiliation. "You're not freaked?"

"Nope. I'm too turned-on to be freaked."

Her focus dropped to his groin, which confirmed his admission. He was thick and hard, a sight that caused every last drop of hesitation and embarrassment to drain from her body like water from a tub. That spot between her legs began to ache, pushing her to action.

"Keep your arms just like that," she ordered, drifting toward the walk-in closet. She grabbed what she needed from the top drawer of the built-in dresser and sauntered over to the bed.

Brody looked at the sheer panty hose in her hands and he grinned. "No fuzzy pink handcuffs?"

"Sorry, I left them in California."

"Pity."

Laughing, she looped the panty hose around his wrists, brushing her fingers over the calluses on his palm. His hands were so strong, fingers long and tapered. A thrill shot through her as she tied those sturdy hands to the headboard. That he let her do it, without moving, without complaining, only deepened the thrill.

She liked it, this feeling of control, something she'd never really felt in the bedroom before. She was all about control when it came to her life, her job, her goals. But sex? Not so much.

With Brody, she was discovering a part of herself she'd denied for a long time. That first night when she'd propositioned him, then letting him touch her in a public bar, now tying him up to her bed—how on earth had he managed to unleash this passionate side of her?

"So what now?" he said hoarsely. "How does this bondage fantasy of yours play out?"

"Well, the fantasy includes some payback actually." She made sure his hands were secure, then straddled him, still fully clothed. "You tortured me last night, Brody."

"You seemed to enjoy it," he teased.

"But you enjoyed it, too, didn't you? You loved having that control over me, driving me wild with your fingers and knowing I wasn't going to fight it." She arched one slim eyebrow. "It's my turn."

He tested the bindings. The headboard shook. "I could easily get out of this position, you know."

"But you won't."

"You sound sure of that."

She bent down and pressed a kiss to his jaw, then licked her way to his earlobe and bit it. He shuddered, his cock jutting against her pelvis. "You're dying for it," she mocked.

A crooked smile stretched across his mouth. "Do people out on the West Coast know how deliciously evil you are, Hayden?"

"They don't have a clue," she said with a self-deprecating sigh.

He threw his head back and laughed. The desire and awe dancing in his eyes sent a wave of confidence rushing through her. Brody made her feel that she could do anything she wanted, be anyone she wanted, confess to any naughty longing she wanted, and he wouldn't judge her.

"Well, it's your turn, as you said," Brody told her. "Let's see what you've got. I warn you, I don't lose control easily."

"We'll see about that."

She pressed both palms to his chest, relishing the hard feel of him, running her fingers through the light sprinkling of hair covering his golden skin. Dipping her head, she traced his collarbone with her tongue.

Brody chuckled. "You can do better than that."

She narrowed her eyes. Was he really convinced he could stay in control? Arrogant man! She'd just have to show him, wouldn't she?

Not rising to his bait, she bent down and covered one flat nipple with her mouth.

He drew in a breath.

She ran her tongue down his chest, scraping her nails along his skin. He tasted like heaven—salty, spicy, masculine—and the hair leading to his groin tickled her lips as she kissed her way south. Her mouth finally reached his erection, but she made no move to wrap her lips around it. Instead she gently flicked her tongue against his tip then blew a stream of air over the moisture she'd left there.

Brody jerked and let out a soft curse.

"Everything okay?" she asked politely, lifting her head just in time to see the arousal creasing his rugged features.

"Is that all you've got?" he groaned.

"On the contrary." She licked her lips and sent him a heavy-lidded look. "I'm just getting started."

Oh, boy, there was nothing more empowering than driving a man as *manly* as Brody Croft into sheer and total orgasmic oblivion. Flames of arousal and satisfaction licked through Hayden's body as she circled the tip of Brody's cock with her tongue, savoring the taste of him.

Curling her fingers around his shaft, she licked him again, then sucked him into her mouth, trying not to smile when he released a low moan of pleasure. God, why hadn't she done this before? She wanted to berate herself for everything she'd been missing.

In the back of her mind a little voice suggested that perhaps she'd never admitted this fantasy because she hadn't found the right man to admit it to, but she forced the voice and its unsettling implications out of her brain. No more thinking. She didn't want to analyze anything about this.

She moved her mouth up and down his shaft, and when she reached one hand down to cup his balls, he shuddered and grew even harder. Her mind was spinning from the incredible feel of him against her lips.

Lightly stroking his rock-hard thigh, she kissed his sensitive underside, then pumped him with her hand while she took him deep in her mouth again.

"You're evil," he wheezed out.

She lifted her head. "What happened to the master of control?"

"He didn't stand a chance."

She laughed. With one final kiss to his tip, she moved up to straddle him. She could feel the heat of his naked body searing through her clothing, making her pants feel like a tight, hot nuisance. But she didn't undress. Not yet.

Leaning forward, she pressed her lips to his and deepened the kiss. He made a frustrated sound and yet again tugged at the bindings constricting his hands. He was right—one forceful tug and the knots would come apart—but he continued lying there at her mercy. His biceps flexed as he tested the knots again. He let out a soft curse.

"Damn it, Hayden, I need to touch you."

"Touch? Nope, sorry."

She lifted her tank top over her head and threw it aside, baring her breasts. "But I'll let you taste." Bending closer, she offered him a sampling, and drew in a breath when he captured one nipple in his mouth and began feasting. He sucked on the rigid bud, hard, biting it gently until she cried out with pleasure that teetered toward pain.

"More," he rasped, pulling away and staring at her pleadingly.

She laughed. "Define more."

His gaze lowered to her thighs, a clear message of what he desired, and her sex instantly throbbed in response. If she gave him what he wanted, what *she* wanted, then the domination game would be shot to hell...but did she really care at this point? Could she last one more second without having this man's hands all over her?

The moisture between her legs provided the answer to that question—a big fat no.

As he inched down a little, so that his head was flat on the pillow, she quickly slipped out of her pants, tore off her panties and knelt over him.

His tongue darted out and flicked over her clit.

"Oh," she moaned, nearly falling backward at the jolt of excitement that ran through her. She was closer than she'd thought. The rippling wave of pleasure swelling inside her confirmed that she was on the brink, her orgasm about to crash to the surface.

Her thighs trembled as she tried to move away from his probing tongue, but he wouldn't let her.

"I want you to come in my mouth," he murmured, the husky sound reverberating against her flesh.

She reached for the headboard, gripped his bound hands

and twined her fingers with his. Her heart thumped, her knees shook, and the moment she leaned into his warm lips again, the second he suckled her clit, she exploded.

Her climax tore through her, fierce, reckless. She gasped, sucking in oxygen as shards of colorful light danced before her eyes and prickled her flushed skin. Still shaking, she sagged against the headboard, struggling to regain her sense of equilibrium while she fumbled with the knots on his hands.

"I need you inside me. Now," she squeezed out, finally untying him.

With a grin, he rotated his wrists to get the blood flowing again, but made no move to flip her over and plunge into her as she'd requested. "It's your show, remember?"

He curled his fingers around her waist and pushed her down so she was straddling him again. From the end table, he swiped a condom she hadn't even noticed him bring into the bedroom and handed it to her. "Do with me what you please."

Swallowing, she rolled the condom onto his erection and shifted her legs. She was wet and ready for him, more than ready, but she didn't guide him inside her. Instead, she brushed her nipples over his chest, enjoying the way his eyes narrowed with pleasure.

She ground her pelvis against him, teased him by pushing against his tip and then edging away from it. Feeling bold and wanton, she leaned forward, let her breasts graze his mouth, and murmured, "Tell me what you want, Brody."

His voice hoarse, he said, "You."

"Me what?"

A wicked gleam flashed in his eyes. "What was it you said to me that first night? Oh, right. I want you to fuck me."

Oh, my.

Without another word, she lowered herself onto him, taking him all the way in, and began to ride him. The pleasure cascading through her body was almost too much to bear. He felt so good inside, so right and perfect.

She increased her pace, moving over him faster, harder, his husky groans urging her on.

He lifted his lean hips and met her thrust for thrust. Then he grasped her ass and rolled her over, his powerful body covering hers as he drove into her. *Yes.* Her insides clenched, pleading with her for release.

"Will you come for me?" he murmured, slowing his pace.

She made an unintelligible sound.

He chuckled. "What was that?"

"Yes," she choked out.

With a satisfied nod, he plunged into her, hard, rough, stealing the breath right out of her lungs. He reached down and stroked the place where they joined, continuing to pump inside her until she finally exploded again.

She gave herself to the orgasm that raced through her body. In the heavenly haze she heard Brody's deep groan, felt his fingers dig into her hips as he jerked inside her.

Struggling to steady her breathing, she ran her hands up and down his sweat-soaked back, enjoying the hard planes and defined muscles under her fingertips. "God, that was…" She trailed off.

He touched her chin, lightly dragging his thumbnail over her jaw. "That was what?"

"Incredible." A laugh flew out. "And to think I was going to spend the evening watching a documentary on a guy who cut his own ear off."

CHAPTER SEVEN

"LET'S ORDER ROOM SERVICE," Brody said a few minutes later, slipping his boxers on.

He watched as Hayden put on her tank top and then attempted to fix the ponytail that had seen better days. Wayward strands of hair fell into her eyes and he smiled at the knowledge that her disheveled state was the result of rolling around in bed with him. She looked rumpled and beautiful and so damn cute he marched over and planted a kiss on her lips. She tasted of toothpaste and popcorn and something uniquely Hayden.

With a little whimper, she pulled his head closer and sank into the kiss, flicking her tongue against his in a tantalizing way that made him hard again.

Just as he lowered his hands to her breasts, she pushed him back. "What happened to room service?" she teased.

"Screw it."

"Knock yourself out. I, for one, am starved." With a grin, she brushed past him and left the bedroom.

He stared down at the erection poking against his boxers. Damn, how did this woman turn him on so fiercely? He felt like a horny teenager again.

He put on his jeans, used the washroom then drifted toward the living room.

"How do cheeseburgers sound?" she called when she spotted him lingering in the hallway.

His stomach growled with approval. "Great."

He joined her on the couch. As she dialed room service and placed their order, he noticed a stack of papers sitting on the table. Curious, he leaned forward and examined the first sheet. It looked like a biography on Rembrandt, neatly typed. The margins were full of handwritten notes.

"What's this?" he asked when she'd hung up the phone.

"Ideas for the Color Theory class I'm teaching in the fall. I plan to focus on Rembrandt for a few lectures."

"Rembrandt, huh? I thought all of his paintings were pretty dark and foreboding." The snippet of information stored in his brain came as a surprise to him. He hadn't thought he'd paid any attention during art history class his senior year of high school.

Hayden also looked surprised, but pleased. "Actually, that's what I want to focus on, the misconceptions about certain artists and their use of color. Did you know that Rembrandt's *Night Watch* is in fact a day scene?"

A vague image of the painting surfaced in his mind. "I remember it being very dark."

"It was—until the painting was cleaned." She grinned. "The canvas was coated with loads of varnish. When it was removed, it turned out to be daylight. A lot of his paintings ended up looking very different once they were cleaned or restored, proving that he definitely knew what he was doing when it came to color."

She grew more animated as she hurried on. "Same with Michelangelo. People didn't view him as much of a colorist, but when the Sistine Chapel was cleaned, it was so vivid, the colors so vibrant, that everyone was shocked."

"I never knew that."

"It took longer to clean that ceiling than it did to paint it," she added. "It was covered in so much soot and dirt that when they were removed the entire scene looked different. That's one of the things I want to talk to my students about, how something as simple as cleaning or restoring can change your entire view of a piece of art."

He nodded. "Sort of like when the Zamboni cleans the ice during second period intermission. Changes the entire playing surface."

He saw her mouth quirk and suspected she was trying not to laugh. "Yeah. I guess there's a similarity there."

Setting down the papers, he said, "You're really into art, huh?"

"Of course. It's my passion."

A smile reached his lips. He hadn't spent much time with women who were passionate about anything outside the bedroom, and the light in Hayden's green eyes tugged at something inside him. He realized this was the first time she'd opened up to him, engaged in a conversation that didn't include ground rules, and he liked it.

"So do you paint, or just lecture about painters?" he asked.

"I used to draw and paint a lot when I was younger, but not so much anymore."

"How come?"

She shrugged. "I was always more fascinated with other people's work than with my own. My undergrad was mostly studio work, but I did my master's in art history. I discovered I liked studying great artists better than trying to become one myself." She drew her knees up into a cross-legged position and asked, "What did you study in college?"

"Sports sciences," he answered. "You know, kinesiology, sports medicine. And I minored in athletic coaching."

"Seriously?"

He didn't respond. Her expression revealed nothing, but he got the feeling she didn't believe him, which made him feel like he was in high school all over again. The kid who'd been written off by his teachers as a big dumb oaf just because he happened to be good at sports. They'd stuck the jock label on him, and no matter how hard he'd tried to tear it off, the judgmental attitudes remained intact. One time he'd even been accused of cheating on an English test he'd spent hours studying for, all because his teacher had decided that a kid who spent all his time handling a puck couldn't possibly finish a book like *Crime and Punishment*.

Hayden must have sensed his irritation because she quickly added, "I believe you. It's just…well, most of the athletes I knew growing up only went to college for the athletic scholarship and just skipped all the academic classes."

"My parents would have killed me if I'd skipped class," he said, rolling his eyes. "They only allowed me to play hockey if I maintained an A average."

Hayden looked impressed. "What do your parents do for a living?"

"Dad's a mechanic, and Mom works in a hair salon." He paused. "Money was always tight during my childhood." He resisted the urge to glance around the lavish penthouse, which was an obvious sign that Hayden hadn't had the same problem growing up.

He wasn't quite sure why he'd brought up that money part, either. He hated talking about his childhood. Hated thinking about it, too. As much as he loved his parents, he didn't like to be reminded of how hard life had been to them. How his mom used to stay up at night clipping coupons and how his dad walked to work—even when Michigan's winter was at its worst—each time their beat-up Chevy truck broke down. Fortunately, his parents would never have to worry about money again, thanks to his lucrative career.

The phone rang, putting an end to their conversation. Hayden picked up the receiver, then hung up and said room service was on its way.

As Hayden headed for the elevator to greet the bellhop with the cart, Brody turned on the television, flipped through a few channels, then finally stopped on the eleven-o'clock news.

Rolling the cart into the living room, Hayden uncovered their food and placed a plate in front of him. The aroma of French fries and ground beef floated toward him, making his mouth water. Funny, he hadn't even noticed how hungry he was when Hayden had had him tied to her bed. He'd been satisfying a different sort of appetite then.

He'd just taken a big bite of his cheeseburger when a familiar face flashed across the plasma screen. He nearly choked on the burger, as a wave of unease washed over him. Hayden had also noticed her father's image on the TV, and she quickly grabbed the remote to turn up the volume. They caught the Channel 8 newscaster in midsentence.

"—came forward this afternoon and admitted there is truth to the rumors surrounding the Chicago Warriors franchise. The player, who refused to be named, claims that the bribery and illegal betting activities Warriors owner Presley Houston is accused of are in fact true."

Brody suppressed a groan. Next to him, Hayden made a startled little sound.

"An hour ago, the league announced they will be launching a full investigation into these allegations."

The newscaster went on to recap the accusation that Presley had bribed players to throw at least two games, and that he'd placed bets on the outcomes. The divorce was also mentioned, as well as Sheila Houston's alleged affair with a Warrior, but by that point Brody had tuned out the news segment.

Who had come forward? It couldn't be Becker, because his friend would've called him with a heads-up before he did anything like that. Yeah, Becker would've definitely warned him.

Craig Wyatt, though, seemed like a likely candidate, especially after what Brody had witnessed at the arena earlier today. The reporters had been pretty rough on Sheila Houston, many of them holding the firm belief that she was lying. It made sense that Wyatt would step in and try to support the woman in his bed.

The headache Brody had tried to ignore before came back with full force. He reached up to rub his throbbing temples. Damn. He wished he knew which one of his teammates had confessed. Whoever it was, this probably didn't bode well for tomorrow's game. How would anybody be able to focus with a possible criminal investigation hanging over their heads?

"It's not true."

Hayden's soft voice jarred him from his thoughts, and he glanced over to see her big eyes pleading with him. "Right?" she said wearily. "It's not true."

"I don't know." He raked a hand through his hair, then absently picked up a French fry. Not that he had an appetite anymore. That news report had destroyed any desire he had for food. He dropped the fry and looked back at Hayden, who seemed to be waiting expectantly for him to continue. "I really don't know, babe. So far, there's been no proof that Pres bribed anyone."

"So far. But if that report we saw just now is true…"

Her breath hitched, and her pained expression tore at his heart.

"Were you… Did he…" She sounded tortured, as if saying each word took great effort. "Did he offer you a bribe?" she finally asked.

"Absolutely not."

"But he could have bribed someone else, another player."

"He could have," Brody said guardedly.

She grew silent, looking so achingly sad that he reached over to draw her into his arms. Her hair tickled his chin, the sweet scent of her wafting into his nose. He wanted to kiss her, to make love to her again, but it was totally not the time. She was upset, and the way she pressed her head into the crook of his neck and snuggled closer told him she needed comfort at the moment, not sex.

"God, this is such a mess," she murmured, her breath warming his skin. "Dad is already stressed-out because of the divorce, and now…"

She abruptly lifted her head, her lips set in a tight line. "I refuse to believe he did what they're accusing him of. My dad is a lot of things, but he's not a criminal."

The certainty in her eyes was unmistakable, and Brody wisely kept quiet. He'd always admired and respected Presley Houston, but experience had taught him that even people you admired and respected could screw up.

"Whoever came forward has to be lying," Hayden said firmly. She swallowed. "This will all get cleared up during the investigation. It has to."

She slid close to him again. "I don't want to think about

this anymore. Can we just pretend we didn't see that news-cast?" Without waiting for an answer, she went on. "And while we're at it, we can pretend I came home for a vacation rather than to deal with my father's problems." She sighed against his shoulder. "God, a vacation would be so good. I could really use some fun right now."

He smoothed her hair, loving how soft it felt under his fingers. "What did you have in mind?"

She tilted her head up and smiled. "We could go see a movie tomorrow—it's been ages since I've been to the mov-ies. Or we could walk along the waterfront, go to Navy Pier. I don't know, just have fun, damn it!"

As much as he hated disappointing her, Brody smiled gently and said, "I would love to, but I can't. The team's catching a plane to L.A. at 9:00 a.m. There's a game to-morrow night."

The light drained out of her eyes, but she gave him a quick smile as if to hide her reaction. "Oh. Right. Dad men-tioned something about an away game."

His arms felt empty as she disentangled herself from the embrace and inched back, absently reaching for a French fry on her plate. She popped it into her mouth, chewing slowly, not looking at him.

"How about Sunday?" he suggested, anxious to make things right and at the same time not sure what he'd done wrong.

"I have this party to go to." She pushed her plate away, apparently as uninterested in eating as he was. "It's impor-tant to my dad."

"Then another time," he said. "I promise you, I'll take you out and give you the fun you need."

Her expression grew strained. "It's okay, Brody. You don't

have to indulge me. It's probably a silly idea to go out on a date anyway."

He bristled. "Why is it silly?"

She blew out an exasperated breath. "This is only supposed to be a fling. Playing out a few sexual fantasies."

A fling. Something inside him hardened at the word. Casual flings had pretty much been his entire life for the past ten years, serious relationships never even making a blip on his radar. And then he'd met Hayden and suddenly he wasn't thinking about casual anymore. He liked her. A lot. Hell, he'd actually experienced a flicker of excitement when she'd mentioned engaging in normal couple things like going to the movies or walking by the lake. He'd never felt the urge to do stuff like that with the previous women in his life. He hadn't cared enough, and that would have sounded awful if not for the fact that they hadn't cared, either.

Crazy as it was, Hayden was the first woman, aside from a reporter, who'd ever asked him about his parents or his college major. Mundane little questions that people asked each other all the time, and yet something he'd been lacking.

He'd seen the potential when Hayden had first walked up to him in that bar. Somehow, he'd known deep down that this was a woman he could have a meaningful relationship with.

And it was damn ironic that she only wanted a goddamn fling.

"What happened to promising to keep an open mind?" he asked quietly.

"I plan on keeping that promise." She shifted her gaze. "But you can't blame me for being skeptical about this becoming anything deeper."

"You don't think it will?"

"Honestly?" She looked him square in the eye. "No, I don't."

He frowned. "You sound convinced of that."

"I am." Pushing an errant strand of hair from her eyes, she shrugged. "I'm going back to the West Coast in a couple of months, and even if I were staying here, our lives don't mesh."

Irritation swelled inside him. "How do you figure that?"

"You're a hockey player. I'm a professor."

"So?"

"So, our careers alone tell me how different we are. I've lived in your world, Brody. I grew up in it. Dad and I had most of our conversations on airplanes on the way to whatever city his team was playing against. I lived in five states during a fifteen-year period. And I hated it."

"Your father was a hockey coach," he pointed out.

"And the travel requirements are not much different for players. I had no say in the career my father chose for himself. But when it comes to what I want in a partner, I can choose."

"The guy in San Francisco, what does he do?"

Her discomfort at discussing the guy who Brody now thought of as the Other Man was evident as she began to fidget with her hands. She laced her fingers together, unlaced them, then tapped them against her thighs. "Actually, he teaches art history at Berkeley, too."

How frickin' peachy. "What else?" he demanded.

She faltered. "What do you mean?"

"So you're both interested in art. What else makes this relationship so delightfully rewarding?"

He almost winced at the sarcasm he heard in his tone. Damn it, he was acting like a total ass here, and from the

cloudy look in Hayden's eyes, she obviously thought the same thing.

"My relationship with Doug is none of your concern. I promised to remain sexually exclusive, but I never agreed to sit around and talk about him."

"I don't want to talk about him," he growled. "I just want to get to know you. I want to understand why you feel I'm not a good match for you."

"God, don't you see it?" she sighed. "I want, I want. You said so yourself, you always get what you want. And that's why I feel the way I do. I've dated too many guys who *want*. But none of them want to give. They're too concerned with getting *their* way, advancing *their* careers, and I always come in second. Well, I'm sick of it. Doug may not be the most exciting man on the planet, but he wants the same things I do—a solid marriage, a stable home, and *that's* what I want out of a relationship."

A deafening silence fell over the room, stretching between. Brody felt like throwing something. He resented the fact that Hayden was projecting her frustration with her father and the previous men in her life onto him, but, hell, he'd opened this can of worms. Pushed her too far, too fast. Needled her about her on-hold relationship and demanded she give him a chance she wasn't ready to give.

Would he still get that chance now? Or had he blown it completely?

"I think asking you over here was a bad idea," she said.

The answer to his silent question became painfully clear.

He'd blown it, all right.

Big-time.

THE LAST THING Hayden felt like doing on Sunday night was attending a birthday party for a wealthy entrepreneur she didn't even know, but when she'd called her father to try to get out of it, he wouldn't have it. He'd insisted her presence was essential, though she honestly didn't know why. Every time she socialized with her father and his friends she ended up standing at the bar by herself.

But she didn't want to let down her dad. And considering how she'd left things with Brody on Friday night, maybe it was better to get out of that big penthouse and away from her thoughts.

It was just past eight o'clock when she neared the Gallagher Club, a prestigious men's club in one of Chicago's most historical neighborhoods. It had been founded by Walter Gallagher, a filthy rich entrepreneur who'd decided he needed to build a place where other filthy rich entrepreneurs could congregate.

The Gallagher Club was by invitation only, and it took some men decades to gain membership. Her father had inherited the membership when he'd purchased the Warriors from their previous owner, and he loved flaunting it. When Hayden was in town, he never took her anywhere else.

She drove down the wide, tree-lined street, slowing her rented Honda Civic when she spotted a crowd at the end of the road. As she got closer, she noticed a few news vans. The dozen or so people milling by the curb were reporters.

And since she couldn't think of anyone else currently involved in a possible criminal investigation, she knew the press was there because of her father.

This was not good.

Taking a few calming breaths, she drove through the wrought-iron gates leading to the Gallagher Club, turning her head and averting her eyes when a few of the reporters started to peer in at her. She exhaled as she steered up the circular cobblestone driveway and slowed the car behind the line of vehicles waiting near the valet area.

Had the reporters harassed her father when he'd driven in? Had he stopped to speak with them, to deny the absurd news report?

A voice interrupted the troubling thoughts. "Good evening, madam."

She lifted her head and saw a young man in a burgundy valet uniform hovering over the driver's window.

"May I take your keys?" he asked.

Her gaze flitted to the massive mansion with its enormous limestone pillars and the stone statues lining the marble entrance. Her father was probably already in there, most likely smoking cigars with his rich friends and acting as if the presence of the media didn't bother him. But she knew it had to bug him. Presley's reputation mattered to him more than anything.

With another sigh, she handed the valet her keys and stepped out of the car. "Davis will escort you inside," the young man informed her.

Davis turned out to be a tall, bulky man in a black tuxedo who extended his arm and led her up the front steps toward the two oak doors at the entrance.

He opened one door and said, "Enjoy your evening."

"Thank you," she answered, then stepped into the lavish foyer.

Miles of black marble spanned the front hall, and overhead a sparkling crystal chandelier dangled from the high ceiling. When she took a breath, she inhaled the scent of wine, cologne and all things expensive.

She paused next to the entrance of the coat check and quickly glanced down to make sure there were no wardrobe mishaps happening. She'd worn a slinky silver dress that clung to her curves, emphasizing her cleavage and bottom. Not to mention that it was slit up to the thigh, revealing a lot of leg. A light touch of eye makeup and some shiny pink lip gloss, and the ensemble had been complete.

Annoyingly, she'd thought about Brody the entire time she'd gotten ready. How much he'd probably enjoy seeing her in the dress—and how much he'd love taking it off her.

It still bothered her, how they'd left things Friday night. Brody hadn't spent the night, needing to catch his flight in the morning, and he'd headed for the elevator with the air of a man leaving a battlefield in defeat.

She'd felt pretty defeated, too. What had she been thinking, suggesting they go out on a real date? After all, she was the one who'd made it clear she wanted a fling. Yet she'd really enjoyed their conversation—talking to him about art, hearing about his parents. It had been really nice. Comfortable. And before she knew it, she was falling right back into her old ways, looking to embark on a new relationship.

That Brody had to be in L.A. the next day was just the wake-up call she'd needed. It reminded her precisely what she wanted—someone stable. Someone who wouldn't be out of town for half the year, while their relationship took second place. As wildly attracted to Brody as she was, she knew he couldn't be that someone.

"Quade has outdone himself this year," a male voice boomed, interrupting her thoughts and reminding her where she was.

Smoothing out the front of her dress, she followed the group of tuxedo-clad men into the large ballroom off to the left. It was a black-tie event, and she found herself surrounded by beautifully dressed people, some older, some younger, all strangers. A dance floor graced the center of the room, in front of a live band that was belting out an upbeat swing song. Before she could blink, a waiter handed her a glass of champagne.

Just as she was about to take a sip, a familiar face caught her eye.

"Darcy?" she called in surprise.

Her best friend's silky red hair swung over her shoulders as she spun around. "Hey! What are you doing here?"

"My dad demanded I make an appearance." She grimaced. "And to think, I almost believed he wanted to spend some time with me."

Bitter much?

Fine, so she was bitter, but really, who could blame her? She'd come here to support her father and bridge the distance between them, and yet he seemed determined to avoid spending quality time with her.

"What are *you* doing here?" she asked Darcy.

Her friend was clad in a white minidress that contrasted nicely with her bright red hair and vibrant blue eyes. "I know the birthday boy. He's a regular at the boutique and pretty much threatened to take his business elsewhere if I didn't make an appearance." Darcy snorted. "To be honest, I think he's dying to get into my panties. Like *that* will ever happen."

"Who exactly is the birthday boy? Dad neglected to mention."

"Jonas Quade," Darcy answered. "He's filthy rich, calls himself a philanthropist, and spends thousands of dollars on his many mistresses. Oh, and he's also a pompous ass, but I can't complain because those thousands I mentioned, well, he spends them at my boutique. He likes getting his lady friends to try on lace teddies and model for him, that sleazy bastar— Crap, here he comes."

A gray-haired man with the build of Arnold Schwarzenegger and a George Hamilton tan made a beeline in their direction. A plump, blonde woman tagged on his heels, looking annoyed by her escort's obvious enthusiasm for Darcy.

"Darcy!" Jonas Quade boomed, grinning widely. "What a treat to see you here."

"Happy birthday, Mr. Quade," Darcy said politely.

Quade turned to his companion. "Margaret, this is the owner of the lingerie store where I buy you all those *intimate* gifts." He winked at the blonde. "Darcy, this is my wife, Margaret."

Hayden could see the barely contained mirth on her friend's face. Hayden had to wonder if Quade's wife was aware that her husband wasn't buying intimate gifts only for her.

"And who is your lovely friend?" Quade asked, peering at Hayden.

Since she didn't particularly enjoy being ogled, Hayden felt a flicker of relief when, before Darcy could introduce them, Quade's wife suddenly latched on to his arm and said, "Marcus is trying to get your attention, darling." She proceeded to forcibly drag him away from the two women.

"Enjoy the party," Quade called over his shoulder.

"That poor woman," Darcy said. "She has no idea..."

"I'm sure she knows. He might as well have *adulterer* tattooed on his forehead."

She and Darcy started to giggle, and Hayden decided this party might not be so bad after all. She hadn't spotted her father yet, but with Darcy by her side, she might not have such an awful time.

"Can I interest you in a dance?"

Damn, she should've known her best friend, with that indecently short dress, wouldn't be available for long.

The handsome, dark-haired man in a navy-blue pinstriped suit eyed Darcy expectantly. After a moment she shrugged, and said, "I'd love to dance." She handed her champagne flute to Hayden, adding, "I'll catch up with you later, okay?"

"Sure. Have fun."

Hayden's shoulders sagged as her friend followed Handsome Man onto the dance floor. Great. Seeing Darcy had been a pleasant surprise, but now her enthusiasm returned to its original level: low.

Then it swiftly dropped to nonexistent.

"Hayden, honey!" Her father's commanding voice sliced through the loud chatter and strains of music. He strode up to her, a glass of bourbon in his hand and an unlit cigar poking out of the corner of his mouth.

She stood on her tiptoes and pecked his cheek. "Hey, Dad. You look like you're enjoying yourself."

"I am, I am." He squeezed her arm and beamed at her. "You look gorgeous."

Something about his overly broad smile troubled her. She wasn't sure why—he was just smiling. And yet an alarm went off in her head. She examined her father more closely. His face was flushed and his eyes were a touch too bright.

Like an unwanted visit from the Avon lady, Sheila's words filled her head. *Your father's drinking again.*

"Are you okay?" she asked, unable to stop the wariness from seeping into her tone. "You look a little…tense."

He waved a hand dismissively. "I'm absolutely great."

"You sure? Because I saw those reporters outside and…" And what? *And I wanted to make sure that they're all just lying about your involvement in illegal sports betting?*

Presley's eyes darkened. "Ignore those bloodsuckers. They're only trying to cause trouble, conjuring up their delusional stories to sell papers." He took a slug of bourbon. "This isn't the time to discuss this. Martin Hargrove was just asking me about you. You remember Martin, he owns a chain of restaurants—"

"Dad, you can't just ignore this," she cut in. "What about the announcement that one of your players came forward? I tried calling your cell yesterday afternoon to talk about it but I kept getting your voice mail. I left you two messages."

He ignored the last statement and said, "I was golfing with Judge Harrison. No cell service out on the course."

She decided not to mention that she'd also called the house he was renting, knowing he'd probably have an excuse for not answering those calls, too.

God, why was he acting like none of this was a big deal? One of his players had admitted that Presley fixed games, and her father was brushing it off like a fleck of lint on his sleeve. Going to parties, smoking cigars, mingling with friends. Did he honestly think this would all just blow over? Hayden refused to believe her father had done the things he was accused of, but she wasn't naive enough to think they could just close their eyes and blink the whole mess away.

"Did you at least talk to Judge Harrison about what your next move should be?" she asked.

"Why the hell would I do that?"

"Because this is starting to get serious." Hayden clenched her fists at her sides. "You should give a press conference maintaining your innocence. Or at the very least, talk to your lawyer."

He didn't bother replying, just shrugged, then lifted his drink to his mouth. After swallowing the rest of the liquid, he signaled a passing waiter and swiped a glass of champagne.

Hayden took the opportunity to place her and Darcy's drinks on the waiter's tray, suddenly losing any taste for alcohol. Both times she'd seen her father this past week, he'd been drinking, but tonight it was obvious her father was drunk. His rosy cheeks and glazed eyes, the way he was swaying on his feet. The blatant case of denial.

"Dad...how much have you had to drink?"

His features instantly hardened. "Pardon me?"

"You just seem a little...buzzed," she said for lack of a better word.

"Buzzed? Is that California slang for drunk?" He frowned. "I can assure you, Hayden, I am not drunk. I've only had a couple drinks."

The defensive note in his voice deepened her concern. When people started making excuses for their inebriated state...wasn't that a sign of a drinking problem?

She cursed her stepmother for putting all these absurd ideas into her head. Her father wasn't an alcoholic. He didn't have a drinking problem, he hadn't had an affair, and he certainly hadn't illegally fixed any Warrior games to make a profit.

Right?

Her temples began to throb. God, she didn't want to doubt her dad, the man who'd raised her alone, the man who up until a few years ago had been her closest friend.

She opened her mouth to apologize, but he cut her off before she could. "I'm sick of these accusations, you hear me?"

She blinked. "What? Dad—"

"I get enough flak from Sheila, I don't need to hear this shit from my own daughter."

His eyes were on fire, his cheeks crimson with anger, and she found herself taking a step back. Tears stung her eyes. Oh, God. For the first time in her life she was frightened of her own father.

"So I made a few bad investments. Sue me," he growled,

his champagne glass shaking along with his hands. "It doesn't make me a criminal. Don't you dare accuse me of that."

She swallowed. "I wasn't—"

"I didn't fix those games," he snapped. "And I don't have a drinking problem."

A ragged breath escaped his lips, the stale odor of alcohol burning her nostrils and betraying his last statement. Her father *was* drunk. This time there wasn't a single doubt in her mind. As she stood there, stunned, a tear crept down her cheek.

"Hayden...honey...oh, Lord, I'm sorry. I didn't mean to snap at you like that."

She didn't answer, just swallowed again and swiped at her face with a shaky hand.

Her father reached out and touched her shoulder. "Forgive me."

Before she could respond, Jonas Quade approached with jovial strides, clasped his hand on Presley's arm and said, "There you are, Pres. My son Gregory is dying to meet you. He's the Warriors' number-one fan."

Her father's dark green eyes pleaded with her, relaying the message he couldn't voice at the moment. *We'll talk about this later.*

She managed a nod, then drew in a ragged breath as Quade led her father away.

The second the two men ambled off, she spun on her heel and hurried to the French doors leading to the patio, hoping she could keep any more tears at bay until she was out of sight.

CHAPTER EIGHT

"I REALLY WISH you hadn't dragged me here," Sam Becker groaned as he drove his shiny silver Lexus in the direction of the Gallagher Club. "My wife is pissed."

"Come on, Mary doesn't have a 'pissed' bone in her body," Brody replied, thinking of the tiny, delicate woman who'd been married to Sam for fifteen years.

"That's what she wants you to think. Trust me, behind closed doors she's not very nice."

Brody laughed.

"I swear, she almost tore my head off when I told her I was going out with you tonight. It was last-minute, so we couldn't get a babysitter for Tamara. Mary had to cancel her plans. I'll never hear the end of this. Thanks a lot, kiddo."

Sam's words might have evoked guilt in some men, but Brody couldn't muster any. For two days he'd been trying to come up with a way to see Hayden and make things right. Sure, he could've just called her, but the way things had ended at the penthouse the other night left him cautious.

Hayden had mentioned she'd be at the Gallagher Club tonight, and he'd spent the entire afternoon wondering how he could show up there without appearing desperate. The answer had come to him during a call from Becker, who'd phoned to discuss a charity event they were participating in next month.

Brody wasn't a member of the Gallagher Club, but Becker was, so Brody had promptly ordered his best bud to brush the dust off his tuxedo.

He felt bad that Becker had been raked over the coals by his wife, but he'd make it up to him.

"Why didn't you get Lucy to watch Tamara?" Brody asked. He'd been over to Becker's house dozens of times, and had spent quite a bit of time with Becker's two daughters. Lucy was fourteen, ten years older than her sister Tamara, but it had been obvious to Brody how much the teenager loved her baby sister.

"Lucy has a—God help me—" Becker groaned "—boyfriend. They're at the movies tonight."

Brody hooted. "You actually let her leave the house with the guy?"

"I had no choice. Mary said I couldn't threaten him with a shotgun." Becker sighed. "And speaking of shotguns, she told me to put one to your head if you didn't agree to spend a week at our lake house this summer. She renovated the entire place and is dying to show it off."

Brody usually tried to spend the entire summer in Michigan with his parents, but for Becker, he was willing to alter his plans. "Tell your wife I'll be there. Just name the date."

Becker suddenly slowed the car. "Oh, shit."

A small crowd of reporters hovered in front of the gates of the Gallagher Club. A few turned their heads at the Lexus's approach.

Rolling up the windows, Becker turned to Brody and said, "Obviously the vultures are following dear old Pres."

Brody suppressed a groan. "Are you surprised? Someone on the team came forward and confirmed the rumors. The press is salivating."

Becker drove through the gate and stopped in front of the waiting valet. Lips tight, he got out of the car without a word.

The second Brody's feet connected with the cobblestone driveway, one of the reporters shouted at them from the gate.

"Becker! Croft!" a man yelled, practically poking his entire bald head between two of the gate's bars. "Any comment on the allegations that Presley Houston fixed Warriors games and..."

Brody tuned the guy out, choosing instead to follow Becker up the front steps toward the entrance of the club.

"Jeez, I hate this place," Becker muttered as they entered the foyer.

"How'd you get to be a member anyway?" Brody asked the question without caring too much about the answer. He'd much rather talk to Becker about Craig Wyatt and the possibility that he was the one who'd come forward, but Becker's body language clearly said he didn't want to discuss the reporters or the scandal. His massive shoulders were tight, his square jaw clenched. Brody could understand. He'd been feeling tense himself ever since he'd watched that news story with Hayden.

And yesterday's loss in Los Angeles hadn't helped. Losing a play-off game was bad, but losing 6–0 was pathetic. The Warriors had played like a team of amateurs, and though nobody had spoken about the scandal, Brody knew it was on their minds. He'd found himself glancing around the locker room, wondering which one of the guys had confessed to knowing about the bribes.

"My wife is involved with one of Jonas Quade's charity foundations," Becker was saying in response to Brody's question. "When he offered to put in a good word for me with the members' committee, Mary pretty much threatened divorce unless I joined." Becker muttered a curse. "I'm telling you, man, she's not a nice person."

"You must have seen *something* good in her considering you married the woman."

"Yeah, I did see something." Becker's rugged features softened. "My soul mate."

The two men entered the massive ballroom, and Brody's eyes instantly began darting around the room.

"So what's her name?" Becker asked with a sigh.

He blinked. "What?"

"Come on, Croft. Only reason you dragged me here is because I belong to this pretentious society of snobs and you needed to score an invite. And since you're no social climber, that means you came here to see a woman. So what's her name?"

"Hayden," he admitted.

Becker accepted a glass of wine from a passing waiter. "Is she a member of Chicago's high society?"

"Kind of." He hesitated. "She's Presley's daughter."

Becker paused mid-sip. "As in the daughter of Presley Houston, the man who signs our paychecks?"

"Yep."

"Bad idea, man. You don't want to get involved with a Houston, not while this betting bullshit is going on."

Brody's tuxedo jacket suddenly felt too tight. "Hayden has nothing to do with that. She's just visiting from California."

"And if the media finds out you're sleeping with her, they'll start drooling. It'll be all over the headlines, how Pres's daughter is screwing one of the star players on the team in order to shut him up."

The hairs on the back of Brody's neck stood on end. "You say that as if you think there's something I need shutting up about. Sam...do you know something about this bribery crap?"

"No, of course not."

"You sure?" He hesitated. "You didn't...you didn't take a bribe, did you?"

Becker looked as if he'd been shot by a bazooka. His mouth dropped open, his cheeks reddened and a vein popped out in his forehead. "You actually think I'd take a fucking bribe? I've been playing in this league for half my life. Trust me, I earn enough."

Brody relaxed. "I didn't think you took a bribe," he said, trying to inject reassurance into his voice. "But what you just said...it sounds like you know more about this scandal than the rest of us. Did Pres tell you anything?"

Though he looked calm now, the vein on Becker's forehead continued to throb. He seemed uncomfortable, scanning the room like that of a prisoner scouting out an escape route. "I don't know anything," he finally said.

"Well, I think I might," Brody found himself confessing.

Becker's head jerked up. "What are you talking about?"

Although this was probably not the time, and definitely not the place, Brody told Becker about what he'd seen at the arena the other day. He spoke in a hushed tone, revealing his suspicions that Sheila Houston had confided in Craig Wyatt about whatever it was she knew, and that Wyatt was the one who'd spoken to the league. He finished with, "So do you think I should do something?"

The other man released a ragged breath. He looked a bit shell-shocked. "Honestly? I think it would be a bad idea."

"Why do you say that?"

"You don't want to get involved," Becker warned in a low voice. "You'll only cast suspicion on yourself."

He mulled over his friend's advice, knowing Becker did have a point. But then he thought of the team captain, and how subdued Wyatt had been lately. Wyatt had always been serious, but he'd barely spoken a word to anyone in weeks, and when he did, it was to yell at them for making a mistake out on the ice. Brody got the feeling Craig Wyatt might very well be in need of a friend, and as reluctant as he was to get involved, he wasn't sure he could watch a teammate struggle without doing a thing to help.

But Becker remained firm. "Don't confront Craig, kiddo. If it bothers you this much, I'll talk to him, okay?"

He glanced at his friend in surprise. "You'd really do that?"

With a playful punch to Brody's arm, Becker gave a faint smile and said, "Unlike my old-timer self, you've still got a lot of years ahead of you. I don't want to see your career tank just because Presley Houston might've decided he needed some extra cash."

"My two favorite players!"

Speak of the devil. Brody shot Becker a look of gratitude, then pasted on a smile as Presley approached them, holding a glass of champagne in his large hand. Considering there were reporters outside just dying to roast Pres for these bribery charges, the man seemed surprisingly jovial. Either the allegations didn't concern him, or he was doing a damn good job covering up his distress.

"Having a good time?" Pres asked.

"We just got here," answered Becker.

"Well, the party's just getting started." Pres lifted his glass to his lips and emptied it. A second later he flagged down a waiter and promptly received a full glass.

"Is your daughter here tonight?" Brody asked. His voice came out more eager than casual. His peripheral vision caught Becker's mouth creasing in a frown.

Pres looked distinctly ill at ease at the mention of Hayden. "I think she went out on the patio," he said.

And there was his cue.

Brody didn't feel bad leaving Becker in the clutches of the obviously plastered team owner. Sam Becker had been in the business long enough to know how to handle every situation thrown at him, and he usually handled them as well as he did the puck. The man was a pro, through and through.

Brody stepped away, glancing around the enormous ballroom for the patio entrance. Finally he spotted the French doors and made his way toward them.

His breath caught at the sight of Hayden's silver-clad figure. She was leaning against the railing overlooking the grounds of the estate, her long brown hair cascading down her bare shoulders, her delectable ass hugged by the silky material of her dress.

He paused at the doors, admiring her. To his surprise, she turned abruptly as if sensing his presence. Their eyes locked. And that's when he saw that her sooty black lashes were spiky with tears.

He was by her side in seconds. "Hey, what's wrong?" he murmured, resting both hands on her slender waist and pulling her toward him.

She sank into his embrace and pressed her face against his shoulder as she whispered, "What are you doing here?"

"I tagged along with a friend." He gently stroked her back. "And I'm glad I did. You look awful."

"Gee, thanks." Her voice came out muffled against the front of his tuxedo jacket.

"Oh, quit sulking. You know you're the sexiest woman

at this party." He swept a hand over her firm bottom. The feel of her warm, curvy body made his pulse quicken, but he reminded himself that now was not the time.

"Now tell me the reason for *these*." He brushed the moisture from her lashes. "What happened?"

"Nothing."

"Hayden."

She lifted her head, chin tilting with defiance. "It's not a big deal, Brody. Just go inside and enjoy the party."

"Screw the party. I came here to see you."

"Well, I came here to see my dad." She turned her head away and stared out at the landscaped grounds.

The temperature had dipped drastically and the thick gray clouds littering the night sky hinted at a storm. Already the endless carpet of flowers on the lush lawn was starting to sway in the wind, sweeping a sweet aroma in the direction of the cobblestone patio.

It was the kind of night he usually enjoyed, the moistness of the air, the hint of rain and thunder, but he couldn't appreciate it when Hayden looked so distraught.

And beautiful. Damn, but she also looked beautiful. The slinky silver dress, the strappy heels, the shiny pink gloss coating her sensual lips. He wanted her, as strongly and as violently as he'd wanted her that first night in the bar. And not just sexually. Something about this woman brought out a protective, nurturing side in him he'd never known he possessed.

"Please, Hayden, tell me what happened."

She hesitated for so long he didn't think she'd say anything, but then her mouth opened and a string of words flew out like bullets spitting from a rifle.

"I think my father is drinking. He blew up at me when I questioned him about it, and then he made a few remarks about bad investments." She looked up, her eyes wide with anguish. "I'm worried he might have done some of the things everyone is accusing him of. God, Brody, I think there's actually a chance he might have bribed players and bet on games."

Brody's heart plummeted to the pit of his stomach. He shoved his fists into the pockets of his jacket, hoping to bring warmth to hands that had suddenly grown ice-cold. Damn it. He didn't want to have this conversation, especially with Hayden. Not when his own flags were raised.

So he just stood there in silence, waiting for her to continue and hoping she wouldn't ask him any questions that might force him to reveal something she probably wouldn't want to hear.

"I don't know what I should do," she murmured. "I don't know how to help him. I don't know if he's guilty or innocent. I have no proof he has a drinking problem, but it's obvious after tonight that something is going on with my dad."

"You need to try talking to him when he's sober," Brody advised.

"I've tried," she moaned with frustration. "But he's determined not to be alone with me. And if by chance we *are* alone, he changes the subject every time I try to bring up my concerns. He won't let me in, Brody."

They stood there for a moment, silently, his arms wrapped around her slender body, her head tucked against his chest.

"I never thought my relationship with my dad would get to this point," she whispered. "He treated me like a stranger tonight. He snapped at me, *cursed* at me, looked right through me, as if I was just another headache he didn't want to deal with instead of his only daughter."

Brody threaded his fingers through her hair and stroked

the soft tresses while he caressed her cheek with his other hand. "Did you two used to be close?" he asked.

"Very." She gave a soft sigh. "Nowadays, the team comes first."

"I'm sure that's not true."

She raised her chin and met his eyes. "Tell me, in all the years you've played for the Warriors, how many times has my father mentioned me?"

Discomfort coiled in his gut. "A bunch of times," he said vaguely.

Her eyes pierced his. "Really?"

"Fine, never," he admitted. "But I'm just a player to your father. He's certainly never treated me as a confidant."

"My dad is obsessed with the team," she said flatly. "He's always loved hockey, but when he was just a coach, it wasn't this bad. Now that he owns a team, he's almost fanatical. It used to be about the game for him. Somehow it's become about making money, being as powerful as he can be."

"Money and power aren't bad things to want," Brody had to point out.

"Sure, but what about family? Who are you supposed to rely on when the money and power are gone? Who will be there to love you?"

A cloud of sadness floated across her pretty face, her expression growing bittersweet. "You know he used to take me fishing a lot? Every summer we'd rent a cabin up at the lake, usually for an entire week. We moved around so much, but Dad always managed to find a place to go fishing. I hated to fish, but I pretended to love it because I wanted to spend the time with my dad."

She moved out of his arms and walked back to the railing, leaning forward and breathing in the cool night air. Without turning around, she continued speaking. "We stopped going once I moved to California. He always promised we'd go back to the lake during my visits home, but we never got around to it. Though we did go out on the yacht last summer." She made a face. "Sheila spent the entire trip talking about her nails. And Dad was on the phone the whole time."

The wistful note in her voice struck a chord of sympathy in him. Despite his busy schedule, he always made sure to return to Michigan a few times a year to see his parents. In the off-season he stayed with them for a month and spent every available moment with his folks. Although it irked him a little that his mom refused to quit her hairdressing job and take advantage of her son's wealth, he loved being home with his folks. And they were always thrilled to have him. He couldn't imagine his parents ever being too busy to hang out with their only son.

Presley Houston was an idiot. There was no other explanation for why the man would pass up the opportunity to spend time with a daughter as incredible as Hayden. She was intelligent, warm, passionate.

"I don't want to talk about this anymore," she burst out. "There's no point. Dad and I have been drifting apart for years. I was stupid to think he might actually value my support."

"I'm sure he does value it. It's obvious he's been drinking tonight, babe. It was probably the alcohol that made him snap at you like that."

"Alcohol is no excuse." She raked her fingers through her hair and scowled. "God, I need to get out of here. I want to go someplace where I can hear my own thoughts."

He glanced at the watch he'd picked up from the arena earlier in the morning, saw it wasn't that late, and threw an arm around Hayden's shoulders. "I know just the place."

She studied him warily, as if she suddenly remembered

what had transpired between them two nights ago. He saw her hesitation, her reluctance to let him back in, but thankfully she made no protest when he took her hand. Instead, she clasped her warm fingers in his and said, "Let's go."

"THIS IS IT? The place where all my thoughts will become clear?" Hayden couldn't help but laugh as she followed Brody into the dark hockey arena twenty minutes later.

She'd let Brody drive her car, but hadn't thought to ask where he was taking her. She'd been content to sit in silence, trying to make sense of everything her father had said to her tonight. Now she kind of wished she'd been more curious about their destination.

The night guard had let them in. He'd seemed surprised at the sight of Brody Croft showing up at the practice arena way after hours, but didn't object to Brody's request. After digging up an old pair of boys' skates for Hayden from the equipment room, the guard had unlocked the doors leading out to the rink, flicked on the lights and disappeared with a smile.

"Trust me," Brody said. "There's nothing like the feel of ice under your skates to clear your head."

"Uh, I should probably mention I haven't ice-skated since I was a kid."

He looked aghast. "But your father owns a hockey team."

"We're not allowed to talk about my father anymore tonight, remember?"

"Right. Sorry." He flashed a charming grin. "Don't worry, I'll make sure you don't fall flat on your ass. Now sit."

Obligingly, she sat on the hard wooden bench and allowed Brody to remove her high heels. He caressed her stockinged feet for a moment, then reached for the skates the guard had found and helped her get a foot into one.

"It's tight," she complained.

"It belongs to a twelve-year-old boy. No figure skates here, so you'll have to make do."

Brody laced up the skates for her, then flopped down on the bench and kicked off his shiny black dress shoes. He'd retrieved a spare pair of skates from the bottom of his locker, and he put them on expertly, grinning when he saw her wobble to her feet. She made quite a fashion statement in her party dress and scuffed black hockey skates.

She held out her arms in an attempt to balance herself. "I'm totally going to fall on my butt," she said.

"I told you, I won't let it happen."

He stood, took two steps forward and unlatched the wooden gate that ringed the ice. Like the pro hockey player he was, he slid onto the rink effortlessly and skated backward for a moment while she stood at the gate and muttered, "Show-off."

Laughing, he moved toward her and held out his hand.

She stared at his long, calloused fingers, wanting so badly to grab onto them and never let go. Yet another part of her was hesitant. When she'd picked him up at the bar five days ago, she hadn't imagined she'd see him after that first night. Or that she'd sleep with him again. Or that she might actually start to *like* him.

And she did like him. As much as she wanted to continue viewing Brody as nothing more than a one-night stand who'd rocked her world, he was becoming unnervingly real to her. He'd listened when she'd babbled about art, he'd let her cry on his shoulder, he'd brought her to this dark arena just to take her mind off her worries. One-night stands weren't supposed to do that, darn it!

"Come on, Hayden, I won't let you fall," he reassured her.

With a nod of acceptance, she took his hand. The second the blades of her skates connected with the sleek ice, she almost keeled over. Her arms windmilled, her legs spread open, and her skates moved in opposite directions as if trying to force her into the splits.

Brody promptly steadied her. "You're not very good at this, are you?"

"I told you I wasn't," she returned with an indignant glare. "Ask me to lecture you about Impressionist art, I can do that. But skating? I suck."

"Because you're trying to walk instead of glide," he pointed out. He clamped both his hands on her waist. "Quit doing that. Now, take my hand and do what I'm doing."

Slowly, they pushed forward again. While Brody's strides were effortless, hers were clumsy. Every few feet the tips of her skates would dig into the ice and she'd lurch forward, but Brody stayed true to his word. He didn't let her fall. Not even once.

"There you go," he exclaimed. "You're getting the hang of it."

She couldn't help smiling. Once she'd taken his advice and stopped treating the skates as shoes, her movements had become smoother. She felt giddy as they picked up speed, gliding along the ice like a pair of Thoroughbreds rounding a racetrack.

The boards, the benches, the bleachers—it all whizzed by her, the cool air in the arena reddening her cheeks. Although there were goose bumps dotting her bare arms, she didn't mind the cold temperature. The chill in the arena soothed her, cleansing her mind.

She cast a sideways glance at Brody and saw he was enjoying this, too. God, he looked delicious in his tuxedo.

The jacket stretched over his broad shoulders and power-ful chest, and the slightly loose trousers didn't hide his taut behind. She noticed his bow tie sat a little crooked, and resisted the urge to reach out and straighten it. She didn't want to move her arms and risk falling, so she tightened her fingers around his instead.

He looked down at their intertwined fingers, his mouth parting slightly, as if he wanted to speak but was being cau-tious. She knew exactly what was on his mind, because the same thing was running through hers. God help her, but she wanted this man in her bed again.

He was arrogant, yes, and pushy sometimes. But he also turned her on in the fiercest way, and every time he fixed those midnight-blue eyes on her, every time he wrapped those big arms around her, she melted.

They slowed their pace, and she forced her thoughts away from the dangerous territory they'd crossed into and tried to come up with a neutral topic of conversation. One that didn't make her think of Brody, naked and hard as he de-voured her body with his tongue.

"When did you start playing?" she finally asked, decid-ing his career was as safe a subject as any.

"Pretty much the second I could walk, I was learning to skate. My dad used to take me to this outdoor rink near our house in Michigan." He chuckled. "Well, it wasn't much of a rink. Just a crappy pond that froze over every winter. My parents couldn't afford the membership fee for a real arena, so I used to practice my slap shots out on that pond while my dad sat on a folding chair in the snow and read car magazines."

"Did you play on a school team?"

"Uh, what team *wasn't* I on?" He dropped her hand and began skating lazy circles around her. "In high school I played hockey, rugby and baseball in the spring. Oh, and I was on the lacrosse team until the practices started to interfere with my hockey schedule."

"Huh. So you were one of *those* guys. I bet you were voted Most Likely to Become a Pro Athlete in your high school yearbook."

"Actually, I was."

He told her a bit about his early years in the league, then made her laugh with some anecdotes about his parents and their overwhelming pride in him. At times a twinge of bitterness seeped into his voice, giving her the feeling that his childhood was tougher than he let on, but she didn't pry. She remembered him telling her money had been tight for his family, and it was obviously something he didn't like talking about.

A few minutes later, a cramp seized her leg and she wobbled to a stop, leaning against the splintered sideboards as she rubbed the back of her thigh. On the West Coast she jogged every morning before heading over to the university, but she was obviously not in the great shape she'd believed herself to be in. Her legs were aching and they'd only been skating around for twenty minutes.

"Wanna take a break?" Brody offered.

"Please."

They stepped off the ice and climbed up to the bleachers. Brody was an expert when it came to walking on skates. She wasn't so fortunate. She almost pitched forward a half-dozen times before she finally sank down on the bench and exhaled with relief.

"I think I pulled a muscle in my butt," she grumbled.

"Want me to rub the kinks out?"

She stiffened, wishing his voice didn't contain that husky note of erotic promise. Damn it. She couldn't fall into bed with him again. As thrilling as it would be to continue exploring the sexual canvas they seemed so skilled at painting together, she couldn't help remembering what had happened the last time she'd given in.

As if sensing her concerns, Brody let out an unsteady breath. "I'm sorry about the other night, Hayden. I acted like an ass."

She didn't reply, just offered a pointed nod.

"I know I'm rough around the edges. I'm demanding, I like getting my way and I'm definitely not the kind of man who's content with playing second fiddle." He held up his hand before she could cut in. "I shouldn't have hassled you about, you know, *Doug*—" he said the name like it was contagious "—but damn it, Hayden, it drives me crazy knowing there's someone else in your life. I'm not used to sharing."

"You're not sharing. Doug and I are on a break."

"There's a giant difference between a break and a breakup." He frowned. "Do you think you'll go back to him?"

"I don't know." Deep down, though, she knew the answer to that question and it probably wasn't one Doug was going to like. But she couldn't talk about it, not now, and definitely not with Brody.

She could tell he wasn't happy with her answer, but instead of challenging her the way he had two nights ago, he simply nodded. "Guess I'll have to live with it then. And I *can* live with it, especially if it means I get to spend more time with you."

"But why? What do you see in me that makes you so sure we should pursue this?" She wasn't prone to insecurities, but she couldn't quite figure out why this sexy giant of a man wanted *her* and not some supermodel.

"What do I see in you?" He leaned closer. "You want a

list? I can do that. I'll skip how beautiful you are. That's all just superficial."

"I'm not above superficial."

He chuckled. "So you'd like me to start with your wild green eyes that have been knocking me out since the second you strolled up to that pool table?"

She bit her lower lip. "Okay."

Carefully, he took a lock of her hair between his fingers. "Or should I start with this silky brown hair that keeps making me want to reach out and touch it?" His attention dropped to her chest. "Or these breasts I can't get enough of?" The fingers that had been toying with her hair moved to brush over her nipples, which were pushing against the thin fabric of her dress. "Or maybe these lips that keep begging me to taste them?" He brushed a thumb over her bottom lip.

Her lips parted, her eyelids grew heavy, and thankfully she was sitting down because she didn't think she could hold up the weight of her body in her weakened state. This man was one smooth talker.

"Any of those places are fine," she breathed.

Strong hands cupped her face. "Then there's the intelligence that practically radiates from you. Did I ever tell you smart women seriously turn me on?" His thumbs began caressing her cheeks and he bent to whisper close to her ear. "You're a walking contradiction, Hayden. Prim and proper one moment, wild and uninhibited the next. And the more I get to know you, the more I like what I find."

Each of his words softened her heart, and every warm wisp of his breath against her ear made her quiver with need.

"When I left the penthouse the other night you wouldn't let me kiss you," he said, his lips just inches from hers. "I promised myself I wouldn't kiss you again until you asked me to."

"Kiss me, Brody. Please…"

In an instant, his lips touched hers, unleashing a trickle of soothing warmth that rivaled a shot of fine brandy. She moved a hand to his cheek and relished the light prickles of his five-o'clock shadow. And despite his tender touch, the hardness of his chest and the roughness of his cheek reminded her he was all man.

He groaned softly, and deepened the kiss. She parted her lips, inviting him to explore. She wanted to surround herself in his protective embrace. Her father's behavior tonight had frightened her, hurt her, but Brody's kiss made her forget about everything except this moment, the feel of his mouth on hers, the flick of his tongue and warm caress of his fingers on her cheek.

She slid her hand to the nape of his neck, allowing the soft curls to tickle her fingers. She took hold and pulled the kiss deeper. His slow, heavy groan spoke of acceptance and thanks.

His hands moved down her sides, and he lightly caressed the sides of her breasts with his thumbs, sending a pulsing charge through her system. It was the most gentle he'd ever been with her, a stark change from his rough, drugging kisses and eager exploratory hands. And as much as she was enjoying the kiss, she wanted more. She lowered her hands to the growing bulge in his tuxedo trousers, but he moved her hand away and broke the kiss.

For a moment, her eyes wouldn't open and her mouth wouldn't close. She was held in transition, her body still tingling from his touch. As she slowly raised her lids, she saw the deep sense of need in his eyes. Need that matched hers.

"Close your eyes," he murmured.

"Why?"

"Just do it."

Curious, she let her eyelids flutter shut. She heard a rustling sound, felt Brody move closer and lean forward, then
gasped when his hand circled her ankle.

"Don't move." His voice was barely above a whisper.

She swallowed. Waiting. Sighing when he ran his big
warm hand up her leg, bunching her dress between his fingers as he traveled north. His touch suffused her with heat,
made her pulse race. He glided his fingers along her inner
thigh, leaving a trail of fire in his wake. And then his palm
was pressed against her lace panties.

"What are you doing?" she breathed out.

"De-stressing you." His tongue was suddenly on her ear,
flicking against the tender lobe before suckling it.

Silent laughter shook her as her eyes popped open.
"What's with you and your need to intimately touch me
in public?"

He rubbed his palm against her mound, his breath hot
against her ear as he whispered, "Want me to stop?"

"God, no."

"Good."

He moved his hand under her panties and pushed one
long finger deep into her hot channel.

"You're always so ready, so tight and wet," he muttered.

Before she could tell him that *he* was the reason she
was always ready, he covered her mouth with his. The kiss
sucked the breath from her lungs, soft and warm and thrilling, his tongue matching the strokes of his finger. Long,
deep, languid strokes. He slid another finger into her aching
sex, kissing her, murmuring encouraging pleas against her
lips, and then his thumb circled her clit and she exploded.

She cried out against his mouth, rocked against his fingers, her mind nothing but a big pile of mush while her body convulsed.

When she finally came back down to earth, she found Brody watching her with surprising tenderness. "You're gorgeous, Hayden," he murmured, withdrawing his fingers and fixing her dress.

Her heart squeezed. She opened her mouth to thank him—for the compliment, the orgasm, the shoulder to lean on—but he didn't give her the chance. "Will you let me come home with you tonight? No big deal if you say no. I just, uh, thought I'd ask."

He was so polite, so careful, when the heat in his eyes and his unsteady breathing told her he'd probably die from arousal if she said no. But it touched her that he'd asked instead of assumed.

"If we go to the penthouse," she began slowly, "what exactly will we do?"

A sensual twinkle filled his eyes. His voice lowered to a husky pitch as he said, "Well, I noticed there's a removable showerhead in the master bathroom."

She burst out laughing. "Do you make it a habit of scoping out the shower when you use other people's bathrooms?"

"Who doesn't?"

CHAPTER NINE

A FEW DAYS LATER Hayden was standing outside the lavish ten-bedroom home her father had bought for Sheila. It was only a few blocks from the Gallagher Club, in the heart of one of the wealthiest neighborhoods in Chicago.

Hayden had finally decided to talk to Sheila to learn more about her father's drinking problem. Although a part of her still didn't fully trust her stepmother, she knew this conversation was long overdue. If she had more information, maybe she could find a way to help her dad. And if his recent behavior was any indication, her father definitely needed some help.

Sheila answered the door wearing sweats, her expression clearly conveying her surprise at seeing her soon-to-be-ex-stepdaughter standing on the pillared doorstep.

"Hayden...what are you doing here?"

She fumbled awkwardly with the strap of her leather purse. "I think we should talk."

With a nod, Sheila opened the door wider so Hayden could step inside. The enormous front parlor, with its sparkling crystal chandelier, was as intimidating as it had been the first time she'd seen it. The white walls were devoid of artwork, a sight that made her frown. She'd encouraged her father to pick up pieces at auctions she had recommended, but it looked as if he hadn't bothered.

"So what's on your mind?" Sheila asked after they'd entered the living room.

Hayden sat on one of the fluffy teal love seats, waited for Sheila to sink down on the matching sofa, then cleared her throat. "I want you to tell me about my father's drinking."

Her stepmother raked one delicate hand through her blond hair, then clasped her hands together in her lap. "What do you want to know, Hayden?"

"When did he start?"

"Last year, about the same time the pharmaceutical company he'd invested in went bankrupt. He lost a lot of money, tried to recoup it by making more investments, and lost that, too."

Hayden fought back a wave of guilt, realizing that she'd had no idea any of this had been going on. Her father had always sounded so jovial on the phone, as if he had no cares in the world.

Was she a terrible daughter for not seeing through the lies?

"He didn't want to worry you," Sheila added as if reading her mind.

"So that's when he started drinking?"

Her stepmother nodded. "At first it was just a drink or two in the evenings, but the worse the situation got, the more he drank. I tried talking to him about it. I told him the drinking was becoming a problem, but he refused to hear it. That's when…" Sheila's voice drifted.

"That's when what?"

"He went to bed with another woman."

A silence fell between them, but this time Hayden didn't

try to defend her father. That day at the law office, she'd believed Sheila to be a heartless lying bitch, accusing Pres of adultery, but after his blowup at the Gallagher Club, Hayden couldn't deny her dad had a problem. And if that problem had driven him to cheat, she needed to accept it. No point sticking her head in the sand and pretending things were okay, when they obviously weren't.

So she leaned back and allowed Sheila to continue.

"He told me what he'd done the next morning, blamed me for his infidelity, said my constant nagging forced him to do it." Sheila made an exasperated sound. "And he kept denying he had a drinking problem. I might have been able to forgive him for the affair, but I couldn't look away while he destroyed the life we'd built."

"What happened?"

"I confronted him again, ordered him to get help for his alcohol problem."

"I take it he didn't agree."

"Oh, no." Sheila's pretty features twisted in distress and anger. "He only got worse. A couple nights later, I came home from the gym and found him in the study, drunk out of his mind. That's when he confessed about the games he'd fixed."

A rush of protectiveness rose inside her. "It could have been the alcohol talking. Maybe he didn't know what he was saying."

"He knew." Her stepmother offered a knowing look. "And what he said was confirmed to me by a player on the team."

"The one you're sleeping with?" Hayden couldn't help cracking.

Two red circles splotched Sheila's cheeks. "Don't judge me, Hayden. I may have turned to another man, but only after your father betrayed me. Pres pushed me away long before I did what I did."

Her mouth closed. Sheila was right. Who the hell was she to judge? What happened within a marriage wasn't anybody's business but the people who were married, and she couldn't make assumptions or draw conclusions about a situation she hadn't been a part of.

And if she were to draw conclusions, it startled her to realize she actually believed Sheila. She might not approve of Sheila's contesting of the prenup or love for all things luxurious, but Hayden couldn't bring herself to brush off what her stepmother had told her.

If her father had really bribed players, what would happen to him if—when?—the investigation revealed the truth? Would he get off with a fine, or would she be visiting him in prison this time next year? Fear trickled through her, settling in her stomach and making her nauseous.

With a sympathetic look and a soft sigh, Sheila said, "Things aren't always as they seem. *People* aren't always as they seem." She averted her eyes, but not before Hayden saw the tears coating her lashes. "Do you want to know why I married your father, Hayden?"

For his money?

She quickly swallowed back the nasty remark, but Sheila must have seen it in her eyes because she said, "The money was part of it. I know, you probably won't understand, but I didn't have a lot of financial security growing up. My parents were dirt-poor. My father ran off with what little money we did have, and I was working by the time I was thirteen." She shrugged. "Maybe I was selfish for wanting a man who could take care of me, for wanting some security."

Sheila paused, shaking her head as if reprimanding herself. "But the money wasn't the only reason. If it was, I would have married one of the many rich jerks who showed up at the bar I waitressed at, pinching my ass and trying to get me into bed. But I didn't marry one of those guys. I married your dad."

"Why?" Hayden asked quietly, strangely fascinated by her stepmother's story.

"Because he was one of the good guys. I wasted so much time on the bad boys, the guys who light your body on fire but end up burning you out in the end. I was sick of it, so I decided to find myself a Mr. Nice—a decent, stable man who might not be the most exciting man in the world but who'd always be there for me, always put me first, financially and emotionally."

A wave of discomfort crested in Hayden's stomach, slowly rising inside her until it lodged in her throat like a wad of old chewing gum. She'd never thought she'd have anything in common with this woman, but everything Sheila had just said mirrored the thoughts Hayden had been having for years now. Wasn't that why she'd chosen Doug— because he was nice, decent and stable? Because he'd always put her first?

"But nice men aren't necessarily the *right* men," Sheila finished softly. "Nice men make mistakes, too. They can take you for granted and they can play with your emotions, just like those bad boys I wanted so badly to get away from."

She swiped at the tears staining her cheeks and lifted her chin. "Your father hurt me, Hayden. If he'd truly loved me, he would've seen that I was only trying to help him, that I wanted to be there for him the way I thought he'd be there for me. But he wasn't there for me. I feel awful about not being able to get him help for the drinking, I really do, but I couldn't take the way he was treating me. He went to another woman, he lied about his criminal actions, and now he's making me out to be a selfish gold digger."

With a bitter smile, Sheila leaned forward and stared at her with sad blue eyes. "How's that for Mr. Nice?"

HAYDEN LEFT WITH no real idea how to help her dad with his drinking problem, even more concerned about his possible criminal activities. She was just as confused and upset as she'd been when she'd rung the doorbell. Her cell phone rang the second she got into her car, and just when she thought this day from hell couldn't get any worse, it did. The number flashing on the phone's screen belonged to Doug.

Oh, God, she couldn't deal with this right now. But she couldn't keep avoiding her issues any longer, either. Today she'd finally opened her eyes to the downward spiral of her father's life, started to accept that her father might have become an alcoholic, adulterer and criminal.

Maybe it was time to face the other man in her life. She'd called Doug back last week, but she'd phoned in the afternoon knowing he would be in a seminar for one of the summer courses he was teaching. Maybe it made her a chicken but she hadn't been ready to talk to him yet, opting instead to leave a brief message on his machine.

She hadn't mentioned Brody in the message, either, mostly because the thought of telling Doug about Brody—on his answering machine no less—had made her palms grow damp. It would've been one thing if the situation with Brody hadn't gone beyond that first night, but it had. It'd been over a week since she'd approached him in the bar, and somehow, during that time, her casual fling had…changed.

She couldn't pinpoint when the change had occurred. All she knew was that since they'd gone skating after the Gallagher Club party, she and Brody had been having fun not only in the bedroom, but out of it. They'd gone back to the Lakeshore Lounge for dinner, gone skating at Millennium Park. Brody had even taken her to the Art Institute of Chicago, where he'd spent the entire day following her from painting to painting and listening to her rave about each one.

What *wasn't* fun, however, was having him fly to another city every other day. He'd had three away games this past week and each time he'd left to catch his flight she'd had to bite her tongue. Had to remind herself that no matter how much she was enjoying being with Brody, this was still a fling. And flings always came to an end at some point.

Her phone continued to chime, the ring tone speeding up to signal that voice mail would kick in soon.

Hayden took a deep breath.

She had to pick up. Doug had already left her three messages since she'd called him back, his voice growing more and more concerned with each call. He probably thought she was lying dead in a ditch somewhere, and she was disgusted with herself for her inability to deal with this Doug dilemma.

No more stalling. She'd already endured one unwanted confrontation today. Might as well make it two for two.

She hit the talk button on her cell phone.

"Thank God," Doug said when she answered. "I was beginning to think something terrible had happened to you."

His obvious relief caused guilt to buzz around in her belly like a swarm of angry wasps. She felt like total slime for making him worry like this.

"Don't worry, I'm fine," she replied, her fingers trembling against the phone. "Didn't you get my message?"

"I got it, but I've called you a few times since, Hayden."

"I know. I'm sorry I didn't return your calls. Things have been hectic."

"I can imagine." He paused. "Some of the papers here are running stories about your father, honey."

"Yeah, it's happening here, too. I'm starting to get worried," she admitted.

Confiding in him came as naturally as brushing her teeth in the morning. She'd always been able to talk to Doug about everything. Whether it was problems at the university or something as minor as a bad haircut, he was always there to listen. It was one of the things she liked about him.

Liked.

The word hung in her mind, making her tap one hand against the steering wheel. She *liked* everything about this man. His patience, his tenderness, his generosity. And she was certain that once he finally decided the time was right for them to get physical, she'd like that, too. And that was the problem. She wasn't sure she could spend the rest of her life with a man she simply *liked*. Sure, sometimes love took time to develop, feelings could grow, friends could realize they were soul mates...at least that's what she'd always believed.

After meeting Brody, she was starting to reconsider.

She didn't just *like* sleeping with Brody. The sex was wild, passionate, all-consuming. When Brody kissed her, when he wrapped those big muscular arms around her, the ground beneath her feet fell away, her body sizzled like asphalt in a heat wave, and her heart soared higher than a fighter jet.

When Doug kissed her...none of those things happened. His kisses were sweet and tender, and she really did *like* them—damn, there was that word again.

"Honey, are you there?"

She forced her mind back to the moment, to this conversation she'd been putting off for too long. "Sorry, I just spaced out for a second. What were you saying?"

"I want to come visit you."

She nearly dropped the phone. "What? Why?"

There was an annoyed pause. "Because I miss you." Another beat, this time strained. "I was hoping maybe you missed me, too."

"I…" She couldn't bring herself to lie, but she couldn't quite tell the truth, either.

Fortunately, Doug continued speaking. "I keep thinking about what you said before you left, Hayden. I know you asked for space, but…" A heavy breath resonated from the other end of the line. "I think space will only lead to distance, and the last thing I want is distance between us. Maybe if I come out there, maybe if we sat down together and talked this through, we could figure out why you're feeling the way you are."

"Doug…" She searched for the right thing to say. Was there even a right thing? "This is something I need to figure out on my own."

"I'm part of this relationship, too," he pointed out.

"I know, but…"

Tell him about Brody.

Damn it. Why did her conscience have to chime in right now? She already felt terrible enough, sleeping with a man a few short weeks after telling her boyfriend she needed space. Could she really confess her sins, *now,* when Doug was so eager to patch things up between them?

You don't have a choice.

As much as she wanted to fight her conscience, she knew that little voice was right. She couldn't hide something this important from him. He needed to know. No, he *deserved* to know.

"I've been seeing someone," she blurted out.

Dead silence.

"Doug?"

A muffled cough sounded from the other end. "Pardon me?"

"I'm seeing someone. Here, in Chicago." She swallowed. "It's only been a couple of weeks, and it's nothing serious, but I think you should know."

"Who is he?"

"He's… It doesn't matter who he is. And I want you to know that I didn't plan on this. When I asked for space, the last thing I wanted was to jump into another relationship—"

"Relationship?" He sounded distressed. "I thought you said it wasn't serious!"

"I did. I mean, it's not." She tried to control her voice, feeling so unbelievably guilty it was hard to get out the next words. "It just sort of…happened."

When he didn't say anything, she hurried on. The pretzel of guilt in her chest tightened into a vise around her heart. "Are you still there?"

"I'm here." He spoke slowly, curtly. "Thank you for telling me."

Her throat tightened. "Doug…" She trailed off, not sure what to say. Not sure there was anything else *to* say.

"I have to go, Hayden," he said after a long pause. "I can't talk to you right now. I need time to digest all this."

"I understand." She gulped, bringing much-needed moisture to her arid mouth. "Call me when you're ready to…"

To what? Forgive her? Yell at her?

"To talk," she finished awkwardly.

He hung up without saying goodbye, and she sat there for a moment, listening to the silence before her cell phone finally disconnected the call. She shoved the phone back into her purse and leaned against the plush driver's seat, raking both hands through her hair.

Between Sheila and Doug, she felt as if she'd spent the afternoon waving a red flag in front of a bull determined to gore her to pieces.

At least nobody could call her a coward.

CHAPTER TEN

THE ATMOSPHERE IN the locker room was subdued, the usual pregame chatter absent as the players changed into their gear and spoke in hushed voices to one another. Brody would've liked to blame the serious mood on nerves; the series was 3–2, and if they won tonight's game they'd move on to the second round of play-offs. But he knew it wasn't the pressure that was weighing everyone down.

Fifteen minutes earlier, a league executive had informed the team that an investigation into the bribery claims was officially under way. Players would be interviewed privately throughout the week, and if the allegations bore any weight, proper disciplinary actions would be taken.

And possible criminal charges executed.

Lacing up his skates, Brody glanced discreetly over at Craig Wyatt, who was adjusting his shin pads. Wyatt hadn't spoken one word since the announcement, his sharp features furrowed with silent concern, his big body moving clumsily as he dressed. He was definitely worried about something.

Damn, winning this game tonight was going to be seriously tough. The morale was lower than the murky depths of the ocean, the players behaving as if individual axes were hovering over their heads.

Which one of them had taken a bribe? And was it only one? For all he knew, half the guys could be involved. The notion caused his blood to boil. You had to be a real son of a bitch to deliberately throw a game. The media had claimed only one or two games had been fixed, and early in the season, but it didn't matter to Brody when or how many. All it took was one game. One game could be the difference between making the play-offs and ending the season in defeat. It was a good thing they'd played well enough to make up for those early losses.

"Let's give them hell tonight," Wyatt said quietly as everyone began shuffling out of the locker room.

Give them hell? That was the big pep talk for the night?

From the wary looks on the other men's faces, Wyatt's words of encouragement were about as effective as dry glue.

"Craig, wait a second," Brody said, intercepting the team captain before he could exit the room.

"We've got a game to play, Croft."

"It can wait. I just need a minute."

The captain tucked his helmet under his arm. "Fine."

What now? Did he come out and ask Wyatt about the bribery bullshit? Bring up the affair with Sheila Houston?

Brody realized that maybe he should've come up with a game plan before he initiated this conversation.

"Well?" Wyatt said, looking annoyed.

He decided to take a page out of his mom's policy book: honesty. "I saw you with Sheila at the arena last week."

Wyatt's face went ashen. Then he swallowed. "I don't know what you're talking about."

"Don't bother with denial. I *saw* you." The collar of Brody's jersey suddenly felt hot and the padding underneath his uniform became tight. Sucking in a breath, he added, "How long have you been having an affair with Presley's wife?"

The air in the locker room grew tense, stifling. Wyatt's face was still white, but his eyes flashed with anger and indignation. Shoving his helmet onto his head, he shot Brody a frown. "This is none of your business."

"It is if you're the player who came forward and confirmed Sheila's accusations."

A long silence fell, dragging on too long for Brody's comfort. Wyatt's face was completely devoid of emotion, but it didn't stay that way for long. After several more beats, a look of weary resignation clouded Wyatt's eyes.

"Fine. You win. It was me." The captain's large hands trembled as he fumbled to snap his helmet into place. "I went to the league, Brody. I'm the reason this damn investigation is starting up."

Brody swallowed. His gut was suddenly burning, but he couldn't figure out if he felt angry, betrayed or relieved. He studied Wyatt's face and quietly asked, "How did you know Sheila was telling the truth?"

"I had my suspicions at the beginning of the season, when we lost a couple of games we had no business losing. And Sheila confirmed it."

Wyatt exhaled slowly, his breath coming out shaky. "I can't play on the same team as a few assholes that would sabotage us for money. I can't play for an owner who is willing to cheat."

Brody couldn't help but believe him. Wyatt seemed legitimately torn up about all this.

"You know who took the bribes then?" Brody asked.

Wyatt quickly averted his eyes. "Just drop it, Brody. Let the league conduct its investigation. You don't want to get involved in this."

"Wyatt…"

"I'm serious. It'll all get cleared up eventually. Just…drop it," he said again. Wyatt stepped toward the door. "Now get your ass out there. We've got a game to win."

Brody watched the other man stalk off. A part of him wanted to run after Wyatt and shake some names out of the guy, but another part was telling him to let it go. Trying to force Wyatt to confide in him wouldn't achieve anything. Craig would just get angrier, more volatile, and the last thing Brody wanted to do was piss him off. Wyatt was a gifted athlete, one of the best in the league, and with playoffs happening, Brody wanted the Warriors captain focused on the game, not personal junk.

And he needed to focus on the game, too. Lately he'd spent too much time worrying, doubting his fellow players, wondering if his career would be blown to hell by the scandal. He had the truth on his side, the knowledge that he'd played clean and hard all season, but that didn't mean squat. Guilty by association, or whatever the hell they called it.

He would be a free agent in a few months, but another franchise might be loath to pick him up knowing he'd been investigated for bribery. All he could hope was that the investigation was quick, painless, and that his name wouldn't be dragged through the mud for something he hadn't done.

Cursing softly, he left the locker room and headed down the hallway leading out to the Warriors bench. As he entered the arena, the deafening cheers of the crowd assaulted his eardrums. The Lincoln Center was filled to capacity tonight, the bleachers a sea of silver and blue. Seeing the fans supporting the team by donning their jersey warmed Brody's heart, but it also renewed his anger.

All these fans who'd come out here tonight—the people

yelling words of encouragement, the kids clapping their hands wildly —deserved a team they could be proud of.

Unfortunately, there was very little to feel proud about, especially when ten minutes into the first period the Warriors were already down by two goals.

And it was one of those games that went from bad to worse. The Vipers cleaned the ice with the Warriors. By the second period, Brody was drenched in sweat, gasping for air and wanting to bodycheck everyone from the ref to his coach. It didn't even seem to matter how fast they skated, how many times they rushed the net, how many bullets they slapped at the Vipers' goalie. The opposing team was faster, sharper, better. They had the advantage of good morale on their side.

When the third period rolled around, Brody could tell most of his teammates had given up.

"This game blows," Becker sighed once they'd sunk down onto the bench after a line change.

Brody squirted a stream of water into his mouth then tossed the bottle aside. "Tell me about it," he muttered.

"So did you take the advice I gave you?" Becker asked, his eyes still on the game in front of them.

"Advice?"

"About staying away from Presley's daughter," Becker reminded him.

Stay away from Hayden? Brody almost laughed out loud. He was tempted to tell his friend that at the moment he was doing everything in his power to stay *close* to her. And he was succeeding. For the most part, anyway.

No matter how often Hayden called their relationship a fling, Brody couldn't view anything between them as casual. For the first time in his life, he was with a woman he actually liked hanging out with. Sure, he liked the sex, too—fine, he *loved* the sex—but there had been moments during the past week when he was shocked to realize there were other things he enjoyed just as much. Such as watching art documentaries with her. Holding her while she slept. Teaching her to ice-skate even though she wasn't much of a student.

She was funny and smart and her eyes lit up when she talked about something she loved. And it troubled him how that light left her eyes whenever an away game came up. He'd had to leave town three times this week, and although Hayden never said a single word about it, he could tell it bothered her. But he had no idea how to make it better, short of retiring from hockey—and he wasn't about to do that.

Yet he had to do something. Hayden seemed determined to keep him at a distance, at least when it came to admitting they were in a relationship, and he desperately wanted to bridge that gap, make her realize just how important she was becoming to him.

"Are you even listening to me?" Becker's loud sigh drew him out of his thoughts.

Brody lifted his head. "Huh? Oh, right, Pres's daughter. About that… As much as I value your advice, I… I can't stay away from her, man." He shrugged sheepishly. "I'm seeing her tonight, in fact."

Becker frowned, but before he could respond, the ref's whistle pierced the air and both men looked over to see who'd taken a penalty. Wyatt. Big surprise there.

There was no more time for chatting as Stan tossed them both back onto the ice for the penalty kill, and although Becker scored a ridiculously incredible shorthanded goal, it wasn't enough. The buzzer went off indicating the end of the third period and the game. The final score was a pathetic 5–1, Vipers.

IT DIDN'T TAKE a genius to figure out the Warriors had lost the game. Hayden could see it on every face that left the Lincoln Center. Her father was probably dreadfully disappointed.

She was tempted to go up to the owner's box and offer some sort of condolences, but she was in no mood to see her dad right now. If she were, she'd be inside the arena instead of loitering in the parking lot and waiting for Brody.

She leaned against the back of his SUV and scanned the rear entrance of the building, willing him to come out. God, this day had been hell. Listening to Sheila's awful tale of Presley's drinking, hearing Doug's heart break on the other end of the telephone line. She didn't want to think about any of it anymore. That's why she'd left the penthouse and driven over here. The need to see Brody and lose herself in his arms was so strong she'd been willing to wait for over an hour.

When he finally emerged from the building she almost sobbed with relief. And when his midnight-blue eyes lit up at the sight of her, she wanted to sob with joy. Maybe their lives didn't mesh, maybe their careers were colossally different and their goals weren't aligned, but she couldn't remember the last time a man had looked so happy to see her.

"Hey, this is a surprise," he said, approaching her.

"Hi." She paused. "I'm sorry about the game. Does this mean the team is out of the play-offs?"

"No, the series is tied. We've got another chance to win it tomorrow."

"That's good."

For some reason, she couldn't tear her eyes from him. He looked good tonight. His hair was damp, his perfect lips slightly chapped. He'd confessed to licking them too much during games and the first time she'd seen him rubbing on lip balm she'd almost had a laughter-induced coronary. But she liked moments like that, seeing Brody out of his manly man element.

Tonight, though, he was all man. Clad in a loose wool suit that couldn't hide the defined muscles underneath it. The navy-blue color made his eyes seem even brighter, more vivid. Brody had told her that with play-offs around the corner, the league expected the players to look professional on and off the ice and, she had to admit, she liked seeing him in a suit as much as she enjoyed his faded jeans and ab-hugging T-shirts.

Unable to stop herself, she stood on her tiptoes and planted a kiss square on his mouth.

"What happened to not being seen together in public?"

She faltered, realizing this was the first time they'd ever engaged in a public display of affection and startled that she'd been the one to initiate it. "I…had a bad day" was all she could come up with.

Brody grinned. "That's all it takes for us to come out of the closet, you having a bad day? Damn, I should've pissed you off a long time ago." His expression sobered. "What happened?"

"I'll tell you all about it later. Let's get out of here first."

"Meet you at the hotel?"

She was about to nod when something stopped her. "No. How about we go to your place tonight?"

He seemed baffled, and she honestly couldn't say she blamed him. Since she'd agreed to explore this…thing…between them, they'd been doing things her way. Brody had asked her over to his house a dozen times but she'd always convinced him to stay at the penthouse instead. She'd felt that being on her own turf, sticking to familiar surroundings, would stop things from getting more serious than she wanted.

Yet suddenly she found herself longing to see Brody's house, to be with him on *his* turf.

"All right." He unlocked the door of his SUV. "You want to follow me in your car?"

"Why don't we just take yours? We can come back for my rental tomorrow."

His eyebrows soared north again, while his jaw dipped south. "You're just full of surprises tonight, aren't you? You do realize your father will see your car in the lot and know you didn't go home?"

"I don't live my life to please my dad." She sounded more bitter than she'd intended, so she softened her tone. "Let's not talk about him. All I want to think about tonight is you and me."

He gently tucked an unruly strand of hair behind her ear. "I like the sound of that."

The drive to Brody's Hyde Park home was a short one. When they pulled up in front of his place, Hayden was pleasantly surprised to see a large Victorian with a wrap-around porch and a second-floor balcony. Flowers were beginning to bloom in the beds flanking the front steps, giving the house a cheerful, inviting air.

"Weren't expecting this, were you?" he said as he shut off the engine.

"Not really." She smiled. "Don't tell me you actually planted all those flowers yourself?"

"Heck no. I didn't choose the house, either. My mom flew out here when I was drafted by the Warriors, and she found the house. She did all the gardening, too, and she visits once a year to make sure I haven't destroyed her handiwork."

They got out of the car and drifted up the cobbled path

toward the front door. Inside, Hayden's surprise only grew. Decorated in warm shades of red and brown, the interior boasted a roomy living room complete with a stone fireplace, a wide maple staircase leading upstairs and an enormous modern kitchen with two glass doors opening onto the backyard.

"Want something to drink?" he offered, crossing the tiled floor toward the fridge. "I don't have that herbal tea you like, but I can brew you a cup of Earl Grey."

"How about something stronger?"

He gave a faint smile. "You really did have a bad day, didn't you?"

He moved to the wine rack on the counter and chose a bottle of red wine. Grabbing two glasses from the cupboard over the sink, he glanced over his shoulder. "Are you going to tell me about it or do I have to tickle it out of you?"

"Hmm." She chewed on her bottom lip. "I'm kind of leaning toward the tickle." Her expression sobered when he shot her an evil look. "Fine, fine… I'll tell you."

Brody poured the wine, handed her a glass and then led her to the patio doors. The backyard was spacious, adorned with more flowers that Brody's mom must have planted. The fence surrounding the area was so high she couldn't see the neighboring yards, not even from the raised deck on the patio. At the very far corner of the lawn stood an idyllic-looking gazebo surrounded by thick foliage.

They stepped onto the deck, where a surprisingly warm breeze met them. It was a gorgeous night, the warmest she'd experienced since coming home, and she breathed in the fresh air and tilted her head to admire the cloudless sky before finally releasing a long breath.

"I paid a visit to my stepmother today," she said.

She filled him in on the details, leaving her conversation

with Doug for the end. Brody's jaw tensed at the mention of Doug's name, but as he'd promised her that night they'd skated at the arena, he didn't freak out about it. When she'd finished, he set his wineglass on the wide rail ringing the deck and gently caressed her shoulders.

"You didn't have to tell him about us," he said.

The remark surprised her. "Of course I did. I told *you* about *him*. Doesn't he deserve the same courtesy?" She lifted her glass to her lips.

"You're right." He paused. "So it's over between you and Doug?"

"Yes," she admitted. "He hung up on me, which is very uncharacteristic of him. I don't think he's happy with me at the moment."

When Brody didn't answer, she put down her wine and reached up to cup his strong chin with her hands. "You're not happy with me, either, are you?"

He looked her in the eye and said, "I *am* happy, babe."

"You are?"

"I love being with you, Hayden." He blew out a ragged breath. "And I'm glad it's over with Doug. It was frustrating sometimes, knowing there was another man in your life. And not just any man, but a man who works in your field, who shares your passion for art and is probably much better at those intellectual conversations you're always trying to have with me. I feel like a dumb oaf in comparison."

A pained look flashed across his handsome face, and it took her a moment to realize it wasn't really pain she saw in his eyes, but vulnerability. The idea that Brody Croft, the most masculine man she'd ever met, could be vulnerable stole the breath from her lungs. God, did he actually feel inadequate? Had *she* made him feel that way?

Her heart squeezed at the thought and she found herself

reaching for him. She twined her arms around his strong, corded neck and brushed her lips over his. "You're not a dumb oaf," she murmured, running her fingers over the damp hair curling at the nape of his neck.

"Then you won't mind if I make an intelligent, rational point about how difficult you're being."

She raised her chin. "And what on earth am I being difficult about?"

Brody let out a breath. "Come on, Hayden, you think I don't see that look in your eyes whenever I have a plane to catch? Every time I left town this week you withdrew from me. I felt it."

Discomfort coiled inside her belly, causing her to drop her arms from his neck. Why was he bringing this up?

"See, you're doing it again," he pointed out, smiling faintly.

"I just…" She inhaled slowly. "I don't see why it's an issue."

"If it keeps you from entering into a relationship with me, then it *is* an issue."

A tiny spark of panic lit up inside her. "We agreed to keep things casual."

"*You* agreed to keep an open mind."

"Trust me, my mind is very open."

"Your heart isn't." His tone was so gentle she felt like crying.

She drifted over to the railing, curling her fingers over the cool steel. Brody moved so they were standing side by side, but she couldn't look at him. She knew exactly where this conversation was going, and she had no idea how to proceed.

"I think we have something really good here," he said quietly, resting his hand on hers and slowly stroking her knuckles. "You've got to admit we're good together, Hayden. Sexually, sure, but in other areas, as well. We never run out of things to talk about, we enjoy each other's company, we make each other laugh."

She finally turned her head and met his eyes. "I know we're good together, okay?"

It was incredibly hard admitting it, but it was the truth. Brody made her body sing, he made her heart soar, and she couldn't imagine any other man doing that. But she also couldn't imagine them ever having a stable life together.

"But I want someone I can build a home with." Tears pricked her eyelids. "I want to have kids, and a white picket fence, a dog. I did the whole hockey-lifestyle as a kid. I don't want to be sitting on airplanes for half the year, and when I have children, I don't want to be home alone with them while their father is gone."

He was silent for a moment. "I won't play hockey forever," he said finally.

"Do you plan on retiring soon?"

After a beat of hesitation, he said, "No."

Disappointment thundered inside her, but really, what was she expecting? That he'd throw his arms around her and say, *Yes, Hayden, I'll retire! Tomorrow! Now! Let's build a life together!*

It wasn't fair to ask him to give up a career he obviously loved, but she also wasn't willing to give up her own goals and dreams. She knew what she wanted from a relationship, and no matter how much she loved being with Brody, he couldn't give that to her.

"I wish you'd reconsider," he murmured. He shifted her around and moved closer so that his body was flush against hers. "Damn, we fit so well together."

She rubbed her pelvis against his. They did fit. Even

though he was a head taller, their bodies seemed to mesh in the most basic way, and when he was inside her... God, when he was inside her she'd never felt more complete.

A soft moan escaped her lips at the delicious image of Brody's hardness filling her, and suddenly the tension of the day drained from her body and dissolved into a pool of warmth between her legs. Suddenly everything they'd just been talking about didn't seem to matter. Brody's job, her need for stability—it all faded away the moment he pressed his body to hers.

"Let's not talk anymore," she whispered. "Please, Brody, no more talking."

Her arousal must have been written all over her face because he ran his hands down her back and squeezed her buttocks. "You've got a one-track mind," he grumbled.

"Says the man who's fondling my ass," she murmured, relieved that the tension had eased. The heavy weight of the painful revelations they'd just shared floated away like a feather.

Brody bent his head and covered her mouth with his. The kiss took her breath away, made her sag into his rock-hard chest as his greedy tongue explored the crevices of her mouth. Keeping one hand on her ass, he moved the other one to the front of her slacks, deftly popped open the button and tugged at the thin material.

Pulling back, he pushed her slacks off her body, waited for her to step out of them, then tossed them aside. Goose bumps rose on her thighs the second the night air hit her skin. She wore a pair of black bikini panties that Brody quickly disposed of.

"Your neighbors can see us," she protested when he reached for her blouse.

"Not where we're going." He quickly removed her shirt

and bra, then lifted her into his arms and headed for the steps of the deck.

She wriggled in his embrace, self-conscious about her naked body being carried around in his backyard, but he kept a tight grip on her. Quickening his strides, he moved across the grass toward the gazebo, ascended the small set of stairs leading into it and set her on her feet.

Her heels made a clicking noise as they connected with the cedar floor of the little structure. She looked around the gazebo, admiring the intricate woodwork and plush white love seat tucked in the corner. When she turned back to Brody, he was as naked as she was.

She laughed. "Let me guess, sex in the gazebo is one of *your* fantasies?"

"Oh, yeah. I've wanted to do this since the moment this damn thing was built."

"What, none of your hockey groupies ever wanted to do it in the wilderness of your backyard?" she teased.

"I've never brought a woman home before."

She forced her jaw to stay closed. He'd never brought a woman home before? The implications of that statement troubled her, but she didn't feel like dwelling on them now. As she'd said, no more talking.

At the moment, all she wanted to do was fulfill this gorgeous man's fantasy.

CHAPTER ELEVEN

HE'D STARTLED HER with his admission. He'd seen it in Hayden's eyes the moment he'd confessed to never having brought a woman home, but fortunately that flicker of wariness had faded. Her eyes now glimmered with passion, and he loved that she wasn't complaining about the way he'd stripped her naked and carried her out to the gazebo.

Lord, she turned him on in the fiercest way. He'd sensed the untamed passion in her the moment they'd met, experienced it that first night when he'd made love to her on the hallway floor, reveled in it the night she'd tied him up to her bed and devoured his body. She was full of surprises, and he couldn't get enough of her. He loved her sass and her intelligence and her dry humor, the way she challenged him and aroused him and made him feel like more than just a hockey player.

"So what does the fantasy involve?" she asked, resting her hands on her bare hips.

He swept his gaze over her curvy body, trying to put his needs into words. He had no idea how the fantasy played out, only that his hands tingled with the urge to fondle her full, perky breasts and slip between her shapely legs.

The night breeze grew stronger, snaking into the gazebo and making his cock swell and thicken as the warm air caressed it. The wind also succeeded in hardening Hayden's small, pink nipples, which were now standing up as if demanding his attention.

But instead of reaching out to touch her, he cleared his throat and said, "Lie down on the love seat."

There was no objection. Her heels clacked against the floor as she walked over to the small couch and draped herself over the cushions. When she reached for the clasp on her right shoe he held up his hand. "Leave them on," he ordered.

"Why do men always get turned-on by a naked woman in high heels?"

"Because it's damn hot," he replied with a roll of his eyes.

"So are you just going to stand there and watch me, or do you plan to join me?"

"Eventually."

They were the same words they'd spoken to each other the night she'd admitted her taste for bondage, only this time he was the one in charge. He leaned against the railing of the gazebo and crossed his arms over his chest. "You've gotta give me some incentive, babe."

"Hmm. Like this kind of incentive?" She slid her hands to her breasts.

His breath hitched when she squeezed the lush mounds with her palms, the motion making her tits look bigger, fuller. With an impish smile, she stroked the underside of each breast, circling her nipples with her fingers and then dragging her thumbs over each hard bud.

He almost fell over backward at the sight of Hayden fondling her own breasts. His mouth was so dry he could barely swallow. He allowed her to play for a bit, then narrowed his eyes and muttered, "Spread your legs."

She did, and his breath caught in his throat again. From where he stood he could see every tantalizing inch of her glistening sex. He wanted to lick those smooth pink folds, shove his tongue inside that sweet paradise and make Hayden scream with pleasure, but he held back. His erection throbbed as he curled his fingers over his shaft.

Making slow, lazy strokes to his cock, he gave her a heavy-lidded look and said, "Touch yourself."

"Sure you don't want to do that for me?" Her voice came out throaty, so full of unbridled lust he almost came on the spot.

"Humor me," he squeezed out.

"It's your fantasy." She shrugged, grinned, and promptly lowered her hand between her legs.

Oh, man, this woman was incredible. His eyes nearly popped out of his head as she dragged her index finger down her slick folds and rubbed her swollen sex.

"That's it," he said hoarsely. "Get yourself nice and hot, Hayden."

She replied with a soft whimper. Her cheeks grew flushed the more she kept stroking herself. The hazy look in her eyes told him she was close, but her fingers continued to avoid the one place he knew would drive her over the edge.

She lifted her hand. "Brody," she murmured anxiously.

He chuckled. "Uh-uh. You won't be getting any help from me."

Agitation flickered in her eyes but still he remained on the other side of the gazebo. After a moment she gave a strangled groan and her hand returned between her thighs.

And then she came.

His hand froze over his erection. He was one dangerous

stroke from a release he wasn't ready for, but for the life of him he couldn't tear his eyes from the gorgeous woman climaxing in front of him. Arching her back, Hayden cried out, moan after moan filling the warm night. Any neighbor by an open window could've heard her, but she didn't seem to care, and neither did Brody. He was a professional hockey player; his neighbors probably expected female moans of ecstasy to drift out of his house.

He leaned back against the rail and relished every moment, from the contented sighs that slipped out of her throat to the way she'd spread her legs even wider, her heels still strapped to her feet.

When she finally grew still, he crooked his finger at her. Despite the sluggishly sated look in her eyes, she stumbled from the love seat and made her way over to him.

"Has anyone ever told you you're the sexiest woman on the planet?" he murmured before dropping a kiss on her lips.

She responded with a lethargic smile. The remnants of orgasm he saw flashing across her delicate face only made him harder. Suddenly impatient, he bent down and grabbed a condom from the pocket of his jeans, then smoothed it over his throbbing shaft. Without giving her time to recover, he gripped her hips with both hands, maneuvered her around so her ass was pressed against his hard-on and drove his unbelievably stiff cock inside her damp sex.

She moaned, leaning forward and clutching at the railing with her hands. The move caused her bottom to rise, allowing him even better access. He withdrew slowly, rotated his hips the way he knew she liked, then plunged right back in to the hilt.

"This is going to be fast," he warned, his voice sounding gruff and apologetic to his ears. He wanted to make it last for her, but the way his cock kept pulsating, he knew it wouldn't be long before he toppled over that cliff into oblivion.

"I love everything you do to me. Fast, slow, hard, I don't care. Just make love to me."

The whispered reply brought a smile to his lips, but it was the phrase *make love* that caused his chest to tighten. It was the first time she'd referred to what they were doing as making love, and hearing the words brought a rush of pleasure so great his knees almost buckled.

He suddenly felt the primal need to claim this woman. Quickening his pace, he thrust into her, again and again, until his orgasm slithered down his spine, clutched at his balls, and the world in front of him fragmented in shards of light. He shuddered, palming a sweet breast with one hand while stroking the small of Hayden's back with the other, wanting to hold on to her for as long as possible.

He wrapped his arms around her from behind and nuzzled her neck, inhaling the scent of her vanilla and lavender body lotion. She gave a breathy sigh and murmured, "Your fantasies are almost as good as mine."

"Almost as good?" He laughed. "Wait until *I* tie *you* up. Then we'll see who has the hottest fantasy."

She disentangled herself from his embrace and turned to kiss him. Then she drifted to the entrance of the gazebo. "Think any of your neighbors will see me streaking through the yard?"

"*Now* you're self-conscious?"

She offered a rueful look. "I guess you're right. The whole neighborhood probably heard me, huh?"

"You are kinda loud…"

He bent down and grabbed his wool trousers, pulling them up his hips. Finding his shirt and jacket, he tucked them under his arm, walked over to Hayden and extended his arm. "Shall I walk the unclothed lady to the house?"

"You could at least let me wear your shirt."

"Nope. I want to experience the splendor of your body during this evening stroll."

"Screw strolling. I'm running."

Before he could blink she bounded down the gazebo's steps and tore across the yard, her firm ass pale in the moonlight. Laughing, he took off after her, hoping to keep her naked just a little bit longer, but she was already slipping her sweater over her head when he reached the deck.

"Spoilsport," he grumbled.

She put on her panties and slacks, then gestured to the back door. "You still have to give me a tour of the upstairs," she reminded him.

"Any room in particular you'd like to see?"

"Definitely one that features a bed. Or a removable showerhead."

With a grin, he grabbed their wineglasses from the railing and followed her inside. "Do you want more wine?" he asked.

"No, thanks."

She suddenly went quiet as he placed the glasses in the sink, and when he turned to look at her he saw her expression had grown somber.

"You okay?" he asked.

"I'm fine." She let out a breath. "I was thinking about my dad."

Brody made a face. "We just had mind-blowing sex and you're thinking about your dad?"

"It's just...the wine." She gestured to the bottle still sitting on the cedar counter. "It made me think about what

Sheila told me today. You know, about my dad's drinking…"
Her voice trailed, the distress in her eyes unmistakable.

"Are you going to talk to him about it?"

"Yes. No." She exhaled again. "I don't want to confront
him right now, not when he's smack in the middle of this
scandal."

"We're all in the middle of it now. We were told today
that the investigation is under way. All the players are being
interviewed this week."

Her green eyes glimmered with distress. "What kind of
questions will you be asked?"

Brody shrugged. "They'll probably ask us what we know
about the allegations, try to coax confessions out of us, quiz
us about whether we know if another player was involved."

"Are they going to ask about my dad?"

He nodded.

Resting her hands against the counter, she went silent
for a moment, her pretty features shadowed by worry. He
could tell she was upset by all of this, especially with everything she was learning about her father, and though he
had no intention of making her feel worse, he unwittingly
did so with his next statement.

"It was pretty much confirmed to me today that your dad
fixed those games."

Her gaze rose to meet his, her mouth forming a startled
O. "You're saying you know for sure that he did it?"

Damn. Maybe he shouldn't have spit it out the way he
had, but the confrontation with Wyatt had been troubling
him all night and he'd been hoping to talk it through with
Hayden before the league's investigator interviewed him.
He knew he'd have to tell the truth if asked, but he'd wanted
her advice, wanted her to tell him how to handle the time

bomb in his hands without looking like he was betraying his teammates or the team owner.

But he hadn't realized confiding in Hayden meant confirming her doubts about her father. Up until now she'd only suspected Presley had fixed those games, but with that one sentence he'd turned those suspicions into reality, and the crestfallen look on her face tugged at his insides in the most powerful way.

He wanted to comfort her, but he didn't know how.

So he kept his distance, leaned against the counter and released a slow breath. "Yes, he did it. I'm ninety-nine-percent sure of it."

"Ninety-nine percent," she repeated. "Then there's still a chance Dad wasn't involved."

"It's unlikely."

"But there's still a chance."

"Look, Hayden, I know you want to see the best in your father, but you're going to need to accept that he's probably guilty."

Her eyes widened, the color in her cheeks fading fast. "Are you going to tell the investigator that? You're going to say my dad is guilty?"

"I don't know what I'm going to say yet."

He could see her legs shaking as she walked across the tiled floor toward him. Eyes wild with panic, she placed one palm on his bare arm and tilted her head to look up at him. "You can't do it, Brody. Please, don't turn against my father."

HAYDEN DIDN'T KNOW where the words were coming from but she seemed to have no control over her vocal cords. In the back of her head she knew what she was asking of him was wrong, that if Presley was truly guilty he deserved to pay for his crimes. But this was her father, the only parent she had, the only constant in her life.

"You want me to lie?" Brody said flatly.

She swallowed. "No, I…maybe if you just didn't say anything…"

"Lying by omission is still lying, Hayden. And what if they straight-out ask me if Presley bribed anyone? What do I do then?"

Desperation clawed up her throat. She knew she had no right asking him to do this for her, but she couldn't watch her father's entire life shatter before her eyes. "He's my only family," she said softly. "I just want to protect him."

Compassion flickered in Brody's eyes, but it quickly faded into annoyance. "What about me? Don't I deserve to be protected, too?"

"Your career isn't at stake," she protested.

"Like hell it isn't!" His eyes flashed. "My integrity and reputation are on the line here, Hayden. I won't throw away my career by lying to protect the team owner, not even for you."

She nearly stumbled backward, assaulted by the force of his words.

She suddenly felt so very stupid. What the hell had she been thinking, asking him to lie for her dad? Her only defense was that she *hadn't* been thinking. For a split second there, the fear seizing her insides was so strong it had overpowered her ability to think logically. Suddenly she'd been the lonely little girl who'd grown up without a mother, who didn't want to see her father carted off to jail even if it meant breaking the rules to keep him out of a cell.

What was the matter with her? She wasn't the type of woman who broke rules. And she didn't condone lies, either.

God, she couldn't believe she'd just asked Brody to throw away his honesty and honor.

With shaky steps, she walked over to him and pressed her face against his chest. She could feel his heart thudding against her ear like a drum. "I'm sorry. I shouldn't have asked you to lie. It was unfair of me to do that. I'm…" She choked on a sob. "I can't believe I just did that."

His warm hand caressed the small of her back. "It's okay. I know you're concerned about him, babe." Brody pressed a kiss to the top of her head.

"I just wish… Damn it, Brody, I want to help him."

"I know," he said gently. "But your dad is the one who got himself into this mess, and I hate to say it, but he's the one who'll have to get himself out of it."

HAYDEN'S CELL PHONE woke her early the next morning, rousing her from a restless sleep and making her groan with displeasure. She was on her side, her back pressed against Brody's big warm body, one of his long arms draped over her chest. She squeezed her eyes shut, waiting for the ringing to stop. A second of blessed silence, and then it rang again. And again. And again.

With a sigh, she disentangled herself from Brody's arms and slid out from under the covers. The sight of the alarm clock on Brody's nightstand made her grimace. Six o'clock. Who on earth was calling her this early?

"Come back to bed," came Brody's sleepy murmur.

"I will after I murder whoever keeps calling," she grumbled, padding barefoot to the armchair under the window. Her clothes and purse were draped over the chair, and she rummaged around in the pile until she found her cell.

Looking at the display, she immediately recognized

Darcy's number. Uh-oh. This probably wasn't good. Not if Darcy was giving up her own beauty sleep to make a call.

Hayden flipped open the phone and said, "What's wrong?"

"Have you seen the morning paper?"

"That's what you woke me up to ask?" Hayden edged to the door, not wanting to disturb Brody. She leaned against the wall in the hallway and added, "And what are you doing up early enough to read the morning paper? Do you even subscribe to the paper?"

"I never went to bed last night." Hayden could practically see the grin on her best friend's face. "And, no, I don't get the paper. But Marco does. Marco, by the way, is my new personal trainer."

"At the rate you're going, you'll never be able to find a permanent gym, Darce." She let out a breath. "Now tell me what's so important about today's newspaper."

"You."

"Me?"

"You're in it, hon. Front page of the sports section, with your hockey player's tongue in your mouth and his hands on your ass."

She nearly choked. "You're making it up!"

"I'm afraid not."

Horror lodged in her throat. Darcy sounded serious. And if Darcy couldn't make a smart-ass remark about it, then it must be bad.

"I'll call you back in a minute," Hayden blurted, disconnecting the call.

The T-shirt Brody had given her to sleep in hung all the way down to her knees, but her arms were bare and goose bumps had risen on her skin. She wrapped her arms around her chest and hurried down the stairs two at a time. In the front hall, she unlocked the door and poked her head out, darting forward when she saw the rolled-up newspaper on the porch. The wooden floor was cool under her feet, making her shiver. Snatching up the newspaper, she headed back inside, pulling the paper from its protective plastic as she wandered into the living room.

She sank down on the couch, found the sports section, and gasped. Darcy was right. The first page boasted a large photograph of her and Brody in the Warrior arena parking lot. It must have been taken the moment she'd stood up on her toes to kiss him, and there was no mistaking it, his hands really were on her butt.

The caption read, "Warriors forward cozies up to team owner's daughter."

But it was the article beneath it that drained all the color from her face. She read it twice, not missing a single word, then set the paper on the cushion next to her and dropped her head into her hands.

"What happened?"

She jerked up at the sound of Brody's drowsy voice, to see him standing in the doorway wearing nothing but a pair of navy-blue boxers and a concerned expression.

Without a word, Hayden pointed to the newspaper beside her. After a second of hesitation, Brody joined her on the couch and picked up the section.

She watched his face as he read the article, but he gave nothing away. Blinked a couple of times, frowned once, and finally rose slowly to his feet. "I need coffee," he muttered before walking out of the room.

Hayden stared after him in bewilderment, then shot up and rushed into the kitchen. Brody was already turning on the coffeemaker, leaning against the counter with a look of utter disbelief in his gorgeous blue eyes.

"They're saying I took a bribe," he said softly.

She moved toward him and rested her hand on his strong bicep. "It's just speculation, Brody. They don't have any proof."

"They have a *source!*" he burst out, his voice resonating with anger. "Someone actually told that reporter I took bribes from your father. This isn't a tabloid, where the so-called reporters make up sources to suit their story. Greg Michaels is an award-winning sports journalist—and someone on the team told him I took a goddamn bribe!"

Hayden's mouth went completely dry. She could barely keep up with the range of emotions flashing across Brody's face. Anger and betrayal and dismay. Shock and disgust. Fear. She wanted desperately to hold him, but his posture was so tense, his shoulders stiff, his jaw tight, every aspect of his body language screaming *back off!*

"Someone is trying to ruin me," he snapped. "Who the hell would do that? I know Wyatt is up to his ears in this mess, but I can't see him casting suspicion on me. He told me to stay out of it."

His eyes were suddenly on her, focused, sharp, as if realizing she was in the room with him. "They think you're sleeping with me to shut me up about your father's part in it." He laughed humorlessly.

Sympathy welled up inside her, squeezing her heart like a vise. "It's going to be okay, Brody. Everything will get cleared up when you meet with the interviewer."

Another chuckle, this time laced with bitterness. "All it takes is one black mark on your name and teams look at you differently."

The coffeemaker clicked, and Brody turned his attention to it. Grabbing a mug from the cabinet over the sink, he slammed it down on the counter, filled it to the brim with coffee and swallowed a gulp of the scalding liquid, not even wincing.

Hayden had no idea what to say. How to make this better for him. So instead she just stood there, waiting, watching his face, trying to anticipate the next outburst.

But she wasn't ready for what he said next.

"I think maybe we should cool things off for a bit."

Shock slammed into her. "What?"

Setting down his mug, Brody rubbed his forehead. "I can't be dragged down along with your father," he said, so quietly she barely heard him. "If you and I are seen together, the rumors and suspicions will only grow. My career..."

He let out a string of curses. "I've worked my ass off to get to where I am, Hayden. I grew up wearing second-hand clothes and watching my parents struggle to afford anything. And finally, finally, I'm in a position to support myself, to support them. I can't lose that. I *won't* lose it."

"You're breaking up with me?"

He dragged his fingers through his hair, his eyes tortured. "I'm saying maybe we should put...us...on hold. Until the investigation concludes and the scandal blows over."

"You want to put us on hold," she echoed dully.

"Yes."

She turned away, resting her hands on the kitchen counter to steady herself. He was breaking up with her? Sorry, putting things on *hold.* Not that it made a difference. Regardless of the way he wanted to word it, Brody was pretty much telling her he didn't want her around.

Everything he'd said last night about how good they were for each other, how well they fit...what had happened to all that, huh?

The memory of the words he'd spoken only yesterday caused the bitterness swimming through her body to grow stronger. It was like a current, forcing all reason from her mind and pushing her into an eddy of resentment she knew too well. How many times had her father chosen his hockey team over her? How many times had the men in her life let their careers take the front seat while she sat in the back begging to be noticed?

"All right. If that's what you want," she said, unable to stop her tone from sounding clipped and angry. "I guess you need to look out for yourself, after all."

His eyes clouded. "Don't make it sound like that, Hayden. Like I don't give a damn about you. Because I *do* give a damn. You can't fault me for also giving a damn about everything I've worked so hard for."

She edged away from the counter, suddenly wanting to flee. Maybe it was for the best, ending it now. They'd already reached an impasse yesterday, when she'd told him his lifestyle didn't fit what she wanted in a relationship. Maybe it was better to break things off now, before it got even harder.

But although it made sense in her head, her heart couldn't stop weeping at the idea of not being with Brody.

Silence stretched between them, until Brody released a frustrated curse and raked his hands through his dark hair. "I care about you, Hayden. The last thing I want to do is end this." He shook his head, looking determined. "And I don't see it as an ending. I just want this mess to go away. I want my name cleared and my career unaffected. When it all dies down, we can pick up where we left off."

She couldn't help but laugh. "Because it's that easy, right?" Her laughter died, replaced with a tired frown. "It would have ended anyway, Brody. Sooner or later."

Anguish flooded his gaze. "Come on, don't say that. This break doesn't have to be permanent."

"Maybe it should." A sob wedged in her throat and it took every ounce of willpower she possessed to swallow it back. "We're probably doing ourselves a favor by letting go now. Maybe it will end up saving us both a lot of heart-ache in the future."

He opened his mouth to respond, but she didn't give him the chance. Blinking back the tears stinging her eyelids, she headed back to the bedroom to find her clothes.

CHAPTER TWELVE

THE CAB RIDE to the arena, where she'd left her car, was probably the most mortifying experience of Hayden's life. Somehow, while she'd gotten dressed, called the cab, murmured a soft goodbye to Brody, she'd managed to rein in her emotions. But the second she slid into the backseat and watched Brody's beautiful house disappear in the rearview mirror, she'd burst into tears.

Looking stunned, the taxi driver handed her a small packet of tissues then promptly ignored her. Despite the tears fogging her eyes she noticed the man shooting her strange looks in the mirror. Apparently it wasn't every day that a brokenhearted woman in tears rode in his cab.

And *brokenhearted* was the only word she could come up with to describe how she felt right now. Although she'd told Brody the breakup was for the best, her heart was aching so badly it felt like someone had scraped it with a razor blade. All she wanted to do was go back to the penthouse, crawl under the covers and cry.

The cab driver dropped her at the arena, where she got into her rental car, swiped at her wet eyes and took a few calming breaths.

Fifteen excruciatingly long minutes later, she was walking into the hotel, hoping nobody noticed her blotchy face. In the lobby, the clerk behind the check-in desk gestured at her. She reluctantly headed over and was surprised when he said, "There's a man waiting for you in the bar."

Hope and happiness soared inside her. Brody? He would've definitely had time to get here before her, since she'd had to pick up her car. Maybe he realized how foolish it was to end things because of something a reporter had written.

She hurried across the marble floor toward the large oak doors leading into the hotel bar. Only a few patrons were inside, and when she searched for Brody's massive shoulders and unruly dark hair, she came up empty-handed. Disappointment crashed into her like a tidal wave. Of course he wasn't here. He'd made it clear back at his place that he couldn't risk his career by being seen with her.

She glanced around again, then gasped when her attention landed on a man she'd dismissed during her first inspection.

Doug.

Oh, God. What was *he* doing here?

"Hayden!" He walked toward her with a timid smile.

She stared at him, taking in the familiar sight of his blond hair, arranged in a no-nonsense haircut. His pale blue eyes, serious as always. That lean, trim body he kept in shape at the university gym. He wore a pair of starched tan slacks and a crisp, white button-down shirt, and the conservative attire kind of irked her. Everything about Doug was neat and orderly and unbelievably tedious. She found herself longing for even the tiniest bit of disorder. An undone button. A coffee stain. A patch of stubble he'd missed while shaving.

But there was nothing disorderly about this man. He was

like a perfectly wrapped gift that only used three efficient pieces of tape and featured a little bow with the same length tails. The kind of gift you hesitated to open because you'd feel like an ass messing it up.

Brody, on the other hand... Now he was a gift you tore open the second you got it—the exterior didn't matter because you knew what it contained inside was a million times better anyway.

Tears stung her eyes at the thought.

"Hi," Doug said gently. "It's good to see you."

She wanted to tell him it was good to see him, too, but the words refused to come out. They stared at each other for a moment, and then he was pulling her into an awkward embrace. She halfheartedly hugged him back, noticing that the feel of his arms around her had no effect on her whatsoever.

"I know I shouldn't have come," Doug said, releasing her. "But after the way we left things... I thought we needed to talk. In person."

"You're right." She swallowed. "Do you want to come up?"

He nodded.

Without a word, they walked out of the bar and headed for the elevator. Silence stretched between them as they rode the car up to the penthouse. Hayden wanted to apologize to him again, and yet she wasn't sure she felt apologetic anymore. She and Doug had been on a break when she'd started seeing Brody, and though she regretted hurting Doug, she couldn't will up any regret about what she felt for Brody.

"I was shocked when you told me that you were seeing someone else," Doug began when they stepped into the suite.

"I know." Guilt tugged at her gut. "I'm sorry I just dropped it on you like that, and over the phone, but I had to be honest."

"I'm glad you were." He stepped closer, his eyes glimmering with something she couldn't put a finger on. "And it was the kick in the behind I needed, Hayden. It made me realize how much I don't want to lose you."

He reached out and tenderly stroked her cheek.

Discomfort crept up her spine.

"I love you, Hayden," Doug said earnestly. "I should have said it a long time ago, but I wanted to go slow. I guess I was going *too* slow. I'm sorry."

He moved closer, but he didn't touch her again, or kiss her, just offered an affectionate smile and said, "I decided we've waited long enough. I want us to cross that bridge. I want us to make love."

No, not the intimacy bridge. Hysterical laughter bubbled inside her throat. "Doug—"

"It's finally the right time, Hayden."

Maybe it's the right time for you, she wanted to say. But for her, that perfect moment she might've shared with Doug had slipped away the second Brody Croft had walked into her life.

He reached out for her again, but she moved back, guilty when she saw the hurt in his eyes.

"It's not the right time," she said quietly. "And I think there's a reason we never got to this point before, Doug. I think...it wasn't meant to be."

He went still. "I see," he said, his voice stiff.

She took hold of his hand, squeezing his fingers tightly. "You know I'm right, Doug. Would you honestly be saying all of this, now, if I hadn't met someone else?"

"Yes." But his voice lacked conviction.

"I think we got together because it was comfortable. We

were friends, colleagues, two people who liked each other well enough…but we're not soul mates, Doug."

Pain circled her heart. She hated saying these words to him, but there was no other choice.

Being with Brody had made her realize that she wasn't going to settle for a man just because he happened to be nice and dependable. As wild and sexy and unpredictable as Brody was, he was also honest and tender, more intelligent than he gave himself credit for, strong, funny, generous… Oh, God, had she fallen in love with him?

No, she couldn't have. Brody was just a fling. He might have some wonderful traits, but his career would constantly keep him away from her. She wanted someone safe, someone solid. Not someone who was so big and bold and arrogant and passionate and temporary and— Damn it!

She loved him. And wasn't it ridiculously ironic that she'd figured it out the day he broke up with her.

"Hayden? Please don't cry, honey."

She glanced up to see Doug's worried expression, then touched her cheeks and felt the tears. She quickly wiped them away. "Doug… I'm sorry," she murmured, not knowing what else to say.

He nodded. "I know. I'm sorry, too." He tilted his head, looking a bit confused. "But I don't see what's so wrong with comfortable."

"There's nothing wrong with it. But I want more than comfort. I want…love and passion and… I want *earth-shattering.*"

He gave her a rueful smile. "I don't have much experience in shattering a woman's world, I'm afraid."

No, but Brody did.

Unfortunately, he also had plenty of experience in shattering a woman's *heart*.

TWO DAYS LATER Hayden woke up feeling confused, devastated and angry. The anger surprised her, but most of it was directed at herself anyway. She'd tossed and turned all night, thinking about what a mess she'd gotten herself into since she'd come back to Chicago. She'd propositioned a stranger, then proceeded to fall in love with him. She'd hurt Doug. Discovered her father had a drinking problem and was probably a criminal.

And what exactly are you doing to fix any of it? a little voice chastised.

She forced herself into a sitting position, her anger escalating. What *was* she doing to fix it? She'd spent all day yesterday lying on the couch in her sweatpants. She'd watched the Warriors play the Vipers, trying to catch glimpses of Brody. And when the team had lost, her heart ached for him. The Warriors were officially out of the play-offs, and she knew how disappointed Brody must be. She'd been so tempted to call and tell him she was sorry. Instead, she'd devoured a carton of ice cream and gone to bed at ten o'clock.

How was that going to help anything? She wasn't the type to let problems pile up without looking for solutions, and although she might not be able to "fix" Doug's broken heart or Brody's decision to stay away from her, she sure as hell could do something about her father.

Jumping out of bed, she threw on some clothes, headed for the bathroom to wash up, then stepped into the elevator with renewed energy and determination.

Enough was enough. She needed to look her dad in the eye and demand the truth from him. This scandal was affecting her, too, and she deserved to know whether or not the trust and faith she'd placed in her father was justified. Presley's mess had taken her away from Doug and brought her to Chicago, it had broken up her and Brody, caused stress to tangle inside her. It was time to quit avoiding her father and try to make sense of everything that had happened.

She drove to the Lincoln Center with a heavy heart, knowing her dad was scheduled to be interviewed by the league investigator today. Come to think of it, Brody was being interviewed, too. She hoped she wouldn't run into him. If she did, she'd be tempted to hurl herself into his arms, and she had no desire to be pushed away again.

Ironic that she'd been fighting this relationship from day one, set on keeping it a fling, and in the end he'd been the one to break things off.

And she'd been the one to fall in love.

Forcing the painful thoughts from her mind, she parked the car and walked to the arena's entrance. After greeting the woman at the lobby desk, she rode the elevator up to the second floor, which housed the franchise offices.

Her father's office was at the end of the hall, through a pair of intimidating wood doors more suited for a president than the owner of a hockey team. Tucked off to the right was the desk of her dad's secretary, a pleasant woman named Kathy who was nowhere to be found.

Hayden walked up to the doors, but stopped when her dad's voice practically boomed out of the walls. He sounded angry.

She slowly turned the knob and inched open the door, then froze when she heard her dad say, "I know I promised to cover your ass, Becker, but this is getting out of hand."

Becker... Becker...hadn't Brody shown up at the Gallagher Club with a player named Becker?

Her blood ran cold. She knew she shouldn't stand there and listen, but she couldn't bring herself to announce her presence.

"I don't give a damn about that...they won't trace the money..."

Enough. She'd had enough.

Feeling sick to her stomach, Hayden pushed open the door and strode into her father's office. He was standing behind his desk, clutching the phone to his ear, and he nearly dropped the receiver when he saw her enter.

"I have to go," he said into the phone, hanging up without giving the other person—Becker?—a chance to respond.

Hayden inched closer, fighting the urge to throw up as she stared into her father's eyes. His face had gone pale, and she could see his hands trembling as he waited for her to approach.

"So it's true," she said flatly, not bothering with any pleasantries.

Her dad had the nerve to feign ignorance. "I don't know what you're talking about, sweetheart."

"Bullshit!" Her voice trembled with anger. "I heard what you said just now!"

Silence hung over the room. Her father looked stunned by her outburst. After a second, he lowered himself into his leather chair, gave her a repentant look and released a heavy sigh. "You shouldn't have eavesdropped, Hayden. I didn't want you involved in any of this."

"You didn't want me involved? Is that why you asked me to come home? Is that why you practically forced me to give a deposition in your divorce? So I wouldn't be involved? Too late, Dad. I already am."

Her legs barely carried her as she stumbled over to one of the plush burgundy visitor's chairs and sank into it. It was hard to think over the roar of her pulse in her ears. Anger and disgust and sadness mingled in her blood, forming a poisonous cocktail that seared through her veins. She couldn't believe this. The signs and suspicions had been there from the start, but hearing her father confirm his criminal actions was like a switchblade to the gut.

If someone had told her that the father she'd loved unconditionally, whose flaws she'd always ignored, whose attention she'd always craved, could be capable of such dishonesty, she would've laughed in their face. And yet it was true. Her father had broken the law. He'd lied. He'd probably cheated on his wife.

When had this man become a stranger to her?

"Honey…" He gulped. Guilt etched into his features. "At least let me explain."

"You committed a crime," she said stiffly. "What's there to explain?"

"I made a mistake." He faltered. "I made some bad investments. I…" Desperation filled his eyes. "It was only two games, Hayden. Only two. I just needed to recover the losses, and… I… I screwed up."

Her belief in him slowly began to shatter, tiny jagged pieces of trust and faith chipping away, ripping into her insides as they sank down to her stomach like sharp little razor blades. How could he have done this? And why hadn't she seen it, damn it?

"Why didn't you call me?" she whispered.

"I was too ashamed." His voice cracked again. "I didn't want you to know I'd destroyed everything I'd built." His eyes looked so tortured Hayden had to turn away. "I never wanted another woman after your mother died. None of the ones I met even compared to her. So I focused on my job instead, first as a coach, and then as an owner. Money was tangible, you know? Something I didn't think I could lose."

When she looked at him again, she was stunned to see tears on her dad's cheeks. "But I did lose it. I lost it and I got scared. I thought I'd lose Sheila, too." He swiped viciously at his wet eyes. "I know part of the reason she married me was for my money. I'm no fool, Hayden. But Sheila and I also loved each other. Sometimes I think I still love her. She's so full of...*life*, I guess. And after so many years of feeling dead, I needed that. I didn't want to lose her. I started drinking too much, trying to forget about what was happening, I guess. Sheila tried to help me, but I wouldn't listen. I didn't want her to think I was weak..."

His voice drifted, his eyes glistening with pain, shame and unshed tears. Tears sprang to Hayden's eyes, too.

She'd never seen her father cry before. It broke her heart. And it hurt even more knowing that she hadn't even noticed while his life was spinning out of control. She knew how much his career and reputation and, yes, his wealth, mattered to him. The threat of losing it had driven him to make such hideous decisions. And she'd been so busy living her own life that she'd failed to be there for her father. Because no matter how dishonorably he'd behaved, he still was her father, and she couldn't write him off just because he'd screwed up.

She rose slowly from the chair and rounded the desk, placing her hand on her dad's shoulder. His head jerked up, his eyes wide with surprise, and then the tears flowed in earnest down his cheeks.

"I'm sorry, Hayden," he choked out.

She wrapped her arms around him and hugged him tightly. "I know you are, Daddy. Don't worry. We're going to get you some help." She swallowed. "And you're...you're going to have to tell the truth today, okay?"

Dropping her arms, she stared into her father's eyes, seeing the remorse and guilt flickering in them. After a moment, he nodded. "You're right," he whispered. "I know I need to face the consequences of my actions."

"I'm here for you, Dad. And if you want me to go to the interview with you, I will."

He shook his head. "It's something I need to do alone."

"I understand."

Her father rubbed his cheeks, then looked up at her and sighed. "Don't you think it's time for *you* to explain?"

"Explain what?" she asked in bewilderment.

"I do read the newspapers, Hayden." He shook his head. "How long have you been seeing Croft?"

Heat flooded her cheeks. "Not long."

"And this affair…you think it's a good idea? Croft isn't your usual type, sweetheart."

"It's not an affair," she blurted out. "I… I love him." She couldn't fight the tears that stung her eyelids. "I want to be with him, Dad."

She paused as the words settled between them. *I want to be with him.* And then she thought of what she'd told her father, just a moment ago. *I'm here for you.*

Why was it so easy for her to say that to her father, but not to Brody? He might not have the stable life she'd always longed for, but didn't he have so many other incredible qualities that more than made up for having to travel every now and then?

She suddenly realized how unfairly she'd treated him, wanting to keep everything on her terms. Fighting him when he tried to make her see they were good for each other.

Well, he was right. They *were* good for each other. Brody was the first man she'd ever been truly herself with. He made her laugh. He drove her wild in bed. He listened.

God, she didn't deserve Brody. All she'd done since the day they'd met was set boundaries, have expectations, find reasons why he wasn't right for her. Yet he'd stayed by her side. Even when she came up with silly rules, or told him he was nothing but a fling. Wasn't that what she claimed to want in a man? Someone solid to stand by her?

And didn't Brody deserve the same thing, a woman who stood by him? He cared about her, she *knew* he did, and if he thought putting their relationship on hold until the scandal blew over was best, maybe she needed to trust him.

She stumbled away from the desk, suddenly knowing what she had to do.

"Hayden?" her dad said quietly.

"I need to take care of something," she answered, inhaling deeply. "We'll talk after your interview, okay? We'll talk about everything."

Her father nodded.

She was halfway out the door when she glanced over her shoulder and added, "And, Daddy? I hope you remember to do the right thing."

BRODY STOOD OUTSIDE the conference room, anxiously tugging at his tie as he waited. Damn, he hated this tie. It was choking the life out of him. Or maybe he found it so hard to breathe because any minute now he'd be sitting in front of three people who could very well destroy his career.

Both explanations were logical, but deep down he knew there was only one reason for the turmoil afflicting his body—Hayden.

He hadn't thought it was possible to miss someone this much. He hadn't been able to stop thinking about her from the second she'd left his house two days ago. Which was probably why his performance during that final game against the Vipers had been less than stellar. But even though the team was out of the play-offs, Brody's disappointment wasn't as great as it should have been. His season had officially ended, and yet he hardly cared. How could he, when his entire body ached for Hayden? Although his brain insisted he'd done the right thing by distancing himself from her, his heart refused to accept the decision. In fact, his heart had been screaming such vile things at him for two days now that he was beginning to feel like the biggest cad on the planet.

Had he made a mistake? He hadn't wanted a permanent break, hadn't intended to end the relationship; he'd just wanted the investigation to be done with, the scandal an unpleasant blip on his memory radar. But Hayden, well, she'd gone and made it permanent. Reverted to her belief that a relationship between them could never have lasted anyway.

Yet he couldn't bring himself to agree. She was wrong about them. If she'd only let down her guard and open her heart she'd see that the two of them could be dynamite together. Not just in bed, but in life. So he traveled for work. He'd have to retire sooner or later, and when he did, he planned on settling down in one place and opening a skating arena that didn't require a membership fee, so that kids from poorer families would have access to the same facilities as those who were better off. He might even coach a kids' team. It was an idea he'd been tossing around for years now.

But instead of planning a future with Hayden, he'd lost her. Maybe he'd never really had her to begin with....

"Croft."

He raised his head, frowning when he spotted Craig Wyatt walking toward him.

Wyatt's massive frame was squeezed into a tailored black suit, his shiny dress shoes squeaking against the tiled floor. The captain's blond hair was gelled back from his forehead.

"What's up?" Brody couldn't stop the twinge of bitterness in his voice.

A muscle twitched in Wyatt's square jaw. "I saw the article about you and Presley's daughter, Brody. You have no reason to be nervous. We both know you didn't do anything wrong."

"You're right, I didn't." He couldn't help adding, "But how did you know?"

Wyatt jerked his finger to the left and said, "Follow me. We need to have a chat."

Brody glanced at his watch, noting he had another twenty minutes before they called him in for his scheduled interview.

They walked silently toward the lobby, then exited the front doors and stepped into the cool morning air. Cars whizzed by in front of the arena. Pedestrians ambled down the sidewalk without giving the two men a second look. Everyone was going about their day, cheerfully heading to work, while Brody was here, waiting to be questioned about something he wanted no part in.

With a strangled groan, Wyatt ran one hand through his hair, messing up the style he'd obviously taken great care with. "Look, I'm not going to lie. I've been seeing Sheila, okay?" His voice cracked. "I know it's wrong. I know I have no business sleeping with a married woman, but, goddammit, I was a goner from the moment I met her. I love her, man."

"Sheila told you who took bribes, didn't she?"

Wyatt averted his eyes. "Yes."

"Then who, damn it? Who the fuck put us in this position, Craig?"

There was a beat of silence. "I don't think you want to know, man."

Another pause. Longer this time. Brody could tell that the last thing Craig Wyatt wanted to do was name names.

But he did. "Nicklaus did. And—" Wyatt took a breath. "I'm sorry, Brody, but…so did Sam Becker."

CHAPTER THIRTEEN

THE GROUND BENEATH Brody's feet swiftly disintegrated. He sagged forward, planting both hands on his thighs to steady himself. Sucked in a series of long breaths. Waited for his pulse to steady.

"Those are the only two Sheila knows about," Wyatt was saying. "There could be more."

Brody glanced up at Wyatt with anger. "You're lying. Nicklaus maybe, but not Becker. He wouldn't do that."

"He did."

No. Not Becker. Brody pictured Becker's face, thinking back to the first day they'd met, how Sam Becker had taken Brody's rookie self under his wing and helped him become the player he was today. Becker was his best friend on the team. He was a stand-up guy, a champion, a legend. Why would he throw his career away for some extra pocket money?

"He's retiring at the end of the season," Wyatt said, as if reading Brody's mind. He shrugged. "Maybe he needed a bigger nest egg."

Brody closed his eyes briefly. When he opened them,

he saw the sympathy on Wyatt's face. "I know you two are close," Craig said quietly.

"You could be wrong about this. Sheila could have lied." Brody knew he was grasping at straws, but anything was better than accepting that Becker had done this.

"It's the truth," Wyatt answered.

They stood there for a moment, neither one speaking, until Wyatt finally cleared his throat and said, "We should go back inside."

"You go. I'll be there in a minute."

After Wyatt left, Brody adjusted his tie, wondering if he'd ever be able to breathe again. His head still spun from Craig's words. And yet he couldn't bring himself to believe it. Damn it, he needed to talk to Becker. Look his friend in the eye and demand the truth. Prove Wyatt wrong.

Then he looked up and realized he was going to be granted his wish sooner than he'd expected. Samuel T. Becker had just exited the arena.

Becker spotted him instantly, and made his way over. "You done already?"

"Haven't even gone in yet." He tried to mask his emotions as he studied his old friend. "Are you scheduled to be interviewed today?"

"Yep," Becker said. "And as a reward, I get to take Mary shopping afterward. What fun for me."

Brody smiled weakly.

"What the hell's up with you?" Sam demanded, rolling his eyes. "Don't tell me you're still gaga over Presley's daughter. I told you, man, you shouldn't be seeing her."

Yeah, he had told him, hadn't he? And Brody now had to wonder exactly where the advice had stemmed from. Had Becker really been looking out for him, or had he wanted to keep him away from Hayden in case Presley decided to confide in his daughter? In case Brody learned the truth about Becker's criminal actions. The thought made his blood run cold.

"Let's not talk about Hayden," he said stiffly.

"Okay. Whatcha want to talk about then?"

He released a slow breath. "How about you tell me why you let Presley bribe you?"

Becker's jaw hardened. "Excuse me?"

"You heard me."

After a beat, Becker scowled. "I already told you, I wasn't involved in that crap."

"Someone else says otherwise."

"Yeah, who?" Becker challenged.

Brody decided to take a gamble. He felt like a total ass, but still he said, "Presley."

The lie stretched between them, and the myriad of emotions Brody saw on his friend's face was disconcerting as hell. Becker's expression went from shocked to angry. To guilty. And finally, betrayed.

And it was all Brody needed to know.

With a stiff nod, he brushed past his former mentor. "I'm needed inside."

"Brody, come on." Becker trailed after him, his voice laced with misery. "Come on, it wasn't like that."

Brody spun around. "Then you didn't sell out the team?"

Becker hesitated a little too long.

"That's what I thought."

"I did it for Mary, okay?" Becker burst out, looking so anguished that Brody almost felt sorry for him. "You don't know what it's like living with a woman like her. Money, power, that's all she talks about. She's always needling me to be better, richer, more ambitious. And now that I'm retiring, she's going nuts. She married me because of my career, because I was at the top of my game, a two-time cup winner, a goddamn champion."

"And you could've retired knowing that you *are* a champion and a two-time cup winner," Brody pointed out. "Now you'll go out a criminal. How's Mary going to like that?"

Becker said nothing. He looked beaten, weak. "I messed up, kiddo, and I'm sorry," he whispered after several moments had passed. "I'm sorry about the games and the article and—"

Brody's jaw tightened. "The article?"

His friend averted his eyes, as if realizing his slipup.

Brody stood there for a moment, wary, studying Becker. The article...the one that had been in the paper two days ago? The one that featured a source who insinuated Brody had taken a bribe?

His blood began to boil, heating his veins, churning his stomach, until a red haze of fury swept over him.

"You spoke to the reporter about me," he hissed.

Becker finally met his eyes. Guilt was written all over his face. "I'm sorry."

"Why? Why the *hell* would you do that?" Brody clenched his fists, knowing the answer before Becker could open his mouth. "To take the blame off yourself. You were too close to being caught, weren't you, Sam? You thought my relationship with Hayden would get the press going, put some pressure on me instead of you."

The sheer force of Brody's anger was unbelievable. He wanted to hit the other man, so badly his fists actually tingled. And along with the rage came a jolt of devastation that torpedoed into his gut and brought a wave of nausea to his throat.

"I'm sorry," Becker murmured for what seemed like the millionth time, but Brody was done listening to his friend's apologies. No, not his friend. Because a true friend would never have done what Sam Becker had.

Without another word, he brushed past Becker and stalked into the arena.

He felt like slamming his fist into something. Becker, his best friend, had betrayed him. Becker, the most talented player in the league, had cheated. And why? For money. Goddamn *money*.

Money. Power. Ambition. She married me because of my career.

And suddenly Brody found himself sagging against the wall as the truth of his own stupidity hit him. Didn't he, too, place importance on financial success? Hadn't he just thrown away the woman he loved because of his damn career?

And, God, but he did love Hayden.

He loved her so damn much.

Maybe he'd fallen for Hayden when she'd first strolled up and proceeded to wipe the pool table with him. Or maybe it happened the first time they'd kissed. Or the first time they'd made love. It could've been the night she'd put on the pair of skates and stumbled all over the ice, or the day she'd dragged him around the museum talking passionately about every piece of art.

He didn't know when it happened, but it had. And instead of clinging to the woman whose intelligence amazed him, whose passion excited him, whose soft smiles and warm arms made him feel more content than he'd ever felt in his life—instead of hanging on to her, he'd pushed her away.

And why? Because he'd been implicated in a crime he hadn't committed? Because his family never had money when he was growing up? So what? His parents loved each other, and their marriage had thrived despite their financial difficulties. What did money and success really matter when you didn't have someone to share it with, someone you loved?

A laugh suddenly slipped out of his mouth, and he noticed the receptionist giving him a funny look. Releasing a shaky breath, he crossed the lobby toward the hallway off to the left and walked back in the direction of the conference room. Lord, he was an ass. He'd been searching for a woman who'd look at him and see past the athlete, and, damn it, but he'd found her. Hayden didn't care if he was a star and she didn't care how much money he made, as long as he was there for her.

He wasn't willing to lie to protect Hayden's father, but he should have told her he'd stand by her no matter what happened with her dad. His relationship with the team owner's daughter might place a negative spotlight on him, but wasn't it worth it if it meant keeping Hayden in his life?

"Brody?"

He almost tripped when he saw Hayden standing at the end of the hall, right in front of the conference-room door.

"What are you doing here?" he asked.

She stepped toward him, and he noticed her red-rimmed eyes. Had she been crying?

"I came to talk to my dad," she murmured. "And then I remembered that you were being interviewed, too, so I thought I'd find you before you had to go in…" Her voice drifted, and then she cleared her throat. "I'm sorry the team didn't make it to the second round."

"So am I… But to be honest, it doesn't seem all that important anymore, considering everything else that's going on."

"I know." She gave him a sad smile. "A criminal investigation kind of casts a shadow over things, doesn't it?"

The pain in her eyes tore at his insides. He hated seeing her this way, and he knew why she'd been crying.

Resting his hand on her arm, he slowly pulled her away from the conference-room door and led her to the end of the hall. "I'm not going to lie," he said softly.

She tilted her head to meet his eyes, her gaze confused, then opened her mouth to speak.

"Wait," he cut in. "I want you to know that just because I won't lie doesn't mean I won't be there for you. Because I will, babe. I don't care what the papers write about us, I don't care how my career is affected. I don't care about anything but you. I'll stay by your side, Hayden. I promise, I'll be here for you, as long as you need me."

He blew out a breath, waiting for her to reply, praying she didn't say, *Well, I don't need you, Brody. It was just a fling.*

But she didn't say that. She didn't say anything, in fact.

Instead, she burst out laughing.

HAYDEN COULDN'T STOP the giggles from escaping. She'd come down here to tell Brody she was willing to wait until the investigation ended, that she would do anything it took to keep him in her life, even if it meant staying apart for a while. And here he was, telling her he wanted to stay by her side.

"You think it's funny?" Brody said in annoyance, raking both hands through his dark hair. "Remind me never to make a grand romantic gesture again."

She chuckled. "I only think it's funny because I came to tell you I'll stay away from you until the investigation is finished."

"What?"

"I respect your decision. If you want to lie low until this blows over, I'll do that." She curled her fingers over his arm and looked at him imploringly. "But I don't want it to be permanent. I don't want us to end, Brody."

His features softened. "Neither do I." He paused. "I also don't want us to lie low."

"Are you sure?"

He moved closer, bent down and planted a soft kiss on her mouth, right there in the hallway. Then he pulled back, smiled, and dipped his head to kiss her again, this time slipping her a little tongue.

Flushed, she broke the kiss and stepped back before she gave in to the urge to pull him into the restroom and fulfill yet another kinky fantasy. "Come to the hotel when you're done," she said, her voice coming out breathy.

He grinned. "I'll be there with bells on."

"No bells. But naked would be good." Her heart did a crazy little somersault. "And don't keep me waiting too long." She drew in a breath. "There are definitely a few things I still need to say to you."

AN HOUR LATER, Brody stepped into the elevator at the Ritz. He waited for the bellhop to turn the key that gave him access to the penthouse floor, and when the guy left, Brody sagged against the wall of the car, feeling as if he'd just run the Boston Marathon and followed that up by climbing Everest. The interview with the league investigators had been pure torture. He'd sat there in his suit, with his oxygen-depriving tie, and had had to sell out a man he'd once considered a friend and another he'd respected as a boss.

Thank God this day from hell was over. He didn't know what the investigation would turn up, how it would all end, but a load had been lifted off his chest. One load, at least. He still hadn't quite faced the fact that Becker had betrayed him. He knew it would take more than one afternoon to come to terms with it. But he'd walked out of that conference with his conscience clear, and now he couldn't wait to lose himself in Hayden's arms and forget about everything except the love he felt for her.

"Hayden?" he called as the elevator doors swung open and he entered the living room.

Her voice drifted out from the bedroom. "In here."

He found her in the bedroom, sitting cross-legged in the center of the bed, still clad in the flowy green skirt and yellow silk top she'd been wearing earlier. Damn. He'd been hoping to find her naked.

Ah, well, that could be easily amended.

She slid off the bed, her skirt swirling around her firm thighs as she moved toward him. "How was the interview?"

"Terrible. But I think I convinced them I wasn't guilty of any wrongdoing."

Relief flooded her features. "Good." Then, looking somber, she added, "I found out something about Becker that you're not going to like."

He swallowed. "I know already. Who told you?" he asked after exhaling a shaky breath.

"I overheard my dad talking to him on the phone. So it's true? He really did do it?"

"Yes." He swallowed. "Nicklaus took a bribe, too—he's our goalie." His anger returned like a punch to the gut. "I can't believe they would do that. Especially Sam."

"I'm sorry," Hayden said again, reaching up to touch his chin with her warm fingers. "But I think forgiveness will come in time. If I can forgive my dad, maybe you'll be able to forgive your friend."

Brody faltered. "And if I can't?"

"I'll help you." She smiled glibly. "I'm good at forgiveness. After all, didn't I forgive you for dumping me?"

"I panicked, okay? And I only suggested we put things on hol—" He stopped when he saw the amusement in her eyes. "You're not mad," he said.

"Of course not." She ran her index finger along the curve of his jaw. "I can't stay mad at the man I love."

He held his breath, not daring to give in to the sheer bliss threatening to spill over. "You mean that?"

"Yes." She lifted her other hand and cupped his chin with both her hands. "I love you, Brody. I know I kept fighting you whenever you said we were perfect for each other, but... I'm not fighting anymore." She exhaled slowly. "I've fallen for you, hockey star. The earth moves when we're together and I love it. I love you."

The joy in his heart spilled over, warming his insides and making his pulse skate through his veins like a player on a breakaway.

"I'm willing to be part of the hockey lifestyle for as long as it takes," she added, certainty shining in her eyes. "I'll even go to your games." She chewed on her bottom lip. "But I'll probably bring some lecture notes to work on, you know, because I still don't particularly like hockey, but I'll make an effort to—"

He silenced her with a kiss, but pulled away just as she parted her lips to let him in.

"I won't play hockey forever, Hayden," he said softly. "And I'm already trying to work on the possibility of signing with a West Coast team next season. That way you can keep teaching at Berkeley, and we could—" his voice cracked "— we could get started on building a life together. A *home*."

As he said the words, he knew without a doubt that's what he wanted. A home with Hayden. A life with the one woman who looked past his uniform and saw the man beneath it.

He'd been searching for her for so long, and now that he'd found her, he wasn't about to let her go. Ever.

"I love you, Hayden," he said roughly. "More than hockey, more than being successful, more than life. I want to wake up every morning and see one of your sleepy smiles, go to bed every night pressed up against you, have kids with you, grow old with you." He put his hands on her slender hips and pulled her toward him. "Will you let me do that?"

Twining her arms around his neck, she leaned up and kissed him, a long, lingering kiss that promised love and laughter and hot, endless sex. Pulling back, just an inch, she whispered, "Yes," and then raised her lips to his again.

"Should we seal the deal?" he murmured against her hot, pliant mouth.

"God, yes."

Deepening the kiss, he untucked her shirt from the waistband of her skirt and slid his hands underneath, filling his palms with the feel of her silky skin. His tongue sought hers. His hands found her breasts.

Hayden moaned. "No, not here." Breaking contact, she darted over to the nightstand and pulled out a condom. Without another word, she grabbed his hand and dragged him out of the bedroom to the middle of the narrow hallway.

"Here," she said, a playful light dancing in her eyes.

He looked at the spot she'd chosen, chuckling when he realized this was the first place they'd made love. On the hallway floor, while Hayden writhed beneath him and squeezed his ass and pushed him into her as deep as he could go.

"Here is perfect," he answered huskily.

He drew her into his arms, claiming her with his mouth, and they were both breathless by the time the kiss ended. Gently stroking her cheek, he gave her another soft kiss, then began peeling her clothes from her body. First her shirt, then the bra, the skirt, the panties, until she was standing naked in front of him, a vision of perfection. He marveled at her silky curves and perfect skin, those beautiful breasts, the shapely legs... God, he couldn't believe she was his. All his.

"I love you, Hayden," he said, his throat thick with emotion. "I love everything about you."

She gave a soft sigh of pleasure as he cupped her breasts, tenderly stroking the swell of each perfect mound.

He hastily removed his own clothes, kicked them aside, then dropped to his knees and peppered little kisses on her flat abdomen before moving to nip at her inner thigh. He loved the sweet little moan she responded with, loved the way she tangled her fingers in his hair and guided him to the spot between her legs that he knew ached for his touch.

He kissed her sensitized nub, flicked his tongue over her sweetness. He would never be able to get enough of her, even if he spent the rest of his life trying. With a small groan, he planted one last kiss on her soft folds and then pulled her down to the carpet.

With a look of pure contentment swimming in her forest-green eyes, Hayden lay back, spread her legs and offered him a wicked smile.

"Don't keep me waiting," she said with just a hint of challenge in her throaty voice.

"I don't intend to."

He covered her body with his, his shaft, hot and hard, pressed up against her belly. He shifted so that his tip brushed her wet sex, but didn't plunge inside.

First, he kissed her again, a long, lazy kiss, and then he pulled back and said, "No ground rules this time."

Her eyelids fluttered open. "What?"

"That second night, you said there were ground rules." He nipped at the hot flesh of her neck. "No rules this time.

You're getting not only my body, but my heart and my soul, every night for the rest of your life. Got it?"

She raised her brows. "Again with the demands, huh?"

"You got a problem with that?"

With a laugh, she gripped his hair with her fingers and pulled his head down. Slipping her tongue into his mouth, she kissed him until he could barely see straight, then reached between them, circled his shaft and guided it to her opening, pushing herself down over his length.

He gasped.

"I don't have..." she moaned as she took him in deeper "...a single problem with that." With a breathy sigh, she wrapped her arms around his neck and pressed a kiss to his collarbone. "I love you, Brody."

He slowly withdrew, then plunged back in, filling her to the hilt. "It drives me wild when you say that," he squeezed out.

"What, I love you?"

His cock jerked in response. "Yes, that."

She lifted her hips off the ground, and hooked her legs around his lower back, holding him prisoner with her wet heat. "Good, because I plan on saying it often. I love you, Brody Croft."

Staying true to her word, she brushed her lips over his ear and said it again. And again. And again. With a groan, he buried his head in the crook of her neck, inhaled her sweet scent and sent them both to heaven.

And when they were sated and happy and lying there on the carpet, Brody could swear that the earth had moved.

EPILOGUE

One year later

"SERIOUSLY, BABE, WE need to do something about that shower," Brody grumbled as he stepped out of the bathroom.

Hayden couldn't help but laugh at the aggravation on his ridiculously handsome face. "The plumber will be here on Monday, *babe*. Quit getting your panties in a knot."

He strode into the recently painted master bedroom of their San Diego home, his frown deepening. "It really doesn't bother you?"

"No, Brody. It doesn't. It's just a removable showerhead, for Pete's sake. We'll live without it for a couple more days."

She rolled her eyes and rose from the bed. They'd purchased the house two months ago, at a bargain since the rambling three-story Victorian was in desperate need of renovations. So far, they'd painted every room, gutted the living room, retiled the kitchen—and Brody was worrying about a showerhead. Her husband definitely had a one-track mind. Of course, she'd known that when she'd married him.

"We should head over to the restaurant," she said, swiftly

putting an end to the subject Brody refused to drop. "Darcy will be wondering where we are."

Brody snorted. "Darcy is probably having sex with one of the waiters as we speak."

She wagged her finger at him. "Be nice. She's taken a vow of celibacy, remember?"

Another snort. "Yeah, and I'm sure that'll last for, oh, ten seconds. No, make that five."

Hayden laughed, knowing he was probably right. Leopards couldn't get rid of their spots, lions weren't about to grow horns and Darcy White certainly couldn't "quit" men. But Hayden was glad her friend was finally able to take time off and visit them. Darcy was actually considering moving to the West Coast, and Hayden was avidly encouraging her friend to do so. She would love having Darcy around on a more regular basis, especially since she wouldn't be able to travel with Brody to his away games for much longer.

Although the Warriors hadn't made it far in the play-offs last season, Brody's standings had impressed the Los Angeles Vipers' general manager, who'd made him an offer, to both Hayden and Brody's relief. It put an end to the "where do we live" dilemma that had been plaguing them since the engagement. Brody signed with the Vipers, and since the commute to San Francisco had been too much for her, she'd agreed to teach courses at Berkeley during the hockey season as well as a few summer courses. The arrangement worked for both of them; the online seminars gave her the time to work on her Ph.D. at the University of San Diego, and getting to L.A. from San Diego would be easier for Brody.

They'd married in Chicago, though, deciding it was fitting to say their vows in the city where they'd met and fallen in love. Brody's parents had flown in for the wedding; Darcy had been the maid of honor, and the guests were a mixture of academics and athletes, including Brody's former captain Craig Wyatt, who'd brought Hayden's ex-stepmother. Shockingly, Wyatt and Sheila were now engaged, and Sheila was happily planning the wedding and enjoying the money she'd gotten from her divorce; she'd eventually settled for half of Presley's estate.

Hayden's dad hadn't been able to make it to the wedding—the rehabilitation facility he'd checked himself into hadn't allowed it—but he'd sent her a beautiful letter that stated how happy he was she and Brody had found love. He'd also thanked her for supporting him through everything, and Hayden had been in tears when she'd read his heartfelt words.

"Hey, you okay?"

Brody's concerned voice drew her from her thoughts. She managed a nod. "Yeah. I was just thinking about my dad."

Brody moved closer and wrapped his strong arms around her. "I know you wish he would move out here, but you can't monitor every move he makes, Hayden. He's sober now. Just have faith that he'll stay that way."

"I know." She sighed. "At least he's not in jail."

Last year's league investigation had resulted in criminal charges being brought up on her father, as well as the players he'd bribed, but Presley had gotten off with a fine and four years' probation. Since her dad hadn't been involved in a gambling ring or organized crime, he'd been lucky with his punishment. He'd lost the team, though, and Hayden knew that had been a big blow for her dad. The Warriors were now owned by none other than Jonas Quade, the man of many mistresses and that god-awful tan.

Sam Becker had wound up with probation, too, but Brody still couldn't seem to forgive his former friend. Hayden hoped that in time the two men might reconcile.

"Last time he called he mentioned he's thinking of buying a place by Lake Michigan," Brody was saying, still talking about her dad. "Did he tell you that?"

"No, he didn't mention it." She suddenly smiled, wondering if maybe there was hope for her dad after all. He might have lost the team, but he seemed much happier lately, and the two of them were on their way to regaining the close relationship they'd had when she was younger.

"I told you he used to take me fishing when I was a kid, right?" she said.

Her husband kissed her on the cheek and took her hand. "Come on, we should go."

"You're right. Darce will freak out if we don't show up soon. She's been really bitchy lately. You know, the lack of sex and all."

They headed for the doorway. "Actually, I think she'll freak out when she sees *this*." Brody rubbed her protruding belly with his palm.

Hayden sighed. She was only five months along, and already she felt huge. "Remind me again how you knocked me up when we'd decided to wait a couple years?"

He shot her a cocky grin. "I told you. I never miss. It's my fatal flaw."

"No, your fatal flaw is not getting me the ice cream I asked for last night."

They left the bedroom and walked down their brand-new winding staircase. The floor in the front hall still needed to be laid down, but Hayden didn't care as long as the renovations were done before the baby came. She grabbed her purse from the hall table and slipped into her flat sandals.

She followed Brody out on the porch, lifting her head to the late-afternoon sun and breathing in the warm San Diego air.

"I told you why I didn't pick up the ice cream," Brody grumbled. "You've got to eat healthy, babe. You're carrying a future champion in that belly of yours. Our son needs proper nourishment."

Oh, brother. Not again.

"I only need one champion in my life, thank you very much." She shot him a sweet smile. "Our *daughter* is going to be a Nobel Prize winner."

"It's a boy," he said confidently with a charming smile of his own. "Haven't you figured out by now that I always get what I want?"

"God, you're arrogant."

"Yeah, but you like it." His grin widened. "And if it weren't for me, you'd still be hiking across some intimacy bridge—"

"I should never have told you about that!"

"And deprive me of endless bridge jokes?"

She tried to scowl but ended up laughing. "Fine. I surrender. The intimacy bridge is funny. Now let's go before Darcy really does sleep with a waiter."

Brody held her arm as they walked to the car. He opened the door for her, then rounded the vehicle and got into the driver's seat.

She stretched the seat belt over her stomach and buckled up, then tucked a strand of hair behind her ears. Suddenly she became aware of Brody watching her, and when she turned her head, her breath caught at the awe, love and passion she saw shining in his eyes.

"Have I told you today how beautiful you are?" he asked.

"Twice, actually." Warmth suffused her body. "But feel free to say it as many times as you'd like."

"Believe me, I will." He shifted closer and stroked her cheek. "You know, the happiest day of my life was when you walked up to that pool table and asked me back to your hotel."

"You're not going to tell our daughter that, are you?"

"Nah. We'll tell *our son* we met at a museum and it was love at first sight."

He cupped her jaw and ran his thumb over her lower lip, sending a wave of heat and desire through her. She could never get enough of Brody's touch, not even if she lived to be a hundred.

"Let's skip dinner," he murmured, then dipped his head to kiss her.

Her pulse raced as his tongue teased hers with long, sensual strokes.

It took all her willpower to pull back. "We can't." When he grumbled, she added, "Come on, it's one little dinner. I'll make it worth your while…"

His eyes lit up. "How?"

She laughed. "You'll just have to wait and see."

"For you, I'd wait forever. In fact, I'd do just about anything you asked." His gaze softened. "I love you that much, Mrs. Croft."

She leaned closer and brushed her lips over his. "I love you, too…so let's get this dinner over with so I can get you home and show you *exactly* how much."

* * * * *

Winning Ruby Heart

Jennifer Lohmann

ABOUT THE AUTHOR

Jennifer Lohmann is a Rocky Mountain girl at heart, having grown up in southern Idaho and Salt Lake City. When she's not writing or working as a public librarian, she wrangles two cats and a flock of backyard chickens; the dog is better behaved. She lives in Durham, North Carolina, and runs regularly (when the dog looks up for it and it's not raining, or too hot or too cold).

Dear Reader,

Few beginnings of books have as clear an "aha" moment as *Winning Ruby Heart*. I was in my car, listening to *Born to Run* by Christopher McDougall on audiobook when I switched over to the radio in time to catch a piece on Lance Armstrong. Voilà, Ruby Heart was born. I'd wanted to have a female athlete as a heroine for a long time, and running was the perfect sport. There's an active amateur community, there are races all over the country and it's feasible for Ruby to be twenty-nine and only starting to be at the top of her game.

I imagined Ruby, sitting in an interview chair and absolutely not understanding what she'd done wrong, throwing mud on her reputation with every excuse. The man interviewing her was destined to be her perfect match. All it would take was a second chance.

If you've read my books, you know I like to recommend a book in my letter (often it's a cookbook) and this recommendation is my favourite so far. While researching spinal cord injuries, I came across the book *Moving Violations: War Zones, Wheelchairs, and Declarations of Independence* by John Hockenberry. Micah's character was already established as a cosmic twin of Hockenberry's. Confident and conquering, all wrapped up with a sense of humour and an eye for the absurd. What more could a reader ask for?

Enjoy,

Jennifer Lohmann

To the Romance Lovers Book Club.
The first Thursday of the month is always my
favourite day.

CHAPTER ONE

THE WOMAN IN the neon green baseball hat looked familiar to Micah Blackwell. There was a loose-limbed smoothness to the way she milled among the other racers at the starting line that tapped at a memory in his brain. He drummed his fingers against the side of his wheelchair, waiting for her to turn her head and let the little bit of sun prying its way through the cloud cover onto her face. He wanted to see her eyes.

The woman, bib number 86, caught him staring at her. She twitched as if to dart off in another direction and then seemed to calm herself. The brim of her cap threw her entire face and neck into shadow when she turned her head from his gaze, and Micah saw the lips of the man next to her moving, apparently in response to number 86's question. The movement of her head was smooth as she looked around, but the bounce of her pigtails on her shoulders exposed her nervous energy, as did the way she shook out the muscles in her arms and legs. Even the shaking seemed familiar.

Micah was so focused on the ripples of muscles in her sleek, powerful thighs that he almost missed her skittish look over her shoulder and the way she tried to ease through the other runners out of his sight. With only a hundred people in this race, the crowd wasn't so big that he couldn't follow the green bounce of the hat.

"Amir," Micah called to his photographer without taking his eyes off the woman. "There's a runner in the crowd—bib number 86. I want you to make sure you get video of her."

Amir's thin face emerged from behind his camera. Sports was a world of big—big men, big egos, big cameras—and Amir always seemed lost among the oversize swagger. But big men often forgot that small men could be a threat, and before they knew it, Napoleon was their emperor. Amir could stand there with the gargantuan camera on his shoulder while the men who Micah interviewed forgot the camera even existed. Which made Amir one of the best photogs in the business. And he was Micah's photog. Two physical misfits working their asses off amidst a world of Achilles' and Hercules'.

"I thought we were covering Currito." The problem with having the best photog in the business was that Amir knew he was the best and so he felt comfortable arguing. The National Sports Network had sent them here to cover Currito, a Mexican-American runner who had seemingly come out of nowhere to finish in the elite pack at Western States and then gave a colorful interview about painting and mystic visions to the local sports guys. Despite Micah's multipart series on ultramarathoners being only in the planning stages, when Currito had told them he was running a race within driving distance of the NSN campus, they'd signed out a production van and driven to Iowa.

Neither Currito nor Amir nor bib number 86 knew it, but the ultra series now had its new star—and it wasn't Currito. Luck favored the watchful, and Micah had been watching. "We are, but I've got a feeling about that runner.

There's something about her...." His jaw tightened as his brain nearly spit out the memory and then yanked it back before a name came to him. "Get Currito, too, but..." The drizzle was obscuring more than his view of the runners.

Amir looked as if he was going to argue again, but Micah raised an eyebrow. "Okay." Shrugging with one shoulder while the heavy news camera was balanced on the other nearly toppled the small man.

Micah caught a low flick of green through the legs of the runners, then followed the arc of the throw back through the crowds, which parted in time for him to see a head of unremarkable brown hair parted into pigtails. Runner 86 lifted her chin in a self-confident, defiant gesture as the gun went off.

"Aah..." The memory exploded into Micah's conscious with a golden flash. "Ruby Heart, I've got you now."

The drumming of his fingers against his chair quickened along with his heart rate as Ruby ran past him, her stride shorter than he remembered from watching the Olympics five years ago. She seemed to be trying to disappear into the crowd, instead of bursting out of it. Noting the angle of her knee as she kicked behind her with each step, Micah wondered if he was right about her identity. The stride didn't look quite right. But the comparative power of Currito as the star of the ultra series balanced against disgraced Olympian Ruby Heart running again was worth the risk. Rumor had it an anchor position at NSN was about to open up, and Micah wanted it.

"Amir, I need to do some research at the hotel, so it'll just be you and King." Micah cocked his head toward the other reporter from NSN who had made the trip out of curiosity to watch, quote, "pain freaks run."

"What?" The one eye of Amir's that Micah could see was wide with horror.

"He'd probably leap at the chance to have input into the story."

His cameraman choked. "Sure. And when I use the camera to beat him to death for his input, I'll make sure NSN sends the bill for a new camera to you. And I'll expect you to post bail."

"Okay," Micah said with a shrug and a smile. King was not a popular figure with the support staff at the network, but Amir would get the footage Micah asked for, King's interference aside.

"Why can't..." Amir stopped. Micah finished the question in his head. *Why can't you send King back to the hotel in your car to do the research so I'm not stuck in the production van with him?* One of the great conveniences of a hand-driven car was that no one could borrow it. "King's gonna want to know why we're waiting to film that woman after Currito runs by."

"If I'm right, you won't have to wait long." Listening to Kingston "Call Me King" Ripley howl with pain when he realized that one of the biggest sporting news stories of the year had run right past him and *he'd* missed it would feel almost as good as the ratings Micah knew were coming his way—as well as that anchor position.

"King won't like it," Amir said. But this argument flopped on the dirt, sucked in a few last gasps of air and then stilled like the dead fish it was.

"King will like it *too* much." The man would think he had a chance to take over this story, and he didn't even have the foresight to know what the real story was. "Look, King is loud, obnoxious and he can't withstand a direct charge. Ignore his bluster and any advice he gives you and stick to getting the footage I want. Half Currito, half that woman. Good shots of the face. I don't want anyone to doubt who she is when I'm done." Micah thought for a minute, then added, "And try to make it look as if you're not focusing on her. I don't want to spook her."

"Who is she?"

"And give you a name for King to weasel out of you? Hell no." If rumors about the upcoming anchor opening were true, King would be fighting Micah to the death for it, and getting an interview with Ruby Heart would be equivalent to securing the nuclear arsenal. "Get the shots—I'll confirm the name afterward." The rough, wet dirt stalled his exit, but Amir knew better than to offer help. Micah wheeled himself over the rocks and sticks in the trail to his car and drove off.

Back at the hotel, he connected to the wireless and started digging. Most of the pictures he found were of Ruby as the world had known her—sharp points of her short platinum hair aimed directly at her painted red lips, looking more like a younger, edgier version of Marilyn Monroe than an athlete. But buried on her college's website was a team photo from her freshman year. There, Ruby Heart looked like the girl next door. Her hair was still short, but it lacked the snap of her Olympic haircut and was the same mousy brown he'd seen today. The eyes clinched it. Without the heavy makeup, there was nothing to hide those doe eyes gracing the face of the girl who would become America's Darling two years after this photo was taken. Even in the picture of her during his interview, after her cheating had been revealed to the world, her brown eyes had dominated her face, giving her an aura of innocence.

"You understand what I'm going through, right?" she had asked him after the camera stopped rolling on that memorable interview. "We both had our passions taken from us." Her voice had sounded so young, adding to the blameless look she'd had on her face and almost making him agree with her. As if their careers had ended the same way. "It wasn't fair." He'd added *whiny* to the list of her defects. When he'd told her that her entire athletic career hadn't been fair to her competitors, she'd jumped back as if he'd swung a fist at her.

Micah pulled himself away from the memory, found the list of participants in today's run and looked for the name. According to the website, no Ruby Heart had registered, but there was a Diana Heart. A Wikipedia page didn't offer Ruby's full name, only a short summary of the girl's soaring rise to greatness and her crashing fall. Icarus, with his wax wings climbing higher and higher toward the sun until the lies he'd woven into the wings melted from the heat. Only Ruby had been the genuine flying article and she'd strapped wax wings onto her back anyway.

Her stupidity left a foul taste in his mouth the bitter coffee couldn't overpower.

The current Wikipedia photo was Ruby at her apex, with the American flag raised high over her head in a stadium of adoring fans. No amount of makeup could hide the pure joy overtaking the exhaustion on her face. The other photo on the page was a still from his interview of her—Ruby's blond hair looking limp and fake, her eyes hurt and confused. Micah wondered how often the pictures were swapped out as the remaining few who cared—both fans and detractors—battled it out in cyberspace. Someone had cared enough about her to note that her suspension for doping was over.

While he didn't recall the specifics of her complicated settlement, after she'd provided enough information to close several clinics, her lifetime ban had been converted into a suspension from all non-Olympic sports. Micah had a vague memory of the prep material he'd gotten for that interview, which had included Ruby's full name and the fact that she went by her middle name.

Pitiful, really, to have disappeared from the American psyche so completely that all it took was a set of pigtails and different first name for people in your own sport not to recognize you.

CHAPTER TWO

BACK IN HER hotel room, Ruby Heart turned the television on for company, tossed the remote onto the bed and then eased her tired body into the chair at the small desk and prepared to indulge in her grocery store sandwich and chocolate milk. Her medal for finishing sat piled atop its ribbon, its tacky glitter weighing down her race bib. When she flicked at the medallion, her fingernail bounced off the cheap metal with a mournful *ting,* which her favorite medal—the gold one she'd had to give up—hadn't had. She picked the medallion off her bib and turned it over in her hand. It might lack the sparkle of the Olympic gold, but no one could argue that Ruby hadn't earned this one.

She had crossed the finish line of the fifty-kilometer race on her own two feet—which had been her number-one goal—in four hours and forty-three minutes, which was short of her second goal by three minutes. The race medal clinked against the desk when she dropped it. Three measly minutes. It had taken being handed a beer by a volunteer for Ruby to remember that she wasn't competing against anyone other than herself. And still those minutes rankled. She allowed herself thirty seconds to clench her teeth before she took a deep breath and focused on what her goals had been. New goals for a new Ruby Heart.

As long as Micah Blackwell hadn't recognized her, then she only had to prove something to herself, and crossing the finish line had done that, even if she'd skipped out on the postrace festivities. She hadn't wanted to risk him catching sight of her again.

The short cameraman standing next to Micah at the start had been filming at several points along the race, but the camera had been rolling long before she'd run past it and had kept rolling; she'd looked over her shoulder several times to make sure. The cameraman was probably getting filler for whatever story they were planning to run on Currito. Ruby was nothing. Less than nothing. Her past was forgotten and her future was nonexistent. Even if Micah had recognized her, no one would be interested in her story. She was the detritus of American sensationalism.

Today was also proof that she could stay that way—run a competitive race, return home and not hear her father say, "Do you know what it's like for me at the office?" Or her mother complain about the gossip at the salon. Or her sister about the rumors on campus. Or any number of the other places her family had gone during the two weeks when the cameras had been camped outside her house and she'd been trapped inside.

She swallowed a bite of her sandwich, chewing through the bread and the ideas of risking another race. She'd finished, but there were those three minutes... She bit her lip, then licked the little bit of mayo off. Had today proved it could be done, or had it only been proof it could be done *once*?

Micah's warm, confident voice came over the television, and Ruby rolled the desk chair back to watch. After Micah introduced him, Currito talked about his race and his training. His black curls bounced about his face and his dark skin was shiny with sweat. "It's all mental," the runner said. "I'm not saying anyone can run one of these things, but it's your mind that works hardest."

"You're also an accomplished artist," Micah said on the television as he leaned back in his chair and opened his arms, inviting the world in. A trademark move, and she'd fallen for it along with a hundred other interviewees. After an interview during the Olympics, one of the gymnasts had said it felt as though he was inviting her onto his lap to whisper intimacies in his ear.

He smiled at the runner and, even though she knew better, Ruby leaned forward, pulled into Micah's magnetic orb. "Could you tell us a little about how your art affects your running? Or your running affects your art?" After seeing him in a thousand interviews, Micah's shallow dimples remained a surprise in an otherwise stern face and clearly disarmed the last of Currito's natural reserve. Ruby sympathized with the runner; she, too, had fallen victim to those dimples, thinking they offered sympathy when they were simply a weakness in the muscles of the cheek.

"Oh, yeah, man. Painting is what I think about while running. The pain, it takes on colors and strokes."

Ruby almost didn't hear the knock on the hotel room door over the runner describing an injury and the painting that had resulted from it. The shuffle of her bare feet was silent on the carpet. Through the peephole she only saw the door of the hotel room across the hall and the thick fingers of a man's hand, distorted by the glass. She was debating ignoring the prank when she heard, "Ruby Heart, I know it's you." It was Micah.

Her shoulders fell, causing a ripple of soreness through her body. *I almost got away with it.* The story of her life.

Before she opened the door, she closed her eyes for a moment and tried to pull her muscles together around her heart. She was allowed to run in non-Olympic competitions again. They hadn't banned her for life from all sport. With as many defenses banded around her as possible, she twisted the lock, opened the door and looked down.

His eyes flickered over to the television, still playing his long interview with Currito. It was what Micah was known for—long, in-depth, personal interviews with sports figures who told those dimples all their secrets, forgetting they were being filmed. The National Sports Network's Barbara Walters. He looked up at her, then rolled his wheelchair forward, and she had to step back or be run over.

"I'm sorry, but you have the wrong room."

"Shut the door, Ruby." He sounded exasperated, with a tinge of disgust. "I assume you don't want people to realize who you are." No disarming interview face for her. Instead, his mouth was pursed and his blue-gray eyes hidden in the shadows of the room's poor lighting. That this was her hotel room with her sweaty running clothes on the bed didn't matter; with his broad shoulders and expectant gaze, he commanded the room as he'd once commanded entire college football stadiums. The spell he'd cast over her through the television danced about on her skin, tempting her to dump all her secrets onto the floor for him to rummage through and find wanting.

The crunch of her teeth slamming together when she snapped her mouth closed reverberated through her head.

Ruby stood, her hand on the door handle, debating her options. Sadly, Micah was right. She would prefer him in her room to the entire hotel learning that Diana Heart was a poorly constructed alias for Ruby Heart. It was unlikely that anyone other than Micah cared who Ruby Heart was, but unlikely wasn't the same thing as impossible. She shut the door and looked at the reporter who had forced her to look at the ugliness of herself.

You didn't have your passion taken from you. You had someone shove your failure into your arm and then you pissed your dreams away. Five years later the scorn was as fresh as rotted meat. The sensation of being both mud on the bottom of someone's shoe and the most fascinating thing in the world was as strange now as it had been back then.

The television flickered. Ruby stood by the door, watching Micah watch the end of his interview with Currito. The runner talked about joy, about blasting past personal limits and about purity. After a short mention of some special on ultra running, the interview cut to a commercial. Micah backed his wheelchair up to the bed, grabbed the remote and turned off the television. "Interesting man, Currito." Micah rolled his *r*'s when he said the man's name. He'd grown up in Arizona, she remembered, and had learned Spanish as a child. "He's got a compelling background, the kind that makes for good interviews and inspires Americans to root for him. A fighting spirit—constantly pulling himself up with his bootstraps. *And* he still believes in the purity of the sport."

Ruby heard the condemnation in what Micah left unsaid. Currito hadn't grown up in an upper-middle-class suburb of Chicago. He hadn't gotten a scholarship to the University of Illinois and he hadn't had a mother standing behind him, providing for him, seeing to his every need so that all he had to think about was racing. Currito worked for a living; he raced for fun. And Currito hadn't cheated.

"Yes. He's a very nice man." She didn't need to be told

what advantages she'd had and what gifts she'd thrown away. Micah may have been the first to explain this to her, but he hadn't been the last. "Did you come here just to talk about Currito?"

"Why are you running?"

Because she'd seen the Christmas letter her mother had put together with glowing reports of her brother Josh's engagement to the perfect Christine and her sister Roxanne's appointment as editor of a top economics journal—"an honor at any age, but especially when she's so young." At the bottom of the letter had been that one sentence, "Ruby is doing well and still at home." She'd read that one line over and over, wishing her mother had found something else to say about her youngest child. Then Ruby had realized she didn't have anything else to say about her life, either.

She could continue to define herself by her sins or do something else.

But Micah's velvet voice couldn't fool her into any more confessions, so she said only, "It's good exercise." She'd had plenty of one-liners ready to tell a curious person if someone realized who she was, but none of them were appropriate for the man who'd barged into her hotel room. She hadn't seen the cameraman, but that didn't mean he wasn't waiting around some corner. Cameras flashing. Microphones shoved in her face again. Her mom's nerves sending her back to the hospital. And the never-ending stream of comments from people judging her. Not just her doping, which deserved judgment, but her hair and her lack of breasts and her thighs and the way she smiled.

Male athletes who slip and repent seemed to receive forgiveness from the American public fairly easily. Maybe it was her perspective, but Ruby had never seen a famous woman forgiven, only hounded.

In her irritated state, she couldn't resist uttering her next statement. "It's very meditative," she said. "You should try it."

Her parting shot hung in the air above Micah's head. If she reached out, could she snatch the words back? No such luck.

He chuckled, which made her feel worse. "Running isn't really the sport for me anymore, though you're right, it was meditative. Wheelchair marathons serve a similar purpose for me now."

"I'm sorry. That wasn't, well…" She knew about his marathons. Four years ago, she'd been in Grant Park during the Chicago Marathon, pretending she was enjoying a day in the city. The wheelchair marathoners had flown by in a blur of wheels, helmets and arms. One in particular had caught her eye and she'd stood at the top of the bleachers to watch him speed to the finish.

The marathoner had been so full of movement, so alive, and she hadn't been sure if the need that had filled her body had been desire for movement or desire for the man. Until he'd taken off his helmet and she'd realized the surge of lust had been for a man who hated her.

"It's wasn't a nice thing to say," she finished lamely. *It's not a nice thing for you to be here,* her fear whined in her head, but that was an excuse, and she had been done with excuses for five years.

"No, it wasn't." His biceps bulged when he crossed his arms over his chest.

"I've seen you. At the marathons." Her voice hitched, dammit.

The brief flicker of openness on his face disappeared. "You didn't answer my question. What are you doing here, Ruby?"

"You asked why I was running. I did answer that question."

His face remained impassive, though his arms tightened about his chest, the line between his biceps and triceps clear. He had good definition, and she wanted to know what lifts he did and how he did them.

How would that ridge where the deltoid led into the biceps feel under the pads of my fingers? And down the arm, where the brachialis meets the brachioradialis. She had to shut down those thoughts immediately. Wondering about his exercise routine could be justified as an athlete's curiosity. The other...well, the other wouldn't and couldn't happen.

Her head jerked up from his arms to his face when she realized he was talking and she hadn't heard a word. She could tell by the raise of his eyebrows that he hadn't missed her singular focus on his arms, though he didn't say anything. To her relief, he repeated his question. "Why did you compete in a race?"

Ruby is doing well and still at home. "I get sick of running by myself."

His sigh was heavy, disgusted. "That's not an answer."

"If you have questions that you want answers to, ask me for an interview."

The way he seemed to grow taller in his chair could be a trick of the eyes, but she didn't mistake the way his dimples deepened, beckoning her into his sphere. *Come into my lair, my pretty.* "Since you conveniently raised the subject, NSN is actually working on a series about ultra runners—and I would like to interview you. Amir is down the hall and the hotel would be happy to provide us with an appropriate space, I'm sure."

Of course they would. The clerk downstairs was a woman, and she knew how quickly female defenses fell at the siege of Micah's charms.

For those athletes still enjoying their glory, Micah's interviews were probably warm, intimate experiences. For her, it would be a poison-filled trap.

"No," she said, certain of this one thing, if only this one thing.

He huffed in response, his eyebrows raised in surprise—faked, she was sure. She ignored his act and continued, "I came here to run in a race and see how I did." Those three minutes poking at her pride nearly overwhelmed Micah's presence, but she shook off her disappointment before he could sniff it out. "If I'd wanted to be interviewed by Micah Blackwell of the National Sports Network, I would have called you up and let you know I'd be here. I didn't, so I don't." Because she managed to make those words come out strong, unlaced by her fears, she straightened her shoulders and looked him in the eye.

"USA Track & Field deserves to know who you are and what you are doing. The American public deserves to know."

"No!" She'd surprised them both by yelling the word and she took a deep breath to calm herself. "For years, the press and the American public had their nose in every little thing I did. My haircuts. My nail polish. The color of my sports bra. And, only during Olympic years, my running. You've had your rule over my life. You're all vultures—you can find another scandal to pick at. I wanted to run in a race with other people. I did that today, along with ninety-nine others. I'm no different from any of them."

Even under the brunt of her anger, Micah's face was open and placid. Whatever emotion had driven him to her door he'd buried deep inside, where she couldn't see it, replacing it with curiosity. *Share your intimacies with me. Confession is good for the soul.* What a liar his face was. Confession opened wounds from which fresh blood poured. It riled up the vultures until they circled over her life and waited for it to be destroyed. "You didn't seem to mind the press's attention until you got caught doping and they took away your gold medal."

Her jaw clenched and she had to spit out her response. "You're here because you think I will get you good ratings, which means you're no better than I am. And before you lecture me—" Ruby put her hand on the doorknob "—I sure as hell know more about my sins and their consequences than you do." She opened the door. "Now get out, before I call the front desk."

"I still want an interview." Micah didn't appear to be going anywhere. His hands weren't even on the wheels of his chair. "You should think about it. I'll be far kinder to you than King Ripley will be if he figures out who you are."

Except Ruby was certain she could outsmart King Ripley. "I am sure it's considered bad etiquette to wheel you out of my room against your will, but I didn't invite you in here, so I don't really care."

Micah cocked his head and regarded her, his scorn caressing every square inch of her bare skin. The sensation was familiar enough that she relaxed her shoulders. He was nothing she hadn't endured before and couldn't endure again. Besides, she was smarter this time. A different and better person. He didn't have to know that Ruby Heart was a new person because *she* knew.

"I think I could stop you," he said. Several long seconds went by with his arms still crossed over his chest, the bulges of his deltoids straining his T-shirt sleeves. Would he call her bluff? Finally, he put his hands down and left her room without saying another word. Ruby shut the door with a soft click, then leaned her forehead against the wood and took a deep breath, closing her eyes against the memories of a phone constantly ringing and camera flashes invading her peace.

She breathed deep into her abdomen before she opened her eyes again. This was the only race she was allowing herself to run. Without an interview, any story Micah did about her was dead as soon as she drove home.

She turned back to her desk, the egg-salad sandwich—now warm as well as soggy—wilting on its plastic wrap next to a small bag of potato chips and some carrots. She was no longer hungry, but she'd been an athlete for too long to confuse food with emotions. Besides, she thought as the bag of chips wrinkled when she cracked it open, she didn't have to taste the food to gain nourishment.

MICAH HADN'T GONE five feet when he stopped and reflected back on Ruby, both the woman in the hotel room and the girl he'd interviewed five years ago. Despite being twenty-four when she'd won her gold medal, and in the public spotlight off and on for the previous four years, after she had captivated the world by winning the silver medal in a sport Americans hadn't known they'd cared about, Ruby had been a girl existing in a silly, cloud-filled dream world where putting one step in front of the other until her chest broke the finish line was the only thing that mattered.

The juxtaposition between the Ruby of then and the Ruby of now was jarring. If she'd denied being Ruby Heart, he might have even believed her. Five years ago, Ruby's hair had been bleached blond and razor sharp at her chin. She'd worn heavy black eyeliner and bright red lipstick. Everything about that Ruby had been composed to catch—and hold—your attention. Like the rest of America, the costume had fooled Micah into believing Ruby was slicker and worldlier than she actually had been. Not until he'd re-watched his interview with her on YouTube with five years of distance could he see the bewilderment in her eyes under all that makeup.

This Ruby Heart, with her pigtails, wide brown eyes and smattering of freckles, had all the innocence of the clichéd girl next door, designed to be forgotten once your front door shut. Only now Ruby's eyes had the harshness of a woman who knew what it felt like to have a knife in the back combined with a sense of resignation, as if she expected another stab at any moment.

Had she really changed from that attention-seeking girl she'd been? She'd turned down an interview, but Ruby was a runner, and she might also be the kind of person who liked to be chased. Which was fine; Micah still enjoyed a good hunt.

One thing was certain, she still had the same glorious body. Her T-shirt and gym shorts meant there had been plenty of bare skin for him to appreciate. When she'd moved her arms, her biceps had expanded and collapsed and he wished he'd managed to make her take a step toward him. With so little body fat, her legs were a lesson in muscle anatomy, and they rippled when she moved.

Micah had always been a leg man, and his tastes hadn't changed just because his own legs were now the downstairs neighbor he waved at but who never waved in return. Calves made shapely by high heels were not the legs he fantasized about. He liked the condensed power in a female athlete's thighs—a ham man, his teammates had said. His college girlfriend had played tennis, but her thighs in that swinging white skirt had nothing on Ruby in gym shorts. All that power in a sleek, racing version.

Micah rubbed his face, then squeezed the bridge of his

nose, forcing himself to remember why Ruby was in that hotel room and not fresh off another Olympic triumph. Pigtails were as much a costume as the red lipstick had been. She needed no pity. And she didn't deserve his admiration of her body. She'd been given the opportunity to compete on the greatest stage the world offered her sport and she'd responded by filling her veins with the blood of another person. Blood doping was a gruesome way to cheat, making a mockery of both the sport and the people for whom that blood meant the difference between life and death. A vampire, draining the sport and the athlete of all its integrity. A monster.

And, after her interview, she'd had the audacity to expect pity from him.

He put his hands back on the wheels of his chair and refused to think of Ruby's thighs in any way other than belonging on the hot seat while Amir filmed the interview of Micah's career. He would show the world how little a doping athlete changed, no matter the tears they produced in a confessional. And then he'd take the promotion NSN offered.

CHAPTER THREE

MICAH HAD ARRIVED back in Chicago late Tuesday night and wasn't expected in the studio until after lunch on Wednesday, so he stopped at his favorite restaurant for a bite to eat before work. The lunch hour meant Micah had to force his way through the other regulars, all of whom greeted him, to get his wheelchair to a table. But Sheila, the hostess, always took special care of him and got him a table for four, which was great until King showed up. "Is this seat taken?" the other reporter asked while pulling out a chair and sitting down. Micah didn't bother to say no; King would only pretend that the restaurant was too noisy to hear.

After asking the waitress, Patty, for a beer, King turned to Micah with the manly joie de vivre that could lure inexperienced athletes into ignoring the cameras and pretending they were in a high school locker room. Savvy athletes, however, treated the wink-wink, nudge-nudge with the same distant professionalism they offered reporters in the locker room after a game, making the majority of King's interviews some of the most boring two minutes of sports reporting on television. The man kept his job only because the few times he got an athlete to confide, internet GIF memes were sparked and YouTube hits records set. Often, those athletes didn't have long careers. Micah tapped his fingers against his chair and waited for the inevitable intrusion that would come after the small talk.

King took a long pull on his beer and set the bottle down with a thunk. "Amir says you spent the entire race in your room and then the night in a runner's room." Micah didn't believe Amir would sell him out, especially after King turned his head to one side, as if offering up his left ear for girlish intimacies, and nodded knowingly.

"I think," King said, tapping his index finger against his lips, "that you knew this runner before you met her at the race."

Micah threw the man a bone, since King didn't have the investigative skills to do anything with this conversation. "I did know her before."

"From college?"

"No."

King lifted his brow for an elaboration, but Micah didn't offer one. The other reporter shrugged off the small insult, took another long pull of his beer and then signaled for another. "A friend, then. Your connection to the elusive Currito?"

Micah had long since stopped being amazed that King couldn't conceive of a nonplatonic reason for Micah to interact with a woman. In an industry dominated by men who didn't even bother looking to see whose dick hung the lowest—because, of course, they would win—Micah knew his supposed celibacy was a curiosity. He had heard all the rumored reasons for why he never had a date at office parties, ranging from some sort of self-imposed sexual exile out of a dislike of women with strange kinks to the ongoing question of how well his plumbing worked. The folks in the first camp would probably be disappointed to learn that there weren't hundreds of women lined up outside hotel rooms across America with fetishes for men who couldn't wiggle their toes. The one woman with such a kink who'd found Micah had been *strange* in bed. It was not an encounter he wanted to repeat.

Lack of imagination generally meant his coworkers credited Micah's physical body for his sparse sex life instead of recognizing that Micah worked too damn much. At least, that was the reason most of his girlfriends never made it far enough past "short-term" for his coworkers to meet them.

King, Micah knew, fell firmly into the camp that believed Micah couldn't get it up anymore. Much to Micah's amusement—and many women's disappointment, he was sure—King didn't seem to understand how a woman could find sexual pleasure unless a man stuck an erect penis into her vagina and then bounced his ass up and down in the air. Once, after ten hours of drinking on a flight to Sydney, King had told Micah that lesbians had to use "accessories." Micah had yet to decide if King's indirect approach was better or worse than the strangers who flat out *asked* intrusive questions.

The memory of the conversation reminded Micah that he didn't want to be sitting in public with King and alcohol. Unfortunately, Micah had talked himself into a King-created corner. Denying now that he hadn't spent the night in Ruby's bedroom would only push King and his beers into asking what Micah *hadn't* been doing when he *hadn't* been in the room—wink-wink, nudge-nudge. Saying that Ruby hadn't been his connection to Currito would also stretch King's imagination to the breaking point.

"A friend," Micah said simply, before pulling his cell phone out of his pocket and checking the time.

"You are a mysterious man, Micah Blackwell."

Micah nodded, the statement overwhelmingly true from King's point of view. "And, given that I overestimated how much time I have for lunch, I'm likely to stay that way." When the waitress arrived at his signal, he asked for his lunch to go.

King peered across the small table at Micah and harrumphed. "You think you can keep this a secret." The ensuing silence would *almost* have been suspenseful if King hadn't been flicking his index finger from his lips to point at Micah and back again, over and over and over in some falsity of a knowing gesture. "Now I am interested and on your trail."

"Okay." Micah backed his chair away from the table and swore under his breath when he hit the chair behind him. The benefit of King moving the chairs out of his way as he navigated through the restaurant was overshadowed by the exaggerated way in which the man drew attention to what a stand-up guy he was by "helping."

"Micah, man, stay longer next time," said one of the cooks from the kitchen, who met him at the front door to drop a sack of food in his lap. "None of this eatin' and rollin' when I've got a fantasy baseball team to manage."

Micah handed Patty a wad of bills before turning to the cook. "Frank, you know I'll be back for lunch tomorrow and you can pick my brain then." They exchanged a few more pleasantries, and then Micah was out the door with a wave.

As he made his way to his car, he wondered if he should track down Ruby and warn her of King's interest. Not that King was likely to remember the rise and fall of Chicago's native gazelle. He'd been busy working his way up the sporting news food chain covering high school football in Texas during that time. However, it was a convenient excuse to ask her for that interview again. No way was he letting her play the part of reformed recluse.

MICAH ENTERED HIS office on the sprawling suburban Chicago campus of the National Sports Network to find the message light on his phone blinking and no fewer than five sticky notes on his monitor. Since all the notes were from his boss, Micah listened to the phone messages first. There were the usual calls from publicists and agents looking for spotlight stories, two from viewers who had managed to bluff or gruff their way past the operator and one call from King, assuring Micah that he was onto him and would solve the mystery of the female racer.

Micah wouldn't give King the chance. King wouldn't even think to ask the interesting questions, like how she'd managed to negotiate her lifetime ban down to five years. The details of her settlement with the governing body were locked up in a nondisclosure agreement, but whatever she'd done for the reduced sentence, her coach had been arrested and the once-great sports agency run by her agent had been dismantled in disgrace. Suggestions that the governing body had gone easy on her because she was white, young, cute and rich had been the dominant theme in any conversation about her punishment.

Micah logged on to his computer and hunted around the old news stories about Ruby, an itch at the back of his brain. The Ruby he remembered had been completely focused on running, but selling out an entire system of cheaters implied that she'd been listening when the people around her talked about the supply chain. She'd claimed not to have been included in the decision making and had simply followed the recommendations of her coach. If Micah was willing to grant her the benefit of the doubt in order to follow his train of thought, then everyone around Ruby had assumed she was too dumb to be a liability and she'd proved, to herself if to no one else, that they'd all underestimated her.

Micah's realization only made him more determined to prevent King from getting that interview.

He didn't have time to return the calls, and there was no need to go see what his boss wanted, because Dexter, one of NSN's executive producers, sauntered up to Micah's door and leaned against the metal jamb, his arms crossed and curiosity etched across his dark skin. "King Ripley came back from lunch telling everyone you got lucky while in Iowa."

"As usual, he had access to all the facts and came to the wrong conclusion."

"But you did have Amir take video of Ruby Heart running."

That explained why there had been five stickies on his monitor instead of one. When Micah had first started at NSN, he'd been surprised at Dexter's clairvoyance. Now it was both a blessing and a curse. "I did."

Dexter's dreadlocks swayed as he nodded. "And you're sure it's her?"

"She didn't deny it, though she said she'd never do another interview." The anger he'd seen in her face when she talked about press intrusion into her life had to be a part of whatever new role she was playing.

"And you want her to be in the ultra series."

"The feature," Micah said. Ruby may not wish for the spotlight, but the spotlight wished for her.

"Get the interview first. We'll run that and see how interested people are."

As soon as Dexter left the office, Micah searched through his contacts until he found Mike Danforth's number. Five years ago, Mike Danforth had worked in the same office as Ruby's agent. Mike also owed him a favor and would probably see nothing wrong with Ruby sweating under the hot lights of another interview.

CHAPTER FOUR

RUBY WALKED INTO her parents' large Lake Forest home and put her running bag on top of the washing machine. Neither the clunk of the bag on the appliance nor the buzz of the overhead lights were enough to distract from the usual deathly silence of the house. Not that the house was emotionless, because cold was an emotion, at least as Ruby had experienced it for the past five years.

She grabbed a towel from her bag, wiping the sweat from the back of her neck. Running had been her passion, her chore and her job. Now it was a gift she both gave and received, and she didn't ever take it for granted. She'd been itching to get out and run again after a few days' rest, and today's volunteer shift at the animal shelter had been especially lovely with the warmer weather and partially cloudy skies. By the third dog she took out for a run, Ruby had settled into a routine and had been able to banish the constant specter of Micah Blackwell.

Her daydreams were nightmares where an interview reinvigorated press attention. At night, though, Micah's chocolaty voice invited her into his world and she dreamed about what his deltoids and trapezius must look like to support his pecs. She explored the rest of his body in her dreams, too, only to wake up hot and excited.

She walked to the kitchen and got herself a banana and a glass of chocolate milk. When she turned to head down to the weight room for some stretching, she found her mother floating in the doorway, the light linens she wore given a weightless quality with the slight breeze of the fan. Her mom looked thin, which wasn't unusual, but the black circles were back under her eyes and her cheeks had a sunken quality Ruby didn't remember having been there this morning.

"You promised." Her mom's fingers fluttered together with the same airy quality of her clothes, giving the impression that her mom had so little substance the air from a fan could blow her away.

Her mom's voice was also several octaves above normal, a sign her mother was more wounded than hurt, so Ruby only asked, "What did I promise?" before taking a gulp of her milk. In another lifetime, she would have rushed to her mother to apologize and beg forgiveness, even before knowing her crime. Also in another lifetime, she would fear finishing a race without knowing her mother would be at the finish line.

In this lifetime, her mom didn't even know there was a finish line.

"Running." Her mother's voice cracked between the two *n*'s. "You've been running."

"Mom, I've been volunteering at the shelter for three years. Why are you complaining about it now?" Ruby's running used to be a source of pride for her mother. At track meets, in church, and at the grocery store, her mother had always been the first person to exclaim over her daughter's athleticism and how her daughter was going to be an Olympic champion. Ruby had won her first big race by running right into her mother's open arms.

Now every time Ruby returned from her shift at the shelter, her mother eyed the running shoes left by the door with the same disgust she gave an errant cuticle. One of the many hard things Ruby had learned five years ago was that her mother's love was conditional on Ruby's success.

Ruby didn't even know what success looked like anymore. Three measly minutes. If she'd run each kilometer only four seconds faster she'd have been looking at her goal from over her shoulder rather than staring at its butt.

"Where were you last weekend?"

"I was visiting Haley." Her cousin had been pushing Ruby to move on with her life for years and had been more than willing to provide an alibi.

"Shopping for wedding dresses, you said." Her mother's voice lost its tremble, becoming sharp and pointed. "I called Marguerite and she didn't see either of you."

Ruby nearly choked on her banana. Both Haley and Ruby had been certain her mother wouldn't do more than call Haley to confirm. Since Ruby had started to express interest in a life outside of this house, her mother had become more concerned with her whereabouts, but she'd never gone this far. Chewing and swallowing her food gave Ruby time to come up with an answer. "We weren't looking for her *real* wedding dress. We went to the big bridal outlet to get a sense for what Haley might like."

"I don't see how that took all weekend." The quiver was back.

Something specific had sparked her mother's paranoia, but Ruby would play along with this game as far as she could. She took another bite of her banana and waited.

"Mike Danforth called." *Ah*. Well, if anyone was going

to call from the agency she'd destroyed, Mike was the best option. "Micah Blackwell—" the name hissed out of her mother's mouth as if it were a name that should never be spoken "—wants an interview with you. Why?" The fear on her mother's face didn't surprise Ruby—the year after the scandal had been scary for everyone—but the concern did.

"Who can say?" She shrugged. "March Madness is over. Maybe NSN needs to fill airtime."

"You know what your, your…"

Mistake? Scandal? Embarrassment? Failure? Sin? Crime?

"…*incident* cost the family. You wouldn't want to put us through that again."

"I remember. And I don't." Her father knew—to the penny—how much the legal bills would have been, *if my firm hadn't taken care of it for you.* The pill bottles left scattered around the house were a reminder of the emotional cost to her mother. Ruby's sister, Roxanne, was still miffed that her research had been overshadowed by questions from even the crustiest academic about her infamous sister. And Josh was kind enough to regularly mention how much experience his sister's problems had given him as a young associate. Josh also said those words while giving Ruby a hug, so she knew her brother's sarcasm wasn't mean-spirited.

Ruby rinsed out her glass and put it in the dishwasher, then threw out her banana peel. "Mom, I really need to stretch. Did you want anything else?"

"Don't forget how important it is to all of us that you stay out of the spotlight."

What about me and my life? Ruby knew saying those words would prompt her mother to talk about the sacrifices the family had made for Ruby's sport, the energy and money they'd thrown away and how her brother and sister had had to fend for themselves. Ruby knew the resources her family had put into her running, but in hindsight she wondered if it had all been for her.

Down in the weight room, Ruby laid out her mat and began her regular series of stretches. The room had been built for her when she was in high school and college coaches had started showing up at her meets. And after college she'd gotten new weight benches and a private coach. The room was the temple to her success and the dumbbell racks her altar.

She'd stayed away from her weight room for an entire year after the Olympics. It had taken another year after that for her to feel comfortable being surrounded by herself in all the mirrors. Now, checking the alignment of her spine as she reached forward and grabbed her toes, Ruby wondered if the room was more a cloister than a temple, designed to keep her in and obedient. She'd only started coming into this room regularly when her father had reminded her how much it had cost the family. "Your brother always wanted a game room," her dad had said, as if her brother hadn't already been off at college and done living at home when the weight room had been put in.

Regardless of everything, she loved this room. She loved the smooth wood under her feet and the way the light bounced off the mirrors. She loved how the mats gave gently under the pressure of her feet when she pushed a loaded bar over her head, and the sharp smell of iron against iron when she pushed another weight plate onto the metal bars. She loved how the speakers drowned out her anxieties when she plugged in her iPod. The room was a sanctuary and also one of the reasons she hadn't moved out of her parents' house yet.

But why *should* she feel trapped here? She wasn't just a

runner, she was *the* runner. The runner who'd made Americans care about middle-distance running again. The runner who'd graced the covers of *Sports Illustrated, ESPN The Magazine* and *People.*

Someone else's blood in her veins hadn't been the only reason for her success. Ruby's best skill when running had always been her ability to escape from the crowd, no matter how tightly others tried to box her in. She'd been the story of her first Olympics because in her first heat, she'd slipped through gaps no one else could see to beat the favorite.

Intrusive Micah, her anxious mother, stupid Mike Danforth, this beloved room—she realized now that they were all trying to box her into the role she'd accepted. Disgraced Olympian. Someone who should hide from her past. Someone who should be ashamed for the rest of her life because there were no second chances and there was no forgiveness.

Ruby could stay in this room, in this house, for the rest of her life. Or she could duck out of the trap and find something new.

Ruby cut her stretch session short, rolled up her yoga mat and headed to her room.

CHAPTER FIVE

"HOW WAS THE ultramarathon?" Micah's father asked as they left his hotel and headed for the lakeshore. His father still traveled too much on business, though he regularly stopped on his way back home to visit Micah.

Parking his son at the child's grandmother's and sending regular checks had been a coward's way of fathering, but they'd both decided it was better to forgive. After Micah's accident, when his father had been the only person to look him in the eyes as the doctor told him he would never walk again, Micah had understood that brave men faced their past and letting go of childhood hurts didn't make him weak.

The other pedestrians gave them a wide berth, like a school of fish parting around a video camera in a nature documentary. The unfamiliar object seen and its foreignness avoided because it couldn't be ignored.

At the crosswalk, Micah handed over a couple bucks to the *StreetWise* vendor before answering his father. "It was fine." He debated elaborating. When they reached the other side of the street and Grant Park, he said, "Ruby Heart was there."

"With her mother?"

An enveloping hug between mother and daughter had been one of the iconic photographs of Ruby's stratospheric rise to fame. After Ruby's cheating had been revealed, Mrs. Heart had vanished and Mr. Heart had appeared as the parent of supreme importance.

"No. She was alone."

His dad snorted. "Her mother always did look too brittle to survive adversity."

"Brittle?" The woman had been thin, with a cutting quality to her face that Micah had always associated with wealthy women and crystal champagne glasses, neither of which he would ever identify as *brittle*.

"Yeah, I got the sense—even in photographs—that if Ruby fell, her mother would break."

They stopped at another light, the traffic on Columbus speeding past them. Micah looked up at his father, who didn't appear to be joking. "I always got the sense her parents supported her." Actually, at the time of her scandal, Micah had found the closeness of her parents in her life— she'd been twenty-four and still living at home for God's sake—to be a sign of weakness.

His father shrugged before stepping forward to cross the street. "I guess they filled the role of a track team for her once she left college, but all I saw was a mother seeking fame through her daughter. Maybe I'm not being fair to the woman."

"She isn't your mother," Micah replied, directing the conversation away from anything resembling sympathy to Ruby Heart.

"No, but the benefit of my mother is that once you realized she couldn't be pleased, you could stop trying."

His father hadn't reached that point until Micah was nineteen, and it had taken a crippling accident for Micah to get there. From what Micah knew of his own mother, part of the reason she'd run off had been because she hadn't even wanted to try to live up to his grandmama's strict standards. *Grandmamas love little boys who win football games.*

"She's dead now, so I guess I don't have to worry about it."

They crossed the rest of the park in silence. Only when they stood at the crosswalk on Lakeshore Drive, the whoosh of cars and busses nearly drowning out his voice, did his father respond. "I'm sorry, you know."

"I know." His father apologized anytime grandmama was brought up in conversation. He had never claimed he didn't know what he'd left his son to deal with, but he'd also never shied away from any punishment Micah dealt out during his rehabilitation. And the first time his grandmama had said, "Cripples belong at home," and Micah had been too doped up to do more than grunt, his father had ordered her barred from the hospital.

The light changed and they crossed the wall of revving car engines and exhaust before arriving at the lakeshore.

"Ruby looked good," Micah said, changing the subject. With her natural plain hair, she'd looked fresh and warm and healthy. A Midwestern milkmaid whose slender figure hid muscles that could bench-press a cow before outrunning all the boys. Weak women were for weak men.

She'd gained some weight in her five years out of the public eye, adding a suggestion of curves to what would otherwise be a stick-straight figure. She looked less of a fantasy and more of a real person one would want to sit across a table from and share a meal with. *A crazy dream.* She was also a cheater.

"Yeah?" his father said, the question in his voice the only acknowledgment either of them would give to the interest

Micah had given Ruby's career before her doping was revealed.

His father had to slip behind him on the path to make room for some bicyclists. After the bikes passed and he caught up with Micah, he asked, "Are you going to interview her again?"

"She said no, but I'm not giving up." Not to mention that Micah had determined the anchor spot was his and Ruby was the key. Despite the paucity of current information available online, he didn't think Ruby was truly forgotten in the public's mind. After all, the American public loved two stories more than any other: Judas's downfall and the possibility of his redemption.

His father stopped to look out over the blue of Lake Michigan. "If I were her, I doubt I'd want to be interviewed by a man who couldn't take no for an answer."

"She'll come to me." Micah let the fact that he'd had Mike call her stay buried under the surface of the rippling water.

THE NEXT DAY Micah was sitting in his office when the phone rang and he knew, without recognizing the number on the caller ID, what voice he would hear on the other end.

"What part of no didn't you understand?" The words were tight—angry—and Micah imagined the clench of her jaw as the words punched their way past her teeth. Well, she couldn't fake doe-eyed innocence anymore. Indignation was probably as close as she could get.

"The part where *you* call *me*."

"Yeah, to tell you to leave my mother alone. To tell you to tell Mike to leave my mother alone. I have no interest in helping NSN pay their satellite bills. Did that once, don't plan to do it again."

"Not even to show the world how you've reformed?" He

threaded the carrot on the rope and dangled it in front of her. "A new person with new hope and new dreams and no needles sticking out of your arm. The TV-viewing public will eat that up."

"Lance Armstrong might be free. Or a baseball player, any baseball player."

"But none of them ever graced the cover of *People* with the headline Meet America's Darling."

"You have me mistaken with someone who wants to return to their past. Find another redemption story. I'm not biting."

The phone clicked and Micah stared into the silence of the receiver. What did she think running a race was if not an attempt to return to her past? When he set the phone back down in the cradle, he knew he had her. He simply needed the right bait.

"YOU CAN'T PLAY that trick a second time," Ruby's cousin Haley said, the exasperation in her voice loud and clear, even over an echoing cell connection. "You know Aunt Julie called my mom, right?"

"There has to be something else you need to do for the wedding that your favorite cousin and best friend is essential for."

"Aunt. Julie. Called. My. Mom." Haley huffed. "Like I was a teenager sneaking out to a college party."

"And the dress shop."

"What! Really?"

"I should have foreseen that, honestly. Mom has always been thorough." Only as Ruby realized that neither her brother nor her sister had managed to sneak out of the house as teenagers did she wonder if her mother had been as ignorant of the doping as she'd claimed.

"I can barely stand this sneaking around, and you live it every day, Ruby."

"I rarely have to sneak." Like the crazed wife in the attic, unless she threatened to make the papers, her parents simply pretended she wasn't there.

"You really should move out."

"I know." Haley had been telling Ruby to get out on her own for years now, since that first sponsorship offer had come in. Ruby was more tempted now than she had ever been. She could make friends other than her cousin. Maybe even invite a man over, if she could find one who wasn't constantly trying to one-up her, or one who didn't lord her past over her.

Micah? No, he failed the second criteria. And he could probably fake liking her enough to interview her, but not beyond the cameras rolling. She wasn't sure she'd trust him even if he *were* nice to her.

Who was she kidding? It wasn't as though she could afford to move out on her own. Her only skill was winning middle-distance races. And all the money she had from sponsorship was frozen while the two lawsuits against her by a shoe company and a sports-drink company moved through courts at their glacial pace. She'd question the credentials of any school that wanted her for a coach, and any private athlete who hired her would be tested for drugs so often their veins would collapse. Her college major and the degree it was printed on would be worth money only if she put it on eBay and accepted bids.

None of which she would say out loud, even to her cousin, who already knew it all. "My parents were there for me when I needed them. And they still want me here." A close-enough interpretation of the look of panic her mom got whenever Ruby mentioned looking for an apartment.

"Your dad went all lawyer-happy when you needed him. And your mom fell apart. And they want you at the house because they fear the gossip, not because they like your company."

In this, her cousin was both right and wrong. Both her parents *had* been available and supportive—or at least available—when Ruby had needed them. But the last time their support had come in the form of a hug was five years ago. All of which only made Ruby more determined to run another race. No matter what her parents thought, running had always been for her.

"Plus," Haley continued, "before you run another race, how do you know that reporter isn't looking for you?" Was her cousin trying to convince her to move out or to hide in a bunker?

"According to NSN's website, he'll be at a Brewers game that weekend because they're honoring some ex-player he's going to interview. In fact—" Ruby's excitement grew with every word she spoke, both at the thought of another race and beating Haley in this argument "—because the Brewers are in Milwaukee and I'll be in Indiana, I'll be *farther* away from Micah than I have knowingly been in five years."

Haley let out a big puff of air. "Fine. But I think you're overplaying your hand. Move out of that house. Get a job. Live a normal life."

"Just one more race."

"Said the addict to the heroin needle."

As MICAH REWATCHED some of the film Amir had taken of Ruby, an itch developed between his shoulder blades. There was something off about her stride and a look of pain on her face that couldn't be the fifty-kilometer run, because she was only five kilometers into the race, which had been her best distance as an Olympian. He looked at her finishing time, which he'd written on a sticky note and stuck on a printout of the photo of her with the American flag high over her head. The itch paced in a circle between his scapulae, nearly wearing a line in his skin.

Ruby had been slow. Even assuming she was trying to get her ultra legs under her, she had still run a slow race. And if she was only running one race—as she claimed—he thought she would have put everything she had into getting the best time possible. Four hours and forty-three minutes was *someone's* best time for a fifty-kilometer race, but it sure as hell wasn't Ruby Heart's best time.

Micah shifted his shoulders around but couldn't get the itch out of his back. He drummed his fingers against his desk, then pressed Play on the film again. Ruby had tossed her hat in an attempt to hide from him and Amir, which meant the camera had much better shots of her face, even through the drizzle that had plagued the race. He slowed the film, reassessing what he saw. The look on Ruby's face wasn't pain—it was restraint.

Even if she was consciously holding herself back, he knew top athletes as well as he knew his own grandmama, and she couldn't have been happy with that time. The four hours and forty-three minutes would needle at her brain and pride until she *had* to see if she could finish better. And even if she was curtailing her normal power for a very good reason, her natural competitiveness would win out. A woman who cared enough about an Olympic gold medal to stick a needle in her arm wasn't going to let such a poor time stand as the only record of her ultra career.

He stopped the video and opened a browser. She had run one 50K race and he would guess she would run another. Micah navigated to an ultramarathon website and started searching. He stopped when he came to the trail run in Indiana in three weeks. A 50K, with at least a few spots still open. Easy driving distance from Chicago. The arrow of the mouse twitched on the screen as he considered the chances she wouldn't be there.

If he was wrong, well, he and Amir would have more footage for NSN's series, so the entire trip wouldn't be completely wasted. But he wasn't wrong. He would see Ruby's tight ass and sleek thighs encased in running shorts as certain as the yuppies at Wrigley Field would spend more time on their cell phones than watching the Cubs play. Micah picked up his phone and called his boss.

THREE WEEKS LATER, Amir slid into the driver's seat of the production van with a huff that Micah ignored. His photographer was a baseball fan and had found the last trip out to an ultramarathon—this one in Idaho to film Currito—to be "about as fun as watching a slug climb a rock."

Despite Micah being a sports guy, Amir's slug description sounded more interesting than a baseball game to Micah, a secret he would take to his grave. Watching the ultramarathoners push their bodies to the limit of possibility fascinated Micah, and he felt a certain kinship with a sport based on the idea of giving the middle finger to the world's perception of what was possible for one body to achieve.

What had possessed Ruby to even try an ultramarathon?

They were on I-94 when Amir asked the question that must have been gnawing at his brain since he'd learned about the change of plans. "If this Ruby Heart really is an—how did you say it?—embarrassment to everything sports stands for, why are we skipping out on what should be a great baseball game, not to mention the festivities afterward, to drive to Indiana and watch people run on dirt for eight hours?"

"We don't have to stay for the whole race. Just until Ruby finishes."

"Five hours, then."

This race was hillier than the one in Iowa had been, but Ruby would be trying to run faster. "No more than four and half." Micah had also looked at the race times for the top runners for this race. Ruby wouldn't be at that level yet, but she would be gunning for it, even if she didn't realize it, and those runners did this race in four hours.

"Still, there's nothing interesting anywhere near this race." Amir braked to avoid hitting the car in front of them, then moved to the left lane and passed a long line of cars while muttering under his breath about stupid drivers and stupid Indiana. He had made the same complaint in Iowa and Idaho and would probably repeat it again if they watched the ultramarathon in Chicago. "Why lower your standards to follow this fraud?"

"You never complain when I interview baseball players. And you didn't complain about the Tour de France, either."

"Sure." Amir shrugged. "I like baseball and I'm not foolish enough to complain about a trip to France." Amir had been his photog for almost three years and remembered those interviews as well as Micah did, though through a different lens. "But while the baseball players and the cyclists both wear tight pants, none of them have pigtails."

Micah didn't say anything. The pigtails probably spoke to some disturbing fetish hidden deep within, but he thought they were hot.

CHAPTER SIX

RUBY STOOD AMONG the other racers at the starting line, tapping at the dirt with the toe of her running shoe. The weather was perfect. Most of the race would be spent in the trees, so the bright overhead sun would be welcome, rather than a hindrance. The temperature was cool enough that she shouldn't overheat at kilometer twenty and there was—thankfully—no rain in the forecast. Her main concern was that the loop crossed two streams and she'd not had much practice running with wet feet.

Still, she thought, lifting her head to look at the morning sky visible through the bright green spring leaves above her, she'd invited the deities Nike and Hermes along for the journey and they'd obliged. She could feel them crouching among the other racers. There would be no measly three minutes to haunt her drive home this weekend.

Haley had flatly refused to provide an alibi for another weekend. Her cousin had said she didn't have a problem lying to Ruby's parents, but Haley was all out of plausible excuses and she didn't have the energy to think of implausible ones the Hearts would believe. Ruby had been about to forfeit her entry fee when her mom had announced that she was taking a spur-of-the-moment spa weekend, which meant her father would use the opportunity to stay in the city and work. Or whatever else he did.

She shifted her weight from side to side, partially to keep muscles pliable and partially to move the uncomfortable knowledge of how naive and self-centered she'd been far enough into the back of her head that she didn't have to stare at it throughout the race. When she'd been training she'd been so focused on herself. Her entire family had been focused on her. All the spare resources went to Team Ruby. She hadn't even noticed how unhappy her family was until she didn't have anything else to occupy her mind and they no longer had her to rally around any. Her career hadn't been the glue that held them together; it had been the butterfly bandage barely keeping them from falling apart when really they'd needed stiches. Now they were left with a scar that would never go away.

This time around she was racing on her own, with her own meager resources. Even though she wasn't doing it to win, her entire family—maybe not Josh—would say she was being selfish. And they'd be right. She was here to find the good parts of Ruby Heart again. She hadn't realized that for her first race, but she knew that now. Ruby Heart had been a scandal and she'd done something horrible, but she couldn't be all bad.

She shivered as it felt as if a mouse ran down her spine. The crowds were sparse enough that she could glance around and see each and every person waiting for the gun to go off. Including the man she wanted to see least, the man who could wreck her whole plan to rediscover Ruby Heart. Micah Blackwell was watching her from the sidelines with his head cocked, a vague smile on his face and his hands on the wheels of his chair as if he were going to dart away from the sidelines to race after her at any moment. Right behind him stood his cameraman and the giant camera stared at her with its black, unblinking eye.

The starting gun boomed and Ruby burst forward. *Try to catch me,* she wanted to yell. She wanted to laugh. Micah could chase her all he wanted, but she was Ruby Heart, and he would never catch her.

MICAH SAT ON the sidelines, tapping his fingers against the wheel of his chair and watching Ruby work to keep her muscles warm for the race. The neon green hat Ruby had been wearing at the first race must have been completely abandoned in Iowa, because she wore a different hat today. The mud-brown canvas wasn't nearly as eye-catching as the neon had been, but it didn't need to be. The set of Ruby's shoulders would attract as much attention as any ugly hat. Her hot pants were a velvety gray, and she wore a tight yellow running shirt. When she moved, he thought he saw a gray parrot silhouetted in the fabric of the back of her shirt. Not quite trying to hide in the crowds today. People would remember the parrot. He was going to remember the way her muscles shifted and moved, like watching a panther stretch.

Her body stilled. She had seen him watching her. Then she straightened and her shoulders rolled back. As the countdown got closer to one, Ruby tilted herself forward. When the gun went off, her muscles contracted for a blink of an eye before she burst forward. Ruby Heart was back. And different.

SHE FINISHED IN just under four hours, fifteen minutes, smashing her past race time and on a harder course, and all that was left to do was to enjoy the euphoria of finishing a race and eat her banana before she fell over. Instead, she took a sip of her beer and looked around. The congratulations friends and family offered other runners boomed over the clamor of the band onstage. The spectators also offered assistance. "How do you feel? Have a seat, I'll get you some chips. The guac is real good."

The top finishers in the race hung around, chatting with one another like old friends and cheering for the runners crossing the finish line. Step over that line from pain into party, their cheers promised. Supportive. Encouraging. A reminder of what it had been like to be a member of a team, even though these were all individual racers.

Her runner's high put a goofy smile on her face and she stood there, not certain where to put her hands, where to look, wishing she had someone to hold a plate of chips and guacamole for her. Finishing one small plate of food was enough to make her feel ready to take the shuttle back to her hotel, so Ruby left the postrace celebration.

She, Ruby Heart, used to being surrounded by coaches and her mother at the end of a race, accustomed to the cheers of an Olympic stadium, had been the only racer on the bus ride back. Of course, old Ruby Heart had been accustomed to winning, not achieving personal bests.

The last of her race euphoria abandoned her when she crossed the threshold into her hotel room. As the sweat crystalized on her body in the dry hotel room air-conditioning, she wondered, *who is Ruby Heart?* Whoever she was, she needed to find dinner and rest, or else it wouldn't matter who Ruby Heart was, because she'd be as stiff as a stadium seat in the morning and would have to drive like a zombie with her joints all locked up.

The phone next to the bed rang and Ruby had the relief of having something to do. "Hello?"

"Ruby?"

The velvet voice said her name, like it did in her dreams before turning on her. *You had someone shove your failure into your arm and then you pissed your dreams away.* When she hadn't seen Micah at the finish line, she'd convinced herself that his presence at the starting line had been a figment of her imagination. And been disappointed that he'd given up so easily.

A part of her—one larger than she cared to admit—wished Micah were at her door. Company, any company, would be nice, but especially company that understood what it meant to create and then smash a personal goal.

But those desires were overshadowed by terror that the press wolves were only waiting for the call of their leader to descend upon her. With no talking, not even the television, to drown out the beats, the drum of her pen tapping the hotel pad filled the room.

Ruby put the pen down. Pretending to be someone she wasn't, lying to herself and everyone around her about her true nature, isolated her. Cabin fever, only without the fresh pine scent of the woods.

Lying created multilevel problems, like the fear deep in her breast that her falsehood would be found out. Because she knew what happened when the world discovered you'd been lying to them. Only this would be worse, because their anger would be unleashed at Ruby's true self, rather than a publicity designed cover girl.

These ultra runs were about conquering your mind as much as your body, so she drew on the reserves of mental energy that kept her putting one foot in front of another and responded without a hint of fear in her voice. "Hello, Micah. Couldn't get the hotel staff to give you my room number this time?"

"Didn't have Amir follow you to your floor." His tone was gentle and correcting, but also offered something. He was playing nice today.

She wondered what else he would offer in exchange for her story and how hard she could push him away before he snapped. "That you did that is incredibly creepy."

He chuckled. "You're right. In this case, the bald truth serves me better than a well-crafted story. In Iowa, Amir was on the same floor and discovered your room number by sheer luck. Luck failed me this time. But that's okay, because I'm not calling for business."

She picked up the pen. Put it down. Stood to walk around the room, only to be stopped by the cord. The last phone in the world to have a cord was in her hotel room. The bed squeaked when she sat back down on the brown-and-orange-striped comforter. "And I'm not the same naive fool I was five years ago, so tell me a story I might believe."

There was silence on the line for a while before Micah said, "Okay. I'm here on business, but I know I'm not going to get an interview today. Amir is still partying with the racers, so a camera isn't even available. But I'd like the chance to convince you to sit for an interview. And not just an interview—an entire feature series where you can tell your story."

"Over the phone?" She could leave the receiver sitting on the bed, take a shower and he could try to persuade her all he wanted. If she turned the volume on the phone all the way up, maybe she could listen to his voice stroke her skin while the water rushed over her.

"Over dinner."

Ruby was so shocked she couldn't say anything for several seconds. *He really thinks I'll say yes to dinner?* Then she opened her mouth to say no, and the intake of her breath was the loudest sound in the room. The joyous group in the hall, probably a runner and her family celebrating the finish, had passed out of her hearing. If she said yes, she would be eating dinner with Micah Blackwell, who probably still hated her. If she said no, she would be eating dinner alone.

"Okay." Regret and her teeth chewed at her bottom lip, but she didn't take back her answer. She was intimate with the sound of her own chewing. Even when sitting around the table with her parents, there was rarely any talking. Just forks scraping across plates and the booming way *you disappointed us* echoed through a room, even when no one said a word. Dinner with Micah would at least be *different*. "Where should I meet you?"

"Tell me your room number and I'll bring dinner to you."

"I'd rather go out."

"We can do that, but I get recognized, especially at sporting events. Do you really want to sit at a table with me and have someone ask who you are?"

No. But neither did she want the memory of him lingering in this room, even if only for one night. "I just have one chair."

"Lucky for both of us that I bring my own."

Right. "I'm in room 415."

"There's a Mexican restaurant that is supposed to do good takeout. Give me some idea of what you like and I'll be at your room in about an hour."

Ruby gave him a couple generic Mexican-food suggestions, said what she didn't like, and he hung up, leaving her to be grateful she only had one change of clothes and couldn't fret about what to wear. The warmth in his eyes would relax her shoulders. His smile would invite her to share intimacies. And all of those were professional tricks designed to lure unsuspecting athletes into his trap. She wouldn't fall for them.

Which meant she had to push her curiosity and interest in the power of Micah's shoulders out of her head. She was never going to see him shirtless. *And I don't want to!* she told herself, though not strongly enough to believe it. It was just a professional interest in his physique, was all. One athlete to another. She'd ask him about his weight-lifting regime. They could compare notes.

Despite her promises to herself, she took the time to blow-dry her hair after her shower.

CHAPTER SEVEN

RUBY WAS MOVING the small hotel table and chair around to accommodate dinner and a wheelchair when she heard a knock at the door. She looked through the peephole, saw a hand and opened the door. On Micah's lap was a bag of takeout, and balanced on top of that was a tray holding two plastic cups with what looked like slushies inside.

"Margaritas." He lifted one of the cups up to her with a smile after she had turned back from closing the door. "To loosen you up."

"This is not an interview," she insisted, not even questioning how he managed to get to-go margaritas. She had been right not to want him in this room. He took up too much space. He smelled too good. "And how do you know I drink? Maybe I don't."

"Another's blood was fine, but alcohol is forbidden?" The tone sounded innocent enough, but the words stung. At least he didn't dance around her crime with euphemisms. *The incident,* her mom called it, which blanketed the severity of her crime with blandness and implied that if they never called it what it was, it hadn't happened.

Still, she didn't need to have her face rubbed in it. Again.

She was moving to reopen the door and push him out of her room when he opened his mouth again and said, "That crack was uncalled-for."

"Especially if you want my participation in any kind of story." She put her hand on the doorknob.

"I apologize."

Her hand stopped on the door handle, the metal warming under her palm. She'd expected something less than an apology out of the great Micah Blackwell, especially for a crack about her blood doping. Silly Micah—she'd have accepted less. Her hand lifted off the handle and rested at her side.

"May I pull up a seat to dinner?" He waved to the table with one hand, the other on the wheel of his chair.

He was here now, and if he left, she'd know he'd been here by the smell of his cologne, the Mexican food on the table and the browsing history on her phone where she'd looked up the mechanics of sex with a paraplegic. God, she couldn't even blame that thought on an athlete's curiosity about the body. She pasted a bland smile on her face. That last thought was just her contrary, competitive nature talking anyway. He didn't like her, and that made him a challenge. Contemplating the feel of his skin against hers was proof that approaching life as one contest after another was stupid. A middle ground existed somewhere between competition and the hollow life she was living now and it didn't involve seeking out the one man who hated her above all else. That was perversity, pure and simple.

He smiled at her silence, completely unconcerned with the mental acrobatics she had to go through to take a step forward. And not to rush at him.

"You may pull up a seat," she said, her haughtiness no compensation for her nerves. Then she slipped into the chair and let him pass out their supper. She choreographed the movements of her hands above the table so that hers never brushed his. The awareness she felt and her body's intense curiosity each time their hands came within a hairbreadth was because she'd been living the life of a nun for five years. It was absolutely not because of Micah.

You tell yourself another tall one.

It couldn't be Micah. She'd never survive.

The aroma of spice and beans wafting from the food overpowered the generic hotel room smell. While he opened the bag of tortilla chips and cup of salsa, she shoved a fork and napkin under his makeshift plate. Swallowing a sigh, she prepared herself to pretend that interrogation and attempted coercion was the same thing as conversation. Second to running, weathering a cross-examination might be her greatest skill.

When he smiled and asked about her drive down here, she realized she'd underestimated Micah. He was practiced at making people feel comfortable. As they made small talk about the changes to Chicago's lakefront, the weather and the possibility of either baseball team making the playoffs, Ruby wondered if Micah's skill at easing people's anxiety had come after his disability, was part of his training to be a sportscaster, a natural trait that had helped make him a star football player or all of the above. Being a sportscaster had a least helped with the magic spell he was trying to weave and she was trying to resist. As far as she remembered, he hadn't been nearly so charming five years ago.

He also hadn't been *trying,* because who would waste the effort charming the sporting princess who'd had it all and been stupid enough to throw it all away? He hadn't needed to try. She'd fallen prey to his face with probably little effort on his part. A walking, talking, *running* doll, with little else to recommend her.

"Do you hate me?" she asked, interrupting his story about meeting his childhood hero, Joe Montana.

She saw by his face that he was considering answering her question with a meaningless *of course not,* when he set his fork down, folded his arms on the table and looked at her. His eyes darkened as he regarded her and thought about her question. She would not squirm. She was not afraid of him any longer. Wary—but caution came from experience and was not the same as fear.

Finally, he said, "Why are you asking that question? Do you mean, do I hate that you can walk and I can't? Do I hate that you are trying to return to your sport, even if only as an amateur, when I must report from the sidelines? Instead of hating, I could resent—"

She held up a hand to stop him. He might come up with reasons she hadn't thought of yet and she wasn't sure her tender decision not to be caged could withstand rough treatment. "Do you hate me for cheating? For throwing away a career and a life and a dream? For disgracing my sport? Can I be forgiven for that?"

The combination of exhaustion, tequila and heavy hotel drapes protecting her from the outside world must have made her willing to ask such a question. If she had let the world into this room by opening her blinds or turning on the television, she'd realize she was opening her heart to this man—again—and inviting him to stick a stake in it. But Micah had made her feel safe, so she'd stuck her neck out and was now waiting for him to drop the guillotine.

Instead, he was silent for several seconds. Ruby was about to tell him to forget she asked when he said, "Why are you asking *me* this question and not someone else?"

"Because when everyone close to me was telling me that blood doping was *no big deal,* you came right out and told me that I was the emperor wearing no clothes." After that interview, faced with his scorn, she'd been naked, shivering with exposure. "If I specifically ask you for the truth, you won't lie to me."

Micah drummed his fingers on the table as he regarded her, again stripping away the protective layers she'd so carefully constructed over the past several years until her raw nakedness was exposed. She shivered.

"Do people lie to you regularly?" he asked.

"Forget it." She shoved a heaping pile of refried beans onto her fork. It was more than she could fit in her mouth, but the protein in the beans would help her build back the layers she needed to protect herself. "Despite you pretending earlier, this isn't a conversation. Hell, it's not even an interview. This is turning into some weird therapy session."

"You're the one who asked the question."

"And you've only answered with questions of your own. And how did it make you feel knowing that the people you trusted most said, 'everyone does it,' and you wanted to win so badly that you believed them? How does it make you feel that people call you a lying bitch at the grocery store for cheating *and* a betraying bitch for confessing?" she mocked.

Suddenly cold, she pushed her chair back from the table, using so much force that the back legs caught on the carpet and she had to grab on to the table before she toppled over. Once she'd righted herself, she rooted around in her bag for a sweatshirt, desperate for more cover. But she wasn't going to run away and hide from him. When she returned to the table, she lifted her chin and looked him directly in the eyes.

The drumming of his fingers irritated her to no end. So did his placid face. He should be angry. Or something. Not this provoking openness that made her ask such questions in the first place. She pushed her beans around the takeout container. Forgive her or yell at her. None of this mid-dle-ground crap.

"So people do lie to you."

"I assume the ones calling me a bitch are expressing their true feelings. It's the people who tell me, 'it's not so bad,' that I doubt." He was doing it again—getting her to answer a question without answering one himself. She scooped beans onto her fork and took a bite, again getting more beans than were possible for her to swallow easily. Maybe now she'd think and chew before giving in to his questions.

Micah took a big sip of his drink. Ruby mashed the beans with her tongue, wishing she were eating something chewy, like bread, so she could pretend her food needed several good chomps and fight her body's reflex to swallow. Could she outchew him?

Just as she decided he wasn't going to answer, Micah spoke. "I did hate you. After that interview, when you were so naive and stupid and blind about the trust you'd abused. And you had the audacity to compare your cheating to my disability. Like a freak accident that changed my body for-ever is the same thing as your calculated decision to modify yours. You hid out in your parents' house, coming out only when it was convenient for you and, for the most part, your world has not changed. Meanwhile, I have to fight for the world to recognize that my life has as much worth now that I can't wiggle my toes as it did when I could."

She swallowed, the taste of her food overwhelmed by the bitterness of her past ignorance. "Yes, I'm…"

"Stop." Weariness overcame his face. "Apologizing only makes it worse."

"Can I agree that I was stupid?"

To her surprise—and apparently to his, as well—Micah smiled. "Yes, you can agree with me on that." He cocked his head to the side and the pendant lamp caught a twinkle in his eyes. God, he was good-looking. "I like to be agreed with."

"When you said hate, you used the past tense."

"I have better things to spend my energy on than keeping alive a feeling as powerful as hate for you."

About as much worth hating as a pebble stuck in his tire, she was sure. "So why interview me about ultramarathons? Why not Geoff Roes or Jenn Shelton or Currito?"

"Geoff has his own movie and Jenn her own book. Currito is an interesting guy, but you getting back into running would be the story of the year. Everyone would be wondering if America's Darling had really reformed. You'd be back on the cover of *People. Sports Illustrated* would do another story on you. If Oprah were still on, you'd be invited to sit on her couch. And you know it, too."

He was right, she did know it. And it was part of the reason she would say no to his requests until cows came home bearing her gold medal. "Since I've only recently been replaced as the sports villain du jour, I'm going to keep saying no to this idea you have of a feature on me, no matter how many times you call my mother."

"Let's make a deal." Damn his wide, inviting eyes. He didn't beg or make her beg, but there was something in the cast of his features and the assurance with which he carried himself that made her want to talk to him. "I'll answer one of your questions for every one of mine you answer."

She suppressed the feeling of small victory by clinging to reality. "You didn't answer the second half of my first question."

"Do you need my forgiveness to move on with your life?" His left dimple deepened as one side of his mouth kicked up in a smile.

"That's a really annoying habit, you know." She refused to be as amused by him as he was by himself.

"If you'd agreed to the bargain, then that would count as one of my questions." He opened his arms to her. They looked so strong and protective that she wanted to crawl into them, so she looked away and only half heard what he said next. "The bargain is open-ended. You can keep a tally of questions I ask in your back pocket and use them against me."

The dim hotel room. The buzz of the air conditioner. Light brown eyebrows shadowing blue eyes. She wasn't safe here, as she'd led herself to believe. But she *was* better—in this room, life was certain. Micah couldn't be relied on not to hurt her, but he would be honest with her when she asked, and enough people lied to her while trying not to hurt her that his honesty was enough for right now.

"Whatever I say is off-the-record. This isn't an interview."

"I agree to that."

"Do you swear?"

"You said you wanted my opinion because I wouldn't lie to you. I said I agreed this wasn't an interview. Either you believe me or you don't."

Ruby put her elbows on the small table, wrapping her hands together in front of her mouth, while she thought about his question. *Either you believe me or you don't.* "Trust me enough to close your eyes and leap across the chasm with me," the soft blue of his eyes said. He raised an eyebrow at her and she looked away again.

She didn't want to hide anymore. She didn't want to be hounded, but she didn't think she should have to live in a hole in the ground, either. She lowered her hands so they no longer blocked her face and looked him in the eye. "I don't think I know what forgiveness is, so how do I know if I need it to move on with my life?"

Micah made a low whistling noise. Ruby looked down at her food, pushing the last bits of enchilada and beans around in the take-out container. After such an embarrassing confession, she should want to close the container, open the room door and encourage Micah out. Instead, she wanted to hear what he had to say. His opinion mattered—as it had five years ago. Only then it had sent her scurrying into her parents' house in shame. Now she hoped to use what he told her to bust out forever.

The sucking of air through his teeth that had made the whistle ended, followed by a short laugh. He shook his head. "This is a much weightier conversation than I expected tonight."

"What did you expect?"

"To lower your inhibitions with a margarita, fill your belly and quiet your mind with Mexican food, and get you to confess the secret, nefarious reason that you've started running again."

A hot glimmer of betrayal flickered in her belly. "You said this wasn't an interview."

"*You* said this wasn't going to be an interview and I agreed. I made no promises about not using my knowledge to get an interview later."

His food was mostly eaten, she noticed, compared to the putty she'd made of her meal. She had to eat, so she reached across the table for a chip to dip into her concoction, asking, "And now?" before shoving the mess into her mouth.

"This series can help you."

"Help me what? Help me win, right?" she said, mocking every lie she'd already been told. *This will make you better, stronger, faster.* The easy way her coach had led her from adding protein powder to her breakfast shakes to shoving an oxygen mask over her face to finally sticking a needle in her arm. "Tell me a lie I haven't heard before." The lip-puckering sweetness of the margarita would help wash the taste of deception out of her mouth, so she wrapped her lips around the straw and sucked in, her sip noisy and harsh.

"The whole world has been told their version of the rise and fall of America's Darling. Don't you want the chance to tell *your* side of the story?" He rested his arms on the table and leaned into her, the magnetism of his personality reaching across the table and pulling her into him as easily as if she had a cord coming out of her chest and he held the other end. "Tell the American public why you did it, what lessons you learned and how you're a new and better person. Be an example of how a past can be remade into a stronger future. The public loves a good redemption story. Look at Mike Tyson and his pigeons."

The cord snapped when she laughed. She fell back into her chair, causing the straw to bump her top teeth and the melting lime and tequila to burn the back of her throat. "Did you just compare me to Mike Tyson? He bit off some guy's ear."

"It wasn't a great comparison...."

"He went to prison for rape—it was a terrible comparison." She was silent for a moment. "Though I suppose cheating is cheating, whether it's an ear or a needle."

"And you don't have pigeons."

"I have a flock of backyard hens."

"Really?" A smile as rich and decadent as chocolate melted across his face. Foolish hunger spread across her belly. Why Micah?

"No," she said, reluctant to admit the truth. Seeing him completely reevaluate everything he knew about her had felt good, even if only for a moment. "My parents would never allow it. I've never even had a pet—not so much as a goldfish." Her volunteer work at the shelter was for *her,* so she didn't mention it. Besides, they weren't her pets. "Look, I get that you're trying to help. Or you think you're trying to help. But America's not interested in a redemption story, and I'm only running to prove to myself I still can. And it's great."

"A run around the block can't teach you your feet still work?"

"A block is hardly the same thing as fifty kilometers."

And fifty kilometers wasn't the same thing as fifty miles. There weren't many ultras in the summer, which gave her plenty of time to train for a longer race. Telling herself she was going to casually run a 50K hadn't stopped her from putting together a training schedule for a fifty-mile race. And she'd planned to finish in line with the other elite runners, too. No casual run in the woods; it would be a race to the finish even if she crossed the finish line and fell over.

"And the second race?" His words brought her attention back to the present and the foolishness of the fifty-mile dream, especially if she *did* want to stay away from the attention of the press.

"To prove to myself that my parents couldn't stop me." And those three fucking minutes.

"And what will your excuse for run three be?"

She scowled at him.

"King Ramsey knows I was interested in someone other than Currito. And he's not as oblivious as he seems. He's going to figure out who you are, and he'll be a lot more of a pest than I am. Any interview he gives you is likely to be a trap."

"Getting out of traps is my specialty."

"Don't let your newfound sense of success trick you into being stupid. The interview I'm offering could be gold for your reputation. You could get your life back."

"Said the spider to the fly."

"What happened to trusting me?"

"I never said I trusted you, only that you would tell me the truth, even if your intentions for not lying to me are questionable. Five years ago you showed me the truth about myself, and it was devastating to me." An understatement. "That it was also the kindest thing anyone could have done was an accident that I think you would have prevented had you known."

When Micah reached across the table and took one of her hands in his, the shock waves of his touch reverberated through her body to her belly. His hand was more callused than she had expected. It was also warm and solid and strong. "I'm not sorry that what I said devastated you. But give me a chance to show the world the new person you've made from that devastation."

She wished she could leave her hand in his all night and into the next morning. Crawl into bed with him and feel his strong arms wrapped around her. Find comfort in the warmth of his bare chest against her back. Not just sex, but a night in which she could pretend she was loved. "I hope I'm a new person, but it's been five years and I'm still running and still living with my parents and I'm not sure what parts of me are new."

"Be patient." He gave her hand a squeeze. "One morning, I woke up in a different body than the one I remembered." Then he laughed and gave her a rueful smile. "Of course, when everyone told *me* to be patient, I told them to fuck off, that I'd never been patient before in my life and I didn't intend to start now." He shrugged and his hand tightened against hers once again. "It's still good advice, though."

"You can't run fifty kilometers and not be a model of patience. Or perseverance." Not to mention the fifty miles she was planning in the back of her head. *Stop that, Ruby.* But thinking about Micah was no safer. "And we haven't even talked about how patient I have been and will continue to be about my finances, because I'll probably be dead before the lawsuits against me are resolved."

"Let's both hope it doesn't come to that." Micah slipped his hand out of hers, leaving it feeling limp and empty. "I should go. This has been a far more interesting—and more pleasant—conversation than I expected."

He backed his chair away from the table and was maneuvering himself out of the tight hotel space when she thought to ask another question. "Why did you interview me? That first time?"

Micah moved so that he was looking at her, his face as expressionless as his voice when he answered, "The ratings, of course."

"That's not what I mean, and you know it." She knew—had known at the time—that her father had only agreed to the interview because he'd confused Micah's loss of agility in his legs with a loss of agility in his mind. It was a miscalculation her father regretted to this day, though he blamed Micah for the mistake.

"Yes, I know what you mean." Micah sat, suspended between the table and the door, assessing her yet again. "I was angry at your father and his arrogance. And I could have let my anger get in the way of the fabulous opportunity he offered on a silver platter wrapped up in gold ribbon. Or I could have harnessed my anger to do the best interview of my life. I decided on the latter."

He put his hands on his wheels and the chair rolled forward, just slightly, then stopped. "Halfway through the interview, I was angrier at you than at your father. Your father is nothing. His position in life is due to his parents' money, a good education and other people wilting under his bluster. You, though—you were something special."

She grimaced at the past tense, the mistakes she'd made in her life floating around her. They weren't threatening specters anymore, but they were ghosts all the same, and no exorcism she'd tried had rid her of them yet. "Patience, you said, right?"

"Whatever you remake yourself into, you won't be the same as before. And no distance you run will bring that back."

"I know." She bit back angrier words. Of course she knew. The details of her suspension had been explained to her over and over and over until she could recite them in her sleep. There were no medals in her future, no matter what she did. She took a deep breath; she'd asked Micah for honesty. "I'm running for me."

"I think I believe you." Micah looked at his watch. "I really do have to go."

"Don't leave on my account." She didn't want to be alone in this hotel room again. When he rolled out that door, the promise of friendship would fade into prepared questions, studio lights and a voice-over turning her life into a movie trailer.

"No, I have to go on my account. I have to use the bathroom."

She glanced to the doorway of her bathroom, assessing whether his chair would fit. "You can use mine. If you can't close the door, I'll step outside."

"Ruby, I didn't bring a catheter."

"Oh." She felt stupid for not realizing that. She stepped around him, putting her hand on the doorknob and bracing herself to let him out.

"Maybe the arms aren't so attractive now that you know the details of how I pee?"

Her face got hot, and she was sure she'd turned bright red. "I wasn't..." She didn't realize he'd noticed, but she'd probably all but drooled at the ropy definition in his forearms. He wasn't oblivious.

"Everyone admires my arms. I'm the only person who seems to remember that my legs still exist and are living their own life, even if we're no longer on speaking terms."

She had remembered his legs and wanted to see them, but she couldn't figure out if it was an athlete's natural curiosity about bodies or because of the way her insides tingled and her breath stilled when she thought of him. Curiosity or desire?

Her motivations probably didn't matter to Micah. She shrugged. "I had someone stick a needle in my arm and pump a stranger's blood through my body in order to win a shiny necklace. It would be silly for me to be put off by the plastic you use to pee."

The smile she surprised out of him was as smooth as sin and just as confident. "Good night, Ruby."

When she opened the door, the real world rushed in with the sounds of a couple laughing in the hallway, the beep of the elevator and the false brightness of the light outside her door. Micah wheeled out her door, and she watched until he disappeared around a corner.

CHAPTER EIGHT

MICAH WOKE UP the next morning still thinking about Ruby and their conversation. Not only thinking—which would be acceptable—but *caring*. Much to his surprise, he was beginning to believe her when she said she was doing this for herself and not for notoriety and fame. The lady may be protesting too much, but he now thought she might be doing it because she really didn't want the spotlight on her.

A shame, because he was more convinced than ever that the series he imagined would boost his career, along with rehabilitating her image. And, if he was honest with himself, he liked spending time with her. Worse, he liked the tilt of her nose and the slight curves of her breasts as much as he liked her perseverance.

Well, she wasn't the only one made more tenacious and stubborn by life's experience. So long as Derek didn't pull the plug on the whole enterprise, Micah would keep showing up at Ruby's races with Amir to get footage. Eventually she would say yes. She would cave, if for no other reason than that she would gain enough confidence in her new self that the thought of letting *other* people tell her story would start to piss her off. Hell, by that point he might have so much footage on her that he wouldn't need an interview.

He swung himself out of bed and into his chair, respect for her tugging at his conscious. She was trying to redefine herself and her life with notoriety hanging over her head. Whether or not she should have awakened to her new life five or four or three or two years ago was beside the point. Rebirth was a hard and painful process. It didn't matter if the world was rooting for you or against you, just cracking that old skin and letting the sensitive new bits see the light of day was scary. Many people didn't even try it until it was too late.

Micah dug a pair of jeans and a Texas A&M T-shirt out of his bag, still mulling over his plans for Ruby while getting dressed. Her worry that the world wouldn't accept her redemption story was justified. He could cook the story however he wanted, but the viewing public had to be in a mood to swallow rather than spit it out.

He patted the bed for his belt and didn't feel anything. When he looked up, the silver in his belt buckle glinted at him from the top of his bag, and he weighed vanity against going to get it. Vanity won.

The fact that he'd even forgotten his belt was a sign that Ruby gave him as much to worry about as he gave her. Conflict of interest was spelled out in the lines of her muscles as clearly as his promotion was. He tightened his belt, making sure to note the notch he was using and any pleats or excess in his clothing. The belt was vanity, but it also helped him monitor the condition of his stomach. He'd never have the muscle definition in his abs that he'd had in college, but it was good health practice to make sure he kept up what was physically possible.

If he was smart, he would leave Ruby alone until she

came around to his point of view. And he'd keep all their interactions professional from now on. No more intimate dinners in dark hotel rooms with liquor to loosen inhibitions. Only the great outdoors and blinding studio lights.

None of which stopped Micah, before packing his bag, from writing a short note to Ruby to leave at the front desk.

RUBY HAD PASSED her signed receipt to the desk attendant and was easing her duffel bag onto her shoulder when the clerk said, "Oh, I almost forgot," and slid an envelope across the desk.

The outside read, "Ruby Heart" in forthright printed letters. She flipped the envelope over and ran her finger under the barely sealed flap. There was a phone number followed by a short message. "Interview or otherwise. Micah." The handwriting on the note was the same as the envelope. Honest. Blunt. They were qualities she'd never expected to appreciate in a man, but she'd also never expected to look back on a conversation with Micah Blackwell and hope to have another.

She slipped the note into an inside pocket of her purse before she could consider either the interview or the otherwise.

THREE DAYS LATER, Ruby stood outside the glass doors of the animal shelter and jogged in place to warm up her muscles. In deference to her race over the weekend, she'd made today a short volunteering day. A one-mile loop around a couple blocks times ten dogs would equal ten miles of running. She'd take it easy and slow, making sure her blood flowed through every cell in her body and rinsed out any lingering fatigue. And if a dog wanted to walk, she'd walk.

Three years ago, she'd sought volunteer opportunities because she needed to get out of the house, but every time

she left to even take a walk or go to the grocery store, her
mother fretted about photographers, running, rumors and
scandal. As if they lived in a soap opera. Or like Ruby was
Britney Spears.

Haley was the one who'd suggested the shelter. "They always need people to walk the dogs, and your parents aren't
heartless enough to complain that you're volunteering at an
animal shelter." Her cousin had been right about the first
and mostly right about the second. Ruby's mother had obviously considered complaining and her father had made
a snide comment about people who don't take care of their
responsibilities, but her brother, Josh, had countered by
pointing out how good it would look if the press found out.

After about a month of walking dogs every day, Ruby
had suggested that she take some of the more hyperactive
dogs running. Ruby and the dogs had gone through an adjustment period where, with the help of one of the volunteer trainers, Ruby had learned how to be the alpha dog
and the dogs had learned how to run with a partner. The
idea had been a win for everyone involved. Ruby got out
of the house and back into running on a regular basis. The
shelter had upped their adoption rate of the bigger dogs, for
whom better exercise meant they were less anxious around
potential owners.

And Ruby had watched the shelter employees care for
and be gentle with dogs too sick, too aggressive or too old
to be easily adopted. The employees and volunteers might
have become desensitized to the fate of many of the dogs
and cats brought in, but their hearts hadn't callused over.
And so Ruby learned both what it meant for the careless
to neglect their responsibilities and for the caring to do the
hard thing because it was the right thing. More than Micah's condemnation of her, the articles in the press and the

lawsuits, volunteering at the shelter had taught her the cost of shortcuts in each and every frightened pair of eyes that peered through the cages at her as she walked past them.

Ruby reached down to touch her toes. A pair of boots and white dog feet appeared in her sight line. She looked up. Jodie, the volunteer coordinator, stood holding on to a leash attached to a Dalmatian. Even though the Dalmatian was sitting, the dog's nervous energy was evident in the way it shook and how its eyes darted about. The dog looked young, scared and ready to bolt.

"This is Dotty," Jodie said. "Dotty has just been surrendered to us. She's a year old and needs to be worn-out. If you can stay an extra hour or so, we would appreciate it if you could run her five miles before the other dogs and five miles after."

Which would make today's run twenty miles. She could run twenty miles, but she'd be pushing the boundaries of her recovery. She did a quick readjustment of her training schedule. If she did twenty slow miles today, she could run five tomorrow and five the day after. It wouldn't be a perfect solution, but Dotty's deep black eyes never once came to rest for longer than a second and Ruby could see that she needed this.

"Sure you want me to take her that far?" One of the original concerns the shelter employees had about Ruby running the dogs had been that they weren't used to it, and they feared that long runs would cause injury. One mile seemed enough for most of the dogs, and the ones who needed more were just in the rotation more regularly.

Jodie looked down at the shivering dog. "Isn't she pretty?" she cooed. Dotty licked her lips and Jodie raised her gaze back to Ruby. "Dalmatians are the original coaching dogs. They have been bred to run for miles alongside a horse.

People get them because they're attractive animals. But they don't take them for long-enough walks during the day and then blame the beast when their couch gets destroyed. We're hoping to place Dotty with one of the Dalmatian rescues but, until then, she needs exercise."

"Oh." Ruby looked Dotty over. The dog trembled.

"Dalmatians are willful, so be firm with her." The dog pulled a little on her leash and Jodie tsked at her. "At least her owners had the decency to take her to obedience school, so she knows her commands. Don't let her fool you into thinking otherwise." Ruby thought she heard Jodie muttering about people who don't do their research, but whatever the volunteer coordinator was saying, she was saying it under her breath.

"Dotty," Ruby called hopefully. The dog looked at her. She looked at the dog. "Are you ready to go running?" Dotty quivered. The amount of a sway in the leash from the dog's shivers made Ruby wonder if her arm would be exhausted holding on to the thing. No matter. The dog needed something—probably not to feel abandoned.

Ruby took the leash from Jodie and, at Jodie's suggestions, went through a couple commands with the dog. Then she double-checked her hip for her cell phone in case of trouble and they were off.

"Don't let her run in front of you," Jodie called after them. "She needs to heel or run behind."

"Hear that, Dotty," Ruby said to the dog trotting next to her and beginning to get a couple toes out in front. "Heel." When Dotty didn't back down, Ruby repeated herself in a firmer tone. The dog slowed enough so that her toenails were level with Ruby's heels. And they settled into a rhythm.

Ruby's mind went to the blissful no-man's-land where only the softs sounds of her feet hitting the ground and movements of her legs were allowed to join her. Until they ran past a couple kids tossing a football in their yard and Micah's smiling face popped into Ruby's head. She stumbled, jerking Dotty forward with her, and the dog made a quiet yelp of surprise. Even once they got their tempo back, what she'd hoped to avoid by running with the dogs had already happened. Micah had forced his way into her thoughts, and he was as hard to get out of her mind as he had been to get out of her hotel room.

The kids had an amazing amount of stamina. Ruby had finished her five miles with Dotty and was on her third dog when they'd finally gone inside and she could pass by the house without Micah's voice in her head. *Do you need my forgiveness to move on with your life?*

People said running was perfect for meditation, turning off your brain and focusing on the cadence of your steps instead of your thoughts. Ruby had always been faster than everyone at school, but she'd gotten *much* faster once puberty started and she'd tried to outrun her anxieties. One advantage of training had been that she could focus her thoughts on her form. But the person who cared about form, nutrition and training schedules had also been willing to cheat to win. In the years between her cheating and her decision to run an ultramarathon, Ruby had limited her thoughts to basic meditation and forced away any cares of form.

At least Micah was a pleasant change of pace, especially the Micah who had brought her dinner and talked with her long into the night, and whose self-assurance made her feel as though everything was going to turn out for the best. That Micah seemed to believe she had a future. She wanted to believe she did.

The handoff back to Dotty was a relief, because she was beginning to combine Micah and the idea of a future into a future with Micah and that thought was a fool's errand. Despite his broad shoulders and confident smile, he was no one she could trust. Hell, he'd admitted it himself. Any future she imagined that included taking her clothes off in front of him also included sharing more intimacies with him, and she didn't believe Micah would be above using those intimacies against her to further his career.

She'd be angry if he did, but she wouldn't blame him. If she forgot he had a career and indulged in foolish little-girl fantasies it was her fault, not his. The break in her rhythm allowed her to talk herself down from a future *with* Micah to seeing Micah *in* the future. Where she would be reminded to be on her guard against him and against fantasies that could never become reality.

Dotty slowed down enough to dart behind Ruby so that she was running next to the road. Ruby made a big circle above her head with her right arm to sort the dog, her arms and the leash. Once she and Dotty were back on track, Ruby noticed a dark blue SUV slow down beside her. Dotty's hackles went up in a line of black-and-white on her neck and back.

Ruby looked around her, her heart pounding and her breath short from more than the running. She'd run this same loop five to thirty times a day, five days a week, for three years. Since the industrial buildings and strip malls hadn't changed, she'd stopped paying attention to them, only noticing the activity at the few houses along the route. Few cars traveled these roads and, to her folly, she'd been focused solely on her running and the dog linked to her arm.

Her already fatigued muscles tightened, and she gripped the end of Dotty's leash. Foreboding crushed her lungs, which hurt her speeding heartbeat. Blood pounded in her ears and she had to take a deep breath not to get caught up in her fear. She was Ruby Heart. No one trapped Ruby Heart.

The passenger-side window eased down. Ruby whipped her head to the left and the right. Between two of the buildings to her left was a passageway that looked big enough for her and Dotty, but not big enough for the car. She could speed up, hope the car continued to try to keep pace with her, then stop suddenly, dart behind the car and through the passageway. If she was lucky, there was an exit on the backside. Or at least a place to hide while she called the shelter for help.

"Ruby Heart?" The voice coming from inside the SUV was familiar, but Ruby couldn't get a good angle that let her see the face of the driver. "I'll be damned. That's really you."

The alarm bells that had quieted rang again when Dotty growled. Ruby had never felt so trapped while running. She could see all sorts of places to escape if it were only her, but she couldn't clamber over a fence with a dog. She tried to ignore the man and the car, picking up her pace a little and hoping she would at least make it to the slightly busier road ahead.

"Micah is a cagey son of a bitch."

Hearing Micah's name uttered by the mysterious man was so astonishing that she stopped short, surprising Dotty, who had run ahead. The dog yelped when the leash snapped back. Dotty looked around, then ambled back to Ruby's side when she muttered, "Heel, Dotty, heel."

"He was going to keep the story of the year away from King, and Dexter was going to let him," the voice continued after the car had stopped and backed up. The voice tsked.

Her shoulders eased away from her ears now that she was able to place both the man's voice and the obnoxious reference to himself in the third person. Micah may have ambushed her in her hotel room, but at least he'd had the decency not to pretend to be a royal *we*. "King Ripley, how did you find me here?"

"I called your house, of course."

What had her mother gotten in return for passing on Ruby's side job to the press? A false guarantee of favorable coverage? Tickets to the U.S. Open? Or was King's presence only punishment for Ruby's secrets? If it had been her father who'd sold her down the river, at least she'd know that King was a reminder of whose opinions counted. But her father was so rarely home these days, and she couldn't remember the last time he'd answered a ringing phone. Whatever her mother's reasons, Ruby wished she could see King's face and the inside of the car, but the tinted windows and the shadows meant she only saw flashes of teeth and skin.

Micah may have used his cameraman to seek her out, but he'd approached her face-to-face and been up-front with his intentions. She lifted up onto the balls of her feet and began running again. She went slowly, keeping Dotty tight at her side. "I'm busy right now. Perhaps you could call me later."

"I wanted to see if it was really you."

As if she was some kind of circus freak?

"But since we're talking, I want you to know that I'd be a better choice for an interview than Micah. Just think on it." And with a wave of his hand, a brief flash of skin and the glint off a large ring, he sped off.

Ruby and Dotty were again alone on the road.

"I'd be less likely to say something incriminating if I let King interview me," she said to the dog, who looked up at her and woofed. "But that oaf provides no challenge."

She and Dotty made their way back to the shelter. Once there, Ruby grabbed her purse from one of the offices.

Micah's note was still in the same pocket she'd slipped the paper into before leaving the hotel. She could hear the paper crinkle every time she dug for her keys. She should throw it out.

She had the note memorized anyway.

CHAPTER NINE

AFTER SHE GOT home and showered, Ruby went down the stairs to confront her traitorous parent. She found her mother in the living room, trimming dead leaves off the houseplants and singing softly to them.

"Mom, did you tell a reporter where I volunteered?"

"Hmm? Oh, yes, dear. He was so nice when we spoke on the phone and you looked so irritated about me interfering with Mike's phone call the last time, not getting the reporter's information and all." Her mother's voice poured out soothing innocence, which floated over the hardwood floors before getting lost in the pallor of the wool rugs.

Ruby preferred Micah's flat judgment. At least that was honest. "And?"

"And your father and I decided that if you wanted to be running again—"

Did they know about her two races? If they knew, would they disapprove of her new hobby enough to give out information to every caller in a ploy to force Ruby back into their fold? She shuddered at the idea, but before she accused her mother of something nefarious, reason wrenched back its control over her thoughts. If they knew she was racing again, both her parents would have expressed the full force of their opinions. They would manipulate and maneuver, but she didn't believe they'd do anything to place her in actual harm's way.

Her mother was still talking, still throwing out her attempts to manage her daughter's life in the same way she tossed dead leaves into a bucket.

"...then we would help you navigate the press. King seemed like he would be a good interviewer for you—your father watched some of his old interviews online."

"I can pick my own interviews now." A slice of her forgave her mother for thinking Ruby still needed her interviews and reporters picked out for her. She'd delegated responsibility for her entire life to her parents when she was racing. The very idea that she'd want any independence back was a shock to their system, and neither of her parents, especially her mother, had fully processed the change yet.

But if love resided in Ruby's heart, fear in her lungs, and anger deep in her belly, *forgiveness* had long ago pitched its tent in her Achilles tendon, a vulnerable spot for any athlete and one where an injury could kill a career.

"You're here," her mom intoned. "We can help you."

Yes, I'm here. Why am I still here? Any appreciation she'd felt for having her own bedroom suite and the expansive lawn for barefoot running exercises was long gone. Even her appreciation of the weight room was waning. *Poor little rich girl,* her guilt—which she was pretty sure resided in her liver—mocked. *The gold surrounding you has a smudge and now you don't want it.*

But was guilt a reason to stay?

Before "the scandal," Ruby had *always* credited her parents' managing her every move as a kindness. Female athletes didn't usually make enough money to hire people to take care of the business. It had been a blessing. And she still wanted to credit it as a kindness, but her parents couldn't seem to get out of the habit of running her life, even when she had no life to run. Perhaps their management would smart less if they seemed to take an interest in *her,* as well.

Now their management was intrusive and about them and their needs, rather than about her and her needs. Like her running, her life—both the highs and the lows—had started out about her and had become about her parents and their reputation.

With one finger, Ruby touched the small lemon growing on the tree by the window. Not even a tree, because it was pruned regularly to keep it the perfect size and shape for this corner. And the poor lemon wasn't even destined to be food—her mother didn't like the taste.

Ruby pulled her hand away before she gave in to her urge to pull the fruit off and kill what growth the tree was allowed. She was sick to death of being a stepping-stone for other people's agendas. More accurately, she was sick to death of herself, for not having enough of a backbone to *be* her own agenda.

"You know we always want the best for you. Everything we've sacrificed for your dreams, we wouldn't have done that if we didn't want the best for you." Hearing her mother say they had only ever acted out of Ruby's best interest made her want to vomit. She left the room without saying another word.

BY THE END of the week, Ruby and Dotty had gotten to know each other through their running. They would run for five miles, then Ruby would run with some other dogs and, depending on her training schedule, she might take

Dotty out for another five miles. They'd grown to trust each other. Dotty's quivering was now more excitement than nervous energy. Today the dog had sat on command only to hop up again.

Once running had been an expression of joy for Ruby. It hadn't been about winning but had been about being outside and feeling her legs move and her feet float above the earth. Freedom, pure and simple. She looked at Dotty, who was sitting down, then hopping up, then sitting down, then hopping up, not entirely able to control her eagerness for a run. Ruby bit back her enjoyment of the dog to reprimand Dotty, even though Ruby's heart had swollen and nearly burst her sports bra. For the first time in many years, Ruby wanted to run longer than was on her training schedule. She could put on her shoes and they could go until they couldn't go any longer.

When Micah had asked her why she was racing again, the promise of finding joy mixed with peace that running offered was her real answer. She puffed air out of her mouth, the wisps of her hair dancing in front of her eyes. Even after they'd had that long dinner together, Micah probably wouldn't believe that answer. Which shouldn't bother her, but it did.

Not that it mattered. Dotty wasn't her dog. But she would stick to her training schedule and take this brief moment to be outside her life with Dotty.

When they returned from their second run, Jodie was standing outside with a clipboard in her hand, which was unusual. Together, Ruby and Dotty slowed down their pace and stopped in front of the volunteer coordinator. Ruby pursed her lips in preparation for whatever had sparked Jodie's serious face. Dotty sat close enough to Ruby that she could feel the dog's heat, her tail kicking up dust that stuck to the sweat on her calves. When Jodie looked at the dog, Ruby followed her gaze. All the attention must have made Dotty nervous, because the dog interrupted her panting to lick Ruby's hand.

Jodie looked back up, tapping her pen on the metal of the clipboard. "Have you thought about adopting Dotty?"

Ruby swallowed her first response, which was "Mom and Dad won't let me," because she was twenty-nine and few people understood how a twenty-nine-year-old who'd been on the cover of *Sports Illustrated* could be stuck living with her parents. Instead, she said, "I thought you were going to place her with one of the Dalmatian rescues."

"They're looking for a foster home for her, but they haven't had any luck. Thanks to your regular running, she's stopped chewing on the bars of the kennel and ripping up blankets, but few people have the stamina for a Dalmatian. Every time someone looks into her kennel, I worry they'll want to take her home and we'll see her back in two months. You could take her running with you and she'd be fine. With training, she'll go twenty, maybe even thirty miles with you."

"But what about my volunteer work here?" Most of her running was done at the shelter, with the dogs.

"Dalmatians aren't clever, but they're obedient and generally get along with other dogs. Dotty's no exception. As a shelter employee, I shouldn't say this, but you could train her to run off leash and she could run along with you and any other dog. You'd have to make sure the other dogs also ran at your heels, or she'd get upset at the pack order, but I think you could handle that."

She looked down at Dotty, who looked up at her with large black eyes and a pink tongue lolling out of her mouth. The dog's tail was still wagging. The sun cast a shadow on the ground, even of the tongue and the tail. Happy and carefree. And eager to go running again.

"Okay." Ruby couldn't say no to all the hope bundled up in Dotty's face.

"Do you have a vet?"

"No, but I can get some recommendations." Affording a vet was another question. Ruby would have to figure that out.

Jodie handed Ruby the clipboard. Ruby handed Jodie the end of Dotty's leash.

"Fill out everything you can. We'll add the name of your vet when you pick one. Dotty will need to be spayed." Jodie's disrespect for Dotty's former owners reverberated as she stretched out the syllables in the last word. "I have a guide for new dog owners for you at the desk, and you can pick up Dotty at the end of next week." She clicked her tongue and Dotty stood, ready to follow Jodie into the building.

Ruby looked at the application. She would have to write down her parents' address, but she didn't want Jodie to think she'd been misled. "Jodie, I'll have to find a new place to live."

"Your current place?"

"I can't have dogs. But—" she hurried on before Jodie could interrupt "—I've been meaning to look for a new place to live, and this is the excuse I needed."

"If you're renting, I'll have to call the landlord."

Ruby looked at the Dotty, who was following the conversation with interest, if not awareness. She tried to imagine the dog going back into the kennel with the cold concrete floor and fifth-hand dog bed. Dotty cocked her head to one side and blinked into the sun. If she let the dog down, Ruby didn't know how she'd be able to look at herself in the mirror again. Having already been through one mirror-covering phase in her life, she knew she didn't want to go through another.

"No problem. I'll take care of it." She had no idea how she would *take care of it,* only that she wanted Dotty more than anything she'd ever wanted before, short of a gold medal. Patience, Micah had said. Ruby had been practicing patience for years. Patiently waiting for the lawsuits to be resolved. Patiently waiting for someone—anyone—to say they forgave her. Patiently waiting to forgive herself.

To hell with patience. Her excitement over getting out of her parents' house outran all the objections her fears threw at her. One step in front of the other, over and over and over until she crossed the finish line. The faster she ran, the faster that finish line came into view. Pain only ended when you crossed. "If I'm arranging for a new place to live, I won't be able to come in next week."

Jodie nodded. "We'll find another way to exercise the dogs. And since you have to look for a new place to live anyway, try to find a place with a backyard. You'll both be happier."

CHAPTER TEN

MICAH WAS IN a dressing room washing makeup off his face when his cell phone rang. The number looked familiar, though he couldn't place where he'd seen it before. Setting aside the washcloth, he dried his hands and answered the phone.

"Before I talk to you," Ruby said into his ear, "did you tell King Ripley who I was?"

He smiled, pleased to hear force rather than fear in her voice and amused that she didn't bother with pleasantries. He'd always admired her single-minded focus on her goals, even when they had proved to be self-destructive. "Since I want you to myself, that would be self-defeating."

He didn't realize until after the vague statement of interest came out of his mouth that he didn't only want her for the interview, and he didn't just admire her body as casual interest. Sometime over the dinner conversation in Indiana, he had come to like Ruby. He liked that she was vulnerable and afraid and yet still had the instinct to put her head down and race as fast as she could to her finish line. Under all that fear was a tenacity he both sympathized with and admired.

Admiration or not, the interview was going to happen.

Dexter reminded Micah on a daily basis the cost of the production van and Amir's time for the trip to Indiana, and the reminder would be the least of Micah's problems if he couldn't get the interview. There was absolutely zero room for pondering Ruby's powerful thighs and gritty personality at work. Conflict of interest got a reporter fired, not promoted.

In her single-mindedness, Ruby continued with her interrogation. "*Unless* you hoped to force me in your direction by pointing out that you wouldn't be stupid enough to follow me in your car while I'm out running."

Micah winced. Subtlety had never been King's strong suit. He also didn't have a deep enough soul to realize that someone who had been followed by tabloids everywhere she went for the better part of a year wouldn't take kindly to being tailed by a reporter.

"I did not tell King it was you, though he could have looked at the video from Iowa and figured it out." *Maybe.* Micah balled up the washcloth and threw it into the hamper. Bull's-eye. "And there's also that video from Indiana."

"I want that footage back."

Not going to happen. "You signed a release when you registered for those races." He grabbed the hand towel and lobbed it at the hamper as well, though he misjudged the arc and it landed on the floor to the left of the opening. He'd been remiss in his practices with the hoop above his trash can in his office. Too much time spent looking at the video of his new favorite female athlete.

"I didn't expect you and NSN to be there with a camera. And I'll bet the race organizers didn't, either. Other racers might not want you holding film of them in such a condition. No one looks their best when running a 50K race."

Just because he didn't blame her for being upset didn't

mean he was handing over the tape. Micah had read the release forms of both races very carefully before showing up with Amir, and the races might not have expected NSN, but they also hadn't excluded the type of footage Amir had gotten. "I'm only interested in the film you're in. I'll even edit all the other runners out."

"About King, do you swear?"

Micah squared his shoulders against the insult but didn't say a word.

Finally Ruby spoke again. "You said you'd be honest with me."

"You said that. I only agreed." He liked Ruby with her hackles up, but he kept his tone warm enough so that she wouldn't decide he was the enemy. And he really didn't want to lie to her. Ever.

"Just tell me, does the honesty offer still hold?"

"So many questions." He tsked.

"You told me I could ask you one question for every one you asked me. And you asked me a lot of questions in Indiana. This is my due. I can't afford a lopsided bargain with a reporter. Not now."

She must believe reporters only wanted one thing out of her, and it wasn't the thing her mama had always warned her about. Or, knowing the little he did about Ruby's family, interviews with reporters probably *was* something her mother had warned her about.

"Honesty still holds. As does the question agreement. And yes, I swear I didn't tell King who you were. I don't know how he figured it out." If it had been Amir or Dexter who had told King, then Micah had strong words for them.

"One more thing. Did you tell anyone else I was racing again?" Apparently Ruby trusted no one, and Micah wasn't sure he blamed her.

"My producer knows, but he figured it out on his own from the video footage Amir took. Though I would have told him eventually, since the interview involves the station. *And* I told my father—he wouldn't have told anyone."

Silence beamed through the phone. "Thank you for being honest. You could have lied about telling your father."

"What would lying have gotten me?"

"You might've lied so I'd trust you more."

"And lose that trust if you ever found out? No thanks." He paused before going on. "Why all these questions?"

"My parents think I should go back down into my weight room and be happy with my life as a former track star turned mole rat."

Anticipation made the hairs on the back of his neck stand on edge. "Ruby, I get why you're asking me about the footage and King, but why are you telling me about your parents?"

"I'm moving out of my parents' house." Her voice stilled and he wished he could see the look on her face. He couldn't decide if the stall was anger, sadness or something in between. "I realize its far past time, but…"

This moment of silence carried regret with it, which made him sad. Ruby should give her past a punch in the nose and then dash off to a greater future. "Looking back never helps."

"Right. Well, I got this dog and I know my parents would never let me keep her." Her chuckle was as bittersweet as cheap lemonade. "Maybe King and his creepy stalking was what I needed at the time, because Dotty got her hackles up when she thought I might be in trouble and that was it. I couldn't *not* adopt her."

"Dotty the dog?" He would have thought she'd be more creative in naming a dog.

"Worse. Dotty the Dalmatian."

He laughed, a little in love with the fact that just when he thought he had her pegged, she could do something completely unexpected. "You could have named her Spot, I guess."

"She came with the name—I don't want to change it. And she's perfect. Jodie said that with a little training, she can run twenty miles, no problem. So even if I'm not volunteering at the shelter, I will still have company for my long runs."

"Will she be able to keep up with you when you decide to get serious about the races?"

"I am serious."

He wished he was in his office so he could call up some of the film, from both Indiana and Iowa. "You're holding back. I have the video."

"No, I'm not. I'm doing exactly what I said I wanted to do. Run a race with other people and see how I did." The words tumbled out of her mouth and Micah wondered if she believed them.

"Ruby, why did you call?" He could continue to argue with her or he could press her for the real reason she'd called, because it wasn't to tell him about her dog any more than it had been to ask him about King. Convincing Ruby to race like her body and her spirit wanted to race could wait for another day.

"I'm twenty-nine years old and everyone thinks they know what I need, when really it's just all about them. My parents won't recognize that I need a new life for fear my existence will continue to make theirs more difficult. Hell, even King thinks he knows what's best for me better than I do." Her frustration shuddered through the phone connection in the deep breath she took. "I'm sick to death of it and of hiding. I'm not really sure you're any better, but at least you qualify your offers by admitting to your own self-interest."

Micah needed a moment to rest and slowly fill his lungs with air.

"What I'm saying is that I'll do the interview."

"Gre—"

"I have conditions, though. If I don't want to answer a question, then I won't, and I want you to edit out my refusal."

The carrot she hung in front of him might as well have been plastic for all the use it was. "That's not an honest interview."

"I'll tell you whatever I can about the doping, but no talk of my parents and or my life between the Olympics and now. This is about me getting back into running."

"Viewers will spot a fake interview."

"It won't be fake, and this is the only offer you'll get. Take it or leave it."

"I'll take it." He wasn't a fool, and he was a good enough interviewer to get what the viewers wanted, even with her conditions. The linoleum of the counter was cool when Micah put his hands on it, but it couldn't stop excitement from boiling over in his blood. The story of Ruby's comeback—and that was what this was, even if she didn't believe it yet—was going to be the news story of the year. He closed his eyes and imagined all the ratings, the promotions…and spending more time with Ruby in her tight running pants.

His brain may have actually made squeaking-eraser sounds as he wiped the last thought from his mind. He'd made his choice and he was choosing his professional integrity.

He was so busy convincing himself of the right thing to do that he almost missed that she'd started talking again.

"And I need your help. This is part of the bargain. I have to find a place to live by the end of a week. Which means I also have to figure out *how* to live, and I want a coach. But I don't want to let this get in the way of my training."

Before the consequences had a chance to flash through his brain, he said, "I'll help you any way I can, but I have my own conditions. If this interview gets the attention I think it will, you're going to be the star of the ultra series NSN is working on."

"Fine."

"We tape you training. We tape you at races. When you succeed, we're taping, and when you fail, we're taping."

"You tape the training only. My home life is off-limits. And I won't fail," she said with the single-minded hubris of an elite athlete.

He drummed his fingers on the side of his chair as he considered both what she was offering and what it would cost him. She was offering to grant him near-full access to her life, and he couldn't use any of it for the ultra series. A feature about running or not, America would squirm with twisted pleasure when they realized Ruby Heart had to learn to balance a checkbook.

The ugly side of being incredibly talented at one thing was that the public wasn't very forgiving when they realized you were as human as the rest of the world. Learning that your hero could fuck up wasn't a lesson most people cared to learn, and they usually blamed their hero for their unreasonable expectations.

But Ruby was already dangerous to him, without the added time spent with her. Getting to know her outside of her sport. Learning more about her as a person.... Even if he didn't use the information directly in his series, the feature would be better for it. But the fact that he would become more emotionally attached and risk his career was high.

Of course, maybe he'd learn Ruby had some horrible flaw that would turn him off her forever. Worse than doping, because apparently that hadn't been enough.

Then he realized all she'd said in this one phone call. "Wait, your parents sic King on you, you adopt a dog, you need to find a new place to live and you call *me* for an interview? Don't tell me this was all in the same day."

"Don't be ridiculous. King found me last week."

He laughed again, this time at himself for underestimating her. Ruby never did anything halfway, which was probably why she had been successful as a runner, but this was... ridiculous. Ruby had had the right word for it.

"And you only gave yourself a week to do this?"

The breath she puffed out this time was full of frustration, and Micah thought it was frustration with him. "You told me that patience was overrated. And you were right. I've been trapped by my fall from grace for too long. And *I* let my sins corner me. And that ends now." God help the world, Ruby was coming out with her fists up and ready to fight back.

The vision was such a contradiction to the pigtailed and big-eyed look she was cultivating now. Back when she'd been America's Darling, she'd had a cutting edge to her appearance, but she'd been a naive, fragile girl. Now she looked like that girl, yet she had the fighting spirit of a woman. He appreciated the contradiction. He *liked* the contradiction. He leaned his head back and stared at the ceiling. God help him, he wished he didn't like Ruby Heart.

"So when do we start the Ruby Heart regeneration plan?"

"This is not a joke," she said suspiciously.

"No, it is not. The more successful you are at this, the better the series will be." *Sure, Micah. Those are your reasons. Nothing personal. Maybe you should make a promise not to lie to yourself, too, eh?* Micah backed himself away from the counter and headed to the door. He needed to go to his office, find Dexter and Amir and get this interview underway. Before he headed out the door, he took the phone off speaker and put his Bluetooth in so that he could use both hands on his wheelchair.

"Before I set a time, I need to talk to my parents. They need to be warned, at least."

"You're not going to let them talk you out of it?" Micah asked while he navigated the gap left for him in the cluttered hallway.

"No. I'm committed."

Micah waited a second to respond. "When are you talking to them?"

"Today."

"Ripping the Band-Aid off all in one go?"

"This won't get easier if I run from it."

Micah figured Ruby probably thought running made most things easier.

"I'll call you tonight, then. And we'll set up a time."

She was silent for a moment. He wished he could see her and judge her commitment. "Okay. I want to do the interview soon."

"So do I. And, Ruby?"

"Hmm?"

"Good luck talking with your parents."

She hung up before responding. Micah pushed the call

button for the elevator. As the elevator beeped its way past a couple of floors, he told himself the rise in his blood pressure was strictly due to the excitement of the ultra series and the upcoming interview.

CHAPTER ELEVEN

RUBY EASED HER way through the French doors and joined her parents on the patio by the pool. Her mother sat with her face in the sun, wearing a large straw hat and a breezy white linen dress. When combined with the gin and tonic fizzing away on the table next to her, Ruby had the impression that her mother could float away at any moment. After their last argument about King's phone call, Ruby knew better—under all that linen and straw was a piece of marble too heavy for mere mortals to move. Had her mother turned from flesh to stone in the aftermath of Ruby's career, or had Ruby been too self-absorbed to notice how cold her mother's hugs had always been?

In opposition to her mother's light and airy facade, her father sat hunched under an umbrella, sweat glistening on his brow and dark spots expanding under his arms on his black polo shirt, even though the June sun was mild. He was drinking a whiskey, neat, which probably didn't help cool him off. The still life of the perfect family was completed by her brother and his fiancée splashing each other in the water, seemingly unaware of the resentment and blame that were mixed into the mortar that held the patio stones together. Somehow Josh had always managed to happily live his life in spite of their parents. She wondered at his secret.

The sun glinted off the patio, and the grass was a bright kelly-green. A beautiful prison, but her parole started next week and she couldn't wait.

Even though her shadow blocked her mother's sun, her mom didn't turn to look at her. Nor did her father glance up from his paper. She wasn't ungrateful enough to think her parents wouldn't notice she was gone, but imagining them missing her was a stretch. Josh, at least, waved when he caught a glimpse of her.

In her mind, she added Micah to the patio, then scratched his image out again. His presence wouldn't help her parents notice her. Instead, she'd be the daughter who couldn't even be trusted to bring home a man with the use of his legs. Her mother would cover up her surprise by being overly solicitous. If Ruby was lucky, her father would *only* be rude.

She needed to leave this house before she forgot all that her parents had ever done for her and only remembered the way they'd imprisoned her with the promise of safety. Theirs was a relationship that could only be repaired through the fog of distance.

She plopped Micah back into the scene, this time erasing her parents' reactions. *You were something special.* Micah hadn't said she'd *had* something special, like her family always had. He'd meant *her,* not her medals, not her records and not even her running. She imagined him pulling up a seat, a margarita in his hand and a warm, encouraging smile on his lips. One that reminded her that she could be something special again.

Her shoulders relaxed and set with determination, Ruby walked around her mother's chair to stand in front of her. She didn't look up until Ruby coughed and said hello. The sun was in the other direction, but her mother brought up her hand to shield her eyes anyway, and Ruby felt looked through rather than looked at.

She'd rehearsed this scene. Visualized it as she had visualized hundreds of races. Josh's presence would make it easier. *Other people your age live on their own.* Previously, that thought had been depressing. Now it felt like a challenge.

"I'm moving out. By the end of this week." Her words must have been more interesting than the news, because her dad folded his paper and looked at her.

Christine and Josh stopped their water fight. Her mother picked up her drink and took a long sip, with a short hiccup at the end. Her father scowled.

"Have you found a place yet?" Christine called out from the water.

"No. I'm going to start looking tomorrow. I'm getting a dog, too. Next week."

"How do you expect to pay for this?" The paper made a loud thud when her father threw it to the ground. "Your money's still frozen."

"I have Aunt Ruby's money." The eccentric aunt she'd been named after had left Ruby the money with a note to follow her dream. Apparently her dream was a dog and some freedom.

"Unless you find a job—and I don't know who would hire you—that won't last you more than a year. Two at the most."

"I know." Find a job was next week's activity. One foot in front of the other and she'd make it to the finish. That's how she'd won on every track in every competition. "I'm running races again. Not anything I'm banned from. Ultras," she clarified before her dad could interrupt by reminding her about the ban. "And I've agreed to sit for an interview. With Micah Blackwell."

Her mom took another loud sip of her drink, then shook the ice and drank some more. Finally the crystal hit the mosaic table and her mother's attention turned to Ruby. "This is because I told that other reporter where you were volunteering," her mother accused, too angry to fake weakness.

"No," Ruby replied, surprised that she meant it. "This is because it's far past time for me to figure out how to live on my own." She had concentrated on her fears and her guilt for so long that what could have been easily stepped over at one time had now swelled into a brick wall eight feet tall. Moving out might only be chiseling at that wall with an ice pick, but an ice pick was all she had. It would do until she found a backhoe.

"You're being selfish. You know what this interview will do to us. Your sister. Your brother."

"I know." She'd been selfish all her life.

"You're punishing us for not supporting you enough." Her mother turned her wobbly voice to her husband. "Dennis, I said we didn't support her enough."

"For God's sake, Julie. She's been living here since she left college. We paid for that goddamned weight room. We paid for a private coach—who turned our daughter into a cheater. My firm isn't charging her legal fees. Running camps. Trips to the Olympics. How much more support does she need?"

"Clearly we didn't do something—"

"I'm nearly thirty," Ruby interrupted loudly. "Living on my own and making my own decisions isn't about the weight room, you or Dad. It's not even about the dog. I can't be in prison forever."

Air whistled through her mom's teeth as she sucked all the hurt feelings out of the backyard and concentrated them inside her breast. "Is that what this house is to you? Prison?"

Her mother sniffed, not loud enough to be indelicate, but everyone within earshot knew she was on the verge of tears. She eased her way away from the table. "I'm going to go lie down before dinner. I'll be in my room."

"Julie, she's looking for attention," her father said to her mother's back. "If we ignore her, she'll learn it doesn't work."

Christine had been staring at the entire battle with her mouth open, but she snapped it shut when Ruby looked over to the pool. Astonishingly, Josh looked as if he was about to laugh. Which their father also noticed.

"This isn't funny," he called out to Josh, who shrugged. "And you—" he turned his attention back to Ruby "—if you think you'll get continued support from us on this…adventure, you're wrong. I might even rethink the legal help."

With that as his last word, he left his newspaper on the patio stone, his tumbler half-full of whiskey on the small table, and followed his wife.

For several seconds, the only noise in the backyard was the normally soothing burble of the pool. Even the birds had stopped chirping. Then Josh burst out laughing. He climbed out of the pool and gave Ruby a hug, apparently oblivious to the fact that he was dripping wet from the pool and she was in jeans and a T-shirt.

"I can't believe what I just heard. Ruby Heart, rebelling teenager fifteen years after the fact."

"It's not funny, Josh," Ruby said. Her T-shirt stuck to her chest. Josh had managed to get a couple of spots of water on her jeans, too. She'd have to wash them quickly in case the chlorine bleached them. And add a washer and dryer to the impossible list of things she needed in a new place, right after allows dogs, cheap and available on a week's notice.

"Ah, but it is funny, little sis. I heard crap like that all the time when I was sixteen, but you were their golden child. I guess everyone has to go through their teen years sometime."

I'm twenty-nine! Wanting to move out of my parents' house and get a job and a dog isn't rebelling. It's normal. The absurdity of all this pounded on her skull while her brain shouted thoughts she couldn't say. Protesting her age and normality only made her feel more immature—and weirder.

"Ruby, do you have any idea how to rent an apartment?" Christine had joined them on the patio and was drying off her hair with a large green towel.

Josh looked as though he was going to laugh again, but his mouth pursed and he stopped. Ruby didn't miss the dart of Christine's hand out from under her towel to Josh's back to, Ruby assumed, pinch the dickens out of him.

"I have to rent a house. Jodie at the shelter said Dotty would do better in a house, with a yard."

Christine and Josh exchanged looks and Ruby felt even more of a fool than before. Then she looked around the perfectly maintained backyard, the pit of her stomach burning. She couldn't say it was unfairness, because she was in her current situation due to her own actions, but she had been raised and coddled to do one thing and one thing only. If she continued to be ashamed that she didn't know how to perform the basic human activities of living, she might as well call the shelter and tell them she couldn't take Dotty. And letting down the dog would really be something to be ashamed of.

"Look, I know this is stupid, but I've got to get out of here. Moving out will never get any easier and we all know my running money is gone. The firm is fighting a losing battle."

"An expensive one, too." Josh's smirk faded. "I'll talk to Dad about the legal bills. He's not actually going to saddle you with them."

Ruby shrugged. "Most athletes in my position have to pay their own legal bills. I'm not sure why I should be so special."

Her brother opened his mouth to argue, then changed his mind. "I'll still talk with him."

"What can we help you with?" Christine asked. She was always kinder than her actual family.

"See if anyone you know has a place for me to rent. Even a room, so long as they don't mind a Dalmatian as a roommate."

"Ruby." Josh's voice was serious. Caring. "I think the interview is a good idea, but is Micah Blackwell really the best choice?"

She caught her brother's gaze. "Yes." She didn't lie and say that he wouldn't hurt her or that the interview wouldn't go against her, but Micah wouldn't *try* to manipulate her. "I've got to get these pants in the wash and I have some calls to make."

Up in her room, with a bowl of ice cream cold on the bare skin of her legs, Ruby called him to set up the interview.

CHAPTER TWELVE

FOR SOME REASON, Micah had expected Ruby to fidget. She didn't, of course. While other people battled their bodies through food or exercise, Ruby's body was her machine to control. If he hadn't been watching her so intently when she'd walked into the room, he wouldn't have noticed her blink of recognition at the chair. She'd sat in the same chair in the same studio five years ago, and the only indication she had noticed was the slight catch of her breath and the rise and fall of her tiny breasts hidden under a plain cream blouse. She had on a black skirt, black hose and boring black pumps. Perhaps she was going for the innocent-nun look.

Her mother must have picked out her clothes when she was America's Darling. And Ruby could have benefited from some wardrobe advice for this interview. She looked like a woman hiding secrets in her skirts.

Hose hid the magnificence of her leg muscles. Her skirt needed to be a little shorter and her blouse a little tighter. Show off a little. With her current outfit, there was no risk that she'd shift her legs and he'd get a peek past her thighs to whatever boring panties she was probably wearing.

God, he wanted it to happen, though.

He was a sick bastard to be thinking that while sitting here, the questions he had for her on a teleprompter behind her head. He wanted Ruby to have her chance at redemption, but he also wanted his ratings and the anchor spot. Thinking about how her hamstrings curved into the soft divot on the inside of her hip would only encourage him to play nice—and playing nice wasn't an option today.

It had been Dexter's idea to pull the old furniture out of storage—for a better reaction, he'd said. He didn't understand that Ruby had been living in and amongst the material evidence of her failures for five years and the chair was probably nothing to the trophy room he imagined had to exist somewhere in the Heart house.

Or maybe not. Maybe the Hearts had decided that if the room didn't display a gold medal, then it didn't need to exist. Much like Micah's grandmother. She'd decided that reminders of his former career would only cause him pain and so, she told him proudly one day in the rehab hospital, she'd packed up all of his trophies and awards and put them in the attic. To make his life more comfortable, she'd said. She'd also offered to donate them to Texas A&M or the College Football Hall of Fame. Because he wouldn't have children to leave them to, she'd said.

Since Grandmama had done all the packing, his father had easily collected everything, and the best stuff was now on display in Micah's apartment.

Loud talking by an electrician focused Micah's attention back to the woman sitting across from him. She noticed and lifted her chin slightly, her neck long and thin. Vulnerable. After one of her runs he could kiss her right under her chin and feel her racing pulse on his lips.

Stupid. Admiring her poise was okay; desiring her was the first roll on a short pier that ended with him diving into conflict of interest and no promotion. If they got the green light for Ruby to be the star of the series, he would have to figure out how to push his desire deep down into his body, to his toes, where he wouldn't feel it.

She started when he asked his first question, revealing a fear she'd managed to keep hidden. But when she looked at him—and the camera behind his head—dead-on, her voice was even and strong.

This wasn't an interview where they would joke and laugh and she would talk about the glory of the game, so his second question was, "Tell me about the doping. What led you to do it?"

Her eyes looked tired, and he wondered how much energy she was expending to keep herself from flinching. "I wanted to win. I wanted to make my country proud. I wanted to make my parents proud. A silver medal wasn't good enough." She closed her eyes, and the American public watching would close theirs. "I'm not proud of the decision. It was wrong and I wish I hadn't made it."

"Was it your idea?"

Her fingers pulsed on her legs. "It doesn't matter whose idea it was. It was my body and I should have said no."

The interview wasn't going the way Micah had expected. He knew it had been her coach's idea. He knew the people closest to her had told her that doping wasn't a big deal, and yet on an interview that would be broadcast on *SportsDaily* twice tonight and again in the morning, she was putting the burden solely on her shoulders.

He ignored the next question on the teleprompter. "That answer doesn't square with the fact that your coach went to prison."

"He shouldn't have offered, but it was still my body. And I'm sorry. To everyone."

"Your all-inclusive ban on competition was up this year."

"Yes."

"What did you tell the various governing bodies to get your ban reduced?"

"I'm not legally allowed to say."

"Were there other runners that you knew of involved in blood doping?"

"I signed a nondisclosure agreement as part of my plea. All I can say is that I'm sorry for what I did and the hurt I caused. I'm sorry for shaming my sport."

Suddenly the reasoning behind her clothing made since. She wasn't going for nun or even sexy librarian. Ruby was trying to look nonthreatening. Harmless. Not worth anyone's attention. Her answers would give the talking heads little to chew over. How much time can you spend analyzing someone who says, "I was wrong and I'm sorry," and doesn't offer up any excuses?

He had to try a different tact before the audience got bored. "You're running again."

Pleasure brightened her skin. The audience finally got a reaction. "I am. And it's the most glorious thing in the world."

"You've run two ultra races, and there are more in the future."

"Yes." Energy poured out of her, changing her from meek to a woman people would want to get behind. To root for, if only to be a part of what changed her from rigid to strong.

"Planning on winning any?"

"Right now I'm grateful to be among athletes again." A bullshit answer, the kind every athlete would give. But it didn't matter. Anyone watching her on-screen would be able to see that, yes, Ruby Heart had her eye on a first-place finish. And whether or not they rooted for her or against her, she had their attention now.

"There are plenty of people who say you should have been banned from all competition for life. They won't like that you're running again."

She stiffened, though whether she was pissed at herself or at her naysayers wasn't clear from her expression. Though the fight in her eyes should concern whoever her anger was directed at, even if it was directed inward. "What I did was wrong, but I've served the punishment handed down to me. I love to run. If people who come out to watch an ultra don't want to see me, they can turn their backs as I run past."

Everyone working in the studio blinked in unison. Ruby Heart had given the quote of the interview, and probably the quote of the week.

The rest of the interview finished uneventfully. Whether it would be a success or not depended on whether people watched the interview or listened to it while busying about the kitchen.

He wanted to say goodbye to Ruby, arrange a time for them to talk about the series, see the flush of excitement on her skin up close. But by the time someone removed his mic, she was gone.

Ruby Heart, back to running.

RUBY WAS STANDING in the lobby, scrolling through Twitter comments about the interview that would be aired tonight when Micah caught her. She'd been prepared for the comments. Had known they were coming. And still the vitriol made every breath she took taste like bile. "Thanks a lot, sis," she muttered. Roxanne had sent her the link.

"Bad news?" he asked, sincerity strong across his face.

No, sincerity implied something more tender. He was honestly asking and honest was all she'd asked for.

"Why'd you ask questions you knew I wouldn't be able to answer?"

"So people could see that they'd been asked."

"And that I didn't answer." Once it was posted online, the comments section of the interview would fill up with conspiracies, and she couldn't offer the truth as an alternative.

"I had to ask, Ruby. You know that." He looked disappointed in her hurt, but he'd probably never been stupid enough to read the comments. And in truth she wasn't hurt, just nervous about what was to come. "What's wrong?" he asked again. He'd never allow her to hide again, from herself or anyone else.

She bit her lip. "Comments about tonight's interview are all over Twitter."

"We want people to tune in. What did you expect?"

"Nothing. I guess I'd enjoyed the break."

"We want online discussion." Micah had promised to be honest with her. He'd also promised to rehabilitate her image. She couldn't crawl onto his lap and rest her head on his shoulder; the interview would have to do.

"Sure," she lied.

"Will you watch the interview tonight?"

She scowled. "I'll have to go to my cousin's because I don't have cable yet. And that's another frustration. I've filled out all the stuff online and nothing happens. When I call customer service, they tell me to go online." Besides the joy of having Dotty, her first week living on her own wasn't going smoothly. She couldn't figure out how to get cable, and she'd screwed something up when opening a bank account at a new bank—one separate from her parents—which had led to an hour-long phone call trying to fix it. To remind herself that she was good at *something,* she'd taken Dotty for a long run.

"Come to my apartment and watch it. I'm not working tonight."

"Won't that be weird?" It would be more intimate than dinner in a hotel room because she'd be in his apartment, surrounded by his things and the smell of him. She blinked before desire overtook her.

"No, it'll be fine. I'll order a pizza."

She should say no. "Okay."

He gave her basic directions, then said goodbye and headed back toward the elevators and his work. *His work.* She couldn't forget that. Going over to a man's house to watch television and have pizza may seem normal, but, like everyone else in this world, Micah had an agenda.

RUBY STOOD OUTSIDE Micah's door, telling herself to knock. He knew she was here—he'd buzzed her up. She should have just watched the interview at Haley's house. Then Ruby wouldn't have had to figure out what to wear, before eventually settling on jeans and a peasant blouse.

Because this wasn't a date. This was a trade. Him helping her and her letting him into all aspects of her life. Fading away into the background again was no longer an option, as scary as that sounded. Because while she hadn't been losing for the past five years, she hadn't been winning, either.

Micah opened the door and she jumped. "Coming in?" he asked with a smile on his face that sent a shiver down her spine. He had a nick on his neck from shaving, above the collar of his dark red check button-down. If she put her finger on the cut, she'd be able to feel his pulse. She put her hands in her pockets before she gave in to the urge.

She wanted the chance at normal, which a relationship

with Micah could never be. They had too much history. But here she was at his apartment door. Her mascara and lip gloss shouldn't go to waste, so she straightened her shoulders and stepped through.

His apartment was spacious and open, with a large comfortable-looking couch, man-size recliner and a big TV. The living room smelled like pepperoni pizza and Micah. Spicy. Definitely bad for her.

"Do you want something to drink? I've got beer. Or water. I can make coffee, too."

"Beer, please."

"Help yourself to pizza. I figured we'd eat on the couch and watch the interview."

Ruby did as she was told, anticipation and apprehension mixing deep in the pit of her stomach. But when her fingers brushed his as she took the beer he offered, she didn't run away. Instead, she leaned back, deeper into the couch. She was here and she was going to do this.

The cushions shifted when Micah joined her. His legs had all the energy of an empty sock as they hung off the side. Despite the cool of the air-conditioning, his feet were bare. "My feet don't get cold," he said, catching her staring.

"I guess they wouldn't."

"They don't get hot either, though I have to be careful where I'm barefoot because I wouldn't feel a burn."

"I'm sorry."

"What are you apologizing for?" He was reaching over to the end table for the remote when he asked the question, all casual, but there was nothing casual about his voice.

"I don't know."

"Then stop apologizing. It doesn't suit you."

He clicked on the television, and there she was in the promo material. "I apologize in the interview."

"I know. And you needed to, but it didn't suit you any better there, either."

She chewed her pizza and kept her eyes on the *Sports-Daily* anchors introducing various segments and continuing to promise the viewing audience that an exclusive interview with Ruby Heart was coming up, but she was too distracted by Micah's nearness to pay much attention. She'd sat on the middle cushion of the couch, too close to him, and yet she couldn't scoot to the other side without being obvious. Worse, she didn't want to.

And Micah, because he was Micah and had always been able to see deep inside of her, seemed to know it. Though somewhere over the course of the dinner they'd spent in her hotel room, his insight had stopped bothering her. At least someone could see beyond the doping and the fear to the real Ruby Heart.

"You're up next," Micah said. *SportsDaily* was back from a commercial break and the anchor was introducing the interview.

She closed her eyes.

"I thought you were here to watch."

She opened her eyes. Now Micah was in front of her and beside her and taking over her mind. She needed to run.

"You're not really watching, Ruby."

"My eyes are open."

"Chicken."

She stiffened. Setting her plate of half-eaten pizza on the coffee table, Ruby crossed her legs under her and leaned forward. She was *done* with being a chicken.

When the entire painful interview was over, she uncrossed her legs, picked up her plate and leaned back into the cushions. "What did you think?"

"That it's enough to convince Dexter that you are the new

star of NSN's ultra series. What do *you* think?" His face was serious, the dimples barely visible on his cheeks as his eyes skimmed over her. Even though they didn't travel farther down than her neck, she felt undressed. Leaning over to kiss him felt as natural as answering.

She leaned back into the cushions. "Next time I'm on TV, I'm going to dress less like a mouse." More powerful, less demure.

His dimples deepened with his laugh. "Who used to pick out your interview clothes? Because *those* had quite the effect."

"I'm not interested in looking like a sexpot anymore."

His blue-gray eyes flared with an interest her body recognized, even if her mind didn't fully understand, though all he said was, "There is a middle ground."

Yeah, he didn't want to be attracted to her any more than she wanted to be attracted to him. "I'll ask my cousin for advice next time. If you really think this series is going to happen."

"Trust me," he said. "This will be good for you."

"Good for you," she corrected.

"Not everyone's best interest isn't your worst interest."

She shrugged. "Maybe, but apparently I'm not very good at sorting it out."

"I expected Ruby Heart to have more confidence."

"Ha. Confidence in what?"

"Running, at least."

"Sure. I can still kick your ass at running."

He quirked his lips, but she didn't apologize; he'd told her not to. "Not in my marathon chair."

She bit her tongue before she threw back, "You're on," because he was right. He would kick her ass.

"While you're here, why don't I help you get signed up for cable."

"What I really need is a gym."

"Come with me to my gym." Temptation purred through his voice and his eyes promised the world.

"Okay." She couldn't crawl into his lap, but she could go to his gym. "When?"

"I'll pick you up on Thursday."

"It's a date," she said, then bit her bottom lip before she could take it back.

"It's okay, Ruby," he said. "I won't hold you to it."

Which was how she knew his inviting eyes and that velvet voice were part of the lie.

CHAPTER THIRTEEN

RUBY STOOD OUTSIDE her house, shifting her bag from her left shoulder to her right shoulder and back again. Fluffy white clouds floated above in the bright blue sky. The pleasant weather would soon be hot, and she would need to take even more care with her long runs, especially with Dotty. From inside the house, her dog barked, angry at being left behind.

Somehow the intrusion of Dotty's needs into her training schedule didn't seem like a burden. It would be *easier* to plan her training schedule if she didn't have to worry about cutting back her training for her dog, but caring for Dotty was a *nice* experience. Ruby got as much pleasure out of it as Dotty did.

She pulled her cell phone out of her bag and looked at the time. Micah was ten minutes late. Just as she was about to give up on him and head inside, a car coming down the street slowed in front of her house. Micah rolled down his window, and her excuse to chicken out disappeared along with the glass.

"Coming or not?" She snorted at his tone, as if he hadn't been the late one.

"Coming," she said, walking toward the car with a stride defiant enough to trick herself into believing she wasn't nervous. She opened the back door, tossed her gym bag next to his chair, then slid into the passenger seat next to Micah.

"Ready?" he asked.

Ruby took a deep breath, which came out of her mouth in waves as she moved her head up and down in something she hoped he would mistake for a nod. But she answered honestly. "This is the first time I've worked out in a gym with other people since college."

And then she had been the star, not the pariah. *Don't think that. A new life. A new you and people will either get it or they won't. And if they don't, don't let 'em hold you back.*

"Think of how much fun it will be," he said, his dimples so deep in his cheeks that she believed him.

"House looks nice," Micah said as he pulled out into the road.

Ruby was too busy watching the movements of his hands with interest—she'd never seen a hand-driven car in action—to answer with anything less than the truth. "Roxanne, my sister, found it for me. A professor in her department is spending a year in Oxford and their house sitter fell through at the last minute. I guess I'm as perfect a solution for them as they are for me." She didn't mention how Roxanne had offered the house with the snide comment that some people have all the luck. Her sister was sensitive to being overshadowed by her younger sister's flashier talents, and the homeowners had been tickled that a former Olympian with a scandal hanging over her head was their house sitter.

Some people had a strange sense of pleasure, but Ruby hadn't been in a position to turn the house down, even if she'd wanted to.

"So you get to learn all about living on your own without the burdens of paying your own bills." She must have made a face as horrible as his comment felt, because he held up his hand. "That wasn't a criticism."

"I guess I'm a little sensitive to being twenty-nine and only now moving out of my parents' house." She'd had a privileged upbringing, and rather than using the luxury to become a better person and do great things, she'd wasted it. Gas stations and fast-food places rushing by didn't help reorient her mind to the present, so she took a deep breath.

"Would you rather people judge you for moving out of your parents' house at twenty-nine or for hiding away behind those large front doors and high fences for the rest of your life?"

"I'd rather people didn't judge me at all."

"Not going to happen, Ruby."

Letting out all the air she had been holding felt so good that she did it again, pushing every last breath out of her body until her belly button touched her spine. "I know."

"How did you survive being famous? Every little slip I made was in the college paper and discussed on NSN by at least five talking heads."

"I didn't play football or basketball or even soccer. People came out to meets, but I was only in the paper when I was successful, which was all the time, but the general public didn't know me until my first Olympics. I was unbeatable in the five and ten K's in college. The reason people were surprised that I won the silver in the first Olympics was not because I wasn't the best in the United States, but because the United States hadn't been in serious medal contention for middle distance in the Olympics in years."

Any discussion of her glory years had always felt as if it was accompanied with a giant weight pushing down on her rib cage and shrinking her heart into nothingness. Now, thinking back to what she'd lost—what it had cost her—still made her sad, but the pressure was gone. She took another deep breath and her chest expanded to its fullest.

When Micah made a noncommittal noise in response but didn't say anything, she continued, "And after I graduated from college, I came back to my parents' house and I trained. If there was criticism, they must have filtered it out because I never saw it. Any talk shows I went on, especially in the lead-up to the second Olympics, were carefully vetted. I listened to my coach and I trained and I raced in meets and my parents told me I was great and that was it.

"I wasn't encouraged to socialize with other athletes." Narcissism, both hers and her parents, had made her world a tiny bubble. "It would interfere with my training, they said. And I agreed because I'd stood on that pedestal and seen the flag of another country raised higher than the Stars and Stripes and I heard the anthem of another country instead of 'The Star-Spangled Banner' and I knew—knew!—that I could be on that higher podium in four years."

"And you were," he said, so softly that she almost didn't hear him.

"And I was. And if felt great. If you've never done it, you can't imagine the pride and joy and patriotism and…and, well, I handed over that medal, but they couldn't take away the memory of that podium."

As they waited to turn left at a light, the only sounds were the soft blowing of the air conditioner and the buzz of other cars as they whipped past them.

"Was it worth it?" Micah finally asked once he'd made the turn and they were going straight again. "Was the doping worth that one memory?"

"No. I lost more than a medal when the doping was revealed. I lost my integrity, and no wonderful memory is worth that." She had more to say, more she wanted Micah to know, but the wall of regret was still too high and she wasn't yet a skilled enough climber to scale it.

Then Micah pulled to a stop at another light and he put his hand on her knee. The wall crumbled and her fears of admitting the truth—even to herself—fell to the dirt, mixed with the broken clay.

"And you were right when you said I was something special. That's what hurts the most. With all that training and dedication, I could have won. I was still America's Darling, the unbeatable Ruby Heart." She swallowed, but the lump in her throat didn't disappear. Water filled her eyes, and if she looked in the mirror she would see the lines down her face where the tears ran through the dust of her life, washing off the shame when nothing else could. "I defeated myself, and I have to face that every time I look in the mirror. No talking head can judge me as harshly as I judge myself."

Her cheeks burned with embarrassment as tears slid down them. Never in the past five years had she admitted to herself that final truth. Like Usain Bolt, she had been as sure a bet as there could be in sports. To this day, she couldn't understand why her coach and agent had risked the win. At the time, she'd been naive enough to buy their story of "insurance" and "everyone does it." The court documents revealed that significant amounts of money had changed hands, but it had been a foolish risk for them and plain stupid for her.

She wiped her cheeks with the back of her hand as her youthful and expensive foolishness fogged up the inside of the car. At least, she couldn't see though the droplets on her eyelashes. And yet, even though Micah didn't say a word, his solid, strong presence was as palpable as her regret and just as powerful. She didn't need him to say anything; she only needed to know that he was there.

They drove the rest of the way in silence. Only when Micah turned into the gym parking lot did Ruby speak again. She wanted to know *his* secrets. "I still can't believe you don't work out at home. Wouldn't it be easier?"

He shrugged. "Easier, maybe. But like you said, training as a solitary experience can be dangerous. People help with perspective. And they interact more than a dumbbell rack."

She smiled, and the easy way he had let her spill her guts and then condensed her experience into a manageable mouthful warmed her heart as surely as her shame had warmed her cheeks. She watched his profile as he turned into a parking spot. His nose was a little crooked from where it must have been broken, probably playing football. His lips were a pale pink, full and inviting. He was attractive when he was charming the world with his dimples, but she liked him better now, with the slight indent of his cheeks hinting at the magnetism that lit him from within. His strength was on evidence to the entire world, but his lightness was somehow a secret he shared with few.

She smiled in spite of herself. She wasn't even sure if she had room in her life right now for an affair, serious or not, and he probably had no room in his life for her. She had been the cheater who couldn't face her crimes and now she was the poor little rich girl. Sure, he was being kind to her, but she was allowing him unprecedented access into her life so that he could boost his career. Next time she was tempted to spill her guts, she needed to remember that his kindness had a price.

"What are you smiling about?" he asked, interrupting her thoughts.

"Just that I know how you feel about going to the gym."

She lied. "When I only had my coach for a spotter, lifting weights became less of a game and more of a chore."

"Let's go inside and see if we can make it fun again."

"Okay," she said, but she didn't even put her hand on the door, much less open it.

"You've already done the interview and you can't hide forever. What's the worst they can do?"

She still hadn't gotten her cable or internet hooked up, so she hadn't *seen* the online comments after the interview aired. But she was as familiar with their rhythm as she was with the rhythm of her own running. And part of her was still afraid that Micah agreed with them. But she already knew what he thought of her doping and his opinion of her subsequent hiding out from life. *And* he had picked her up to drive her to his gym anyway. No one else in her life had considered that the exercise was her life and had been her job, so the new gym was almost as significant as the new house and finding a new job.

Another piece in the new-Ruby plan.

"Well, I came here with you, so I can't be that afraid." Her self-doubt would only be answered if she placed herself in a position of competition. And she'd only have a chance of winning if she threw out her self-doubt. Maybe she could pack it up in a box and store it at her parents' house.

"Never show fear. It's like throwing chum to sharks." Then Micah opened the car door and she could either follow him or be left behind.

CHAPTER FOURTEEN

RUBY SAT IN the car thinking about the trip from the parking lot to the door for longer than she should have, and she had to dart to catch up to Micah before he opened the door. Suddenly, they were in the gym, a sprawling single-story building with lots of glass and metal. It wasn't until she saw the pale wood paneling on the wall behind the front desk that she felt at home. She followed Micah up to the counter where he checked in and she handed over her guest pass. On the guest sign-in sheet, she started to write "Diana," then stopped and wrote "Ruby Heart."

The clerk didn't even blink. Ruby chuckled at her own hubris as she waved to Micah and headed into the dressing room to change.

When she came out of the dressing room, Micah was already at the weights. She faltered in the doorway, then remembered who she was and stepped out. First a warm-up on the treadmill, then lifts. She set the program for an easy pace with no incline for twenty minutes and let herself fall into the rhythm of the run.

Five minutes in, a man got onto the treadmill beside her. Seven minutes in, he broke her rhythm completely—mostly because he had none. She glanced at him from the corner of her eye. His legs were okay. He wasn't fully landing with his feet underneath him, but he wasn't fully heel striking, either. His arms were another story; he might as well be a symphony conductor. She would bet that half of his energy was lost in the way he swung his arms about. If he could control his arms, his run would be more efficient and he wouldn't have to breathe so hard.

Ruby forced her eyes forward. This man and his running style was not her business. He was wearing expensive running shoes and clothes, and judging by the definition in his biceps, it looked like he lifted weights—a lot of them. A man used to the gym. He had a shaved head, a full beard and tattoos. This was not a man who would appreciate her interference. She should leave him alone. Plus, running was as much about controlling the mind as controlling the body. If she could block out the pain constricting her hamstrings at mile thirty, she could ignore this man's poor form.

But his breaths were starting to come in loud huffs. She eyed him again, this time noticing how long he had set his treadmill run for. He still had thirty minutes left. He'd be here the entire time she ran, huffing and puffing and flailing. A few pointers and some of the flailing at least would be under control. Ten minutes of peace for her. A lifetime of better running for him. A fair trade.

She slowed her treadmill down until she was at a bare jog. "May I suggest some changes to your running style?"

"Who the hell are you?" he huffed out.

She looked around for Micah and his encouraging, supportive smile. Sometime since she'd gotten on the treadmill, he'd started doing dumbbell curls. He was deep in concentration.

What the hell, she'd already done the interview. "Ruby Heart."

He wasted more of his precious and dwindling energy to blink. Then he hit the emergency-stop button and lurched to a halt. She paused her own run.

"Get out," he said, gripping the rails of the treadmill. He'd caught a breath or two, but his body was still reeling from the erratic movements of his running form.

"I'm afraid it's true. Would you like some pointers?"

"How do I know you're not shitting me?"

For a brief second, Ruby considered backing down. But the only time she hadn't stood tall against a challenge had turned into five lost and lonely years. She should have stood in front of the cameras and microphones and admitted to the magnitude of what she'd done, then gone on with the remnants of her life. Retreat was no longer a Ruby Heart trait. Regret shouldn't be, either. "Would you like a race?"

"On the treadmill?"

"Sure. We each set the treadmill for a 5K race. The first person to finish their 5K wins." Her Olympic time—the silver medal time before the doping—had been fourteen minutes, forty-one seconds, and she'd hit that hundredths of a second right on the bull's-eye. Now she was training for distance over speed, but even if she ran at what she considered an easy pace, she would still beat this guy.

"How do I know you won't cheat?"

She shook off the offense. "Worry more about yourself."

He still looked suspicious, but nodded, and they each set their treadmills. Ruby's breathing was even and calm when the mileage on her treadmill hit 3.1 in seventeen minutes and she began her cooldown. The man next to her was straining hard enough that he had to stare at the screen on her machine several times before he could focus on both her distance and time. He shrugged, then reduced the speed of his treadmill until he was walking next to her, his chest rising and falling in massive, sucking breaths.

"So Ruby Heart, huh?"

"Yup. Did you see the interview on *SportsDaily*?"

"No. I didn't want to give you the time of day." He eyed her to see if she was offended and she shrugged. She'd heard worse. "Did you even struggle at that pace?"

"Not really." An exultant high of pushing herself to win—not finish, but win—lifted her chest and relaxed her shoulders. Stretching herself to win felt different from a runner's high and just as awesome. She knew from experience that when the two highs combined, she was invincible through any amount of fatigue.

Before she grasped on to the feeling and hugged it tight to her chest as if welcoming home a long lost friend, she reminded herself that all she'd done was beat a man with poor form in a 5K on a treadmill, and that success had led her into a moral desert once. Winning may be an old friend, but it was an old friend with very bad habits.

He nodded several times, apparently still processing who she was. Or maybe he couldn't believe that he'd gotten his ass kicked by a girl. "And you offered to give me some pointers?"

"You look like you need some. You waste a lot of energy in how you move your arms. You're not running right to left—you're running forward. Let your arms provide momentum to take you there. Making a fist also takes energy. Loose hands. Not so loose that they flounce, but not so tight that you have to fight your body to keep them closed."

"And this will help?" He sounded skeptical.

"Tell you what—I'm going to go lift weights. Run for ten minutes while thinking about what I said. You'll have to concentrate, so it will be harder on your mind, but easier on your body. When you realize I'm right, come let me know." She considered her offer and every person who'd ever coached her in running, and then she said, "If you decide I'm wrong, let me know that, as well."

She stopped her machine and headed off to get a wipe for the screen and rails. On her way back to the treadmill, she paused to watch the man's form. Better. Far from perfect, but better. She wiped her machine clean, grabbed her towel and set off for Micah and the weights.

The scent of him filled her nose, growing more powerful as she approached. Warm, salty and hardworking. His essence came at her in waves as she stepped closer and he worked the weights. Since he was wearing gym shorts, she saw his legs for the first time. They weren't as atrophied as she'd expected, though they were more bone and skin than muscle. Up close, what she could see of his arms and shoulders through the muscle shirt looked as fantastic as she'd hoped. Those arms would look especially nice wrapped around her. She wished she could see his back muscles as he moved, but he was doing chest flies on the machine. She supposed someone would notice if she crawled behind the machine for a glimpse.

Curiosity about his body, or attraction? Or both—since she'd be curious about the body of anyone she was attracted to.

Rather than make a fool of herself, she waited off to the side. When Micah finished counting, he let go of the pulleys and the weights dropped with a crash. Her curiosity warmed into pleasure as his eyes refocused on her standing next to him and his expression turned luxurious.

"LIKE WHAT YOU SEE?" he asked. He had felt her looking at him as he'd finished his set, her gaze adding extra weight to the rope and making each pull harder. Though he probably couldn't blame that on her gaze but on the dirty thoughts occupying his mind and distracting him from the exercise— much like being near her on the couch in his apartment had meant he had to rewatch the interview after she'd left so he could pay attention.

Her face flushed, but she didn't look away. Neither did she stare at his legs. "Yes, yes. I do. In fact, I'd like to see more."

Her directness surprised a cough out of him. He hadn't expected Ruby to return his interest. Realizing that he was sexually attracted to her, despite her doping and their shared history, had been astonishing. But considering that he had once humiliated her on television and then all but told her what a piece of scum he thought she was…well, he figured their past might have more baggage for her than it did for him.

They both knew this friendship was an exchange. Tit for tat. Innuendo only confused things and sex would make the threads of their relationship damn near impossible to unravel. "Well, you're about to see less of me, because I'm going to get in my chair and set up for the next lift."

"What's next?" She stood, waiting for him to move without trying to push his wheelchair closer or offer to help.

He appreciated the lack of intrusion. When he had finally decided that he didn't like lifting in his apartment and started looking for a gym, he'd worried that his entire workout would be spent fending off help from the well-meaning.

He'd known that the catch would be getting on and off the narrow weight benches without kissing the floor. If he fell during the transition, he'd be slotted into a poor-crippled-guy hole. So he had a bench delivered to his apartment and spent six months getting on and off the damn thing until he could do it thirty times in a row without once landing ass- or face-first on the floor.

He had made it a whole three months without falling when lifting himself from the chair to the bench. The first and only time he'd overshot the bench and hit the floor on the other side in public, the entire weight room had gone silent for several seconds. Finally one of the guys on a simi-lar schedule as Micah said, "Your form on that lift was shit, Blackwell," with the same flat tone he used to correct the strutting teens who came in to lift for the first time. The noise in the gym had picked back up as the rest of the lift-ers decided Micah was just another dude who'd misjudged his lift but not actually done himself any harm. A victory he shouldn't have had to earn, but a victory nonetheless.

Still, Micah waited until he'd swung himself back into his chair before answering Ruby's question. "Preacher curls. And if you're going to stand around, you might as well set the weight plates while I transition onto the seat."

She shrugged and then fell into step beside him as he wheeled himself to the preacher bench. "I'd rather stand around and just watch you, but okay."

He glanced over his shoulder at her, and the heat in her face surprised him so much that he misjudged his transition and had to grab on to the bench before he landed on his ass. "Didn't you come here to lift?" This conversation had to stay professional or they would both be in serious trouble.

Conflict of interest danced in her eyes and she looked both mischievous and inviting at the same time. Young, with more of the fight he remembered from prescandal Ruby and less of the fear. "Sure, but you were using the machine I wanted." She tossed the hand towel he must have left on the other machine at him, smiling when he caught it.

There were many other ways to do chest flies, most of which didn't require a machine, but she stood next to him with a challenge in her eyes. Daring him to argue with her and practically sending out an invitation for continued flirting. Well, if she wanted to slide herself onto a seat covered in his sweat, she was welcome to it. Micah shook his head before the words *slide* and *sweat* combined in his mind to reference anything other than the weights. He almost told her to knock it off, but her outrageous flirtation stroked his ego.

Something must have just happened that buoyed her spirits and put the conquering look on her face, because this was not the same Ruby who'd considered hiding in the car rather than coming through the gym doors.

And if she was going to make comments, he'd never been above showing off. The wheelchair pull-ups *were* pretty impressive.... No, he was being foolish. Best get back to her being in one area of the gym and him in another.

"Before you get too into your lifts, could you set the weight?" Even as he said the words, he knew they wouldn't help get this conversation back where it needed to be.

"Bossy today, aren't we?" she said with a raised eyebrow.

"I'm not complaining, but who added Red Bull to your cereal this morning?"

"Actually, I just helped a guy improve his running form." She was crouched at his feet, spinning a weight plate on the preacher bar. Whether she intended it or not, the pose was incredibly erotic. "He doesn't know it yet, but if he follows my suggestion, I've made his running better by, oh, twenty percent. I also beat the pants off him at a 5K. He was too easy of a target for it to feel so good, but it does and I'm going to let it."

His mind had decided to take after his legs and was ignoring his directive. *Focus! Weight lifting!* Instead, he was admiring the way her moist lips didn't fully close when she stopped talking. When she stood, she made a humming noise in the back of her throat. Closing his eyes helped some, but only some. "You helped some guy with his running form," he repeated, straining to keep his attention on the weight he had to lift.

"Sorry. You're lifting, and I need get on with mine. I'll tell you about it when we're done." She patted him on the shoulder and he almost gave up on the day then and there.

He should be relieved that she had left him alone. But even after she stepped away from him to her own weight bench and set up for her own chest flies, he could feel her. The energy of her soft grunts rippled through his body. And after putting his senses on high alert, she didn't even seem to remember he was in the same room.

Of course Ruby would tempt and pull back. As one of the world's best middle-distance runners, Ruby had two deadly skills. Other runners had never been able to develop a trap that could hold her, and once in front, she liked to hang back enough so second place wasted energy trying to catch her before strengthening her kick and leaving the rest of the pack in the dust. A tease, even on the track.

When he finished his count, he released the bar, which banged against the metal stand. If he was going to think about Ruby, he might as well be looking at her, and being a leg man didn't mean he couldn't appreciate the way her shoulder and back muscles flexed as she pulled her elbow behind her.

"So that really is Ruby Heart," said a voice from behind him. He turned to find the man Ruby had been talking to on the treadmill walking up on his right side.

"If she gave you running tips, take them."

"She did. I did." The man rubbed at the thick beard on his chin. "Do you think she would coach me through a marathon?"

"Best ask her." Judging a man's net worth by the clothes he wore to the gym was tricky business. Still, this man had on expensive running shoes and a full set of sweat-wicking running gear. Plus, expensive headphones. "Be prepared to pay a pretty penny, though. I mean, it *is* Ruby Heart."

"Huh," the man said, before walking toward Ruby.

Micah took a longer rest than he needed so he could watch their interaction. He eavesdropped a little on the man's offer and Ruby's response, but he concentrated on the joy in her face when the man named what he was willing to pay. And, like the fighter she was, she didn't take his first offer, but asked for more. Micah didn't think Ruby noticed the weight of anything she lifted for the rest of the time they were at the gym. Lifting to impress her would be a waste of time. Ruby was too far gone into her own world to notice the rest of the plebs down here on planet Earth. She couldn't look more triumphant if she were standing on the top of Mount Everest with her hands over her head.

SHOWERED AND DRESSED, Ruby opened the car door and hopped in next to Micah. "I feel like I've got an Olympic gold medal hanging around my neck."

"That good a workout, huh?"

"Okay, maybe not *that* good, but still pretty good. And *this* medal won't be taken away. At least, I don't think it will." She rushed out the words before jinxing herself.

"You're going to coach the guy?"

"Yeah. He's run two marathons before, but he wants to better his time. By a lot. He seems pretty committed and he's willing to pay me." Back in the gym, lifting all those weights, the iron might as well have been bubbles. She was going to earn that money through her own hard work and by using skills she'd been blessed with. "It feels so good, you know."

"And this doesn't violate the terms of your ban?"

For one glorious moment she'd forgotten about that damned ban. It was an albatross on her back. "I'll have to check when I go home. It's not as if this would be even close to professional. Eric wants to get under four hours."

Suddenly Micah's car was much too small for them both. She wanted to throw her arms up in the air and scream, or pound on the floor with her feet. Dance. Twirl. Laugh. "I feel like the old Ruby. Only not the old Ruby because the old Ruby would never have been in a public gym, and if she had been in a public gym she would have been annoyed and moved to another treadmill, not offered suggestions to a fellow runner. But that feeling of winning, God, that's good."

"You sure you're going to be all right when I drop you off at home? Not going to float off into outer space, are you?"

"No." She shook off his tease, and the wondrousness floating out of her soul remained. She *owned* this. She *owned* herself. And it felt great. "I'm going to take Dotty out for a slow, easy run and enjoy every minute of thinking about how to explain form, create a training schedule, develop a nutrition plan, the whole bit."

"And then you're going to come home and call me and we're going to talk about filming your training?"

She sank a little closer to the earth. Micah was being nice to her, but their relationship wasn't about friendship—nor was it going to be about anything more. She shouldn't even be upset. She was the one who'd offered the exchange in the first place. Offered herself as a carrot, and now she was disappointed that he was following through.

"I guess." She turned to look at him. "I mean, you're keeping up your end of the bargain."

"Oh, no." He pulled his head back as if distancing himself from her words. "I will not be that person for you. I agreed to the bargain, but if you don't feel good about the series, it will not help you. Your reserve will visible on camera. Hell, even if you're doing this because you want to show your parents that they don't control you, the negativity will come through on film." She was about to interrupt him when he spoke again. "Do it because you believe you are a new person and you want the world to see it. Do it for you, not for anyone else."

She snorted. Telling Eric her name at the gym had been hard enough. Even though she had known what she was getting herself into, letting a camera follow her around and having Micah ask her about the stupidest decision she had ever made in her life would be harder. Owning her exposure was not an idea she could fully get behind. "Hell, I'm lucky Eric didn't spit on me when he decided to believe me. I'm doing this for lots of reasons, Micah, but because I deserve it isn't empowering—it's masochistic."

Micah slowed the car to a stop at a light. The noise of the street poured into the silence in the car. The rev of a motorcycle engine. Some guy on the corner hawking the Word and a conspiracy theory mixed together. The ding of someone's bicycle bell. Then Micah looked at her. "Has it really been that bad?"

The light turned and the car eased forward. "Recently? No. People forgot about me, and those who knew who I was and saw me on a regular basis got used to the crime I carried about me like a heavy chain. But in the beginning? That first year…yeah, it was that bad."

"Someone spit on you?"

"He missed. I almost taunted him about his aim, but I didn't want him to try again." Leaving guilt behind was difficult when it regularly jumped up and curled its claws around her ankles, desperate to pull her back down in the mud as she kicked at its evil grin and pointy teeth. "Being spit at was bad enough. Being spit *on* sounds absolutely terrible."

"It is," Micah said.

"Yeah, when were you spit on?"

"Bad things happen at the bottom of a tackle that the ref can't see. But most players realize that what comes around goes around." Micah looked over at her, the smile on his face almost maniacal.

"Anyway, I'm glad the guy missed me. But the notes, letters and emails were the worst. When I was the golden girl, they *offered* sex. After the doping, they *threatened* sex. It took a long time for another woman to replace me in the Lilith category, and I feel very sorry for the one who eventually did." She had also felt incredibly relieved—another stain on her soul.

"And you're worried they'll start again if you do the series?" To her surprise, Micah was turning onto her street. She'd been so wrapped up in the conversation that she hadn't paid attention to where they were.

She snorted. "When is the last time you read comments on YouTube? Or trawled Reddit?"

"I try not to."

"Yeah, well, they started as soon as the promo for the interview went up. And it will only get more vicious."

He pulled into her driveway behind her car and stopped the engine. This time, when he looked at her, his eyes were kind and caring. "Are they threatening?"

Concern could be as much of a cage as shame. "Nothing serious."

Yet.

He inspected her face, his eyes warm and soft and closing the distance she needed to keep between them. *Believe, please believe. I don't want to be trapped anymore. I don't want to be scared anymore.* "Did the house come with an alarm system?"

"Yes. And I set it."

"And the dog?"

"Dotty is protective. And big, even if she's not too smart. Besides," Ruby said, her tone tinny instead of light, "someone trying to break into my house would give Dotty an activity, and she craves activity."

"That doesn't actually give me any confidence in your safety."

"The worst that has happened is that King Ripley tracked me down. And Dotty growled like a champ, her hackles raised all along her spine. That's it. Nothing else." She didn't want to hide anymore, didn't want to give the world any reasons for her to hide.

She thought he was going to press her for more, but he only said, "Enjoy your run with Dotty. Text me and your cousin your route each time you go."

"It's fine…"

"For me. To make me feel better." He put both his hands on the wheel, and when he looked at her, his expression, dark and unreadable, burned into her skin and she didn't know if it was good or bad. "I don't want to lose my story."

"Okay."

She had meant to get out of the car quickly, before "the story" could orchestrate any more of her life, but the heat in his eyes glued her to the seat. She couldn't look away, and she didn't move as he leaned over the console and pressed his lips to hers. Sweat and warmth and the smell of the gym's soap filled her nose. Micah. Now she wouldn't be able to take a shower at the gym without thinking of him.

His lips were firmer than she had imagined; his lower lip had always looked so full and soft and feminine. The skin covering her clavicle singed when he placed his hand on her shoulder, his grip demanding she give in. He pressed his fingers deeper, pulling her closer, and her desire gave in without checking in with her brain. The moan was hers. Her lips parted at his command when he ran his tongue along the crease. She opened herself to him, and he tasted like lemon-lime Gatorade. Even her toes got in on the action, bending and gripping in her shoes, propelling her forward. Toward him. Against him. Into him and his orbit.

That thought broke his hold on her. She yanked herself away, clocking her head against the passenger window. But the damage had been done. His eyes twinkled, and there was no hiding the heat that had risen through her body. She had flirted because he was safe. Because he'd hated her once and he might like her well enough for television, but surely not for more.

So what had that been?

"It's not just the story, Ruby. I care about *you,* too." The side of his mouth had kicked up like the cocky athlete he was, irritating her further.

"Thanks. Coming in second to ratings is a real compliment." Then, before he could say anything that might change her understanding of their bargain, she slipped out of the car, slammed the door and dashed off into her house.

CHAPTER FIFTEEN

BACK IN HIS office, Micah was failing at all the ways he tried to take his mind off kissing Ruby. Because it had been stupid. Career-suicide stupid.

But lifting weights had warmed her skin and brightened her eyes. The musky, sweaty smell of her had filled the car, buoyed by her determination to find herself again. Her nose, pert and upturned. Her hair hanging in front of her face, limp, as if it, too, had pushed itself to its limit at the bench press. And he'd thought about how he would feel if she disappeared out of his life. Kissing her had been so natural that he didn't remember the thought of it crossing his mind before it happened.

It couldn't happen again.

Micah set aside the questions he'd been working on for an upcoming interview and opened a web browser. This time, when he clicked on articles about Ruby, he skipped directly to the comments. Five years' distance between the time stamp on those comments and now didn't diminish their creepiness. The people—mostly men, if the references to dicks and sticking were to be believed—had obviously written their comments with hate pressing down on the keyboard. Hate for a woman they didn't even know. Hate for a woman who had failed, sure, but the person she'd failed most was herself.

The second-place finisher, a woman from Romania, had been awarded the gold. The Romanian woman, who had the most reason to hate Ruby, had been gracious in her remarks and had gone on to win the gold at the following Olympics, so she'd even had her moment on the podium.

These people commenting couldn't have been angrier if Ruby had poisoned their puppy.

"Oh, Ruby," he said into the buzzing of the office lights. "No wonder you shied away from more press coverage."

Perhaps he shouldn't have been surprised. Any video or article of him had idiocy in the comments, but that was people's fear of someone with a disability. Their ignorance and self-congratulatory pity maddened him, but it never made him fear for his safety. In either case, the commenters seemed to forget that both he and Ruby were people. Or maybe the commenters didn't forget, but wanted to dehumanize them.

Micah tapped his finger on the mouse. Even if his experiences weren't the same as Ruby's, there was a similarity there that he hadn't expected.

He should pull away from the computer and those vicious comments, but he couldn't. Instead, he read each and every one of them until his soul felt as if someone had poured tar over it. And she had received mail like this *at her home*.

Micah picked up his phone to call her, then set the receiver down. What was he going to say? He knew men could be pigs, but he'd never noticed the sheer pile of sexual innuendo and threats poured out on a woman—any woman, but this one in particular. He hunted around until he found some older articles from before her cheating was revealed, and he read those comments, too. Again the volume of sexual offers overwhelmed him. Some suggested she should do porn because she had the name for it. Some suggested that only a lesbian would have thighs like hers. Others remarked on her stamina in bed. And threaded through all the comments was a sense that Ruby needed to be tamed. That she needed a "real man" to teach her. That her spirit needed to be dampened.

And those men had succeeded. She had retreated into her parents' house and hidden from the world for five years.

Micah rolled himself as far away from the computer screen as he could get, anger welling up in his throat and threatening to come out of his mouth in a primal, protective yell. He wanted to call her and tell her never to leave her house. To go back to her parents' and lock herself behind their gates. To get herself over to the NSN campus and never leave his sight. To get a meaner-looking dog and name it Killer.

He looked down to see his hands clenched in tight fists on the tops of his thighs. His quads were spasming, and he'd been so tense that he hadn't noticed the movement under his hands. His first deep breath came out in a hard puff, so he lifted his chin and breathed, unfurling his fingers centimeter by centimeter, despite their protestations. He fought the anger that resisted opening his hands up any farther than claws digging into his thighs. It took another two deep breaths for his fingers to loosen another centimeter.

Finally he had calmed enough to handle the mouse and close browser windows until the offensive shit no longer took up space on his monitor and he could contemplate his options. He could essentially lock her away for her own protection—like his grandmother had suggested be done with him. Given the fierceness in her face when he had expressed worry, he would get as far with that plan as his grandmother had with her suggestion. Though he didn't plan to add, *if you love me, you'll do this,* nor would he wonder aloud in front of her if she would be better off dead.

She had agreed to do this series because she didn't want to be caged any longer. He got that, and asking her to stay indoors for her safety didn't make the iron bars less oppressive.

Of course, between his reaction to the comments and the kiss, he needed to get his priorities back in order and make the best series NSN had ever had.

RUBY HAD LIED when she'd said she was going to think of coaching strategies for Eric while running. She ran for seven miles, her body fatigued after the weight lifting and her mind jumping up and down like a teenage girl after her first kiss. None of the complications of a relationship managed to break through the giddy bubble. She was breaking free, and there was nothing between her and another kiss from Micah.

Next time, she wouldn't be so stunned that she let him take *all* the lead.

Her certainty that there would be a next time made the email she got from him several hours later apologizing for his actions and saying it wouldn't happen again all the more shocking. Not devastating—she wasn't going to allow that feeling to well up in her. But he was right. She had a list of goals, and swapping spit with a reporter wasn't on the page.

If she said that enough times, she would believe it. Visualization was the key to *everything.*

LIKE SHE HAD three days a week for the past several weeks since Micah had kissed her, Ruby slid into the passenger seat of his car with a smile as large and as bright as the neon pink gym bag she threw into the backseat.

He'd tried to ignore it, waiting for her to say something. But the memory of a similar smile during their interview five years ago in a dumbstruck response to his question about her life falling apart around her meant he couldn't hold back any longer. Her uncertain smile couldn't hide the mountains of stress in her eyes. She needed someone to talk to, and she may not want that person to be him, but he seemed to be all she had.

"Living alone is going well?" Micah asked.

"Dotty and I are doing fine. I should have moved out years ago."

"I'd believe you if the shine in your voice wasn't several watts more blinding than your smile."

The fall of the corners of her lips changed her smile from fake to beautiful. Freedom looked good on her. "I still haven't figured out what I'm going to do with this new life. Eric will be finished with his marathon in three months and then what?"

"Train someone else. Why can't you be a personal trainer?"

"No one would hire me to be a coach."

"I didn't say coach, I said personal trainer."

She waved him off. "I only know how to run."

How many times had Ruby been told she was only good at running and not to even try anything else? "You can learn to do more. And for every person who's horrified at the idea of being trained by Ruby Heart, fallen American darling, there are probably more who, like Eric, will pay extra for the privilege."

"I'm not sure how I feel about cashing in on my crimes. It seems—" she paused "—dirty."

Micah opened his mouth to tell her *everyone does it,* then changed his mind and closed it. *Everyone does it* had put a needle in her arm.

They drove the rest of the way in a painful silence as Ruby visibly fought the demons of her past and Micah felt like a shit for introducing the subject. Which didn't stop him from putting a hand on the firm muscles of Ruby's arm after they'd parked. "Ruby, I looked up old articles about you."

"When? Why?" The blinding shine was back in the tone of her voice and it hurt his ears. "I would think you knew everything about the rise and fall of America's Darling."

"After our kiss. I read the comments."

She pulled toward the door but, after Micah's ten years in a wheelchair, even Ruby Heart and her powerful muscles couldn't break his grip. He didn't squeeze, but he also didn't let go. Finally she collapsed back into the seat with a huff. "You should never read the comments. Never." The pain in her voice pierced the dash and shot shrapnel through his car, wounding his heart.

"You've read them."

"Even if I didn't, I'd know what they say. Every famous woman knows what they say. Hell, you don't even have to be famous. A friend posts a picture of you and sixty percent of the men want to fuck you—"

Micah winced at a crudeness he'd never heard from her.

"—and the other sixty percent want to stomp on you."

"Ruby, that's a hundred and twenty percent."

She snorted. "The overlap is the men who want to stomp you while fucking you. And that's the men. The women also want to beat you down."

"Even the old articles have recent comments."

"I *know.*" Her words came out hard and she pushed stray hairs out of her face. "Don't people say nasty things about you?"

"All the time, but they lack the…" Searching for a polite term was stupid, since Ruby knew what people said about her, but he did it anyway. "The sexual edge that the comments people say about you have. Mostly people just try to pretend I'm not a human being or wonder why I didn't kill myself after the accident."

She blinked, clearly startled by his words. "Well, don't worry about me, Micah. People say things. They've always said things and they will always say things, only on the internet they can say them anonymously and they're harder to track. The cops say the person who comments so regularly about me online is getting all his hate out and is unlikely to do something in person. All I can do is stop waving my arms about in front of their face and asking their opinion."

In the haunted depths of her eyes, he saw that her knowledge of the ill will that people bore her was more than just bottomless—it had bubbled up to the surface.

"And has retreating into obscurity worked?"

This time Ruby slipped out of his car before he could grab hold of her again. "That, Micah Blackwell," she said with her head framed by the car, "is none of your business." Then she slammed the door.

Micah had always been a man who tested his physical limitations, but even he knew that chasing after Ruby Heart without his wheelchair under him wasn't possible. He let her go.

But just because he couldn't chase her didn't mean he couldn't catch her.

CHAPTER SIXTEEN

IF THE DAMN receptionist hadn't been so slow, Ruby would have been able to slip into the women's locker room before Micah caught up with her. Instead, he was blocking her exit with his body and his anger.

"Do you feel like a champion now? Running away when I can't chase after you?"

She darted to her right, but Micah was quicker, and his fingers dug into her back when he caught her around the waist. She pushed the balls of her feet into the concrete floor, coiling her legs and preparing to leap from his trap. He was stronger than she'd anticipated.

His nostrils flared. "Is running away all you ever do?"

"What the hell do you know about running?" She stopped pressing forward, testing his resolve. The strength of his forearm hard against her stomach never wavered.

"I was a quarterback. I looked deep into the eyes of men who wanted to break me and I stood my ground."

"Yeah, with the help of an offensive line," she growled.

The fingers gripping her waist relaxed, and he must know her better than she knew herself because she didn't run away. "Ruby, tell me what you want and I'll try to help you."

The honest concern in his voice disarmed her. "I don't want to be scared anymore. I used to be triumphant."

"Triumph doesn't run away."

"Maybe you've forgotten, but I was a track star, Micah. I was triumphant *because* I ran away."

"Bullshit," he said, and she flinched. "You were triumphant because you ran, not because you ran away. Those aren't the same thing and you know it."

"I'm here, aren't I?"

"You're not a coward, Ruby. Don't pretend to be one." His eyes softened and he put his hands back on the wheels of his chair. She missed the feel of him. "And don't run from me. If you're angry or sad or scared, tell me. I can take it."

But could he take it when she was feeling sinful? "I don't know if I can do it."

"You're here, aren't you?"

He moved his chair enough for her to get by, and they stared at each other for several seconds before she hitched her gym bag higher on her shoulder and walked past him into the women's locker room, her spine straight against the disappointment in his eyes burning her back.

Once in the women's locker room, she threw her bag to the floor and took several deep breaths. Micah's cameraman was meeting them here to film her, and any hesitation on her part would scream through the television screen and into America's living rooms—as would her anger and fear. She knew Micah had been right about that; he was right about so many things.

After she changed, she sat on the floor in a back corner. First she did a couple of simple stretches, focusing her mind away from her emotions and onto her body. Once her body was limber and her mind was clear, she crossed her legs, closed her eyes and visualized what she wanted America to see on their screens. When the word *chastened* flitted up to the surface of her mind, she held it up high and examined it before throwing it away. She scrutinized each word as it floated into view, storing some away for future use and discarding others. *Reborn* burst out of the depths. She took another deep breath, opened her eyes and stood, ready to glide out the door.

Conquering her mind was the first step to conquering her body.

Amir and Micah were waiting for her on the weight room floor, along with King Ripley, whom she hadn't expected. The words she'd thrown away in the locker room threated to reappear, and she went back to the place in her mind that had brought forth *reborn,* staying there until the urge to run disappeared.

Micah's eyes were tight with frustration. Some of it might still be directed at her, but most of it was probably due to King, who was saying to Micah, "So where are the weight benches *you* use?" when she joined the trio.

"I use the same weight benches as everyone else," Micah answered, his voice as constricted as his face.

"Huh," the other reporter said. "Can I see?"

"No."

"How about the pull-ups I hear you can do? I want to see those."

Micah didn't even acknowledge that request. He turned to her, the shallowness of his dimples betraying the authenticity of his smile. "Ruby, are you ready?"

She nodded, and her entourage followed her to the squat rack like mismatched ducklings. She was loading weights onto the bar when Micah said, "King, do something useful and move the benches out of the way so Amir can get good video."

Ruby wasn't the only one smiling at that. She might not be able to see Amir's face, but his stance gave away his amusement. Something on Micah's face must have discouraged King's protests because the only sound she heard besides the scrape of the weight plates on the bar was the squeak of the benches being dragged across the floor.

Ruby positioned herself at the rack, the bar resting across her trapezius. Normally she chose her gym clothes for ease of movement and breathability, but today she'd dressed with extra care. She wanted the video to capture her muscles in their movements, which meant showing skin, but, even if it was a failed effort, she wanted to sell power, not sex. Her black tights should show the strength in her legs while the pale blue racer-back top she wore provided plenty of chest coverage while displaying every muscle of her upper back.

Old Ruby Heart had padded her bra and painted her lips to please other people. New Ruby Heart pleased herself first.

She lifted the bar off the safety catches, stuck out her butt as if she was going to sit on a chair and bent her knees. By the count of two, she had blocked the trio of NSN men from her mind and was lost in the movements of her body.

AFTER RUBY HAD showered and changed into khaki shorts and a gray T-shirt, she met the men in the parking lot. The engine of the production van parked behind Micah's car was idling, almost drowning out the men's conversation. Ruby put her gym bag on the hood of the car and joined them.

Amir was telling Micah about the shots he got, both of Ruby and of the weight room. Ruby must have looked quizzical when Amir said, "I got great nats," because Micah leaned into her and said quietly, "Nats are natural sounds. Background noise that brings depth to the video, in this case the grunts of the other lifters and the sound of metal scraping against itself."

Sound waves might not have enough power to blow a single leaf, but Ruby felt Micah's words touch every inch of her body before what he said registered in her ears. The sensation produced both goose bumps and redness in her cheeks. She was hunting for balance in her newly defined life, but with Micah around she might as well be trying to do squats while standing on a water bed.

Which made it all the more aggravating when he said, "We're not done with our conversation about the internet comments," as soon as he'd pulled out of the parking lot.

She should have known he wouldn't let it go. They shared the same tenacity. She had only rediscovered her own stubbornness; Micah had apparently never let his go.

Still, she tried to dissuade him. "*I* was."

"Ruby, the attention NSN is paying to you—that I am paying to you—is sure to attract notice. Half the gym watched you lift. Twenty people came up to me while you were in the locker room to ask who you were and what Amir was doing there. If any of those commenters intend to follow through on their words, a photog's presence is going to make finding you a lot easier."

"I'm not going to let you or anyone else push me back into a cage."

If only Micah wasn't driving. His face was turned to the front and his expression mostly hidden from view. But she understood his strategy behind ambushing her in the car. She'd walked right into the trap and shut the door on herself.

"There's a middle ground between moving back in with your parents and being the feature in an NSN series. You could just run. No spotlight shining on you."

"Been there. Done that." She sneered, angrier with him

than she had even been with her parents. "Why do you travel the world reporting on athletes? I'm sure it's not always easy for you. You could just stay home and cash a disability check."

Micah slammed his hand on the wheel when her sucker punch landed. "Comparing my situation to yours made you a fool before and it makes you a fool now."

Ruby was on solid ground again. She hugged his disdain close to her heart, squeezing tighter and tighter until her anger popped and the noise brought tears to her eyes. "Halfway isn't my style any more than it is yours," she said to the window.

"I'm trying to do the right thing here. I'm trying to give you an out." His fingers curled slowly around the leather wheel cover, the tendons on the backs of his hands standing out in full relief until his fists were clenched and his knuckles stole the show. The pressure of the joints turned his skin white as they threatened to burst through. "Ruby, I care about what happens to you. I don't want to see you get hurt, and I certainly don't want to be a part of anything that puts you in harm's way."

"Is this about a concern for my safety or the fact that you don't want to feel guilty when I get more nasty comments?"

"Dammit, Ruby!" Micah hit the steering wheel again, and the blow rang through Ruby's bones. "I am not your parents or your coach and I'm not trying to control your life for my ends."

She scoffed. "You could have fooled me. First you say this series will help me. Then you say it will hurt me. I *know* that NSN is putting out the money because they think this is going to be a ratings bonanza. You think it's going to catapult your career to another level, like your first interview with me did. Not just the first paraplegic sports reporter, but the first paraplegic anchor on *SportsDaily*. I'll bet that promotion comes with a window office."

When Micah stopped at the light, the tendons on his neck were popping out enough that Ruby wondered if hitting the steering wheel with his hand wouldn't be enough next time. He looked ready to bang his head on it. But then he took a deep breath and turned to face her. "You're right. You said no to an interview in Iowa and I followed you to Indiana because I knew that the Ruby Heart comeback show would give me the type of ratings most reporters can only dream about. And you know what would be even better for my ratings?"

She shrugged, trying to pretend the intensity on his face wasn't scarier than his anger.

"If something tragic happened to you, and, honestly, a debilitating injury would be better than death—something so tragic people could tsk and tell themselves how much *kinder* it would have been if you'd died."

The pain in his words pressed against her skin. She had vague memories of his accident and had probably expressed the very same sentiment to her friends at one time. Cruel and stupid and with a complete lack of understanding of what made life worth living. How many people had said that to his face and how many more had expressed it with their eyes?

"The executive producers at NSN would chew me up and spit me out, wheelchair and all, if this series got canceled. I was told to get you to agree, and I'm pretty sure they'll turn a blind eye to *any* tactic I use."

She was opening her mouth to argue with him, to accuse him of using the kiss as part of his tactics, when he continued in soft voice that wrapped around her insecurities like a wool blanket, "If you want to go through with this, I will, but I want to make sure you know the risks."

She put her hand on his thigh and spent several seconds waiting for him to react before she realized her mistake. When she moved her hand to his shoulder, his muscles tightened. "I know the risks. While it's been a long time since anyone cared enough about me to do more than sabotage my Wikipedia page, I know the procedure, and the police have certainly explained to me what they can and cannot do to help."

Micah took his hand off the wheel and rested it on hers for a brief second that she would tuck in her memory and pull out later. "You're fighting, Ruby Heart, and I've always admired a fighter. If you don't know anything else, know that."

By the time he'd pulled up in front of her house, Ruby's world was upside down. She didn't quite know what to make of Micah. Ascribing selfishness to his motivations made them easier for her to swallow, but it didn't taste right. He might actually have her best interests at heart, putting him in a category previously only Josh and Haley had occupied in her life. And unlike Josh and Haley, Micah had no blood ties to justify his concern.

Once, he had hated her.

They sat in his car at her curb, silence booming all around them. Since that kiss, she'd hopped out of his car and run into her house, splitting the awkwardness in two if not actually alleviating it. She put her hand on his shoulder again, hoping he would turn to face her. He flinched, but his gaze remained fixed firmly ahead. The time in her life when she'd be willing to beg had passed. She slipped her hand from his shoulder.

The energy in the car relaxed. All he said as she eased

her tired muscles out of the vehicle was "I'll be in touch," in a flat, emotionless voice.

Dotty greeted her when she walked into the house, following her to the bedroom and lying on the floor with a huff. Ruby tossed her gym bag onto the bed, but she couldn't throw her sadness away as easily. Her gym clothes felt like lead as she pulled them out of the bag, and her body was so fatigued that she missed the hamper when she tossed them.

She sighed and walked over to the hamper to pick up her mess, Dotty's eyes following her with curiosity. When she picked up her pants, her phone fell to the floor with a clunk. The message light was blinking. A Google alert, which she knew she shouldn't read but did anyway. Apparently someone hated her enough to post a GIF on Tumblr. The picture was an old one, Ruby Heart at her prime with textbook-perfect running form. The sentiment expressed wasn't a new one. "Ruby Heart runs like a girl. I'll teach her to fuck like a woman."

She'd clicked the link and now the stranger had invaded her bedroom. She took slow steps backward until her legs hit the bed and she could sit down. She didn't know how long she sat on the bed fighting the negative images beating at the edges of her mind, but Dotty was whimpering for attention when Ruby finally surfaced, her decision made.

She would train smarter and better than she ever had before. When she won a race, the man who'd made this GIF would learn how fast and hard a girl could run.

BACK ON THE NSN campus, Micah watched the video from this morning, tracking and logging information for the script later and for Amir. They would have to edit out the crowds that had formed around Amir as Ruby had shown off, a move he should have expected from her. Ruby Heart had been a spectacle at the Olympics, and it hadn't just been her flashy clothes and her bright red lips. She'd been supremely confident in her body, and her present anxiety and indecision still rested on a bedrock of confidence.

Derrick came into the editing room in time to catch the best moment of the morning. When Ruby had finished her squats, she'd taken a long drink of her water, then rubbed her hands together. Amir had caught every motion on camera as she'd bent her knees and, in a flash, leaped up to grab hold of the rack bar above her. She'd hung from the bar for a moment before bending at the waist and lifting her legs up in an arc until her toes touched her hands. Then she lowered her legs, neither slowing nor speeding up as her legs went down, down, down. Without even a blink, she repeated the process.

"And she's not doing steroids now? You're sure of that, right?"

Micah couldn't pull his eyes away from her athleticism and grace to look at his boss. "It was blood doping, but yes, this is all Ruby Heart." Including the showmanship.

"No weights on her ankles, though."

"This isn't about strength." Ruby was on her third lift. "This is about control. Not letting her body decide when to stop. Pushing through any fatigue and pain for one more lift."

Together Derrick and Micah watched Ruby do seven more lifts, all with the same amount of control, even as her face scrunched up in fatigue and her muscles shook. Ruby Heart, America's Darling Ruby Heart, hadn't had the maturity not to let her body rush her movements. The feat they were watching on the screen was more than strength and athleticism; it was a full understanding of what it meant to lower your head to the wind blowing in the other direction and power through to the next day.

Her feet hanging under her, Ruby looked up at her hands, pulled herself into a pull-up—one last final show—then dropped to the mat below her.

"That was amazing," Derrick said, leaving the room.

Micah continued watching the tape.

Amir had caught more than Ruby's control on camera. He'd caught Eric rushing over to tell her how cool she was and Amir's own words, said out of the corner of his mouth. "Jealous?"

"Of whom?" Micah's reply was muffled but understandable.

"Ruby."

Even though he was removed from that moment by several hours, Amir's comment still burned. Everyone thought the disabled man would be jealous of Ruby. Not even Amir, who Micah had worked closely with for three years, considered that Micah might be jealous of Eric, the man who could touch Ruby's shoulder muscles in amazement without worrying that his longing would show on his face.

CHAPTER SEVENTEEN

RUBY SAT IN her house, staring at the article on becoming a personal trainer on the database the librarian had shown her. The article didn't really tell her anything she didn't already know, though it did provide a link to a personal trainer program and an application form. Once she'd finished reading the rest of the article, she switched to the website on dog training.

The summer continued the routine she and Micah had set earlier. She met Eric three times a week for his training. She and Dotty did their runs at the shelter. And unless he was out of town on a story, Micah picked her up three times a week and they went to the gym together. A simple life scheduled around two training calendars—hers and Eric's—and occasional dinners with her family and lunches with Haley.

Dotty rested her hand on Ruby's knee, moaning a little when Ruby scratched behind her ear, though never taking her large black eyes off the treats on the desk. Without the dog, Ruby might have considered moving back into her parents' house as soon as the euphoria of living on her own had worn off and reality had set in. The silence of the car rides with Micah had made her old weight room especially tempting.

The argument between her and Micah about her dropping out of the NSN series had been the last time they'd had an "intimate" conversation. And he'd been the one to run away. Since then Micah seemed to have canned answers for every topic she came up with. And no matter what she talked about or what questions she asked, he turned the conversation back to her. One-sided conversations were interviews. Every car ride had started to feel more like Micah was interested in what might make a good story line for his series. Anything else was off the table.

So she stopped talking.

When he pulled up in twenty minutes, he would be so close that she could smell his aftershave and yet far enough away that she would miss him.

Ruby pushed her chair away from the computer, snatched up the pile of dog treats and headed for the living room, Dotty dogging her heels. Jodie had thought Dotty was trained, but it turned out the dog only knew how to sit and heel. Working with her on other tricks had given Ruby something to concentrate on besides her looming need for a job and the Google alerts she had stopped clicking on.

Dotty knew the training drill and sat on the rug before Ruby had to ask her to. Today, they were practicing waiting. Ruby put a treat on the dog's nose, gave the dog the command and then put her hands behind her back, trying desperately not to laugh when Dotty's eyes crossed on the treat. Dotty's desperate whine echoed Ruby's feelings about the change in her friendship with Micah. He hadn't just kissed her, he'd said he cared about her. And then pulled away. The tease.

"Go," she said. Dotty lowered her nose and snapped up

the treat from the rug. Then the dog sat and held her snout steady for the next torture session. Gluttons for punishment, both of them. She set the next treat on Dotty's nose and told her to wait. Then they stared each other down.

"Go," she said again to Dotty. The treat didn't have time to hit the rug before her dog snapped it up. Maybe Dotty could learn how to catch a Frisbee, even if she'd shown no interest in fetch so far. Or dog-agility competitions. Those looked like fun, and Dotty definitely had the stamina for it.

She commanded Dotty to lie down, and Ruby set the treat on the rug, beyond the reach of her dog's shiny black nose. "Wait," she said again. Dotty whined, but she waited.

Fun though it might be, dog-agility training was a distraction from filling out the personal training program application. Self-destruction, a Ruby Heart specialty.

Micah might be using her to further his career, but he was also right. She *liked* physical activity. She liked thinking about training programs and muscle building and nutrition. And from coaching Eric, she'd learned that she liked seeing someone push themselves until they learned they were faster and stronger than they had imagined. Refusing to try it simply because it had been Micah's idea was stupid.

Movement on the rug hauled Ruby's mind back to Dotty, who was still lying on the rug, innocence radiating off her face. The treat was missing. Not even a crumb. Ruby hadn't heard a crunch, which meant Dotty had swallowed the cookie whole—probably before she had a chance to taste it.

Ruby huffed. Dotty blinked more innocence.

At least Ruby could cross professional dog trainer off her list of career options, which wasn't all that helpful. She had only ever been certain about running and she needed to get comfortable with the rest of her life being, well, the rest of her life.

At the blow of a car horn, Ruby patted Dotty on the head, grabbed her gym bag and headed out the door. Micah sat, smiling at her, good-looking, confident and in her life for all the wrong reasons. She got in the car wishing she were less confused about him.

THE SILENCE OF the weekly car rides only tightened the knots in Micah's neck and shoulders. Stretching his neck by holding an ear to his shoulder didn't do anything for the tension in his back.

Throughout his football days, Micah had always been insistent that his teammates take responsibility both for their successes and their slipups. And he had always been strict with himself when assigning blame. Only fair to expect out of yourself what you expected out of your team.

And Micah was responsible for the silence pounding between them.

All of which made the car rides to and from the gym more painful. Ruby's confusion about the change in tone of their car rides was obvious. In every question she asked, he could feel her try to steer their relationship back to the intimate tone it had previously enjoyed. He would open his mouth to respond and then he'd remember their bargain.

That bargain was the only thing keeping him on the correct side of a professional relationship, and each time she slipped her tight butt into his passenger seat, Micah's professionalism tried to slip out the door. Again, dammit. He'd already slipped up majorly once.

The kiss, the way he worried about her, the way he felt her presence in the car and, worse, the way he had to stop himself from leaving his apartment early so he'd be near her sooner... All of it was conflict of interest rearing its ugly head. Temptation to put his relationship with her above the truth of her story hung in front of his eyes, a perfectly formed piece of fruit ripe for the picking.

The devil riding his shoulder cackled in his ear that someone else might pick her if Micah didn't.

But as he already knew, he had to push all thoughts of Ruby that weren't professional out of his head. Besides, she had already expressed her contempt for his concern. In trying to trap and cage her, he was no different than her parents, she'd said. Trying to control her and manipulate her talents for himself, with little regard for what she wanted.

He'd call her out for that piece of revisionist history, except Micah didn't think Ruby was pushing all the responsibility for her successes and her failures onto her parents because she blamed them and only them for her past. He was pretty certain that Ruby Heart didn't know what to make of her own competitive nature and found it easier to pretend it didn't and had never existed than to accept she might want to compete—to win—again.

She needed to accept and embrace her own nature before the fifty-mile race scheduled for October. A top finish by her would be better for his ratings, sure, but he wanted her to want a top-five finish for herself, as well. And he wanted to be there with her when she broke free of her past. Even if he was there as the reporter and not as the friend.

He missed Ruby the friend. Whether the distance he'd put between them was for his own good or hers was irrelevant. He missed sharing with her. And all the blame for the break in their relationship fell squarely on his shoulders. Fine. He could take it.

"How's Eric's training going?" he asked, desperate to fill the silence in the car. He took the opportunity to enjoy the pert upturn of her nose as she stared out the passenger window.

"Good. The Chicago marathon is in a couple weeks and he'll do much better than his time last year." She twisted to look at him and he turned his attention back to the road. "Well, you know when it is—you're racing in it."

"I am."

The silence stretched back into uncomfortable until Ruby finally looked back out the window and started talking again. "Do you do anything to celebrate?"

Whether for his own benefit or hers, Micah let her see a little deeper into his life. Just this once. "My dad comes into town. We'll probably go out to dinner."

"Nice. Haley's going to come out and watch the race with me. So are Josh and Christine. Eric has some friends who will come out, too. This will be my fourth year down by U.S. Cellular Field, cheering."

"You went during your suspension?" Reason number one he didn't want their conversations to get personal. The image of Ruby Heart on the sidelines of the Chicago marathon, banned from the very sport she was watching, not only made for good television, it also made him more interested in her as a person. Dangerous territory.

"I saw you race," she said, and he remembered what she'd said in the hotel room in Iowa.

If he'd known at the time that she was on the sidelines and cheering him on, it would have made him angry. Now he was only angry with himself for caring.

"I used to stay to the bitter end, but Eric apparently has a tradition of going to this place on the South Side for Polish buffet afterward, and I don't want to miss the celebration. Someone else will have to stay and cheer on the stragglers, I guess."

All he could think of to say in response was a lame "I guess." Reporters were probably not wanted at the dinner.

Micah's jealousy was his own damn fault—not that he had a right to any such feeling in regards to Ruby.

"The night before we're doing my tradition—dinner and a game of some sort. You and your dad are both welcome." She gave a pleased little shrug, an oddly feminine move for her. "I always told myself that the games primed my competitive spirit." She laughed. "Which must be true because I hate losing, even at board games. The first time I ever beat Josh at a race was right after he bankrupted me at Monopoly. I think my humiliation at his razzing added boosters to my feet."

The memory danced lightly in her voice; her past seemed to pull her down more than push her up. Every time Micah felt he had the new Ruby pegged, she did something unexpected like laugh or shrug. He could spend decades getting to know her.

"Eric would love to have you there, either before or after the race. I have never heard him talk about a network other than NSN. He even listens to NSN Radio while running."

Jealousy pinged at his brain again. Much like regret, it was an emotion that existed outside himself and, as such, was useless.

As Ruby talked about how she would find the sports radio exhausting to listen to while running, Micah wondered if Eric was interested in having an NSN reporter at his celebration dinner or having the *disabled* NSN reporter at his dinner? Normally he didn't care about a person's motivations because he made what he wanted out of his life, but this was Ruby, and she'd messed with his expectations since the moment he'd met her.

Micah braked at a light, and suddenly the question he'd had since their dinner together in Indiana gurgled up in his throat, and he wasn't able to swallow before it came out.

"Why do you never ask about my paraplegia?" He'd spent ten years trying to get the rest of the world to see a person in a wheelchair rather than just a wheelchair. Ruby had gone the opposite way and not said anything at all. At first it had been refreshing. But after driving to and from the gym together all summer, it had become strange.

He'd interrupted her midsentence and she stared at him openmouthed for several seconds. Only after shutting her lips and several seconds of blinking did she answer his question. "I get the sense you don't like talking about it."

"I've got no problem talking about it. I don't like it when it's the only thing people notice about me. In your case, it seems to be the only thing you *don't* notice about me."

"I notice it about you. If you'll remember, I stupidly commented on it after that first interview."

"I haven't forgotten." Her comparison had been stupid, but also probably smarter than she'd realized. Everyone was defined by their bodies and the ways in which their bodies both enabled and failed them. The difference, of course, was that she could put on jeans and a T-shirt, say her name was Diana and disappear from Ruby Heart and all its associated baggage. Removed from his wheelchair, Micah was a grown man crawling through trash other people stepped over. He could change his name, change his job and go about his life as any other dude gettin' by and he'd still be known first as the paraplegic instead of being just another guy.

"Of course, I want to know all about your body—its limits and how you find a way around them—but I don't want to be intrusive. So I've not said anything. Especially since you've closed yourself off from me."

"So it's my job to make you comfortable with my disability?"

She blinked. "When you put it like that, no. It's my job

to be comfortable with it. With you. But you scare me. Less now than you used to, but…"

Her comment didn't surprise him. He scared lots of people. He'd hoped for better out of Ruby. "Does the whimsy of fate scare you?"

She flinched. "Your disability doesn't scare me. It's a body, just different from mine. The power people have to wound comes first from their minds, not their limbs." Even with his eyes on the road, he felt her gaze on his neck and shoulder. His muscles tightened even more. "You defeated me. On national television. I wasn't used to having my ass handed to me, and I guess I'm still not. I worry what will happen when I slip up." Out of the corner of his eye, he saw her shrug. "But I recovered and got smarter from that defeat, so I guess I can do it again."

He stopped at the light before he turned to face her. "What am I to you?"

Her brows crossed and a little wrinkle appeared above her nose. The shadows of the sunlight shining through the car window deepened the wrinkle. Suddenly she looked older. "Is this a test?"

Her question prickled his skin. "If you love me you'll…" had been the mantra of his childhood. His grandmama had been the queen of conditional love, only it wasn't so much how she proved she loved him, but how Micah would prove he loved her. Succeeding wasn't enough. He had to follow her every whim to prove he loved her.

No matter how much he loved his grandmama, she could never fully love him. The final straw that had broken their relationship had been in the rehabilitation hospital when he'd realized he could either be a cross for her to bear, as he'd been during his childhood, or he could move on with his life. When he'd declined her support, he'd failed her test and she'd never forgiven him for that. He'd never forgiven her for asking.

"I don't think of it as a test."

"Is there a right answer?"

"There's a wrong answer."

"Sounds like a test to me."

Micah pulled into the parking spot at the gym and twisted the key to turn the car off. His movements were jerky and, if he wasn't careful, he would let his irritation get the better of his body and break something. Maybe himself.

Out of the corner of his eye, he saw her reach for his leg. Then her hand stilled inches above his skin as she reconsidered. Finally she rested her palm on his arm, her fingers curling around and singeing his biceps. "I think your first instinct, the one to keep our relationship purely professional, was the right one."

Micah's heart sank deep into no-man's-land when she removed her hand. Her fingers floated away from him, the side-angle view making them look detached from the rest of her body.

She left him alone in the car with his righteous anger, though he couldn't figure out if she'd passed or failed. Which meant she was right; it had been a test. And suddenly it felt like he was the one who'd failed.

CHAPTER EIGHTEEN

MICAH MET HIS dad in the hotel lobby. His father, dressed in a suit and tie for their traditional dinner out at one of Chicago's best restaurants the night before the marathon, raised an eyebrow at Micah's jeans. "Do I need to change?"

"Not if you don't want to." Micah hadn't told his dad about the change in plans, because he hadn't been certain he would go to Ruby's until he'd passed over the suits in his closet for a button-down that flattered his eyes. "We're going to Ruby Heart's for dinner and a board game tonight."

Pretending not to notice the shock on his dad's face wasn't easy, but Micah did so anyway. Finally his dad nodded. "I guess I'll get changed." Then he gestured to the bank of elevators. As the doors closed on them, Micah stared at the ceiling while his father stared at him.

"So Ruby Heart, huh."

"Yup."

"I saw the interview. It was good." His father waited for Micah to respond. Micah lowered his gaze from the mirrored ceiling to the mirrored doors and their stares ricocheted around the tight space. "It's nice that you're getting to know her better."

The elevator dinged to a stop, a grating sound that made Micah's back teeth hurt. "Dad, NSN is doing a series on ultramarathons, featuring Ruby. That's all."

His father was silent for the trip from the elevator to his hotel room, a courtesy that didn't last past the closed door. "It's just that, for example, you've never brought me over to a Blackhawk player's house for board games."

Despite the differences between his father's four-star hotel room and the dumpy, roadside hotel Ruby had been staying in in Indiana, memories of her flooded his mind as he looked around his father's room. The sagging elastic of her gym shorts that had tantalized him with the smooth skin of her stomach when she lifted her arms. The sight of her rumpled, unmade and probably uncomfortable hotel bed. The enchilada sauce at the corner of her mouth and the way he'd had to grip the table to keep from licking it off her.

"Maybe I should." No one would suspect him of a sexual attraction to a hockey player. Though, maybe he was giving his bosses too much credit. They might suspect him of being able to be sexually attracted to Ruby, but they might also *not* believe Ruby could be sexually attracted to him.

But Micah hadn't mistaken the heat in Ruby's eyes when she looked at him. And if she thought she was being subtle when she checked him out at the gym, she was fooling herself.

His dad tossed his suit coat on the bed, followed by his tie, before rummaging around in his suitcase for a change of clothes. "Have you crossed a line?"

"No. At least not one I haven't been able to repair." If the silence of their drives to and from the gym was considered a repair.

"Repair for your career or for your relationship?"

"My relationship with Ruby *is* about my career." And if he said it enough times, he would believe it.

"Well, this is the first girl since college you've brought me to meet, which has to mean something. I spent all of your childhood pretending work was a substitute for meaningful relationships. Don't repeat my mistakes."

"Work is all I've got right now."

His dad tossed his slacks onto the bed and pulled on a pair of jeans. "No, your job is all you've allowed yourself. Hell, even in college I think you only surrounded yourself with pretty women because it was expected for your image as a college football star."

Micah rolled over to the window and looked at the many lights still on in buildings around the Loop. All those other people putting their careers before their personal life. "I can keep any feelings I have for Ruby separate from my job."

His dad placed a hand on his shoulder and they looked out over the city together. "I didn't say you didn't have the ability. I questioned whether or not you *should.* If you care about her, you'll have to choose eventually, or figure out how to have both."

Micah looked at his dad's hand. The skin was old and dry, and he had put on a different watch and changed his shirt. All this effort to meet Ruby, even though Micah said she was only a job.

His father was hoping for too much. Work may be the reason his father was meeting Ruby, but it had also been the reason his father hadn't met any previous girlfriends. By the time Micah had felt serious enough to introduce them to his family, the women had been irritated enough with his work schedule that they'd moved on.

"Well, I'm still curious. The only things I know about

Ruby Heart are what I've read in the papers, and that was all stuff from five years ago."

"She's not what I expected." His father seemed to understand—correctly—that what Micah meant was that *none* of this was what he expected.

THEY APPROACHED THE house together, Micah's trepidations and his father's curiosity as bright as the porch light. The barest sounds of laughter floated from the house. His father rang the bell.

The laughter stopped and Dotty barked. Enjoyment reverberated through Ruby's face as she opened the door, brightening her eyes and flushing her skin, making her look radiant and joyful, much like she looked when running. "Micah! Oh, and Micah's father." She stuck out her hand in greeting. "I, um…well, welcome to dinner."

His father looked at him out of the corner of his eyes, which Micah ignored in favor of pretending to contemplate the single step into the house. By the raise of his father's brow, Micah knew he hadn't fooled the man. At least his father didn't make a face as Micah popped a wheelie to get his front wheels onto the stoop, grasped the doorjamb and propelled himself the rest of the way into the house. The three place settings were a dead giveaway that they hadn't been expected. Uncharacteristically, Micah had acknowledged receipt of her emailed invitation but had not responded yes or no. Rude, but true. Jealousy had driven him here, and the presence of Eric's girlfriend, Taylor, confirmed jealousy as a stupid thing to base any decision on.

"I was just setting another place at the table," Ruby lied. No one bought it, but no one argued with her, either.

Micah looked up at his father, who greeted Eric and Taylor with an enthusiastic handshake to cover up how irritated his father was to have been put in the situation of uninvited guest. How much worse to explain that they were invited but that Micah had been stupid enough not to confirm that they were coming? Helping to set the table wasn't quite enough to make up for his lack of RSVP.

When Eric and Taylor went into the kitchen to help Ruby get dinner, Micah's father asked, "Is there a reason she didn't expect us?" There was a tight scowl in his voice, and he placed a hand on Dotty's head.

"A relationship with her could cost me my job."

"Being achievement driven helped you in college and, later, to figure out what to do with your life after the accident. But a woman who puts you so far off your game only comes along once in a lifetime."

"For most people, a chance to be an anchor at NSN doesn't even come along once."

"Either figure out how to have both, or pick one. Refusing to make up your mind is disrespectful to you both."

No punch could have hurt worse.

AFTER THE INITIAL discomfort of Micah and his father's surprise appearance, dinner relaxed into slurped spaghetti and conversation they could all chew on. Ruby had bought and prepared enough food for five people, continuing to hope until the last minute that Micah would say he was coming.

After everyone helped clear the table, Micah stayed in the kitchen with Ruby while she packed the leftovers and put away the dishes. If he was expecting questions, he was going to get them. "Why didn't you tell me you were coming?"

He shrugged, his lush bottom lip chastened and downcast. "I guess I didn't know myself."

"Why are you here?"

The longing on his face when he looked at her shocked her, echoing the feelings in her heart when she thought about him. "You know we can't have any relationship past my story."

"That doesn't answer why you're here." She rinsed the plates and handed them to him.

He looked from the plate to the dishwasher, the remnants of his gaze still sending shivers down her spine. "You know why I'm here."

"To torture us both? The three days a week we spend at the gym together isn't enough?"

"Is it enough for you?"

"I'm not the one putting barriers between us. I'd give up the series in a heartbeat if you asked."

The plate she held out dripped onto the others already loaded into the dishwasher, the drops seeming to echo throughout the kitchen. Any conversation seeping in from the living room was drowned out.

"The series matters to me. My career matters to me."

Ruby remembered what it was like to want something so badly that you were willing to sell your soul to get it. She also knew that nothing was worth the cost. Of course, she thought, as Micah rolled out of the kitchen and back to the rest of her guests, maybe she was ascribing more to their mutual longing than she should.

She was glad she was only serving as cheerleader tomorrow, because she wouldn't get much sleep tonight.

CHAPTER NINETEEN

"OKAY," RUBY SAID, rubbing her hands as the five of them sat around the dinner table. She looked tired, Micah thought, or at least not as excited as she should be for her precompetition tradition. "The goal is to get points by building medieval France. Everyone has meeples—those are these little people-shaped things—and there's a stack of tiles. Whether your meeple is a knight, a farmer, a monk or a thief depends on whether you put her on a road, in a castle or in a monastery, and all those plays are worth different points. Are we good so far?"

"Can we play a practice round?" Taylor, Eric's girlfriend, asked.

"We won't need one. Plus, the boys need to get to bed early tonight so they'll be ready for tomorrow. With five people, the game will go quickly. It's fun. And it's easy."

Micah watched Ruby finish explaining the rules. She might be tired and she might be keyed up from their discussion in the kitchen, but the more she talked about the game, the brighter her eyes got.

"Now, before I flip the starter tile over, everyone has to pick a team name."

"But one person doesn't make up a team," Eric argued.

"You and your meeples are the team. And you've got to give them a name to rally around." With her fists clenched, she made a rousing, aggressive gesture seen on TV screens during any huddle. Dotty barked.

"Well, I'm out of my league," Micah's father said, "so call me and my meeples the Old Folks. Hopefully experience will help me win."

"I'm gonna be the Packers," Eric said at the same time Taylor said, "Packers." They exchanged smiles dripping with memory and more sentimentality than Micah expected out of the bearded and tattooed marathon runner.

Ruby waggled her finger. "This is Chicago. You're lucky I'm allowing one Packers team—there's no way I'll allow two."

"Brewers, then," Eric said, and he was getting lucky for a week if the smile Taylor gave him was any indication.

Micah was stuck on the other side of the table and the other side of his job from getting a smile like that from Ruby. Dammit, time had not erased from his memory the feel of the lips he wasn't kissing. Shaking his head didn't clear his mind, but he did notice everyone staring at him. "Salt-and-Pepper Potato Chips. Chips for short," he said.

"Oh, I like those, too," Taylor exclaimed. Eric's girlfriend was sweet, but judging by the gleam in Ruby's eye, nice wouldn't help her win the game.

"One Hundred and One Dalmatians," Ruby said for her team name. "Because I'm going to run you all down."

Micah, his dad and Eric laughed. Taylor looked startled.

"So that's how we're going to play the game," Micah said.

"It's a game," Ruby responded with a blink. "You play to win."

"Game on, then," he said, and suddenly wished he'd paid more attention to the rules when she'd explained them.

Ruby put down the starter tile, and it was Taylor's turn. "Okay, connect farmland to farmland. Can I lay down a person?"

"You can claim either a road and be a thief or the farmland and be a farmer." Ruby shoved the scorecard across the table. "And the points for each are different, so take that into account."

They went around the table several times, each person picking a tile and laying it on the board as the game spread out across the table. Ruby answered questions and moved meeples on the scoreboard for all the players. Micah was in the lead. "For all the big talk, Miss Dalmatian, you're in last place."

When she raised her eyebrows at him, the small, dark freckle on the side of her nose stretched. "You, Micah Blackwell, are overconfident. Don't you know it ain't over until it's over?"

"You have half the points of anyone on the board," he pointed out.

"It's part of my strategy. You hang back and let everyone exhaust themselves and then *boom*—" she flashed her fingers out at them with a smile "—you catch 'em from behind where they're vulnerable."

"Same strategy as in your running."

She shrugged, her eyes a little dimmer. "Yeah, well, it wasn't the strategy that was broken there." The smile she offered was one she fought hard for. "And my Dalmatians are going to eat up every last one of your chips, so don't you worry about having to clean up after yourself."

"Oh, I was more worried about you and the dog shit you're spouting."

This time her laugh was genuine.

They continued trading barbs as Ruby got farther and farther behind and Micah got farther and farther ahead, with
Taylor, Eric and the Old Folks trading places in between.
Eventually, Taylor turned over the last tile and played her
last meeple.

"You're still losing, Ruby," Micah said.

"And you—" she waggled her finger at him "—are still
overconfident. You haven't won until we total up the points
on the board."

As Ruby counted the points for their roads, castles and
monasteries, the meeples on the scoreboard got closer and
closer together until Ruby was only three points behind him.
Farms were next, and Micah had no farms. He could only
watch in dismay as Ruby's red meeple overtook his green
one and he finished in last place.

"Next time I'm going to listen to the rules of the game
before I play."

"Excuses, excuses, excuses." She gestured around the
table. "No one else is making excuses."

"I really thought you were going to win," Taylor said,
which didn't make Micah feel any better.

But getting his ass kicked by Ruby Heart turned out to
be better than he thought it would. As she shimmied and
generally made an obnoxious fool of herself, her shirt rode
up, revealing bits of skin and cupping the undersides of her
bouncing breasts. Get her in a short skirt and he would be
willing to lose to her again.

RUBY WAS COLD, even in her jeans and wool sweater with
her hands wrapped around a cup of hot coffee. Haley was
cold and complaining.

"Why are we up this early in the morning and on the South Side?"

"We're up early because the wheelchair marathoners will be past here soon. We're on the South Side because there aren't many spectators down here."

"I'd rather be in bed."

"You didn't have to come."

"How else was I going to see this reporter you've got the hots for?"

"He'll be a blur. And he's working on me for a series. There's nothing more to our relationship."

"Working on you. Heh."

Ruby eyed her cousin and swallowed a smile. Nothing good ever came out of encouraging Haley. "How about you just take this as a break from the never-ending wedding planning?"

"I told Mom we were going to talk about favors in between cheering."

"Are we?"

"No. You're going to tell me what you see in Micah. And I don't want to hear about the sex-denial thing you've got going on. He made you cry on national TV. Why should I forgive him?"

"Because he was right—I failed my sport."

"He's in a wheelchair." Haley put on her rarely used serious voice. "Let's say you finish the NSN thing and you guys start dating. Have you thought about what would happen next?"

"I assume we would keep dating and then we would either break up or we wouldn't. It's been a while since I've had a boyfriend, but I think that's how it works."

"Ruby!"

"If you're asking what I find so attractive about a man

on wheels, then you should come right out and say it." Tires scraped on asphalt and the rhythm of hands pushing at wheels got louder and louder. "But not now. They're coming and I want to watch."

Micah was in the second pack of racers and tenth overall. Even through his sunglasses, the concentration in his eyes made her legs clench and her belly tingle. He had looked at her with the same intensity, and the memory of it shot electricity down her spine. She didn't turn back to Haley until they'd passed.

"His legs are just a part of his body, like my legs are a part of my body. He believes in sports and second chances. And passion. Micah knows what it is to have an all-consuming passion for your job." Ironically, she admired the very thing that kept them at a distance from each other.

"Okay." Haley took a sip of her coffee. "I see why that would be attractive for you. Not for me, but you're not me. But what are you going to do when he gets old. Will he have health problems?"

Haley's fiancé smoked a pack a day, a fact Ruby chose not to point out. "I wonder if Micah's father is asking him if I have enough body fat to menstruate so we'll be able to have children."

"Lay off, is what you're saying."

"Or even the playing field and ask Micah if he's prepared for my possible joint problems."

CHAPTER TWENTY

WHEN SHE CAME home from her shift at the shelter, Ruby collapsed into a chair even before making herself a postrun snack. Everything was tired, not only her body. She was tired of not feeling that she knew who she was and how she was supposed to live. She was tired of being afraid to say her name to strangers. She was tired of being afraid of strangers. Tired of wanting a man who wasn't certain he wanted her.

She leaned her head back against the chair. Apparently, sitting in NSN's hot seat, facing down Micah Blackwell, and daring America to turn its back on her hadn't been as liberating as she'd hoped.

She'd run for so long to please other people that the simple enjoyment of putting one foot in front of the other and letting euphoria fill her mind as her body fought through fatigue felt wrong—as if she shouldn't be allowed to love to run anymore.

The internet was still solidly against her running in competition. No surprise there, no matter what Micah had said about "rehabilitation." Of course, she understood people's feelings about her running in competition. How could she not? But living in the past had nearly suffocated her.

Dotty was still prancing around the living room, expecting *more* after a ten-mile run. Jodie had been correct when she'd said the dog would never stop, though she'd also said that Dotty would calm down around age five. After doing a little research, Ruby had learned that by calm down, Jodie meant that a ten-mile run would be enough to keep Dotty from being destructive. That kind of contract with life should've been offered to Ruby when she was younger— run enough and she wouldn't destroy the world around her. Unfortunately, she'd done the opposite. All she'd done was run and yet she'd still managed to wreck the lives of everyone around her.

Ruby banged her head against the back of her chair a couple times before opening the drawer of the end table and getting Dotty's treats. As soon as she heard the bag crinkle, Dotty sat. Ruby wished she could take a lesson from her dog and let go of the past. Her parents had gone on with their lives. Her sister and brother were just fine. Hell, even her coach had finished his prison sentence.

Ruby gave Dotty one treat for sitting, then made her shake for another and lie down for a third. Dotty loved Ruby for the treats, but her dog loved her more for the running. If Ruby couldn't yet run for herself, she could at least run for her dog.

She'd wrecked her life and disgraced her favorite sport. Those were the crimes she was responsible for, but she couldn't let those hang on to her forever.

Ruby stood and walked into the kitchen for her postrun snack, Dotty plodding along after her, hoping for more excitement. The only excitement Ruby had to offer her was another cookie, which she made the dog wait for. Ruby got her banana and chocolate milk, then pulled out her laptop. She signed in to the registration for the fifty-mile race that was coming up and corrected her name.

It would serve her and her big ego right if no one noticed.

RUBY SAT ON the benches the next afternoon at a high school track waiting for Micah and looking forward to a little friendly sprinting competition. Dotty sat beside her, twitching with the excitement of a new place to run.

Coming to the track had been Micah's idea after she had complained that her sprints weren't up to her standards. "You can race me," he'd said. "We'll go to a track and race for money. Eat dirt in the four hundred, pay the other person a dollar."

The bargain he'd proposed was so unfair that she'd choked. "In your racing chair? You'll beat me every time. I'll be broke after one afternoon."

His eyes had twinkled and his dimples deepened and she'd known that he knew he had her. "But you'll still try to beat me, right?"

She should have refused immediately. But the thought of refusing an issued challenge made her teeth clench. "You might have to carry me off the track, but I'll beat you *once*." As she looked up from tying her shoes to see Micah's car park practically on the field, she wondered if beating him to the track was worth a dollar.

Dotty, however, beat Ruby to the car, where Micah was unloading himself, his wheelchair and his racing chair. The dog was not helping, though she was jumping up and down far enough away from Micah that she wasn't hindering his progress, either.

"Do you need another hand?"

"You can carry my racing chair over to the bench. It's in

my best interest to wear you out before we even get to the starting line. More money in my pocket."

His racing chair was lighter than she'd expected it to be, which was silly, because he wouldn't be able to get the speeds he needed for marathons in a heavy chair. She carried it to the bench while he followed with the rest of his gear. Once he'd gotten everything set up to his preference, she asked, "How do you manage when you're by yourself?"

"You want to do something bad enough, you figure it out. Or you realize it will never happen and you move on before the *nevers* sink you." He shrugged. "I come here because the principal is a huge Texas A&M fan, so he ignores where I park as long as I don't ruin the field. But having my own pack mule will make setup and takedown easier."

He smiled blandly at her when she scowled at him for basically calling her an ass. She wasn't fooled. Once he got strapped into his chair and his helmet on, he looked fearsome and fast. More aerodynamic than she could ever be.

Ruby, Dotty and Micah were lined up at the start when she said, "I don't know why I agreed to this."

"Sure you do. Even though beating me around this track will be like trying to leap higher than Michael Jordan at the height of his career, you're going to try. You'll tell yourself it's stupid and you'll do it anyway, secretly hoping that I eat it on the turns so you have a shot." His glasses and helmet covered much of his smile, but they couldn't hide the amusement and approval in his voice. "And at the end, your body will have rediscovered the mechanics of a sprint. We can even do this again, as often as you want, until your body refinds its speed."

She crouched at the starting line, wishing she had a block for that extra burst at the beginning, even though she would probably trip over it when she crossed the finish. Or maybe

Micah nudging it out of the way would give him something to do while he twiddled his thumbs after beating her.

"On the count of three...go!"

At Micah's signal, Ruby erupted off her feet and ran, pumping her hands for forward momentum and using her feet to shove the track behind her. A controlled fall essentially, and at this speed, the emphasis felt more on the *fall* than on the *controlled.* The grass around the edges of the track blurred into one green streak. The cold wind of mid-October made her eyes water. And still she threw herself forward, grasping on to every second.

As predicted, Micah and Dotty were both waiting for her at the finish. Micah had his glasses sitting in his lap and Dotty was hopping about at his feet, ready to play the game again. Ruby was panting. She didn't look at her watch to see how long that lap had taken her because she'd only be irritated with herself. Natural talent could only make her so fast. If she wanted to *win,* she needed discipline to get her technique back.

With a sense of mutual understanding, Ruby fell in beside Micah and she walked the track beside him, Dotty trotting along with them. After two laps, Ruby had caught her breath and the grass started to redefine itself into blades. Though by the fifth, she was still wiping tears from her face.

"Are you crying because you didn't bring enough dollar bills?" Micah asked, just as Ruby was about to fall into a funk thinking about her wasted five years.

Only they weren't truly wasted. She may have forgotten some of her running technique in those five years, but she'd learned a lot about herself and the world. And herself *in* the world. In this world, she was going to exhaust herself and give Micah all her money—and she was going to enjoy doing it for herself.

"I brought twenty dollars," she replied with an arch in her voice to match the arch of her neck as she turned to look at him. "I hope you brought some, too. Cockiness is a sure sign of doom."

"You haven't paid me my first dollar yet."

She scowled, then went over to her gym bag, dug out a dollar and grabbed a water bottle. Back at Micah's side, she shoved the crumbled paper into his outstretched hand. "Here."

"Good," he said, tucking the bill into his spandex top. "Now I have a dollar in case you beat me. Is some of that water for me?"

She finished her drink and handed the bottle over. "You're lucky you're cute."

"Have you recovered enough to be beaten again?"

"There's no guarantee you'll win this time."

"True. But I'm willing to bet more than a dollar that I will."

"No," she grumbled. "A dollar bet is fine." She only had nineteen more with her after all, and she had a lot of training to get in.

"How about you give me another dollar if I can toss the water bottle back to the bench?"

Opposing needs warred within her. She *hated* giving up any more dollars than she had to, not because it meant she was handing over money. It meant she was *losing*. But Micah was wearing a muscle-fitting top, and he used to be a quarterback—she'd like to see his throw. She inclined her head. "Okay."

He looked at the bottle, lifting it up and down slightly to judge the weight of it in his hands. Then he made a show of licking his finger and judging the wind.

"C'mon, get on with it!"

"Fine. Don't appreciate the art." And then he threw. The bottle landed on the grass in front of the bench, skidding a bit before finally coming to rest directly under the seat.

"No need to go get another dollar now. I'll add it to your tab." He looked entirely too pleased with himself as he put his goggles back on. But the whole act—and the motion of his arm—had been worth more than a dollar.

Ruby crouched at the starting line and looked at him, not responding to his last jab with anything more than an eyebrow raised in challenge. "All talk, or is there game hidden in that chair somewhere?"

"Oh, there's game. If your britches are ready, we're on at *go*."

The smack talk wasn't only riling up Ruby; Dotty had also noticed something in the air and was hopping around and barking, waiting for action. At Micah's "Go!" Ruby took off, only to look behind her and see Dotty running in another direction.

"Dotty, come!"

Her dog looked confused for a moment, then figured out the correct direction and ran alongside Ruby for a lap. At the finish, Micah was mimicking filing his nails.

"You may have won the race," Ruby said, "but I get karma points for saving a straying dog."

"Dotty would have figured out which way to run, or at least gotten in another lap."

They fell into some slow laps around the track, each one of them catching their breath, with Micah and Ruby arguing about whether or not Ruby got karma points and, if she did, if they were worth a dollar. Ruby lost the argument, as she'd known she would, and interrupted her break to get Micah more money.

"Two dollars," he called, holding up his fingers in a V. "I want my two dollars."

She returned to the track, slapped the bills in his hand and jokingly asked if he was going to follow her to the ski slopes for his two dollars, acknowledging the reference he'd made to *Better Off Dead*.

"Maybe. They make adaptive skis. I grew up in Arizona, so I don't know how to ski, but I'd learn if you were there."

Ruby turned her head so quickly to look at him that she worried she'd strained something in her neck. He'd been hot and cold and hot and cold and she'd been having such a hard time getting a read on him. "If you were there" was definitely hot. Except now he was muttering nonsense to her dog as if he hadn't just implied they should take a ski vacation together.

A ski vacation was not research for any NSN series involving her—it was a futuristic statement about their relationship once this series was over. This stupid series, which she'd agreed to out of spite and was now regretting. Or, not regretting so much as feeling the burden of being on TV again and the exponential increase in awful things said about her on Reddit for the weeks following her small-screen appearance. And this stupid series that had been Micah's excuse for becoming a different person for several months.

Unfair, Ruby. She had been career driven for years. It hadn't served her well, but that wasn't Micah's fault. Only… she wished their relationship wasn't caught in the cross fire. She wished they could always be as free and easy with each other as they were right now.

"Penny for your thoughts?" Micah pulled out the three bills he'd stuffed in his shirt and held them toward her. "I've got three dollars, so I can afford a lot of thoughts."

"Nothing. No thoughts to tell." Which was a lie.

"We have more laps to do," she added. Which was truer than her statement that nothing was on her mind.

Her worrying took all the fun out of the last of their laps. She still lost every race, but the banter was gone and even Micah's wicked sense of humor couldn't bring it back. Every dollar bill she handed over only rubbed salt into the wound.

CHAPTER TWENTY-ONE

"ARE YOU CRAZY? You changed your registration from Diana to Ruby?" Micah stopped undoing his gloves and looked at Ruby, who was seated on the bench at the edge of the track. The crazy woman. Certifiable. With no sense of self-preservation. And in desperate need of a manager or agent. "For your safety, we release information about the races you're running when *I* say we do."

And she had the nerve to lift her head from her shoe-laces, her face tightened in anger. "I thought you said you weren't going to try to cage me."

The Velcro on his right glove made a harsh, satisfying noise as he ripped the fastenings. "I thought you said you would be sensible and not take unnecessary risks."

The line between promoting Ruby's story and having another network at a race, releasing better video, was narrow. Especially since NSN didn't have exclusivity contracts with any ultra race. No network did. King's big mouth didn't help, despite all of Dexter's interference. And the secrecy wasn't just so NSN could sit on one of the biggest sporting news stories of the year until they were ready to milk it for all the ratings it was worth, but also because Micah had argued that maintaining a low profile was for Ruby's safety.

The interview had exposed her, but once the NSN series was filmed and aired, there'd be enough goodwill around her name to offset the negative comments. The NSN story would change how the public interpreted the Ruby story— and public opinion was gold.

"This *is* necessary." She turned her attention back to the knot in her laces, as though this argument wasn't even worth having. "I may be redefining myself and my life, but I know myself well enough to know that Ruby Heart is a runner."

"No one is saying you're not a runner. Between the shelter, coaching Eric and your own training, you run more than ten miles a day. Hell, NSN is banking on you being a runner *and* on people getting behind you being a runner. But we're also invested in your safety." He gritted his teeth against his anger, and a sour taste he recognized as fear. "Controlling the message, Ruby. I'm here to help you control the message." Micah threw his gloves into his kit bag.

"Has it escaped you that *I* am the message and so perhaps *I* should decide what name I'm running under?" She matched his irritation with a throw of her running shoes into her gym bag. After losing to him all afternoon, she won this contest—his gloves couldn't compete with her shoes for irritated-statement power. "And I thought the message was that I'm back and I'm running and I don't care what anyone thinks about it. I thought the message was that I'm reformed and I can take my place in society again."

"That is the message. We're also trying to control *how* it's released."

"How angry do you think people will be when they find out I'm running races as Diana Heart? Do you think they're going to believe in my honesty?"

He ignored both her argument and the perfect reason-
ability of it. "I've had a hell of a time convincing NSN to
sit on this series until after your one-hundred-mile race.
They want to run it now, in bits on *SportsDaily,* without
building in the sympathy story I've been writing for you.
I've had to convince them that this story, my story, would
get better ratings."

She arched her brow at him. "I'm sorry? Better ratings?
When you started this argument, the issue was my safety.
Or is *my safety* code word for 'there's no story if Ruby is
dead'?"

Micah gripped his wheels before he gave in to his urge
to shake them at her. "Don't be stupid. You as my lead is
gold. You as my lead because you're *dead* is the forty-nin-
ers, 'strike it rich never have to work again' kind of gold."

"Sure." She shrugged. "Better ratings for one night, but
not as good long-term."

His hands flew up and out at her. If he couldn't shake
some sense into her, the least he could do was mimic shaking sense into her. "Could we get away from the idea that
this is all about my ratings? I care about more than just the
ratings."

"I remember. You care about me. And you care about
conflict of interest, too. I get that. Buds. We're buds and
that's good. I'm still racing under my own name next week."

Argh. He pulled the skin of his face, stretching it as much
as Ruby was stretching his nerves. "You of all people should
know that one bad moment can ruin a career. And my career is important to me. You should get that, too."

The muscles of her face softened to match her voice. "I
get that. I do. But then you get it *all* and you get it all on
your timetable. And I get buddy Micah because I can't have

Micah *and* be the star of your series. But it's my life, too. At the very least, my name is my own to have control over."

"What's the big deal about running under your own name right now? The big race is in March. Can't you wait until after that?"

"Do you sit in your wheelchair while on camera?"

She might as well have printed out and handed over a map, because he could follow the trajectory of her argument as sure as if she'd given him directions. "Being on camera in my chair was a hard-fought battle, and I'm not even sure I won. It's true, I get to be me on camera and it's important for people to know and see *me,* but every time a NSN reporter who is not me does a story on an athlete with a disability, people email the network to ask if I died and they missed the obit. Because crippled athletes are surely the beat of the crippled reporter and no one else."

"But I'll bet you wouldn't go back. If I'm going to move forward, I can't keep living as if I'm in the past. And that means that for good or bad, I have to perform as me."

"I'm not the one getting rape threats online."

"No one's ever acted on it."

"Yet." Micah said the word he knew Ruby was thinking. "Ultra races have long stretches where it's just you and the trees. That makes you an easy target."

"And he won't be able to catch me." She said the words with all the confidence of an Olympian and medalist and a woman who had run faster than all the boys until she hit college.

"It might not be a footrace, Ruby."

"Look," she said, slapping her hands against her legs, "I refuse to be trapped. Besides, anyone who wants to threaten me can find me here if they really want to. And I'd rather be out running a race."

"Yeah, exposed, tired and possibly hallucinating. At least here you have a dog with you."

"I've not yet hallucinated while racing."

"*Yet* is the key word there again."

"You'll be there."

"I'll be there at the start and at the finish with Amir and a production van. What good are we to you when you're in the woods?"

She shrugged. "I've done it and I'm not undoing it. I don't want to undo it. I'm sick of not being me."

"I just…" He shrugged, not entirely sure how to express what he was feeling because he didn't understand it himself. "I would love to sit in that *SportsDaily* anchor chair, but not if it means you've been discovered dead in a ditch somewhere along the side of the road. Call me crazy for wanting to see you finish the race. For wanting to see you win the race."

"Oh." Her brown eyes got soft and gooey and he could tell that he'd surprised her, especially since he'd been so careful to maintain a professional distance between them.

He didn't even try to follow the uncomfortable unburdening of his emotions with a kiss or a come-on to make him feel more in control of the situation. Because he wasn't in control. Ruby wasn't in control. They had a path laid out in front of them, and anything beyond the next bend was completely hidden. And as risky as it was, he liked traveling on that path with her and he hoped their paths didn't diverge.

And if that wasn't already a conflict of interest, he didn't know what was.

"Yeah. I'm willing to sacrifice my story for your safety. Why are we fighting about this?"

Her nose twitched and her eyes darted around the track as she searched for an escape. Now that Ruby Heart had discovered she'd been imprisoned, it seemed she mistook any attempt to express concern or caring as another steel bar set into her world.

He sped up his words so he could finish what he wanted to say before she accused him of trying to cage her again. "I'm doing my best to respect your right to your decision. I really am, but it doesn't stop me from worrying."

"I'll be fine. Really," she said, though her repeated attempts to reassure him weren't comforting. "I've been here before. And these men, they talk big, but follow-through requires more balls than they've got. The worst that will happen is that one of the other runners will call me a cheat and tell me I don't belong. And they'll be right about at least half of that statement."

But he could tell by the shadows falling across her face that she didn't believe her reassurances any more than he did. "But thanks for caring about me." She reached over and patted his leg, as she had in the car, only this time she didn't remember that she might as well be patting the bench for all the comfort it gave him.

Yet another sign that Ruby Heart thought she was doing something stupid and was determined to do it anyway.

CHAPTER TWENTY-TWO

TWO WEEKS LATER, Micah sat at the starting line watching Ruby shake out her muscles. Though he'd been in this very position before, this time was different. Ruby knew he was watching, and she didn't dart behind other runners or offer him a challenge in her glance before darting off into the distance. If he wasn't mistaken, the look Ruby was giving him after she'd finished warming up could best be described as "come hither."

Damned story. They would be playing games with each other until the stupid series was over...or he broke.

Micah rolled his way over the dirt and rocks through the crowd, the wide berths spectators gave his wheelchair working to his advantage as he scanned the crowd. "For what?" he muttered to himself. "I don't even know what I'm looking for." It wasn't as if he was a cop, or even an investigative reporter.

He supposed he was looking for someone with as much interest in watching Ruby as he had. Maybe more. Being about four foot ten in the chair meant watching people's facial expressions required him to torque his head. One guy in a gray sweatshirt was looking in Ruby's direction, but when Micah turned his head to follow the man's gaze, he saw another man wave, and the gray-sweatshirt man waved back. Not interested in Ruby but in the person *next* to Ruby.

He wove his way in and out of people chatting and pointing, examining each face, so it was pure luck that he noticed one man's hands clenched tightly in two fists. The force with which the man clenched his hands was evident in the tightness of his arms and how his shoulders played patty-cake with his earlobes. The man's muscles twitched and he looked around. Micah didn't bother trying to hide his interest; a man in a wheelchair was only considered a threat when people assumed he was homeless, and even then he would be ignored. This man reacted no differently to Micah. His gaze went right over his head, and so Micah was able to follow the man's interest right back to Ruby.

Could it be this easy?

Micah almost missed the gun's bang that signaled the start of the race. Ruby darted forward, only not nearly with as much push as she usually did. He looked back at The Man, who was watching Ruby intently enough for Micah to almost believe the force of his stare was holding her back. When Ruby was out of view, The Man's shoulders relaxed and he took a sip from his Starbucks cup, and Micah was left wondering if he'd imagined the whole thing.

RUBY HAD PUSHED herself a little and, at the halfway mark, was maybe fifteen minutes behind the lead woman. She was fatigued and her body hurt, but she had run twenty-five miles and she wasn't any more tired than she expected to be. Rethinking her strategy and the finish, Ruby slowed down a little to conserve energy for the end. There were at least three other women between her and the lead woman. She wasn't here to win—she was here to prove that America's Darling could run under her own name and that she could finish with other elite runners.

But every time the words *win* and *finish* flittered through her mind, Ruby's chest puffed out in anticipation. Greater. Faster. As she caught up to three men in front of her, she clamped down on her competitiveness to stay in line with them. At least until the next aid station, and then she'd pass them.

Up around the bend that marked the official halfway point, she spied Micah and waved. He lowered a set of binoculars to his lap and waved back. After she had been weighed, he rolled over to her with a water bottle and granola bar. At the previous aid stations, Ruby had taken her food and run. But this time she decided to stop long enough for support from a friend and to discard the empty water bottles from her belt.

"You're holding back," he said, taking the water bottle from her outstretched hand and handing her another full one to tuck into her belt.

"I need to save my energy for the finish." She shifted her weight back and forth on her feet, trying to keep her legs loose and warm. The weather was cool, and the difference in temperature between the chill of the air and the heat of her body could cause cramping if she wasn't careful. "Besides, I'm not trying to win. I want a competitive time."

He raised both his eyebrows at her, looking thoroughly disgusted with her excuse. "The first time you ran was to see if you *could.* The second time was to beat your time and be competitive. How about trying to win this time? You're not that far behind the lead woman."

Ruby took a large, angry bite of the granola bar and chewed, her irritation coming out in every chomp. "To make your interview a bigger success?"

His only response was a lift of his eyebrows.

"Let me worry about my strategy," she said, which was as close to a peace offering as she could handle right now.

"I hope your anger fuels you to run faster," he said evenly, as if she'd never spoken in anger. "I can sell your story no matter how you finish, and if that's all I cared about I wouldn't be at this station—without Amir—handing you a granola bar."

"You're right," she said, before taking another bite. Micah was here with water and food. He'd given her a lift to the race. And, most important, she wouldn't be on her own for dinner tonight. "I've not had the luxury of running one of these races with a support team before. I do appreciate it."

She hadn't been keeping an eye on the trio of men she'd headed into the aid station with the way she should have. When she looked up, they were out of her view, so she took a last swig of water and shoved the bottle and the granola wrapper at Micah, then took off, going slightly faster than she had before without ruining her rhythm. If she was steady but faster, she'd catch them.

Delicate business, this ultra running. The struggle wasn't just in getting her body to run through fatigue and pain, but also training her mind not to give in to its pulsing siren's song for a break. The mind was harder to train than the body. A devious creature, always looking for a shortcut and easy way out.

She turned another bend and the route changed from a dirt trail to some kind of access road. Her feet kicked out behind her and put distance between her and Micah and his kindness. Despite how short she'd been with him, seeing him waiting for her had lifted her spirits, and now each step felt a little lighter. He seemed to believe in her. Not in the created, fake America's Darling her, but in the Ruby who had given up both fake blood and fake hair to become the Ruby who was vulnerable and flawed—both things he seemed to appreciate rather than condemn. She settled back into the rhythm of her running, letting her thoughts on Micah distract her from the spreading fatigue in her legs and pull her back into the space in her mind where she loved running. So caught up was she in her mental push that she didn't notice the man she'd gained ground on until she was even with him. A baseball cap blocked his eyes, but she saw the moment he recognized her in the sneer on his lips.

Then she heard, "Cheating bitch, you don't belong here," and his arm came out from his side. Fatigue and being caught between steps caused her to stumble as much as his strike did. She landed hard on her left foot, then took another step before the asphalt rushed at the side of her face.

To her surprise, she bounced the first time she hit the ground. The second time, the pain radiated through her eyes as her head hit. The piece of asphalt she landed on had been in the sun and was warm, much like the hand that had pushed her. She closed her eyes and hugged the warmth to her, but it did nothing to push the pain away.

"Hey! Are you okay?" The voice came through the smog of her mind in slow motion. She pictured the slow motion running scene from *Chariots of Fire,* and she suddenly giggled. Then she moaned as painful icicles stabbed her hip and ankle.

Please don't let anything be broken.

Crouching above her was a young female runner with spiky black hair and deep brown eyes soft with concern. Ruby shifted, moaned again, then sat up. Her head lolled back and she swung her arms back behind her to steady her body before she fell over again. The woman put a hand on her shoulder to steady her. The hand was damp from sweat.

Ruby's eyes hurt too much to keep them open, so she shut them, but they only hurt more. She opened them again. The front of her body looked okay. There was dirt on her running shorts and a nasty bit of road rash on the side of her knee, but otherwise she looked whole. She wiggled her toes, and her toenails hit against her socks and the tips of her shoes like they should. She swayed her feet from side to side and her ankles seemed to work, too. She ached, but there wasn't any spiking pain.

"I think I'm okay." Her head was still crowded with the thick cotton of cheap running socks, but the pain behind her eyes wasn't enough to make her wince when she gave her head a slight shake. She tucked her legs under her so that she sat cross-legged, pushed herself up off her hands and leaned forward.

"Do you see stars? Are you dizzy at all?"

Ruby gave her head a tentative nod, then a shake. "I was dizzy when I first sat up, but I'm okay now. No stars."

"Headache?"

"Yes, but I did get pushed and hit the ground. It's no worse than I would expect."

"Ears ringing? Nausea?"

"No." Ruby waited a moment to see if her stomach rolled. It didn't. "And no."

"Fatigue?"

Not enough that Ruby didn't give her rescuer a dirty look.

"Fair enough," the woman said. "Just checking you for concussion symptoms. Do you need me to check your ankles?"

Ruby stuck her legs out in front of her again and gave everything a wiggle before answering, "No. I'm okay."

The woman stood, offered her hand and hauled Ruby to her feet. While Ruby shook out her limbs and ran her hands over her body checking for any other damage, the other runner put her hand on Ruby's back and waited. She didn't take it off until Ruby said, "No, really, I'm fine," with the full force of her voice.

"Can you run?" the woman asked.

Ruby took a hesitant step forward. "I think…maybe if I walk a bit first."

"I'll walk with you." They took small, slow steps together. "I'm Patrice, by the way."

"Ruby Heart," she said, feeling it was a risk even though her name was on the roster of runners. Patrice had already helped her up off the ground. She was unlikely to push her over now.

MICAH WASN'T LISTENING as the man next to him explained a miracle cure for spinal cord injuries. Normally he didn't put up with such intrusive comments from strangers, but he and Amir had a prime spot to view the finish line of the race, and they weren't willing to give it up, even at the cost of Micah's sanity or jail time for assault.

Ruby was late. He drummed his fingers against the wheel of his chair, the noise barely making a dent in the onslaught of miracle cures from his newfound friend. Even accounting for a change in pace due to the increased length of this race, she was still thirty minutes late. She'd been dead-on for time at the aid station. After he'd harassed race officials several times, even trading on his NSN credentials—which he almost never did—they told him the only runner found in need of rescue so far had been a man. Ruby was built strong and powerful, but no one would mistake her for being a man.

So why hadn't she finished yet? He drummed his fingers harder, letting the clings of his nails against the metal drown out his neighbor's nonsense about a disk and some sort of magical fluid. Over the years, other people's obsession with *fixing* him had grown more annoying than the fact that he couldn't use his legs. Easier for people to assume *Micah* needed to be fixed than to bother rethinking their own assumptions.

The man had started talking about the benefits of turmeric for inflammation when Micah's post at the finish line paid off. He signaled to Amir, who signaled back that he was getting the video. Rounding the corner was Ruby, her braided pigtails bouncing against her collarbone and her bangs plastered against her forehead. Her face was flushed red, but her eyes were bright and Micah didn't think he'd ever been happier to see her.

The man was midstream into his turmeric lecture when Micah put his hands on his wheels and took off toward Ruby, darting through the small crowds of supporters and runners until he was at her side. Heat radiated off her body and she smelled like salt, which would probably turn sour after she'd started to cool off, but he was so relieved to see her that he didn't care. Conflict of interest, cheating and scandal be damned, Micah wanted to reach up, grab her face between his hands and pull her in for a kiss. A warm, salty, sweaty, celebratory kiss.

When she caught his eye, she smiled softly. Micah's shoulders relaxed, but his mind raced with ideas of what he could do *to* and *for* and *with* a hot, sweaty woman in bed. She had long, lean, strong muscles, and the image of them wrapped around him was imprinted permanently in his brain.

He loved her. The realization slammed into him and he had to grab on to the wheels of his chair to stay balanced.

She reached out a hand to him. Her palm was rougher

than normal, and when he squeezed it, she winced. Only then did he notice that her hand was scraped. Not badly, but she'd clearly skidded across some asphalt on it. When he looked her over more carefully, he found road rash on the side of her legs and on both her knees. And a bruise was beginning to form on her cheek, under a spot of blood.

The heat rising in his body this time wasn't sexual attraction, it was anger, which boiled away the icy cold fear that he'd felt before.

"What happened?" he asked, certain he knew the answer.

She was hunched, likely in both fatigue and pain, and he almost missed the way her eyes darted about. He steeled himself for the lie.

"I caught up to some guy after the aid station and he pushed me."

If she was going to lie to him, he'd expected her to make up something better. "Just some guy? You don't know who he was or what he looked like? Did you tell race officials?"

"I don't know anything more about him and, no, I didn't tell race officials. I don't want some guy pushing me to be the story of my race." She pulled away from him, limping around and looking for a chair. A spectator hopped out of a camp chair and gestured to her. She half sat, half collapsed into it. "I was running along, fully into my rhythm when I came up behind him. He looked at me, knew who I was and stuck his arm out. I don't think he meant for me to go down."

"It doesn't matter...."

But Ruby was too far into her story to listen to him. "Another runner stopped to help me up. Patrice. I'd like to wait for her actually." She leaned her head back and closed her eyes, turning her face to him to say, "Can you get me some food?"

He looked around him. The aid station wasn't far away, and Ruby needed food more than he needed to argue with her. "You'll promise to talk to race officials after you tell me everything?"

Apparently she was too tired to argue.

On his way to the food, Micah stopped to tell Amir to get them some satellite time. Ruby getting hurt was big news; they would have to use a quick segment on *SportsDaily* to tease about the upcoming series—and Ruby would have to be talked into it. He returned with a plate full of boiled potatoes, guacamole, jelly beans and a banana, as well as a couple of bottles of water and a beer.

"You know I have to get a story ready for *SportsDaily*. Right after you tell the race officials what happened."

Ruby glared at him, a mess of everything that had been on her plate piled onto a fork and about to go into her mouth. Guacamole mixed with jelly beans sounded nasty, but he supposed his body wasn't the one craving sugar and salt in any form available.

"I shouldn't have told you."

"I'm interested to hear how you would have kept the bruises on your face from me."

She took a big bite of her postrace food and shrugged. She must have gotten a guac-covered jelly bean, because her shrug was quickly followed by a grimace. "What happened to me keeping a low profile?"

"You're the one who registered for the race as Ruby Heart."

"This had nothing to do with how I registered my name. I surprised the guy and he reacted." Her adrenaline must be wearing off. Even though she kept shoveling food into her mouth, her movements slowed down to a precise crawl.

"You said another runner stopped to help you? Do you

think that runner is going to be able to keep your accident a secret? Tell the officials. And then it's either I run the story now or another news station knocks on your door."

"Those are my choices? Either I give in to you now or I give in to another station later? Those are terrible choices. Let's go with your original plan of running the series all at once rather than feeding them bits of my story one piece at a time. I liked that idea better."

"That idea isn't an option any longer."

"What if I don't give you more detail? You have all that video you can use and I can just sit here in mute protest."

"Come on, Ruby." He held out his hands in supplication. "Don't make me choose between my career and you."

"Fine." She put her plate on the ground and shivered. "Go get a race official. I'll even answer some questions for you. It's not like I'm going anywhere."

She was only agreeing because she was too tired to argue, but Micah wasn't going to look a gift horse in the mouth. In this case, he was going to get his interview with the horse while she was still willing to talk. "I'll grab your gym bag with your warm clothes when I get Amir."

Ruby managed to put on her warm clothes while talking to a race official and without standing fully upright while Amir set up for the interview. Once they got it going, the interview was short. Ruby told him the same thing she'd told the official—which wasn't much—and she was too fatigued to put much energy into her story. Not that he blamed her; she hadn't even had an hour to rest after running fifty miles. At least Amir had gotten good video, and the story would be compelling.

He had to get this video done and in before some other network, even a Podunk local network, sniffed out the story. Otherwise Dexter would have his head for dinner.

623

Before he went back to the van to track the interview and log any sound bites, Micah rolled closer to Ruby and rested his hand on her knee. "I'll take you back to the hotel now if you want."

"No." He blinked away surprise at her answer. She'd completely disappeared from the two previous races, heading to the hotel as soon as she could catch a shuttle bus. "I'm going to wait for Patrice to finish. In fact," she said, easing out of the chair, "I'm going to get up and walk around a little before I cramp up, and then you can find me at the finish."

After Ruby dismissed him, Micah wrinkled his nose and looked over at Amir, who shrugged. Micah made his way to the production van to get his part of the story ready as quickly as possible.

He'd asked her not to make him choose between her and his job and she hadn't. She was letting him alone.

So why did he feel like such a shit?

RUBY WAITED AT the finish for Patrice, shifting her weight from side to side, trying to walk a line between her fatigue and keeping her body from losing heat too rapidly and cramping. She was already stiff, and walking was an idea best approached with caution and undertaken gingerly.

She didn't wait alone, and that wasn't a metaphorical statement, either. Both finishers and supporters stood around the finish with her. And the fact of her existence at the race had spread quickly from the thirty-mile mark where she'd left Patrice to the bright sign flashing Finish and the time of each runner as they crossed under the line. Several people had come up to her, asked her if she really was Ruby Heart, made a noncommittal noise of some kind and left. One person had told her that she outright didn't belong here. She didn't see the guy who'd pushed her, though she also wasn't sure if she'd recognize him if she did.

Much to Ruby's surprise, the top female finisher welcomed her back to the sport and said she was looking forward to the added competition. If the other woman had meant to leave the *don't cheat again, you cheater* heard but unspoken, she hadn't expressed herself very well.

Ruby shoved jelly beans and gummy bears into her mouth, letting the sugar drip down as she mulled over what she'd set herself up for. Micah had offered to help her minimize the impact of her identity until the big, hopefully sympathetic story aired. And she'd turned him down, saying she was ready for whatever happened. And then that guy had happened. How many people watching the short interview she'd done with Micah would think, "bitch got what she deserved"? *Do I care?*

The production van was barely visible through the crowds and the trees. She could make it over there and ask to review Micah's script to make sure she came off well. Or she could continue to stand at the finish and cheer as loud as her tired voice would let her when Patrice came into view. Ruby made her way through the spectators for another plate of food—this time less candy—and returned to the finish to wait for Patrice.

When Patrice came into view, her feet were dragging and she was moving barely faster than a walk, but Ruby rushed to the fencing and yelled as loud as if her rescuer was crossing the finish in an Olympic stadium. Patrice was half enveloped, half held up by a dark-skinned man dressed as though he'd also run the race, a young girl and an older woman, who looked enough like Patrice that she had to be Patrice's mom.

The family, except for Patrice and her husband, who both

looked too tired to contemplate anything but a nap, jumped up and down in celebration. Ruby hung back, the loneliness she'd kept at bay walloping her on the back. Again she was alone at the finish. Micah was here, but he was off finishing his story on her. He wasn't *here* with her.

She scrubbed at her face with the heel of her hand, trying to press reality into her brain. Micah had asked her not to make him choose between his career and her. She'd done the interview. He was with Amir getting it ready to air, as was his job. For her to be cranky about it after she'd said it was okay was unfair of her.

Not to mention that she'd insisted she was running for her and no one else. Which should mean she didn't *need* anyone else at the finish with her. That didn't mean she didn't *want* someone here at the finish with her. Or that she didn't want that person to be Micah.

Just as she was about to turn away from Patrice and her family, Ruby heard a noise behind her. Micah was rolling toward her, his face suspiciously clean and fresh. Only when she saw a lingering bit of foundation on his chin did she realize that he'd been on camera and so had had on makeup.

"Story done?" she asked, tamping down any irritation still lingering within her. *You're running for yourself, remember. Micah's a nice bonus.*

"Amir's got it for cuts now and we feed it to the bird at five." She must have looked confused, because he added, "The satellite. The video is scheduled for satellite at five to get it to the station."

"Oh. Okay."

"It'll be on tonight and tomorrow morning's *SportsDaily*. It was good. You looked really strong in the video."

Strong was good, but did she look forgivable? Not that it

mattered. That story was out of her control. Running was the only thing in her control.

Out of the corner of her eye Ruby saw Patrice pull away from her family and limp toward her. The woman was stiffening up fast and looked as though she would be incredibly sore in the morning.

When Patrice reached them, Ruby was holding both her arms out for a hug. "Thank you again for your help," Ruby said. "Are you doing okay?"

Patrice looked up from her curious glance at Micah to answer Ruby's question. "Yeah, this was my first fifty-miler and I ran above my pace for most of it. I hit a wall at mile forty and limped my way to the finish. Which, of course, means I finished after my goal."

Ruby laughed. "I sympathize, but sometimes the finishing has to be accomplishment enough."

"I'll try to remember that, even though I don't think you hold yourself to that standard."

"No." The words came out behind a chuckle. "Not usually, but it's good to say." Patrice's gaze had gone back to eyeing Micah. Ruby remembered that she hadn't yet introduced them. "Micah Blackwell, meet Patrice. Micah, Patrice is the woman who looked me over for injuries after helping me up off the asphalt."

"Nice to meet you, Patrice," Micah said.

"Oh." Patrice seemed to have just noticed Micah's face. "Didn't you… I mean…" Patrice stopped talking, and by the look on her face Ruby could tell she was trying to place distant bits of past gossip and news together. "Right. I don't generally like sports casting, but I've enjoyed many of your interviews."

"Thanks," he said, before turning to Ruby. "Come on, let's go get some dinner and I'll drive us back to the hotel."

They said their goodbyes, and Patrice and Ruby exchanged phone numbers. "If you need me for anything," Ruby said, hugging the woman one more time.

Micah and Ruby were headed to his car when she said, "One of these days, I'm going to drive and you'll sit in the passenger seat."

"I like to be in control. I won't pretend otherwise." He shrugged.

"Has your controlling mind come up with dinner plans yet?"

"No," he said with a smile and those deep dimples. "She who expended the most calories gets to decide how to replace them. But I did investigate your options. Pizza or burgers."

"Pizza, then." Ruby brushed Micah's shoulder with her hand and the warmth of him pushed away the last of her postrace chills.

CHAPTER TWENTY-THREE

RUBY WAS STIFF as she walked down the hotel hallway ahead of Micah and their dinner. His chair made a noise she hadn't expected on the tight, low carpeting. Actually, she didn't know what kind of noise she thought a wheelchair would make. But the long, low sound of the chair, the institutional smell of the hotel fighting with the spiciness of the pizza and the din of the fluorescent lights highlighted how unreal this entire day felt.

A push by one stranger and a rescue by another. Micah and dinner in her hotel room. And she wasn't glad Micah was here because she was lonely and wanted company, but because she wanted *his* company. It put a whole different spin on things, this spending time with someone because you wanted to.

Old Ruby Heart hadn't spent much time reveling in her successes. She hugged her mom at the end of a race, then immediately reevaluated her strategy, training and caloric intake. An unasked question always accompanied her mom's hug: What if I don't win another race?

She hadn't won this fifty-mile race. And she was unlikely

to win the hundred-mile race she'd signed up for. Yet Micah was here, with her, just the same.

The point wasn't whether or not she liked winning, because she did, but whether or not her life depended on it. And it didn't.

She would work on a training schedule in the morning for the hundred-mile race she intended to win next fall. Or maybe she'd wait a couple of days before she thought about her next race. Because she had a life to live right now, and winning was only a small part of it. Perhaps when the NSN series was over, Micah could be a larger part of this life. His solidness could become a constant presence.

She stuck her key into the door and opened it. The light from the overly bright bulb in the bedside lamp glinted off the golden highlights in Micah's hair as he went past her into her room.

"No dinner table in this room," he said, his words shrinking the room around them until she could feel his breathing deep in her bones.

"No. Just a desk, the two beds and a television. Bare bones down here in Missouri." A couch would have been nice. She wanted to sit down, and sitting on the bed with Micah seemed…well, the ideas that single piece of furniture put in her head loomed large in the tight space. Even larger because she wasn't sure of Micah's feelings and wasn't sure how sex would or could happen. If she knew the answer to the first question, she'd feel confident enough to ask the answer to the second.

And this all assumed that she wouldn't fall asleep the instant she was in any position other than standing. She stood, not sure what to do with her hands because the pizza box was on Micah's lap, held there by his large, strong hands. Her head darted up and she looked around the room.

"Which bed are you sleeping in?"

"That one." She pointed to the bed closest to the window.

"Okay. That desk will make using my chair as a dining seat difficult and you don't want to sleep on pizza crumbs. So we'll have a little bed picnic here—" he gestured to the bed closest to the door "—and we can move to the other bed to watch *SportsDaily*. Go shower. I'll wait for you. And then you can serve me dinner." Their hands brushed as she took the pizza box that he shoved into her hands. The secrets in his smile made her shiver. "I like the idea of America's Darling serving me dinner."

Her awkwardness and fatigue had been replaced by a heightened awareness of Micah and his movements. Nonchalance was getting harder and harder to fake. "I'm hardly America's Darling anymore."

"You're darling enough," he said as he transitioned from his chair to the bed. Despite having seen him transition several times, the grace of his movements still struck her. Silly, because he had been paralyzed for ten years, and before that he'd been a quarterback known for his grace on the field. No reason to think his athleticism would disappear with the use of his legs.

He had scooted up, his back against the headboard, when she realized what he'd said. "What did you mean by that? 'You're darling enough'?"

"Exactly what I said. No matter what the rest of the world thinks, I like you. Anyone who doesn't like you is missing out."

Ruby left it at that. She rushed through her shower, Micah's words louder than the sound of the water pressure as it beat against the tile. She was off balance when she got out of the bathroom as she fumbled with the pizza box while she plated. The room was still small, but Micah's words meant her world had gotten a whole lot bigger. "How many pieces do you want?"

He laughed. "I was going to tease you for running away when I said I liked you, but you came back, so I'll tease you for thinking only of pizza instead."

"I'm still thinking about what you said. And I need food."

"Don't think too much, Ruby. There are more fun ways for us to get in trouble together." His half smile eased some of the tension in her body, and he gestured for his plate. "Two, for starters. I may have you get me more, though."

She set their plates on the bedside table. His breath brushed her face as she crawled over him to the other side of the bed. She stilled, straddling him on her hands and knees, their faces only inches apart. The small streak of foundation still dotted his chin. Funny, she'd never thought of the attraction of a man in makeup.

Sitting back on her heels, she reached out with her thumb and touched the spot of makeup. His skin was smooth and his jaw sharp. Her breathing slowed. Her heart raced. The corners of the room blurred before fading completely as Micah took over her world. When she'd rubbed the makeup off, she leaned forward again, desperate for the connection of his mouth to hers. Her knee hit the remote and the *Sports-Daily* intro music made them both jump. A reminder of the real world—and their bargain.

"This is a rerun from last night. It's too early for your story to be on." His breath danced on her neck. Lips fluttered across hers. "And if you're not ready to eat, I can think of more fun ways to pass the time than watching NSN."

Temptation. She slid off him to the rough polyester of the comforter.

"I don't know why I had to serve the pizza, since I'm

the one who ran fifty miles," she said after he handed her a plate.

Micah put his pizza slice down onto the plate and looked at her, the charm she'd come to expect from him when they were alone replaced by the tangible pull on her soul that had marked their interviews. She knew he wielded the same magnetism against all his interview subjects, but somehow it seemed to affect her at the cellular level.

"Because you don't expect to have to serve me. And so I'll let you."

Like he had at the last race, Micah took charge of the conversation, though this time he never let the conversation ease her anticipation. Or maybe she was too keyed up for even the magic of Micah to work its spell.

Despite her fatigue, Ruby's eyes were wide-open. And she was functional enough to eat four slices of pizza. Physical exhaustion also didn't stop her from noticing the fine hairs on Micah's wrists as he took a bite of his pizza. Or the way he ate to the very edge of his crust but didn't eat the crust. Or how his tongue licked sauce from the corner of his mouth.

Ruby slid off the bed to throw away their plates and get Micah another beer. She got water for herself. Beer sounded good, but a second one was liable to hit her upside the head like a shot put to the jaw.

Micah's neatly trimmed nails stood out against the dark brown of the beer bottle as he wrapped his hand around his drink. He had hair that never seemed to grow longer and a face that never seemed to need shaving. He was precise, without being uptight or oppressive about it. The kind of person who would make you want to be precise, as well.

"You have the hots for me, Ruby Heart," he said, eyeing her over his beer bottle. "Don't think I can't tell."

"I…" But denying the truth was stupid. "Sure."

"Are you going to do something about it?"

She had to put her glass on the nightstand before she dropped it from coughing. When she looked at him, her eyes were watering and she still couldn't speak, but the confusion must have been obvious in her eyes because he shrugged and said, "Or we could not do something about it."

When she was finally able to say something, she asked, "What about all that stuff you said about conflict of interest?"

"Yup. I said that."

"You still believe it?"

"I do. And I also believe that seeing your scraped-up legs and bruised face was one of the scariest moments of my life." His eyes slipped over her body, leaving goose bumps in their wake. "The conflict of interest already exists. I might as well enjoy the benefits."

"Rationalization and I used to be good friends, but he got me into a lot of trouble." The bed shifted and creaked as she moved to sit cross-legged. "I stay away from that crowd as much as possible now."

"But you're interested."

His arm muscles flexed as he lifted over her. The tendons in his neck stretched tight with pleasure. Grunts, moans and nails digging into skin. Any sex they had would be…*athletic*. Yeah, that seemed to be the right word. And therein lay an easy excuse to put him off. And the troubles that anything he suggested might cause her heart. "I don't have the energy for anything I'm interested in."

"Are you awake?"

"Yes," she said, suspicious. "Though shouldn't more be expected of me?"

"And you're likely to remain awake?"

"Until I fall asleep. And," she said, holding up one finger in warning, "I don't want you to think that me falling asleep couldn't happen at any time. Because it could. And without warning." At least she hoped it could, because her body really needed it, no matter that her brain was up to running another fifty miles.

"Your body looks like it could melt into a puddle, but I've got to say, your eyes look wide-awake."

She eyed him, still not sure what his point was.

"Here's the thing. We could scoot over to the sleeping bed, turn on the television and I can find something boring enough to put you right to sleep. Or I can help you relax another way. I'm voting for option two."

"Do I get to know what option two is before I choose?"

If his smile was any indication, option two would turn her into a pile of goo. "I've got strong hands and a quick tongue. What more do you need to know about option two?"

CHAPTER TWENTY-FOUR

MICAH DIDN'T NEED to actually follow through with his words, because Ruby was pretty sure she was already a pile of goo. *Strong hands and a quick tongue.* Her insides didn't know whether to combust or melt. Given the number of butterflies in her stomach, they were leaning toward combustion. The very core of her, on the other hand, might melt before explosions could detonate.

"And your conflict of interest?" At this point she was only offering up obstacles as a matter of course. Unless he got into his wheelchair and left her room, she was picking option two.

"We're at a cheap hotel in the middle of nowhere in Missouri. Who's going to know?"

Ruby remembered a similar argument being made by her coach. "I will. You will."

"I'll also know what you taste like. And if I die tomorrow, that's more important to me right now."

Her resistance melted to a puddle on the floor. "Option two," she said. She'd be a fool to turn down strong hands and a quick tongue.

Though she was also probably a fool not to.

"I get to be the boss for the rest of the night."

"From now until I fall asleep," she said, unwilling to cede too much power to him.

"Oh, I'm not worried about that until I'm done. And then I promise you'll sleep like a baby."

"Okay."

Micah folded his arms across his chest, surveying the room and all that was in it. Supposedly it was her room, but Micah owned any room he went into, and this hotel room was no exception. "Take off your clothes and fold down the sheets. Then get into bed. I'll join you there."

"In that order?"

"I said I'm the boss."

"Okay, boss. How quickly am I to accomplish these tasks?"

"You can take as long as you want, but option two doesn't start until you're on that bed, naked, with your legs spread wide."

"No foreplay?"

His raised eyebrow was enough to scoot her off the bed. "Do you need foreplay?"

The bed skirt brushed the tops of her bare feet, but that wasn't what sent shivers down her spine. No, between the hardness of her nipples poking against her T-shirt and the dampness between her legs, the foreplay was already happening.

"Well?" He looked both expectant and as if she'd disappointed him by not being naked already.

"Ask and you shall receive." She tried to tell herself that she was lifting her shirt slowly as a tease and as a way to prove further control over her own body, but really it was because she was too sore to move quickly. Whatever her reasons, the short tease must have been effective, because

Micah let out a sigh that rippled through her own skin as soon as her T-shirt hit the floor.

Even though she was feeling a little wobbly on her feet, she stayed standing and well in Micah's sight line as she stripped her shorts from her body. Warm fingers touched the inside of her thighs when she turned to pull the sheets down. Micah's fingers drew a light line up her thigh, tracing around the underside of her buttocks and then back, grazing the soft folds between her legs. She pulsed in response. When she looked over her shoulder, his eyes were focused on something she couldn't see and he had the otherworldly look of someone mesmerized.

How much more than *I like you* had been beneath the surface of his teasing and flirtations over the past couple months?

She slapped his hand away, unwilling to think too much about the look of rapture on his face and what that meant. This was supposed to be light and fun. This was supposed to be for her. The expression on his face changed the rules.

"I thought option two didn't start until I was naked on the bed and my legs were spread wide."

He visibly pulled himself together, but the smile he gave her wasn't playful. Whatever he meant tonight to be for her, it was serious for him. "Think of this as a bonus." He ran his palm up the back of her thigh, cupping her buttocks in his hand and squeezing the muscle. "This is my appetizer, not yours."

Ruby scrambled away from the emotion in his voice, climbing on the bed with as much energy as she could muster, trying to get the lightness back. By his half smile, he knew what she was up to. She scooted up against the headboard and looked over at him, realizing all of a sudden that she was very naked and he was very not. She shoved her feet under the sheets and kept her legs together. It took all her self-control not to cross her arms over her chest.

"Self-conscious all of a sudden?"

"Only one of us is naked!"

"And we're going to stay that way."

"You could at least take off your shirt." She was exposed and vulnerable, the stale hotel air cold on her body.

The smile of pure sin and pleasure was back on his lips. "Our bargain at the track worked so well, I'm willing to try another one. I'll raise my shirt an inch for every inch you open your legs."

"Like the bargain at the track, I'm destined to lose." But she put an inch between her ankle bones. "It should at least be half an inch to an inch. You have farther to go than I do."

"I know. But I'll take that movement as acceptance of the bargain."

One glimpse of skin between his pants and his shirt and Ruby no longer had the patience for this game. She opened her legs as wide as they would go, clenching against the rush of cold air between her thighs. Micah would be there. Soon.

Anticipation made the time between Micah removing his shirt and him placing his hot, moist mouth against her feel like an eternity. Cold against the outside of her legs. Hot Micah along the inside. The combination was exquisite. With his lips pressed against hers, he hummed, so softly that she could barely hear him, though she could feel the vibrations all the way from her head to her toes. All the hairs on her body answered his call.

Then he got to work, his strong fingers moving in concert to create pleasure in her body. Ruby angled her pelvis toward him for better access, her head falling back into her pillow, her body tense and relaxed all at the same time. The movement lifted her breasts up to the air, and he cupped one in his palm, his thumb flicking her nipple at the same tempo his tongue flicked her clitoris.

She needed to be closer to him. She pushed her hips forward. To his mouth, his tongue, his hands and to him. Micah. He was drawing every last bit of energy down to her pussy and concentrating it there as he sucked. Ruby's muscles might still be fatigued, but any soreness was overshadowed by the pleasure shooting up her spine with each lick. Her fingers crawled down the sheets, clutching the cotton. Holding on before she drifted off into space.

Micah walked on his hands up from her pelvis, holding on to her hip and squeezing, just slightly. His grip was strong and firm, and his fingers pressed a magic button in her belly she hadn't even known was there. Her abductor muscles flexed around his head in response and he chuckled, which only made her thighs grip harder. *Keep him there doing that,* her body screamed. She moved her hands from the sheets to his shoulder, clasping on to him for fear he'd disappear on her. Or that she might float away and disappear on him.

Finally, as it seemed her body might curl up inside itself—her extremities drained of all feeling because her energy was concentrated in a couple square inches near Micah's tongue—everything released in a bang and she cried out. He didn't stop his attentions, even as the waves of pleasure washed over her. Only when her soul returned to her body and her limbs weighted themselves into the mattress did Micah pull away.

"Good?" he asked.

"Great." She looked down the long line of her body to see his face propped up on his hands above her pubic hair.

"Is your mind as relaxed as your body? Because that was part of the goal."

She lay still, waiting for her mind to send signals in and around her body to move. The signals never came. Stillness washed over her and she sunk farther into the mattress. "I may never move again. That was better than a bath with Epsom salts."

Hovering at the edge of her silent mind, not quite willing to intrude but making sure she knew he was there, was the knowledge that she would wake up in the morning and wonder what she had been thinking, letting herself be open and vulnerable to Micah. But she shut the door on those darker thoughts now and released herself into the moment. She closed her eyes. The bed shifted as Micah moved off it.

Somewhere outside herself, Ruby heard Micah's voice ask, "Can I sleep over?" and she was aware enough to scoot to one side of the mattress to make room for him. Any consciousness beyond that moment was gone.

MICAH CRAWLED OUT of bed and headed for the bathroom, the doorway just barely big enough to get his chair through. Unfortunately, the space was definitely not big enough for him to shut the door. He didn't have his toothbrush and he didn't want to go to his room to get it, so he settled for using some of Ruby's mouthwash. For a brief moment he considered waking Ruby so that she could brush her teeth, but by the soft snores coming from the bed, that was probably a lost cause. They would both have one-night-stand breath in the morning and could fix it then, though the addition of cheap hotel room coffee wouldn't help. But she'd be awake for him to kiss her, which was a plus.

Was this a one-night stand? That was the question of the hour. He had meant it when he'd said that seeing her banged up had been one of the scariest moments of his life that he could remember. And at that moment, he'd thought, *If I don't do something about this now, I may never have the chance.* That had been an easy thing to say in the heat of the moment, or even a couple hours afterward while holed up in a dark hotel room sharing spicy pizza and hot looks.

Tomorrow morning would be a whole different story.

And, of course, there was the question of Ruby's feelings. No matter that she'd been absent from competition for five years, she was still an elite athlete, and there was a self-centeredness that elite athletes couldn't help. Accepting a one-sided intimacy for a little deeper sleep after a hard competition was one thing. Returning his affections was another. But begrudging her the selfishness would be like begrudging a cat for stalking laps.

Regardless, he still wanted to know. If he were to do it all again, well… Looking back on the what-ifs of life was self-defeating at best and dooming at worst. He'd risked his career for this one night, whatever the consequences. He would know what it felt like to be between her legs, and men had risked more than a job for that kind of knowledge of a woman.

Shaking those thoughts from his head, Micah finished getting ready for the night and then rolled his way back to the bed. Ruby's initial acquiescence had ended, and she was again sprawled out over the entire mattress. He gave her leg a tap and she scootched over to one side of the mattress, though she left free the side of the bed that would be hardest for him to get to. Since she'd proved to be malleable once, he gave the other side of her leg a tap, this time a little harder. She snorted, shimmied a bit under the covers, then moved over to the opposite side of the bed, leaving her hand in his way.

And he didn't begrudge the hand any more than he begrudged her selfishness, because when he climbed into bed, she used the arm to pull him closer.

THE NEXT MORNING, after Micah and Ruby had been able to ignore the lingering implications of the night because of late sleeping, quick packing and cowardliness on both their parts, Micah and Amir waited next to the production van while Ruby drove out of the parking lot. As soon as her brake lights released and she pulled onto the road, Amir smacked Micah on the shoulder, exclaiming, "What the fuck were you thinking?"

"How do you mean?"

"How do I mean?" Amir mocked. For a small man, he packed a lot of sarcasm. "I came by your room last night to show you the cuts and you didn't answer. Were you in the bathroom?" He shrugged. "Maybe, but I've been the photog assigned to you for most of your career, and this is the first time you've shown up at the hotel breakfast not showered and not wearing a fresh shirt. So I'm asking again, what the fuck were you thinking?"

The same thing every heterosexual man is thinking when confronted with the naked body of the woman he loves. "Are you going to rat me out?"

"And risk being assigned to King Ripley for the rest of this story? Not on your life. But you should turn yourself in and see if you can save your job."

Micah looked in the direction of Ruby's car, but it was far gone. So, the morning after, the status of their relationship was still unsettled. He rubbed his face against the reality glaring at him through the dull autumn sunlight and waited for regret.

It never came. And that fact was as frightening as it was exhilarating.

CHAPTER TWENTY-FIVE

As MICAH DROVE past his apartment building the next evening, he was pretty sure he spotted Ruby's car sitting on the street. He pulled into the cavernous parking garage, took the elevator up to the lobby instead of his floor and rolled his way onto the sidewalk. It was Ruby's car. She was in it, tapping her fingers on the steering wheel and looking around.

He rolled over to the passenger-side window, and she jumped at his knock before rolling down the window.

"Are you looking for me, Ruby?"

"Yes. Well, specifically right now I'm looking for parking. But then I was going to look for you."

Micah didn't know what he had been hoping for today—or even what he might be hoping for tomorrow, or next week, or next month or next year For one of the few times in his life, he'd made a rash decision based on immediate gratification. Even if he wanted something long-term with Ruby, Amir wasn't the only one hoping King didn't get any closer to the ultra series than spectator. Micah's father had said he would either have to choose Ruby or his career, or fight for both. Right now, Micah was fighting for both.

"What can I help you with?"

"Well, I'm not supposed to pick Dotty up until tomorrow morning and that house is empty without my dog. I was thinking…well, maybe we could get some dinner?"

"Do you mean go out?"

She shrugged. "Or we can stay in. Whatever requires less movement would be better for me, but I'm the one surprising you, so you can pick. Or not. You might be busy." Her lips twisted with uncertainty. "That didn't occur to me."

Ruby may have grown a lot over the past five years, but the coddled, expectant athlete was still inside her. Not that he could blame her. An intense focus on herself had been required to get to the Olympics, doping or no doping. It was probably a part of her personality that would never go away, and everyone close to her would have to learn to deal with it if they couldn't learn to admire the power that came out of it.

"I can go," she said, misinterpreting his thinking as a polite refusal.

"No. I'll get you a visitor's parking pass. Be right back."

He returned from the lobby with a parking pass. "I'll meet you there," he said, hoping he had enough time to double-check that his apartment wasn't a complete disaster. He should at least be able to pick up the clothes off the floor.

When his doorbell rang, he opened the door to find Ruby standing on the other side. The jeans and slick track jacket she wore weren't nearly warm enough for tonight's forecast. She moved gingerly as she stepped into the foyer and looked around. Then she spied the recliner and her shoulders dropped from around her ears.

"Can I?" she asked, her eye on the chair.

"Sure. Would you like something to drink?" He still wasn't sure why she was here. If his read on her was correct, she wasn't sure why she was here, either.

"Yes, please." She put her hands on the armrests and was pushing herself out of the chair when he waved her away. "Thanks." She closed her eyes and became absolutely still, her body melting into the cushions of the chair. "I'm sure it's rude of me to invite myself over to your apartment, take the most comfortable chair and then make you get me a drink, but I'll get the next."

Sure you will, Micah thought but didn't say. He returned with a tray of drinks, including water and beer for both of them. She perked up immediately at the sight of the beer. Even though she continued to not move, her body seemed to have more life in it.

"I was more awake when I came up with the idea to come over here. This chair is really comfortable."

"I know." Its knobbly fabric massaged sore muscles, and it had a perfect view of his television. "Ruby, why are you here?"

"I didn't get to see the clip last night."

"No. You fell asleep before your spot was on." Micah had turned the television on for a couple hours after Ruby had fallen asleep. She hadn't even twitched at the noise.

"I thought maybe we could watch it together." Her pink lips twitched from side to side, and he only now noticed how bow-shaped her upper lip was. "If you don't mind watching it again."

She was lonely, he realized. He'd known she was lonely before, but this was the first time she'd sought out his attentions. Wanting her, respecting her, realizing that he loved her didn't stop him from wondering if she was here because...hey, any port in a storm.

"The clip's probably on YouTube. You could've watched it at home."

"Yeah, but..."

Micah only raised his brow. He was going to make her say it. No use risking his career on ethical charges to be nothing more than a convenient warm body.

"I'm tired. I'll be tired no matter where I sit, but last night, being tired with you was better."

"Me or…"

Confusion overrode the exhaustion on her face for a moment before she figured out what he meant. "You. I'll grant that I don't have many friends, but I'm sure I could find someone to celebrate with me tonight. People love spending time with someone they can say is a winner. I'm over here because I wanted to spend time with *you*."

"Okay."

"Okay?"

"Sure. You're still suspicious enough of my motives not to say something like that unless you mean it." The realization that he was more than simple company stroked his ego, and he reevaluated the entire night ahead of them. Ruby really was here for him as much as for herself. The night could turn very interesting if he let it.

As FAR AS Ruby could tell, the one good thing about recovering from an ultramarathon was that she was too tired to show how awkward and embarrassed she felt sitting in Micah's armchair with him looking at her and clearly trying to figure out what she was doing here. If he figured it out, she hoped he'd tell her. Thinking to herself "it seemed like a good idea at the time" didn't actually clarify what the good idea had been or why.

Plus, the chair was comfortable and Micah knew enough about ultra running not to expect much out of her the day after a big race. She'd considered going over to Haley's house or calling Josh to see if he wanted dinner, but she'd dismissed those ideas as quickly as they'd come. Both Haley and Josh would expect movement out of her, and she had to save everything she had to pick up her hyperactive dog tomorrow morning. But that reasoning sold Micah—and the feelings Ruby had for him—short. When she said she was here because she wanted to be around *him,* she meant it. Anywhere he was, Ruby Heart could just *be.*

"You make me feel like a whole person, not Ruby the athlete or Ruby the cheater or any of the other bits and pieces of me that people see instead of the whole. And I like that."

And he made her laugh. And he thought she looked hot when she did squats, and he looked hot doing preacher curls. Smart, driven, independent and not afraid to call her a self-centered idiot when she was being one. What more could she want out of a guy?

Probably one who didn't say "conflict of interest" every time their relationship teetered into something more than friends. And even that wasn't so bad, because she admired someone who made the right decision, even if she wasn't crazy about the decision.

Though last night their relationship *had* taken a nosedive out of the friend category, and neither of them had wanted to face that fact in the morning. She still didn't want to face the consequences, wishing instead that they could be back in a cheap hotel room, far away from any barriers to *more than friends.*

"So dinner out or dinner in?" Micah asked, pleasure setting the warm tones of his voice on fire. His change of subject was fine. Ruby didn't think she'd be comfortable baring any more of herself. Not yet. When she opened her eyes, he was looking at her with a slight smile on his face, his dimples barely visible in his cheeks. "Looking at you, I'm thinking in," he said. "What would you like?"

"I picked last night."

"No complaints about what I pick, then."

Ruby eased her head to the left, then slowly lifted her eyebrows. "Does it look as if I'm going to complain?"

"Good point."

She was dozing when he returned.

"Did you come over here to sleep?" he asked with a smile in his voice. He parked his chair next to the couch, and with interest she watched him maneuver from his chair to the couch.

She liked seeing his body move. She liked watching bodies move and muscles interact in general, but both Micah's limitations and his athleticism made his body all the more interesting. Like the way he controlled the swing of his legs by the movements of his upper body—and how he made it look effortless and an everyday occurrence. Which, she reminded herself, it was for him. To be too impressed—to focus on him being unusual—was to miss the point that this was his life and he was going about it. He winked; she'd been caught staring again.

"*No,* I didn't just come here to sleep. I'll perk up with a little food." She scooted up higher in the recliner, as if her sitting position would emphasize her point.

"I'll turn on the race interview and you can doze through that for a second time." She cocked her head at him in confusion and he laughed. "Last night, I watched some television after you fell asleep. Come sit by me." He patted the cushion beside him. "Tonight's TV options will be more exciting."

"Okay. I promise to stay awake through something more exciting."

"If you're really good, maybe we can up the excitement level even more."

"A board game?"

"That's not really what I had in mind."

CHAPTER TWENTY-SIX

IT BECAME CLEAR to Micah that he may have had all sorts of interesting ideas in mind, but Ruby wasn't going to be able to participate in any of them. She stayed awake as they watched the interview about her assault, but she moved through the air in his apartment with the dogged determination of someone trying to trudge through waist-deep mud. They could have a repeat performance of last night, but if Micah was going to risk his career again, he wanted Ruby able to participate. When he'd suggested they go to bed, she hadn't argued.

Once on the bed, Micah lowered his shoulder and lifted his head so he could kiss Ruby softly on her lips before she tucked herself into the crook of his arm. The bed creaked as she rolled over onto her side, throwing her arm around him and shifting it to find her most comfortable spot. Her arm started as a heavy weight between his collarbone and his nipples, changed to a bare tingle and then disappeared.

In the ten years since his accident, he had become accustomed to many things. He didn't wonder "what if," because what-ifs had always driven him mad. Better to push forward than to look back. But he remembered the feeling of sharing a bed with someone and being aware of them along the whole length of your body. Sometimes it was a spark, sometimes it was a warmth and sometimes it was softness. He had liked it best when it was all three.

"You're so quiet all of a sudden." Ruby's voice was soft next to him.

"I thought you wanted to sleep."

"That's not why you're quiet."

Was she going to ask the dreaded question?

"What are you thinking?"

Apparently she was and she did. He'd promised to be honest with her. "It has been a long time since I shared a night's sleep with a girlfriend."

She started moving her hand up and down the side of his body. Feeling. Silence. Feeling. Silence. Then she drew her hand across his nipples and they hardened. Strangely, he missed her hand across his stomach. He might not be able to feel her hand there, but that part of his body wasn't dead. It deserved Ruby's attention as much as the rest of him did.

"Really? How long has it been?" Her fingernails trailed patterns across his pectoral muscles, twirling around in his chest hair. All innocent and guileless. Like the old Ruby, only he knew them both better now.

"Are we really going to talk about this?"

"I'm sorry. I guess I feel like you've seen all my dirty laundry. Even helped me pack it up and move it to a new house." He stopped her before she could pull her hand away. "I want to know about yours."

"My last serious girlfriend was two years ago. We dated for six months and were talking about moving in together when it ended."

"What happened?"

"Do you really want to know all this? Now?" He'd had

many awkward conversations with women while lying in bed, but this beat them all. Most women seemed to know what was and what wasn't appropriate pillow talk.

"I like to know my competition."

Most women were not Ruby Heart.

"She says she left because I worked too much, but I don't know if it would have lasted much longer, despite our attempts to salvage it. She never really stopped seeing me as her disabled boyfriend. She couldn't see me as simply her boyfriend. It got old."

"That's funny. I'm always afraid most men will see me as Ruby Heart, some speedy, doped-up freak. And yet the first man I end up in bed with in five years—"

She hadn't had sex in five years?

"—sees me *only* as Ruby Heart."

"Ruby's not so bad." He pulled a hand out from between them, running it down the length of his own body until he could maneuver it to her leg. "She's got a lot of fight left in her, and she's got great legs—I've always been a leg man." He squeezed her thigh. One bonus about being in bed with an athlete was that he never had to wonder if he was touching his leg or hers. His leg muscles hadn't been that solid in a decade. Her quads twitched. Power pulsed under his hand.

"I wondered if I would ever be able to see you as anyone other than the man who defeated me. I hate to lose, you know."

"I am aware."

"Do you miss it?"

Micah bristled. He didn't ask what *it* was. *It* was only ever one thing. This conversation was usually a prelude to some comment about how his body was less than, or wondering if he ever thought about suicide, or if he could have his legs back or a billion dollars which would he choose. No one who asked this conversation could stretch their imagination far enough to see that his life was pretty damn good, thank you very much. They never realized how their offensive and intrusive questions suggested they pitied him enough that they would rather be dead if in his situation.

He didn't expect to be lying in bed next to Ruby when she disappointed him by falling into the question trap. He'd thought they'd made it past this. But he was tired, she was warm and her thigh muscle under his hand was an object of beauty, so he kept his calm when he said, "Why do you ask?"

"I've only ever been appreciated for my body and what it could do. When I was on the cover of *Time,* I mistakenly thought, 'Oh, how nice. Someone is interested in me.' But being America's Darling was never about people being interested in me as a person. They weren't even interested in the runner so much as the body. Like, no one ever asked me what my favorite book was."

She said the last sentence with such sadness that Micah winced. He'd been as guilty as every other person. He assumed she *could* read, but he didn't assume she *did* read. And he should know better than to stereotype an athlete, though it hadn't been her athleticism that led him to underestimate her. She'd had, and still had, a lightness about her that he didn't associate with someone who spent their free time reading.

And again, he was judging her.

"Yeah, what does the great Ruby Heart read anyway?"

"British Victorian literature." His body must have given away his shock because she laughed. "No one ever remembers that I was an English major. I got C's, but I was still an English major."

The tips of her fingers tickled as she trailed them along

the inside of his arm and to his armpit. His body was so heavy with relaxation he felt he could sink through his bed, through the floor and into the apartment below. Hypnotized by her touch.

"I used to wonder what it would be like to be introduced at a party as 'Ruby Heart, the great chess player' or 'Ruby Heart, librarian.' Or really anything that suggested I possessed a gift other than my two legs. I just wonder if you miss not being defined by your body."

Micah had no idea what to make of this. "When I played quarterback, I was also defined by my body. I'm no longer revered for my body, but my other talents are still ignored by those too ignorant to see past the functionality of my legs. So *how* I'm judged has changed, but I don't miss it. I worked hard for my life and I wouldn't trade it." Other possibilities to her question suggested themselves. "Are you saying you're jealous of people less talented than you? Because that's nuts."

Her wandering fingers stopped at the crook of his elbow and she seemed to think for a minute. "No. Jealousy implies some desire to trade places. And I don't want to do that."

"I can tell you for certain that a spinal cord injury only increases people's interest in your body."

This time her fingers skipped a beat before starting their route around his arm again. "Like I'm doing to you. Although," she said, and giggled, "I am interested in your body for other reasons, too."

"Quite." The last lingering bit of tension in his shoulders drained away. "And, for your information, I like to read true stories of the feats of man. Shackleton's adventures in Antarctica. The climbing of Mount Everest. Stuff like that."

"Man versus nature." Again he must have twitched with surprise because she said, "Hey, I said I was an English major. I was a C student because I had more important things on my mind than studying, not because I didn't like the subject."

Again he was confusing naive with simple and stereotyping where he shouldn't. He knew as well as anyone that no one expected the pretty-boy quarterback to study either, but he'd gotten his master's degree, and everyone, including himself, had forgotten that he was supposed to be stupid. "I'm sorry. You're right. I did make judgments when I shouldn't. I think of the books as man versus nature, man versus self and man versus man all rolled into one. That's part of their appeal."

She kissed his shoulder. "I forgive you for making judgments. You have had so little good of me to go on."

"Is that what you think of yourself?"

"I was only ever valued for my running. When I threw that away, I didn't have anything left. Even now I'm only able to make a new life for myself by running." Despite the snuggles and the warmth of the bed, he heard bitterness in her voice. "Any personal training job I ever get is going to be about me the runner and not me the person."

"Why don't you own it?"

"Excuse me?"

"What's stopping you from winning one of those ultra-marathons?"

She pulled back from him and cooler air rushed in to fill the void. "Can you imagine what would happen if I won?"

"You would be the comeback story of the year."

"Women don't get comeback stories. Once they fall, they fall. So long as I was America's Darling, being competitive was acceptable. Being America's Doping Case, anything I do for the rest of my life is suspect." She sighed. "I'm not blaming anyone but myself for that. Many roads and many people led me to doping, but I'm ultimately responsible for saying yes."

"How do you handle it?"

"Handle what?"

"I've not only seen you run, but I've lost to you at board games. You're a competitive person, and yet when you step up to that start line at the races, you do so planning to lose."

"I finish the race and my times keep improving. That's not losing."

"Do you try to win?"

"I'm not a masochist."

Knowing what ultramarathons did to the mind and body of the runner, Micah doubted this statement. But she was referring to her fear of being in the public spotlight again, not the physical toll of the sport on her body. Ruby was an athlete and would think nothing of pushing her body to its limit. "You should go for it. We both know you would have a chance."

"I can't do what you do. I can't look at the world and see anything other than walls."

Now it was his turn to be offended. "You think it's easy for me to scale walls? That I just use my massive wheelchair arm strength to pull myself over heights on a rope?"

"That's not what I…"

"Lying in a hospital bed ten years ago, I had to make a decision." His jaw tensed with disappointment and it was hard for him to get out the rest of the words. "I could either look back on what had happened or I could go forward with what had changed. I decided to go forward. You're still looking back."

"But when you do look back, what do you see?"

He wanted to get in his chair and roll away from her

question, but he didn't run from challenges—either figuratively or literally.

"That was another life, in another body. I got a spinal cord injury that left me paralyzed from the nipples down. Everyone sees that injury as a tragedy, but my former teammates have had their heads bashed in week in and week out. When I'm fifty, I won't be able to walk, but I'll be independent—they might be in a nursing home." He took a deep breath. "So when I look back and then look forward to that other life—which is what you're really asking about—I don't necessarily see glory and the good life. Changing one small decision, taking one different step that day, doesn't mean my life would have been better in that other future. It is what it is and you go on with it."

"I can't help but think I would have that gold medal."

"Does it ever occur to you that without the blood doping, you might not have won?"

"No."

Her unencumbered honesty and self-confidence surprised a snort out of him. "No?"

"I was the best middle-distance runner in the world. Bar none."

"Why did you do it?"

"I didn't think it was a big deal. I had hair out of a bottle. I either wore sports bras or push-up bras—no one ever saw my real tits. Fake eyelashes and fake lips. What was someone else's blood?"

"And the real you?"

"The real me is here in bed with you right now."

"Does the real you think of winning?"

"All the time. But I'm not sure the real me deserves it. When will I have repented enough?"

They were back to that question of forgiveness. The one

that had haunted their first dinner together and never left
Ruby's shoulder. If forgiveness danced on her right shoul-
der, what devil danced on her left? Responsibility? Regret?
Shame?

He reached an arm around to pull her so that she snuggled against him, then kissed the top of her head and her
real, mousy-brown hair that was luscious in the morning,
stringy by the evening and always smelled a little salty from
sweat. He supposed perfect, wavy locks of hair were important to some men, but he'd always been a leg man. And
the strength in her thighs was all her own.

"Do you have to know the answer to that question now,
Ruby?"

"No, I guess not."

"Good, because I'm tired now and would like to fall
asleep. You'd probably think it rude if I fell asleep while
you were still talking. Besides, I thought you were too tired
for anything more active."

In the dim light through the window, he could see her
head tilt up. He angled his face down to meet her lips and
indulged in the kind of luxurious, long, good-night kiss
one only gets when you know the person will also be there
when you wake up.

She shifted against him, his pillow collapsing and rising
as she moved. When her breathing became slow and steady,
Micah sighed and stared at the ceiling. By encouraging
Ruby to fall asleep so he could think, he'd told his first lie.

CHAPTER TWENTY-SEVEN

MICAH LAY IN his bed, wide-awake and haunted by the idea of repentance and forgiveness. He had no answers. The questions Ruby asked were not the same questions he asked of himself, but they had been asked of him. For the month he had been in the hospital, Dominick Carter's name had been conspicuously absent from conversation when other players visited him. In the rehabilitation hospital that followed, only the shrink had been willing to mention Nick's name. No one thought Micah should see the footage of the tackle that forever split his life into pre and post. The shrink had wanted to talk about his *feelings* without ever giving him a context for those feelings.

His father had finally snuck the footage in. Every night for a week Micah waited until the last check, opened up his laptop and watched the tackle until he couldn't keep his eyes open. He measured the distance between steps, the number of steps, the dart to the right, Nick's arm position, *his* arm position. Micah memorized each movement in such detail and with such precision that he could have drawn a cartoon. Right leg, there. Left knee bent at a twenty-degree angle. Right hip forward. Back arched.

Boom! Nick was a solid defensive tackle who, for the first and only time in his career, had made a late and high hit. Micah was lucky, they said, that his back had broken and not his neck. It could have so easily been his neck. And if it had been his neck, Micah might not be lying here in bed with Ruby. He definitely wouldn't be able to put his arm around her without help. Able to feel her hair tickle his chest and the soft puffs of her breath across his shoulders.

One inch. Millimeter even, together with the pads, made the difference between minor injury, paraplegia and quadriplegia. And Micah could have placed his body an inch differently. The late hit was all Nick, but that inch... They shared that inch.

Once Micah had realized that, forgiveness was easy.

The concepts of restitution and redemption had been harder on both of them. When Nick had finally worked up the courage to see Micah, once Micah had moved out of the rehabilitation hospital and into his father's apartment, Nick had prostrated himself at Micah's feet for forgiveness. Easy. But Nick couldn't accept a handshake and a "don't worry about it, man," and then move on to talking about the next game. He circled around and around his own guilt until he was a large black vulture riding the air currents. And Micah wasn't carrion.

Eventually Micah had been "busy" whenever Nick wanted to come over and flagellate himself on Micah's behalf. Then Micah had gone to graduate school, gotten his job at NSN and moved on with his life. Nick still played, but the aggressiveness that had made his career was gone.

Forgiveness had come so naturally to Micah that Nick's restitution or repentance had never been an issue for him. And so it was the only issue for Nick.

Was Ruby Nick, or was she Micah? Probably both and neither at the same time.

The sporting world had been out for her blood. The networks, the magazines, the gear companies—none of them stopped to consider that she'd made them millions and all it had cost her was a life. Maybe it took a person examining their own culpability before offering forgiveness. Maybe forgiveness meant only that a person turned their head to face them back. The former was something Ruby was never going to get from the American public; the latter was still possible.

The ends of Micah's fingers began to tingle, so he shifted Ruby's head on his arms a little. She gave a soft, warm sigh and snuggled closer to him, using his chest as a pillow. With the extra freedom in his arm, he traced the angle of her spine as far down her back as he could, not quite able to reach the curve of her butt. Her knees were probably butted up against his thighs down in the silence. He liked to think his legs enjoyed the sensation.

She stirred more in her sleep, let out a couple hard snorts and then settled down again. The embargo of information between his brain and his legs meant that if she were a kicker, he'd never know. Though, because it was Ruby, she would probably leave bruises. He wrapped his arm more tightly around her, enjoying her warmth. Any more thoughts he had on Ruby could wait until morning. It had been over a year since he'd shared a bed with a woman, and he was going to eke every last bit of enjoyable sleep out of it.

RUBY WOKE UP the next morning to the smell of bacon and pancakes, with a second note of coffee in the air. She stretched her arms above her head, luxuriating in the comfortable bed, slick sheets and the warmth Micah had left behind. The coffee was inviting, but she pulled her hands back under the sheets anyway and turned over onto her side. Two days ago, she'd run fifty miles. She could laze in bed and let a handsome man bring her breakfast in bed. Or at least a cup of coffee.

Every muscle in her body was tired. The muscles that weren't tired were sore and would be tired tomorrow. Skipping any aerobic activity last night had been a good idea. Probably also this morning. She needed to conserve energy so she could actively participate next time.

She closed her eyes until she heard the sound of Micah rolling down the hall and into the bedroom. When she could feel him in front of the bed, she eased her eyes open and looked into his warm blue eyes. Balanced on his lap was a wooden tray, and on top of that tray sat a steaming cup of coffee and a plate brimming with food. She counted six pancakes in the stack and an equal number of pieces of bacon. She assumed one of the little pitchers had cream and she hoped the other had real syrup.

"Are you going to sit up so I can put your food on your lap?"

"Yes!" Her stomach muscles protested her attempt to scramble up in bed. Chastened by how quickly steady soreness had turned into pain, she eased herself up into a sitting position.

"Thank you for the food." The tray pressed down on her legs. Her thighs weren't a fan of the weight pinning her to the bed, but she ignored them. Her stomach's loud growls took precedence, silencing even the aches in her abdominal muscles.

"There's more where that came from."

She'd eaten after the race and yesterday, more because she knew she had to than because she'd been hungry. The mental, physical and emotional strain of the race had over-whelmed all other bodily urges. The only thing she'd felt hungry for at the time had been Micah's touch, and she felt she'd only been able to handle that because he'd done all the work. This morning, she was ravenous.

"Thank you for everything. For the help at the race, the breakfast and taking such good care of me."

"If you're talking about your orgasms, you're welcome." Then he smiled and put the late-morning sun shining through the curtains to shame. He cocked his head and ex-amined her from head to toe. The T-shirt of Micah's that she wore and the thick sheets covering her weren't enough to shield her from the heat of his eyes on every inch of her skin. The warmth in her blood relaxed some of her most tense muscles when she blushed.

"You're welcome for the rest of it, as well. We could do it again. I can take the tray back to the kitchen and be back here in a flash."

Maybe a morning of sex wouldn't be such a bad idea after all. She lifted up the tray to hand back to him and nearly dropped it. Not only were her arms tired, but her hands were feeling the effects of holding them in a fist for seven hours, even if they had been loose fists. A little cream had spilled out of one pitcher onto the tray and syrup was drip-ping from the other. Looking down at the mess, she couldn't help but laugh as she put the tray back on her lap. "Give me at least a couple hours, unless the idea is that I lie back and possibly fall asleep."

He laughed. "That sounded okay, except for the fall-asleep part. Eat your breakfast. We have time."

She crumbled the bacon into pieces over the stack of pan-cakes, and she poured syrup over the whole plate. "I have to go get Dotty," she said before taking a bite. Salty-sweet and starchy goodness filled every corner of her mouth. She moaned.

"How are you going to keep her active enough while you're recovering?"

"My plan is to sit in a comfortable chair in the backyard with a beer and throw a tennis ball until my arm falls off. Unless you have another idea."

"If she'll stay with me, I can take her when I train."

"Oh, she's a good dog. She'll stay. Thank you."

"No problem, but I expect you to bring me breakfast in bed the morning after my next marathon."

"Deal." Micah's next marathon. Future plans. As though they were a real couple. The idea energized her more than any amount of coffee or sugary food could.

When he reached out to touch her face, the flirtation in his eyes turned to concern. She flinched before the pads of his fingers touched the road burn on her cheeks, and he pulled his hand back so that it hovered over her skin.

"How does it look?" she asked. Her skin itched as if she'd washed her face with poison ivy. The itch might be a sign she was healing, but it was more irritating than the aches in her muscles.

"Like shit, but I've seen worse."

"You've probably had worse."

"True. Though I didn't shake the cobwebs out of my head and run another twenty-five miles. That was hard-core, Ruby." Electricity buzzed between his hand and her skin as he moved his hand down the side of her body before his touch settled on her hip. If she was sore there, she didn't notice.

He cupped her hip bone in his fingers and gave a squeeze she felt deep in her core. It took her abdominals clenching in pain again to remind her why she was supposed to rest her body. He must have noticed, because he pulled his hand back to rest on his lap.

"I'll tell you what, you go get Dotty and give her as much exercise as you can. Take a shower, and I'll pick you up later. We can go to a movie. Then you can sit, fall asleep and we can pretend it was a date. Maybe dinner afterward?"

"Sounds perfect."

The glow of a good breakfast and a hot date to look forward to lasted until she drove out the parking garage and was blinded by the sun reflecting off paparazzi cameras. Digital cameras didn't make the snap that a film camera did, but she flinched anyway.

"Were you with Micah Blackwell?"

"Ruby, is Micah helping you challenge your Olympic ban?"

"The lawsuits, Ruby! Is Micah helping you settle the lawsuits?"

The questions blurred together in one long yell of what, who and how much. Because of course she should only want to spend the night with Micah if she was getting something out of it. Because she was Ruby Heart, runner, cheater, user and villain. And Micah was the man who'd called her out for it all.

She could retreat into the building and find sanctuary or she could roll up her window and drive past them like she hadn't done anything wrong. Because she hadn't.

But back at home she stepped out of the shower to find a message on her phone from Micah saying he'd been called into work, didn't know when he'd be done and he had to cancel their date. No matter how quickly she ran to edge past her crimes, the world and its punishments kept pace.

CHAPTER TWENTY-EIGHT

RUBY SAT ON her couch, petting Dotty and completely at a loss with what to do now that a date was no longer in her future. Anything strenuous in the next couple weeks might kill her recovery and make the one-hundred miler an impossibility. Sitting around wondering about the paparazzi was doing her no good, either.

Ruby got up off the couch and walked stiffly to the dining room and her laptop. She eased herself into a chair and started looking for the picture. One Google search was all it took to find the photo on a trashy internet gossip site. She may have felt euphoric as she left Micah's, but her face was scuffed up, she was hunching her sore muscles and her eyes were bloodshot. She looked like something the cat had chewed up and barfed out. The site made a brief mention of whose apartment building it was, referenced the interview from five years ago and took a swipe at Micah's disability that implied their relationship must be the most bizarre kind of twisted. Micah's natural charm was reimagined as a twisted ability to manipulate her into self-harm—the explanation for the road burn on her face, she assumed. She finally had some understanding how complicated people will make their thoughts to deny a disabled person agency. If the site wanted to hint that she had been abused, the simplest thing to do would be to accuse Micah of it, but they couldn't even grant him the power to do his own dirty work.

The author of the short paragraph really should be given some kind of writing prize, because he or she had crammed the motive for Micah's abuse into the small space, too. Micah, of course, was jealous that she had managed to come out of her suspension with her physical body intact. No mention was made about how he was a successful sports reporter for the largest sports network on the planet or how he competed in his own marathons. There was no discussion of how Micah had created a future for himself after his accident while Ruby had responded to her crimes with a self-imposed house arrest—or that maybe she might be jealous of *him*.

Ruby could walk. Micah could not. Obviously, the jealousy must only go one way.

She was angry. Micah would be furious.

Her phone rang and she answered without looking at the caller ID, expecting to hear Micah's voice on the other line. Instead, her mother's voice trembled out, "Will we have to go through this again?"

Ruby blinked, not believing what she was hearing. The photo had been taken a couple hours ago. She had just found it. How had her mother known to scour the internet for gossip? As far as Ruby knew, she hadn't made a gossip page in years and she thought her family had all canceled their Google alerts.

"Go through what?"

"Seeing pictures of you on the internet. Hearing people gossip about you at the salon? Your father's colleagues insinuating that we didn't teach you any morals."

You didn't teach me any morals. You taught me that running and winning made me special and you would only love me if I did those two things. She couldn't have that conversation over the phone. She was too exhausted to have that conversation at all.

"How did you find the picture?"

"Is it true?" Her mother's voice was so weak Ruby had to turn the volume up on her phone as high as it would go. "You and that reporter who ruined your life? Is it true?"

Ruby sighed. Exhaustion or not, the conversation needed to be had. "Mom, are you home? Is Dad home?"

"Your father is on the phone, trying to do damage control."

What damage had been done to her parents? This wasn't even about them. God, her mom hadn't even asked the essential question of whether or not the abuse allegation was true; she'd just complained that they would be humiliated at the office and the salon.

"Mom, I'm coming over. We need to talk."

"Do you need Josh to go there and help you pack?" Hope wavered through her mom's voice.

"I'm not moving back. I'm visiting. So we can talk. Dotty and I will be over shortly."

"You know your father doesn't like animals in the house."

"You have a patio. Wear a sweater." Ruby wasn't certain she could face this conversation without her dog's comforting chin resting on her knee. She would call Micah and ask for his support as well, but if her parents had heard about the photo, then surely NSN had heard about it, which explained why Micah had been called to the studio.

Ruby got Dotty into the car and, on the drive over, told her dog everything she was going to tell her parents. With her head almost completely out the back window, Dotty probably couldn't hear Ruby, though she wagged her tail when her name was said. And Dotty didn't disagree with Ruby, which was good enough for now.

Ruby parked her car by her parents' front door rather than pulling through to the garage. She didn't live here any longer and she didn't want her parents thinking she was considering a move back. She even rang the doorbell. The thick wood of the doors couldn't hide the way the ding echoed through the emotionally empty spaces and high ceilings. Despite the warning that Ruby was coming over, her mother looked shocked to open the door and find her daughter and her daughter's dog standing there.

Her mom looked down at Dotty, who looked up with her pink tongue out and her black eyes deep with love. The dog was going to be disappointed; this conversation wouldn't end in hugs and cookies. Dotty was still wagging her tail when Ruby's mom raised her gaze from the dog to Ruby's face and opened her mouth in shock.

When several seconds had gone by in silence, Ruby said, "I can take the dog through the back gate."

"What happened to your face?"

"I was pushed, and *not*—" Ruby rushed to clarify before her mother could accuse Micah "—by the reporter. Can we sit down? I wasn't kidding when I said we need to talk."

Her mom stepped back, and Ruby unhooked Dotty from her leash as soon as the dog's nails clicked on the white marble floor.

"The dog..." her mom started.

"Is as well trained as I ever was. She'll stay by my side unless told otherwise."

Her mom nodded. "Your father's waiting on the patio. He fixed us some drinks."

Her mom trembled as she walked past the expensive furnishings. For the first time in her life, Ruby was far enough removed to wonder at her parents' relationship. They had always seemed locked together on the same side of every memory in her childhood, though her mom provided the pull and her father the push. But as her mom glanced several times over her shoulder both at Dotty and at Ruby's face, Ruby wondered how much of the great plan of the Heart family had been ruled by her father, with her mother going along because it was easier that way. Ruby thought she saw curiosity about the dog in her mother's many glances, and maybe a hand twitch to touch Dotty's magnificent coat. But each time she thought she might have seen in her mother's movements a desire to break her father's rule about animals, her mom shook her head and faced resolutely forward.

Out on the patio, her father greeted her mother by giving her a tumbler of whiskey and placing a hand on her back. "When you told us about the interview with NSN, you promised we wouldn't have to go through this again," her father said, his only greeting for Ruby. "We shouldn't have given you permission to run again." They were much the same words her mother had said over the phone, only her father's voiced boomed where her mom's had quivered.

"I never agreed not to run." Another whiskey sat on the bar cart, presumably for her, though Ruby had never liked her alcohol neat. She poured herself a glass of water instead. "I agreed to abide by the terms of my suspension, which was full disclosure of what I knew about doping clinics that Coach was involved in, no participation in any athletic competition for five years and no participation in any competition related to the Olympics for the rest of my life. Until there is a 50K or 50-mile race in the Olympics, I have followed the terms to the letter. I haven't even signed up for a turkey trot."

"And what about your promise to your family?"

Ruby turned her attention away from the glass of water to look her father in the eyes. Her mother looked off to the side. Her father squared his shoulders and puffed his chest out into the wool of his sweater, clearly expecting his daughter to retreat. Ruby set her glass down and took a step forward instead.

"We remember the conversation differently, Dad. You said you never wanted to hear me speak of running again. And so I haven't. Not to you and not to Mom." Her father had probably also meant that she was never to run outside of the neighborhood, but he had obviously assumed she would obey the spirit of his law out of fear and that he didn't need to specify each letter. His mistake, not hers.

"Not only do you ignore the terms with which we had agreed to keep you under our roof, but you get yourself back into the spotlight. With the same reporter who ruined your career."

Her muscles ached to sit down and her knees might collapse on their own, but she remained standing. A hundred-mile race was waiting for her in the spring. She would stand during this confrontation with her parents, no matter how long it took.

"Make no mistake, Dad. I ruined my own career."

"Your coach…" her mom protested.

"My coach, the man Dad picked out and told me to obey, certainly led me to believe that doping was no big deal. And you and Dad taught me that I was only special as long as I was winning, but *I* was the one who agreed to have someone else's blood pumped into my body. Whatever the circumstances that created the opportunity for doping and led me to say yes, I still said yes. That responsibility lies with me. I own it and my guilt and my shame, and you can't take them away from me. But I won't let you use them against me anymore."

"I forbid you from running again."

"And I'm telling you that you don't get to dictate my life. Not whether I run and not who I spend time with." Like running fifty miles on already fatigued legs, saying those words exhausted her as well as filling her with a triumph that would keep her standing until the earth shook under her feet.

"My firm will stop defending the cases against you. We're close to settling such that you get to keep any money made before your second Olympic trials. If my firm pulls out, how do you think you'll find the money to pay back everything?"

"I can hope my memoir sells as well as my agent thinks it will," she lied.

Her parents' faces turned white against their matching navy sweaters. "You wouldn't!" her mom said, her voice as firm as Ruby had ever remembered it.

"I need money to live. As Dad said, I might need far more money in the near future."

"How could you do this to your family? Even if you hate your father and I—after all we've done for you—at least think of Josh and Roxanne."

Roxanne would again suffer through faculty parties where people asked more questions about her infamous sister than her research, but that wasn't under Ruby's control and she wasn't going to disappear for the sake of her sister's ego.

And Josh had always loved her no matter what. He would always love her no matter what. His love didn't come with a condition of good behavior. Hell, he hadn't even tried to define good behavior for her since the one disastrous time their parents had assigned him to babysit.

Then she softened the anger in her voice, because the people standing in front of her were still her parents. They had not always been there for her and had certainly failed her when she'd needed them most, but she couldn't let their failures define her future any more than she could let her own failures define her.

"The thing is, since it became clear that I had a gift, my running stopped being about me and started being about everyone else. I made you—" she nodded toward her mother "—the talk of everyone at the spa and you—" she nodded to her father "—the only man at the office with a daughter who was an Olympian."

The words sounded more selfish coming out of her mouth now than they had when she was driving over here and saying them to Dotty. People would argue that she had always been selfish, and they would be right. *No one* made it to the Olympics without sacrificing their friends and family to their dreams, and America's Darling had sacrificed more than most. But she had done it for the look of pride on her parents' faces and now she was doing it for herself. Embracing Ruby Heart, warts and all, meant embracing her gifts and her sins and recognizing that the same womb had birthed them both.

"And now I'm running for me. Because I can and I want to and I'm good at it and I like winning. I hope to win again. I will win again."

"The press will say terrible things about you."

"They have and, yes, they will. In a couple hours, that site you saw with my picture will be pages deep with comments, most of them wishing me harm." The knowledge of what people would say made her weak at the knees, but Ruby kept her joints locked. If she sat down, she might fall down. Weakness was not something she'd allow other people to witness, especially not now. Not until she could see Micah.

"And no matter how many drug tests I submit to and how open I am about my life and my training, some people will assume I'm only a success because I'm doping. And I can't do anything about them. But I can put one foot in front of the other and I can do it again and again and faster and faster until I cross that finish line. I can do it for me."

CHAPTER TWENTY-NINE

IF SHE'D EXPECTED her parents to clap after such a rousing speech of independence, she'd been mistaken. Despite repeatedly saying she was running and racing for herself, her mother took a sip of her drink, turned to her husband for reassurance—her father's slight nod was impossible to miss—then said, "It's this man, isn't it? This reporter whose apartment you were coming out of. He's somehow convinced you to feel sorry for him because of his accident."

Ruby might as well not have come over, except now at least she knew she'd said her piece to her parents and would make what she could out of the rest of her life. Hell, at least if she were talking to Dotty, the dog would wag her tail. Still, Ruby tried. "I know you can't believe it, but if anything, Micah feels sorry for me, not the other way around."

"Your face." It was his father's turn to show how little he'd listened to her. "Your face is a mess. Something clearly happened and I'll bet *that reporter* was involved."

Did her father even remember Micah's name, or was he only the disabled reporter on TV? The weak one he thought he could push around because Micah sat in a chair with wheels.

"Over the weekend, I went to Missouri and ran a fifty-mile trail race. Someone pushed me and I hit the asphalt pretty hard. I have worse scrapes on my legs and arms. Micah was at the race, but wasn't involved in the accident." She couldn't make the truth any clearer.

"See, we knew something like this would happen if you got back into sports. Didn't we, Dennis? We knew people would be jealous of her success and unable to let her participate fairly."

Who was she kidding? This conversation was already off track. "First of all, people aren't jealous of my success—they are pissed off because I *didn't* play fairly. I cheated!" A deep breath failed to calm her, though it did lower her voice. "That's the very point of why I was suspended. Second, being pushed was terrible. It hurt, and I don't like facing the world knowing that people might be out to get me. It's *scary.* But you know what? Living here and being afraid of my own shadow was worse. If something happens to me, it will be because I'm out doing something I love, not hiding in my own room afraid someone will jump out and say *boo.*"

She took another deep breath, both to calm herself and to calm Dotty, who had started licking her lips and panting. "Micah helped take care of me, Mom. He put Bactine on my scrapes and made sure I ate something even though I felt too exhausted to chew." She didn't mention his creativity in putting her to sleep. "Isn't that why you decide to be with someone? Besides their sense of humor or their intelligence or their good looks? When you're too worn down to take care of yourself, that special person will make you a cup of tea."

"It's all well and good for him to get you dinner, but can he provide for you?"

The scratches Ruby was giving Dotty's head sped up until she could probably produce fire behind the dog's ears. But Dotty didn't seem to mind, and it was better than shaking her hands up and down and yelling, *He's got a job! It's me who can't pull my own weight right now.*

Instead, she said, "I'm more worried about my ability to provide for myself, especially if Dad's firm does pull their support." Stab and twist. "In any case, Micah has been making a minidocumentary about me and my return to running. Up until last night, that's all our relationship was about. We have not talked about anything beyond who buys dinner, and I don't know that either of us is interested in that conversation yet."

"Can he provide... I mean, can he father children?" Her mom held her clutched hands together by her chin, almost in prayer.

"I don't know, Mom. I haven't asked him. When I do, I probably won't tell you about it. But that conversation is even further away than who buys the groceries. Can I just have this, for me? Running and a man in my life who seems to like me for me and not because I was America's Darling? Please?"

Both of her parents stood, their faces impassive, her mom's whiskey glistening over on the small table, her dad's warming as he clutched his tumbler in his hands. Neither of them had consumed more than a sip of their liquor. "It's not what we wanted for you," her mom said finally.

"I ruined what you wanted for me. And I ruined what I had wanted for myself. But that doesn't mean I can't want something new, nor does it mean that the new thing I want can't also be great. It means it's different, Mom."

"Josh and Christine are coming over for dinner. You could stay," her mom implored. "Maybe we can keep talking?"

"You need to think about what I said more than I need to say it again." And again and again. "I'm taking Dotty to the dog park for the remaining hour or so of daylight and throw the ball around until she's exhausted." *Or I fall over.* "I'll eat dinner at home."

CHAPTER THIRTY

WHEN MICAH HAD first gotten a call from Dexter to get his ass to the office immediately, he hadn't thought much of it; Dexter approached everything in the world from needing a cup of coffee to breaking sports news with the same urgency. Until he'd rolled into Dexter's office to find Dexter, the sports director and another executive producer all seated around Dexter's small table waiting for him. Micah squared his shoulders and rolled toward the table, the extra bulk of his chair forcing the three bigwigs to scoot closer together. They may have ambushed him, but he knew how to own a space, no matter whose space it was. Micah stuck his elbows out and laid his folded arms on the table, taking up even more space. Sports reporting was a battle of inches, much like football had been.

Dexter slid a piece of paper across the table. Micah stared at the expanse of white, then flipped the page over and stared some more. There was Ruby, leaving the parking garage of his apartment building.

"Where did you get this?" Micah asked.

"What's wrong with her?" Dexter asked.

Micah looked back down at the printout. The scrapes

on her face made it look like someone had rolled her along the asphalt, mostly because someone *had* tried to, not to mention that her face was long and worn. She looked like a survivor.

"She's fatigued from running fifty miles and scraped up because someone assaulted her along the trail, which you know because I did a segment on *SportsDaily* about it. Given all that, I think she looks pretty awesome." Even through her fatigue she'd cried out with pleasure at the movements of his tongue. Knowing that made her look even better.

"This is your apartment building?" the sports director and Micah's immediate boss asked.

"You know it is."

"What do you think this looks like from an outsider's point of view?"

Micah took another long look at the photo, this time evaluating the fatigue and exhaustion on Ruby's face without the knowledge that she'd competed yesterday. If he came across this image on Jezebel's Twitter feed, he would think the worst of the man whose apartment she was leaving.

But being pulled into Dexter's office for this interrogation was ridiculous. "You're not that stupid. And besides—" he was loath to admit the next part, but better said by him than one of the men at the table "—if people know it's my apartment, no one is going to believe *I'm* capable of abusing her. She's Ruby Heart and I'm in a wheelchair, for God's sake."

Whether or not he would be physically able to abuse a woman wasn't the issue, but much of the nondisabled world underestimated his ability to do great things, so surely they'd underestimate his ability to do evil, as well. Unless they thought he had minions in his apartment to perform his physical abuse for him.

"This isn't about the actuality of the thing but about its perception," Dexter said. His voice left no room for humor or Micah's frustrations. "Did you sleep with her?"

The full weight of what he'd sworn he wouldn't do crashed down on his shoulders. He'd avoided all physical contact with her because he knew a relationship with her would compromise his objectivity. When he'd seen her limp past the finish line, blood on her face, knees and arms, objectivity had been the least of his worries.

"It won't happen again," he said, knowing that promise wouldn't be enough, even if he could keep it.

Dexter's dreadlocks swung about his face as he shook his head. "It doesn't matter if it won't happen again. It matters that it happened this once and some parasite caught it on camera. We were asked to comment on whether we know that you were having a sexual affair with America's ex-darling and, if we did know, how long it had been going on."

Dread pooled in the base of Micah's throat. He'd gotten Ruby Heart into his bed, and it was going to cost him the making of his career. "Pulling the plug on the ultra series would be monumentally stupid. Especially after this photo and the assault piece, everyone who remembers her Olympic performances would tune in to watch the series, hardcore sports fans or not."

It was the sports director's turn in this tag team. "Micah, you mistake what is happening. We've already sunk a good deal of money into this series. And you're right, it's ratings gold. We're not pulling the feature. We're firing you."

His teeth ground together, and the only way to release the pressure would be to tip the table over and hope the men sitting across from him went down with it. Instead, he said, "Who are you giving the feature to?"

"King Ripley."

"Fuck no!" He brought his hands down hard on the top of the table and the trio of bosses flinched. "You know he'll mess this up. Ruby will come out of this with her reputation in worse shape than it already is."

"Objectivity, Micah," his boss said. "You lost it. King hasn't."

"King's a dick."

"Ah, but he's a dick who knew how to keep his in his pants."

"He has no respect for the sport you're asking him to cover. That's not the same as objectivity. I get that you're firing me, but at least give Ruby's story to someone else. Anyone else."

"You know as well as I do that it's not so much the actuality of objectivity that matters but the appearance of it," Dexter said. "We can all continue to pretend King's objective. There's no idiot on earth who will believe it of you."

Micah knew they were right. Just because they weren't covering wars and natural disasters didn't mean they didn't have to keep their noses clean. "I can freelance and write the script."

"If you'd wanted to stay involved in this series, you shouldn't have gotten involved with Ruby Heart. And if you wanted to keep your job, you should have pulled yourself from the story as soon as your objectivity was questionable. This is damage control."

He sank back in his chair, all the pressure of what he'd ruined both for himself and for Ruby pushing against his shoulders. "And all that footage I've gotten? The interviews we've done so far?"

"The footage is still good. King can redo the interviews after Ruby's final race. No matter the outcome, her words will have more meaning then. And he'll have time to pre-pare."

Eternity would not offer King enough time to pull his head out of his ass, even with the help of gallons of mayon-naise. But that wasn't Micah's problem any longer. It was NSN's problem when the series was a disaster. And Ruby's problem, because it was her life.

Which made it his problem again.

Micah backed away from the table and made his way to his office to pack up.

He'd get Amir to squirrel away the footage. Then he would go home and decide what to do next. Did he call Ruby? Could he call Ruby and keep the blame creating a bitter taste in his throat out of his voice?

A dangerous question he didn't know the answer to.

CHAPTER THIRTY-ONE

THE BOX FULL of stuff from Micah's office made the roll from the elevator to his apartment awkward. What was he going to do with all this crap? What was he going to do with himself? For as long as he could remember, he'd been pushing for the next and the biggest thing. Starting quarterback. College scholarship. NFL draft. The accident had only pointed the drive in a new direction.

Now what?

He was fumbling with the box and the keys to his apartment when the door opened and Ruby stood there. *You're going to have to tell her.* Light in the entryway highlighted Ruby against the darkening sky outside, but she didn't look happy. She looked as sad as he felt. They were both going to feel worse by the time the night was over.

"I hope you don't mind," she said, helping him with his coat, gloves and scarf. "The doorman let me in. I really needed to see you. I'm sure you heard about the paparazzi at your door. My parents found out about our relationship. I talked with them today. About my running. About us."

She was talking too much. He wanted to sit on the couch,

wrap his arms around her, smell her hair and be in a perfect moment, even if it was short-lived.

"They wondered if you hit me." Her voice followed him as he rolled to his recliner. "And they doubted your ability to take care of me. Can you believe them? My father told me his firm was dropping my lawsuits and they had the nerve to doubt how *you* would pay for a dinner out."

Micah didn't say anything as he swung himself into the recliner, letting go of all his energy and leaving no room for the angry, massive Ruby standing in front of him, hands on her hips and indignation in her eyes.

"I guess so long as I'm not doing their bidding, we'll never understand each other." God, she was even pacing. She was supposed to still be exhausted, not worked up even further.

"Maybe I will—"

"Ruby," he said.

"—sell my memoir, like I threatened to do."

"Ruby." He said her name louder this time.

"Though I'll need an agent. Can you help me find an agent?"

Now he had her attention on him because she needed something from him.

"Ruby, I was fired today."

"But what about the series?"

"That's it? I was fired and all you can ask about is the series?"

"I'm sorry you got fired." Her brows furrowed together and he was too angry to find it cute.

Instead, her expression infuriated him. "I'll bet you're sorry. King has control of the series now. And there goes your redemption story."

"You didn't..."

"Didn't what, Ruby? Was I supposed to be looking out for your reputation and that *fucking series* while I was packing up my office?"

By her expression, the answer was yes.

"You know what? I was an elite athlete in college, too. I should have known better than to get mixed up with one. All you can think about is yourself."

"I'm… I'm… I'm sorry. I didn't know. You didn't tell me."

"I didn't have a chance to tell you because the moment I rolled into *my* apartment, you started talking about *your* problems." He wanted to close his eyes and disappear. He wanted to launch himself at her in anger.

He wanted her gone.

"Worse than realizing I lost my job is realizing that I lost my job because of a woman who can't even see far enough past her own nose to ask how I'm doing."

"I'm just…"

"You're just not used to having to think about anyone else. All this talk of 'running for yourself' and 'living for yourself' is bullshit. You've only ever lived for yourself. And no matter what happens, Ruby Heart is the only person you'll ever live for."

She recoiled as if he'd hit her. "Let me help you."

Her offer was the last straw. "Get out."

"I have to be able to do something for you."

Micah scrambled out of his recliner, willing to drag her out if she didn't leave on her own. In his anger and exhaustion, he'd forgotten to set the brakes on his chair, and the chair slipped out from under him, leaving him grasping on to the arms of the recliner, his legs uselessly dragging on the ground and his chair out of reach unless he let go and crawled to it. Not in front of Ruby. He wouldn't be vulnerable in front of Ruby.

"Get out," he said again.

"Let me…"

"Ruby, what do you think your parents will say when the gossip sites report that I locked you out of my apartment? Or that the doorman had to call the cops? King couldn't redeem you after a story like that hits the papers, even if he wanted to."

She backed away from him, her tears running down her face in torrents that matched the gush of blood in his ears. "I would've asked how you were. I would have."

Micah had managed to set the brake on his chair and do the difficult transition of getting himself off the floor. He looked her in the eye, no longer the man begging at her feet. "You cost me my job, Ruby. Asking how I am doesn't matter anymore."

Clenching his jaw so hard his teeth hurt, Micah stared Ruby down until she backed up to the door and left. Running. Like the coward that she was.

ONLY WHEN RUBY got down to the parking garage did she realize that she'd played right into Micah's expectations of her. *You have to stop escaping your problems by running away.* Instead of getting out of the elevator, she pressed the button for Micah's floor. Her courage and stomach sank as she rose higher and higher into the air. And when the doors opened with a ding, she stepped onto the carpet in the hallway and dragged her feet to Micah's door.

He didn't answer her first knock. Or her second. She leaned her forehead against the wood, determined to say her piece, even if she spoke into emptiness.

"Micah, I'm sorry." The metal of the eyehole—at a useless height for Micah—dug into her skin, but she didn't move from her position. "You're right. I'm selfish. Narcissistic, even. I opened the door and I knew something was wrong with you. Knew, and I didn't ask what was wrong because I had stuff I wanted to talk about with you."

Still no answer, though she thought she felt him behind the door. Smelled him, even. Gym soap...and castor oil for his chair.

"I'm trying not to run away. I'm trying to learn." She tapped on the wood with her fingers. "Selfishness is who I am, but I love you. And I'm slowly learning not to see the world as my own little bubble because I want to. For you." The door tore into her fingernail as she scratched at it. "But for me, too."

She'd battered her heart and soul against the door. Now there was nothing to do but wait and hope he was on the other side. That he could hear her.

"Do you hear me, Micah? I was wrong. And I'm sorry."

The words hadn't worked when she'd said them to the American public on national TV, either. And still Ruby waited, her head pressed against the door until she either had to curl up and sleep in his hallway or go home.

MICAH SAT ON the other side of the door, listening to Ruby apologize. When she stopped talking, he could hear her breathing on the other side of the wood. And he still didn't open the door. He had his own anger to deal with. He didn't need Ruby's easy apologies.

CHAPTER THIRTY-TWO

MICAH'S FATHER WAS walking toward him when his phone rang. Again.

"Someone important?" his father asked.

"No." *Yes.*

"Aren't you going to answer it? What if it's about a new job?"

"It's not." He'd halfheartedly applied for sportscaster positions around the country and the studios had wholeheartedly turned him down. Except for one, who'd asked him to cover an adaptive skiing event in Colorado as a freelancer. When Micah had asked if there would be other events—not *just* the disable beat—the network had responded, "Not at this time." Micah had turned that offer down in a flat second.

"Ruby?" his father asked, though it wasn't really a question. Ruby called several times a day, but all her calls went to voice mail. Micah deleted them without listening.

"Probably."

Micah rolled easily across the hard marble floor of the lobby, his father having to keep pace with long strides, until they got out onto the sidewalk and there was a crowd to deal with. They were headed to the lakeshore. Again. Once Ruby was out of his mind, Micah was never going to come to the lakeshore with his father again. Let the memories be ridden over by a million different bicyclists, all with no respect for sharing the path.

His father had been on an afternoon flight. Night was falling. Maybe the fresh, cold winter air would freeze her out of his mind.

"Have you talked with her since you were fired?"

"No."

"Why not?"

"Busy."

"All you ever did was work. What has been keeping you busy now?"

Taking stock of his life. Thinking about work. Missing his desk and the camaraderie of his office. Wondering where he had gone wrong. Thinking about buying a fish because he'd no longer have to worry about being sent off to cover the national championship in New Orleans at the last minute.

All he told his father was, "I've been looking for jobs."

"Are you still upset with her?"

"Yes." Micah paused. "And no."

He was more upset with himself. As tempting as it was to continue blaming Ruby, he just couldn't. For one thing, she had nothing to do with the fact that he'd let his work and his desire to stay in sports eliminate everything else in his life. And second, she literally hadn't done anything to compromise his integrity. She had been tired and sore and he had been the one to offer a better solution than a massage.

A bicyclist buzzed by them, cursing. Micah returned the curse with a gesture. Coming out on the lakeshore and cursing out bicyclists who thought they owned the path helped with some of his anger, but it hadn't answered any of his questions.

"Any good jobs out there?" His father asked, jump-starting the conversation again and probably hoping Micah would give more than a one-word answer.

"I don't want to be a sportscaster for some Podunk network. I wanted to be a *SportsDaily* anchor. I've worked toward that goal for ten years."

"No. First you wanted to survive graduate school. Then you wanted a beat job. Only when you realized it was possible did you want the anchor position. And there's nothing wrong with wanting something big, but what if, along the way, you've lost sight of the smaller pleasures of life? A wife. Kids."

"You didn't marry again after Mom left."

"No. If I married again I'd have to be home more. Or abandon another wife. Just because I didn't like either of those options doesn't mean I made the right decisions. Or that they're the right decisions for you." His father stepped off the path to allow a group of women to run past. None of the women was Ruby. "Maybe if I'd let myself be open to it, I would have found a different woman. One I wanted to be home with or one who ignored my mother. Or maybe I would have taken you and moved to another city. But I only had one goal, and so I didn't see the other possibilities."

"So what am I supposed to do?" Micah asked when they started forward again.

"Well, do you love her, or did you lose your job over a relationship that would have failed anyway?"

"It might have failed anyway, Dad. She can't see past her own nose."

"Neither could you, when you were the quarterback everyone wanted in the draft. You were always a fighter, but your accident taught you to see the battle in a new way. A way that included the whole battlefield. Don't retreat into headquarters now."

"Am I supposed to arrange a broken back for Ruby so she'll think of someone other than herself?"

"Obtuse is an ugly look on you." His father stopped short and Micah had to back up to continue the conversation. "Talk to her. If you can't make something happen, at least you'll have talked to her."

"She's lived her whole life on the other side of the camera. What advice can she offer me about what to do next?"

"She's been in the spotlight since she was, what, twenty years old? And her *job* crashed around her—also through her own fault—when she was twenty-four. She can probably understand your predicament better than your dear old dad, who's been a boring sales manager for the same company for his whole life."

Remarried or not, in a job rut or not, his father had pinpointed one of the sources of Micah's unease. Reassessing his life with someone wasn't enough. He wanted to talk with Ruby. And not just about his life but hers, as well. Even if both of them were little more than bodies to the rest of the world, they also had strong minds and could figure something out. And they would be better together.

THE NEXT EVENING, Ruby opened the door to her house with a nervous smile and stuck a hand out for the Chinese takeout Micah handed over. Then she and Dotty backed up to let him in.

Micah hadn't been in her house since he and his father had come over for the game night, which meant he hadn't seen the new furniture arrangement that made it easier for him to get from the living room to the dining room. During the month of Micah's silence, Haley had told her to move the furniture back. Advice Ruby had ignored.

"The house looks nice."

"Thanks. I was hoping you'd be back to see it. I'll have to move all the furniture back when the owners return, but for now…" A shrug didn't cover up her nervousness.

Ruby waited for him to tell her again how she'd cost him his job. A job he loved. He'd been so angry the night they'd fought, and as he'd hung off the recliner, she'd been frightened. For her. For their relationship. But mostly for him. She'd been slow to catch up to what was happening, but she knew what it meant to lose a job you loved. Knew that hopelessness as well as she knew the back of her eyelids.

"I missed you." The bag of takeout thumped as it hit the table and she almost didn't hear him.

"I missed you, too. I'm sorry…. I'm trying."

"I know."

They stared at each other for several long seconds, steam and the sweet smell of orange chicken filling the air between them.

"I have some ideas for you on how to beat King at the game I'm sure he's going to want to play."

"Oh. Is that all you came over for?"

"I brought dinner, too." His smile was halfhearted.

"Why?" She wrapped her arms around her body, tucking her cold hands under her pits.

"I'm bored. I need something to do."

"Am I supposed to offer you something in return? Another bargain?"

"No. I'm not offering to help as part of a bargain."

"Am I to become your lifeline, then? My redemption will become your purpose?" She couldn't say the words quietly enough to hide her horror.

"No." He shook his head. "I'm looking for another job. Thinking of another life. Of reinventing myself again. But if I'm going to reinvent myself, I guess I'd rather do it with you in it. And if we're together, I might as well help you with King."

"Okay." When she untied the plastic bag, more steam and spicy smells escaped in a puff. She laid out the chopsticks and napkins.

Micah returned from the kitchen with plates. "All you can say is *okay*?"

"I've not run away, have I?"

This smile wasn't halfhearted. "No, Ruby. You've not run away."

"So serve yourself dinner and explain."

He folded his arms on the table, leaned toward her and started talking. And Micah Blackwell was back in her life. His eyes were hot with determination. His face warmed with affection, and her body was set to boiling by the same lust she'd felt as far back as when she'd seen him in that first marathon.

Their plans made, Dotty fed and the leftovers stored in the fridge, Ruby stood facing Micah, shifting from one foot to another. The tenor of their relationship was completely different. Not only was the business deal out the window, but what was emerging in its place was a team. She'd never played team sports—not even relays—and she wasn't sure how to stop acting as one person cooperating for her own benefit and become two people cooperating for mutual benefit.

"Why did you really call me?" She waved her hand when he opened his mouth. "And don't say because you're bored or you missed me. Why else?"

"You and me, Ruby, we're the same. We want and we

want and we push and we push and we keep aiming for number one. When I get back to number one, it will be better with you there. And I'd like to think, maybe, when you win your hundred-mile race, the victory will be sweeter because I'm waiting for you at the finish."

"Oh."

"I love you, Ruby."

He loved her.

She was afraid to breathe too strongly and push the feeling away. Then she said, "I love you, too," and her breath grew, filling the room before sneaking out through the drafty windows and into the sky. Suddenly her world was much bigger than she'd ever thought possible.

She'd never really been a fan of the unexpected before, but she could learn to look forward to conversations like this.

"Can I ask a question?"

"You look as if you might burst if you don't."

"When I talked with my parents, about us, they asked me all kinds of intrusive questions about you that I didn't know the answers to, even if I didn't think it was any of their business."

"Like?"

"Like if you could provide for me—which is hilarious since I've never had a job in my life and still haven't registered for the personal trainer classes. If anyone's worried about their kid being provided for, it should be *your* dad." She treaded carefully, not fully trusting that there wouldn't be another big fight. Micah had been fired from a job he loved. He was likely still grieving. "They also asked if you have the ability to father children."

"Does that matter to you?"

"If you can father children? I don't think so. I mean, I

think I'd like kids. They sound like a challenge and I like challenges. But I don't know if I care so much about their genes. It seems as if I could mess up my children no matter whose blood they carried."

"Then…"

She waved him off. "I don't want to know the answer now, not unless you want to tell me. But I would like to have the conversation with you—when we're ready."

He laughed. "You want to schedule a conversation about children down the road, already assuming we'll be ready for it someday. Why not do it now?"

"We can, but I figured we should take things one step at a time."

"My sperm have forgotten how to swim, but they still function as sperm. It will take doctors, but I can father children."

"Oh." That was better news than she'd expected. "Thank you for the answer. But didn't we skip a step?"

"I don't know, Ruby. What did you think the next step was?"

"You can sleep over with me and Dotty. If you brought catheters, of course."

The corners of his mouth lifted in a smile that was so full of pleasure and anticipation that Ruby was almost tempted to figure out the mechanics of sex with a paraplegic on a kitchen counter. "Plenty. And disinfectant. I came prepared."

"Then that's what I've got next in the Micah-Ruby calendar."

He gestured wide with one arm. "Lead the way."

CHAPTER THIRTY-THREE

MICAH FOLLOWED RUBY through her living room and back into her bedroom, which wasn't entirely what he'd expected. The rest of the house wasn't reflective of Ruby—she was house-sitting, of course—but she'd placed her stamp on this room. There was nothing of Ruby in the sleigh bed, the tan coloring of the walls or the antique dresser with an ornate mirror, but she was still in the room, under all the furnishings and beyond.

He looked at the line of running shoes under the window. In the dim light of the lamp, he could barely make out the markings on the heel of each shoe, designating pairs of the same styles and probably helping Ruby keep track of how many miles of running she'd put on each shoe.

She had walked farther into her room and must have sensed his halt, because she turned back to look at him and then followed the line of his gaze to her parade of shoes. "Would you believe I still don't have to buy running shoes?"

"But…" Confusion cocked his head to the side so his ear almost touched his shoulder. "I can't imagine any running company would still send you samples."

"They don't. This is evidence of how many samples they

sent me. All of these styles are at least five years old, and I'm sure a sales person at a running store would tell me that the plastic has gone stale, but I couldn't very well ask my parents for new shoes. And, I'm still a twenty-nine-year-old without a real job, so I have to watch my pennies." She let out a breath, and he thought it was a laugh because the corners of her mouth had gone up. "The shoes are okay, I mean, I have to wear shoes, but I had to give all the branded running clothes away. One of the conditions of the many lawsuits against me is that I can't go out in a branded shirt. The company won't want to risk being associated with me."

"I'm risking it."

This time she laughed outright. "Yes. I wonder what they'll do if we go out together and you're wearing a New Balance shirt. They could not have foreseen you."

It was Micah's turn to laugh. "Neither of us could have foreseen us."

"When life gives you lemons, make lemonade, but no one gets to dictate where you get your sugar. I'm glad you're my sugar." Who knew Ruby Heart could be cheesy?

"So," he said with a lift of his eyebrow, "did you invite me here to talk about your shoes and to sleep in that bed, or are we going to do something else?"

"Else. But you did all the work last time. I'd like to do some of the heavy lifting this time, but I'm not sure what that entails. I remember a fantastic orgasm on my part the last time, but if I asked you any logistical questions, I was too out of it to remember the answers."

He wheeled himself forward, past Ruby to the side of the bed, and transferred himself out of his chair. When he'd gotten himself into a balanced position with the help of some pillows, he caught her attention and she walked over to him. She walked between the thighs he'd pushed out wide. The points of her hip bones pressed into his palms. His fingers rose and fell with the movement of her belly. Intimacy was here, in their bodies finding a rhythm together, more than it had or ever would be in the mechanics of sex. He opened his heart and his mind to the sensations, both physical and emotional, that would follow, then looked up at her, completely aroused by the simple act of watching their bodies move together.

"Logistics. My lower body functions in every important way but ejaculation." He kept his eyes locked with hers, both because the intensity of her warm brown eyes was incredibly erotic and in order to keep a read on her reactions to their frank conversation. She wouldn't be the first woman he'd been in this position with who ended the evening with hurt feelings because she believed a lack of ejaculation was about them and not about his body.

Ruby lowered her head slowly, her eyes still locked with his. Deep breaths allowed oxygen to fill every part of his body. Ruby's ever-present salt smell filled his nostrils. Before his head could float away, he ground his attention down to the present. One thing he understood, in a way he could never have understood in his preaccident body, was that intimacy was not two naked bodies rolling around together. Intimacy—real, deep sexual intimacy—was communication.

Scary, intense shit.

"And my lower half still feels pleasure—it just doesn't communicate the feeling to me anymore. Touches to my upper half feel good, sure, but the real pleasure is in my mind." Micah grinned, open, wide and feral, while he tapped his head. "I like to watch."

This time she lifted and lowered her head slowly several times as the import of what he was saying settled on her. Finally she removed her hands from his shoulders and placed them over his hands, still resting on her hips. "What do you like to watch?"

Ruby guided one of his hands off her hip bones, under her T-shirt and onto her taut belly. "This?" she asked as she steered his hand under her shirt to her breast.

Her shirt still covered her skin, so he could only see the lump their hands made together under the fabric. He could also feel the peak of her nipple and they sucked air between their teeth in tandem when she directed his fingers around her nipple and pinched.

"Or do you like to watch this?" she asked. She pulled their hands still resting on her belly into a claw shape and walked them under the waistband of her gym shorts and down the crease where her thigh met her belly. Again the fabric covered their hands, and watching the lumps of their hands aroused him to the point of bursting. He knew what her skin looked like there. When their joined fingers tiptoed lower, he could picture her brown curls against the white of her thighs and the pink of her labia.

She led his finger between the lips of her pussy and he licked his lips, remembering the taste of her. The warmth and dampness of her folds and the changing rhythm of her breaths under his hand cried out her arousal. His breaths slowed, becoming deeper and filling the scent of her into his soul.

"Or is this a better view?" She gave each of his hands a pat, which he understood as a directive that they were to stay where they were and continue what they were doing. He was happy to oblige.

Ruby flung her shirt across the room in one quick movement. One instant he had been looking at a lump under a gray T-shirt. The next instant he was staring at her pale skin. One of her nipples was a deep pink, hard and pointed;

the other was covered by his hand. He moved his palm so it didn't completely cover her breast, and this time when he pinched the nipple, he saw the flush of her areola while air whistled between her teeth. Blood pounded in his ears.

"That's a good view," he choked out.

She slipped her thumbs under her waistband and lowered the elastic of her shorts a quarter of an inch, his eyes tracking each extra cell of skin she revealed. He licked his lips again, desperate to taste her. Her answering smile was wicked, her mouth wide-open and her tongue swiping across the edges of her lips while her shorts bared only that extra tantalizing inch of skin.

Anticipation pounded fire in his ears until he could hear little more than the music of his arousal. The view of Ruby half-naked was intoxicating, as her nipple poked out between the fingers of his one hand while his other hand made light circles between her legs.

When he eased one finger forward a little to find her clitoris, her head fell back, her hands locked in the waist of her shorts. Her thighs twitched against his hand, clasping his hand with the power of her muscles. In an experiment, he brought his thumb to meet his finger and rolled her nub between them, like he had with her nipples, not taking his eyes off her face. Her eyelids flittered. Her nostrils flared. He did it again, this time easing his middle finger inside her.

Her hips jutted forward with such ferocity that Micah lost his balance and fell backward onto the bed with an "oomph." As they were still attached, Ruby fell on top of him, her breasts landing on the line of demarcation so he could feel one of her nipples against his though not the other.

"I don't think I used enough pillows," he said to the top of her head, short wisps of her hair moving with his breath and sticking to his damp lips.

When she looked up at him, her eyes seemed to have a line of demarcation as clear as the one across his chest. Above hot, below startled. Unable to help himself, Micah burst out laughing. He untangled his hands from between their bodies, gripped her under her arms and slid her up his body until her face was level with his. Once she was where he wanted her to be, he put his hands on either side of her face, lifting his head up to meet hers. His tongue answered the invitation of her parted lips, slipping in and around her mouth.

Between the shifting of the bed and the movement of her upper body against his, he was pretty sure she was grinding her hips against his. He sucked her tongue deep in his mouth before taking it lightly in his teeth and drawing his head back to the mattress, her tongue gliding along the tops of his teeth until they were unlocked from each other.

Arousal had taken control of her eyes again.

"So what's next in the Ruby Heart plan of attack?" He matched his question with a smile and a raised eyebrow.

"Who says I have a plan?"

He raised his other eyebrow.

"Okay. I was going to slip off my shorts and then take extra care undressing you. Me naked and presenting as many full views of myself as possible to you." She cocked her head at him, certain she was back in control. "Maybe touch myself while considering what piece of your clothing to remove next."

In demonstration, she slid her hand between their bodies and it passed from where he could feel to where only his lower body could enjoy the movements. But her wicked smile gave away what she was doing, especially as she drew her hand back out and pressed a glistening finger to his lips.

"And after that?"

"Sharing my game plan with the other team?" It was her turn to raise a brow at him. "I don't think so."

"Does it involve my mouth where your hand was?"

"It could." Her voice rolled with suggestion.

"I want that."

"You are a bossy man."

"And I expect my whims to be catered to."

She used her finger, the one that had been inside her, to trace a line down his jaw. "I'll think about it."

He craned his neck to watch her slide her body down the length of his. Freed from the grip of his hand and the cover of her T-shirt, her breasts jiggled as she shimmied out of her shorts and panties. Hypnotic. And he was going to get to play.

Together they stripped the clothes off his body in record time. In a hurry to get where they were going so they could spend more time there, Micah grabbed as many pillows as he could and shoved them to the headboard and scooted himself to the head of the bed, in a sitting position. It was Ruby's turn to watch him and she stood at the side of the bed, eyeing the movement of his limbs, both controlled and not.

For about two years after his accident, the continued atrophy of his legs had bothered him. The doctors said it would stop and that spastic movements of his muscles would keep some muscle tone.

This was the first time Ruby had seen him laid out in full view, no clothes in the way. And he might not worry about the state of his legs any longer, but all men liked for their lovers to look upon them with pleasure. Ruby's eyes were still dilated and her lips plump and wet, but she also looked uncertain for the first time that night. He patted the side of the bed and she sat down.

"Can I answer any questions for you?" Sex required trust, no matter the partners, and after the fifty-mile race, Ruby had put all her trust in him to both relax and give her pleasure. He had to trust her to do the same. Trust and communication went hand in hand.

He put his hand on her thigh, with enough pressure in his grip that he could see shadows in the indentation of her skin but not so much that he couldn't move his hand around. She tightened her quads and he gripped the strength hidden beneath the soft surface of her skin. Her nipples, which had relaxed, began to harden into peaks again. He moved his hand around to her inner thigh, brushing against her soft folds before pulling his hand back. Her mouth parted. Micah had to concentrate on his breathing to keep the pleasure from flooding his mind. Just because his orgasms were all in his head didn't mean he wanted to come prematurely.

"I don't mind repeating myself in the name of hot sex. In fact, talking about sex while you're sitting there naked and glorious is almost as erotic as watching." This time, when he moved his hand to her inner thigh, his fingers breached the folds of her skin again and the musky smell of her filled his nose. He slipped his fingers back out and rubbed them together, reveling in the slipperiness of her juices.

Another truth his preaccident, young-stud self had not realized was that sex may be the act of insertion, but intimacy and eroticism were the smells, the sounds, the mind, the emotions, the trust, the connection—everything about sex that nineteen- and twenty-year-olds tended to forget about in the rush for the big O.

"You said you like to watch because the orgasm happens in your mind." Despite her evident attempt to control her breaths, they were short and shallow. The conversation and connection between them was as arousing to her as it was to him. "And you said that your lower body feels pleasure, but doesn't tell you. Where can and should I concentrate my attentions? Maybe more important, are there parts of you that you want me to stay away from?"

He opened his arms wide and gestured down to the rest of his body. "Have at it. Just don't do something where I can't see it, because I definitely can't feel from about here—" he put his hand below his nipples "—down, and if I can't feel it or see it, you're doing it only for you. Which is fine—"

"But I want to do this for you," she interrupted. "With you."

Ruby slipped her naked form off the side of the bed, eyeing his body up and down, forming a strategy, as he had known she would. Then she smiled, a wicked smile that lit up her face and was more for herself than for him. He took several deep breaths to calm his overactive mind and focus on her. Their connection. The thing that would make this interaction different from closing his eyes and simply imagining.

Ruby licked her lips until they glistened in the lamplight. If Micah wasn't careful, he would catch his breath while watching her trace the bedcovers next to his legs, and in catching it, he'd lose it completely. His legs must have sensed something was near them because his right calf muscle twitched, a movement that traveled up his thigh.

She climbed onto the bed. His legs lowered slightly from her weight. The hairs on his arms stood on end. A bomb could explode in the next room and he wouldn't be able to look away, especially after she cocked her head at his reactive legs and said, "Interesting? Good or bad, I wonder?"

"Good. I don't think my taste and the interests of my lower limbs have diverged much since we stopped talking to one another, and *I* think it's good."

"Huh. I wonder…" She straddled his feet, with knees wide, her face pointed toward his toes and her firm ass in the air as if she was presenting herself to him. Then she leaned forward, and he could see her breasts brush his legs and the lights dance across her glistening pussy.

As she walked back on her arms and knees, he could see *everything.* Her breasts bounced above his legs, her nipples brushing against his skin, which jumped in reaction. Hair interplayed with rosy folds of skin, open, deep and on display for him. The muscles of her hamstrings and her arms bent and flexed. And—he drew his gaze back up to her bottom hanging in the air—*she was open to him.* When she scooted up until her mouth was level with his dick, her pussy was practically in his face.

The view wasn't entirely perfect. Despite her intentions, her hair and breasts were in the way, so he couldn't see all of what she was doing. But when he reached his hand out to stroke her, she gasped, and the muscles of her upper thighs quivered. He moved himself higher on the pillows, grasping on to her hips and swinging her ripe ass until he could lean forward and press his mouth against her. She didn't even question.

He spread the cheeks of her ass wide, providing his tongue direct access to her core and enveloping himself in the smell of her. She shuddered and moaned, giving herself completely to him. He still couldn't see what she was doing to his lower half, but positive energy came up through his body in waves, flooding his mind with images, colors and sounds. As she moved, her breasts bounced and brushed against the edges of his hand. Her breaths got increasingly shorter. Her knees tightened around his chest, squeezing every last breath out of him.

"Turn around," he said, unable to see farther than a couple inches of her skin. "Ride me."

The mattress depressed under her knees as she moved and shifted around to reach into her bedside table. Together they rolled a condom onto his erection. As he held his erection in his hand, pleasure only traveled one way, but he guided her onto him. The skin on his legs was red with pleasure and interest. Her nipples were hard peaks and her mouth was soft.

She lifted herself up off him, coming down with such intensity that both their thighs twitched. He gripped her waist, keeping her movements steady so he could watch. Pressure mounted in his mind, emotions flying at him from all directions. If he tried to avoid them, this moment would be lost. The most frightening part of orgasm was right before it happened, when Micah felt splayed wide and vulnerable. But Ruby's sharp gasping breaths kept him as pinned open as she was, unable to stop the mounting weight of sight, sound, taste, touch and smell.

When orgasm started to overtake her, she leaned forward and he caught her shoulders in his hands, keeping her aloft so he could continue to watch. Her long hair bounced against his chest.

"Oh!" She sat up so quickly she nearly unbalanced herself. All her muscles seemed to tense at once. Then she finished her "oh!" with a breathier "Micah," and she fell forward again.

Before he caught her, he relaxed the grip he'd had on his mind. Everything he'd experienced burst through him like a geyser. He closed his eyes and shuddered, riding the waves of emotions until he crashed onto the shore in exhaustion.

Physically and emotionally depleted, Micah opened his eyes. Judging only by the exhaustion evident in her thighs,

Ruby probably felt the same. His fingers creaked as he loosened his grip on her hips, and he gave a tired smile when her hips wavered, this time from weariness rather than arousal. He patted her behind. The bed rocked as she shifted her weight to climb off him, a small groan escaping her lips.

He removed the condom and tossed it into the trash, then scooted over until he was on one side of the bed. She took advantage of the space he'd made to collapse next to him. Was she a postsex talker? The last time hadn't been a good measure because she was recovering from a fifty-mile run. Maybe he wouldn't be able to judge accurately this time either, since that bit of sport had apparently exhausted them both.

The mattress swayed under Ruby's changing weight as she got comfortable. She tucked her head on his chest, her soft breaths dancing across his skin. Her breathing was slow, but it wasn't even enough for him to be certain she was asleep, plus her head didn't press down onto his chest. She was awake enough to hold herself up a little. He put one arm around her, resting his hand on her moist back. The other hand he walked down the length of his body until his fingers came across her leg, which was draped across him. He took a moment to let his fingers explore the different textures of their skin before resting his hand on her knee. He closed his eyes, too tired to express anything that had just happened, though his mind was still racing from the experience.

Love was more exhausting than he'd thought.

CHAPTER THIRTY-FOUR

MICAH'S NEWLY FREED-UP schedule meant he and Ruby had gotten to spend more time with one another outside of trips to the gym. They went on dates and spent nights together. Fortunately, Micah had done most of the work for the ultra series already, leaving only this final hundred-mile race for King and Amir to film before the series was over. In theory, there wasn't much for King to fuck up. In practice, Micah didn't trust the man at all. Especially since the race was about to start and King was nowhere to be found.

Amir stood at the starting line with his camera and a large spotlight targeted on Ruby. Micah looked through the dark and the crowds for King. Not being present at the start of the big race, the climax of this entire series that NSN had put staff hours and lots of money into producing was inexplicable and inexcusable.

The announcer began his countdown and Micah turned his attention to the woman he couldn't have ever dreamed he would love, watching her shake her muscles and herself awake. Her goal was to run the hundred miles in seventeen hours, which would put her in line with the best ultra runners in the Midwest.

After the NSN interviews, her presence in the sport was no longer a secret. A man Micah had remembered from the Missouri race greeted Ruby and seemed genuinely interested in the competition she would provide. Everyone else did their best to ignore her, though they gave her long glances out of the corners of their eyes.

Ruby Heart, America's Darling, was impossible to ignore.

The starting gun went off and Ruby leaped in front of the male runner who'd been talking to her, her back straight, her arms pumping and bliss on her face. Micah wouldn't see her again until the third aid station. The first and second aid stations had been deemed inaccessible, even by Micah's standards. Josh would be waiting at those. Glancing at his watch, Micah judged that he had enough time to head back to the hotel and grab breakfast before he could reasonably expect Ruby at mile forty.

Back at the hotel, he slipped his room key into the slot and opened his door. One of the benefits of being fired and having his relationship with Ruby out in the open was that hotel rooms, especially cheap hotel rooms, were better when shared. He wheeled himself through the door, smiling at Ruby's clothes piled on the floor.

A rustling noise came from the bathroom and Micah gripped the wheels of his chair, then quickly relaxed his hands, taking a deep breath. Whatever was in the bathroom was better handled with loose, agile muscles than clenched shoulders up around his ears. His wheels barely made a noise as he traversed the room to the bathroom, though whoever was in there seemed too engaged to notice anything. Hell, the person hadn't even heard the door open.

Before he had gotten into a position where he would be visible from the bathroom, Micah looked back over his shoulder and considered the door. If it had been open, maybe housekeeping was here. Only it was six in the morning and no hotel by the freeway supplied housekeeping this early in the morning. And the door had been shut. Sticking his key in the door to unlock it hadn't been a figment of his imagination.

Micah used his arms to push himself forward enough to be able to peek into the bathroom, then pulled back. King's presence in his bathroom was as inexplicable as his absence had been from the race. However, King's absence from the race could be explained away by incompetence—his presence in the bathroom could only be due to malice of some kind. Micah eased his phone out of his pocket and dialed nine-one-one. Then he set his phone on his lap and pushed himself into King's view.

King was so engrossed in his task that he only turned when a barely audible voice said, "Nine-one-one, what is your emergency?"

Micah replied in an even, clear broadcaster's voice. "Someone has broken into my hotel room. They are still here."

King dropped what he had been holding and it shattered on the floor. His gaze was wild around the bathroom, not even stopping at Micah. Finally King said, "It's not true. He broke into *my* hotel room."

"I'd love to hear you explain to the cops why you were assigned to a wheelchair-accessible room and how both my clothes and Ruby's clothes came to be in here."

The operator's voice said, "The police are on their way. Please identify which hotel room."

Micah said, "Four-oh-six" at the same time King said, "The police aren't needed." King kicked a large shard of glass over to Micah's chair. "Look, Micah, we can discuss this on our own."

"Discuss what? You breaking into my room?"

"You girlfriend is doping again and you know about it. The proof is in this room. And the cops are coming. Good." King brightened. "I'll call Amir and he can be here when they arrest her."

Micah examined the bathroom, taking in all the details, including the small addition of a needle package and some medical tubing. Not enough to be absolute proof, but enough to be damaging to Ruby's reputation. And his. "How much effort did you put into this frame job, King Ripley?" Micah enunciated his coworker's name, all the better for the taping device to capture in the nine-one-one office. "Is there a needle in the trash with Ruby's DNA on it? Or is this just to tarnish her reputation, not to actually put her in jail?"

"You're the only person who gives a fuck about Ruby's reputation. She's another in a long line of doping athletes. But she will make my career. And it could have been your career, but you were stupid enough to climb into bed with her. How long did it take her to convince you to help her with the transfusions after you started sleeping together? She had you pegged. All that medical knowledge you've acquired with your, your..."

"*Disability* is the commonly accepted word. *Paraplegia* would be medically accurate." Micah shut his mouth before King remembered the phone was still on and the operator on the other end was still listening. The man was doing a fine job talking himself into a hole without Micah getting in the way.

"Whatever. You don't really belong at NSN, you know. A pity hire who kept getting promoted. You only got that original Ruby story because of the chair. It should have gone to me."

"So this whole thing is about me?"

That a couple people around the office agreed with King's rant was no secret—no matter that Micah had never shied away from a story, had never been late with a story and generally worked as hard if not harder than his colleagues. The pity-hire charge would hang over him until the end of his days.

"I hope you never work in broadcasting again, Micah."

"Getting fired from NSN wasn't enough for you? Taking over *my* story?"

"Ruby wasn't even supposed to be a story."

"You were at the same race I was. You could have seen her, and then maybe you would have earned the story instead of getting my sloppy seconds. Think how much better you would feel about your life right now if you had paid attention to sports history." Needling King was unnecessary, but Micah was too pissed off to control himself.

A knock came to the door. "Police." Another knock, this time accompanied by shuffling and the scraping of the key in the lock. From his position at the threshold of the bathroom, Micah could see a hotel employee jump aside and two uniformed policemen enter.

"Is everything okay here?" one of the cops asked. The cop was young, with his shoulders thrown back to puff out his chest and a wide-legged swagger.

"Officer, I came into my room and this man had broken in. I found him in the bathroom."

The second officer, a man who looked too old for his crisp uniform and acted like he knew it, looked at Micah, then up and around the room. "This here's your room? Whose bra, then?"

"Pete, that's Micah Blackwell," the younger cop hissed at his partner. "The other guy is King Ripley."

"Am I supposed to know who they are?" The older man couldn't take his eyes off the bra.

"*SportsDaily* reporters. You know, the one who was…" The young cop looked at Micah and Micah shrugged, still too angry to say anything that wasn't rude, and so he kept his mouth shut. "Micah is the one who was fired."

"That's right, I saw those pictures of that woman leaving your apartment building. A runner or something."

"Officer," King said, seizing the advantage, "wait until you see what's in the bathroom."

"Like a man who was *breaking into my hotel room,* lest we all forget why I called nine-one-one."

"Right." Finally the older cop pulled his attention away from the bra and looked at King skulking in the doorway. "The manager said this was Mr. Blackwell's room. Why are you here?"

"If you watch NSN, and it sounds like you two officers do, then you'll know I was assigned the Ruby Heart story after Micah's suspension. Well, I became suspicious and so I came here looking for evidence of doping. And I found it. Micah was even helping."

"I suggest we all retire to the station," the older cop said, "where we can sort this out."

"Officer, Ruby's running the race over at the state park today. I'm supposed to be at the third aid station for her. I'd like to be there at the finish."

"I'm afraid that won't be possible…" the older cop said. At the same time, the younger one said, "We'll see what we can do."

"Can I at least text her brother so *he* can be at the aid station for her?"

The younger cop spoke before the older one could open his mouth. "I don't think that will be a problem."

The older cop was apparently unwilling to argue with his colleague in front of the suspects, but he clearly wasn't happy with that answer. Micah took what he could get and texted Josh the barest bit of information. Anything more would sound ridiculous, which this situation clearly was. Then Micah put his phone away and agreed to talk with the cops at the station, so long as he could drive himself over there.

King was making arguments of his own, talking about the importance of the story and how he was the innocent one and he didn't need to come down to the station.

It was going to be a long morning.

CHAPTER THIRTY-FIVE

RUBY SLOWED AS she entered the aid station. Carter, a runner she'd met in Missouri and one of the top runners in the Midwest, had about a five-minute lead on her. But she'd also seen the extra effort he put into his kick to pull away from her. He wasn't at a pace he could sustain—at the end of the race he'd have to slow down. While Ruby would still have enough left in her to speed up.

She climbed onto the scale, not paying attention to the weight. The volunteer declared her good. While she went through the medical check, Ruby found Josh, who handed her a water bottle and a granola bar. "Where's Micah?" she asked, not bothering to swallow her food before talking. She may have enough juice left in her to catch Carter, but that didn't mean every last second didn't count, even in a seventeen-hour race.

"All I got is a text from him saying something happened in your room having to do with King. And that's why Micah couldn't make this aid station. He hopes he'll be at the finish, but he wasn't certain."

"What the… Never mind. I can't worry about this right now. I have a race to win."

Ruby shoved her questions out of her head and her trash at her brother. She couldn't fix whatever was happening in their hotel room, but she could beat Carter. The rustling of the trail under her feet and the rhythm of the running drowned out everything but the push inside her.

RUBY CROSSED OVER the finish line thirty-nine seconds after Carter did. The last two miles had been an all-out sprint between the two of them and, in the end, he'd been a half minute stronger than she was. She staggered to the medical check with Josh at her elbow. It wasn't until she'd completed the final medical check that she realized Micah wasn't by her side.

She'd been running for herself, sure, but it had been nice knowing there was a person waiting for her at the end. Just any person wasn't enough, though. She was glad to have Josh by her side as she congratulated Carter on his win, but she wished Micah were here instead of her brother. As she collapsed in a chair, she wished she knew where Micah was.

Amir and his camera came into view. No Micah. No King either, which was a good thing. She didn't have the energy to put up with him. Bells announced the coming of another runner. Ruby gestured to Josh to help her up. Getting her standing required effort on both their parts, and she staggered to the finish line to start cheering.

Micah didn't show up until the fifth finisher had crossed the line, a full forty-five minutes after Ruby. "I missed your finish," he said, reaching his arms up for a hug.

She bent down and embraced him, too worried about him to be upset. "If it had taken you another forty-five minutes, I'm not sure I would be able to bend down."

His hands were warm on her face. His grip was strong and there was something urgent in the way his fingers clasped her jawbone. No matter how tired her body was, she recognized the relief in his kiss. She didn't pull away until bells announced the coming of the next runner, and then she had to brace her back to stand up straight. When Micah held out his hand for assistance, she took it and didn't let go.

In between cheering for the finishers, Micah told Ruby what had happened in their hotel room and about his multi-hour adventure at the police station and the accompanying call to the NSN offices. "King is suspended pending further inquiries, and I'm back on your story. Freelance until paperwork goes through."

"Do we need to do an interview now, then?" She was exhausted in mind, body and spirit, and the news of King's attempt to sabotage her fledging reentry into running didn't help. Come morning, exhaustion would probably hit her like a ton of bricks. It might be days before she had the energy to fully process what had happened.

"No. We can wait." A pleased expression must have crossed the fatigued muscles of her face because he gave her hand a squeeze and said, "And it's not me putting you and our relationship in front of my career—NSN will have their hands full firing King. Your story can wait until tomorrow."

"What comes after that? For you? For us?"

"How does Southern California sound? For me and for us?"

They paused to cheer for three runners who finished all together.

"What do you mean?"

"I didn't just get your story back. I also got offered an anchor position at the new *SportsDaily* studio in Los Angeles."

"Can we live closer to the mountains so I can train there?"